Acclaim for Mark Mazower's

Salonica, City of Ghosts

Winner of
The John Criticos Prize
The Runciman Award
The Duff Cooper Prize

"In a remarkable display of historical craftsmanship, he resurrects the city's manifold ghosts. . . . Mazower's scrupulous witness to the experiences of each major group that made up the fabric of Salonica is an act of compassion for their suffering, a recognition of their gifts and aspirations, an acknowledgment of their common humanity."
—*Los Angeles Times*

"Mark Mazower's new book is a necessary masterpiece; necessary because it fills a gap, and a masterpiece because it fills that gap so well."
—*The Times* (London)

"An extraordinary book by a historian with a wonderful appetite for complexity."
—*Newsday*

"Enthralling. . . . Tragic, hopeful and beautifully written, *Salonica, City of Ghosts* shows how cities, as much as people, can be seduced by the prospect of escaping their own past and remaking themselves in ways unrecognizable to old friends."
—*The Times Literary Supplement* (London)

"Mazower . . . is a champion of the cosmopolitan. He tells his history with sweep but doesn't neglect the human side." —*The Miami Herald*

"[A] tremendous book about a city unique not just in Europe, but in the entire history of humanity. . . . What [Mazower] does to perfection is to express the historical meaning of Salonica down the generations, authenticating his story with a multitude of contemporary quotations, from the fifteenth to the twentieth century, and scrupulously explaining it all out of his profound scholarly knowledge."
—*The Guardian* (London)

"Mazower has made a major contribution. . . . A book worth reading by anybody interested in the coexistence of Islam, Judaism, and Christianity—and interested in a single small but glorious place."
—*The Weekly Standard*

"A brilliant reconstruction of one of Europe's great meeting places between the three monotheistic faiths."   —*The Economist*

"[Mazower] sensitively analyses the internal debates and divisions which could be found within all the major communities."
—*The Sunday Telegraph* (London)

"Masterly. . . . A brilliant and timely reminder that cities have played as important a role as states in the lives of their inhabitants."
—*The Spectator* (London)

"Mazower has succeeded so well that scholars of all nationalities and religions will refer to this book as their principal source on the city."
—*The New York Times Book Review*

"Mazower is a formidable historian. He has produced a majestic work: the biography of a city, complete with soul and ichor."
—*The Independent* (London)

"This exploration into the soul of a Balkan city is both evocative and profound, a masterful addition to Mazower's work."
—*BBC History Magazine*

"*Salonica, City of Ghosts*, is a wonderful evocation of the complex, glorious and tragic history of a city, with lessons both positive and negative for our present age. The author, as always, writes with compelling clarity and penetrating eye for detail. If the past is another country, the author allows us to travel there."
—"Books of the Year," *The Sunday Telegraph* (London)

MARK MAZOWER

Salonica, City of Ghosts

Mark Mazower is professor of history at Columbia University and Birkbeck College, London. His books include *Dark Continent: Europe's Twentieth Century* and *Inside Hitler's Greece: The Experience of Occupation, 1941–44*, winner of the Fraenkel Prize in Contemporary History and the Longman/History Today Award for Book of the Year. He lives in New York City.

Salonica,
City of Ghosts

Salonica, City of Ghosts

*Christians, Muslims
and Jews, 1430–1950*

MARK MAZOWER

VINTAGE BOOKS

A DIVISION OF RANDOM HOUSE, INC.

NEW YORK

FIRST VINTAGE BOOKS EDITION, MAY 2006

The Library of Congress has cataloged the Knopf edition as follows:
Mazower, Mark.
Salonica, city of ghosts : Christians, Muslims and Jews, 1430–1950 /
Mark Mazower.
p. cm.
Includes bibliographical references and index.
1. Thessaloniki (Greece)—History. I. Title.
DF951.T45M39 2005
949.5'65—dc22
2004057690

Vintage ISBN-10: 0-375-72738-8
Vintage ISBN-13: 978-0-375-72738-2

Author photograph © Jerry Bauer
Book design by Virginia Tan

www.vintagebooks.com

Printed in the United States of America
10 9 8 7 6 5 4

To Marwa

Contents

Contents

Acknowledgements

In the twenty years I have been working on this project, I have been helped by so many people that I fear I may not remember them all. To everyone who has discussed their experiences of the city with me, provided me with documents, advice or support, I am deeply indebted. In particular I would like to thank the following: Miko Alvo, Georgios Angelopoulos, Albertos and Leon Arouch, Efi Avdela, Rika Benveniste, Moise Bourlas, Steve Bowman, Peter Brown, John Campbell, Jean Carasso, Richard Clogg, Erika Counio-Amariglio, the late Nancy Crawshaw, the late Mando Dalianis, Nicholas De Lange, Katy Fleming, Ben Fortna, Norman Gilbertson, Eyal Ginio, Jacqueline Golden, Dimitri Gondicas, Vasilis Gounaris, Ashbel Green, Eleni Haidia, Bill Hamilton, Renée Hirschon, Elliott Horowitz, the late Judith Humphrey, Sukru Ilicak, Cemal Kafadar, Mike Keeley, Nikos Kokantzis, Toga Koker, John Koliopoulos, Basil Kontis, Kostas Kostis, Antonis Liakos, Heath and Demet Lowry, Rena and Meir Molho, Yannis Mourellos, Barbara Politi and Walter Lummerding, Maria Seremetis, Nikos Stavroulakis, Charles Stewart, Alexandre Toumarkine, Karen van Dyck, Maria Vassilikou, Mike Vogel, Johanna Weber, Maria Wojnicka, Andrew Wylie and Onur Yildirim.

Mike Fishwick has been from the outset a wonderfully enthusiastic and supportive editor. Thanks to him, Vera Brice and Kate Hyde, I felt in good hands. Maria Vassilikou, Bea Lewkowicz, Bernard Pierron, Rena Molho, Dimitris Livanios and Iakovos Mihailidis were kind enough to provide me with copies of their unpublished dissertations. In Athens, Aegina and Tinos, Fay Zika, Haris Vlavianos and Katerina Schina have made Greece a home from home. I must also acknowledge a debt to the extraordinary array of devoted scholars—among them Alexandra Karadimou-Yerolympou, Georgios Anastassiadis, Vasilis Colonnas, Vasilis Dimitriades, Evangelos Hekimoglou, Rena Molho, Albertos Nar, Sakis Serefas, and the late Kostas Tomanas—whose writings have done so much to bring the city to life.

I am grateful for their assistance to the librarians of the following institutions: the Institute for Balkan Studies, the Centre for the History of the City of Thessaloniki, the Newspaper Library in the Thessaloniki Municipal Library, the Historical Archives of Macedonia; in Athens, the Greek Literary and Historical Archives (ELIA), the Archive of Contemporary Social History (ASKI), the Newspaper Library, the Gennadios Library, the Jewish Museum of Greece and the Central Board of Jewish Communities of Greece; in London, the Public Record Office, the School of Oriental and African Studies, Birkbeck College London and the Wiener Library; in the USA, the American Joint Distribution Committee and the United Nations, as well as the university librarians at Berkeley, Princeton, Columbia and Harvard. My research was also supported by the Central Research Fund of the University of London.

Among those who read drafts and gave me the benefit of their scholarly expertise, I would like to thank Fred Anscombe, Selim Deringil, Ben Fortna and Heath Lowry for helpful counsel on matters Ottoman and their patience with an interloper. Philip Carabott, Vasilis Gounaris and Dimitris Livanios made many valuable comments, corrections and suggestions and helped me with their deep knowledge of the Balkan context and contemporary Greece: I thank them for the time and attention they generously gave me. Nikos Stavroulakis gave me precious guidance on the complexities of Marrano and *Ma'min* identities, not to mention food. My parents, Bill and Miriam Mazower, and my grandmother, Ruth Shaffer, read the early chapters closely for style and were both critical and supportive. And I am hugely indebted, not for the first time, to Peter Mandler, for ploughing through the entire manuscript and giving me the benefit of his encouragement, thoughtfulness and invaluable critical eye. Above all, I would like to express my deep gratitude to Marwa Elshakry, who, despite living with the subject for much longer than anyone would consider reasonable, never betrayed impatience at hearing yet another story about Salonica, being shown another document or driven down another side-street. Her challenging suggestions and queries opened up exciting new perspectives for me. What is more, she went rigorously through the text line by line, and made innumerable scholarly and stylistic improvements. In this as in everything else, I owe her more than I can put into words. This book is dedicated to her with the author's love.

Illustrations

BLACK AND WHITE

Yane Sandanski

Hilmi Pacha

Ioacheim III

Albanian Ottoman irregulars

Regular Ottoman infantry arrive in Macedonia

Cretan gendarmes *(Imperial War Museum)*

Venizelos arrives by sea to lead Greece into the First World War, 9 October 1916 *(Imperial War Museum)*

A German biplane attracts crowds along the front

A refugee camp inside the city, 1916 *(Imperial War Museum)*

Devastation in the town centre following the 1917 fire *(Imperial War Museum)*

First meeting of the town planners, 1917

Ernest Hebrard leads a dig in the precinct of the Rotonda *(Courtesy of Mr. H. Yiakoumis and Editions Potamos)*

The new city

Huts of Asia Minor refugees beneath the old walls, *c.*1960

The Upper Town, *c.*1960

Rosa Eskenazi, Dimitrios Semsis and Tombol, *c.*1930

An interwar dandy

The Hamza Bey mosque in its postwar incarnation as the Alcazar Cinema, *c.*1960

The round-up of Jewish men by German troops, July 1942

University buildings going up on the site of the old Jewish cemetery, 1950s

Salonica 1910

Salonica, fifty years later in 1960 *(Reproduced from A. Karadimou-Yerolympou, I anoikodomisi tis Thessalonikis meta tin pyrkaia tou 1917, by permission of University Studio Press and the author)*

1962 parades to mark half a century of Greek rule

The planned city centre: Plateia Aristotelous and the seafront *(Reproduced from A. Karadimou-Yerolympou, I anoikodomisi tis Thessalonikis meta tin pyrkaia tou 1917, by permission of University Studio Press and the author)*

Maps

Salonica,
City of Ghosts

Introduction

> Beware of saying to them that sometimes cities follow one another on the same site and under the same name, born and dying without knowing one another, without communicating among themselves. At times even the names of the inhabitants remain the same, and their voices' accent, and also the features of the faces; but the gods who live beneath names and above places have gone off without a word and outsiders have settled in their place.
>
> ITALO CALVINO, *Invisible Cities*[1]

THE FIRST TIME I visited Salonica, one summer more than twenty years ago, I stepped off the Athens train, shouldered my rucksack, and left the station in search of the town. Down a petrol-choked road, I passed a string of seedy hotels, and arrived at a busy crossroads: beyond lay the city centre. The unremitting heat and the din of the traffic reminded me of what I had left several hours away in Athens but despite this I knew I had been transported into another world. A mere hour or so to the north lay Tito's Yugoslavia and the checkpoints at Gevgeli or Florina; to the east were the Rhodope forests barring the way to Bulgaria, the forgotten Muslim towns and villages of Thrace and the border with Turkey. From the moment I crossed the hectic confusion of Vardar Square—"Piccadilly Circus" for British soldiers in the First World War—ignoring the signposts that urged me out of the city in the direction of the Iron Curtain, I sensed the presence of a different Greece, less in thrall to an ancient past, more intimately linked to neighbouring peoples, languages and cultures.

The crowded alleys of the market offered shade as I pushed past carts piled high with figs, nuts, bootleg Fifth Avenue shirts and pirated cassettes. Tsitsanis's bouzouki strained the vendors' tinny speakers, but it was no competition for the clarino and drum with which gypsy boys were deafening diners in the packed ouzeris of the Modiano food mar-

The topography of the Balkans

ket. Round the tables of *Myrovolos Smyrni* (Sweet-Smelling Smyrna), its very name an evocation of the glories and disasters of Hellenism's Anatolian past, tsipouro and *mezedes* were smoothing the passage from work to siesta. There were fewer back-packers in evidence here than in the tourist dives around the Acropolis, more housewives, porters and farmers on their weekly trip into town. Did I really see a dancing bear performing for onlookers in the meat market? I certainly did not miss the flower-stalls clustered around the *Louloudadika* hamam (known also according to the guidebooks as the Market Baths, the Women's Baths, or the *Yahudi Hamam*, the Bath of the Jews), the decrepit spice warehouses on Odos Egyptou (Egypt Street), the dealers still installed in the old fifteenth-century multi-domed *bezesten*. This vigorous commercialism put even Athens to shame: here was a city which had remained much closer to the values of the bazaar and the souk than anything to be seen further south.

Athens itself had eliminated the traces of its Ottoman past without much difficulty. For centuries it had been little more than an overgrown village so that after winning independence in 1830 Greece's rulers found there not only the rich cultural capital invested in its ancient remains by Western philhellenism, but all the attractions of something close to a blank slate so far as the intervening epochs were concerned. Salonica's Ottoman years, on the other hand, were a matter of living memory, for the Greek army had arrived only in 1912 and those grandmothers chatting quietly in the yards outside their homes had probably been born subjects of Sultan Abdul Hamid. The still magnificent eight-mile circuit of ancient walls embraced a densely thriving human settlement whose urban character had never been in question, a city whose history reached forward from classical antiquity uninterruptedly through the intervening centuries to our own times.

Even before one left the packed streets down near the bay and headed into the Upper Town, tiny medieval churches half-hidden below ground marked the transition from classical to Byzantine. It did not take long to discover what treasures they contained—one of the most resplendent collections of early Christian mosaics and frescoes to be found anywhere in the world, rivalling the glories of Ravenna and Istanbul. A Byzantine public bath, hidden for much of its existence under the accumulated topsoil, still functioned high in the Upper Town, near the shady overgrown garden which hid tiny Ayios Nikolaos Orfanos and its fourteenth-century painted narrative of the life of Christ. The Rotonda—a strange cylindrical Roman edifice, whose multiple re-incarnations as church, mosque, museum and art centre encapsulated the city's endless metamorphoses—contained some of the earliest mural mosaics to be found in the eastern Mediterranean. Next to it stood an elegant pencil-thin minaret, nearly one hundred and twenty feet tall.

Like many visitors before me, I found myself particularly drawn to the Upper Town. There, hidden inside the perimeter of the old walls, was a warren of precipitous alleyways sometimes ending abruptly, at others opening onto squares shaded by plane trees and cooled by fountains. One had the sense of entering an older world whose life was conducted according to different rhythms: cars found the going tougher, indeed few of them had yet mastered the cobbled slopes. Pedestrians took the steep gradients at a leisurely pace, pausing frequently for rest: despite the heat, people came to enjoy the panoramic views across the town and over the bay. Down below were the office blocks and multi-storey apartment buildings of the postwar boom. But here there were few signs of wealth. Abutting the old walls were modest whitewashed homes in brick or wood—often no more than a single small room with a privy attached: a pot of geraniums brightened the window-ledge, a rag rug bleached by the sun served as a door mat, clotheslines were stretched from house to house. Their elderly inhabitants were neatly dressed. Later I realized most had probably lived there since the 1920s, drawn from among the tens of thousands of refugees from Asia Minor who had settled in the city after the exchange of populations with Turkey. Their simple homes contrasted with the elegantly dilapidated villas whose overhanging upper floors and high garden walls still lined many streets; the majority, once grand, had been badly neglected: their gabled roofs had caved in, their shuttered bedrooms lay open to public view, and one caught spectacular glimpses of the city below through yawning gaps in their frontage. By the time I first saw them most had been abandoned for decades, for their Muslim owners had left the city when the refugees had arrived. The cypresses, firs and rosebushes in their gardens were overgrown with ivy and creeping vines, their formerly bright colours had faded into pastel shades of yellow, ochre and cream. Here were vestiges of a past that was absent from the urban landscape of southern Greece—Turkish neighbourhoods that had outlived the departure of their inhabitants; fountains with their dedicatory inscriptions intact; a dervish tomb, now shuttered and locked.

With later visits, I came to see that these traces of the Ottoman past offered a clue to Salonica's central paradox. True, it could point, as

Athens could not, to more than two thousand years of continuous urban life. But this history was decisively marked by sharp discontinuities and breaks. The few Ottoman monuments that had endured were a handful compared with what had once existed. The old houses were falling down and within a decade many of them had collapsed or been demolished. Some buildings have been recently restored and visitors can see inside the magnificent fifteenth-century Bey Hamam, the largest Ottoman baths in Greece, or admire the distinguished mansion now used as a local public library in Plateia Romfei. But otherwise the Ottoman city has vanished, exciting little comment except among preservationists and scholars.

Change is, of course, the essence of urban life and no successful city remains a museum to its own past. The expansion of the docks since the Second World War has obliterated the seaside amusement park—the Beshchinar gardens, or Park of the Princes—where the city's inhabitants refreshed themselves for generations; today it is commemorated only in a nearby ouzeri of the same name. In the deserted sidings of the old station, prewar trams and elderly railway carriages are slowly disintegrating. Even the infamous swampy Bara—once the largest red-light district in eastern Europe—survives only in the fond memories of a few ageing locals, in local belles-lettres, and in its streets—still bearing the old names, Afrodite, Bacchus—which now house nothing more exciting than car rental agencies, garages and tyre-repair shops.

But ridding the city of its brothels is one thing and eradicating the visible traces of five centuries of urban history is quite another. What, I wondered, did it do to a city's consciousness of itself—especially to a city so proud of its past—when substantial sections were at best allowed to crumble away, at worst written out of the record? Had this happened by accident? Could one blame the great fire of 1917 that had destroyed so much of its centre? Or did the forced exchange of populations in 1923—when more than thirty thousand Muslim refugees departed, and nearly one hundred thousand Orthodox Christians took their place—suddenly turn one city into a new one? Was the sense of urban continuity, in other words, which had so powerfully attracted me to Salonica at the outset, an illusion? Perhaps there was another urban history waiting to be written in which the story of continuity would have to be told rather differently, a tale not only of smooth transitions and adaptations, but also of violent endings and new beginnings.

For there was another vanished element of the city's past which I was also beginning to learn about. On the drive into town from the airport, I had caught intriguing glimpses of substantial nineteenth-century villas hidden behind rusting railings and overgrown weeds amid the rows of postwar suburban apartment blocks. The palatial three-storey pile in its own pine-shaded estate, now the main seat of the Prefecture, turned out to have been originally the home of wealthy nineteenth-century Jewish industrialists, the Allatinis; this was where Sultan Abdul Hamid had been kept when he was deposed by the Young Turks and exiled to the city in 1909. Along the same road was the Villa Bianca, an opulently outsize Swiss chalet, home of the wealthy Diaz-Fernandes family. On the drive into town, one passed a dozen or more of these shrines to the eclectic taste of its fin-de-siècle elite—Turkish army officers, Greek and Bulgarian merchants and Jewish industrialists.

Turks and Bulgarians figured prominently in the histories of Greece I had read, usually as ancestral enemies, but the Jews were in general remarkable only for their absence, enjoying little more than a bit-part in the central and all-important story of modern Greece's emergence onto the international stage. In Salonica, however, it would be scarcely an exaggeration to say that they had dominated the life of the city for many centuries. As late as 1912 they were the largest ethnic group and the docks stood silent on the Jewish Sabbath. Jews were wealthy businessmen; but many more were porters and casual labourers, tailors, wandering street vendors, beggars, fishermen and tobacco workers. Today the only traces of their predominance that survive are some names—Kapon, Perahia, Benmayor, Modiano—on faded shopfronts, Hebrew-lettered tombstones piled up in churchyards, an old people's home and the community offices. There is a cemetery, but it is a postwar one, buried in the city's western suburbs.

Here as elsewhere it was the Nazis who brought centuries of Jewish life to an abrupt end. When Kurt Waldheim, the Austrian politician who had served in the city as an army officer, was accused of being involved in the deportations, I came back to Salonica to talk to survivors of Auschwitz, resistance fighters, the lucky ones who had gone underground or managed to flee abroad. A softly spoken lawyer stood with me on the balcony of his office and we looked down onto the rows of parked cars in Plateia Eleftherias (Freedom Square), where he had been rounded up with the other Jewish men of the city for forced labour. Two elderly men, not Jewish, whom I bumped into on Markos Botsaris Street, told me about the day the Jews had been led away in 1943: they were ten at the time, they said, and afterwards, they broke into their homes with their friends and found food still warm on the table. A forty-year-old woman who happened to sit next to me on the

plane back to London had grown up after the war in the quarter immediately above the old Jewish cemetery: she remembered playing in the
wreckage of the graves as a child, with her friends, looking for buried
treasure, shortly before the authorities built the university campus over
the site. Everyone, it seemed, had their story to tell, even though at that
time what had happened to the city's Jews was not something much discussed in scholarly circles.

A little later, in Athens, I came across several dusty unopened sacks
of documents at the Central Board of Jewish Communities. When I
examined them, I found a mass of disordered papers—catalogues,
memoranda, applications and letters. They turned out to be the
archives of the wartime Service for the Disposal of Israelite Property,
set up by the Germans in those few weeks in 1943 when more than
forty-five thousand Jews—one fifth of the city's entire population—
were consigned to Auschwitz. These files showed how the deportations
had affected Salonica itself by triggering off a scramble for property
and possessions that incriminated many wartime officials. I started to
think about deportations in general, and the Holocaust in particular,
not so much in terms of victims and perpetrators, but rather as chapters
in the life of cities. The Jews were killed, almost all of them: but the city
that had been their home grew and prospered.

The accusation that Waldheim had been involved in the Final Solu-
tion—unfounded, as it turned out—reflected the extent to which the
Holocaust was dominating thinking about the Second World War.
Sometimes it seemed from the way people talked and wrote as though
nothing else of any significance had happened in those years. In
Greece, for example, two other areas of criminal activity—the mass
shootings of civilians in anti-partisan retaliations, and the execution of
British soldiers—were far more pertinent to Waldheim's war record.
There were good reasons to deplore this state of cultural obsession. It
quickly made the historian subject to the law of diminishing returns. It
also turned history into a form of voyeurism and allowed outsiders to
sit in easy judgement. I sometimes felt that I myself had become com-
plicit in this—scavenging the city for clues to destruction, ignoring the
living for the dead.

Above all, unremitting focus upon the events of the Second World
War threatened to turn a remarkable chapter in Jewish, European and
Ottoman history into nothing more than a prelude to genocide, over-
shadowing the many centuries when Jews had lived in relative peace,
and both their problems and their prospects had been of a different
kind. In Molho's bookshop, one of the few downtown reminders of ear-

lier times, I found Joseph Nehama's magisterial *Histoire des Israélites de Salonique*, and began to see what an extraordinary story it had been. The arrival of the Iberian Jews after their expulsion from Spain, Salonica's emergence as a renowned centre of rabbinical learning, the disruption caused by the most famous False Messiah of the seventeenth century, Sabbetai Zevi, and the persistent faith of his followers, who followed him even after his conversion to Islam, formed part of a fascinating and little-known history unparalleled in Europe. Enjoying the favour of the sultans, the Jews, as the Ottoman traveller Evliya Chelebi noted, called the city "our Salonica"—a place where, in addition to Turkish, Greek and Bulgarian, most of the inhabitants "know the Jewish tongue because day and night they are in contact with, and conduct business with Jews."

Yet as I supplemented my knowledge of the Greek metropolis with books and articles on its Jewish past, and tried to reconcile what I knew of the home of Saint Dimitrios—"the Orthodox city"—with the Sefardic "Mother of Israel," it seemed to me that these two histories— the Greek and the Jewish—did not so much complement one another as pass each other by. I had noticed how seldom standard Greek accounts of the city referred to the Jews. An official tome from 1962 which had been published to commemorate the fiftieth anniversary of its capture from the Turks contained almost no mention of them at all; the subject had been regarded as taboo by the politicians masterminding the celebrations. This reticence reflected what the author Elias Petropoulos excoriated as "the ideology of the barbarian neo-Greek bourgeoisie," for whom the city "has always been Greek." But at the same time, most Jewish scholars were just as exclusive as their Greek counterparts: their imagined city was as empty of Christians as the other was of Jews.[2]

As for the Muslims, who had ruled Salonica from 1430 to 1912, they were more or less absent from both. Centuries of European antipathy to the Ottomans had left their mark. Their presence on the wrong side of the Dardanelles had for so long been seen as an accident, misfortune or tragedy that in an act of belated historical wishful thinking they had been expunged from the record of European history. Turkish scholars and writers, and professional Ottomanists, had not done much to rectify things. It suited everyone, it seemed, to ignore the fact that there had once existed in this corner of Europe an Ottoman and an Islamic city atop the Greek and Jewish ones.

How striking then it is that memoirs often describe the place very differently from such scholarly or official accounts and depict a society of almost kaleidoscopic interaction. Leon Sciaky's evocative *Farewell to Salonica*, the autobiography of a Jewish boy growing up under Abdul Hamid, begins with the sound of the muezzin's cry at dusk. In Sciaky's city, Albanian householders protected their Bulgarian grocer from the fury of the Ottoman gendarmerie, while well-to-do Muslim parents employed Christian wet-nurses for their children and Greek gardeners for their fruit trees. Outside the Yalman family home the well was used by "the Turks, Greeks, Bulgarians, Jews, Serbs, Vlachs, and Albanians of the neighbourhood." And in Nikos Kokantzis's moving novella *Gioconda*, a Greek teenage boy falls in love with the Jewish girl next door in the midst of the Nazi occupation; at the moment of deportation, her parents trust his with their most precious belongings.[3]

Have scholars, then, simply been blinkered by nationalism and the narrowed sympathies of ethnic politics? If they have the fault is not theirs alone. The basic problem—common to historians and their public alike—has been the attribution of sharply opposing, even contradictory, meanings to the same key events. Both have seen history as a zero-sum game, in which opportunities for some came through the sufferings of others, and one group's loss was another's gain: 1430—when the Byzantine city fell to Sultan Murad II—was a catastrophe for the Christians but a triumph for the Turks. Nearly five centuries later, the Greek victory in 1912 reversed the equation. The Jews, having settled there at the invitation of the Ottoman sultans, identified their interests with those of the empire, something the Greeks found hard to forgive.

It follows that the real challenge is not merely to tell the story of this remarkable place as one of cultural and religious co-existence—in the early twenty-first century such long-forgotten stories are eagerly awaited and sought out—but to see the experiences of Christians, Jews and Muslims within the terms of a single encompassing historical narrative. National histories generally have clearly defined heroes and villains, but what would a history look like where these roles were blurred and confused? Can one shape an account of this city's past which manages to reconcile the continuities in its shape and fabric with the radical discontinuities—the deportations, evictions, forced resettlements and genocide—which it has also experienced? Nearly a century ago, a local historian attempted this: at a time when Salonica's ultimate fate was uncertain, the city struck him as a "museum of idioms, of disparate cultures and religions." Since then what he called its "hybrid spirit" has been severely battered by two world wars and everything they brought with them. I think it is worth trying again.[4]

IN THE 1930s, the spirit of the Sufi holy man Mousa Baba was occasionally seen wandering near his tomb in the upper town. Even today house-owners sometimes dream that beneath their cellars lie Turkish janissaries and Byzantine necropoles. One reads stories of hidden Roman catacombs, doomed love-affairs and the unquiet souls who haunt the decaying villas near the sea. One hears rumours of buried Jewish treasure guarded by spirits which have outwitted the exorcists and proved themselves too strong for Mossad agents, former Nazis and anyone else who has tried to locate the hidden jewels and gold they protect.

But Salonica's ghosts emerge in other ways too, through documents and archives, the letters of Byzantine archbishops, the court records of Ottoman magistrates and the hagiographies of the lives and extraordinary deaths of Christian martyrs. The silencing of the city's multifarious past has not been for lack of sources. Sixteenth-century rabbis adjudicate on long-forgotten marital rows, business wrangles and the tribulations of a noisy, malodorous crowded town. The diary of a Ukrainian political exile depicts unruly Jewish servants drunk in the mud, gluttonous clerics, a whirl of social engagements, riots and plague. Travellers—drawn in ever-increasing numbers by the city's antiquities, by the partridge and rabbits in the plains outside, by business, art or sheer love of adventure—penned their impressions of a magical landscape of minarets, cypresses and whitewashed walls climbing high above the Aegean. From the late nineteenth century—though no earlier—there are newspapers, more and more of them, in half a dozen languages, and even that rarity in the Ottoman lands—maps. As for the archives, they are endless—Ottoman, Venetian, Greek, Austrian, French, English, American—compiled conscientiously by generations of long-departed foreign consuls. Drawing on such materials, I begin with the city's conquest by Sultan Murad II in 1430, delineate its daily life under his successors, and trace its passage from the multi-confessional, extraordinarily polyglot Ottoman world—as late as the First World War, Salonican boot-blacks commanded a working knowledge of six or seven languages—to its role as an ethnically and linguistically homogenised bastion of the twentieth-century nation-state in which by 1950, more than ninety-five per cent of the inhabitants were, by any definition, Greek.

The old empires collapsed and nations fought their way into being, identities changed and people were labelled in new ways: Muslims turned into Turks, Christians into Greeks. Although in Salonica it was the Greeks who eventually got their state, and Bulgarians, Muslims and Jews who in different ways lost out, it is worth remembering that elsewhere Greeks too lost out—in Istanbul, for example, or Trabzon, Alexandria and Izmir, where thousands died during the expulsions of 1922. Cities, after all, are places of both eviction and sanctuary, and many of the Greek refugees who made a new home for themselves in Salonica had been forced from their old ones elsewhere.

Similar transformations occurred in cities across a wide swathe of the globe—in Lviv, for instance, Wroslaw, Vilna and Tiflis, Jerusalem, Jaffa and Lahore. Each of these endured its own moments of trauma caused by the intense violence that has accompanied the emergence of nation-states. Was the function of the Israeli Custodian of Absentee Property after 1948, for example, handing out Arab properties to new Jewish owners, very different from that of the Greek Service for the Disposal of Jewish Property founded in Salonica five years earlier? Both systematized the violence of dispossession and sought to give it a more lasting bureaucratic form. Thanks to their activities, the remnants of former cities may also be traced through the trajectories of the refugees who left them. A retiree clipping her roses in a Sussex country garden, an elderly merchant in an Istanbul suburb and an Auschwitz survivor in Indianapolis are among those who helped me by reviving their memories of a city that is long gone.[5]

By 1950, when this book concludes, Salonica's Muslims had been resettled in Turkey, and the Jews had been deported by the Germans and most of them killed. The Greek civil war had just ended in the triumph of the anti-communist Right, and the city was set for the rapid and entirely unexpected pell-mell postwar expansion which saw its population double and treble within thirty or forty years. A forest of densely packed apartment blocks and giant advertising billboards sprouted where in living memory there had been cypresses and minarets, stables, owls and storks. Its transformation continues, and today Russian computer whiz-kids, Ghanaian doctors, Albanian stonemasons, Georgian labourers, Ukrainian nannies and Chinese street pedlars are entering Salonica's bloodstream. Many of them quickly learn to speak fluent Greek, for the city's position within the modern nation-state is unquestioned: the story of its passage from Ottoman to Greek hands has become ancient history.

PART I

*The Rose
of Sultan Murad*

I

Conquest, 1430

BEGINNINGS

BEFORE THE CITY FELL IN 1430, it had already enjoyed seventeen hundred years of life as a Hellenistic, Roman and Byzantine metropolis. Sometimes it had flourished, at others it was sacked and looted. Foreigners had seized it and moved on. Throughout it remained a city whose inhabitants spoke Greek. But of this Greek past, only traces survived the Ottoman conquest. A few Christian survivors returned and saw their great churches turned into mosques. The Hippodrome, forum and imperial palace fell into ruins which gradually disintegrated and slipped beneath the slowly rising topsoil, leaving an invisible substratum of catacombs, crypts and secret passages. In a very different era, far in the future, archaeologists would assign new values to the statues, columns and sarcophagi they found, and new rulers—after the Ottomans had been defeated in their turn—would use them to reshape and redefine the city once more. One thing, however, always survived as a reminder of its Greek origins, however badly it was battered and butchered by time and strangers, and that was its name.

SALONICCO, SELANIK, Solun? Salonicha or Salonique? There are at least thirteen medieval variants alone; the city is an indexer's nightmare and a linguist's delight. "Is there really a correct pronunciation of Salonika?" wrote an English ex-serviceman in 1941. "At any rate nearly all of us now spell it with a 'k.' " His presumption stirred up a hornet's nest. "Why Saloneeka, when every man in the last war knew it as Salonika?" responded a certain Mr. Pole from Totteridge. "I disagree with W. Pole," wrote Captain Vance from Edgware, Middlesex. "Every man in the last war did *not* know it as Salonika." Mr. Wilks of Newbury tried to calm matters by helpfully pointing out that in 1937 "by Greek royal decree, Salonika reverted to Thessaloniki." In fact it had been officially known by the Greek form since the Ottomans were defeated in 1912.[1]

It is only foreigners who make things difficult for themselves, for the Greek etymology is perfectly straightforward. The daughter of a local ruler, Philip of Macedon, was called Thessaloniki, and the city was named after her: both daughter and city commemorated the triumph (*niki*) of her father over the people of Thessaly as he extended Macedonian power throughout Greece. Later of course, his son, Alexander, conquered much more distant lands which took him to the limits of the known world. There were prehistoric settlements in the area, but the city itself is a creation of the fourth-century BC Macedonian state.

Today the association between the city and the dynasty is as close as it has ever been. If one walks from the White Tower along the wide seafront promenade which winds southeast along the bay, one quickly encounters a huge statue of Megas Alexandros—Alexander the Great. Mounted on horseback, sword in hand, he looks down along the five-lane highway (also named after him) out of town, towards the airport, the beaches and the weekend resorts of the Chalkidiki peninsula. The statue rises heroically above the acrobatic skateboarders skimming around the pedestal, the toddlers, the stray dogs and the partygoers queuing up for the brightly lit floating discos and bars which now circumnavigate the bay by night. It is a magnet for the hundreds who stroll here in the summer evenings, escaping the stuffy backstreets for the refreshment of the sea breeze as the sun dips behind the mountains.

But in 1992, after the collapse of Yugoslavia led the neighbouring republic of Macedonia to declare its independence, Alexander's Greek defenders took to the streets in a very different mood. Flags proliferated in shop-windows, and car stickers and airport banners proclaimed that "Macedonia has been, and will always be, Greek." Greeks and Slavs did battle over the legacy of the Macedonian kings, and Salonica was the centre of the agitation. In the main square, hundreds of thousands of angry protestors were urged on by their Metropolitan, *Panayiotatos* (His Most Holy) Panteleimon (known to some journalists as His Wildness [*Panagriotatos*] for the extremism of his language). The twentieth century was ending as it had begun, with an argument over Macedonia, and names themselves had become a political issue in a way which few outside Greece understood.

The irony was that Alexander himself never knew the city named after his half-sister, for it was founded during the succession struggle precipitated by his death. He had a general called Cassander, who was married to Thessaloniki. Cassander hoped to succeed to the Macedonian throne and having murdered Alexander's mother to get there, he founded a number of cities to re-establish his credentials as a statesman. The one he immodestly named after himself has vanished from the pages of history. But that given his wife's name in 315 BC came to join Alexandria itself in the network of new Mediterranean ports that would link the Greek world with the trading routes to Asia, India and Africa.

As events would prove, Cassander chose his spot well. Built on the slope running down to the sea from the hills in the shadow of Mount Hortiatis, the city gave its inhabitants an easy and comforting sense of orientation: from earliest times, they could see the Gulf before them with Mount Olympos across the bay in the distance, the forested hills and mountains rising behind them, the well-rivered plains stretching away to the west. Less arid than Athens, less hemmed in than Trieste, the new city blended with its surroundings, marking the point where mountains, rivers and sea met. It guarded the most accessible land route from the Mediterranean up into the Balkans and central Europe, down which came Slavs (in the sixth century), and Germans (in 1941) while traders and NATO convoys (on their way into Kosovo in 1999) went in the other direction. Its crucial position between East and West was also later exploited by the Romans, whose seven-hundred-kilometre lifeline between Italy and Anatolia, the Via Egnatia, it straddled.

Poised between Europe and Asia, the Mediterranean and the Balkans, the interface of two climatic zones brings Salonica highly changeable air pressure throughout the year. Driving winter rains and fogs subdue the spirits, and helped inspire a generation of melancholic modernists in the 1930s. The vicious north wind which blows for days down the Vardar valley has done more damage to the city over the centuries than humans ever managed, whipping up fires and turning them into catastrophes. A bad year can also bring heavy falls of snow, even the occasional ice in the Gulf: freezing temperatures in February 1770 left "many poor lying in the streets dead of cold"; in the 1960s, snow-drifts blocked all traffic between the Upper Town and the streets below. Yet the city also enjoys Mediterranean summers—with relatively little wind, little rain and high daytime temperatures, only slightly softened by the afternoon breeze off the bay.[2]

This combination of winter rains and summer sunshine makes for intensive cultivation. Apricots, chestnuts and mulberries grow well here, as do grains, potatoes, cucumbers and melons. Fringed now by the Athens motorway, vegetable gardens still flourish in the alluvial plains—"our California," a farmer once happily told me. "There is excellent shooting in the neighbourhood," noted John Murray's *Handbook* in 1854, "including pheasants, woodcocks, wildfowl etc." Cutting wide loops through the fields the Vardar river to the west runs low in summer, sinuous and fast in the winter months, too powerful to be easily navigable, debouching finally into the miles of thick reedy insect-plagued marshes which line its mouth. All swamp and water, the Vardar plain in December reminded John Morritt at the end of the eighteenth century of nothing so much as "the dear country from Cambridge to Ely." For hundreds of years it emanated "putrid fevers," noxious exhalations and agues which drove horses mad, and manifested themselves—before the age of pesticide—in the "sallow cheeks and bloodless lips" of the city's inhabitants.[3]

"From water comes everything" runs the inscription on an Ottoman fountain still preserved in the Upper Town. Fed by rivers and rains and moisture rising from the bay, water bathes the city and its surroundings in a hazy light quite different from that of parched Attica, softer, stranger and less harsh, shading the western mountains in grey, brown and violet. After days of cloudy and stormy weather, the Reverend Henry Fanshawe Tozer realized "what I had never felt before—the pleasure of pale colours." Artesian wells are dug easily down to the water table which sits just below the surface of the earth, and there are plentiful springs in the nearby hills. Winter rains have etched beds deep into the soil on either side of the town, torrents so quick to flood that well into the nineteenth century they would carry away a horse and rider, or sluice out the poorly buried bones of the dead in the cemeteries beyond the walls.[4]

From earliest times, too, fresh water has been channelled through fountains, aqueducts and underground pipes, attracting the rich and the holy, plane trees, acacias and monasteries, wherever it bubbles to the surface. Archaeologists have traced the remains of the Roman, Byzantine and Ottoman mills which dotted the water-courses leading down into the city's reservoirs. Until the 1930s, villagers on nearby Mount Hortiatis produced ice from water-bearing rocks in the thickly forested slopes above the town, kept it in small pits cut into the hillside and brought it down by donkey into the city each summer. With nearby salteries vital for preserving cod and meat, abundant fish in the bay, partridge, hare, rabbits and tortoises in the nearby plain, and oaks, beech and maple in the hills above, it is not surprising that the city flourished.

ROMANS

A HELLENISTIC DYNASTY gave Salonica birth but it was under the Romans that it prospered. Shrines to Macedonian and Roman rulers intermingled with temples to Egyptian gods, sphinxes and the city's own special tutelary deities, the mysterious Samothracian Kabirii. They were probably worshipped in the Rotonda, the oldest building still in use in the city, whose holy space has since attracted saints, dervishes and devotees of modern art and jazz. Even before the birth of Christ Salonica was a provincial capital with substantial municipal privileges. Later it became the base of Emperor Galerius himself. By the side of the main road running through town the carved pillars of a massive triumphal arch still commemorate Galerius's defeat of the troublesome Persians. His own urban ambitions, influenced by Syrian and Persian models, were extensive. Today students sun themselves on the walkways above where his now vanished portico once connected the triumphal arch with an enormous palace and hippodrome. Meanwhile, in what is still the commercial heart of the city, archaeologists have uncovered a vast forum, a tribute to Greco-Roman consumerism, with a double colonnade of shops, a square paved in marble, a library and a large brothel, complete with sex toys, private baths and dining-rooms for favoured clients.

This was, in short, a flourishing settlement of key strategic significance for Roman power in the East. We may find it puzzling that Greeks even today will call themselves *Romioi* (Romans). But there is nothing strange about it. The Roman empire existed here too, among the speakers of Greek, and continued to exert its spell long after it had collapsed in the West. Yet we need to be careful, for when Greeks use the term *Romios*, they do not exactly mean that they are "Roman." Hiding inside the word is the one ingredient which has shaped the city's complex cultural mix more strongly than any other—the Christian faith. The Ottomans understood the term this way as well: when they talked about the "community of Romans" (*Rum millet*) they meant Orthodox Christians, not necessarily Greeks; *Rum* was Byzantine Anatolia; *Rumeli* the Orthodox Christian Balkans. Until the age of ethnic nationalism, to be "Greek" was, for most people in the Ottoman world, synonymous with belief in the Orthodox Christian faith.

With this Christianization of the Roman Greek world few cities are as closely identified as Salonica. In the days when the Apostle Paul passed through, Christians were merely a deviant Jewish sect, and members of the two faiths were buried side by side. By the late fourth century, however, Christianity had triumphed on its own terms and turned itself into a new religion: the Rotonda had been converted from pagan use, and chapels, shrines and Christian graveyards were spreading with astonishing speed across the city.

The figure who came to symbolize Christ's triumph in Salonica, eventually outshining even the Apostle himself, was a Roman officer called Dimitrios who was martyred in the late third century AD. A small shrine to him was built alongside the many other healing shrines which studded the area around the forum. After a grateful Roman prefect was cured by his miraculous powers, he built a five-aisled basilica to the saint, which quickly became the centre of a major cult, attracting Jews as well as Christians and pagans. The adoration of Dimitrios swept the city, and by the early nineteenth century—the first time we have a name-by-name census of its inhabitants—one in ten Christians there were named after him.[5]

Like the other major early Christian shrines—the massive, low-sunk Panayia Acheiropoietos (the Virgin's Church Unmade by Mortal Hands), the grand Ayia Sofia and the Rotonda itself—Dimitrios's church shows how deeply the city's Greco-Roman culture had been impregnated with Christian rituals and doctrines. Although the fire of 1917 caused irreparable damage to the priceless mosaics that line its colonnades, enough has remained following its restoration to illuminate the imperial-Christian synthesis: the saint is shown heralded by toga-clad angelic trumpeters, receiving children, or casting his arms around the shoulders of the church's founders. Another saint, Sergios, is depicted in a purple chiton with military insignia around his neck. The city's devoted inhabitants are Christians, but they are also recognisably Romans. Incorporated into the church's structure is part of the original baths, the place of the saint's martyrdom, which became a site of pilgrimage in the following centuries. And crowning the pillars which line the nave are marble capitals whose writhing volutes and acanthus leaves, doves, rams and eagles, sometimes taken from earlier buildings, sometimes carved specially for the church, cover the entire range of Roman design in the centuries when Christianity began to take hold of the empire. Byzantium is the name we have given to a civilization which regarded itself, and was regarded by those around it, as the heir to the glories of imperial Rome. Its character was defined by its cultural synthesis of the traditions of Greece, Rome and Christianity, and Salonica was one of its bastions.

INVADERS

"GUARDED BY GOD, greatly surpassing every city in Thrace and in all of Illyricum as to variety of wealth," the city was superbly protected by its towering walls, by its fortress perched commandingly above the bay and even by the spit of land which guarded the entrance to the gulf itself. It needed all the divine protection it could get, however, for through the centuries its riches and location seemed to attract one invader after another. In the sea raid of 904 an assault by Sudanese, Arab and Egyptian soldiers, led by Byzantine converts to Islam, left the city strewn with corpses and thousands of its inhabitants were sold into slavery. But that remained an isolated event, for Macedonia was far from the centre of the long-running Byzantine-Arab land war, and in eastern Europe—unlike in Syria and Anatolia—the men of Christ had several hundred more years to proselytize before confronting a serious rival in Islam.

Infinitely more important in the long run than the booty-hunters were the nomadic tribes who found Salonica on their path as they migrated from the central Asian steppes to the verdant lands of Europe. Some passed through before veering off to the north and settling elsewhere. But starting in the mid-sixth century, Byzantine military experts became aware of a new threat—the Slavs. According to the contemptuous court historian, Procopius, they lived in miserable huts, were often on the move, and went to war mostly on foot and armed only with small shields and javelins.[6] Yet despite their poverty and their crude weaponry the Slavs had numbers on their side, and quickly became a serious threat to Byzantine rule. In the late sixth century, they reached the walls of Salonica for the first time, and a huge army gathered on the plains outside the walls.[7] Only Saint Dimitrios saved the day: thanks to his inspiration, the defenders suspended curtains below the ramparts to blunt the shock of the missiles hitting the walls, while armed sorties frightened the attackers into retreat. Again and again the Slavs laid siege to the city; each time, Saint Dimitrios, it was said, kept them at bay in a series of miracles which were collected, written down, and re-told over centuries.

The Slav tribes did not disappear. They settled as farmers and traders in villages across Greece and down into the Peloponnese, and the fundamental ethnographic balance between Salonica and its hinter-land over the next fourteen hundred years was henceforth established: a predominantly Slavic peasantry cultivated the soil and was kept under the political and economic control of non-Slav elites based in the city.[8] But frontiers are places of interaction, and few frontiers were more per-meable or symbiotic than that between the Slavs and the Greeks. The former trickled into Salonica, drawn by the seductive power of a Hel-lenic education and the upward mobility this bought. Only nineteenth-century romantic nationalism turned the porous boundaries between Slav and Greek into rigidly patrolled national cages.

Moreover, the city did not only take in the Slavs, but it reached out to them too, and converted them, through the Church, into members of its own civilization. It was two brothers from Salonica, Constantine (better known to posterity by his later name, Kyrill) and Methodius, themselves possibly of Slavic descent, who drew up a new alphabet, adapted from Greek, translated the Christian liturgy into Slavic and spread Christ's message across eastern Europe. The extent of their suc-cess was matched only by that with which others were spreading the word of Mohammed in the Middle East. The seeds of their mission were planted in Dalmatia, Hungary, Moravia and Poland; by the end of the ninth century the pagan Bulgars too had been converted. As a result, a version of the Cyrillic alphabet first devised by these two sons of a Byzantine officer from Salonica is taught today in schools from the Adriatic to Siberia.

THE COMING OF THE OTTOMANS

OVER THE NEXT six hundred years, the city became a centre of humanistic learning and theological debate. Many new churches were established, turning it into a treasure-house of late Byzantine art. Monasticism spread to the Balkans from Egypt and Syria, and the great foundations of Mount Athos attracted pilgrims, scholars and benefac-tors to the city as they made the journey to the Holy Mountain just to its east.

Yet amid this cultural ferment, the Byzantine emperors were staggering from crisis to crisis. Ambitious Bulgarian and Serb rulers were—despite their shared Christianity—more of a threat than they were allies. In 1185 Salonica was pillaged by Norman invaders. In 1204 Catholic crusaders—*Franks*, as they were contemptuously known in the Orthodox world—sacked Constantinople itself and carved up its possessions. To the east, Byzantine power was largely spent. Turkish tribes had moved in from central Asia, and the rise and fall of the Seljuk sultans turned Anatolia into a battleground between competing emirates. That the empire survived at all was owing to the weakness of its enemies, and the judicious bribery of foreign allies.

In the early fourteenth century, however, as Catalan mercenaries, Genoese, Venetians, Serbs and others fought for mastery in the eastern Mediterranean, an entirely new power began the remarkable ascent which would turn it within two hundred years into the greatest force in the world. Osman Ghazi, the founder of the Ottoman dynasty, initially ruled a small emirate on the frontier with Byzantine territory in Anatolia. To his east lay more powerful Muslim emirs, and behind them the mightiest state of all, that of the Mongol khans. By comparison, fighting the fading Greeks was easy. In 1302 Osman defeated a mercenary army sent out by the emperor and by the time of his death in 1326 he had established his capital in the former Byzantine city of Bursa. Feuding between the Byzantine Palaeologues and Cantacuzenes gave his successors their chance in Europe. In 1354 his son Orhan won a foothold at Gallipoli and less than twenty years later the Byzantine emperor Jean V Palaeologue made his submission to his successor Murad I. By the end of the century, Murad's successor Bayazid I—the Thunderbolt—was styling himself Sultan.

Thanks to the distortive effects of both sixteenth-century Ottoman ideology (when the empire's rulers were keen to demonstrate the purity of their Sunni credentials, following the conquest of the Arab provinces) and nineteenth-century Balkan nationalism, the character of the early Ottoman state remains poorly understood. The Ottomans were Muslims, but their empire was built as much in Europe as it was in Asia. In fact before the sixteenth century they probably ruled over more Christians than they did Muslims. Their form of Islam was a kind of border religion spread both by warriors dedicated to Holy War and through religious fraternities which took over Christian shrines, espousing a surprisingly open attitude to Christianity itself. They were in many ways heirs to central Asian Turkic versions of Islam, like that embraced by the Grand Khan Mongha, for whom the religions of his empire "are like the five fingers of the same hand." They followed the Hanafi school of Sunni law, the most tolerant and flexible in relation to non-Muslims, their rulers married Serbian and Greek princesses—which meant that many Ottoman sultans had Christian mothers—and their key advisers and generals were often converts recruited from Byzantine service.[9]

One historian has recently argued that before the fifteenth century, the empire was actually what he terms a "raiding confederacy," in which the Ottomans joined with several other great families in the search for land and plunder. Ghazi (frontier warrior) Evrenos Bey, the leader of the most feared squad of raiders, was a former Byzantine military commander who converted to Islam. Evrenos acted in a way which suggested he was virtually a junior partner with the Ottoman emirs, and when he spearheaded the Ottoman assault on northern Greece the value of his support was recognized by them with huge grants of land. The fiefdoms his family won in the vicinity of Salonica made them among the largest land-owners in the empire and a dominant force in the city well into the twentieth century. His descendants included Ottoman pashas and Young Turks, and his magnificent tomb was a place of pilgrimage for Christians and Muslims alike.[10]

The Turks' attitude to religion came as a pleasant relief to many Orthodox Christians. Held captive by the Ottomans in 1355, the distinguished archbishop of Salonica, Gregory Palamas, was surprised to find the Orthodox Church recognized and even flourishing in the lands under the emir. Prominent Turks were eager to discuss the relationship of the two faiths with him and the emir organized a debate between him and Christian converts to Islam. "We believe in your prophet, why don't you believe in ours?" Muslims asked him more than once. Palamas himself observed an imam conducting a funeral and later took the opportunity to joust over theology with him. When the discussion threatened to overheat, Palamas calmed it down by saying politely: "Had we been able to agree in debate we might as well have been of one faith." To which he received the revealing reply: "There will be a time when we shall all agree."[11]

As Byzantine power waned, more and more Orthodox Christians felt caught between two masters. Faced with an apparent choice between the reviled Catholics (their sack of Constantinople in 1204 never to be forgotten) and the Muslim Turks, many opted for the latter. Written off as an embarrassment by later Greek commentators, the pro-Turkish current in late Byzantine politics was in fact a powerful one for the Ottomans, who could be seen as protectors of Orthodoxy against the Catholics. The hope for political stability, the desire for wealth and status in a meritocratic and open ruling system, admiration for the governing capacities of the Ottomans, and their evident willingness to make use of Christians as well as Muslims explain why administrators, nobles, peasants and monks felt the allure of the sultans and why many senior Byzantine noble families entered their service. Murad II's grand viziers were well known for their pro-Christian sympathies; Murad himself was influenced by dervish orders which preached a similarly open-minded stance, and the family *sheykh* of the Evrenos family was reputed to be a protector of Christians. In the circumstances, it is not surprising why surrender seemed far more sensible an option than futile resistance against overwhelming odds, and why the inhabitants of Salonica themselves were known, according to at least one Byzantine chronicler, as "friends of the Sultan."[12]

In the second half of the fourteenth century, one Balkan town after another yielded to the fast-moving Ottoman armies; the Via Egnatia fell into their hands, and even the canny monks of Mount Athos submitted. Salonica itself was blockaded for the first time in 1383, and in April 1387, surrendered without a fight. On this occasion, all that happened was that a small Turkish garrison manned the Acropolis. The town's ruler Manuel Palaeologue had wanted to resist, but he was shouted down by the inhabitants, and forced to leave the city so that they could hand themselves over. Manuel himself paid homage to the emir Murad, and even fought for his new sovereign before being crowned emperor.

Had the city remained uninterruptedly under Ottoman control from this point on, its subsequent history would have been very different, and the continuity with Byzantine life not so decisively broken. Having given in peacefully, Salonica was not greatly altered by the change of regime, its municipal privileges were respected by the new rulers and its wealthy monastic foundations weathered the storm. The small Turkish garrison converted a church into a mosque for their own use, and the *devshirme* child levy was imposed—at intervals Turkish soldiers carried off Christian children to be brought up as Muslims—which must have caused distress. But returning in 1393, Archbishop Isidoros described the situation as better than he had anticipated, while the Russian monk Ignatius of Smolensk who visited in 1401 was still amazed by its "wondrous" monasteries. Christians asked the Sultan to intervene in ecclesiastical disputes, bishops relied on the Turks to confirm them in office, and one "said openly to anyone who asked that he had the Turks for patriarchs, emperors and protectors."[13]

Unfortunately for Salonica, the Byzantine emperor Manuel could not resist taking advantage of the Ottomans' own difficulties to try to wrest the city back for himself. For in 1402, the Ottoman army suffered the most crushing defeat of its entire history at the hands of the Mongol khan Tamurlane. Sultan Bayazid died in captivity and his defeat led directly to a vicious Ottoman civil war which lasted nearly twenty years. Exploiting the dynasty's moment of weakness, Manuel got one of the claimants, Suleyman, to marry his daughter, and to agree at the same time to return Salonica to Byzantine rule. Local *ghazis* like Evrenos Bey were not pleased, but apart from delaying the withdrawal of the Ottoman garrison they could do nothing. But in 1421 a new ruler, the youthful Murad II, fought his way to the throne, and determined to put an end to the confusion and internecine bloodletting which had divided the empire.

THE SIEGE

IN 1430 Sultan Murad II was "a little, short, thick man, with the physiognomy of a Tartar—a broad and brown face, high cheek bones, a round beard, a great and crooked nose, with little eyes." Only twenty-six, he had already established his place in history by restoring the authority of the Osmanlis after the defeat by the Mongols. Hard-living, hard-drinking and a keen hunter, he enjoyed the affection of his soldiers and the respect of diplomats and statesmen who encountered him. He was a brilliant warrior, who spent much of his reign building up Ottoman power in the Balkans and Anatolia, but he preferred a life of spiritual contemplation, tried twice to withdraw from the throne, and was eventually buried in the mausoleum he had designed himself at Bursa, a building of austere beauty, with an earth-covered grave open to the skies. The much-travelled Spaniard, Pero Tafur, described him as "a discreet person, grave in his looks, and . . . so handsomely attended that I never saw the like."[14]

According to an Ottoman legend, the sultan was asleep in his palace one night when God came to him in a dream and gave him a beautiful, sweet-smelling rose to sniff. When Murad asked if he could keep it, God told him that the rose was Salonica and that he had decreed it should be his.

In fact Murad had set his heart on the city from the start. So far as he was concerned, it was not only a vital Mediterranean port, but belonged to him by right since it had already submitted to Ottoman rule. After 1422 his troops besieged it, and with the hinterland also under his control, there was little the Byzantine emperors could do. The empire itself was dying. The city's inhabitants invited the Venetians in, thinking they at least would bolster the defences, but the situation went from bad to worse. By 1429 urban life had virtually collapsed, three-quarters of the inhabitants had already fled—many into Ottoman-controlled territories—and only ten thousand remained. Despite occasional Venetian grain convoys, food was scarce. Some defenders let themselves down by ropes to join the Turks. Others passed messages saying they wished to surrender: the pro-Ottoman faction within the walls was as powerful as it had ever been, its numbers swelled by Murad's promises of good treatment if the city gave in.

To the aged Archbishop Symeon, the defeatism of his flock came as a shock. "They actually declared they were bent on handing over the city to the infidel," he wrote. "Now that for me was something more difficult to stomach than ten thousand deaths." But angry crowds demonstrated against him. When he invoked the miraculous powers of their patron Saint Dimitrios, and talked about a giant warrior on horseback coming to their aid, they heard nothing but empty promises. God had preserved the city over the centuries, he told them, "as an acropolis and guardian of the surrounding countryside." But the Turks were outside the walls, and the villages and towns beyond were in their hands. Their mastery of the hinterland had turned the fortified city into a giant prison. Resistance meant certain enslavement. In 1429 Archbishop Symeon died, but the Venetians brought in mercenaries to prevent the defenders capitulating and the siege dragged on until in March 1430 Murad determined to end it. He left his hunting leopards, falcons and goshawks and joined his army before the city.

Combining levies from Europe and Anatolia, his troops gathered outside the walls, while camel-trains brought up siege engines, stone-throwers, bombards and scaling ladders. The sultan took up a position on high ground which overlooked the citadel, and sent a last group of Christian messengers to urge surrender. These got no more favourable a response than before. Prompted by the sight of a Venetian vessel sailing into the Gulf, and fearing the garrison was about to be reinforced, Murad ordered the attack to begin.

For two or three days the desperate defenders managed to hold out against the assault troops and sappers. But then Murad galvanized his men. "I will give you whatever the city possesses," he pledged them. "Men, women, children, silver and gold: only the city itself you will leave to me." At dawn on 29 March, a hail of arrows "like snow" forced the defenders back from the parapets. Crowds of *ghazi* fighters, spurred on by the sultan's words, attacked the walls "like wild animals." Within a few hours, one had scaled the blind side of the Trigonion tower, cut off the head of a wounded Venetian soldier and tossed it down. His fellow *ghazis* quickly followed him up and threw open the main gates.

The Venetian contingent fought their way to the port and boarded the waiting galleys. Behind them the victorious Turks—"shouting and thirsting for our blood" according to the survivor Ioannis Anagnostes—ransacked churches, homes and public buildings, looking for hidden valuables behind icons and inside tombs: "They gathered up men, women, children, people of all ages, bound like animals, and marched them all to the camp outside the city. Nor do I speak of those who fell and were not counted in the fortress and in the alleyways and did not merit a burial," continues Anagnostes. "Every soldier, with the mass of captives he had taken, hurried to get them outside quickly to hand them over to his comrades, lest someone stronger seize them from him, so that any slave who as he saw from old age or some illness perhaps could not keep up with the others, he cut his head off on the spot and reckoned it a loss. Then for the first time they separated parents from their children, wives from their husbands, friends and relatives from each other . . . And the city itself was filled with wailing and despair."[15]

As ever, Murad followed the customary laws of war. By refusing to surrender peacefully, after they had been given the chance, Salonica's inhabitants had—as they knew well—laid themselves open to enslavement and plunder. Had they been allowed to follow the path of non-resistance that most of them wanted, the city's fate might have been less traumatic. A few months later, Ottoman troops went on to besiege the city of Jannina, and their commander, Sinan Pasha, advised the Greek archbishop to surrender peacefully "otherwise I will destroy the place to its foundations as I did in Salonica." "I swear to you on the God of Heaven and Earth and the Prophet Mohammed," he went on, "not to have any fear, neither of being enslaved nor seized." The clergy and the nobility would keep their estates and privileges, "rather than as we did in Salonica ruining the churches, and emptying and destroying everything." Jannina obeyed and remained an important centre of Hellenic learning throughout the Ottoman period: indeed one of Murad's generals actually founded a Christian monastery there. Salonica's fate was very different: ruined and eerily quiet, its streets and buildings lay empty.[16] In the Acheiropoietos church the sultan held a victory thanksgiving service. Then he had the building turned into a mosque, and ordered a laconic inscription to be chiselled into a marble column in the north colonnade of the nave. There it survives to this day, and if your eyesight is good enough, you can still make out in the elegant Arabic script: "Sultan Murad Khan took Thessaloniki in the year 833 [=1430]."

2

Mosques and Hamams

THE MIGHTIEST WAR

CENTRES OF TRADE, learning, religious piety and administrative control, cities were essential for the prosperity of the Ottoman lands. Yet as the sultans knew, it is one thing to conquer a city, another to restore it to life. In 1453, Mehmed the Conqueror called the task of reviving Constantinople after its conquest the "mightiest war" compared with which the business of taking it had been merely one of the "lesser wars." Twenty years earlier his father, Murad, had viewed Salonica in a similar light. The man who for all his military genius was reputed "not to love war" now pondered how to return it to its former glory. No other city in his domain matched its imposing fortifications or its commercial possibilities. It was the key to the Balkans, and the Balkans were fast on their way to becoming the economic powerhouse of his empire. According to Anagnostes: "When he saw a city so large, and in such a situation, next to the sea and suitable for everything, then he grieved and wanted to reconstruct it."[1]

The first thing he did was to chase out the looters, camp-followers and squatters. "The money and slaves which you gained should be enough," he told his troops, "I want to have the city itself and for this I made many days' march and tired myself, as you know." He began by repairing the damaged walls and ordered the new garrison commander to modernize the fortress. Less than one year later, an inscription above the entrance to the newly built main tower marked the swift completion of his work. "This Acropolis," it runs, "was conquered and captured by force, from the hands of infidels and Franks, with the help of God, by Sultan Murad, son of Sultan Mehmed, whose banner God does not cease to make victorious. And he slaughtered and took prisoner some of their sons, and took their property."[2]

Murad's initial thought was "to return the city to its inhabitants and to restore it just as it had been before." Anagnostes tells us that he would have even liberated all the captives had not one of his senior commanders prevented him. As it was, he personally ransomed members of some of the city's notable Byzantine families (as was his custom after a siege), and his vassal, the Serbian despot George Brankovich—whose daughter Mara he married a few years later—paid for others. In all, about a thousand Greek ex-prisoners were thus rescued from slavery and returned to their homes. They were joined by refugees who had fled the siege earlier and were now ordered back. Shocked by the scenes of devastation that greeted them, they blamed Archbishop Symeon for having blocked a peaceful outcome to the siege, and some even questioned the powers of Saint Dimitrios himself. Gradually, the Byzantine *caravanseray*, public baths, old manufactories, tanneries and textile workshops were brought back to life. The Venetians patched up their relations with the sultan and were allowed to set up a consulate one year after the conquest. But the city was a shadow of its former self, a mere vestige of the flourishing metropolis of forty thousand inhabitants which had existed a decade earlier.

In fact, once Murad realized the extent of its depopulation, he changed his mind and decided to bring in Muslim settlers as well. He handed over many properties to senior officials at his court, and craftsmen, attracted by tax breaks, were resettled from the nearby town of Yannitsa and from Anatolia. Their arrival injected new blood into the urban economy. But it was a major blow to the city's Christian identity and the Greek survivors were shocked. Salonica, wrote Anagnostes, "wore this ugliness like a mourning garment . . . The hymns to God and the choirs have fallen silent. In their place one hears nothing but *alalagmoi* [the sounds of Allah] and the noise of the godless who make Satan rejoice. And yet no sign of divine anger has appeared to punish the unbelievers who defiled the churches, made families and houses vanish, looted and destroyed churches and the city."[3]

Thousands of the city's former inhabitants were still enslaved. "On numerous occasions we saw Christians—boys as well as unmarried girls, and masses of married women of every description—paraded pitiably by the Turks in long lines throughout the cities of Thrace and Macedonia," wrote the Italian merchant-antiquarian Cyriac of Ancona. They were "bound by iron chains and lashed by whips, and in the end put up for sale in villages and markets . . . an unspeakably shameful and obscene sight, like a cattle market." (Cyriac's sorrow did not prevent him buying a young Greek slave and sending her home to his mother's household.) Some converted to Islam in the hope of better treatment; others, yoked to one another by the neck, could be seen begging for alms in the streets of the capital, Edirne, where they were brought to be sold off, or entered the imperial service.[4]

Yet the Sultan certainly did not intend to wipe out Christianity from the city. It was not only that this would have been economically harmful; it would also have been contrary to Ottoman practice and his own beliefs. In fact, he quickly appointed a new archbishop, Gregorios, and his Serbian Orthodox wife, Mara, herself became a notable benefactress. Churches and monasteries were reconfirmed in their possessions (in one case perhaps, as a malicious fifteenth-century chronicler alleged, because the monks had helped the Turks conquer the town). In keeping with the Muslim custom in cases where towns had been won by force, a few churches were converted into mosques, looted for building materials, turned into private homes or abandoned. But how many were taken over at the start is hard to say. Anagnostes claims that only four remained in Christian hands: yet even after Murad began to bring in Muslims in 1432 many ecclesiastical foundations continued to collect substantial revenues from their estates. After all, there was no point converting churches into mosques if there were not the congregations to use them: the wave of conversion thus followed the slow expansion of the Muslim population. Of the city's noblest buildings, Ayios Dimitrios was converted into a mosque only in 1491, Ayia Sofia and the Rotonda a century later.[5]

The real problem for the Christian survivors was not so much the expropriation of places of worship—for scores of them had lain within the walls before the conquest, and enough survived even after 1430 to serve the city's sharply reduced population—as the lack of priests to run them. Many had fled or were still enslaved. Laymen were still having to chant the hymns in the church of Ayia Paraskevi twenty years after the conquest since, as one local Christian sadly noted, "the majority of the clergy and of the others were then still in captivity and this condition prevails up to today." Orthodoxy—though recognized by the Ottoman authorities—was scarcely flourishing. "One can hear only from the more elderly people," wrote Anagnostes after his return from captivity, "that such and such a church was here, another one was there, and what the beauty and charms of each had been."[6]

As it spread into Europe, Ottoman conquest brought the Islamiciza-
tion of urban life. The centre of gravity of Balkan Christianity shifted
into the rural areas where monasteries, especially in Mount Athos,
prospered. The cities were more deeply altered. With the newcomers
came their faith, their places of worship and characteristic institutions
of their way of life. A few Christians converted to Islam, both before
and after the conquest, but it was chiefly through the settlers from Anatolia that Salonica was transformed—in the words of the chronicler
Ashikpashazadé—from a "domain of idolatry" to a "domain of Islam."
The sounds of Christian worship—the bells, processionals and Easter
fireworks—were replaced by the cry of the muezzin, the triumphant
processions which celebrated a new conversion, and (later) the firing of
guns at Bairam. At Ramadan, the bustle of the markets subsided, and
even non-Muslims avoided eating in public, and waited for the sound of
the fortress cannon at dusk to mark the onset of the nightly street
feasts, parties and Karaghöz shadow puppet shows whose obscenity
shocked later travellers. Minarets—spiralling, pointed, multi-coloured
or unadorned—dominated the skyline and became landmarks for visitors, lit up during holidays and imperial celebrations. In 1853 the
Oxford geographer Henry Tozer saw them each "circled by a ring of
glittering lamps"; as he sailed away by night "they formed a delicate
bright cluster, like a swarm of fire-flies on the horizon."[7]

Murad's use of the Ottoman colonization technique of forced resettlement worked: the settlers kick-started Salonica's economy and more
than doubled its population within a few years. The first extant
Ottoman records, from 1478, show that unlike the Christian population, who were almost entirely descended from pre-conquest families,
the Muslims were new arrivals. They were grouped in communities,
each with their own place of worship. With a total of twenty-six imams,
they had one religious leader for each 166 Muslims, compared with
an average of one priest to every 667 Christians. Islam, newly established though it was, was thus far better served than Orthodoxy. If
the urban grid—the course of the walls, the main roads, the location
of markets—remained recognizably Greco-Roman, the demands of
Ottoman power and the Islamic faith were nevertheless changing Salonica's physiognomy.[8]

An imperial decree of 14 December 1479 appointing a teacher to a
city *medrese* informs us about the spread of Muslim learning there. The
appointee, *mevlana* Qivam ed-Din, was granted a salary of 20 aspers
daily and instructed to pray "for the continuity of the State." He was to

teach "sciences related to religion, to resolve the difficulties of the branches of religious law, the subtleties of the tradition and the truths of the exegesis of the Quran." He was not only to give lessons to students, but also to look after their welfare and ensure they were properly fed "so that religion finds its glory and learning its splendour and the position of *ulema* attains the highest degree."[9]

Despite the existence of this and other schools, however, Salonica never became a major centre of Muslim piety or learning. It seems to have lacked sufficiently illustrious historical, religious or emotional associations. Its *medresas* remained relatively small and undistinguished, its mosques never rivalled the soaring masterpieces of Edirne, Bursa and Istanbul—the three imperial capitals—and its *mufti* (chief religious adviser) was ranked only in the fourth class of the hierarchy, below his colleagues in the empire's eight leading cities. Was it the vast nearby estates of the Evrenos family which reminded the Ottoman sultans uncomfortably of their early years in partnership, and led them to bestow their favour and money elsewhere? Its Balkan location probably did not help either, since Muslims there felt the presence of an alien Christian hinterland even when they controlled the towns. Mehmed the Conqueror had to remind the Muslims of Rumeli to pray five times a day—an indication that the climate of observance in the Balkans was rather different from that in Anatolia. But elsewhere in the Balkans, the towns themselves at least were emphatically Muslim—90% of Larissa's population by 1530, for instance, 61% in Serres, 75% in Monastir and Skopje, 66% in Sofia. In Salonica, on the other hand, Muslims never dominated the city numerically, and slipped from just under 50% to 25% of the population between the mid-fifteenth century and 1530. At the time of the first census of modern times—in 1831—Salonica had the smallest Muslim population of any major Ottoman city. Yet to outsiders, its Islamic character was immediately evident. The city acquired a *sheykh* of the ruling Hanafi school of Islamic law, who acted as the chief *mufti* of the town, and, after the empire expanded into the Arab lands in the sixteenth century, jurists from the other three main schools as well. There were soon more mosques than there were churches, and *tekkes* (monasteries) were eventually established by the main mystical Sufi orders, nearly one for every neighbourhood. To the seventeenth-century geographer Hadji Chalfa, the city was "a little piece of Istanbul."[10]

MOSQUES AND *VAKFS*

IN MODERN SALONICA, where classical and Byzantine monuments have been shorn of the houses that surrounded them to make them stand out more prominently, one has to search for remains of the early Ottoman years. Most mosques perished in the great fire of 1917 and the surviving minarets were torn down shortly afterwards. Nevertheless, at the busy central junction of Egnatia and Venizelos streets, small shops, a disused cinema, and tourist boutiques still cling to the sides of an elegantly domed mosque, one of the last in the city. Hamza Bey was one of Murad's military commanders, and his daughter built a small neighbourhood prayer hall in his memory in 1468. As the city expanded and prospered, Hamza Bey's mosque grew too: it acquired a minaret (now gone) and a spacious columned courtyard.[11]

One other fifteenth-century mosque survives, similarly impressive in scale, though in better condition. This is the Aladja Imaret, which peeps out of a gap between rows of concrete apartment blocks above the bus stop on Kassandrou Street. The Aladja complex served as school, prayer-hall and soup-kitchen for the poor and illustrates the way older Muslim architectural forms were reworked by Ottoman builders in territories which lacked any tradition of Islamic architecture. In the original Arabic-Persian type of *medrese*, or religious school, students and teachers took their lessons in rooms arranged around an open-air courtyard. The Seljuk Turks adapted this model for the harsher conditions of central Anatolia by covering the courtyard with a dome, often adding a small prayer room at the back. Over time, the domed prayer-hall became larger still and was integrated into the main body of the building—the shape chosen by the unknown architect of the Aladja Imaret. A large airy portico runs the length of the façade, and once sheltered refugees and beggars, though it is now abandoned and covered with graffiti. The multi-coloured minaret, ornamented with stones in a diamond pattern, which gave the whole building its name (*Aladja* = coloured) has long gone, though visitors to the nearby town of Verroia will find a very similar one, half-ruined, in a side-street off the main road. This style of minaret was a last faint Balkan echo of the polychromatic glories of central Asian and Persian Islam, whose influence, as the historian Machiel Kiel points out, extended from the towns of Macedonia in the west to the north Indian plains and the Silk Road to the east.[12]

Fifteenth-century records identify other newly founded mosques by the names of local notables—Sinan Bey, the fisheries owner Mehmed, the teacher Burhan, Mustafa from Karaferiye, the pilgrims Mehmed, Hasan, Ismail, Kemal, Ahmed and the judge Abdullah. Their neighbourhood mosques or *mescids* must have been relatively humble sites, and the main Friday services for the city were held in "Old Friday"— the name given to the mosque founded by Sultan Murad in the Acheiropoietos Church where he had held his victory service. More substantial foundations, like the Aladja Imaret, usually required the kind of financing affordable only by notables. In this case the benefactor was another of Murad's commanders, Inegöllü Ishak Pasha, whose illustrious career ended as governor of Salonica. Ishak Pasha spent his fortune on many noble edifices including several mosques, a *hamam*, a bridge over the Struma River, fountains and a dervish *tekke*. He was not alone. Koca Kasim Pasha, who started life as slave of an Egyptian scholar, before rising in the imperial civil service to become grand vizier, founded another mosque-imaret in the city. Yakub Pasha, a Bosnian-born vizier renowned both for his poetry and for his victories against the Austrians and Hungarians on the Croat border, endowed a mosque named after himself.

What is striking about these large-scale building projects—especially when compared with western Europe—is the speed of their construction. Often only a few years were necessary for their completion. Such efficiency implied not only plentiful skilled labour and highly developed architectural traditions, but the means to accumulate and concentrate funds for such purposes much more quickly than most European states could manage at this time. The highly centralized nature of Ottoman authority helped, but the real vehicle of urban renewal was the pious charitable foundation known as the *vakf*.

The *vakf* was a well-established Muslim institution. By endowing a property with revenues from rents on shops and land, the founder of a *vakf* relinquished his ownership of the property and its endowments but in return received compensation in the afterlife, and the blessings of later generations. For the tenants of the properties and lands involved, *vakf* status was no hardship: on the contrary, exempted from the often burdensome irregular state taxes, *vakf* properties thrived and contributed to the city's prosperity. For the donor, turning his (or her— the donors included many wealthy women) possessions into a *vakf* was also a way of ensuring that wealth passed down through the family, since relatives could be nominated as managers and trustees of the foundation, and receive payment. Benefactors spelled out the running of their institutions down to the smallest details—saffron rice and honey on special holidays, a (lavish) evening meal of meat stew with spices and onions, boiled rice and bread for students attending school regularly.[13]

The imperial family set the example: Murad II himself, despite the distractions of almost incessant campaigning and his focus on the old capital Bursa and the noble mosque he was building in Edirne, commissioned the construction of several fountains in the upper town, as well as the great central *hamam* complex. He also repaired the city's old Roman and Byzantine aqueduct system and settled colonists to look after it. His son, Mehmed the Conqueror, although hostile to the *vakf* idea in theory because it alienated land and resources from the control of the state, encouraged his viziers to build market complexes and other buildings of public utility. Bayazid II, who wintered in Salonica during his Balkan campaigns at the end of the fifteenth century, erected a new six-domed stone *bezesten* (market building), for the storage of valuable goods which is still in use today. Across the road from the Hamza Bey mosque, this elegant structure quickly became the centre of commercial life. The sultan endowed it with rents from premises selling perfumes, fruits, halva and sherbet, cloth, slippers, knives and silks, and also used the income to support the mosque he created when he ordered the church of Ayios Dimitrios to be turned over to the faithful in 1492.[14]

In addition to numerous chapels, schools, soup kitchens and Sufi lodges, *vakfs* financed the spread of the wells and fountains necessary both for performing ablutions and for keeping the city alive. Public baths were constructed near places of worship and religious study so that people could fulfil their obligation to make sure they were clean before entering the mosque to pray. Murad II built the sprawling *Bey hamam* as a place to prepare for the city's main mosque, only a stone's throw away. Its steam-filled rooms and private suites, where young *masseurs* pummelled and oiled their clients as they stretched out on the hot stones, were also a place for sexual and social interaction in an urban environment with few public spaces. Bath-attendants always had an ambiguous reputation, but work in the *hamam* offered access to the powerful and a step onto the ladder of imperial service. Salonica's *Bey hamam*, with its separate baths for men and women, is one of the outstanding examples of early Ottoman architecture in the Balkans. Until the 1960s, travellers could still wash themselves in what were latterly called the *Paradise Baths*. Today the constant flows of hot and cold water mentioned by seventeenth-century travellers have dried up, but thanks to the Greek Archaeological Service it is possible to walk through the narrow passages from room to room, and admire the intricacy of its internal decorations, the marble slabs where clients were massaged, and the cool vaulted rooms with their stucco honeycombed *muqarnas* illuminated only by bright shafts of light which burst through holes cut deep into the domed ceiling.[15]

Vakfs fostered trade too. In addition to Bayazid's central market building, and quarters for flour, textiles, spices, furs, cloth and leather goods, there was the so-called "Egyptian market" just outside the gate to the harbour, which (according to one later traveller) contained "all the produce of Egypt, linen, sugar, rice, coffee." Nearby were the city's tanneries, which were already flourishing by the late fifteenth century. Ship's biscuit was produced here, and later on coffee-houses and taverns sprang up to cater to the needs of sailors, travellers, camel-drivers, porters and day-labourers. At the heart of this bustling district lay the Abdur-Reouf mosque—"a beautiful and most lovely sanctuary, a place of devotion, respite and recovery"—founded by a *mollah* of the city, who built it to serve the traders, since there was none other outside the walls, endowing this too as a *vakf*. "Day and night," reports a seventeenth-century visitor, "the faithful are present there, because Muslim traders from the four corners of the globe and god-fearing sailors and sea-captains make their prayers in that place, enjoying the view of the ships in the harbour."[16]

It is worth pointing out that Christians could form *vakfs* as well as Muslims and indeed had had a similar institution in Byzantine times. By 1498, the canny monks of the Vlatadon monastery, for example, owned properties throughout the town: they had one shop in the fish market (next door to that owned by someone the scribe referred to only as "the bey") as well as another seven nearby, (adjacent to the premises of a Christian, "Kostas son of Kokoris"). They also had three stalls in the candle-makers' market, and two cobblers' workshops next to those owned by "Hadji Ahmed" and "Hadji Hassan." They rented out cookshops, wells and outbuildings in the old Hippodrome quarter, watermills outside the walls, and a vineyard on the slopes of Hortiatis. With the revenues from these, they supported the life of the monastery and acquired yet more properties.[17]

Further afield, *vakfs* financed the construction and maintenance of bridges, post-houses, stables, caravanserais and ferries, all of which were essential both for trade and for the speedy military advances through which Ottoman power was projected into south-eastern Europe. Robert de Dreux, a seventeenth-century French priest, was impressed by the *khans*, hostelries as large as churches, "which the Bachas and other Turkish *signors* build superbly to lodge travellers, without care for their station in life or religion, each one being made welcome, without being obliged to pay anything in return." As the key naval, mercantile and military strong-point for the sultans' fifteenth-century advance westwards, Salonica benefited from the pacification of the countryside and the consolidation of Ottoman authority along the old Roman Via Egnatia. For the first time in centuries, after the acute fragmentation and instability of the late Byzantine era, a single power controlled the region as a whole.[18]

RUNNING THE CITY

IN THE BALKANS the Ottomans conquered a region whose cities were already in decline as a result of the political and military instability of the previous centuries. They had, therefore, not only to repopulate them but to reorganize them administratively as well. Salonica itself was brought under the direct control of the sultan and placed by him under the supervision of appointed officers. There was no clear legal or institutional demarcation between the city and its rural hinterland—the same officials were often responsible for both and in contrast to the Romano-Byzantine tradition there was no municipal government in the strict sense. City-based tax farmers controlled the local salteries and city officials were instructed to look after the mines in the Chalkidiki peninsula. Moreover large areas within the walls were given over to vineyards, orchards and pasture, so that the countryside came within the city as well: indeed the Christians who patrolled the sea-walls nightly, as ordered by Murad (in return for tax exemptions) were mostly local shepherds and farmers. Nevertheless, the needs of the urban economy and rhythms of urban life themselves required special attention.[19]

We lack documents which would show us precisely how Salonica was run in the fifteenth century. But on the basis of what was happening in other provincial towns we have a good idea. There would have been a governor who combined military and urban functions—overall responsibility for the garrisoning of the fortifications, gates, local troop contingents and horses on the one hand; and on the other, keeping an eye on the local tax officials, especially those who had bought concessions for customs duties, and on the needs of the city in general. The collection of taxes and the running of the market were the Ottoman state's priorities. It laid out, in enormous detail, the duties to be levied on each good brought into the city, and the governor was supposed to check that these were properly paid. The guardian of the gates examined the produce and animals brought in by farmers and traders. Another official regulated the buying and selling of "all that God has created." He and his assistants paid weekly visits to the flour market and the slaughter-houses, checking weights and measures and monitoring the price and quality of silver. He also kept an eye on the behaviour of slaves and made sure they prayed regularly, looking out for any signs of public drunkenness or debauchery. Production itself was organized in trade guilds, some—like the butchers, confined to one religion—others (like the shoemakers), mixed. But guild members did not cluster together in the same residential areas as they did elsewhere.

The Ottoman legal system was one of multiple legal jurisdictions. The governor and several of his subordinates had powers of arrest and imprisonment. The city's chief law officer and public notary was the *kadi* but there was sometimes another judge, subordinate to him, whose remit covered "everything that could trouble public order"—murders, rape, adultery, robberies—crimes which in the Balkans at least were often judged not according to the divine law but "on the basis of custom" or royal decree. For the empire had a triple system of law with the *shari'a* providing a foundation, alongside the body of customary law—*adet*—which varied from place to place, and the decrees and regulations issued by the sultan himself—the *kanun*.[20]

With no municipal authority to watch over the city, it was up to the governor to organize its policing, fire prevention, sewage disposal and hygiene. Policing came out of the pockets of merchants and local people who paid the *pasvant* (from the Persian word for nightwatchman) to patrol their neighbourhood. Four hundred years later, visitors to Salonica were still being kept awake by the unfamiliar sound of his metal-tipped staff tapping out the hours on the cobbles as he made his rounds. Householders also paid for rubbish to be collected, and were supposed to be responsible for the condition of pathways outside their homes. Guilds had the responsibility to provide young men for fire duty, but the frequency with which the city was hit by devastating conflagrations was testimony to their ineffectiveness. On the other hand, the water system was surprisingly sophisticated—early travellers commented on the abundance of public wells and fountains—and the flow could be controlled and directed in an emergency to where it was needed.[21]

Thanks to the survival of a 1478 cadastral register, the third which the conscientious Ottoman scribes had prepared since the conquest (but the first to survive), we have a fairly precise picture of who was living where roughly half a century after the conquest. The pattern of settlement indicates a kind of transition from the Byzantine period to the Ottoman city in its heyday. A total of just over ten thousand people lived there—so the population had barely recovered to the level it was at when the Ottoman army burst in—roughly divided between Christians and Muslims, with the former still very slightly in the majority. The Muslims were immigrants and there do not appear to have been many converts from among the Christians, in contrast with some other former Byzantine towns.

The Byzantine past lingered on, and could be discerned in the Greek names which continued to be used for neighbourhoods and districts. The Ottoman scribes faithfully referred to *Ayo Dimitri, Ofalo, Podrom* (from the old Hippodrome), *Ayo Mine, Asomat* after the old churches. Even *Akhiropit* (Acheiropoietos) was mentioned although the church had been converted into a mosque; it would be replaced by a Turkish name only in the next century. Large churches—such as Ayia Sofia—and the Vlatadon Monastery still lived off their estates. The garrison was made up of Ottoman troops, but Christians were assigned the responsibility for maintaining and even manning the sea-walls and the towers—an arrangement which a later governor at the start of the seventeenth century regarded as a security risk and put an end to. As the details of the Vlatadon monks' property portfolio show, Muslims and Christians lived and worked side by side, probably because Murad had settled newcomers in the homes of departed or dead Christians. Indeed Christians still outnumbered Muslims in the old quarters on either side of the main street.

Only in the Upper Town—a hint of the future pattern of residence—were Muslims now in the majority. There they enjoyed the best access to water and fresh air. The poor lived in humble single-storey homes whose courtyards were hidden from the street behind whitewashed walls; the wealthy slowly built themselves larger stone mansions with overhanging screened balconies and private wells in their extensive gardens, connected to the city's water system. Cypresses and plane trees provided shade, and there were numerous kiosks which allowed people to escape the sun and drink from fountains while enjoying the views over the town. The highest officials were granted regular deliveries of ice from Mount Hortiatis, which they used mostly in the preparation of sherbets. In the eighteenth century if not before, they started painting their houses and ornamenting them with verses from the Qur'an picked out in red.[22]

Imperial edicts had successfully replenished the city with the trades for which it would shortly become renowned—leather and textile-workers in particular—together with the donkey and camel-drivers, tailors, bakers, grocers, fishermen, cobblers and shopkeepers without which no urban life could be sustained. The city was now producing its own rice, soap, knives, wax, stoves, pillows and pottery. Saffron, meat, cheese and grains were all supplied locally. Fish were so plentiful that local astrologers claimed Selanik—as it was now known—lay under the sign of Pisces. Scribes provide one badly needed skill; the fifteen *hamam* attendants—a surprisingly high number at this early date—another. And the presence of merchants, a furrier, a jeweller and a silversmith all indicate the revival of international trade and wealth.

Yet the city was still far from its prime. Many houses lay abandoned or demolished, and great stretches of the area within the walls, especially on the upper slopes, were given over to pasture, orchards, vineyards and agriculture. Two farmers are mentioned in the 1478 register, but many more of the inhabitants tended their own gardens (the word the Ottoman scribe uses is a Slavic one, *bashtina*, a sign of the close linkage between the Slavs and the land) or grazed their sheep, horses, oxen and donkeys on open ground. Centuries later, when the population had grown to more than one hundred thousand, the quasi-rural character of Salonica's upper reaches was still visible: Ottoman photographs show isolated buildings surrounded by fields within the walls—the Muslim neighbourhood inside the fortress perimeter was virtually a separate village—while the city's fresh milk was produced by animals which lived alongside their downtown owners right up until 1920. In fact, most of the time under the sultans there was more meadow within the walls than housing. A Venetian ambassador passed through at the end of the sixteenth century and what struck him—despite the "fine and wide streets downtown, a fountain in almost every one, many columns visible along them, some ruined and some whole"—was that the city was "sparsely inhabited."[23]

Yet not nearly as sparsely in the 1590s as it had been a century earlier. For after 1500 Salonica's population suddenly doubled, and soared to thirty thousand by 1520, putting pressure on housing for the first time, and necessitating the opening up of a new water supply into the city. The newcomers emanated from an unexpected quarter—the western Mediterranean, where the Spanish monarchs Ferdinand and Isabella were taking Christianization to a new pitch by expelling the Jews from their kingdom. Attracted by Bayazid's promises of economic concessions and political protection, Spanish-speaking Jews arrived in droves. Some went on to Istanbul, Sarajevo, Safed and Alexandria, but the largest colony took shape in Salonica. By the time the Venetian ambassador passed through, it was a Jewish guide who showed him round, and the Jews of the city were many times more numerous than in Venice itself. Of the three main religious communities contained within the walls—Muslims, Christians and Jews—this last, which had been entirely absent from the population register of 1478, had suddenly become the largest of them all. The third and perhaps most unexpected component of Ottoman Salonica had arrived.

3

The Arrival of the Sefardim

WHEN EVLIYA CHELEBI, the seventeenth-century Ottoman traveller, came to describe Salonica he provided a characteristically fantastic account of its origins. The prophet Solomon—"may God's blessing be upon him"—had been showing the world to the Queen of Sheba when she looked down and saw "in the region of Athens, in the land of the Romans, a high spot called *Bellevue*." There he built her a palace "whose traces are still visible," before they moved on eastwards to Istanbul, Bursa, Baalbec and Jerusalem, building as they went, and repopulating the Earth after the Flood. Chelebi ascribes the city's walls to the "philosopher Philikos" and his son Selanik "after whom it is named still." Later, he says, Jews fleeing Palestine "slew the Greek nation in one night and gained control of the fortress." Hebrew kings did battle with Byzantine princesses, the Ottoman sultans eventually took over, and "until our own days, the city is full of Jews."[1]

Evliya's tall tale conveys one thing quite unambiguously: by the time of his visit in 1667–68, the Jews were such an integral part of Salonica that it seemed impossible to imagine they had not always been there. And indeed there had been Jews in the city before there were any Christians. In Byzantine times there were probably several hundred Greek-speaking Jewish families (or Romaniotes); despite often severe persecution, they traded successfully across the Mediterranean, at least to judge from the correspondence found in the Cairo Genizah many years ago. Shortly before the Turkish conquest, they were joined by refugees fleeing persecution in France and Germany. Whether or not they survived the siege of 1430 is not known but any who did were moved to Constantinople by Mehmed the Conqueror to repopulate it after its capture in 1453, leaving their home-town entirely without a

Jewish presence for perhaps the first time in over a millennium. This was why in the 1478 register they did not appear. But then came a new wave of anti-Jewish persecution in Christendom, and the Ottoman willingness to take advantage of this.[2]

FLIGHT ACROSS THE MEDITERRANEAN

WHEN THE ENGLISH expelled their Jews in 1290, they inaugurated a policy which spread widely over the next two centuries. In 1492 Ferdinand and Isabella's edict of banishment forced thousands from a homeland where they had known great security and prosperity. Sicily and Sardinia, Navarre, Provence and Naples followed suit. By the mid-sixteenth century, Jews had been evicted from much of western Europe. A few existed on sufferance, while many others converted or went underground as Marranos and New Christians, preserving their customs behind a Catholic façade. The centre of gravity of the Jewish world shifted eastwards—to the safe havens of Poland and the Ottoman domains.[3]

In Spain itself not everyone favoured the expulsions. (Perhaps this was why a different policy was chosen towards the far more numerous Muslims of Andalucía who were forcibly converted, and only expelled much later.) "Many were of the opinion," wrote the scholar and Inquisitor Jeronimo de Zurita, "that the king was making a mistake to throw out of his realms people who were so industrious and hard-working, and so outstanding in his realms both in number and esteem as well as in dedication to making money." A later generation of Inquisitors feared that the Jews who had been driven out "took with them the substance and wealth of these realms, transferring to our enemies the trade and commerce of which they are the proprietors not only in Europe but throughout the world."[4]

The expulsion of the Jews formed part of a bitter struggle for power between Islam and Catholicism. One might almost see this as the contest to reunify the Roman Empire between the two great monotheistic religions that had succeeded it: on the one side, the Spanish Catholic monarchs of the Holy Roman Empire; on the other, the Ottoman sultans, themselves heirs to the Roman Empire of the East, and rulers of the largest and most powerful Muslim empire in the world. Its climax, in the sixteenth century, pitted Charles V, possessor of the imperial throne of Germany and ruler of the Netherlands, the Austrian lands, the Spanish monarchy and its possessions in Sicily and Naples, Mexico and Peru, against Suleyman the Magnificent, who held undisputed sway from Hungary to Yemen, from Algiers to Baghdad. Ottoman forces had swept north to the gates of Vienna and conquered the Arab lands while Ottoman navies clashed with the Holy League in the Mediterranean and captured Rhodes, Cyprus and Tunis, wintered in Toulon, seized Nice and terrorized the Italian coast. The Habsburgs looked for an ally in Persia; the French and English approached the Porte. It was an early modern world war.[5]

In the midst of this bitter conflict the Ottoman authorities exploited their enemy's anti-Jewish measures just as they had welcomed other Jewish refugees from Christian persecution in the past. They were People of the Book, and they possessed valuable skills. Sultan Murad II had a Jewish translator in his service; his successors relied upon Jewish doctors and bankers. Those fleeing Iberia would bring more knowledge and expertise with them. In the matter-of-fact words of one contemporary Jewish chronicler: "A part of the exiled Spaniards went overseas to Turkey. Some of them were thrown into the sea and drowned, but those who arrived there the king of Turkey received kindly, as they were artisans."[6] The French agent Nicolas de Nicolay noted:

[The Jews] have among them workmen of all artes and handicraftes moste excellent, and specially of the Maranes [Marranos] of late banished and driven out of Spain and Portugale, who to the great detriment and damage of the Christianitie, have taught the Turkes divers inventions, craftes and engines of warre, as to make artillerie, harquebuses, gunne powder, shot and other munitions; they have also there set up printing, not before seen in those countries, by the which in faire characters they put in light divers bookes in divers languages as Greek, Latin, Italian, Spanish and the Hebrew tongue, being to them naturell.[7]

The newcomers were not enough in numbers to affect the demographic balance in the empire—the Balkans remained overwhelmingly Christian, the Asian and Arab lands overwhelmingly Muslim. But they revitalized urban life after many decades of war.

And of all the towns in the empire, it was Salonica which benefited most. Since 1453, while Istanbul's population had been growing at an incredible rate thanks to compulsory resettlement and immigration by Muslims, Greeks and Armenians, turning it into perhaps the largest city in Europe, Salonica lagged far behind. Bayezid had been concerned at its slow recovery and had been doing what he could to promote it himself. Did he order the authorities to direct the Jews there? It seems likely, although no such directive has survived. According to a later chronicler, he sent orders to provincial governors to welcome the new-comers. Since Salonica was the empire's main European port, many were bound to make their way there in any case. As wave after wave of Iberian refugees arrived at the docks, the city grew by leaps and bounds. By 1520, more than half its thirty thousand inhabitants were Jewish, and it had turned into one of the most important ports of the eastern Mediterranean.[8]

Perhaps only now did the real break with Byzantium take place. In 1478 Salonica was still a Greek city where more than half of the inhabitants were Christians; by 1519, they were less than one quarter. Was it a sign of their growing weakness that between 1490 and 1540 several of their most magnificent churches—including Ayios Dimitrios itself—were turned into mosques? A century later still, if we are to judge from Ottoman records, the number of Christians had fallen further, both in absolute terms and as a proportion of the whole. While Istanbul remained heavily populated by Greeks, local Christians saw Salonica re-emerging into something resembling its former prosperity under a Muslim administration and a largely Jewish labour-force.

Not surprisingly, Greco-Jewish relations were infused with tension. Occasional stories of anti-Jewish machinations at the Porte, long-running complaints that the newcomers paid too little tax, bitter commercial rivalries between Christian and Jewish merchants, the emergence of the blood libel in the late sixteenth century, even the odd riot, assault and looting of Jewish properties following fire or plague—these are the scattered documentary indications of the Greeks' deep-rooted resentment at the newcomers. It cannot have been easy living as a minority in the city they regarded as theirs. Jewish children laughed at the Orthodox priests, with their long hair tied up in a bun: *está un papas* became a way of saying it was time to visit the barber. We learn from a 1700 court case that the Greek inhabitants of Ayios Minas were so fed up with Jewish neighbours throwing their garbage into the churchyard, and mocking them from the surrounding windows during holiday ser-vices, that they appealed to the Ottoman authorities to get them to stop. The balance of confessional power within the city had shifted sharply.[9]

For the Jews themselves, a mass of displaced refugees living with other recent immigrants among the toppled columns, half-buried temples and ruined mementoes of the city's Roman and Byzantine past, this Macedonian port was at first equally strange and alienating. Lost "in a country which is not theirs," they struggled to make sense of forced migration from "the lands of the West." Some were Jews; others were converts to Catholicism. With their families forced apart, many mourned dead relatives, and wondered if their missing ones would ever return or if new consorts would succeed in giving them children to replace those they had lost. The trauma of exile is a familiar refrain in Salonican history. One rabbi was forced to remind his congregation "to stop cursing the Almighty and to accept as just everything that has happened."[10]

If Europe had become for them—as it was for the Marrano poet Samuel Usque—"my hell on earth," we can scarcely be surprised: Salonica, by contrast, was their refuge and liberation. "There is a city in the Turkish kingdom," he wrote, "which formerly belonged to the Greeks, and in our days is a true mother-city in Judaism. For it is established on the very deep foundations of the Law. And it is filled with the choicest plants and most fruitful trees, presently known anywhere on the face of our globe. These fruits are divine, because they are watered by an abundant stream of charities. The city's walls are made of holy deeds of the greatest worth." When Jews in Provence scouted out conditions there, they received the reply: "Come and join us in Turkey and you will live, as we do, in peace and liberty." In the experience of the Sefardim, we see the astonishing capacity of refugees to make an unfamiliar city theirs. Through religious devotion and study, they turned Salonica into a "new Jerusalem"—just as other Jews did with Amsterdam, Vilna, Montpellier, Nimes, Bari and Otranto: wrapping their new place of exile in the mantle of biblical geography was a way of coming to feel at home. "The Jews of Europe and other countries, persecuted and banished, have come there to find a refuge," wrote Usque, "and this city has received them with love and affection, as if she were Jerusalem, that old and pious mother of ours."[11]

Indeed, only a few devout older people, usually men, were ever tempted to make the journey southeast to Jerusalem itself, even though it formed part of the same Ottoman realm. As in Spain, the Jews came to feel—as one historian has put it—"at home in exile" and had no desire to uproot themselves once more, not even when the destination was the Land their holy books promised them. For this home was not only their "Jerusalem"; it was also a simulacrum of the life they had

known at the other end of the Mediterranean. They worshipped in synagogues named after the old long-abandoned homelands—Ispanya,
Çeçilyan (Sicilian), Magrebi, Lizbon, Talyan (Italian), Otranto,
Aragon, Katalan, Pulya, Evora Portukal and many others—which survived until the synagogues themselves perished in the fire of 1917.
Their family names—Navarro, Cuenca, Algava—their games, curses
and blessings, even their clothes, linked them with their past. They ate
Pan d'Espanya (almond sponge cake) on holidays, *rodanchas* (pumpkin
pastries), *pastel de kwezo* (cheese pie with sesame seed), *fijones kon karne*
(beef and bean stew) and *keftikes de poyo* (chicken croquettes), and gave
visitors *dulce de muez verde* (green walnut preserve). People munched
pasatempo (dried melon seeds), took the *vaporiko* across the bay, or
enjoyed the evening air on the *varandado* of their home. When Spanish
scholars visited the city at the end of the nineteenth century, they were
astonished to find a miniature Iberia alive and flourishing under Abdul
Hamid.[12]

For this, the primary conduit was language. As a Salonican merchant, Emmanuel Abuaf, tried to explain in 1600 to a puzzled inter-
rogator of the Pisan Inquisition: "Our Jewish youngsters, when they
begin from the age of six to learn the Scripture, read it and discuss it in
the Spanish language, and all the business and trade of the Levant is
carried on in Spanish in Hebrew characters . . . And so it is not hard for
Jews to know Spanish even if they are born outside Spain."[13] In
Salonica, there was a religious variant—Ladino—and a vernacular
which was so identified with the Jews that it became known locally as
"Jewish" (*judezmo*), and quickly became the language of secular learning and literature, business, science and medicine. Sacred and scholarly
texts were translated into it from Hebrew, Arabic and Latin, because
"this language is the most used among us." In the docks, among the
fishermen, in the market and the workshops the accents of Aragon,
Galicia, Navarre and Castile crowded out Portuguese, Greek, Yiddish,
Italian and Provençal. Eventually Castilian triumphed over the rest.
"The Jews of Salonica and Constantinople, Alexandria, and Cairo,
Venice and other commercial centres, use Spanish in their business. I
know Jewish children in Salonica who speak Spanish as well as me if not
better," noted Gonsalvo de Illescas. The sailor Diego Galan, a native of
Toledo, found that the city's Jews "speak Castilian as fine and well-
accented as in the imperial capital." They were proud of their tongue—
its flexibility and sweetness, so quick to bring the grandiloquent or
bombastic down to earth with a ready diminutive. By contrast, the Jews

further inland were derisively written off as *digi digi*—incapable of speaking properly, too inclined to the harsh *ds* and *gs* of the Portuguese.[14]

SERVING THE IMPERIAL ECONOMY

EARLY IN THE SIXTEENTH CENTURY, the Porte entrusted the Jews of Salonica with the responsibility of manufacturing the uniforms for the janissary infantry corps, and over the next century this turned the city into one of the principal producers and exporters of cloth in the eastern Mediterranean. Wealthy Jewish merchants bought up the local supply of wool, imported dyes, and set up poorer Jews with equipment and wages for weaving, brushing, dyeing and making up the finished material. Ottoman authorities banned all exports of wool from the region until the needs of the manufacturers had been met and tried to chase back any weavers who sought to leave. By mid-century, the industry was not only supplying military uniforms, but also clothing the city itself and sending exports to Buda and beyond.[15]

Another imperial *corvée* a few years later jump-started silver-mining outside the city—crucially easing the desperate Ottoman shortage of precious metals. Because the silver shortage was one of the main constraints on Ottoman economic growth, Grand Vizier Maktul Ibrahim Pasha brought in Jewish metallurgists from newly conquered Hungary, and within a few years the Siderokapsi mines had become one of the largest silver producers in the empire, with daily caravans making the fifty-mile journey to Salonica and back. Bulgarian and Jewish miners did the hard work, and rich Jewish merchants were commanded to bankroll operations. To be sure, running the economy by imperial fiat in this way was not popular with the wealthy. The bankers complained bitterly at an obligation which was not shared by the community as a whole, and which more often than not led to losses rather than profits. They bribed Ottoman officials, hid or fled the city. The industry itself became such a drain on resources that Salonican Jews shunned the miners when they came into town: "They would rather meet a bear that lost its cubs than one of those people."[16]

In order to curb the impact of such obligations and to allow for greater fiscal predictability, the city's Jews sent a delegation to Suleyman the Magnificent in 1562 to plead for a reform of their overall tax burden. The move indicated the surprising degree of self-confidence with which the Sefardim dealt with their Ottoman masters. It took many visits, several years, and at least one change of sultan, before an answer was forthcoming. It could easily have resulted—had the imperial mood been rather different—in the delegates losing their lives, as happened to another rabbi when he tried to negotiate a later reduction in the tax burden. But in 1568, it still seemed vital to the Porte to stay on good terms with Salonica's Jews and the principal delegate, Moises Almosnino, was able to return with welcome news: in return for the abolition of many special taxes, the community committed itself to collecting and handing over an agreed sum annually to the authorities.

For the Ottomans were not modern capitalists. They did not aim at unlimited growth in unrestricted markets but rather at the creation and maintenance of a basically closed system to keep towns alive—in particular the ever-expanding imperial metropole—and to guarantee the domestic production of commodities essential for urban life and the provisioning of the military. Salt, wheat, silver and woollens were what they needed from Salonica, a list to which they occasionally added gunpowder and even cannons. The primary value of the Jews lay in their ability to provide these things, thereby freeing Muslims for other occupations. After a century of Ottoman rule, more than half of the latter were now imams, muezzins, tax collectors, janissaries or other servants of the state and its ruling faith. They administered the city; the Jews ran its economy. It was a division of labour which suited both sides and the city flourished.[17]

For the rich, the buoyant Ottoman economy allowed them to invest their funds in attractive and profitable outlets such as the tax farms and concessions upon which the sultan relied for the gathering of many of his revenues. Salonican Jews thus came to play an important part in the regional economy of the Ottoman Balkans. Local Jewish *sarrafs* (bankers) collected taxes from drovers, vineyards, dairy farmers and slave dealers. They bankrolled prominent Muslim office-holders such as the *defterdar* and local troop and janissary commanders, and farmed the customs concession for Salonica itself—one of the most important sources of revenue for the empire—and the salt pans outside the city, where at their peak more than one thousand peasants worked. Many had interests in the capital, in Vidin, and along the Danube. Much of the wealth of the Nasi-Mendes family—the most politically successful and prominent Jewish dynasty of the sixteenth century—was invested in concessions of this kind.[18]

Capital accumulation was easy because Salonica was such a well-placed trading base. It reached northwards into the inland fairs and markets of the Balkans, south and east (via Jewish-Muslim partnerships) to the Asian trading routes that led to Persia, Yemen and India, and westwards through the Adriatic to Venice and the other Italian ports. Italian, Arab and Armenian merchants all participated in this traffic: but where the crucial Mediterranean triangle with Egypt and Venice was concerned, no one could compete with the extraordinary network of familial and confessional affiliates that made the Salonican Jews and Marranos so powerful. Shifting between Catholicism (when in Ancona or Venice) and Judaism (in the Ottoman lands), they dominated the Adriatic carrying trade, helped to build up Split as a major port for Venetian dealings with the Levant, and wielded their Ottoman connections whenever the Papacy and the Inquisition turned nasty. They combined commerce with espionage and ran the best intelligence networks in the entire region. So confident did they feel, that some threatened a boycott of Papal ports when the authorities in Ancona started up the auto-da-fé in 1556, and one even talked about spreading plague deliberately to frighten the Catholics in an early attempt at biological warfare.[19]

Greeks and Turks must have been astonished at the assertiveness of the newcomers, for the Romaniote and Ashkenazi Jews they had known had always kept a low profile. In the early years, it is true, the Sefardim tried to tread cautiously. Congregants were reminded by their rabbis to keep their voices down when they prayed so that they would not be heard outside. In external appearance, synagogues were modest and unobtrusive and even larger ones, like the communal Talmud Torah, were hidden well away from the main thoroughfares, in the heart of the Jewish-populated district. Thanks to the benevolence of the Ottoman authorities, however, more than twenty-five synagogues were built in less than two decades. After the fire of 1545, a delegation from Salonica visited the Porte and quickly obtained permission for many to be rebuilt.[20]

But the Iberian Jews had always known how to live well, and their noble families had been unabashedly conspicuous, with large retinues of servants and African slaves. Even before Murad III introduced new sumptuary legislation in the 1570s to curb Jewish and Christian luxury in the capital, the extravagant silk and gold-laced costumes of rich Salonican Jews, the displays of jewellery to which the wealthier women were prone—they were particularly fond of bracelets, gold necklaces and pearl chokers worn "so close to one another and so thick one would think they were riveted on to one another"—the noise of musicians at parties and weddings, where men and women danced together—to the dismay of Greek Jews—were all attracting unfavourable comment. In 1554 a rabbinical ordinance ruled that "no woman who has reached maturity, including married women, may take outside her home, into the markets or the streets, any silver or gold article, rings, chains or gems, or any such object except one ring on her finger." Murad himself had, according to an apocryphal story, been so angered by Jewish ostentation that he even contemplated putting all the Jews of the empire to death. Fear of exciting envy often lay behind the rabbis' efforts to urge restraint. It took more than rabbinical commands, however, to stop women wearing the diamond *rozetas*, *almendras* ("almonds"), chokers, earrings, coin necklaces and headpieces which still awed visitors to Salonica in the early twentieth century.[21]

It must have been as much the sheer number of the newcomers as their behaviour which struck those who had known the town before their arrival. The once sparsely populated streets filled up and population densities soared. At first Jews settled where they could, renting from the Christian and Muslim landlords who owned the bulk of the housing stock. The very first communal ordinance tried to prevent Jews outbidding one another to avoid driving up prices. But the continuous influx led to many central districts becoming heavily settled. Muslims started to move up the higher slopes—enjoying better views, drainage and ventilation, more space and less noise—while the Greeks—mostly tailors, craftsmen, cobblers, masons and metalworkers, a few remaining scions of old, distinguished Byzantine families among them—were pushed into the margins, near Ayios Minas in the west, and around the remains of the old Hippodrome.[22]

South of Egnatia, with the exception of the market districts to the west, the twisting lanes of the lower town belonged to the newcomers. Here wealthy notables lived together with the large mass of Jewish artisans, workmen, *hamals*, fishermen, pedlars and the destitute, cooped up in small apartments handed down from generation to generation. The overall impression of the Jewish quarters was scarcely one of magnificence. Clusters of modest homes hidden behind their walls and large barred gates were grouped around shared *cortijos* into which housewives threw their refuse. As the city filled up, extra storeys were added to the old wooden houses, and overhanging upper floors jutted out into the street. Every so often, the claustrophobic and airless alleys opened unpredictably into a small *placa* or *placeta*. Rutted backstreets hid the synagogues and communal buildings.

These were the least hygienic or desirable residential areas, where all the refuse of the city made its way down the slopes to collect in stagnant pools by the dank stones of the sea-walls. The old harbour built by Constantine had silted up and turned into a large sewage dump, the *Monturo*, whose noxious presence pervaded the lower town. The tanneries and slaughter-houses were located on the western fringes, but workmen kept evil-smelling vats of urine, used for tanning leather and dying wool, in their homes. People were driven mad by the din of hammers in the metal foundries; others complained of getting ill from the fumes of lead-workers and silversmiths—like the smell of the bakeries but worse, according to one sufferer. Living on top of one another, neighbours suffered when one new tenant decided to turn his bedroom into a kitchen, projecting effluent into the common passageway. The combination of overcrowding—especially after the devastating fire of 1545—and intense manufacturing activity meant that life in the city's Jewish quarters continued to be defined by its smells, its noise and its lack of privacy. Why did people remain there, in squalor, when large tracts of the upper city lay empty? Was it choice—a desire to remain close together, strategically located between the commercial district and the city walls, their very density warding off intruders? Or was it necessity—the upper slopes of the city being already owned and settled, even if more sporadically, by Muslims? Either way, the living conditions of Salonican Jewry provoked dismay right up until the fires of 1890 and 1917, which finally dispersed the old neighbourhoods and erased the old streets from the map so definitively that not even their outlines can now be traced amid the glitzy tree-lined shopping avenues which have replaced them.

THE POWER OF THE RABBIS

HISTORIANS OF THE OTTOMAN EMPIRE often extoll its hierarchical system of communal autonomy through which the sultan supposedly appointed leaders of each confessional group (or *millet*) and made them responsible for collecting taxes, administering justice and ecclesiastical affairs. The autonomy was real enough, but where, in the case of the Jews, was the hierarchy? It is true that in 1453, after the fall of Constantinople, Mehmed the Conqueror appointed a chief rabbi just as he had a Greek patriarch: the first incumbent was an elderly Romaniote rabbi who had served under the last Byzantine emperor. But this position probably applied only to the capital rather than to the empire as a whole, did not last for long and was then left vacant. Once Salonica emerged as the largest Jewish community in the empire, dwarfing that in Istanbul itself, the authority of the chief rabbi of the capital depended on obtaining the obedience of Salonican Jewry. But this was not forthcoming. "There is no town subordinated to another town," insisted one Salonican rabbi early in the sixteenth century. What he meant was that his town would be subordinated to no other.[23]

The usual rule among Jews was that newcomers conformed to local practice. But the overwhelming numbers of the immigrants, and their well-developed sense of cultural superiority, put this principle to the test. The Spanish and Italian Jews regarded the established traditions of the *Griegos* (Greeks) or the *Alemanos* (Germans), as they were now somewhat dismissively known, as distinctly inferior. "Ni ajo dulce ni Tudesco bueno,"—neither can we find sweet garlic nor a good German (Jew)—was a local saying. No one likes being condescended to. Outside Salonica, the French naturalist Pierre Belon witnessed an argument that flared up around a fish-stall. Did the *claria* have scales or not? Some Jews gathered and said that as it did not, it could be eaten. Others—"newly come from Spain"—said they could see minute traces of scales and accused the first group of lax observance. A fist-fight was about to erupt before the fish was taken off for further inspection.[24]

Rabbis took the same unbending line over the superiority of the Sefardic way that their congregants had done in the fish-market. As early as 1509, one wrote:

> It is well-known that Sephardic Jews and their *hakhanim* [rabbis] in this kingdom, together with the other congregations who join them, comprise the majority here, may the Lord be praised. The land was given uniquely to them, and they are its majesty, its radiance and splendour, a light unto the land and all who dwell in it. Surely, they were not brought hither in order to depart! For all these places are ours too, and it would be worthy of all the minority peoples who first resided in this kingdom to follow their example and do as they do in all that pertains to the Torah and its customs.[25]

Less than twenty years since the expulsions, this was a stunning display of arrogance—turning the Romaniotes (Greek-speaking Jews), who had lived in those lands since antiquity, into a subservient minority. Such an attitude created friction with Istanbul where Romaniotes were more numerous and not inclined to bow so easily. In Salonica itself, the argument for Spanish superiority was repeated over and over again until it needed no longer to be made. "As matters stand today in Salonica," commented Rabbi Samuel de Medina in the 1560s, "the holy communities of Calabria, Provincia, Sicilia and Apulia have all adopted the ways of Sefarad, and only the holy community of Ashkenaz [Germany] has not changed its ways." Thus it was not only because of the lack of a Jewish hierarchy comparable to that which structured the Orthodox Church that the model of communal administration suggested by the patriarchate was bound to fail. Salonica's largely Sefardic Jewry never for a moment contemplated allowing itself to fall under the guidance of a Romaniote chief rabbi.[26]

Yet not only did the Ottoman authorities apparently not bother with a centralized imperial Jewish hierarchy based in the capital, they scarcely bothered to formalize how the Jews organized themselves in Salonica either. Under the Byzantine emperors, there was apparently a Jewish "provost." No such post was established by the Ottomans. The community could not fix upon a single chief rabbi, and its early efforts to set up a triumvirate of elderly but respected figures met the same fate as the chief rabbinate in the capital. There was thus not even a Jewish counterpart to the city's Greek metropolitan. For a time, the local authorities appointed a spokesman for the Jews to act as intermediary between the community and themselves. But the only mention of this figure in the historical record paints him as an unmitigated disaster, who used the position for his own advancement, insulted respected rabbis and eventually, through his blasphemous conduct, brought down the wrath of God in the shape of the fire and plague of 1545. We do not hear about a successor: if he existed, he was of no importance. More or less all that mattered for the local Ottoman authorities was that taxes were regularly paid to the court of the *kadi* or to the assigned collectors. The community as a whole gathered as an assembly of synagogue representatives to apportion taxes. When there were difficulties it sent elders to Istanbul to plead at court, or contacted prominent Jewish notables for help.[27]

In fact, in many ways it is misleading to talk about a Jewish community in Salonica at all. From the outside, Jews could be identified by language and officially imposed dress and colour codes. But with the exception of a small number of institutions which *were* organized for the common good—the redemption fund that ransomed Jewish slaves and captives, or the Talmud Torah, the community's combined school, shelter (for travellers and the poor), insane asylum and hospital—what the Sefardim created for themselves was a highly de-centralized, indeed almost anarchic system, in which Jewish life revolved around the individual synagogue, and Jews argued bitterly among themselves as to what constituted right practice. Fifteenth-century Spain had in fact been not a unitary country so much as a collection of disparate cities, regions and states united eventually under the authority of a single monarch; it was this keenly local and often rivalrous sense of place that was reproduced in Salonica.

From the outset, congregations guarded their independence jealously from each other. Synagogues multiplied—a fundamental principle of Jewish life was that everyone *had* to belong to one congregation or another—and within half a century there were more than twenty. Not all were of equal standing or size and many of the larger ones were constantly splitting apart thanks to the factionalism which seemed endemic to the community: before long, the Sicilians were divided into "Old" and "New" as were the "Spanish Refugees." But the congregation was, at least at first, a link to the past and a way of keeping those who spoke the same language together. No significant differences of liturgy or practice divided the worshippers in the New Lisbon or Evora synagogues; only the small Romaniote Etz Haim and the Ashkenazi congregations might have pleaded the preservation of their traditions. Nevertheless whether the differences were liturgical or purely cultural and linguistic, each group preserved its autonomy as passionately as if its very identity was at stake. "In Salonica each and every man speaks in the tongue of his own people," wrote the rabbi Yosef ibn Lev in the 1560s. "When the refugees arrived after the expulsion, they designated *kehalim* [congregations] each according to his tongue . . . Every *kahal* supports its own poor, and each and every *kahal* is singly recorded into the king's register. Every *kahal* is like a city unto itself."[28]

This then was what the city actually meant for most Jews—a *kahal* based in a squat and modestly decorated building, unobtrusive from the street and plainly adorned inside, from which they ran their charity funds, their burial societies and study groups. There they organized the allocation and collection of taxes and agreed salaries for their cantor, ritual slaughterers, the *mohel* (responsible for circumcisions) and rabbi. Since usually only the taxable members of the community voted on communal policies, the domination of the notables was a frequent bone of contention with the poorer members.

Not surprisingly, such a system was highly unstable. Indeed the Jews were well known for their dissension and often bemoaned the lack of fellow-feeling. Acute tensions between rich and poor, extreme factionalism, and the lack of any central organization made wider agreement very difficult and delayed badly needed social reforms: marriages took place with startling informality outside the supervision of rabbis, leading unfortunate girls astray; conversions—especially of slaves—to Judaism were perfunctory; moreover, any rabbi was free to issue ordinances and excommunications, and some on occasions evidently abused these rights. In 1565 it was finally agreed that an ordinance could be applied to the community as a whole only when it was signed by a majority of the rabbis in the city.[29]

Rabbis formed a privileged ruling caste free of communal or government taxes. There was, of course, an Ottoman court system, presided over by the *kadi*, an appointed official, who dispensed justice throughout the city. The *kadi* courts, though designed primarily for Muslims (who were treated on a different footing than non-Muslims), were considerate of Jewish religious demands: they never obliged a Jew to appear on the Jewish Sabbath, and sent Jewish witnesses to the rabbi when it was necessary to swear an oath. But the *kadi* did not try to monopolize the provision of justice, and it was the rabbinical courts which constituted the chief means through which Jews settled their differences. Because they were never given any formal legal recognition, these existed for centuries in a kind of legal limbo sanctioned by the force of custom. It was an extraordinary state of affairs and one which offers an important clue into the way the Ottoman authorities ran their state: strictly regimented where taxes and production were concerned, in other areas—such as law—almost uninvolved and only sporadically prescriptive.[30]

Interventions by the Ottoman authorities in rabbinical affairs were rare. It is true that a *kadi* would be deeply displeased to learn that rabbis treated his court with disdain, or to be informed that Jews were being urged by their rabbis not to use them. But only rarely did he stir into action. In one case, a dispute between two contenders for the position of rabbi in the Aragon synagogue led to the *kadi* stepping in and making the appointment himself; but this rendered the victorious candidate so unpopular with his congregants, who were after all paying his salary, that he was forced soon after to move on. Another *kadi* dismissed a rabbi for instructing his congregants not to have recourse to the Ottoman courts. But in this case it was the congregants themselves who had shopped their rabbi by bringing his alleged remarks to the attention of the authorities so as to get rid of him, and in any case he was employed soon after by another congregation.[31]

In fact Jews did attend the Muslim courts, despite rabbinical injunctions against their doing so, usually to register commercial agreements, or divorce settlements in case of future legal disputes (for which the rabbinical courts were useless precisely because of their unofficial status). Jewish workers ran to the courtroom to disclaim responsibility when a soldier's gun accidentally went off in their yard and killed someone: only a judgement from the Ottoman judge could help them escape paying a blood price for a death which they had not caused. Otherwise, the Ottoman authorities seemed happy for the rabbis to run the legal affairs of their community, cooperating with them and giving them support, for instance, in enforcing sentences, an area where the rabbis often felt their weakness. Without this backing, the rabbinical courts could not have functioned.[32]

For the main point about this system was the enormous power it gave to the rabbis themselves. Although they were appointed and paid by the lay notables who ran the synagogues, Ottoman practice in effect turned them into something approximating Jewish *kadis*—religiously trained lawyers. But this is not really so surprising when one bears in mind how, over time, Salonica's Jews were beginning to adapt some Ottoman legal institutions to their own needs—for instance, the charitable foundation (*vakf*) and inheritable usufruct (*yediki*)—and starting to follow Muslim custom by growing their beards longer, wearing turbans, robes and outer cloaks, and making their women cover themselves more than in the past. In the law, as in other areas of life, the Jews of Sefarad were becoming Ottoman.[33]

The range of issues rabbis pronounced on was vast: tenancy disputes, matrimonial, probate and commercial law made up the bread and butter business, but there were also medical matters—what kinds of venereal disease justified a woman in divorcing her husband; or when abortion was permissible. The traumatic rupture of family life experienced by the refugees was reflected in various dilemmas: Could the son of a Jewish man and a black slave inherit his father's estate? What was the situation of women whose husbands had converted to Christianity and had remained in Spain? How many wives was a man allowed to take? To help decide, entire libraries were brought over from Spain and Italy, and merchants paid scribes and copyists to transcribe rare manuscripts and translate Hebrew texts into Ladino. In fact, rabbis felt at a disadvantage when forced to rule without the judgements of their predecessors to guide them. One, caught outside the city by a supplicant at a time when the plague was raging, apologizes in advance for offering an opinion without having his books at his elbow.[34]

Controlling power and resources unmatched by their peers elsewhere, Salonica's rabbis possessed a degree of training and a breadth of outlook which made the city a centre of learning throughout the sixteenth-century eastern Mediterranean. An extraordinary centre of print culture too: Jewish books were printed there centuries before any appeared in Greek, Arabic or Ottoman Turkish where religious objections to seeing the sacred texts in print held things back. Equipped with the wide-ranging interests of the Spanish rabbinate, exploiting the familiarity with the holy sources that their availability in translation offered, these scholars simultaneously kept in touch with the latest intellectual fashions in western Europe and pursued extensive programmes of study that took them far beyond the confines of scriptural commentary. They applied Aristotle and Aquinas to the tasks of Talmudic exegesis, engaged with Latin literature, Italian humanism and Arab science, and were not surprisingly intensely proud of the range of their expertise. Insulted by charges of parochialism, for instance, one young scholar challenged an older rabbi from Edirne to an intellectual duel:

> Come out to the field and let us compete in our knowledge of the Bible, the Mishnah and the Talmud, Sifra and Sifre and all of rabbinic literature; in secular sciences—practical and theoretical fields of science; science of nature, and of the Divine; in logic—the *Organon*, in geometry, astronomy *Physics*; . . . *Generatio et Corruptio, De Anima* and *Meteora, De Animalibus* and *Ethics*. In your profession as well, that of medicine, if in your eyes it is a science, we consider it an occupation of no special distinction and all the more in practical matters. Try me, for you have opened your mouth and belittled my dwelling-place, and you shall see that we know whatever can be known in the proper manner.[35]

All this was not love of learning for its own sake—though that there was too—so much as the fruits of the sophisticated curriculum required by the city's scholar-judges, and their response to the opportunities created by Ottoman policy.

Nor did the rabbis, left to their own devices as they mostly were, ignore the fact that they lived in a state run on the basis of the *shari'a*: Jews might be represented by Muslims professionally if they lived in certain neighbourhoods or belonged to certain guilds; Jewish men (like Christians) converted to Islam for financial advantage or to marry—even on one occasion to get the help of the authorities in wresting another man's wife away from him; some Jewish women married Muslim men, or converted to facilitate a divorce when their husband was reluctant to grant it. All these situations made a knowledge of the *shari'a* desirable on the part of the rabbi-judge. But if a degree of familiarity with secular Ottoman law, the Qur'an and the *shari'a* was common practice in many Ottoman Jewish communities, a few Salonican scholars took their interest in Arab thought even further. "I will only mention the name of Abuhamed and his book, because it is very widespread among us," notes Rabbi Isaac ibn Aroyo, referring to the philosopher al-Ghazali. Rabbi David ibn Shoshan, blind and wealthy, was said to have been not only "a master of all wisdom, both Talmud and secular studies, astronomy and philosophy," but also "very familiar with books on the Moslem religion to such an extent that Moslem scholars and judges used to visit him to learn their own religious tomes from him." When he moved to Istanbul, "the greatest Arab scholars used to honour him there greatly because of his great wisdom." One of his students, Jacob HaLevi, translated the Qur'an, a book which we know other Jewish scholars too kept in their libraries.[36]

WHERE SALONICA WAS CONCERNED, the Ottoman strategy proved highly effective, and by attracting a large number of Jews and Marranos, the sultans succeeded in revitalizing the city. By the mid-sixteenth century its population had grown to thirty thousand and it generated the highest per capita yield of taxes in the Balkans and the largest revenue of any urban settlement to the west of Istanbul. It would not be going too far to say that this economic success provided much of the fiscal sinew for the sultan's military triumphs. The Jewish immigrants embraced the opportunity Bayezid II had given them and brought an entrepreneurial and productive energy which astonished the city's existing residents. The resulting Hispanization of its culture was long-lasting: although there were ups and downs in the state of the economy, and in standards of rabbinical learning, the cultural imprint of Judeo-Spanish was felt right up to the end of the empire. In 1892, on the four-hundredth anniversary of the edict of expulsion, Spanish journalists and politicians visited the Macedonian port. There they found a continuing link to their own past, an outpost of Iberian life which had been forgotten in the home-country for centuries. In the words of the Spanish senator Dr. Angel Pulido Fernandez, they were *Spaniards without a Homeland*; but this was not quite true. Their homeland was Salonica itself.[37]

4

Messiahs, Martyrs and Miracles

When I was in Salonica the second time, I received an order to
perform contrary deeds and so when I met a Turk on a Greek
street I drew my sword & forced him to speak the name of the
First and the Second and to make the sign of the cross, and then
I did not let him go until he did it; similarly, having met a Greek
in a Turkish street I forced him to say the words "Mahomet is
the true prophet," and also the names of the first two & ordered
him to lift one finger upward according to the Mahometan custom. And again, when I met a Jew he had to make the sign of the
cross for me, and also to pronounce those two names when this
happened in a Greek street, while when I met him in a Turkish
street he had to raise one finger upward & name those two
names. And I was performing those deeds daily.

YAKOV FRANK (1726–1791), Autohagiography no. 15[1]*

IN THE OTTOMAN EMPIRE religious affiliation provided the categories according to which the state classified its subjects. Muslims had
to be readily distinguishable from non-Muslims, who existed in a position of legal inferiority. "Their headgear is a saffron yellow turban,"
wrote the French agent Nicolas de Nicolay of the Salonican Jews in the
mid-sixteenth century, "that of the Greek Christians is blue, and that of
the Turks is pure white so that by the difference in colour they may be
known apart." Yellow shoes, bright clothes and white or green turbans
were reserved for members of the ruling faith, as were delicate or
expensive fabrics. A later traveller, Tournefort, found "the subjects of

---

*Frank, a messianic figure in his own right, was a follower of Sabbatai Zevi, and
Barouch Russo (see below).

the Grand Signior, Christians or Jews, have [their slippers] either red, violet or black. This order is so well-establish'd, and observ'd with such Exactness, that one may know what Religion any one is of by the Feet and the Head."[2]

But regulations were one thing, and what people did in real life was another, especially when out of sight of the imperial capital. Boundaries were constantly being subverted by accident or design and in a bustling commercial port in particular, religious communities could not be impermeably sealed from one another. Young Muslim boys served as apprentices to Christian shoe-makers; Jewish and Muslim *hamals* and casual labourers scoured the docks together for work. When well-off Muslim families employed Jewish and Christian servants and milk-nurses, the children of the families intermingled and the boys often became "milk-brothers," a relationship which could endure for many years. In Salonica, with its unique confessional composition, there thus arose what a later visitor described as "a sort of fusion between the different peoples who inhabit the place and a happy rapprochement between the races which the nature of their beliefs and the diversity of their origins tends to separate."[3]

The stress Islam laid on the unity of God made possible what was, within its own self-imposed limits, an inclusive attitude to other religions of the Book. For unlike the Jews, who regarded themselves as a chosen people, and the Christians who repudiated and distanced themselves from their origins by focusing on the charge of deicide against the Jews, Muslims explicitly acknowledged their own connection to the earlier monotheistic faiths. Christ himself, though not regarded as divine in nature, was celebrated as a prophet—one particularly stern preacher is even reputed to have had someone executed for blaspheming against his name. The adaptation too of churches and Christian shrines for Muslim use could be seen not as deliberate humiliation and desecration—though it was naturally seen that way by Christians—but as a recognition by Muslims that God lingered already in the holy places of their predecessors.[4]

One should not, obviously, ignore the powerful evidence for the mutual contempt and hostility that could be projected across the religious divides—the janissaries who beat a Christian arms merchant to death in the market, shouting, "Why are you an unbeliever? So much sorrow you are!"; the Jewish householders who mocked Christian worshippers during holy festivals; the stuffed effigies of Judas burned with much glee by the Orthodox during Easter. (Muslims were occasionally

mocked in public too, but only by those who wished to become martyrs.) Popular hostility was palpable against those who converted and
abandoned their ancestral faith. Yet even—perhaps especially—when
confessional boundaries were not crossed, the daily life of the city fostered a considerable sharing of beliefs and practices.[5]

For contrary to what our secular notions of a religious state might
lead us to believe, the Ottoman authorities were not greatly interested
in policing people's private beliefs. In general, they did not care what
their subjects thought so long as they preserved the outward forms of
piety. This attitude was shared by many non-Muslims too. Visiting
Catholics, for whom doctrine mattered a great deal, were struck by the
perfunctory character of Orthodox observance. "Among this people
there is immense ignorance not only of councils but of the Christian
faith," noted a Ukrainian Catholic in the early eighteenth century.
"They retain the name of Christ and the sign of the cross but nothing
else." Such accusations of doctrinal ignorance said as much about the
accuser as about Salonica's Christians, for the latter tenaciously
observed the feast-days and customs they felt to be important. But it is
true that there was far less theological policing under the Ottomans
than there was in Christendom at this time, and this laxity of atmosphere and absence of heresy-hunters fostered the emergence of a popular religious culture which more than anything else in the early modern
period united the city's diverse faiths around a common sense of the
sacred and divine.[6]

MARRANOS AND MESSIAHS

ON SUNDAY, 2 JANUARY 1724, a Jewish doctor was chatting with
one of his Christian patients and telling him his life story. He had
grown up a Catholic in the Algarve where he had been baptized and
went to church regularly. But his parents had also secretly instructed
him in the tenets of Judaism as well and "inside he was a Jew." At the
age of thirty, after constant harassment and petty persecutions, he had
left Portugal, and for the past fourteen years he had been settled in
Salonica, where he had returned to his family's original faith. "So stubborn are heathens in their unbelief," his shocked patient confided to his
diary.[7]

It was not only Jews who had remained true to their ancestral faith
that took the path of exile from the Iberian lands to Salonica, but also

large numbers of so-called Marranos and New Christians—in other words, those who had already converted to Catholicism, in some cases many generations before leaving. Some of them—like the doctor—had kept Jewish customs alive secretly for decades, and equipped their children with two names ("If you ask one of their children: 'What's your name?' " reported one observer, "they will respond: 'At home they call me Abraham and in the street Francesco.' "). On the other hand, many others were fully observant Catholics who had been forced from Spain and Portugal by the Inquisition, essentially on the grounds of race rather than religion. In Salonica, this group had trouble adjusting to rabbinical Judaism, and the rabbis in turn found it hard to make their minds up about them. The question of whether or not they were "still" Jews divided learned opinion. Several leading rabbis thought *not*, since many Marranos had only abandoned Iberia (and Catholicism) when forced out. The 1506 Lisbon massacre of Portuguese "New Christians" induced a more sympathetic attitude, but many of Salonica's Jews and their rabbis, even those descended from Marrano families themselves, remained highly suspicious of the latters' motives and regarded them as apostates.[8]

For as they well knew, religion could often serve simply as a flag of convenience. Catholics returned to Judaism as they had left it, to protect their wealth or to inherit property from relatives; in Italy Jews allowed themselves to be baptized for similar reasons. Traders even switched between faiths as they sailed from the Ottoman lands to the Papal states. One seventeenth-century Marrano, Abraam Righetto, in his own words, "lived as a Jew but sometimes went to church and ate and drank often with Christians." Another, Moise Israel, also known by his Christian name of Francesco Maria Leoncini, was baptized no less than three times as he shifted to and fro, and "was making merchandise of sacred religion" in the graphic words of an outraged commentator. Such men were dismissed by contemporaries as "ships with two rudders," but they were not particularly uncommon. A certain Samuel Levi went even further, converting to Islam as a boy in Salonica—mostly, according to him, to avoid punishment at school—then reverting to Judaism once safely across the Adriatic to marry an Ottoman Jewish woman—*la Turchetta*—in the Venice ghetto, before ending up baptized as a Catholic by the Bishop of Ferrara.[9]

Salonica offered the Marranos the possibility of a less concealed, perilous and ambiguous kind of life, and the activities of the Portuguese Inquisition after 1536 led many to make their home there. Yet even those who returned to Judaism for good preserved characteristic features of the old ways. Their past experience of the clandestine life, their inevitably suspicious attitude towards religious authority, as well as their exposure to Catholic illuminism, inclined them to esoteric beliefs and mysticism. Salonica became a renowned centre of Kabbalah where eminent rabbis were guided by heavenly voices and taught their pupils to comprehend the divine will through the use of secret forms of calculation known only to initiates.

And with Kabbalah came the taste for messianic speculation. Each bout of persecution since the end of the thirteenth century had generated prophecies of imminent redemption for the Jews. Their exodus from Spain, the Ottoman conquest of the biblical lands and the onset of the titanic struggle between the Spanish crown and the Ottoman sultans stoked up apocalyptic expectations to a new pitch. The learned Isaac Abravanel, whose library was one of the most important in Salonica, calculated that the process of redemption would begin in 1503 and be completed by 1531. Others saw in the conflict between Charles V and Suleyman the Magnificent the biblical clash of Gog and Magog which according to the scholars would usher in the "king-messiah."[10]

In 1524, a mysterious Jewish adventurer called David Ruebeni arrived in Venice and presented himself as prince of one of the lost tribes of Israel. He gained an audience with the Pope and told the Holy Roman Emperor to arm the Jews so that they might regain Palestine. Crossing his path was an even less modest figure—a Portuguese New Christian called Diego Pires. After rediscovering his Jewish roots and changing his name to Solomon Molcho, he studied the Kabbalah in Salonica with some of the city's most eminent rabbis and gradually made the transition to messianic prophet. He predicted the sack of Rome—which occurred at the hands of imperial troops in 1527—and then declared himself to be the Messiah, and went to Rome itself, in accordance with the apocalyptic programme, where he sat for thirty days in rags by the city gates praying for its destruction. Before being burned at the stake, Molcho saw the future: the Tiber was flooding over, and Turkish troops were bursting into the seat of the Papacy. The truly striking thing about Molcho is how many people believed in him and preserved and reinterpreted his messianic timetables. Relics of the martyr were carried across Europe and a century after his death, they were still being displayed in the *Pinkas Shul* in Prague.[11]

By the mid-seventeenth century, millenarian fever had grown, if anything, more intense. In the centres of Jewish mysticism, Salonica and Safed in particular, scholars prepared for the coming of the Messiah. The apocalyptically minded saw positive signs in the murderous wars of religion in central Europe, the Turkish campaigns in Poland and the Mediterranean, the admission of Jews into the Protestant lands, and the persecution of east European Jewry by the Cossacks. Expectations—both Jewish and Christian—focused on the year 1666. "According to the Predictions of several *Christian* writers, especially of such who Comment on the *Apocalyps*, or Revelations," wrote one commentator, "this year of 1666 was to prove a Year of Wonders, and Strange Revolutions in the World." Protestants looked forward to the Jews' conversion, Jews themselves to their imminent return to Zion. Rumours ran across Europe, and it was reported "that a Ship was arrived in the Northern parts of *Scotland* with her Sails and Cordage of Silk, Navigated by Mariners who spake nothing but *Hebrew*; with this Motto on their Sails, *The Twelve Tribes of Israel*."[12]

That winter a forty-year-old Jewish scholar from Izmir headed for Istanbul with the declared intention of toppling the sultan and ushering in the day of redemption. Sabbatai Zevi had been proclaiming himself the Messiah on and off for some years while he wandered through the rabbinical academies of the eastern Mediterranean. Helped by wealthy Jewish backers in Egypt, and by a promotional campaign launched on his behalf by a young Gaza rabbi, he was mobbed by supporters when he returned to his home-town. According to one account "he immediately started to appear as a Monarch, dressed in golden and silken clothes, most beautiful and rich. He used to carry a sort of Sceptre in his hand and to go about Town always escorted by a great number of Jews, some of whome, to honour him, would spread carpets on the streets for him to step on."[13]

It was only, however, once he headed for the capital, announcing he was planning to depose the sultan himself, that the Ottoman authorities became alarmed. By this point, he had thrown the entire Jewish world into turmoil. From Buda to Aleppo and Cairo, thousands declared their allegiance and shouted down the doubters. "It was strange to see how the fancy took, and how fast the report of *Sabatai* and his Doctrine flew through all parts where *Turks* and *Jews* inhabited," noted an English observer. "I perceived a strange transport in the *Jews*, none of them attending to any business unless to wind up former negotiations, and to prepare themselves and Families for a Journey to *Jerusalem*: All their Discourses, their Dreams and disposal of their Affairs tended to no other Design but a re-establishment in the Land of Promise, to Great-ness, Glory, Wisdom, and Doctrine of the Messiah."[14]

Nowhere was the frenzy greater than in Salonica, where Zevi was a well-known figure. He had spent some years studying there with local scholars, and preached regularly in the synagogue of the Marranos. In 1659 he had outraged his audience by pronouncing the divine name and was excommunicated and forced to leave. Now, however, the city was gripped by millenarian hysteria. Anticipating the Messiah's arrival, rabbis ordered acts of penance and fasting; in their enthusiasm some acolytes starved themselves to death, or whipped themselves till their backs were bleeding. "Others buryed themselves in their Gardens, cov-ering their naked Bodies with Earth, their heads onely excepted remained in their Beds of dirt until their Bodies were stiffened with the cold and moisture: others would indure to have melted Wax dropt upon their Shoulders, others to rowl themselves in Snow, and throw their Bodies in the Coldest season of Winter into the Sea, or Frozen Waters." Preparing to go and meet him, shopkeepers sold off their stock at bargain prices, parents married off their children and all sought "to purge their *Consciences* of Sin." Christians and Muslims looked on in bemusement and scorn. When a French onlooker smiled at the wild abandon of the crowds, a young Jewish boy told him "that I had noth-ing to smile about since shortly we would all become their slaves by the virtue of their Messiah."[15]

Even Zevi's arrest en route to the capital, and his subsequent deten-tion, did not diminish his influence. To the Grand Vizier he denied ever having claimed he was the Messiah; but at the same time, he addressed the Jews of the capital as "The Only Son and Firstborn of God, Mes-siah and Saviour of the World." Delegations visited him from as far afield as Holland, Poland, Germany and Persia, and hundreds of pil-grims made their way to see him. A light—so bright as to blind those who looked upon it—was said to have shone from his face and a crown of fire was seen above his head. He was dressed in expensive garments paid for by his admirers; in return, he sent out instructions for new fes-tivals to be celebrated in his honour. Only in Istanbul did doubters pub-licly resist his claims. In the Balkans his supporters held sway; women dressed themselves in white and prepared to "go and slay demons." His fame even prompted another Kabbalist, a Polish Jew named Nehemiah, to make his way to Gallipoli, where Zevi was being held, to tell him that the books foretold the arrival of a *second*, subordinate Messiah, which unsurprisingly he proclaimed himself to be.[16]

Zevi and Nehemiah quickly quarrelled, no doubt because Zevi suspected the newcomer of trying to steal his thunder. But the quarrel had fateful implications, for Nehemiah went straight to the Ottoman authorities and revealed the full extent of what Zevi had been saying to his followers. For added effect, he accused Zevi of lewdness and immorality, charges which his ecstatic conduct—and his well-known views that "God permitteth that which is forbidden"—made highly plausible. Although Mehmed IV's first impulse seems to have been to have Zevi executed, the hunt-loving monarch, who rarely attended too closely to matters of state, was persuaded by his advisers to give him the chance to convert to Islam. The *ulema* were conscious of the danger of turning him into a martyr; the Grand Vizier agreed. Zevi was interrogated in the sultan's presence where one of the royal physicians, Hayatizade Mustafa Fevzi Efendi—a convert whose original name was Moshe Abravanel—translated for him from Turkish into Judeo-Spanish, and said he could get his supporters to follow him if he became a Muslim. To the astonishment of Ottoman Jewry, Zevi agreed, taking the name Aziz Mehmed Efendi and being honoured with the title of Chief Palace Gatekeeper and a royal pension. For the next six years, he lived in Edirne, Salonica and Istanbul under the eye of the Porte, receiving instruction in Islam from—and offering insights into Judaism to—the Grand Vizier's personal spiritual adviser. Sometimes Zevi issued commands which encouraged his followers to convert; at others, he behaved as though still a Jew at heart. In 1672 he was banished to a remote port on the Albanian coast where he died four years later. Despite the temptation to take stern action against the Jews, even apparently considering at one stage to force them to convert *en masse*, the Ottoman authorities adroitly allowed the movement to fizzle out.[17]

The Messiah's conversion was not the end of the matter, however. After his apostasy, there were ceremonies of expiation, contrition, and later of excommunication, but even then many of his followers remained undeflected: they argued the Messiah had converted to test the strength of their faith, or perhaps to bring the Turks themselves onto the right path—for was the Messiah not to care for humanity as a whole, and not just the Jews? Reading things in this way did not seem perverse to them: interpreting events so as to distinguish their outward meaning from their true, inner significance was, after all, at the heart of the Sabbataian teaching, while dissimulation and deliberate self-abasement in the eyes of the world had a positive value for mystics of all kinds—Jews, Christians and Muslims. Zevi's apostasy was recast in

Kabbalistic terms as an act of virtue, a way to redemption, gathering in the sparks of the Divine that had become scattered throughout the material world of sensory perception and matter itself. Zevi may have confirmed that those who thought this way were on the right path when he stopped briefly in Salonica the year after his conversion. He certainly got a number of leading notables and rabbis to follow him, provoking further fratricidal rage, brawls and even killings which the community managed to hush up. Eventually he was forced out of the city for the last time, and a triumvirate of chief rabbis took control and attempted to avert any further disturbances. Henceforth there was a deep suspicion of mysticism. Yet most of Zevi's followers—like his right-hand man, the Gaza rabbi Nathan—never did convert and subterranean Sabbataian influences could be found among Jews as far afield as Poland, Italy and Egypt. In Salonica they lingered on for decades and only disappeared after the Napoleonic wars.[18]

THE *MA'MIN*

HUNDREDS MORE, HOWEVER, did actually follow Zevi into Islam—some at the time, and others a few years later—and by doing so they gave rise to what was perhaps one of the most unusual religious communities in the Levant. To the Turks they were called *Dönmehs* (turncoats), a derogatory term which conveyed the suspicion with which others always regarded them. But they called themselves simply *Ma'min*—the Faithful—a term commonly used by all Muslims.* There were small groups of them elsewhere, but Zevi's last wife, Ayse, and her father, a respected rabbi called Joseph Filosof, were from Salonica, and after Zevi's death, they returned there and helped to establish the new sect which he had created. By 1900, the city's ten-thousand-strong community of Judeo-Spanish-speaking Muslims was one of the most extraordinary and (for its size) influential elements in the confessional mosaic of the late Ottoman empire.

Schism was built into their history from the start. Not unlike the Sunni-Shia split in mainstream Islam, the internal divisions of the *Ma'min* stemmed from disagreement over the line of succession which followed their Prophet's death. In 1683 his widow Ayse hailed her

---

*In Hebrew, the term is *Maminim;* in Turkish *Mümin*. *Ma'min* was a Salonica derivation.

brother Jacob—Zevi's brother-in-law—as the *Querido* (Beloved) who had received Zevi's spirit, and there was a second wave of conversions. Many of those who had converted at the same time as Zevi regarded this as impious nonsense: they were known as *Izmirlis*, after Zevi's birthplace. Jacob Querido himself helped Islamicize his followers and left Salonica to make the *haj* in the early 1690s but died during his return from Mecca. As the historian Nikos Stavroulakis points out, both the *Izmirlis* and the *Yakublar* (the followers of Jacob Querido) saw themselves as the faithful awaiting the return of the Messiah who had "withdrawn" himself from the world; it was a stance which crossed the Judeo-Muslim divide and turned Sabbatai Zevi himself into something like a hidden Imam of the kind found in some Shia theology.[19] A few years later, a third group, drawn mostly from among the poor and artisanal classes, broke off from the *Izmirlis* to follow another charismatic leader, the youthful Barouch Russo (known to his followers as Osman Baba), who claimed to be not merely the vessel for Zevi's spirit but his very reincarnation.[20]

Although they differed on doctrinal matters, the three factions had features in common. Following the advice of Zevi himself, whose eighteen commandments forbade any form of proselytism, they preserved an extreme discretion as a precaution against the suspicions and accusations which they encountered from both Turks and Jews. Even their prayers were suffused with mystical allusions to protect their inner meanings from being deciphered by outsiders.[21]

Over time they developed a kind of mystical Islam with a Judaic component not found in mainstream Muslim life. While they attended mosque and sometimes made the *haj*, they initially preserved Judeo-Spanish for use within the home, something which lasted longest among Russo's followers. They celebrated Ramadan, and ate the traditional sweets on the 10th of *Moharrem*, to mark the deaths of Hasan and Huseyn. Like their cooking, the eighteen commandments which they attributed to Zevi showed clearly the influence of both Muslim and Talmudic practice. (Was it coincidence that eighteen was also a number of special significance to the Mevlevi order?) They prayed to their Messiah, "our King, our Redeemer," in "the name of God, the God of Israel," but followed many of the patterns of Muslim prayer. They increasingly followed Muslim custom in circumcizing their males just before puberty, and read the Qur'an, but referred to their festivals using the Jewish calendar. Some hired rabbis to teach the Torah to their children. Although the common suspicion throughout the city—certainly well into the nineteenth century—was that they were really Jews (if of a highly unreliable kind), in fact they were evolving over time into a distinctive heterodox Muslim sect, much influenced by the Sufi orders.

The Ottoman authorities clearly regarded their heterodoxy with some suspicion and as late as 1905 treated a case of a *Ma'min* girl who had fallen in love with her Muslim tutor, Hadji Feyzullah Effendi, as a question of conversion. Yet with their usual indifference to inner belief, they left them alone. A pasha who proposed to put them all to death was, according to local myth, removed by God before he could realize his plan. In 1859, at a time when the Ottoman authorities were starting to worry more about religious orthodoxy, a governor of the city carried out an enquiry which concluded they posed no threat to public order. All he did was to prevent rabbis from instructing them any longer. A later investigation confirmed their prosperity and honesty and after 1875 such official monitoring lapsed. *Ma'min* spearheaded the expansion of Muslim—including women's—schooling in the city, and were prominent in its commercial and intellectual life. Merchant dynasties like the fez-makers, the Kapandjis, accumulated huge fortunes, built villas in the European style by the sea and entered the municipal administration. Others were in humbler trades—barbers, coppersmiths, town-criers and butchers.[22]

Gradually—as with the Marranos of Portugal, from whom many were descended—their connection with their ancestral religion faded. High-class *Ma'min* married into mainstream Muslim society, though most resided in central quarters, between the Muslim neighbourhoods of the Upper Town and the Jewish quarters below, streets where often the two religions lived side by side. "They will be converted purely and simply into Muslims," predicted one scholar in 1897. But like many of Salonica's Muslims at this time, the *Ma'min* also embraced European learning, and identified themselves with secular knowledge, political radicalism and freemasonry. By a strange twist of fate it was thus the Muslim followers of a Jewish messiah who helped turn late-nineteenth-century Salonica into the most liberal, progressive and revolutionary city in the empire.

The juxtaposition of old and new outlooks in a fin-de-siècle *Ma'min* household is vividly evoked in the memoirs of Ahmed Emin Yalman. His father, Osman Tewfik Bey, was a civil servant and a teacher of calligraphy. Living in the house with him and his parents were his uncle and aunt, his seven siblings, two orphaned cousins and at least five servants. "The strife between the old and the new was ever present in our house," he recollects. His uncle was of the old school: a devout man, he prayed five times a day, abhorred alcohol, and disliked travel or innovation. For some reason, he refused to wear white shirts; "a coloured shirt with attached collar was, for him, the extreme limit of westernization in dress to which he felt that one could go without falling into conflict with religion . . . He objected to the theatre, music, drinking, card playing, and photography—all new inventions which he considered part of Satan's world." Yalman's father, on the other hand—Osman Tewfik Bey—was "a progressive, perhaps even a revolutionary," who wore "the highest possible white collars," beautiful cravats and stylish shoes in the latest fashion, loved poetry, theatre and anything that was new, taking his children on long trips and photographing them with enthusiasm. He adorned his rooms with their pictures and prayed but rarely.[23]

Esin Eden's memoir of the following generation shows Europeanization taken even further. Hers was a well-to-do family of tobacco merchants which combined a strong consciousness of its Jewish ancestry with pride in its contemporary achievements as part of a special Muslim community, umbilically linked to Salonica itself. The women were all highly educated—one was even a teacher at the famous new Terakki lycée—sociable, energetic and articulate. They smoked lemon-scented cigarettes in the garden of their modern villa by the sea, played cards endlessly and kept their eyes on the latest European fashions. Their servants were Greek, their furnishings French and German, and their cuisine a mix of "traditionally high Ottoman cuisine as well as traditional Sephardic cooking," though with no concern for the dietary laws of Judaism.[24]

When the Young Turk revolt broke out in Salonica in 1908, *Ma'min* economics professors, newspaper men, businessmen and lawyers were among the leading activists and there were three *Ma'min* ministers in the first Young Turk government. Indeed conspiracy theorists saw the *Ma'min* everywhere and assumed any Muslim from Salonica must be one. Today some people even argue that Mustafa Kemal Ataturk must have been a *Ma'min* (there is no evidence for this), and see the destruction of the Ottoman empire and the creation of the secular republic of Turkey as their handiwork—the final revenge, as it were, of Sabbatai Zevi, and the unexpected fulfilment of his dreams. In fact, many of the *Ma'min* themselves had mixed feelings at what was happening in nationalist Turkey: some were Kemalists, others opposed him. In 1923, however, they were all counted as Muslims in the compulsory exchange of populations and packed off to Istanbul, where a small but distinguished community of businessmen, newspaper magnates, industrialists and diplomats has since flourished. As the writer John Freely tells us, their cemetery, in the Valley of the Nightingales above Üsküdar, on the Asian side of the Bosphorus, is still known as the *Selanikliler Mezarligi*—the Cemetery of Those from Salonica.[25]

Meanwhile, in the city which nurtured them for many years in its curiously unconcerned atmosphere, little trace of their presence now remains. Their old quarters were destroyed in the 1917 fire, or in the rebuilding which followed; their cemetery, which lay next to the large Sephardic necropolis outside the walls, became a football field. Today their chief monument is the magnificent fin-de-siècle *Yeni Djami*, tucked away in a postwar suburb on the way to the airport. Used as an annexe to the Archaeological Museum, its leafy precinct is stacked with ancient grave stelai and mausoleums, and its airy light interior is opened occasionally for exhibitions. Built in 1902 by the local architect Vitaliano Poselli, it is surely one of the most eclectic and unusual mosques in the world, a domed neo-Renaissance villa, with windows framed in the style of late Habsburg Orientalism and pillars which flank the entrance supporting a solid horse-shoe arch straight out of Moorish Spain. Complete with sundial (with Ottoman instructions on how to set your watch) and clocktower, the Yeni Djami sums up the extraordinary blending of influences—Islamic and European, Art Nouveau meets a neo-Baroque Alhambra, with a discreet hint of the ancestral faith in the star of David patterns cut into the upper-floor balconies—which made up the *Ma'mins'* world.[26]

THE SUFI ORDERS

THE CITY, DELICATELY POISED in its confessional balance of power—ruled by Muslims, dominated by Jews, in an overwhelmingly Christian hinterland—lent itself to an atmosphere of overlapping devotion. With time it became covered in a dense grid of holy places—fountains, tombs, cemeteries, shrines and monasteries—frequented by members of all faiths in search of divine intercession. One of the most important institutions in the creation of this sanctified world were the heterodox Islamic orders—known to scholars as Sufis and to the public, inaccurately, as dervishes—who played such a pivotal role in consolidating Ottoman rule in the Balkans. Western travellers to the empire never, if they could help it, lost the opportunity to describe these mysterious and otherworldly figures with their whirling dances and strange ritual howlings. But dwelling on such eccentricities—abstracted from their theological context—turned their acolytes into figures of fun and overlooked their central role in bridging confessional divides during the Ottoman centuries.[27]

Many of these mystical orders borrowed heavily from the shamanistic traditions of central Asian nomad life and from the eastern Christianity they found around them. But by the fourteenth and fifteenth centuries they were powerful forces in their own right, supported by— and supportive of—sultans like Murad II, who founded a large Mevlevi monastery in Edirne. When Ottoman troops conquered the Balkans, they were accompanied and sometimes preceded by holy men who spread the ideas of the missionary-warrior Haci Bektash, the poet Rumi and Baha' al-Din Naqshband. Their highly unorthodox visions of the ways to God were shared in religious brotherhoods financed by pious benefactions. Some of their leaders—men like the fifteenth-century heretic *sheykh* Bedreddin—saw themselves as the Mahdi, revealing the secret of divine unity across faiths, and legalizing what the *shari'a* had previously forbidden. From the early sixteenth century, as the Ottoman state, and its clerical class, the *ulema*, conquered the Arab lands and became more conscious of the responsibility of the caliphate and the dangers of Persian heterodoxy, these unorthodox and sometimes heretical movements came under attack. In the mid-seventeenth century, Vani Effendi, the puritanical court preacher who converted Sabbatai Zevi, was outraged by the permissive attitude of some of them to stimulants such as coffee, alcohol and opium, as well as by their worship of saints and their pantheist tendencies. Murad IV took a dim view of such practices, and at least one tobacco-smoking *mufti* of Salonica got in trouble as a result. In practice, however, many leading statesmen and clergymen were also "brothers" of one group or another, and generally they prospered.[28]

Most major orders had their representatives in a place as important as Salonica where there were more than twenty shrines and monasteries, guarding all the city's gates and approaches. We know of the existence of the Halvetiye, who expanded into the Balkans in the sixteenth century and gave the city several of its *muftis*. Even during the First World War, the Rifa'i were still attracting tourists to their ceremonies: Alicia Little watched them jumping and howling, and was struck by their generous hospitality and their courtesy to guests. One nineteenth-century Albanian merchant, who made his fortune in Egypt, allowed his villa in the new suburb along the seashore to be used as a Melami *tekke;* among its adepts were the head of the Military School, an army colonel, a local book-dealer and a Czech political refugee who had converted to Islam.[29]

There were *tekkes* of the Nakshbandis, the Sa'dis and many others. The magnificent gardens and cypresses of the Mevlevi monastery, situated strategically next to a reservoir which stored much of the city's drinking water, attracted many of the city's notable families and appear to have been popular with wealthy *Ma'min* as well. The Mevlevi were extremely well-funded, and controlled access to the tomb of Ayios Dimitrios and many other holy places in the city. They retained close ties with local Christians and were reportedly "always to be found in company with the Greek [monks]." One British diplomat at the end of the nineteenth century recounts a long conversation with a senior Mevlevi *sheykh*, a man whose "shaggy yellow beard and golden spectacles made him look more like a German professor than a dancing dervish." Together, in the *sheykh's* office, the two men drank raki, discussed photography—local prejudices hindered him using his Kodak, the *sheykh* complained—and talked about the impact a new translation of the central Mevlevi text, the *Mesnevi*, had made in London. "He did not care about the introduction of Mohammedanism into England," noted the British diplomat, "but he had hoped that people might have seen that the mystic principles enunciated in the *Mesnevi* were compatible with all religions and could be grafted on Christianity as well as on Islam."[30]

Of all the Sufi orders in the Balkans, however, perhaps the most successful and influential were the Bektashi. They had monastic foundations everywhere and they were very closely associated with the janissary corps, the militia of forcibly converted Christian boys which was the spearhead of the Ottoman army. Often they took over existing holy places, saints' tombs and Christian churches, a practice which had started in Anatolia and continued with the Ottoman advance into Europe. In the early twentieth century, the brilliant young British scholar Hasluck charted the dozens of Bektashi foundations which still existed at the time of the Balkan Wars as far north as Budapest, most of which (outside Albania, which is even today an important centre) have long since disappeared. In such places, people came, lit candles and stuck rags in nearby trees—a common way of soliciting saintly assistance. In Macedonia, the Evrenos family supported the order; in Salonica itself, it owned several modestly appointed *tekkes*.[31]

The Bektashi themselves had a close connection with the worship of Christ. Their use of bread and wine in their rituals, their stress on the twelve Imams (akin to the twelve apostles), and many other features of their rites all bore a close resemblance to Christian practice. In southern Albania, according to Hasluck, legend claimed that Haji Bektash was himself from a Christian family—he had converted to Islam before coming to recognize the superiority of his original faith, whereupon he invented Bektashism as a bridge between the two. The lack of any basis in fact for the story should not disguise its symbolic truth. As one close observer of the movement explained: "It is their doctrine to be liberal towards all professions and religions, and to consider all men as equal in the eyes of God."[32]

THE POWERS OF THE CITY

BENEATH THE CONFESSIONAL divides and helped by such creeds, there existed a kind of submerged popular religion, defined by common belief in the location and timing of divine power. Take the calendar itself: whether under their Christian or Muslim titles, Saint George's Day in the spring and Saint Dimitrios's Day at the end of autumn marked key points in the year for business and legal arrangements affecting the entire society, the dates for instance when residential leases expired, shepherds moved between lowland and upland pastures, and bread prices were set by the local authorities.

Salonica's Casimiye Mosque, which had formerly been Saint Dimitrios's church, saw the cult of the city's patron saint continuing under Muslim auspices. Casim himself was an example—one of many in the Balkans—of those holy figures who were Islamicized versions of Christian saints, and Dimitrios's tomb was kept open for pilgrims of both faiths by the Mevlevi officials who looked after the mosque. Near the very end of the empire, a French traveller caught the final moments of this arrangement and described how it worked. He was ushered into a dark chapel by the *hodja*, together with two Greeks who had come for divine help. This conversation followed:

> "Your name?" asked the Turk . . . "Georgios," replied the Greek, and the Turk, repeating "Georgios," held the knot in the flame,

then commented to the Greek with an air of satisfaction that the knot had not burned. A second time. "The name of your father and your mother?" "Nikolaos my father, Calliope my mother." "And your children?" And when he had thus made three knots carefully, he put the sacred cord in a small packet which he dipped in the oil of the lamp, added a few bits of soil from the tomb, wrapped it all up and handed it to the Greek who seemed entirely content. Then he explained: "If you are ill, or your father, your mother, your children, put the knot on the suffering part and you will be cured." After which, turning to me, the Turk asked "And you?" I shook my head. The Greek was amazed and believed I had not understood and explained it all to me. When I continued to refuse he seemed regretful. "Einai kalon" [It is good] he told me sympathetically . . . and the two Greeks, together with the Muslim sacristan, left the mosque happily.[33]

These rituals were not especially unusual, though the setting was. "If your heart is perplexed with sorrow," the Prophet Mohammed is said to have advised, "go seek consolation at the graves of holy men." Muslims—especially women—made the *ziyaret* at times of domestic need, and the Arabic term was taken over by Salonica's Jews, who spoke of going on a *ziyara* to pray at the tomb of rabbis or deceased relatives. Christian women used both the Jewish cemetery and Muslim mausoleums when collecting earth from freshly dug graves to use against evil spirits. Mousa Baba, Meydan-Sultan Baba and Gul Baba gathered pilgrims to their tombs, even after the twentieth-century exodus of the city's Turks. In the 1930s, Christian women from nearby neighbourhoods were still lighting candles at the tomb of Mousa Baba and asking his help (against malaria), to the surprise of some Greek commentators who could not understand how they could do this "in a city where hundreds of martyrs and holy saints were tortured and martyred in the name of Christ." The answer was that for many of those who came to seek his help, Mousa Baba was not really a Muslim holy man at all. Rather he was Saint George himself, who had metamorphosed into a Turk with supernatural powers: "I heard this when we refugees first came here from Thrace, from a Turkish woman, who told me she had heard it from elderly Turkish women who had explained it to her." Why had Saint George assumed this disguise? For the same reason that Sabbatai Zevi had converted, according to his followers: to make the unbelievers believe.[34]

Power to keep the dead at rest was one of the chief attributes of religious authority, the reverse side of the power to curse or excommunicate. Both powers formed a key weapon in the armoury of the city's spiritual leaders but also transcended the bounds of religious community. According to a local story an archbishop converted to Islam and became a leading *mollah*. While he was still a Christian he had, in a moment of anger, cursed one of his congregation: "May the earth refuse to receive you!" The man died and after three years passed his body was exhumed. Of course it was found in pristine condition "just as if he had been buried the day before"—the power of the excommunication had evidently endured even though the cleric himself had since converted, and only he could revoke it, even though he was now a Muslim: "Having obtained the Pasha's permission, he repaired to the open tomb, knelt beside it, lifted his hands and prayed for a few minutes. He had hardly risen to his feet when, wondrous to relate, the flesh of the corpse crumbled away from the bones and the skeleton remained bare and clean as it had never known pollution." Christian, Muslim or Jew, one looked wherever it was necessary to make the spell work and bring peace to the living and the dead.[35]

For the city was peopled by spirits—evil as well as good. "There are invisible influences everywhere in Turkey," writes Fanny Blunt, a long-time resident of Salonica, in her classic study of Ottoman beliefs and customs—vampires in cemeteries, spirits guarding treasures buried in haunted houses, djinns in abandoned *konaks*, and enticing white-clad *peris* who gathered anywhere near running water. Fountains were dangerous, especially at certain times of the year, and antiquities like the Arch of Galerius were well known to possess evil powers, if approached from the wrong angle. Church leaders tried to draw doctrinal distinctions between acceptable and unacceptable forms of the supernatural, but Salonica's inhabitants did not bother. If the rabbi or bishop could not help them, they appealed to witches, wise men or healers. The religious authorities never felt seriously threatened by such practices, and it is a striking difference with Christian Europe that there were never witchcraft trials in the Ottoman domains. Devils, demons and evil spirits—euphemistically termed "those from below," or "those without number," or more placatingly, "the best of us"—were a fact of life.[36]

"*De ozo ke lo guadre el Dio*—May God guard him from the eye," elderly Jewish ladies muttered. Was there anyone in the city who did not fear being jinxed by the evil eye—*to mati* for the Greeks, the *fena göz* for the Turks—and sought remedies against it? All avoided excessive compliments and feared those who paid them, cursing them under their breath. Moises Bourlas tells us in his wonderful memoirs how his mother was sitting out in the sun one fine Saturday with her neigh-bours, gossiping and chewing pumpkin seeds, when some gypsy fortune-tellers passed them and shouted: "Fine for you, ladies, sitting in the sun and eating pumpkin seeds!" To which his mother instantly and pru-dently replied—*sotto voce* in Judeo-Spanish, so that they could not understand: "*Tu ozo en mi kulo*" (Your eye in my arse).[37]

Fanny Blunt lists accepted remedies: "garlic, cheriot, wild thyme, boar's tusks, hares' heads, terebinth, alum, blue glass, turqoise, pearls, the bloodstone, carnelian, eggs [principally those of the ostrich], a gland extracted from the neck of the ass, written amulets and a thou-sand other objects." She tried out the ass gland on her husband, the British consul, when he was ill, and reported it a success. For keeping babies in good health, experts recommended old gold coins, a cock's spur or silver phylacteries containing cotton wool from the inaugura-tion of a new church (for Christians), bits of paper with the Star of David drawn on them (Jews), or the pentagram (Muslims). Holy water helped Christians, Bulgarians were fond of salt; others used the heads of small salted fish mixed in water, while everyone believed in the power of spitting in the face of a pretty child.

Spells required counter-spells. Mendicant dervishes and gypsy women were believed to know secret remedies, especially for afflicted animals. *Hodjas* provided pest control in the shape of small squares of paper with holy inscriptions that were nailed to the wall of afflicted rooms and Jews wore amulets containing verses from the Torah to ward off the "spirits of the air" which caused depression or fever. Blunt describes some striking cases of cross-faith activity: a Turkish woman snatching hairs from the beard of a Jewish pedlar as a remedy for fever; Muslim children having prayers read over them in church; Christian children similarly blessed by Muslim *hodjas*, who would blow or spit on them, or twist a piece of cotton thread around their wrist to stop their fever. Doctors were not much esteemed; the reputation of *la indul-cadera*—the healer—stood much higher. Against the fear of infertility, ill health, envy or bad luck, the barriers between faiths quickly crum-bled.

ORTHODOXY:
TAX-COLLECTORS AND MARTYRS

BUT WE SHOULD NOT PAINT too rosy a picture of the city's religious possibilities under Ottoman rule. Life was clearly better for some than for others. Muslims were in the ascendant, and the assertive Sefardic Jews, who dominated numerically, found their rule welcoming and were duly grateful. Mosques and synagogues proliferated as a result of official encouragement, and even the extraordinary episode of Sabbatai Zevi can be seen as illustrating the Ottoman state's flexibility with regard to the Jews, who lived in Salonica, as a Jesuit priest noted in 1734, with "more liberty and privileges than anywhere else."[38]

For the city's Christians, on the other hand, Ottoman domination was very much harder to accept. The Byzantine scholar Ioannis Evgenikos lamented the capture of "the most beautiful and God-fearing city of the Romans," and a sense of loss continued to flow beneath the surface of Orthodox life. After all, not even Saint Dimitrios, Salonica's guardian, had saved it from "enslavement." Catholic visitors to the Greek lands often saw their plight as a punishment for their sins, but so did many Orthodox believers. An anonymous seventeenth-century author even pleaded in tones of desperation with the city's saint:

> O great martyr of the Lord Christ, Dimitrios, where are now the miracles which you once performed daily in your own country? Why do you not help us? Why do you not reappear to us? Why, St. Dimitrios, do you fail us and abandon us completely? Can you not see the multitude of hardships, temptations and debts that crowd upon us? Can you not see our shame and disgrace as our enemies trample upon us, the impious jeer at us, the Saracens mock us, and everybody laughs at us?[39]

The small size of the surviving Orthodox population, its lack of wealth, and the constant erosion of its power left none in any doubt of its plight. The Byzantine scholars who had made its intellectual life so vibrant fled abroad—Theodoros Gazis to Italy, Andronikos Kallistos ending up in London—where they helped hand down classical Greek texts to European humanists. Within the city, while rabbinical scholarship flourished, the flame of Christian learning flickered tenuously through the eighteenth century. Such intellectual and spiritual discussions as were taking place within the empire were going on in the monasteries of Mount Athos itself, in the capital, or in the Danubian Principalities to the north. Salonica—the "mother of Orthodoxy"— became a backwater. Bright local Christian boys usually ended up being schooled elsewhere. It is scarcely a coincidence that one of the best-known works to have been composed by a sixteenth-century scholar from the city, the cleric Damaskinos Stouditis (1500–1580), was a collection of religious texts put into simple language for the use of unlearned priests. Stouditis himself had been educated in Istanbul.[40]

First among the temptations that afflicted its Christians, of course, was Islam itself. During the prosperous sixteenth century, in particular, many poor young villagers flocked into the city from the mountains, and these newcomers soon formed a very large part of the local Christian population. Some of them, finding themselves adrift and vulnerable to the dangers facing those far from home, converted for the sake of greater security. Other converts were Christian boys apprenticed to Muslim craftsmen, or girls who had entered Muslim households as domestic servants: in both cases the economic power of the employers paved the way to conversion. But this was a dramatic step at the best of times and one which laid the individual open to unrestrained criticism from his relatives and community. Relatively few Christians (or Jews) with families in Salonica appear to have abandoned their faith. To judge from the mid-eighteenth century, which is when the first data became available, the overall numbers of converts were not great—perhaps ten cases a year in the city and its hinterland.[41]

Even so, Orthodox clerics were always deeply anxious about this. A monk called Nikanor (1491–1549) travelled in the villages to the west of the city, urging the inhabitants to stay true to Christ: "by his sweet precepts and the shining example of his virtuous conduct," we are told by his hagiographer, "he was able to hold many in Christ's faith" before retiring to the solitude of an inaccessible cave high above the Aliakmon River. Nikanor also built a monastery nearby, and in his will urged the monks to refrain from begging for alms without permission, not to mix with those of "another faith" and to avoid seeking justice in Turkish courts, stipulations which suggest the extent to which monks and other pious Christians were usually interacting with the Ottoman authorities in one way or another.[42]

In fact, the very manner in which the Church's ecclesiastical hierarchy was brought within the Ottoman administrative system added to Christian woes. Patriarchs paid an annual tribute to the Porte and acted as tax-collectors from the Christians. When one sixteenth-century Patriarch toured the Balkans, Suleyman the Magnificent ordered officials to summon the metropolitans, bishops and other clerics to help him collect "in full the back payments from the past years and the present year in the amounts which will be established by your examination." In the early eighteenth century, the city's *kadi* was told to help when it turned out that "Ignatius, the metropolitan of Salonica, owes two years' taxes and resists fulfilling his obligations towards the Patriarchate." Fiscal and religious power were separated in both the Muslim and the Jewish communities (where rabbis were salaried employees of their congregations); for the Orthodox they overlapped, damaging the clergy's relations with their flock.[43]

The buying and selling of ecclesiastical favours and offices did not help either: in the seventeenth century alone, there were sixty-one changes of Patriarch. Most Metropolitans of Salonica had run up debts to get into office, and one of the earliest records to survive in the city's archives is a 1695 Ottoman decree from the Porte on behalf of a Christian money-lender ordering Archbishop Methodios to pay what he owed him. The problem travelled down the hierarchy. One priest demanded to be paid before he would read the sacrament to a dying man; others were accused of taking payment to hear confession. The more their seniors took from them, the more the priests required.[44]

Money also explained the endless tussles between Salonica's religious leaders and the lay council of Christian notables, the *archons*, which supposedly ran the non-religious side of community affairs. When the *archons* demanded control over management of the city's charitable Christian foundations, the Patriarchate angrily told them "not to involve themselves in priestly affairs." "There is order in everything," they were rebuked, "and all things in the world, heavenly and mundane, royal and ecclesiastical and civil, right down to the smallest and least important, have their order before God and before men, according to which they are governed and stand in their place." The message was simple: there was no way that "lay people," whatever their motivations, would be allowed to "become rebels and controllers of church affairs." Ironically, the main defence against the rapacity of the clergy were the Ottoman authorities themselves. In 1697 Salonica's Christians complained directly to the Porte about the demands of their bishops, and the *kadi* was instructed to look into the matter. Twenty years later, their anger was so great that they even got the local Ottoman officials to throw one archbishop in jail until he could be removed.[45]

Three hundred years after the conquest, the city was still suffering from a dearth of priests, and lay figures regularly performed ecclesiastical duties. "Not many years ago," reports the Jesuit Father Souciet in 1734, "a lay figure married with children not only had charge of the revenues of the archbishop but acted even as a kind of vicar, giving the priests permission to celebrate and confess, and preventing them as and when he saw fit. I am not even sure he did not claim to be able to carry out excommunications." The underlying problem was economic, for until the commercial boom of the mid-eighteenth century, the Christians of the city were, on the whole, of modest means. Only a few descendants of the great Byzantine families still lived there; most were artisans, shopkeepers, sailors or traders.[46]

For them, faith was not really a matter of theology. Poorly educated, few could bridge the gap between the complex formal Greek of the church and the language of daily life, which for many Orthodox Christians was often not Greek at all, but Slavic or Vlach. "The priests and even the pastors—the metropolitans, archbishops and bishops—are extremely simple and unlearned men, who do not know the Hellenic language and have no explanations in the vulgar tongue, so that they don't know and don't understand anything they read," noted a visiting Ukrainian notable. "The people don't know anything at all except the sign of the cross (and this not everyone). When we asked them about the Our Father, they would answer that 'this is the priest's business, not ours.' "[47] Sometimes this uncertainty could be taken surprisingly far, as when a young Greek village priest asked whether Jesus was really God (though perhaps the questioner had been influenced by the scorn with which both Muslims and Jews treated such a claim).[48]

On the other hand, Salonica's Christians were deeply attached to their traditional customs—especially fasting, about which they were extremely conscientious—and to the observance of local festivals, which were celebrated vigorously in the city and the neighbouring countryside, combining spiritual and commercial satisfaction. On Saint Dimitrios's Day a majestic service was attended by all the suffragan bishops. There was also a rapidly developing cult of Gregory Palamas, the fourteenth-century archbishop of the city, whose mystical and political views had made him a highly controversial figure in his lifetime. To the surprise of visiting Christians, who knew him for his much-disputed theology, his memory was revered as that of a saint and his mummified body, laid out on a bier, attracted increasing numbers of worshippers.[49]

Orthodox Christians were constantly reminded that theirs was a second-class faith: they were not allowed to ring church bells or even beat wooden clappers to bring the faithful to prayer. Yet so far as the Ottomans were concerned, they were a people of the Book and one distinctly superior to the Catholic Franks. During the long wars with both Venice and Austria, Catholic missionaries were accused of leading the local Orthodox astray, and introducing them to "polytheism, cunning and craftiness." When an early-eighteenth-century visitor discussed Christianity with one of Salonica's *mollahs*, the latter told him "that the three faiths, the Papist, the Lutheran, and the Calvinist are the worst, while the Greek is better than all." According to him, many of the town's Muslim scholars studied the Gospels in Arabic and valued the Greek Church above the rest because "the Greeks don't depart from evangelical teachings and from church traditions and . . . they don't introduce anything new into their religion or remove anything." The very conservatism denounced by visiting Jesuits was thus understood and appreciated by Muslims.[50]

This sympathy, however, had its limits. The primacy of the ruling faith was axiomatic, and any public assertion of the superiority of Christianity over Islam was punished with severity. But even here Ottoman and Orthodox interests fitted strangely together, since the church, itself founded through an act of martyrdom, regarded the public suffering of new martyrs as a way of demonstrating the tenacity of Christian belief. Priests or monks instructed would-be candidates who then presented themselves to the authorities, or carried out acts designed to lead to their arrest, dragging crosses through the streets, or loudly insulting Mohammed. Seeing apostates—in particular—return to the fold was, wrote one priest, "as if one were to see spring flowers and roses bloom in the heart of winter."[51]

Those who died for their faith were the popular voice of spiritual protest—the senior church hierarchy, by contrast, were servants of the sultan—and their deeds were carefully recorded by monks at the time. Even today modern editions of these "witnesses for Christ" circulate within the Orthodox world, with stories which are well worth reading for their unexpected insights into Ottoman religious culture. Like most Christians in Salonica, the city's "neo-martyrs" were humble men (and a few women)—a painter, a coppersmith, a fisherman, gardener, tailor, baker and a servant to take just a few of them. Michael, for instance, who was executed in 1547, was one of the many Christian immigrants from the mountains; a baker, he had got into trouble after chatting about religion with a Muslim boy who came to buy bread. Kyrill's father died young and he was brought up by his uncle, who had converted to Islam. Alexandros, who also converted, had wandered the Arab world as a dervish, and made the pilgrimage to Mecca, before returning to his ancestral faith, and testifying—in the words that distinguished Christians from Muslims—that "one is three and three are one." Although many of these martyrs had converted to Islam before seeing the error of their ways, what had induced their initial apostasy did not matter to the church—it might have been nothing more noble than the desire to pay lower taxes or to escape punishment for earlier crimes. All their sins were wiped out by their intention to repent and to testify to the superiority of the true faith.

Nor were all martyrs apostates. Some sought to emulate the martyrs of the early Church, or wanted to blot out the stain on the family name caused by the conversion of relatives. Aquilina's mother had remained a Christian when her father had converted to Islam and brought shame on them. Nicetas was outraged when relatives became Muslims and he decided on martyrdom as a way of upholding the family honour. Pilgrimage to the Holy Land inspired one or two to follow in the footsteps of the Lord. In 1527 the noble Macarios, a monk on Mount Athos, became "completely consumed with the heartfelt desire to finish his life with a martyric death." He went into the streets of Salonica and began to tell a large crowd of Muslims about the teachings of Christ. Brought before the *kadi*, Macarios prayed that the judge might come "to know the true and irreproachable Faith of the Christians" and "be extricated from the erroneous religion of your fathers by the Holy and Consubstantial Trinity." His martyrdom followed.[52]

The path to death could be very dramatic indeed. An eighteen-year-old French convert to Islam repented of his apostasy, confessed to a Greek priest and then—this appears to have been exceptional even among the neo-martyrs—put a crown of thorns on his head, a small cross round his neck, thrust small spikes into his limbs and paraded in public, whipping himself and shouting, "I was an apostate but I am a Christian." He was arrested, rejected various attempts to get him to return to Islam and was put to death. Christodoulos, a tanner, was so disturbed to hear of a fellow-Christian planning to convert that he took a small cross, entered the tavern where the convert's circumcision was about to take place and tried to stop the ceremony. He was arrested, beaten and hanged outside the door of the church of Ayios Minas.[53]

Executions were as public as the celebrations which marked conversion itself. In fact vast crowds gathered to witness the last moments of the dying and to pick up relics of martyrdom. Following the Frenchman's death, "the Christians took away his corpse and buried it with honour in a church." Many people carefully collected drops of his blood and pieces of his clothing, just as they did with the holy remains of other martyrs: the Ottoman authorities respected this practice and made no attempt to stop it. When a young Bulgarian girl who had spurned the advances of a Turk died after being thrown into prison falsely accused of having pledged to convert to Islam, the guards noticed a great light emanating from the room, and were so struck by the miracle that they spread the news around the city. Once again, the clothes of the martyr were carefully parcelled out as relics.

Ottoman reactions generally ranged from bewilderment to anger. Officials considered would-be martyrs insane, and hence not responsible for their actions. Romanos was regarded as mad and consigned to the galleys the first time round. Cyprian was dismissed as a lunatic by the pasha of Salonica and having "reasoned that he would not receive the martyric end he desired at the hands of the Turks in that unbelieving city" took himself off to the capital, where by writing an anti-Muslim epistle to the grand vizier and having it specially translated into Turkish, he achieved the desired goal. The biographer of Nicetas recounts an extraordinary conversation that took place in 1808 between that would-be martyr and the *mufti* of Serres. After offering him coffee, the latter asked Nicetas if he had gone mad, coming into the town and preaching to Muslims that they should abandon their faith. Nicetas explained that it was only zeal for the true faith that motivated him, and he began to debate the merits of the two religions. Other Turks asked him if he had been forced to do this, and this too he denied. But the *mufti* only became truly angry when Nicetas described Mohammed as "a charlatan and a sensual devil." "Monk!" said the *mufti*. "It is obvious you are an ill-mannered person. I try to set you free, but by your own brutal words you cause your own death." To which Nicetas replied: "This is what I desire, and for this have I come freely to offer myself as a sacrifice for the love of my Master and God, Jesus Christ."[54]

What is surprising in many of these accounts is how reluctant the *kadis* were to order the death sentence. They could be forced to change their minds by local Muslim opinion, but they must have been conscious of the power of religious self-sacrifice and unwilling to add to the list of victims. As it is, martyrdom was not a common choice, and the vast majority of Christians who converted to Islam evidently never returned to the fold. The hagiographer of the martyr Nicetas suggests that by the early nineteenth century a note of scepticism was beginning to prevail among Christians themselves. A Salonica merchant, he tells us, cast doubt on the merit of what Nicetas had done, saying "it is not necessary to go to martyrdom in these days, when there is no persecution of the Christian church." Only after a terrifying dream, in which a

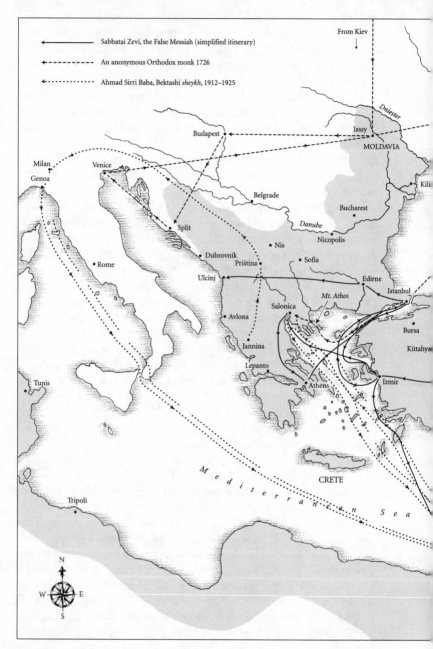

Salonica's sacred geographies

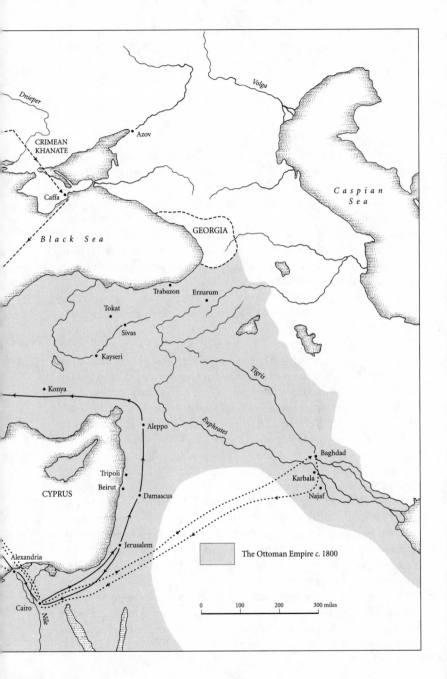

Dnieper

Volga

CRIMEAN
KHANATE

Azov

Caffa

_Caspian
Sea_

Black Sea

GEORGIA

Trabazon

Erzurum

Tokat

Sivas

Tigris

Kayseri

Konya

Aleppo

Euphrates

Baghdad

CYPRUS

Tripoli

Beirut

Damascus

Karbala

Najaf

Alexandria

Jerusalem

The Ottoman Empire _c._ 1800

Cairo

Nile

0   100   200   300 miles

loud voice told him that Nicetas was indeed a true martyr, did he change his mind. Following British pressure in the 1840s, capital punishment for apostasy was abandoned, and the need for such dreams ceased.[55]

SACRED GEOGRAPHIES

IN 1926, an eminent Albanian Bektashi *sheykh*, Ahmad Sirri Baba, stopped for a rest in Salonica during arduous travels which took him from Albania to Cairo, Baghdad, Karbala and back. By this point, the city's Muslim population had been forced to leave Greece entirely as a result of the Greco-Turkish 1923 population exchange, and the *tekkes* had been abandoned. The *sheykh*'s journeys, as he moved between the worlds of Balkan and Middle Eastern Islam, were a last indication of channels of religious devotion which had once linked the city with extraordinarily diverse and far-flung parts of the world.

For centuries, Muslims from all over the Balkans congregated in Salonica to find a sea passage to Aleppo or Alexandria for the *haj* caravans to Mecca. Christians followed their example, acquiring the title of Hadji after visiting their own holy places. Others came to visit the remains of Saint Dimitrios before travelling onwards to the Holy Mountain. A Ukrainian monk, Cyril, from Lviv, arrived to raise money for the monastery in Sinai where he worked, and brought catalogues of the library collections there which he passed on to the head of the Jesuit mission in the city, Père Souciet, whose brother ran the royal library in Paris. For Muslim mendicant dervishes and Christian monks, the region's network of charitable and hospitable religious institutions offered a means of permanent support, especially in the cold winter months when work and money were hard to come by. "One monk, almost a vagabond, came from Kiev to Moldavia," noted a Salonica resident who met him in 1727, "and from there wandered aimlessly through Hungary, Croatia, Dalmatia, Venice, then returned from that unnecessary peregrination to Moldavia, and from there to the Zaporozhian Sich whence, by way of the Black Sea, he came to Constantinople and to Mount Athos."[56]

In short, the city found itself at the intersection of many different creeds. Through the Sufi orders it was linked to Iran, Anatolia, Thrace and Egypt; the Marranos bridged the Catholicism of the Iberian peninsula, Antwerp and Papal Italy; the faith of the Sabbataians was carried by Jewish believers into Poland, Bohemia, Germany and eventually North America, while the seventeenth-century Metropolitan Athanasios Patellarios came to the city via Venetian Crete and Ottoman Sinai before he moved on to Jassy, Istanbul, Russia and the Ukraine, his final resting-place. Salonica lay in the centre of an Ottoman *oikumeni*, which was at the same time Muslim, Christian and Jewish. Perhaps only now, since the end of the Cold War and the re-opening of many of these same routes, is it again possible to calculate the impact of such an extensive sacred geography and to see how it underpinned the profusion of faiths which sustained the city's inhabitants.[57]

5

Janissaries and Other Plagues

IF SCARCELY ANY BUILDINGS from Ottoman Salonica survive today, this cannot easily be blamed on the effects of war. Before the Ottoman conquest, the city had suffered one siege after another; after it, there were none. A visitor to the fortress vaults in the early nineteenth century found chests of rusting Byzantine arrows, their feathers worm-eaten: they were the long-forgotten remains of the ammunition left behind by the defenders of 1430. Every so often, hostile fleets approached the Gulf and on one occasion Venetian shells landed in the port. But apart from sporadic pirate raids, and a spot of gunboat diplomacy in 1876 which ended without a cannon being fired, that was all the fighting Salonica saw, before the Greeks marched in to end Ottoman rule in 1912.[1]

The early Ottoman rulers never imagined how little actual danger the city would face, and for three hundred years they kept the walls, gates and port in good order. Bayazid II wintered there. Suleyman the Magnificent built the White Tower at the end of the sea-wall, and another tower, now vanished, on the other side of the city. Both men were engaging the Venetians by land and sea, and Salonica was a crucial staging-post for their forces and a major manufacturer of gunpowder. They added batteries—like the "mouths of great lions"—at key points, and a new fortress between the harbour and the land walls. The traveller Evliya counted a tower every five hundred paces, and spent five hours pacing the entire perimeter across the hilly ground. Each night, he writes, "the sultan's music" is heard within the walls, while the garrison patrols shout: "God is One!" No houses were permitted to be built on the far side of the walls for security, and even today a tiny lane, barely a car's width, snaking round the outside perimeter past the shacks which cling to the steep northwest side of the ramparts, traces what is left of the invisible outline of this policy.[2]

But by the start of the eighteenth century, there were signs of imperial over-stretch. In 1732 a commissioner of the Porte reported that many of the towers were badly neglected. Within decades, the walls were of antiquarian interest only. An emissary of Louis XVI described the city as "of no importance" from a military point of view—"an enceinte of ramparts without moats and badly linked, even worse defended by a very small number of poor artillery pieces." In 1840, the British army captain who drank sherbets and lemonade with the artillery commander found the troops excellent but the batteries "defenceless in themselves." When the guns sounded, as they often did, it was to mark nothing more than the breaking of the Ramadan fast, the strangulation of a janissary or imperial celebrations.[3]

Until the demolitions of the 1870s, however, which got rid of gates, towers and entire stretches of the *muraille*, the ring of ramparts held the city tight—marking the boundary between residents and strangers, the living and dead. The claustrophobic airless warren of lanes within contrasted with the dreary expanses of open country—"a mournful and arid solitude" wrote a nineteenth-century French visitor—on the far side of the walls, studded with water-mills, cemeteries, plague-hospices and monasteries. On the approach to the gates, the dangling corpses of criminals hung from trees to remind passers-by of the virtues of obedience. "We enter the Vardar-kapesi, or gate of the Vardhari," wrote the imperturbable Leake. "In a tree before it hangs the body of a robber." The gates themselves were manned by guards who checked the passes of non-residents and collected merchandise duties from farmers and traders. Come nightfall, tardy visitors were left outside, and everyone else kept in. The sharp sense of a division between city-dwellers and non-residents reflected the prevailing Ottoman conception of a close link between foreigners and crime. Vagrants, migrants and strangers were the cause of insecurity: the gates helped to keep them at arm's length.[4]

For even if it was never itself invaded or attacked, in other ways Salonica was deeply affected by the numerous disorders which punctuated the seventeenth and eighteenth centuries. With every campaign, rumours swept in: invading Austrian armies were approaching from the north, hostile Russian flotillas were just off Cape Caraburnu, a column twenty thousand strong of Napoleon's troops was marching down from Bosnia. Wars against European states aroused the anger of local Muslims and jeopardized the position of the Christians. In 1715, during the war with Austria, the French consul reported that "terror has spread among the Greeks, who fear being chopped to pieces in their churches, and the Franks, who have a reputation for wealth, are worried about a population which does not reason and cannot distinguish between the French and the [Austrians] who are only five or six days' march from us."[5]

War brought the burden of extra taxation to pay for new galleys, uniforms, and provisions. In 1702 the orders were for gunpowder, in 1714 biscuit and flour, and in the great campaign of the following year, which drove the Venetians out of the Aegean, the city contributed the equivalent of 40,000 sheep and 150,000 kilos of flour as well as workers to repair the roads and bridges along which the Grand Vizier's army passed. In 1734 lead, powder, iron, medicines and thirty cannons were demanded, in 1744 pack-animals. By 1770, during the war with Russia, the Greeks were "so exhausted from constant requisitions that they don't know how they will manage." Yet seventeen years later, the Greek and Jewish communities were instructed once again to find two hundred ox-carts and three hundred camels—or the equivalent sum in silver.[6]

For many Muslims, there was also military service, disrupting trade and family life for up to six months in the year. Town criers publicizing the sultan's demand for extra troops found little enthusiasm. When decrees were read out in the mosques calling for volunteers, angry voices shouted that Greeks and Jews should enlist too. Most of Salonica's seven thousand janissaries were in theory liable to serve, but their commanders often claimed they could not be spared. In January 1770, an imperial decree called on all who believed in Mohammed to march on the Moldavians and Wallachians and to annihilate them for daring to rise up in rebellion against the Emperor. They were given licence to act as they would, and to take slaves.[7] Yet many preferred to give money and to shut themselves away in their houses. Another appeal for Muslims to enter the ranks explicitly allowed elderly and wealthy Turks, as well as the *Ma'min*, to make a monetary contribution instead. The city's growing prosperity was creating new, more sedentary interests which clashed with the old *ghazi* warrior ideals.[8]

For troops levied in the hinterland, Salonica was a mustering point whether they were marching by land or sailing across the Mediterranean. The Grand Vizier's 1715 campaign against the Venetians in the Peloponnese was probably the last time the imperial army as a whole gathered in its full glory outside the walls. But in 1744 at least twelve thousand landed cavalrymen embarked there for the Persian campaign, and three thousand *yürüks*—settled nomads liable for military service—gathered from the surrounding villages. Albanian contingents from the mountains arrived en route to campaigns in the Crimea and Arabia, and so many men of arms-bearing age flocked to the city that north African recruiters and privateers combed it for volunteers: at least five hundred took the coin of the Bey of Algiers on one recruiting drive in May 1757 alone.[9]

Since there were no proper barracks, thousands of these unruly, poorly paid and ill-disciplined fighting men lodged in the city's great *khans* and *caravanserais*. Their arrival invariably sent a shudder of apprehension through the town. In 1770, news that local levies might be ordered into the city provoked the Venetian consul to despair: "As soon as they enter the town, God knows what ill deeds they will perform and getting rid of them will be very hard." Made up of poor villagers, who associated towns with authority, judges and tax-collectors, these troops often found it hard to stomach the wealth they saw around them. In 1788, a levy of fifteen hundred men, destined for the "German" front, "committed much disorder" and the shops were closed for two months until they left.

Merchants and tavern-keepers were at greatest risk. In April 1734, to take a typical episode, the city was immobilized by the violent behaviour of Bosnian irregulars en route to Syria. As usual, wine shops and taverns were a magnet for trouble. In one they killed the owner, a baker and a Greek wine salesman. Others robbed the house of a Muslim woman, "raped her and tormented her cruelly until she died." Armed with stones, knives, sabres and revolvers, they swaggered through the streets in gangs of as many as fifty, holding up anyone they met. "We are all locked inside our houses and well guarded until they depart for Syria," writes the Venetian consul. Even the Pasha remained in his palace, since he lacked sufficient troops to keep order.[10]

THE JANISSARIES

ANYONE OF ANY WEALTH hired bodyguards, usually janissaries, whose fearsome reputation and well-organized networks were usually sufficient to ward off troublemakers. Yet if eighteenth-century Salonica was what one resident described as a *malsicura città*, where one hesitated to travel except with an escort, and where one foreigner kept his own private priest at home to spare his family the unpredictable mile and a half journey to the church, the main reason was the unrestrained and increasingly arbitrary violence of the janissaries themselves. They guarded the city's gates and towers, patrolled the markets to ensure fair trading and were in theory at least one of the police forces of the Ottoman state. In practice, however, the fighting prowess and internal discipline of what had once been the mainstay of the Ottoman infantry had degenerated over the years until the chief threat they posed was to the empire's own subjects.

As the janissary corps expanded in the seventeenth and eighteenth centuries, recruitment, which had once been through levies of Christian boys, became hereditary and very much less selective; membership was often transferred from father to son, or simply through the sale of the pay slips to which they were entitled. Their training had been so drastically cut that as Paul Rycaut, a well-informed English observer, wrote in 1668, some "neither know how to manage a Musket, nor are otherwise disciplin'd to any exercise of Arms." In the capital, they were renowned for their mutinous making and breaking of viziers and even sultans. "As there is no question," Rycaut noted, "but a standing Armee of veteran and well-disciplined Souldiers must be always useful and advantageous to the Interest of a Prince; so, on the contrary, negligence in the Officers, and remissness of Government, produces that licentiousness and wrestiness in the Souldiery, as betrays them to all the disorders which are dangerous and of evil consequence to the welfare of a State."[11]

In Salonica, the janissaries fell into two categories. There were the heavily armed infantrymen, who formed the town garrison, a total of somewhere between twelve hundred and two thousand men. In addition, there were thousands more Muslim men and boys—mostly shopkeepers and tradesmen—who were enrolled purely nominally in one or other of the four local janissary companies. Although some of the officers controlled the customs house, the city gates, the tanneries, slaughter-houses, and the pasturing lands which they made available to shepherds when they brought their flocks down each autumn, official perquisites were distributed only irregularly by the Porte. Many janissaries enjoyed an uncertain living as bodyguards or fruit-sellers, and observers grouped them together with "poor Greeks and the Jews" as "ordinary types who are obliged to make savings."[12]

In their own minds, the janissaries were the protectors of the masses, the voice of hard-working Muslim artisans and traders, stepping in when the rich—be they land-owners, Ottoman officials or Frankish merchants—tried to exploit the poor. Baron de Tott, a knowledgeable observer of the empire, saw them as the natural opponents of "despotism." And it is true that whenever a sudden downturn in the market or a failure of the harvest threatened the city with starvation, the janissaries found themselves speaking for its consuming classes. The state was supposed to ensure the regular supply of affordable, high-quality daily bread, and it tightly regulated both prices and trade in grain and flour. But caught between the great land-owners, who controlled (and often speculated in) the local grain supply, and the sultan's civil servants, whose duty was to make sure enough food reached Istanbul, the poorer inhabitants of Salonica often needed the janissaries to defend them. Why should they starve solely to swell the profits of the wealthy, or to allow precious wheat to be shipped to Istanbul? In August 1753 there was a "popular revolt" as a janissary-led mob burned down the bakeries in the Frankish quarter, suspecting them of contributing to the scarcity of bread. Six months later, export of grain from the city was still forbidden. In September 1789 there was a far more serious uprising against the *mollah* and the *mufti* for allowing grain to be sent to the capital. An enraged mob went after the *mollah*, then dragged the *mufti* into the streets, beat him and shaved off his beard. Only the resolute action of the *janissary agha*, who ordered the immediate arrest and strangulation of the ringleaders, restored order.[13]

Yet the janissaries made unconvincing Robin Hoods. With their violent tempers, esprit de corps, rivalrousness and swaggering aggression they were as liable to fall on each other, beat up innocent Christians or ransack taverns as to worry about the food supply. "The government, properly speaking," wrote a visitor, "is in the hands of the Janissaries who act here like petty despots." They rarely had anything to fear from those above them for the pashas appointed from Istanbul came and went—sometimes three in one year—and often did not even bother to turn up at their new posting. The *janissary agha* himself often enjoyed only a nominal authority over the rank and file, and a prudent *kadi* would steer clear of trying to punish them: usually a few ounces of coffee were enough to buy him out of a guilty verdict. About the only voices they were likely to heed belonged to the senior men of their own company.[14]

To make matters worse, through the eighteenth century Istanbul was exporting its own janissary problem, as it expelled troublemakers into the provinces. In April 1743 Salonica was witnessing "daily murders by Turks, either of each other or against Greeks and Jews," and a janissary killed the *kahya* of Ali Effendi, one of the leading men of the city. Rabbis and bishops prayed to be rid of them; community leaders sent petitions to the emperor to take action against them.[15] By 1751 they were said to "rule" the city, ready to kill "a man for a salad." The following year, a crowd of five hundred gathered to demand that certain particularly extortionate officials be handed over to them; when the *janissary agha* refused, they turned their fire on him. He managed to escape on a ship bound for Constantinople, but they then mounted a noisy guard outside the pasha's palace, while others opened the wine shops and drank themselves into a stupor. Terrified by the violence which had already led them to three murders, everyone else kept off the streets.[16]

Yet their bitterest hatred was reserved for each other. In 1763 a good-looking young Jewish boy was seized by a member of the 2nd *orta* (company) and men from the 72nd were called in to help recover him. Clashes continued throughout the city for three days till the sultan ordered forty men from each company to be put to death, and the *janissary agha* demolished four cafés which the troublemakers were known to frequent.[17] But although a determined pasha with his own men might frighten the locals into temporary obedience, janissaries could play at court politics too and often engineered the recall of officials they disliked. By the end of the century, the problem had become so bad that even the older janissary officers were losing control over the younger men. Salonica is "not a city but a battlefield," wrote the Venetian consul despairingly in March 1789. It remained that way until they were finally massacred by Sultan Mahmud II in "the auspicious event" of 1826 which eradicated them forever.

ALBANIANS

IN THE MEANTIME, the remedy for janissary violence was often worse than the disease. Unable to rely on the troops supposedly under their command, many pashas kept armed retinues of their own. Mostly they recruited young Albanians from impoverished mountain villages, who brought with them an aggressively uncomplicated approach to life. An Ottoman traveller among them a century earlier had warned others what they might expect in the way of Albanian greetings and salutations. His list had included the following useful expressions: "Eat shit!" "I'll fuck your mother," "I'll fuck your wife" and "I'll fart in your nose."[18]

Salonica lay between the southern Albanian lands and Istanbul, and by the mid-eighteenth century, several thousand worked there as attendants in the *hamams*, *boza* sellers, gunsmiths, stonemasons and bodyguards. Others found seasonal work as shepherds, or drovers. Most official entourages relied on them, and they provided the strength which enabled large land-owners (*ayans*) in the regions to the north of the city to accumulate more and more power for themselves. One redoubtable land-owner of Doiran, for instance, who had most of the pashas of Salonica in his pocket, was able to put three thousand Albanians into the field against his enemies—easily a match for the *yürük* troops whom the Porte ordered against him. Indeed many of the leading beys in the Macedonian hinterland were themselves of Albanian origin.[19]

The Ottoman authorities, with their fundamental dislike of migrants, were deeply suspicious of the Albanians (despite the fact that many of the most senior officials were themselves of Albanian descent). Exceptionally in an empire which recognized only distinctions of religion, they were singled out by name—*arnavud*—and in 1730 the emperor ordered all Albanians, both Muslim and Christian, to be expelled from Istanbul. Such measures simply intensified the problem in the provinces, increasing brigandage and crime, and slowly the government's attention turned there too. After the long mid-century war with the Russians, when Albanian troops served the sultan in the Peloponnese, they continued plundering the Greek lands, until Sultan Abdul Hamid I, backed by his reforming admiral Gazi Hasan Pasha, decided to take action against them.[20]

To the French consul in Salonica at the time, they were more than a mere irritant. In fact, the stakes for the empire itself could not have been higher. As he wrote to Paris:

> All men of sound sense here hope that the Capudan Pasha follows the example of Topal Osman Pasha who . . . covered Albania in rivers of blood on the orders of Sultan Mahmoud in 1731. Without this it is to be feared that this nation, which is very numerous and very poor at the same time, will abuse her habit of bearing arms and become powerful and dangerous for this Empire. All the open cities of Rumelia are exposed to its devasta-

tions, which could lead it to the gates of Constantinople, if some ambitious man knows how to profit from the number, the courage and the natural discipline of this nation.

Thus in 1779, the Ottoman admiral led a force of more than thirty thousand men against them. En route to the Peloponnese, in an operation impressive for its speed and brutal decisiveness, he personally decapitated two leading land-owners, and shot dead their main rivals: thirty-four heads were despatched to Constantinople and their lands were handed over to members of the Evrenos and other loyalist families. Hasan Pasha also gave the green light for Turks and Greeks to take whatever action they pleased against any Albanians they found: killing them was not a crime. Continuing his march, he executed all the Albanians he encountered, setting fire to a monastery where others were hiding and offering five sequins for every Albanian head brought him. In Salonica the governor expelled more than four thousand within five days, including several hundred in his own entourage, and permitted only a few long-time residents to stay.[21]

This was only a temporary remedy, however, and it did nothing to reconcile the Albanians to Ottoman rule. Many of them were Muslims, but their shared religion could not override the contempt they now felt for the Turks. "The Albanians do not any longer recognize the authority of the Grand Seigneur," wrote an observer a few years later, "nor by extension that of the pasha of Salonica whom they regard as an odious enemy."[22] In 1793 the pasha of Shkodra defeated an Ottoman army, captured several senior officers, and sent them back with their beards shaved to show his disdain for the sultan. And in Salonica itself, they were soon causing trouble again. When the pasha attempted to arrest a known troublemaker called Alizotoglou in 1793, his house turned out to contain more than 150 of them, amply supplied with food and arms. The pasha, having called on "all true Muslims" to come to his aid, used cannons to fire on Alizotoglou's house, but his opponent only left the city after taking hostages for his security, and threatening defiantly to return with 2000 men if an official pardon was not forthcoming. A decade later, yet another edict had to be issued ordering local officials to clear the city of "an unknown number of Albanians and others belonging to the same category who are not fulfilling any service, without any proper occupation and who are gathering incongruously."[23]

And, just as the French consul had predicted, much more powerful Albanian leaders did indeed become a genuine threat to the empire. At the start of the nineteenth century Mehmed Ali, an Albanian soldier from Cavalla, became ruler of Egypt, founder of a royal dynasty, and creator of a short-lived empire in Africa and the Arab lands. Closer to home there was Ali Pasha—the "Muslim Bonaparte" as Byron called him—who ruled the entire west coast of the Balkans from his Jannina stronghold. His writ ran almost to the gates of Salonica and nearby monasteries found he provided more effective protection against brigands than the city's governor himself, supplying them with small handwritten notes written in "extremely bad Greek" on "a small square piece of very dirty paper," which threatened any Turk who maltreated the monks with execution. Here was an Albanian pasha building his own state and offering protection for the region's Christians whose safety the sultan could no longer guarantee. There could be no clearer illustration of how fragile the authority of the Ottoman state had become.[24]

PRISONERS AND SLAVES

THE INCESSANT STRUGGLES waged between the Ottomans and the Venetians, the Habsburgs, Russians and Persians, left their mark on the city in other ways. In August 1715, after the Venetians had been driven out of the Peloponnese, six thousand Ottoman troops "dispersed into the regions of Larissa and Salonica, causing much harm along the road to the inhabitants of the country." The head of the city's janissary corps was told to scour the area for "evil-doers" and to imprison any he found. When more than one hundred Venetian deserters were rumoured to be making their way there, the town governor was so alarmed at the potential for disorder that he arranged for them to be seized and sold back to their commanding officers. Every campaign brought problems of this kind. In September 1769—during the war with the Russians—it was reported that "the countryside was filled with deserters, ragged, killing."[25]

For war also meant booty, prisoners and slaves. As Busbecq noted in the sixteenth century, "slaves constitute the main source of gain to the Turkish soldier." Edward Browne, the travelling son of Sir Thomas Browne (author of the *Religio Medici*), was moved "by the pitiful spectacle of Captives and Slaves" when he passed through northern Greece in 1668, men like the polyglot Hungarian Sigismund, a learned man who spoke "Hungarian, Sclavonian, Turkish, Armenian and Latin" and had served a Turk, a Jew and an Armenian before being manumitted. French and Venetian consuls tried to get imprisoned or enslaved prisoners of war released and helped others escape: in 1700 the consulate gave a list to Paris of "all the soldier deserters, French, Italians, Spaniards etc., Catholics, Huguenots and infidels" he had sent on to Marseilles. The Alsace man redeemed by another French consul in 1792, or the deserter who fled his master and made his way to Cavalla, were among the dozens of fortunate individuals who were thus returned to Christendom many years after failed campaigns had first brought them to the Ottoman lands.[26]

The fog of war enshrouded this human traffic in a penumbra of legal uncertainty. Two Hungarians sold in the Larissa market in 1721 had to be released on the emperor's orders after it turned out that they were not captured in battle but had merely been seized by some enterprising janissaries while about their master's business. In fact, peace treaties often stipulated that prisoners of war were *not* to be sold. "I learned ten days ago that in Larissa there are two Venetians, prisoners of some Albanians, who are negotiating their sale," writes the Venetian consul in 1739. "I immediately sent a trustworthy man there to the *kadi* with a letter informing him that they are Venetians and that according to the terms of the peace they cannot be sold as slaves. The *kadi* read the letter, imprisoned the Albanians and gave up the two men into my care."

But because so many of the sultan's troops saw the acquisition of slaves as their right, official orders were often ignored and the problem of illegal enslavement persisted, complicating efforts by the Ottoman state to organize prisoner exchanges. After the Russo-Turkish war of 1768–74, with a large number of Ottoman troops in Russian captivity, the sultan ruled that all Russian prisoners still in Ottoman hands should be released. Only those "Muslims willingly staying in Russia and embracing Christianity" and "those Christians willingly embracing Islam in My supreme empire" were to be exempt. One year on, however, few of the "Russians, Poles, Moldavians, Vlachs and Moreotes" in Turkish hands had been liberated. The sultan accused Turks and Jews in Salonica of holding on to their captives out of sheer greed, and warned them that until they handed them back, the religious obligation to free "brothers of the faith" in Russian hands remained unfulfilled. As in so many areas of eighteenth-century life, what the sultan ordered and what actually happened were two quite different things.[27]

The traffic in bodies formed part of the Mediterranean economy until late into the nineteenth century. During the long and complex struggle between Muslim and Catholic powers all sides bought and sold slaves, and the markets of the Barbary coast had their counterparts in the little-studied dealers of Christendom. Salonica's own inhabitants had been sold into slavery after 1430, but as the Ottoman city grew and flourished, its new residents—Christians, Jews and Muslims—all bought slaves for domestic use, many of whom settled there in their turn. Poland, Ukraine, Georgia and Circassia, the Sudan and north Africa were the main sources of supply, and slaves from all these regions were to be found there. We do not know where its slave market was located but wars kept it well stocked. Large numbers of Christian women and children were sold off in 1715, after the Venetian campaign, and again in 1737 after the Habsburg invasion.[28]

This was not, as in the Americas, a cheap route to the plantation economy, but rather a feature of the domestic household life of the well-to-do in an empire where slaves had until very recently occupied some of the highest positions in the state. In Salonica, slaves cost far more than domestic servants, especially if the latter were children; there is no evidence for their being used as cheap labour en masse in public works in the way that occurred in north Africa. Some accumulated money of their own, enabling them to buy their way out of service. Others were freed with a legacy on their master's death. Probably worst off were those who had fled their employer's service, or were released from the galleys with no money to support them: such individuals eked out a very precarious existence on the margins of society, joining the beggars, gypsies and wandering dervishes at one of the city's half a dozen soup kitchens. Groups of African beggars roamed around the city and its hinterland, and these were almost certainly manumitted slaves, banding together for protection. Those on their own, in particular women, were frequently kidnapped to be sold as slaves by dealers. This happened, for instance, to Amina bint Abdullah, a convert from Christianity, despite the fact that "she did not have anything to do with slavery in her genealogy."[29]

What worried non-Muslims was not so much the idea of slavery itself—for this they were familiar with—as the prospect that enslavement might lead to conversion and the loss of Christian (or Jewish) souls. "Various Turks have come here," reports the Venetian consul in June 1770, following unsuccessful Greek uprisings in the islands and on the mainland, "with twenty of those children, male and female, and they sell them to other Turks, who make little Turks [*tourkakia*] of them." The Jesuits and Jews had organizations devoted to redeeming slaves who were of their faith. Other Christians handled matters more informally. In the 1720s, for instance, a female Ukrainian slave who had been badly treated by her captors was brought to Salonica to be sold. She had some hidden savings and sought help in arranging a ransom, or at least a Christian buyer, "so that she does not fall into the hands of a Turk." Because the woman belonged to the Orthodox rite, some of the town's European merchants questioned whether, being Catholics, they should be involved and proposed that "Mikalis, the Greek physician," should take responsibility, especially since he knew that "she can sew and embroider excellently and weave and can cook in the Turkish style very well." But Mikalis did not want to pay the asking price, and anyway the Greeks had a reputation for being more reluctant than the Turks to manumit their slaves, "especially when the slaves are Polish or Kazak or of any different nation." The Catholic Father Superior found a solution by organizing a lottery among the French merchants in the city: within three days he had raised the money and arranged for the woman to be bought and given to the winner. The sale was completed and the necessary deed of sale was signed by the local customs officer, handed over with the woman herself. She was lodged in a French-owned house "until she learns the catechism and other mysteries of the Christian confession, which the priest promised to teach her in Turkish, because [she] speaks only Turkish and Russian." She had not been freed, but her soul at least was safe.[30]

Captives of a different kind, fewer in number but equally reliable indicators of far-off troubles, were the distinguished guests whom the authorities in Istanbul sent to Salonica as political exiles. The city provided a suitable home where they could live in some style, hunt if they wished and hold court at official expense, remaining all the while under the watchful eye of the authorities. At a time when many were living on the margins, they were treated extremely well. We still have the list of foods provided for Mirza Safi, a Persian pretender, when he was held there in 1731. It includes "bread, rice, clarified butter, yoghurt, cumin, sugar, starch, boiled grape-juice, clove, cinnamon, chicken, eggs, almonds, pistachios, pepper, saffron, coffee, coriander, olive oil, flour, honey, bees-wax, grapes, salt, chick peas, vinegar, onions, lemon-juice, black cumin, chestnuts, quinces, tobacco (from Shiraz), soap, meat, barley, straw and vegetables"—a respectable diet by any standards.[31]

Patriarchs and grand viziers were parked there when their careers suffered eclipse. Sultan Abdul Hamid II himself was deposed by the

Young Turks in 1909 and sent into gilded captivity. Hungarian aristocrats passed through, as did the Pole Jan Potocki, the multi-talented
author of that remarkable novel *The Manuscript Found in Saragossa*, who
blew his brains out with a silver bullet a few years later. Following the
suppression of the Wahhabi uprising in 1814, the Sherif of Mecca
arrived with an entourage of forty and was treated with the greatest
honour: he lasted a few years before succumbing to the plague. His son
and successor, Abdul Muttalib—"a grand old man of sixty, tall, but slender, with the grand manner, distinguished in every way, of very brown
colour, almost black, fine skin, a long blue robe, a Kashmir turban"—
eventually followed in his father's footsteps and even erected a domed
tomb in his father's memory which survived into the early twentieth
century.[32]

Among all these, however, the man who stayed the longest and left
the most important record of his experiences was a little-known early-
eighteenth-century Ukrainian political emigré called Pylyp Orlyk.
After years fighting against the Muscovite tsars, Orlyk fled first to Sweden, and then passed through central Europe to the relative safety of
the Ottoman lands. On 2 November 1722—in the month of *Moharrem*
1135 according to the dating of the imperial firman—the fifty-year-old
Orlyk was ordered by the Porte to Salonica. There this cultivated and
warm-hearted man spent no less than twelve years in exile, watching
the twists and turns of European politics from the sidelines while his
impoverished wife remained in Cracow and his eight children were dispersed throughout Europe. Only in March 1734 was he released,
thanks to French intervention, and allowed to move north; still trying
to organize an uprising in the Ukraine, he died in poverty nine years
later.[33]

Orlyk's misfortune has proved to be the historian's gain, for from
the day of his arrival he kept a diary which offers a unique insight into
the eighteenth-century city. No other journal of comparable detail
from Salonica has survived. His urgent scrawl gives access not merely
to his voluminous political correspondence, most of which—in Latin,
French, Polish and Ukrainian—was duly copied into his journals, but
also to the rigours of daily life in his place of exile. The misbehaviour of
his loutish servants, the local fare, his bag after a day's shooting in the
plains, stories told him by tailors, interpreters and bodyguards enliven
its pages. Jesuits, consuls, doctors, spies and the Turkish judges and
governors who ran the city all encountered the busy exile.

Much of the time, he lived well, considering his predicament. He hunted partridge, hogs and hares, which he distributed generously among his acquaintances. There was a lot of drinking, especially among the Christians—the French wandered drunkenly through the streets of the European quarter during Carnival, while parties at the house of the Greek metropolitan apparently went on for days at a time, with chicken, salted olives and lemon jam washed down with copious quantities of vodka, wine and coffee. Orlyk and his entourage were fond of the bottle too and he coped easily enough with his often inebriated Jewish interpreter and his manservant "Red," found more than once sprawled in the gutter after a hard night. But the dangers and risks of urban life hemmed him in. At the minor end of the scale they included frequent indigestion from over-eating, the "horrid muck" of the city streets and the bribery necessary to smooth relations with Greek and Ottoman officials alike. He was shocked by the corruption of the church and the readiness of Christians to use the Ottoman courts when it served their interests. His diary is also sensitive to disturbing portents—a full moon cleft with deep black fissures, earth tremors and "great lights flying in the air like a big lance." Meanwhile, crimes went unpunished, pirates threatened voyagers by sea, and as the streets echoed with the sounds of gunfire, janissaries and irregulars acted much as they wished. Of all the numerous dangers Orlyk's diary describes, however, none was more frightening, murderous or unpredictable than what an earlier traveller described as "the terrour of horrid Plagues." Arriving in the city in the aftermath of the epidemic of 1718–1719, Orlyk quickly became familiar with the biggest killer of the early modern Ottoman world.[34]

PLAGUE

"THANK GOD THE PLAGUE IS NOT HERE!" wrote a relieved traveller arriving in Salonica in 1788. Borne on the trade routes from Central Asia and the Black Sea through to the Mediterranean, it could come by both land and sea. A century before Orlyk, an epidemic in Istanbul had killed one thousand a day, according to the British ambassador there, and forced more than two hundred thousand to flee into the countryside. Izmir lost perhaps one-fifth of its entire population in 1739–41, and as many as a quarter may have died between 1758 and 1762: the historian Daniel Panzac estimates it lost the equivalent of its entire population to the plague in the course of the century. At such times, one saw "the Streets . . . filled with infected bodies as well alive as dead; the living seeking remedies either from the Phisitians or at the Bathes, the Dead lying in open Beers, or else quite naked at theyr dores to be washd before theyr buryalls."[35]

In Salonica, athwart the empire's main carrying routes, warm summers and a humid climate offered the plague bacillus a near-ideal environment in the lethal months from April to July. Compared with Izmir, with 55 plague years in the eighteenth century, and Istanbul (65), Salonica got off lightly: even so plague struck one year in three. Outbreaks in 1679–80, 1687–89, 1697–99, 1708–9, 1712–13—which supposedly claimed 6,000 victims—1718–19, 1724 and 1729–30 were just the start. In 1740, a "bad plague" carried off 1337 Christians, 2239 Turks and 3935 Jews. That was not the only really serious outbreak: in 1762 10–12,000 people, roughly 16–20% of the population, died. The figures were similar in 1781 when as a survivor put it, one could "die of fright," and again in 1814. Over the century, roughly 55–65,000 victims were carried off, something close to the mid-century population of the city itself. Only the constant inflow of new, mostly Christian, migrants from the countryside and high, mostly Jewish, local birth rates can account for the lack of a very steep decline in numbers. It is testimony to the resilience of the city's economy that unlike ports such as Alexandria and Aleppo, its growth was not more seriously checked.[36]

Through Orlyk's entries during the epidemic of 1724—a serious year but not nearly as bad as 1713 or 1762—we can see the astonishingly rapid trajectory from rumour to full-scale panic and mass death. It all started fairly quietly: "On Wednesday morning, after I came back from the Orthodox Church after mass, I was told by my people that the small daughter of a man who lives close by the cemetery at the Orthodox Church is extremely sick with the plague." Hearing this, Greeks from the vicinity had already started moving out to villages in the mountains. And there were omens: "My people told me they heard an owl on my inn, and this is a fatal bird, which is proven by experience."[37]

The next day the girl was dead and the church had closed. Orlyk asked his servant to find lodgings for him in a nearby village, together with the English consul and some other members of the community, in order to escape "God's awful punishment." But the villagers, as often happened, were understandably reluctant to take in refugees from the city and started arming and erecting barricades to prevent them coming. Reportedly they were being encouraged by the pasha of Salonica, who planned to make wealthy foreigners pay handsomely for the privilege of leaving.[38]

As a political exile Orlyk had particular difficulties getting out. When he presented himself to the *mollah*, "this heathen made me more annoyed, telling me there is nothing written down in the emperor's order that I can go wherever I want and choose inns, but that it is written down that I shall stay at the inn in this town and have to stay here. I discussed it a long time with him and put forward lots of arguments; he promised to speak about it with the *aghas* tomorrow and to tell me what they decide at their stupid council." Despite Orlyk's efforts, the *mollah* stuck to his guns, perhaps fearing the consequences if he absconded. Meanwhile, the younger son of his landlord fell ill as well, which scared the household so much "that all of us ran away from the inn, and left our stuff and also the carriage on the street, at which the servants slept the whole night in the rain, and I slept over in some monastery house . . . where I slept in great fear." Two days later, Orlyk tried again and this time he informed the *mollah* that the entire street where he lived was infected, including the house next door, and that he had given up sleeping in the inn. Even this had little effect. Only when the English consul intervened, and promised to be responsible for his eventual return, was he allowed to depart.

After the usual difficulties with the janissaries guarding the gates, who blocked his way until they received payment, he and his party set off, their carriages loaded down with clothes, provisions, guns, books and tents. They had left the walls far behind and were heading for the prosperous little town of Galatista in the wooded hills to the southeast when they heard that its inhabitants were threatening to burn down their own houses and retreat to the mountains if they came. Neither Orlyk nor the British merchants he was travelling with took the threats seriously. Desperate to put the infected city behind them, they travelled together to protect themselves against robbers and sent their Jewish interpreter to deal with the village headman. Eventually they arrived, settled into an inn and over the coming weeks got used to the scanty rations—olives, salted fish—which made up the local diet, passing the time teaching country children phrases in French.

In an effort to stem the plague's progress, the *mollah* had ordered all the inhabitants of the city who had left for the villages to stay where they were. No one appears to have obeyed, however, and into their mountain refuge trickled word of developments eight hours' ride away down in the plain. "A young English merchant who went yesterday to Thessalonica, came back from there this evening and told me that the plague spreads more and more, that every day thirty people die and even more leave the town." The next day they heard of the death of a

Jesuit who had recently arrived from Smyrna. Even more alarmingly, a local peasant had been stricken while in the city and had died since returning to the village. "Others say also that he was carried out of the village while he was still alive so that he doesn't infect the rest." Down in the city "the plague spreads more and more and especially among the Turks and Jews; just yesterday they carried 250 dead out of the town." One could see the sense of the Islamic injunction—derived from a *hadith* of the Prophet, but only partially obeyed by Salonica's own Muslim population—that those living in a place afflicted by the plague should accept whatever their fate held in store for them and not budge. Constant movement between the villages and the city extended the range of the epidemic, for as Orlyk himself noted—"people from here incessantly go to the city to sell their wares, and another village, very close by, is also infected."

There were several reports that it had eased off or abated entirely before Orlyk and his party judged it safe to return. Having escaped the worst, a final frisson of terror awaited him back in Salonica. He had spent the summer months wearing a light coat made for him by his Jewish tailors. Now, as they brought him his new winter furs, they confessed that one of them had already been plague-stricken—the tell-tale swellings had appeared under the arm—when he had delivered Orlyk's summer coat: "He could hardly finish his job for the pain, which tormented him and as soon as he got back home he laid down on his bed. I was thrilled when I heard this and thanked God that he kept me and my son alive. I wore this coat through the whole summer and September too, without knowing about the plague-ridden Jews. When I asked them today why they hadn't told me, these heathens answered that if I had known about it, I wouldn't have wanted the coat."

It was not until a century later—well after quarantine restrictions had become customary in Europe, and imposed upon travellers from Ottoman lands—that the city's vulnerability to plague, cholera and other epidemics began to diminish. Until then, nothing so clearly marked man's vulnerability to the external world. The rabbis often managed to isolate the houses of victims, sometimes barricading them up, at others setting guards at the doors, but since such measures were not implemented comprehensively, those who could leave did. In 1719 two-thirds of the population escaped, and the city was abandoned. The pashas, beys and notables fled into the villages; the poor remained behind and were disproportionately afflicted, especially in the densely packed Jewish quarters of the lower town. "The only prey of the epidemic left are the poor most of whom are dying," writes the Venetian consul in 1781. Many tried prayer, seeing in their sufferings the signs of God's vengeance for their sins. An English merchant reported that some Greek peasants opened up the graves of the victims, and stabbed and mangled the corpses "in a fearful manner" in the belief that the Devil had entered them. Others took a kind of revenge of their own, seizing the opportunity offered by the empty mansions, locked stores and shuttered shops in the markets to loot and steal: "More than a few villains have stayed here and there are fears lest they set fires to create the opportunity for looting the abandoned houses." Orlyk's translator turned out to head a gang of Jewish thieves which plundered unguarded warehouses, and stole jewels and cloth. The first Orlyk heard about it was when he was contacted by his former employee from prison, promising to work free for a year for him if he got him out. Wisely, no doubt, he refused. Meanwhile the cemeteries expanded on the slopes of the Upper Town where the thousands of plague victims were usually buried.[39]

MANAGING THE CITY

ONE OF THE QUESTIONS raised by the Ottoman experience of plague is what it tells us about the attitude of local officials to the management of the city. Although soldiers returning from wars, pilgrims and merchants all carried the deadly disease into the unprotected port, preventative measures were more or less non-existent. Infected houses were sometimes sprinkled with vinegar, limed or even occasionally demolished. But each community took its own measures and there was no overall governmental response. According to the reformer John Howard, who visited Salonica in 1786, the Greeks and the Jews each ran a small hospital, the former enclosed by high walls, the latter "lightsome and airy, and better accommodated for its purpose than any I had seen," situated in the midst of the cemetery, and utilising tombs as tables and seats. But the small European community was far less well equipped than in Izmir, and evidently relied on flight into the countryside. And with no public health service, at least before the administrative reforms of the mid-nineteenth century, Ottoman officials were no better informed than anyone else about where and when the epidemic struck. In 1744 when rumours of plague ran through the town, the only way the Venetian consul could establish their veracity was by approaching the chief rabbi, who got the Jewish grave-diggers to say on oath whether they had observed signs of illness among the deceased. The Ottoman town officials themselves had no idea.[40]

Here as in so many areas, they approached municipal governance in a spirit of extreme disengagement. The plague—like the other risks of urban life such as fire and violent crime—highlighted the limited resources and ambitions of the eighteenth-century Ottoman state. The truth was that the *kadi* and the pasha of the city had few means at their disposal, for the city and its interests were often squeezed between the demands of the capital, on the one hand, and the powerful regional land-owners on the other. Criminal justice was generally solved through mediation and fines, and imprisonment was limited for many years by the lack of a proper prison in the town. The so-called Tower of the Janissaries was usually used for this but rarely had many inmates and was not designed for large numbers. A considerable amount of alcohol, coffee and opium was being consumed. The city was notorious for its dozens of taverns, coffee-houses and drinking shops—Evliya had been astonished at the brazenness of the unbelievers who would openly get drunk on wine or *boza* (a drink made from fermented millet)—but they too were largely outside official control, and frequented by janissaries who did much as they pleased. Taxes and the setting of market prices did concern the authorities. But even there, as we have seen, the resources they commanded were limited.

In general, whilst not quite as anarchic as some other Ottoman cities—Aleppo, for example, seems to have been in a state of virtual civil war as notable families and local power-brokers fought out their differences—eighteenth-century Salonica was a place where the authority of the central state could only be enforced sporadically and intermittently. When events threatened to spiral into large-scale violence, the strangulation of janissary ringleaders or the expulsion of troublemakers restored order for a time. But so long as the city fulfilled its role as provider of grain and wool for the capital, the Porte was prepared to tolerate high levels of street violence, and substantial power remaining within the hands of local elites. Food riots were the townspeople's way of signalling that local land-owners and merchants needed to remember the poor. Controlling the janissaries themselves was almost impossible, and together with the Albanians, they were the main internal challenge to imperial rule. As soldiers rampaged through Salonica's streets, and the plague carried off thousands a year, it could seem as if this was a city on the verge of chaos. Yet this was a chaos of vitality, not decline.

6

Commerce and the Greeks

THE ROUTES OF TRADE

ACCORDING TO THE SIXTEENTH-CENTURY Ottoman cartographer Piri Reis, Salonica's harbour could hold at least three hundred vessels. A hundred years later ships were calling from "the Black Sea, the White Sea [the Aegean], the Persian Gulf, Egypt, Syria, Algeria, Suez, Tripolis, France, Portugal, Denmark, England, Holland and Genoa," while the languages used by the city's traders and shopkeepers included Italian, French, Spanish, Vlach, Russian, Latin, Arabic, Albanian and Bulgarian as well as Greek and Turkish. None of this sounds like a city in the doldrums. And indeed, despite plague, war and the janissaries, the population rose steadily—after stagnating throughout much of the seventeenth century, it was up to 50,000 by 1723 and around 70,000–80,000 by the 1790s. The motor of trade was humming, and even with the decline of the traditional cloth manufacturing industry, and the emigration of some Jewish weavers and businessmen, it was bringing new prosperity.[1]

The Russian monk Barskii, who visited in 1726, was impressed. "They come to Salonica from Constantinople, Egypt, Venice, France, by English trading vessels, and by land," he wrote. "Germans, Vlachs, Bulgarians, Serbs, Dalmatians, people from the whole of Macedonia and the Ukraine, traders in wholesale and retail visit here to import grain and every kind of good." The bazaars themselves were extensive, well-stocked and "perpetually crowded with buyers and sellers" and the shops contained abundant manufactured goods and colonial produce. The city's inland trade flourished, there was a carrying trade to the thriving regional fairs in the hinterland, and increasingly, a longer-range overland traffic to the expanding markets of Germany and central Europe. Once Catherine the Great conquered the Tatar lands and founded Odessa, the Black Sea grain trade took off as well, passing through Salonica on its way to southern Europe.[2]

By the century's end, the old, small wooden landing stage, unable to handle more than two or three vessels a day, was clearly insufficient for the volume of traffic. Goods lay for weeks in the open, quickly ruined by winter rains, the customs officials were notoriously corrupt, and the Jewish and Albanian *hamals* had a reputation for helping themselves. Yet despite these obstacles, some merchants amassed substantial fortunes; they were, wrote one observer, the "possessors of the treasures of Egypt." The city could not compete with Izmir, still less Naples or Genoa. Nevertheless, when one Ottoman official compiled a geography of Europe, he mentioned Salonica as one of the three key ports of the northern Mediterranean, along with Venice and Marseille. Henry Holland visited in 1812 and was impressed by the "general air of splendour of the place": "We passed among the numerous vessels which afforded proof of its growing commerce," he wrote, "and at six in the evening came up one of the principal quays, the avenues of which were still crowded with porters, boatmen and sailors, and covered with goods of various descriptions."[3]

Intra-imperial trade—with north Africa, the Black Sea and the Middle East—still overshadowed the markets of Europe. The Ottoman economy was a closed circuit, efficient and prosperous on its own terms, only gradually becoming linked to the wider, global economy. Macedonian tobacco went to Egypt and the Barbary coast, even though demand was growing in Italy and central Europe. Armenian merchants travelled to and from Persia with jewellery and other precious goods. Thick woollen capots from the Zagora went mostly to the islands, Syria and Egypt, though some were exported as far afield as the French West Indies. In addition, the obligatory grain shipments to Istanbul were often accompanied by other orders—for silver and metal tools. In return, the city was importing blades and spices from Damascus and further east, coffee, slaves and headgear from the Barbary coast, flax, linens, gum and sugar from Egypt, soap, wood, pepper, arsenic and salted fish from Izmir. From the islands came lemons and oil from Andros, and wine from Evvia. Much of this trade remained in the hands of Muslim merchants and the demand was so substantial that the city ran a deficit on its trade with the rest of the empire. Perhaps we can understand why a well-travelled Ottoman diplomat, Ahmed Resmi

Effendi, was so scathing about commerce in Europe. "In most of the provinces, poverty is widespread, as a punishment for being infidels," he wrote: "Anyone who travels in these areas must confess that goodness and abundance are reserved for the Ottoman realms."[4]

Nevertheless, during the eighteenth century, the balance of economic activity within the empire was changing as wars with Persia hit the Anatolian trade and Europe's new prosperity made Rumelia more commercially important. Salonica, as the chief port for the Balkans, was poised to profit. Izmir was busier, but a much higher proportion of Salonica's traffic was directed west and north and its trade deficit with Asia and the Middle East was more than outweighed by its surplus on the growing exchange with Europe. Exports of locally produced grain, cotton, salt and tobacco as well as wax, hides, furs and fats from the Danubian Principalities and Russia paid for Murano glass, books, fine velvets, Italian paper and even furniture. Mid-century also saw a boom in the illegal smuggling of antiquities—one Venetian shipment included five entire columns plus another one hundred "stones"—until the exporters (mostly French and Greek) damaged the roads, houses and even cemeteries so badly that the authorities put a stop to it.[5]

Despite the increasing competitiveness of French and English textiles, indigo and American coffee, the trade gap in Salonica's favour remained. It was filled by coin—Ottoman aspres and piastres, the Cairene *fundukli* and the Stambul *zermahboub* as well as German and Hungarian thalers, Spanish doubloons and Venetian ducats and sequins. Demand was so high that counterfeits entered the market produced in bulk by enterprising villagers in the Ionian islands—under Venetian control—and the towns of western Macedonia. Both the Ottoman and the Venetian authorities tried vainly to stop them. But despite the constant depreciation in the value of the Ottoman piastre, it was generally traded above its official rate, such was the foreign demand.[6]

Some European items did appeal to the elite. Heavy English watches, encased in silver, and preferably made by George Prior or Benjamin Barber, sold thirty dozen annually, reflecting the scarcity of public clocks. Lyons carpets and gold-fringed Genoese damasks adorned the wealthier *haremliks*, while the beys, as they had always done, wintered in caftans lined with Russian ermine, sable, fox and agneline. Tastes were slowly changing. The French consul Cousinéry was impressed by the contrast in living styles between the old Albanian bey of Serres, Ismail, who had "banished all interior luxury," which he regarded as "useless and ruinous," and his son Yusuf, who spent the substantial fortune he acquired as deputy governor of Salonica on his country palace, its walls painted to imitate marble, the whole "a melange of Oriental ostentation and European taste"—elegant divans, richly decorated wood-panelled doors and windows, combined with Bohemian crystal in the window-panes, English carpets and gilt-framed pictures in the harem. Yet someone as wealthy and ambitious as Yusuf Bey—the most powerful man in the city in his heyday—was probably the exception. In general, Muslim taste was far less profligate and directed not to European manufactures but to coffee, fruits, metal-work, spices and fabrics which the empire itself supplied. In fact, according to one irritated consul, the average Salonican Muslim simply did not consume enough:

> Always the same in his way of being, of living, and of dressing, the pleasures and the wants of yesterday are to him the pleasures and wants of tomorrow. Rich or poor, he puts on every morning the same woollen cloth, and lays it aside only when he has worn it entirely out, in order to purchase another of the same quality, the same price, and the same colour. He has drunk coffee in his childhood, he will drink it in his old age. He will not forsake old habits, but he will not imbibe new ones. This stupid monotony in habits and taste must set constant limits to the consumption of our commodities.[7]

It is not hard to see in such language the sterotypes of cultural immo-bility and stagnation which have long underpinned the Western diag-nosis of Ottoman decline. Yet economically, there was nothing wrong with the empire, and if consumption was low—Captain William Leake noted that "Turks as well as Jews" often carried parsimony "to excess"—this may have reflected life under a government "which makes every one feel danger in displaying his wealth and renders property and life insecure even to its most favoured subjects." Wills left half a cen-tury later show that even wealthy members of the city lived a surpris-ingly modest lifestyle, with scanty furnishings—apart from carpets, chests and lamps—adorning their homes, and few other possessions to leave their heirs.[8]

Elsewhere in the city, however, it was a very different story, and new tastes, clothes and manners were leaving their mark upon the tiny but growing European and Europeanizing elite. The French were the first to establish a consulate in the city—in 1685—a sign that the Levant trade now encompassed Salonica on a significant scale. Before 1698 only two Frenchmen actually resided in the city; but by 1721 there were eight French trading houses and about thirty-seven members of the "French nation," including servants, a baker, inn-keepers and a tailor. An English agent of the Levant Company arrived in 1718, and the same year began the commercial boom which followed the ending of the Venetian–Ottoman war and brought more and more European residents and merchants. By the middle of the century, Venice, Naples, the Duchy of Tuscany, Ragusa, Holland had representatives; Sweden, Denmark, Austria, Spain and Prussia arrived a little later. The consuls—symbols of the power of Europe—had appeared in force, even if at this stage they still had to demonstrate their respect for Ottoman power by lavish gifts to the town's chief officials, and humble and respectful behaviour.[9]

Frank Street (Odos Frangōn), now lined with rag-trade outlets and commercial agents housed in gloomy postwar concrete office blocks, still winds past the Catholic church on the western edge of the modern city centre. In this area, taverns opened for foreign sailors, and wine dealers, bakers and butchers provided them with familiar fare. Teachers, doctors, priests, secretaries and housemaids served in the houses of the city's merchants. Overland mails, run by the Neapolitans, the Austrians and the French, made news from central Europe a mere ten days distant from the city. Each group formed, in the parlance of the day, a "nation" unto itself. Yet mostly the European residents of the city got on with one another. Despite the tensions engendered by the Napoleonic wars, wrote John Galt, "their social intercourse is maintained on a pleasant and respectable footing." Henry Holland enjoyed several *conversazioni* at the house of the Austrian consul, where the entertainments included cards and recitals of Greek and Turkish songs, as well as dinner parties hosted by German merchants.

On the other hand, assertive Christians threatened the hierarchies of authority carefully established by Ottoman rule. Through the eighteenth century, even the consuls remained at the mercy of the whims of a pasha or *kadi*, a target of resentment and a useful scapegoat when needed. When over-enthusiastic Jesuits built a church without permission, and, still worse, constructed illegal bells hidden behind a brick wall, the local authorities quickly had them taken down. Venetian sailors celebrated their religious festivals so noisily they woke up the town. Janissary violence often expressed popular anger at such Frankish arrogance, especially when it broke the silence of the Ottoman city at night. In 1752 a Greek Venetian merchant, recently back from Cairo, was dining and singing with friends in his home when a passing city patrol was disturbed by the noise, entered the premises and on being told angrily by the owner that "I am a Venetian, can't I enjoy myself in my own house?" beat him up and threw him in prison.[10]

THE *BERATLI*

THE EUROPEAN TRADERS knew that despite their growing economic influence they could not function unaided. Few spoke the necessary languages, or understood the Ottoman legal system or local patronage networks. Moreover what had basically brought them to Salonica was the wool export trade, to tap which they required the cooperation of local Jews who controlled the regional supply. Without their help, they had no means of purchasing the wool itself, or of getting round the official restraints on the sale and export of this and other commodities such as cotton, leather and wheat. Credit too was short in the city, and this market was also mostly under local control. This was why, in addition to the usual panoply of servants, bodyguards and attendants, every merchant and consul acquired a *dragoman*, or interpreter, as well as a general business agent, or *censal*. These postholders were officially recognized by the Porte through its issue of licences (*berats*) which brought their holder under the protection of the nation concerned and exempted him from Ottoman taxes, justice and—not least—clothing restrictions. As a result, the post of *beratli* became highly sought after, and *berats* changed hands for thousands of piastres. In theory their possessors had obligations to the foreign nationals whom they nominally served; in practice, the consuls competed with each other to issue *berats* to the leading merchants of the place, hoping in this way to gain influence for their country. David Morpurgo, for instance, scion of a distinguished Italian Jewish family, who had settled in Salonica before 1710, was fought over by the French, Dutch and English consuls. Consuls grumbled at the "disgraceful chaffering" of *berats*, but they were all at it.[11]

To almost everyone the *beratli* were soon an anomaly, if not a disgrace. French merchants in Salonica resented their consul making wealthy Livornese Jews honorary Frenchmen, especially as they often decamped to another nation if offered better terms. But the Livornese—the last in the series of Jewish migrations into the city from the

Catholic West—had built up powerful trading houses, dominating the lucrative tobacco trade with Italy, and the consul was not about to lose their goodwill if he could help it. "In this port," wrote one, "the treasury of the French nation would suffer a significant loss if the Jews, who do big business, were obliged to leave their protection."[12]

Many *beratli* demanded exemption from Ottoman taxes: they had, after all, paid large sums to acquire their favoured status. But in this way, despite being among the richest men in the place, they simply increased the tax burden upon their co-religionists. Thus their assertion of European untouchability did not go down well and it is not surprising that they made themselves unpopular. Community leaders sometimes connived with Ottoman officials to have them imprisoned or beaten up. Nightwatchmen knocked their European hats off their heads. When Greek *beratli* started to flaunt their status by wearing expensive woven belts and silks, bishops introduced new sumptuary laws. The newly arrived Livornese Jewish *francos* shocked traditional Jews with their wigs, frock coats and goatees, and rabbis in Salonica and Livorno hotly debated the proper length and shape of beards; some *beratli* were excommunicated for trimming theirs too fine. "These newcomers are dressed like the Franks," wrote a Jesuit missionary in the city. "They have only a moustache not a beard; they do not mind eating with Christians; thus the others regard them only as half-Jews and almost as having deserted the Law."[13]

The Ottoman officials themselves had little sympathy for these upstarts. When a wealthy Greek merchant, Alexios Goutas, turned out to be working for the Venetian consul while claiming English protection, they queried his entitlement to both. Goutas asked to keep his English protection but to pass on his Venetian *berat* to his brother-in-law, and this was eventually done. In fact, the Ottoman authorities at the start of the eighteenth century had been most reluctant to encourage the spread of the consular system, precisely because they feared the abuse of the *berats*, and the consequent drop in their own tax revenues. As a result, they tended to sympathize with local men whenever quarrels arose. In 1732 there was a row between two Livornese *beratli* under French protection and one of the most powerful Jews in the city, Jacob Kapon, who was the pasha's money-lender and chief treasurer. Kapon got the rabbis to excommunicate his rivals, so that their goods were left untouched by the local dockworkers; all the French consul's protests failed to result in his punishment.[14]

In the longer run, however, the *beratli* were unstoppable for they had the prestige of Europe behind them. They were a new power in the city, middle-men between the local Jews and Frankish traders, and soon they were not only assisting European merchants but giving them a run for their money. Among the Jews, it was chiefly the Livornese who profited from the expansion of trade after 1718. A certain Raphael Villareal—whose relatives lived in Livorno and Marseilles—bought a ship, named with admirable *chutzpah* the *Archange-Raphael*, and hired a French captain: this was the kind of competition which frightened French exporters. But there were also men like "Don" Asher Abrabanel, a member of one of the most distinguished Sefardic families in the city and a man who had inherited "houses filled with luxury . . . immense wealth and property." Abrabanel was a leader of the local Jewish community and responsible for the provision of cloth for the janissary corps. From 1738, Jewish *beratli* were attending consular ceremonies, a striking indication of their relative power vis-à-vis the city's Christian merchants, who were shocked to receive them on equal terms, and the English consul was careful to send congratulations on the eve of the Jewish New Year.[15]

Yet the rise of the Greeks threatened to put even the Livornese in the shade. After nearly three centuries on the margins, Salonica's Greek community was reasserting itself. Greeks were rising to high positions in the Ottoman service, where the most successful became *voivodes* of Wallachia, or interpreters (*dragomans*) to the Imperial Fleet; others were powerful tax-collectors around Salonica itself. Hellenized Vlachs from the Pindos mountains traded in tobacco with Vienna, Venice and Trieste, building substantial frescoed mansions which can still be seen in the towns of Jannina and Siatista. With unrivalled connections with Leipzig, the Danubian Principalities and Russia, what one historian once called the "all-conquering Balkan Orthodox merchant" was quick to seek out new opportunities. Russia's rise under Catherine the Great brought a powerful new protector, interested in the Balkans as never before. "Humble, crafty, intriguing and bold" as the French consul described them, the Greeks became an unrivalled force in Salonican commerce.[16]

THE RISE OF THE GREEK MERCHANT

BY SEA THE GREEKS were already making their entrepreneurial spirit felt, becoming successful freebooters and privateers. Starting with the Seven-Year War (1756–63) between England and France, Greek corsairs embarked on an illustrious career in the Eastern Mediterranean that would last nearly a century. Flying English colours, the *angligrecs* preyed on French shipping, while the Ottoman authorities turned a blind eye. The same thing happened in the American war of 1778–83. In between, they participated in the Russo-Turkish war of 1768–74 on the Russian side. Corsairs had always been a nuisance—or rather, part of the Mediterranean maritime economy: Algerians, Tunisians, Dulcigniotes, Maltese, Venetians and other Italians, not to mention the English themselves, had all flourished. But none of them found it easy competing in the second half of the eighteenth century with the Greeks, who were drawn from the impoverished islands of the Aegean and the Adriatic, and adjusted easily to the seasonal nature of professional piracy. During the 1770 Russian campaign, Greek pirates from the islands entered the Gulf of Salonica in armed *caiques*, forcing the imperial grain levy for Istanbul to be sent the long way round along the muddy inland roads. Fifty years later, they were more of a nuisance than ever, not least to their own fellow-Christians. "The troubles and misfortunes that have befallen us and continue now for ten days . . . we cannot relate," wrote three unfortunate Greek victims in 1827. "Beating us and binding our hands, and with cutlasses threatening us that if we did not confess where we had our money they would take our lives with all that they had already taken from us, all our possessions, and they have left us in our shirts."[17]

With some reason, the Porte associated European merchants with piracy, and accused the *beratli* of more than once sharing their profits with them. The lines between legal and illegal trading were always a little blurred at sea. Nevertheless, it was surely a sign of the Greeks' growing prosperity that alongside their piratical activities, they were also increasingly involved in legitimate commerce. In the summer of 1776, an Austrian aristocrat, Baron Starhemberg, tried to set up a large new trading company in the Ottoman lands—the German trade was by far the fastest growing partner for the Levant. His agent arrived from the capital on a boat under a Russian flag, captained by a Greek from Smyrna and crewed by Greeks and Ragusans, to buy tobacco from local Greek merchants and ship it to Trieste for the Austrian and north Italian markets. The Venetian consul was understandably worried and passed on the news to his masters: Starhemberg, he reported, planned to monopolize the export of tobacco and cotton in particular not only to "Germany" but also to Italy. The implications for Venice's traditional predominance in the Mediterranean scarcely needed to be spelled out: "A new flag, the Russian, will come into the harbour, which on the one hand is much more attractive to the fanatical Greeks, and on the other will attract Barbary pirates into the Gulf." But in fact, it was worse than that: the local Greeks soon realized they did not need the Austrians at all, for they were already running the Vienna trade effectively enough without them. Heavily laden caravans of between one hundred and one thousand horses, well-guarded, were regularly making the thirty-five-day journey by land to the Austrian domains.[18]

Under the protection of the Russian flag, which they enjoyed since the 1774 Treaty of Kutchuk Kainardji, Greek merchants supplanted the Jews who had dominated the carrying trade with Venice, and established a network of trading houses between Odessa, Alexandria and Marseille. Men like the tobacco and cotton exporter Andronikos Paikos or "the most illustrious Signor Count Dimitrios Peroulis" paved the way. Their new wealth brought them prominence and allowed them to live in a new style: by the end of the century, the firm of one of the wealthiest Greek merchants, Ioannis Youta Kaftandzoglou, was reputedly the largest in all Macedonia: he supported the publication of scholarly and religious books (mostly in Vienna), and married into the family of a local French trader. Even though he himself was under the protection of the Prussian consul, he was concerned enough about the finances of the Greek community to take action against other *beratli* who were refusing to pay their taxes, and as a result he managed to get the community's tax arrears paid off.[19]

This was the kind of attitude appreciated by the Ottoman authorities. In return, they allowed the centrally located church of Ayios Minas, which had burned down many years earlier, to be rebuilt and later the churches of Panagouda and Ayios Athanasios too. Orthodox Christians were also moving into larger houses, previously owned by Turks. But this was still a sensitive business. When a Greek Venetian *beratli* called Georgios Tsitsis bought a mansion in the centre of town previously owned by a former *mufti*, he took the precaution of obtaining a positive religious opinion, or *fetva*, issued by one of the *mufti*'s successors. Even so, he later ran into trouble with a new pasha who insisted it was against the Qur'an for an unbeliever to live in the house once inhabited by a *mufti*.[20]

THE GROWTH OF RUSSIA offered the Ottoman Greeks more than just prosperity and new trading opportunities. After the string of defeats suffered by Venice in the seventeenth century, the rise of a

Christian Orthodox power also carried the promise of liberation and redemption from the Turks. Greek monks spread the "Russian expectation" from the time of Peter the Great. "The Greeks are persuaded," a French Jesuit observed in 1712, "that the Czar will deliver them one day from the domination of the Turks." Apocalyptic visions foretold the downfall of the empire at the hands of "another Lord, another Macedonian, the monarch of the Russians," in the words of the most popular of these, a collection of prophecies known as the *Agathangelos*. The author, a Greek monk, saw "Christ's victorious banner over Byzantium" and predicted that "then all will be milk and honey. Truth will triumph. And the heavens will rejoice in the true glory. The Orthodox faith will be raised high and spread from East to West."[21]

In this climate of expectation, Catherine the Great realized how useful it might be to play to the Balkan Orthodox audience, and to present her self-styled "Greek project"—as the Russian march south was termed—as the revival of Byzantine imperial glories. The 1768–74 war left the Ottomans worried at the bond of sympathy they discerned between the Russians and the Greeks. In December 1768, they ordered the Christians of Salonica and the surrounding region to hand over all their arms. In 1770, as Russian agents fomented Greek uprisings in the Peloponnese, some Muslims in Salonica were sufficiently worried to contemplate killing or driving the Greeks out. But in fact cooler counsels prevailed, with the result that the janissaries grumbled that the *mollah* and *mufti* were "pro-Greek," and attacked their residences, destroying them and carrying off their possessions. So long as the war lasted, and especially after the crushing Russian defeat of the Ottoman navy off Chios, the Christians of Salonica feared massacre.[22]

The following year, the Eastern Mediterranean was still filled with rumours of imminent salvation. In April 1771, it was reported that on Paros there were Greek and Albanian troops under canvas, serving alongside the Russians. They had built a church there and the former Patriarch Serafeim had celebrated Good Friday mass before departing for Mount Athos. After the service he had blessed the Russians and prayed for their victory, warning them not to accept offers of peace but to continue fighting "until the Greeks had been freed from the heavy Ottoman yoke."[23] Salonica again lay at the mercy of the Russian fleet. Nevertheless, the Russians, despite all the rumours, did not come, the fleet sailed past Athos without entering the Gulf, and when peace was concluded in 1774 the only losers were those few Ottoman Greeks who had been tempted to take up arms in the hope of Russian support.

REBELLION AND REPRESSION:
THE 1821 MASSACRES

HALF A CENTURY LATER, when the Greeks rebelled in earnest, the impact on the city was devastating. How the life of Salonica's Greek community would have developed without the 1821 war of independence we cannot say. The previous decades had brought new commercial opportunities and sources of enrichment—increased exports of Macedonian tobaccos to Egypt, for instance, and wool and cotton to Marseille, while Yussuf Bey requested French glass and Lyons carpets for his new palace. But the same trade routes were also carrying dangerous new political ideals. The outbreak of the French revolution inspired activists like Rhigas Ferraios to propagandize for a future Hellenic Republic; the Napoleonic wars too seemed to presage major political upheavals in the Balkans and left Serbia in turmoil.

When the Greek revolt of 1821 broke out—to Salonica's north (in the Danubian principalities) and south (in the Peloponnese)—some patriotic agents began an uprising in Macedonia as well. Suppressed quickly by Ottoman troops, the consequences were catastrophic: villages were burned down, fields destroyed and families uprooted. In the city itself, the revolt halted the Greek revival in its tracks, and massacre and exile devastated its most prosperous and successful Christian families. It was a blow from which they did not fully recover for the rest of the century.

As it happens, our best account of the uprising and the harsh Ottoman response comes from a most unexpected source. The twenty-eight-year-old Haïroullah ibn Sinasi Mehmed Agha was *mollah* of the city in 1820, where he was accused by some of pro-Greek views. When the revolt broke out, he was dismissed from his post and briefly imprisoned. Later, on his return to the capital, he did something unusual: Shaken by what he had witnessed, he wrote a memoir for the sultan, and his testimony—practically unique as a personal account by a Muslim official on any aspect of Salonica's life in the Ottoman era—was filed away in the archives of the Top Kapi palace, where it gathered dust for more than a century in the royal library before being discovered by a Greek scholar in 1940.[24]

Haïroullah Effendi begins his report with the usual polite disclaimers, excusing his lack of competence and wondering whether he would be up to the expectations placed upon him:

When therefore the faithful slave of your Excellency, and my powerful master, Halet Effendi, communicated to me your order that I should leave for the God-guarded city of Salonica to take up the high office of *mollah*, I estimated the weight of the responsibility which I should have in that position for which you had judged me worthy, I calculated my capabilities, and I saw, that with the help of Allah and with as my infallible guide the sacred and holy Laws of our faith, I would be able to appear worthy of my mission, and I prepared for my long journey. Thus, in the middle of Rebiul-Ahir in the year of Hegira 1235 [August 1820], I started out for my post, and after a somewhat difficult journey of several days, I arrived, on 8 Djemaziul-Evel [September 1820] in Salonica.

The author describes his first impressions of the city—"My God what was my surprise!"—and lauds, in conventional fashion, its wealth and prosperity. "Your Excellency may be proud that among so many cities in His possession, there is included Salonica." Its mosques, *tekkes*, markets and fortifications are all found worthy of praise: "They say that the glory of a city and its strength depends upon the number of its mosques. If this be true—and truly it is a wise saying—then Salonica is one of Your most powerful cities, if not the most powerful." In keeping with the spirit of exaggeration, Haïroullah Effendi goes on implausibly to estimate the number of mosques at seventy, and the inhabitants at one hundred thousand.

But soon politics and contemporary concerns intrude into his seemingly formulaic account. Describing the *Despot-Effendi*—the Greek metropolitan—who governed the "unfaithful," and the churches and schools under his jurisdiction, he mentions the leading church "which they call Mina Effendi [Ayios Minas] and in whose cells all the Christian notables gather and discuss the Patriarchate, the Phanar and the Peloponnese." The ferment among the Greeks was increasingly evident. "Indeed the day I arrived and went to the *Konak* they had brought in to Yusuf Bey, a middle-aged unbeliever, Mestané Effendi, because— they say—he was teaching children a song written by an unbeliever from Thessaly which Your Greatness had condemned in a previous firman and forbidden." (This was almost certainly the revolutionary hymn of the Greek propagandist Rhigas Ferraios, whose execution by the Austrians had helped popularize him among the Orthodox.)

What was as bad if not worse, he went on, the Greeks in the city rang their church bells, rode through the streets on horseback, wore fine clothes and did not step down from the pavement when they passed a Muslim. To us this indicates the extent of non-Muslim influence there; to Haïroullah it was shockingly bold behaviour which would not have been tolerated in Istanbul; prohibited by imperial decree, it was explicable only in terms of the corruption of local police officials.[25]

Despite his dismay, however, at the arrogance of the infidels, Haïroullah did not regard himself as "a fighter of unbelievers"; this was a term he reserved for the high-spending deputy pasha, the notorious Yusuf Bey, whom he also described as "rough and tyrannical," a man who so intimidated the *mufti* and the *janissary agha* that they sat quietly with crossed hands in his presence. Yusuf Bey's father, Ismail Bey of Serres, had been described by Leake as "one of the richest and most powerful of the subjects of the sultan, if he can be called a subject who is absolute here, and obeys only such of the sultan's orders as he sees fit, always with a great show of submission." With wealth based on the booming cotton trade, Ismail Bey was enjoying a quiet retirement while his son exerted an almost unchecked mastery over the city. Haïroullah—according to his own account—dared to challenge him at their first meeting. When Yusuf Bey warned that the Greeks were preparing to rise up and would have to be struck a brutal blow, Haïroullah protested: "My God! Who would dare to revolt against Your just power and strength? Rather than tyrannize them better let us behave towards them as friends, so that they will feel gratitude towards us and will not complain."[26]

Haïroullah clearly saw storm clouds ahead. After consulting the Qur'an, he met with the Greek archbishop and advised him to keep his flock in check, "to be more faithful to the laws of the *shari'a* and to obey the orders of the governor." The two men sat and drank coffee together "like old friends," a fact which spies reported to Yusuf Bey. His suspicions about the *mollah*'s sentiments were strengthened on learning too that one day, sitting at a large café outside the Kazantzilar mosque, Haïroullah had been upset by the sight of the body of a dead Christian being carried past, and had exclaimed, "May God forgive them!" Yusuf Bey accused him of having become a *giaour*—only a Christian, he insisted, would thus have sympathized with the suffering of other Christians—and on 27 February 1821, just as the Greek revolt was about to begin, Haïroullah Effendi was imprisoned in the White Tower. It was from that strategic if unpleasant vantage point—life there was frightening, he wrote, "if one is not accompanied by the thought of all-powerful God"—that he watched the terrifying events of the next months unfold in Salonica.

His fellow prisoners were Christians whose only crime had been to fail to salute Yusuf Bey in the street, or to meet in the cathedral to talk about the Patriarchate, or merely to be a prominent notable in the community. Many were suffering from starvation and thirst. An emissary of the revolutionaries, Aristeidis Pappas, was brought in, badly beaten, before he was handed over to the *janissary agha* to be executed. "Before he left," writes Haïroullah, "forgive me for this, Your Majesty, I embraced him and kissed him, because in truth, he was an honourable man and if he was to blame it was out of the goodness of his heart."

A few days later another Greek, Nikola Effendi, was brought in. He had shocking news: the Morea was in revolt, and there was intelligence that the Greeks in and around Salonica were planning to do the same. Yusuf Bey had demanded hostages, and more than four hundred Christians—of whom one hundred were monks from Athos—were under guard in his palace. All these, naturally, were being beaten and mistreated; some had been already killed.

Shortly after this the order came through from the Porte for Haïroullah's release. Yusuf Bey's attitude towards him now changed entirely, and he was sweetness itself; nevertheless, he would not allow him to leave the city immediately: the countryside was not safe and villagers ready to revolt. To Haïroullah's horror, he learned that Yusuf Bey intended to put the hostages to death and was unable to dissuade him: "The same evening half of the hostages were slaughtered before the eyes of the uncouth *moutesselim*. I closed myself in my room and prayed for the safety of their souls."

"And from that night began the evil. Salonica, that beautiful city, which shines like an emerald in Your honoured crown, was turned into a boundless slaughter-house." Yusuf Bey ordered his men to kill any Christians they found in the streets and for days and nights the air was filled with "shouts, wails, screams." They had all gone mad, killing even children and pregnant women. "What have my eyes not seen, Most Powerful Shah of Shahs?" The metropolitan himself was brought in chains, together with other leading notables, and they were tortured and executed in the square of the flour market. Some were hanged from the plane trees around the Rotonda. Others were killed in the cathedral, where they had fled for refuge, and their heads were gathered together as a present for Yusuf Bey. Only the dervish *tekkes*—whose adepts traditionally retained close ties with Greek monks—provided sanctuary for Christians. "These things and many more, which I cannot describe because the memory alone makes me shudder, took place in the city of Salonica in May of 1821."

IT WAS BY FAR the worst massacre the Greeks of the city ever suffered under Ottoman rule. At other moments of high tension over the centuries, murder had been in the air, or had actually taken place not far away—in Larissa, Serres and Nish, for instance. But to kill perhaps as many as several thousand Christians at one time was unprecedented. It broke with the basic assumptions of Ottoman administration, which dictated that the state care for all those under its sway, and showed how deeply the uprising had shaken the authorities. That spring, Sultan Mahmud II had sent a firman informing the authorities in Salonica of the outbreak of the revolution in Wallachia, and the *sheykh-ul-Islam* had issued a *fetva* saying the revolt could be crushed with all necessary means. As Haïroullah Effendi put it, the Greeks "paid for the errors of the unbelievers of Russia."

In Salonica, Yusuf Bey's superiors had wanted above all to secure the city. They were simultaneously engaged in a demanding campaign on the other side of the Pindos mountains to eliminate Ali Pasha of Jannina, who seemed at the time a far more serious foe. Even after the massacres, the Greek threat preoccupied them, and reinforcements were ordered in from the capital and Anatolia. In March 1822, another pasha, Mehmed Emin Abulubud—a Syrian of an "energetic and sometimes violent" character—ordered a new mobilization: the city forts were inspected, and brief risings in Halkidiki and on Thasos were quickly snuffed out. In the mountains of Olympos and at sea, the insurgency lasted longer. But Ali Pasha was eventually defeated and killed, and Abulubud's forces retook the town of Naoussa, which had been held by Greek rebels.[27]

In the aftermath, the booty looted from Greek homes was sold off, while the severed heads of Christian worthies decorated the *konaks* of the leading beys and the western gates of the city. Caravans of Greek captives were auctioned in the Bosniac Han, and others were sent on to the slave markets of Istanbul, Tripolis and Benghazi: ten years later, British officials were still trying to trace them and secure their release. It is not surprising that the Greeks who survived seriously believed that the Turks planned to kill them or to bring them into a condition of "servitude through the total ruin of their fortune." According to the French consul, Bottu, Abulubud's "system of spoliation" reflected his view that the Greeks had been inspired to fight for freedom by "the increase in their wealth and their industry, as well as the extreme influence they had begun to exert on affairs in Turkey."[28]

But the Ottoman state had no long-term interest in eliminating the Greeks, or in impoverishing them. On the contrary it needed their commercial acumen, as well as their support whenever it decided to curb the always troublesome Albanians. The policy of terror was becoming ever more counter-productive, bringing business to a halt and alarming non-Greeks too as it rippled outwards. Muslims and Jews were plunged into "the most profound misery, irritation and despair." "It is chiefly among the Turks of the town," noted the French consul, "whose self-esteem Mehmed Pasha and the Arabs in his entourage daily affront, and whose livelihood they ruin, that the fermentation is liveliest and most general." One sees here indications of a Turkish-Arab antipathy which rarely surfaces in the documents. News of Abulubud's posting elsewhere in August 1823 was greeted with "astonishment and the greatest joy." Ibrahim Pasha, his replacement, greeted the Greek notables with "sweetness." "We could have believed ourselves transported into another country and surrounded by other men," noted Bottu. Considering that at this time the war with Greek insurgents was in full swing, that Greek pirates had blocked access to the Gulf and that the hinterland was also unsafe, this betrayed striking self-confidence. In January 1824, all non-residents were ordered to leave within three days, following reports that armed rebels had infiltrated the city; two years later, pirates nearly succeeded in firing on the Top Hane munitions dump, which would have taken much of the Frankish Quarter with it had it gone up. But memories of the massacre of 1821 were still vivid, and left both Turks and Greeks in the city unwilling to provoke further conflict.[29]

These bloody events were a turning-point in Salonica's history. In the first place, they led to the shrinking of the city's Greek population and its impoverishment. The loss of several thousand lives, numerous properties and hundreds of exiles continued to be felt for generations. The costs of putting down the revolt were borne by the community itself, a crushing burden, which the Porte was still struggling to apportion in 1827. Five years on, houses still lay empty, at least to judge from an imperial decree permitting the sale of abandoned properties belonging to Greeks, to prevent their dilapidation. The city itself did not recover for more than a decade.

The second momentous development was the emergence, for the first time in Ottoman history, of an independent Christian successor state scarcely one day's voyage from Salonica itself. The very idea was an affront to Muslim sensibilities and to Ottoman pride. An imperial firman from 1828—just two years before the declaration of Greek independence—had warned the emperor's subjects about the extent of the international support for the "Greek revolutionaries of the Morea and the other islands of the White Sea" and underlined the impossibility of ever granting them their goal—"for this would mean—may it never happen—that we set Muslims in the place of *rayah* and the *rayah* in the place of Muslims, something which would touch the entire Muslim people and is impossible from the point of view of holy law, politically and religiously for us to accept, or even countenance." Yet just this came to pass, and Athens—a small town less than half the size of Salonica—eventually became the capital of the new state.[30]

The Kingdom of Greece was too weak to mount a serious challenge to the empire for many years to come. Nevertheless, its very existence was a marker of Ottoman failure and a pointer to the strength of a new force in the eastern Mediterranean—nationalism—especially when this was backed up by the Christian states of Europe. In 1835 the first Greek consul took up residence in the city, placing local Christians in a novel situation. Greeks were henceforth torn between loyalty to the empire, which still contained the overwhelming majority of Orthodox Christians in the Levant, and allegiance to the tiny Kingdom; Slav-speaking Christians would in turn have to decide whether they were merely Orthodox or also Greeks, a choice which pressed heavily upon them as the century closed and new Slavic states emerged as well. Jews, and of course Muslims, felt no such tug, and if anything their attachment to the empire took on an anti-Greek tinge.

But the sick man of Europe was not dead yet, and Sultan Mahmud II was among the first to draw lessons from his defeats. In 1826 he ordered the disbanding of the janissaries and thanks to his ruthlessness succeeded where many of his predecessors had failed. In Salonica, a few weeks after they burned down the pasha's palace, the janissaries were systematically hunted down and many were imprisoned in the Tower of Blood (better known today as the White Tower) and killed. Overnight they were eliminated as a force. Some fled to the same dervish monasteries that had sheltered Greeks five years earlier. Others burned their uniforms and payslips. Only occasionally in the years that followed would an Ottoman official, perhaps justifying his conservatism, let slip his regret at their passing, or perhaps even refer to his own janissary past. With their destruction Mahmud could begin the hard work of administrative reform—improving internal security, re-establishing central authority and banishing the memories of the chaos and anarchy which had afflicted the city through the eighteenth century.

7

Pashas, Beys and Money-lenders

THE SULTAN'S VISIT

SHORTLY AFTER EIGHT O'CLOCK one morning in July 1859, a salute from the town batteries heralded the arrival of Sultan Abdul Mecid. The imperial squadron—a flotilla of paddle-wheel frigates, steamers and cutters—glittered in the bay. On the carpeted wharf stood the heads of the town's religious communities, the governor, notables and consuls; thousands of curious and respectful inhabitants lined the approaches. The sultan—together with his brother, three sons, the grand admiral and Riza Pasha, the minister of war—proceeded through the town. Their passage flanked by detachments of troops, they made their way along streets specially widened for the occasion to the mansion of Yusuf Bey, the most powerful landed proprietor in the region, and one of the wealthiest men in the city.

Over the next few days, the sultan held public audiences in the Beshchinar gardens by the shore. Under the plane trees he received the homage of local Ottoman dignitaries, the chief rabbi and the metropolitan, while hundreds of petitions were handed to him by townspeople and villagers seeking his aid in curbing brigandage, eradicating corruption and guaranteeing just administration. His aides distributed more than sixty thousand piastres for the benefit of local Ottoman, Greek and Jewish schools, hospitals and the poor "of different nations." By night, the town was brilliantly illuminated as lanterns festooned the minarets and ships. When he departed three days later, he took with him not only the cheering memory of his enthusiastic reception but also an attack of the local fever, brought on by exposure to Salonica's notoriously unhealthy summer climate (and—so it was whispered among observers—"to his imbibing other things besides bad air when sitting there" for he was known for his fondness for alcohol). Two years later, he was dead, not yet forty years of age.[1]

This was the only royal visit paid to Salonica, the empire's most important and prosperous European city, during the whole of the nineteenth century, and probably the first such since Mehmed IV wintered there in 1669. But then Abdul Mecid was not a man overly concerned with convention: he had shocked people a few years earlier by attending the wedding of the daughter of one of the leading Christians at his court, and had even graced with his presence a ball held by the British ambassador. Twenty years earlier, his Gulhané (Rose Garden) decree had ushered in far-reaching changes to the way his empire was ruled, and in 1856, following the Crimean War, a second proclamation had spelled out the need for modernization and religious equality in even greater detail. Breaking the isolation which had come to surround the figure of the sultan, Abdul Mecid naturally wanted to see for himself the results of his reforms.

For the Ottoman empire was never the static and unchanging entity its critics (and idealizers) insisted it was. After the Napoleonic wars, its sultans learned an important lesson from the success of imperial rivals like Russia, the Habsburgs and Prussia: no state could hope to survive without centralizing military, judicial and fiscal authority. Mehmed Ali's regime in post-Napoleonic Egypt had begun this process, demonstrating that an Islamic country was capable of modernizing itself along European lines. Indeed so successful was the experiment that by the 1830s Egypt had emerged as a serious threat to the empire itself.

It was in the midst of this Egyptian crisis that Abdul Mecid came to the throne and that his reforms—the "Auspicious Reorderings" (Tanzimat i-Hayriye)—had their origins. Mehmed Ali, a servant of the sultan, had been bitterly disappointed that the help he had provided against the Greek rebels had not been better rewarded, and once the Greek crisis was over, he sent his new French-trained army into the sultan's Syrian provinces. In June 1839, just after Mahmud II's death, the Ottoman grand admiral surrendered the entire fleet to the Egyptian upstart, and when the youthful new sultan, Abdul Mecid, offered to make Mehmed Ali hereditary governor of Egypt, the latter demanded Syria and Adana too. Faced with humiliation, the Ottoman foreign minister was sent to London to secure British backing. A joint British-Austrian and Ottoman fleet bombarded Beirut and forced the Egyptians out of Syria and in 1841 Mehmed Ali backed down, accepting hereditary rule over Egypt under the nominal suzerainty of the Ottoman crown.

During the crisis, the influential British ambassador in Istanbul, Stratford Canning, and reformist Ottoman diplomats had both become convinced that the only hope for the survival of the empire lay in sweeping institutional change. Mustafa Reshid, the Ottoman foreign minister, led this movement and it was in November 1839, while the delicate negotiations for British help were continuing in London, that from his residence in Bryanston Square he sketched out a draft of new legislation fundamentally altering the constitutional basis of the Ottoman state. The draft itself became the famous decree of Gulhané in which Abdul Mecid declared his intention to safeguard the security of life, honour and property of his subjects, to do away with tax-farms and state monopolies, to bring in a regular system of tax assessment and collection, and to introduce a new means of conscription into the army.[2]

Even though the proclamation was short on specifics, it was an astonishing departure from tradition, for in outline the Gulhané decree projected an entirely new relationship between the sultan and his subjects. His pledge that "the Muslim and non-Muslim subjects of our lofty Sultanate shall enjoy our imperial concern" marked, at least in embryo, a policy of formal equality of all Ottoman subjects, regardless of religion, a policy which would transform the very foundations of Ottoman rule. In addition, it defined relations between ruler and ruled in a completely new way: the empire's subjects were no longer merely the sultan's property, governed through a range of intermediaries, contracts and special concessions; they were now individuals bound politically in a direct relationship with the head of the state. Thus began the transformation of Ottoman administration, law, economy and politics which reached its apogee in the 1876 constitution and the short-lived parliament of the following year.[3]

Thanks to the support of the Great Powers, especially the British, the Near Eastern crisis of 1839–41 removed the Egyptian threat to the Ottoman dynasty, and Sultan Abdul Mecid could begin the difficult task of realizing the promises he had made. Imperial ministries were established and expanded, and the new civil service became the generator of change. An invigorated central government started to re-assert its power over the provinces. The tax system was reformed so that collection no longer lay, at least in theory, in the hands of the provincial governors and their tax-farmers but by salaried tax collectors sent out from Istanbul. Administrative boundaries were re-drawn to clarify the chain of command. Governors were supposed to pay more attention to local advisory councils, marking the first time the principle of representative government had been acknowledged. New criminal and commercial tribunals came into existence alongside the older *kadi* courts. And finally, the military and civilian functions of provincial administrators were separated, and the army itself was reorganized, with new supply services and an autonomous military school system. It was, on paper, a radical transformation.

The challenge was to sell it to the populace. In April 1840, therefore, the governor of Salonica, Namik Pasha, called a meeting of leading inhabitants to explain the principles behind the new decree. The Christians appeared pleased, but the beys were annoyed by the idea that Muslims and non-Muslims might pay the same taxes. Over the coming months, it became clear that opposition to the reforms was mobilizing. On the other hand, support for them was discernible too among the peasantry, shopkeepers and guilds. By the end of 1842, the British consul was optimistically noting "a more correct system of administration in all the branches of the Local Government, less oppression, less plundering, and everyone being free, it may be said, to dispose of his own."[4]

Yet in fact, it was early days and the struggle was just beginning: the central government might propose, but it was those with power in regional centres like Salonica who disposed. The destruction of the janissaries had removed one of the most unruly obstacles to the authority of the sultan, and brought relative peace to provincial society, but other interest groups and powerful classes remained. In mid-century Salonica, three centres of influence predominated—the governor, the local landed elite, and the private bankers and money-lenders who controlled the supply of credit. The success or failure of the Ottoman state's attempt to reform itself depended on the relations between them.

THE PASHAS

IT WAS SURELY NOT BY CHANCE that Sultan Abdul Mecid did not stay in the governor's residence on his 1859 visit. A sprawling wooden building in the centre of the town, in a walled enclosure with gardens, outbuildings and offices, it was not a particularly grand or awe-inspiring affair. Its imposing fin-de-siècle replacement—a palatial neo-classical pile designed by an Italian architect at the end of the nineteenth century—was very different, and showed how far the power and majesty of the Ottoman state had grown. Today this building still houses the offices of the pasha's Greek equivalent, and the car-parks, widened streets and open spaces which detach it from its surroundings signal its authority. But at the time of Abdul Mecid's visit, the pasha's *konak* was surrounded by narrow twisting streets, inns, stables, a *hamam* and the Saatli (Clocktower) mosque, its theological school and cemetery: it was not left in majestic isolation, and had not yet succeeded in imposing its demands on the urban space around it.

The pasha's divan, however, was the administrative heart of the city: through the double-guard at its gates thronged all those seeking an audience. When summoned they removed their shoes and walked down carpeted corridors to a large, light reception room lined with sofas and stools. Here petitions were presented, complaints aired and information passed on, all in full hearing of the many other supplicants seated and awaiting their turn: news of everything that had been discussed at the divan spread through the coffee-houses of the town within hours. Access was surprisingly easy, and restricted neither by religion nor status. The wealthy Omer Pasha, "though as fond of pomp and show as most pashas," nevertheless ensured that "the most humble individual may at any moment obtain an interview." Distinguished visitors were greeted by the pasha in person, and invited to seat themselves beside him. Sweetmeats, coffee, sherbets, cigarettes and fine *chibouks* with amber mouth-pieces were handed round, and newcomers were engaged in polite conversation, or encouraged to report the news they brought with them. Hierarchy and informality were blended in ways unfamiliar to Western visitors: Ottoman Christian subjects displayed servility, like the elderly *dragoman* from the consulate, who "raised his hand to his head" each time he addressed the pasha. On the other hand, Muslims of all ranks behaved with greater ease, and village peasants spoke as freely as dignitaries visiting from the capital.[5]

If he was conscientious or prudent, the governor did not remain in the seclusion of his *konak*. Hadji Ahmed Pasha perambulated incognito, chatting with shopkeepers, and acquiring local knowledge which he put to use establishing a short-lived police force to patrol the streets. Sali Pasha personally inspected the state of the prisons, while his successor, a keen reformer, "visits every corner of the town . . . instead of passing his leisure in the corner of his divan," and as a result ordered prisoners to sweep the streets and organized monthly inspections of the fire brigades. Another pasha wandered the streets disguised as a farmer, and mingled with the peasants outside the town walls, encouraging them to submit petitions to himself.[6]

This was still a personalized system of rule in which temperament

counted for much. Husni Pasha headed off a riot by promptly announcing lower prices for flour, while Akif Pasha won praise for his "timely
and vigorous measures" to check an outbreak of cholera. During a fire
in 1840, Omer Pasha "was immediately on the spot" to check the
flames by ordering all the shops near the fire to be pulled down. By
contrast, Yusuf Pasha was "not respected owing to his indolence" and
the former vizier Riza Pasha made it obvious that he felt he was parked
there in exile.[7] Only a year or so before him, in 1846, Yacoub Pasha had
sat and watched as more than fifteen hundred houses were burned. As
the British consul reported:

> His Excellency Yacoub Pasha evinced the most extraordinary, if
> not cruel, apathy, smoking his pipe and quietly looking at the fire
> without giving one single para to urge the people to exert them-
> selves. Most of the fire engines were taken away from the fire to
> be ready to protect the Konak of the Pasha and the Greek Arch-
> bishop's palace, the consequence was that the fire made dreadful
> ravages till it reached these two extremities.
>
> In one instance, when an Engine was required which had
> been taken by some Greeks to protect the church of St.
> Theodoro (when all danger for the safety of the edifice was
> passed) I urged His Excellency Yacoub Pasha to send and take
> the Engine to save the upper part of the Town, his reply was
> "What can I do, it is a Frank engine." Astonished at such a reply,
> I said: "The engine may be a Frank engine but Your Excellency
> must not forget that you are a Governor, and that as it is neces-
> sary for the safety of the Town, you should send and seize it."
> Yacoub Pasha then sent some of his people to take it, but they
> returned saying that it was a Frank engine and that they will not
> give it up.[8]

The mid-nineteenth-century Ottoman state, as this example may suggest, was still suffering more from chronic weakness than from excessive despotism. The pasha had no greater resources at his direct
disposal than his eighteenth-century predecessors had commanded—
usually only small detachments of *zaptiehs*, or gendarmes, who were
quartered at his palace, or companies of artillerymen manning the batteries in the fort. In 1843, the departure of troops to the capital left only
five hundred artillerymen to police the town and keep order throughout the *pashalik*. There was no regular municipal police force till late in

the century, and the streets were patrolled infrequently. Night patrols and nightwatchmen were often armed with nothing more than the large stick they used to beat on the cobbles, and frequently stood aside rather than get involved in brawls which they had not been ordered to stop; many neighbourhoods effectively policed themselves, with the local headman organizing bands of young men, especially in the Jewish quarters of the lower town. As a result, the market attracted thieves and pickpockets, and there were even gangs of child-prostitutes, armed with pistols and rifles, who roamed the streets near the port, clustering around the *hamams*, and soliciting sailors from visiting naval vessels. The public baths themselves were, according to the experienced British consul, "full of children who act as Fellachs, or washers . . . the resort of all the most depraved, and where the crime is openly tolerated." But as with abortion—another technically illegal but widely tolerated social practice—little was done to end the scandal. On one occasion, a sweep was made of the baths, and all workers there under thirty years old were dismissed; but as soon as the pasha responsible was disgraced and sent on elsewhere, they came back.[9]

Lack of police hampered the monitoring of known trouble spots—casinos, cabarets and cafés "where all the wicked subjects gather together to drink, play cards and gamble, and then prowl the streets." It also made it harder to disperse the kinds of mobs that still formed when grain prices rose and rumours of scarcity spread through the lower quarters—as when one thousand poor Jews stormed grain warehouses in February 1847. Until late in the century, criminal investigation continued to be based upon the principle of collective neighbourhood punishment: thus after two women and their children were brutally killed not far from the pasha's residence in 1839, the entire street was jailed in an effort to find the culprits. The prison itself was squalid and overcrowded, its Jewish jailers notorious for their use of the heavy three-inch collar which they fixed around an inmate's neck. Occasionally, public executions took place without ceremony, sometimes outside the Vardar Gate, at others in the midst of the city, the rope hung from a convenient signpost, a stool borrowed from a nearby café, the dead man left hanging with a placard around his neck. Lack of statistics makes it impossible to know how often the Ottomans resorted to capital punishment, though it was almost certainly far less than the Christian states of north and western Europe. The real difficulty for the Ottoman authorities was asserting their power, not limiting it.[10]

The destruction of the janissary corps in 1826 eliminated the pasha's chief challengers. But disorderly soldiers were still a problem. In 1855 troops en route to the Crimean War were abducting people for ransom, throwing stones at houses in the Greek quarter and frequenting the bath-houses in search of young boys. During the great fire of the following year, eight hundred Albanian irregulars en route to the Arab provinces plundered the bazaar freely, knowing that no one—least of all the pasha—would dare to arrest them. The year before Abdul Mecid's visit, more irregulars swaggered around with their arms; having refused to stay in the barracks outside the walls they had to be lodged in the khans. The pasha, who did not have "more than a few artillerymen," was powerless. Salonica's inhabitants were always surprised when there were "no robberies, no insults"; or when troops did nothing more than wander in great numbers through the bazaar "expressing surprise at what they see." Badly paid and lodged in flea-ridden caravanserais or, later, in the vast, insanitary warehouse-like barracks built thoughtlessly above a former graveyard on the city's outskirts, the under-age conscripts and irregulars were so poorly looked after that it is extraordinary they did not cause more trouble than they did.[11]

With few forces at his disposal, the governor remained constantly attentive to the prestige of his office. When the French consul accidentally struck Namik Pasha on the arm—the latter had intervened in a quarrel between him and a Jewish neighbour—the governor immediately withdrew from the scene as a mark of his displeasure: in the face of the growing assertiveness of European powers, upholding the authority of the Ottoman state was more important than ever. Husni Pasha imprisoned two elderly men for "the trifling offence" of failing to salute him as his carriage passed by. But maintaining the dignity of the office was one thing, arbitrary violence another, and if a pasha's behaviour slipped over into needless cruelty, it was openly criticized. After Salik Pasha, "whose equal in anti-Christian feeling it would be difficult to find in any country," ordered the harsh treatment of some Albanian Catholic families suspected of having abandoned Islam and had them embarked for Constantinople with such brutality that several died, "all classes Christians, Turks and Jews cried 'Shame' " and the Turkish captain of the port confided to the British consul that "such acts are contrary to the Law of God and our Prophet." Eventually Salik Pasha was recalled by the Porte.[12]

Underlying the Ottoman state was a fundamental paradox. As the chief government official, the pasha was the single most powerful influence on the success or failure of the whole reform effort. Yet the temporary and unstable character of his position militated against effective long-term governance. How does the sultan ensure the obedience of his governors? asked David Urquhart, a sympathetic observer of the empire. His answer: by "the perpetual possibility of losing their fiefs, their life, their fortune, possibilities to which no other Muslim, no other subject of the Porte is exposed to the same degree . . . Their services are neither assured nor recompensed; their fall must come and is usually more rapid than their rise." Political appointees who owed their posting to court connections, largesse and vizierial favour as much as to their own abilities, pashas rarely stayed more than a year in the city before their next posting came. This speedy rotation ensured they would not turn into powerful challengers to their master; but equally it made it hard for them to carry out his policies effectively.[13]

In order to prevent them treating their assignment as a fiefdom to be ransacked, the new reforms had supposedly created a caste of salaried officials; in reality, their pay was so low that into the 1860s little changed. "I have no inducement to be honest," one pasha confessed. "If I attempt to rule justly all the other pashas will combine against me and I shall soon be turned out of my place, and unless I take bribes I shall be too poor to purchase another." Each year Salonica's inhabitants hoped they would be assigned a man rich enough to ignore the many opportunities for personal gain, a man "whose eye is full" as the saying went. Ibrahim Pasha's sole redeeming feature was that he was "sufficiently rich to pay for the situation he holds." Omer Pasha's first term as pasha in the city had been marked by his rapacity; seven years later, he had become "a man of great wealth which may help him withstand bribery."[14]

Unfortunately, money was no guarantee of restraint. It was a good sign that Bekir Pasha, for example, who arrived in August 1813, was "very rich"—he owned huge estates in the Peloponnese—but it turned out within the year that his avarice had not been satisfied and that though "master of a considerable fortune, he was none the less passionate about money and all means for extorting it are legitimate in his eyes." In the hands of men such as these, it became clear that the creation of new bureaucracies, laws and taxes would not suffice to transform Ottoman life. First the Porte would have to work out whether or not it trusted its own officials. So long as the pasha himself was a deliberately weakened force, little prevented others from challenging and subverting his authority.[15]

THE BEYS

THE POLICY OF REFORM was driven from the centre, and forced on the provinces. As an imperial emissary, almost always brought in from outside, without prior knowledge of the city, and bound to leave before long, the pasha had to measure himself against, and work alongside, those men who by their position, wealth and long residence in Salonica wielded real power locally. With the sultan deliberately keeping his pashas on a tight rein for his own reasons, it was the landed Muslim elite who benefited. Leake noted in 1807 that "a few great proprietors" in the city "usurp such an influence that the pasha is a mere cypher, unless he comes accompanied by a sufficient body of attendants to enforce his authority." Urquhart, a little later, saw him as a "marionette," a puppet whose strings were pulled by others. Compared with the Bey of Serres, an independent landowner, whose "authority in the districts he commands is unlimited" and who could draw if necessary upon as many as fifteen or twenty thousand troops, the pasha of Salonica was hamstrung by his dependence on orders from the capital, his unfamiliarity with the local scene, and his lack of men or money. Salonica might have been the largest city in the area, but neighbouring Serres and Yennidje, home of the illustrious Evrenos family, were power-bases whose leading families possessed dozens of villages. There, away from the pasha's gaze, they had grown accustomed to total mastery. They regarded their villagers—Muslim and Christian alike— as their possessions, and unlike their equivalents in Anatolia, they were never dispossessed of their hereditary estates by the Porte.[16]

For much of the nineteenth century, this was the city's real ruling class, and no reform effort could succeed without their cooperation. A local council of six leading land-owners had existed since the early eighteenth century to advise the governor. When a new advisory council was set up as a result of the Tanzimat reforms they dominated that too, and more often than not they ensured that members of their families held the crucial lower-level judicial, administrative and economic posts through which real power was deployed. In such circumstances even the toughest-minded pasha found it difficult to make headway against them. This would not have mattered if the interests of the pasha and the beys had converged. But in fact the opposite was the case. After the great crisis of the 1820s and 1830s—the loss of Greece, the Russian invasion and Mehmed Ali's insubordination in Egypt—the declaration of equality for Christians and Jews, the attempted abolition of peasant forced labour and the establishment of a standing army with regular troops all implied a challenge to the power of the Muslim landed elite. As Christian confidence grew and peasant expectations of reform rose, the beys fought back to defend their place in the old order.

Even before the first reform decrees were proclaimed in 1839, the villagers—both Christian and Muslim—had begun speaking out with a new freedom about the beys' ill-treatment of them. "We know it to be the will of the sultan," they now declared, "that we should enjoy our rights ... As subjects of the sultan, we demand justice." The beys reacted to these developments with undisguised hostility. When the pasha instructed them to treat the local Christians with courtesy they did not disguise their irritation. They also criticized Namik Pasha for having returned the visits of European consuls, another mark of humiliation, so far as they were concerned. A later pasha, Yusuf Mehmed, arrived with a show of firmness, imprisoning one bey for debt and shouting down a deputation which came to plead for his release: "Our laws are for the rich as well as the poor," he told them. "They who incur debts must sell their property and satisfy their creditors." But he too was soon having to backtrack, his position undermined by his corrupt subordinates.[17]

For the beys themselves had powerful weapons at their disposal. They had their own supporters at court, whose favours they secured by regular supplies of honey, oil and flour. "Up to the present moment," noted an observer in 1837, "Any Pasha of Salonica who possessed sufficient nerve to remonstrate with the beys did not remain in power. For being united, the beys by their joint means were enabled to offer such bribes to some of the parties in power at the Sublime Porte." And if bribes failed, defamation and intrigues usually did the trick. Control of local grain supplies made them—not the pasha—the crucial figures in ensuring an affordable local supply of flour through the year. Their henchmen could be sent off on plundering raids by land or sea which exposed the pasha to accusations that he was failing to act against brigands and pirates. The reforming Namik Pasha regretfully came to the conclusion that "there is no one to second me."[18]

Yet already by the mid-1840s, some of the more far-sighted and politically adroit land-owners had come to appreciate the advantages of participating in the new reforms. At first this was an obstructive strategy, a way to monopolize positions of influence and control the flow of information to Constantinople. Shortly after the Gulhané decree, it was reported that the most influential beys "being members of the [local] Council, have become more powerful." They also packed a provincial deputation sent to the capital in 1845 to advise the Porte. As a result, forced labour dues continued to burden the peasantry, money-lending remained a curse on the local economy and the beys effectively ran their own affairs: peasants both Christian and Muslim quickly became gloomy at the prospect of any real improvements in their lives. It was only from the 1860s onwards—and in particular following new laws on provincial administration in 1864—that the reform movement gathered momentum. As the city prospered, and Greeks and Jews began to make substantial fortunes, the new capitalist economy swept away the old closed Ottoman system and non-Muslims started to invest in estates around the city, especially after foreigners were allowed to own property. Gradually the beys—like landed classes across Europe—realized that land itself was no longer necessarily the best repository of their fortunes. More and more made their way into the rapidly expanding imperial bureaucracy whose rapid growth from roughly 1,000 to nearly 100,000 over the century was an important means of reconciling them with the regime. They entered municipal and national politics, became mayors and ministers, and in 1908 when the first parliamentary elections were held for a constitutional assembly, three out of the eight deputies elected locally were drawn from the landed class. In this way they safeguarded their power and their estates whilst contributing to the modernization of their city and country.[19]

The most distinguished landed family in the Balkans—the descendants of Ghazi Evrenos Bey, the conqueror of Macedonia—had little difficulty making this transition. Their staying power and flexibility was impressive. In the eighteenth century they had been tax-farmers on a huge scale. Yet Evrenoszade Pasha was among the deputies sent to the first-ever parliament in 1877 and his descendants were prominent members of the imperial bureaucracy. Even after the Greek army marched into Macedonia in 1912, they managed to collect their rents. Would not the first Evrenos Bey, to whose tomb Muslim and Christian pilgrims still flocked, have admired the foresight of his descendant Mustafa Rahmi, an influential and early member of the Committee of Union and Progress in Salonica when it was still in its coffee-house and beer-garden phase, deputy in the Ottoman parliament in 1908 and 1912, and governor of Izmir in 1914–15, where he resisted pressure from his former co-conspirators to drive the Armenians of the city out to certain death in the interior? True to his familial tradition, this scion of the great dynasty preferred, despite the events of the war, to maintain good relations with the Greeks and Armenians, a humane policy which may not have been unconnected with his efforts to exchange the hereditary estates around Salonica with those owned by a Greek landowner outside Izmir. For even Rahmi Bey could see that his family's long connection with the Salonica region was inevitably coming to an end. Later, between the two world wars, he was pushed to the margins of Turkish political life, forced into exile, and sentenced *in absentia* on trumped-up grounds of attempting to plot against Mustafa Kemal.[20] Meanwhile the Evrenos estates were taken over by the Greek state in the aftermath of the vast migration of peoples which followed the collapse of the empire. The great land-owners had been able to survive both the weakening and the subsequent regeneration of the Ottoman state, but as in every empire, their wealth was ultimately bound up with the fate of the imperial system itself, and could not survive long into the era of nation-states, mass movements of populations and land reform.[21]

THE MONEY-LENDERS

IT WOULD BE A COMPLETE MISREADING of the realities of life in mid-nineteenth-century Salonica to assume that the only people to wield power there were Muslims. In September 1840 extraordinary fly-bills were pasted to the walls of the main churches and other buildings in town. Curious passers-by found a satire, written in Greek, which directed the pasha's attention to the misdeeds of both the archbishop of the city and his Muslim colleagues on the local advisory council, and stated that their acts were not in accordance with the imperial instructions contained in the Gulhané proclamation of the previous year. The anonymous writer called on God to witness that he would expose their unjust doings if there was not immediate reform.[22]

The accusations referred specifically to machinations to thwart the Porte's anti-corruption drive. As everyone in Salonica knew, the culprits were doing this because they themselves had been bribed by the local bankers and usurers whose business depended on supplying vast sums to everyone from peasants to high-ranking office-holders and tax-farmers. In the old Ottoman economy, control of the supply of credit was at least as important as ownership of land—more important perhaps, since it was scarcer. The first Western-style bank, the Ottoman Bank, was founded by imperial decree only in 1863: before that date, money-lenders and private bankers wielded huge power. In complete contrast to the land-owning class, they tended not to be Muslims at all, but Jews, Armenians and Christians. In 1738, as we saw in the last chapter, the Jewish *sarraf* (private banker), Jacob Kapon, the pasha's money-lender and chief treasurer, was a man powerful enough to get the rabbis to issue excommunications against his rivals and bring their business affairs to a halt. A century later, Izzet Pasha's *sarraf*, also Jewish, was said to have interests in two-thirds of the monopolies of the city. According to the British consul, the pasha "entertains too high an opinion of his Jew Bankers. They are the cause of much evil," and had the pasha's entire entourage in their power. Firmans outlawing excessive bribes to *mollahs* and *kadis* were ignored because the officials demanding the bribes needed money to pay off their debts to such men.

It was because money-lending and corruption were closely connected that this class of men formed one of the principal targets of the reforms. In 1851 the government sent a commissioner, Sami Pasha, to investigate. "I hardly ever witnessed in this Town so great a concourse of people collected for the arrival of any Ottoman authority," noted a foreign eye-witness. Money-lending, the extortionate rate of interest, the mortgaging of estates and the damaging impact on cultivation were pressing issues. Everyone knew the fate of the bishop of Kassandra who tried to make credit available to his parishioners at a mere 8½ per cent interest annually. Powerful local money-lenders had managed to get him recalled so that they could continue lending at their usual 20–25 per cent. During his stay in the city, Sami Pasha—who like many Ottoman civil servants spoke Greek as well as Ottoman Turkish—received numerous petitions calling for regulation. A little later it was announced by the governor, Yacoub Pasha, that lending money to villages was no longer legal without the permission of the regional advisory council.[23]

But then Yacub Pasha himself fell into disgrace and was replaced by someone far worse. Sadik Pasha, a sixty-year-old Salonican bey with a bloody past, had borrowed £25–30,000 to secure his appointment to the *pashalik* and as a result owed a huge sum to his bankers. The relevant calculations were easily made: his total income, one observer noted, "does not amount to half of the interest due at the end of the year"; as a result, "plunder and corruption may be anticipated." Within a short space of time, the city was enduring an "unprecedented" level of extortion, by the police, government officials, and by the pasha himself. Guilds were having to hand over a monthly allowance and men were being cast into prison solely in order to force them to pay large fines: the pasha's private secretary was reputed to have raised "about £24,000" in this way.[24] An official enquiry later established that as many as 250 had been unlawfully killed during Yusuf Sadik Pasha's tenure as governor: but his grip over the town, and the fact that most of the advisory council were related to him, meant that no one had been able to prevent his crimes.[25]

Memories of this "unprecedented plunder" must have still been alive six years later when Sultan Abdul Mecid made his visit to the city. For it was during the few days he remained there that an episode occurred which through its sheer emblematic power gripped Salonica's imagination for generations. Told and re-told many times, this was the story of how the sultan met with Sadik Pasha's chief local banker, a man called Jackie Abbott, a Levantine businessman and money-lender, the man in other words whose money had been responsible for so much suffering. The embodiment of Ottoman authority and the architect of reform thus came face to face with the figure who represented as well as anyone the old system and its defenders.

John "Jackie" Abbott was "Greek by religion, British by nationality." His family had been settled in the city for over fifty years but he had been the real architect of its rise. A mid-century photograph shows a plump man in a morning coat, his large necktie carelessly knotted, staring aggressively at the camera as though keen to get back to work. His fortune came originally from cultivating and trading in leeches, an indispensable commodity for local healers. But the leeches signified something else as well, for Abbott had used his wealth to turn himself into one of the region's chief money-lenders by "corrupting the authorities and thereby committing all kinds of acts of injustice." In addition to Sadik Pasha, Abbott also had the city's Greek metropolitan in his debt, and several of the leading beys—a majority, in fact, of the advisory council. He was a good example of what Urquhart called "the hidden mechanism which sets the administrative machine of Turkey in motion." His lavish bribes to successive pashas and their secretaries included money, snuff boxes and diamond-studded pipes, sufficient to get his rivals thrown into jail and making him a dangerous man to cross (according to one apocryphal version of the tale he had started out in life by murdering a competitor, the Jewish owner of the finest local leech-farm). By the time of Abdul Mecid's visit, his interests extended to more than twenty-five landed estates and numerous villages whose peasants laboured to repay the extortionate interest rates he charged.[26]

On the slopes of Mount Hortiatis above the town, Salonica's consuls had been building themselves country retreats for several decades to flee the fevers, plague, mud and dust of urban life. From the little hamlet of Urendjik the panorama across the Gulf to Mount Olympos was superb, the soil fertile. Over six years, with the help of hundreds of workers, and at a cost of one million Turkish pounds (according to the legend), Abbott built himself the grandest villa of all. In its private chapel, a mass was celebrated every Sunday. A fountain cast a jet twenty metres high in the courtyard. Extensive gardens, tended by foreign specialists, were planted with dozens of species—including cedars, cypresses, elms, oaks, persimmons from America, mulberries, figs, apples, pears, plums, almonds, chestnuts and pines.[27]

During Abdul Mecid's visit, Abbott took the liberty of inviting the sultan to his country estate. He could not have been accused of stinting for the occasion. He had the road widened and new bridges built. Carpets were bought up from local dealers to cover the entire stretch—six or seven miles—along which the imperial carriage would have to travel. Within the house itself, a Turkish bath was added for the sultan's use. Abdul Mecid was delayed by the many petitions presented to him, but eventually his carriage drew up outside the gates to Abbott's property. He was just about to place his foot on the carpeted ground when the skies clouded over, and there was a clap of thunder: a superstitious man, he immediately refused to descend. Abbott begged the padishah to accept a coffee, and when the gold stove was brought up, the flames were fed by banknotes (the sultan is supposed to have asked whether coffee thus heated tasted better). Abbott then again proffered the keys to his property, but Abdul Mecid, after turning them over for some time, handed them back, telling the disappointed owner merely that "your fine property will be exempt from taxes so long as you own it."

At least in the telling, the story marked heaven's displeasure at Abbott's sins and pride, the triumph of true majesty over the corrupt parasites who had been feeding off, and contributing to, the city's impoverishment. The Abbott family remained powerful in Salonica for another generation but they were a lavish and cantankerous lot, and their money was soon gone. The villa itself lay in ruins by 1895, though when the British were stationed there in the First World War, the remains of the Turkish bath built for the sultan were just visible as were the overgrown but still impressive gardens. And when the new Imperial Ottoman Bank took over the Abbotts' palatial townhouse in the Street of the Franks a few years after the sultan's visit, it was another sign that the age of money-lenders was coming to an end and being replaced by the power of international capitalism. Most of the city's inhabitants probably welcomed the change. Money-lenders like Abbott had profited from the system of state monopolies and the acute shortage of local capital. The unflattering image of the "King of the Leeches" which is preserved in the city's old folk memories speaks as eloquently as any of the petitions presented to the sultan and his servants of the power of this class and the lack of regret which accompanied its passing. Today in a corner of the garden on Odos Frangōn, on the site of the old Imperial Ottoman Bank building, the curious passer-by can make out, peering through overgrown ferns and acacias, an abandoned neo-classical monumental statue of a seated woman: it is the last remnant of the Abbott estate.[28]

8

Religion in the Age of Reform

REFORM

THE OTTOMAN EMPIRE was an Islamic state and the Ottoman sultan was also Warrior of the Faith, Custodian of Sacred Relics, Protector of the Pilgrimage and Servitor of the Two Holy Cities. As for the governor of Salonica, his most prized symbol of authority was the silver-bound Qur'an known as the "cherished book of the province." For all the licence shown to the other People of the Book—especially in the Balkans, where Muslims were a minority of the population—it was always clear that Sunni Islam was the ruling religion. Yet in the nineteenth century, Islam's primacy came under challenge. Nowhere was the impact of the reforms more keenly felt than in the transformation of the relationship between the empire's faiths.[1]

Reform meant, in the first place, a new attentiveness on the part of the sultan and his ministers to Ottoman Christians. The empire remained an important centre of Orthodox life and mid-century Salonica alone had at least twice as many inhabitants as Athens—Izmir, Alexandria and the capital itself many more. In 1830 Sultan Mahmud II ordered any Greek captives who had been seized in the course of the revolt to be released and made it clear he still counted on the support of his Christian subjects. In a radical departure from older imperial political tradition, he encouraged new churches to be built, replaced the established official dress codes with uniforms based on European models, and introduced the red fez for all his subjects in place of the old colour-coded turbans, a huge symbolic step forward for non-Muslims. As for his successor, Abdul Mecid, his Gulhané decree promised the empire's inhabitants that "of whatever religion or sect they may be;

they shall enjoy them without exception." Although principles took a long time to be translated into practice, the position of Christians was unmistakably improving.[2]

If Christian Europe welcomed these developments, many Muslims deplored the way the *shari'a* had been dethroned and replaced with new laws, institutions and procedures slavishly adopted from the Franks. The state had been captured, according to one critic, by a coterie of "Frenchified playboys," who were little more than a voice for foreign interests. By crushing the janissaries, a small unelected group of reformers had destroyed defenders of Muslim interests, and by incorporating the *vakfs* and their revenues into a new official Ministry of *Vakfs* they hoped to control the religious establishment as well. The *kadi* courts were slowly being deprived of their old administrative functions and replaced by tribunals manned by poorly trained pen-pushers ignorant of religious law. Village heads were informed that the Sultan's reforms did not contravene the Qur'an, but resistance on religious grounds persisted. As an anonymous scholar wrote in 1870: "Only those that come from the ranks of the *ulema* deserve to be called clerks."[3]

Most Muslims remained loyal to the imperial house, but in the 1830s some were momentarily tempted to look elsewhere in defence of their faith. After all, from Algeria to Persia, the Caucasus and Mughal India, Islam seemed to be under assault from Europe. Within the empire, there was enormous enthusiasm for Mehmed Ali's new Egyptian regime, a regime described by one historian as "the last Oriental effort to found a power on the shores of the Mediterranean which should be independent of the West." In Salonica, there was an "Egyptian party" that waited eagerly for Ali's troops to arrive. Pamphlets urged "all good Musulmans . . . to hold themselves ready to take arms in defence of their faith," and reports that an Egyptian fleet had been spotted off the coast of Macedonia were greeted with joy before it turned out the ships were British. But the resolution of the crisis in 1841, when Ali submitted to the sultan, dulled the lustre of his name. When he paid a visit to his birthplace in nearby Kavalla a few years later, the ruler of Egypt returned to Cairo disappointed by his reception. Many of the local beys had not even bothered to await his arrival, and had gone back to their farms.[4]

After Mehmed Ali, there was no one to turn to. Yet the weight of Muslim opposition to any alteration in the place of traditional institutions remained. In the 1850s Christians round Salonica still found it almost impossible to obtain justice against Muslims in criminal cases, and murders and robberies routinely went unpunished. In 1851 Christian testimony was admitted in a local criminal court for the first time, but it was not for another decade that it was given decisive weight when contradicted by Muslim witnesses. "Are we the masters of this empire or not?" demanded some of the beys, protesting on the "part of Islamism" against the constant infringement by foreign powers of the "rights of the Turkish nation." A visiting dervish preached that Europe was "devoted to the extermination of Muslims," and claimed that the sultan, by giving in to their demands, had shown himself to be no more than a *gavur.* "Let us massacre the infidels whom the Prophet and our first Sultans conquered," he went on, "And then we will go throughout *Frenghistan* [the land of the Franks] sword in hand, and all will be well with us." When Abdul Mecid died in 1861, the view in the local coffeehouses was that he had been "too favourably disposed to Christians," and many of Salonica's Muslims, including highly placed functionaries, openly hoped that his successor would bring back the janissaries and revoke the reforms.[5]

This did not happen. Instead the number of non-Muslims in the civil service rose, and in 1868 a Council of State with non-Muslim members was created. In the provinces progress was slower: as late as 1867, justice in Salonica was still loaded against non-Muslims, taxes remained inequitable and the clause relating to Christians being appointed to official positions remained a "dead letter." Ibrahim Bey, the *mufti,* resisted reform of the local courts, and as he was very popular among the poorer Muslims of the city, Salonica's governors hesitated to take him on. But the lead from the top was clear: the Porte instructed Salonica's *mollah* to speak respectfully when he addressed the Greek metropolitan, and to refer politely to the "Christian" religion. "Looking at things reasonably," wrote the British ambassador, Sir Henry Bulwer in 1864, "it is but just to observe that this government is about the most tolerant in Europe."[6]

The old ideology of the sultan as Defender of the Faith was now no longer appropriate for the new-look empire. It was supplanted by a new creed of Ottomanism, an allegiance to the dynasty itself that supposedly crossed religious boundaries. As the government gazette for the province declared in May 1876:

Even though for centuries among us there has not existed something we might call public opinion, on account of our different religions, nonetheless Ottomans, Christians, Jews and in a word all those bearing the name of Osmanli and living under the sceptre of His Imperial Excellency have lived as faithful subjects of all ranks, as patriots and as a single unit of nationalities, each lending a helping hand to the other as brothers, none ever daring to attack the honour, property, life or religious customs of the other, and everyone enjoying complete freedom in the exercise of his social privileges.[7]

The new policy was underlined in religious holidays and official ceremonies. After the Ottoman fleet arrived in port, Greek priests from the city performed mass for its Christian sailors in the Beshchinar gardens, and Turkish naval officers complimented the archbishop on a "very appropriate sermon." When the chief rabbi Raphael Ascher Covo died at the end of 1874 after twenty-six years in office, his funeral was attended by the staff of the governor, the president of the town council, the Greek archbishop, consuls and other notables: the procession was "one of the largest ever witnessed in European Turkey." All shops were closed, Jewish firemen in the service of the North British and Mercantile Insurance companies provided the guard of honour lining the streets, and bells were rung as the bier passed the Orthodox cathedral." A century earlier, such an occasion would have been inconceivable.[8]

EXCOMMUNICATION:
THE CHIEF RABBI ASCENDANT

FOR THERE WAS A STRIKING ASYMMETRY in the impact of the reforms. Whilst they brought the *ulema* more tightly under the state's control and curbed the power of Muslim religious elites, they actually increased the administrative power, authority and prestige of the non-Muslim religious leaders. Ottoman modernization was not, in other words, about the construction of new French-style secular citizens, for whom religion would be an entirely private matter, and the old collective identities did not vanish into a bright new dawn of European individualism: on the contrary, the equality under the law promised by the reforms was for communities, not individuals. As Muslims lost power, Christians and Jews gained it. More than ever, therefore, it was to the leaders of their communities, rather than to the Porte or the pasha, that most of Salonica's non-Muslims turned.

Where the city's Orthodox flock, still approximately one quarter of Salonica's population, was concerned, the 1839 decrees did little to change its basic administrative structure: on the one hand, a committee of bishops governed ecclesiastical affairs; on the other, a mixed council of churchmen and laymen dealt with secular matters. Both were presided over by the metropolitan bishop, who remained responsible to the Patriarchate in the capital. This was basically the old system, scarcely altered either by the 1821 massacres or by the reforms of the first half of the nineteenth century.

For Salonica's Jews, it was a different matter since the position of chief rabbi of the city was recognized officially only in 1836. The religious, legal and administrative head of the community, he was responsible for the collection and allocation of taxes, the interpretation of laws, and the punishment of offenders. He could call on the Ottoman authorities for assistance, and he had the right to ride on horseback when visiting the governor. Saul Molho, the chief rabbi between 1839 and 1849, took every opportunity to assert his prestige, and made sure he was always accompanied by a large crowd of followers. "His gestures have a symbolic value," writes the historian Joseph Nehama, "all his utterances are impregnated with sanctity. His acts too reverberate in people's souls. He is very choleric and his rages—very frequent—make people tremble." "The influence which the chief rabbi has here is truly astonishing," missionaries reported. "Besides the power which he possesses in secular affairs, by virtue of his appointment by the Sublime Porte, he exerts no less influence in matters purely religious. His advanced age, his rigid abstemiousness, his using no spectacles when reading, though aged ninety-six, and such qualities, go very far with the superstitious Jews of this place. He is greatly feared by them, and almost adored. Some affirm that if the world possessed another rabbi like him, Messiah would have come long ago."[9]

The chief rabbi could imprison Jewish offenders and also had another weapon at his disposal—excommunication (*herem*). The mild form of this lasted thirty days, and required the guilty party to repent, to wear old clothes and to leave his beard unshaven and his feet bare. There was also a more serious version. "A Jew, my Lord," Blunt explained to his ambassador, "who suffers excommunication, must either become a Christian, turn Turk, or die, for whilst under that edict they cannot purchase food, no Jew can speak to them, and they are not allowed even the solace of seeing their wives, children or relatives." Not infrequently—if local Jewish opinion was to be believed—this resulted in the speedy death of the sinner.[10]

Excommunications had been frequently issued by rabbis in the past. But the chief rabbi profited from the centralization of communal power, the waning of Greek influence after 1821 and the growing grip of the Jews on the city's economy. "The Bankers, Cashiers, Buyers and Sellers of imports and exports are Jews, the Porters, Boatmen and persons necessary to employ in preparing wools, cottons, silks, grain and seeds of all Kinds for exportation are all Jews, and very many of the Shops, where all the necessities of life are to be purchased, are kept by Jews," reported the British consul. In these circumstances, even the threat of excommunication could bring the city to a halt. In April 1839 a Jewish child was abducted near a church and it was announced that any Jew who did business with a Christian before the matter was resolved would be cast out. The town came to a standstill, the bazaar closed, and merchants found their accounts frozen. Poor Jews threatened to march into the European quarter to "set fire to every house" if the child was not handed over. Significantly, only the intervention of the British ambassador ended the affair and brought the town back to life.[11]

What is striking is that at no stage had the local Ottoman authorities seen a challenge to their own authority. On the contrary, the governor refused to get involved and left matters to the chief rabbi himself. Only the damage to a higher power—European economic interests—forced the latter to back down and rescind his *herem*. This whole affair looks at first sight like something old-fashioned and antiquated, for at a time when western Europe was experiencing class conflict and challenges to established religion, Salonica's rabbis were asserting their power over the laws of the market. But in fact it would be more accurate to see it as a mark of the extraordinary degree of power Salonica's chief rabbi had acquired thanks to the sultan's reforms. For nearly half a century, he was unquestionably one of the most powerful men in the city.

GREEKS AND JEWS

RELATIONS BETWEEN GREEKS AND JEWS were better in Salonica than elsewhere, but troubled even so. The suspicion between them was reflected in local Jewish proverbs: "to go to Prodrom" (the Hippodrome: a Christian quarter), for instance, was tantamount to finding yourself far from home. The Greek war of independence had been accompanied by massacres of Jews as well as Muslims, and at Easter anti-Jewish feelings often surfaced. In Athens a mob ransacked the house of a Maltese Jew during an Easter riot in 1847: because he was a British subject, London was drawn in and the so-called "Don Pacifico affair" eventually led to a British blockade of Piraeus. "The Christian populace generally allow no opportunity to pass of insulting their Jewish fellow-citizens, who as a rule submit humbly to this contumelious treatment," wrote the ethnographer Lucy Garnett, who knew Ottoman society well, "except at Salonica where their superiority in numbers gives them greater assurance." It did not help that by a quirk of fate, the Orthodox cathedral and the adjoining residence of the metropolitan were situated in the very heart of the Jewish lower town: this gave rise to frequent tensions and quarrels.[12]

In December 1852, at a time of mounting hostility internationally between Greece and the Ottoman empire, two Greeks the worse for drink—a certain Costandi from Mytilini and Panayiotis from Edirne—triggered off a major brawl—a "fearful, fanatical excitement"—when they passed through a Jewish quarter one Sunday afternoon and insulted a local man. When the latter protested, Costandi hit him and Panayiotis drew his knife and stabbed him twice, killing him on the spot. A "low rabble" of Jews—mostly slaughterers, wood and charcoal porters who had finished work for the day—fell on the two men. More joined in on both sides with knives and pieces of firewood, and by the end, after the outnumbered Greeks had been surrounded and disarmed, one Greek had been killed and several others were wounded. The Ottoman police merely looked on, saying that they "could do nothing without firing their pistols which they were not authorized to do."[13]

The next day, the furious archbishop went to the pasha to warn him that the Jews were planning to burn the Greek quarters of the town and to "murder the Christians." The chief rabbi, Ascher Covo, tried to calm matters by issuing a *herem* forbidding Jews from any dispute "however trifling" with Christians and prohibiting any mention of the affair on pain of expulsion from the community. But the archbishop wanted revenge and kept things at boiling point. His anti-Jewish preachings inflamed feelings so much that Jewish fishermen and traders feared to leave the protection of the city walls; inside the city there were fights and fisticuffs. The pasha was unnerved, and turned to his astrologer for guidance. Accused by the British consul of having released the Greek murderers because he was afraid of the Christians in the town, he responded: "Decidedly I am!" Not the lower orders, he went on, but only the Frankish consuls and the wealthier Greeks.

Indeed the Greek consul tried to keep up the pressure by urging the pasha to take further measures against the imprisoned Jews, and when he ignored this advice, turned to the foreign consuls for support.

What had started out as a drunken brawl thus quickly turned into a dispute between the two communities at the highest levels exacerbated by the pasha's ineptitude and uncertainty, and fuelled by the actions of the Greek consul. The following month, the archbishop announced he would excommunicate any Christian who attended the annual soirée given by the Allatinis, the leading Jewish family in the city. Even the blood libel entered the scene when a respectable Greek surgeon saw a suspicious huddle of Jews around an Albanian man and reported to the police that some Jews were planning to seize a Christian to murder him for his blood. The police arrested all concerned and brought them before the pasha where it was discovered that the explanation was quite different. "What am I arrested for?" the Albanian exclaimed. "I have nothing to fear from the Jews, for I gain my bread by lighting the fires of these people on a Saturday!"[14]

Shortly after this, new communal leadership brought an improvement in relations. In the longer run, the rise of Bulgarian nationalism changed Greek attitudes towards the Porte, and as these became more friendly, so did feelings between Greeks and Jews. In the 1870s, Chief Rabbi Gattegno and Metropolitan Ioacheim patched things up, Greek and Jewish notables attended each other's official functions and in 1880 the most powerful lay Jewish figure in the city, Moses Allatini, was decorated by the Greek government. Nevertheless a residue of suspicion remained and gangs of Greek and Jewish boys held weekly stone-throwing "battles" to the annoyance of respectable society. Everything depended on the city's communal elite: when their inter-relations were good, harmony prevailed. For better or worse, the reforms had turned the city's ecclesiastical leaders into political factors of considerable weight and by increasing their powers over their respective flocks had had the effect of turning street fights into contests of strength, prestige and political influence between the two religions.[15]

MISSIONARIES

OTTOMAN OPPONENTS OF REFORM saw the pernicious hand of Christian Europe everywhere, dethroning Islam, protecting Christians, forcing change upon the old order. European diplomats and travellers agreed but believed they were engaged not in Christianization but in the work of social and political improvement. For some Europeans, however, civilization did indeed require the spread of Christ's message. The reform era was also the age of the missionaries, the "Bible-men," who introduced a new and potentially destabilizing element into the balance of power between the faiths of the empire. Discouraged by the Porte from trying to convert Muslims, their energetic efforts among Christians and Jews, their distribution of thousands of Bibles translated into local languages from Bulgarian to Judeo-Spanish and their links with European diplomats all increased their impact far beyond the rather small numbers of converts they actually won over, and marked a new kind of European (and American) assault upon Ottoman religious practices and sensibilities.

It was their stridency and lack of tact—what one British ambassador denounced as their "violent and provocative methods"—that made the missionaries so controversial. The problem was not the Catholics who had maintained their small presence in Salonica since the late seventeenth century and formed a tiny and accepted part of its complex confessional mosaic, but rather those American and British Protestants who were energetically penetrating the eastern Mediterranean from the early 1800s on behalf of groups like the Church Missionary Society, the British and Foreign Bible Society and the American Board of Foreign Missions.[16]

Protestant missionaries seemed magnetically drawn to the numerous Jews of Salonica who offered them the chance to continue where Saint Paul had left off. There was "great eagerness for the Scriptures," reported one missionary in 1826, after he had distributed several hundred copies of "the Word of God" printed in both Greek and Judeo-Spanish. "If anything is to be done for the Jews in this land of barbarism," he declared, "Thessalonica offers a fine field ... May it please the Disposer of all things to moderate his wrath and give them a helping hand to extricate them from their present errors and enable them to walk once more in the ways of the Lord."[17]

Four years later, in the summer of 1830, the missionary Joseph Wolff arrived on behalf of the London Jews' Society. Wolff was a former German Jew who had converted to Catholicism before becoming an Anglican curate. Married to a Walpole (a kinswoman of the prime minister), this extraordinary figure—later he would take to styling himself "the Apostle of Our Lord Jesus Christ for Palestine, Persia and Bokhara"—specialized in converting Jews, or trying to. He had been thrown out of Egypt after announcing that according to the Book of Daniel the Jews would be restored to power in Jerusalem and the Turkish empire would collapse. At sea he had been pursued by pirates, ending up on the Macedonian shore two days' south of Salonica without shoes, coat or money. Undaunted, he began his holy work the day he arrived, preaching in the city and disputing with its rabbis. According to John Meshullam, a Salonica Jew who later converted to Protestantism, Wolff "came into their synagogue, on the Sabbath, and began to address the Jews, on the subject of Messiah and his kingdom." He distributed his Bibles and put up posters predicting the Messiah's arrival. Adolphus Slade, an English naval officer who was also present, recorded his impressions:

> I have listened with delight to Mr. Wolff. He is eloquent and persuasive, with four languages—Hebrew, Italian, German and English—in which to clothe his thoughts gracefully; besides having a tolerable knowledge of Arabic and Persian. But on one subject his enthusiasm rather taxes his auditor's patience, if not precisely of his opinion. He has published, and he believes, that in the year 1847 Christ will come in the clouds, surrounded by angels and commence his reign in Jerusalem for one thousand years.[18]

Wolff's activities soon attracted a huge crowd and he had to pay a Turkish guard to watch over his poster in order to prevent it being torn down. As he reported proudly back to London: "In a few hours 2000 Jews were assembled around it, who read it. A Turkish soldier stood near it, in order that no one might tear it up. The chief of the soldiers, who placed a man there, desired an Arabic Bible as a reward." This was exactly the kind of action that was likely to cause trouble. "The whole city was upside down," reported Slade. According to Meshullam, some Jews were so "enraged" that they asked the pasha to execute him. Others reacted cautiously, waiting to see what their elders would decree, or opining that as there were still seventeen years to wait, they would make up their minds in good time since "few men are so old as not to hope for as many as seventeen years more life." Slanderous rumours started to circulate—hotly denied by Wolff—that he had been offering four thousand piastres to anyone who converted. Very soon, the chief rabbi ordered all Jews who had received Bibles from Wolff to burn them, and the unfortunate missionary was ordered to cease disturbing the peace by the pasha himself who told him that he considered it "highly improper" to invite people to change their religion. The final ignominy was when his own superiors in London publicly disowned his tactics. After a fortnight, in which he failed to make any conversions, he set sail for Smyrna.[19]

More discreet than Wolff, others continued to distribute their Bibles: over the coming decades, the offices of the American Bible Society in the Levant sent out copies in Hebrew, Judeo-Spanish, modern Greek and Turkish. Twenty years after him, these labourers for "the Book of Life" still found Salonica's Jews "shrewd disputants and bitter opponents . . . bigoted and self-righteous, and priding themselves especially on the long renown their city has had in the Jewish World for learning and Rabbinical Lore." Although they held theological discussions together in private, in public missionaries were fiercely opposed by the religious leaders of the community: Chief Rabbi Saul Molho established Bible-reading groups to refute passages cited by the missionaries in favour of Christianity, published pamphlets against the New Testament, and issued excommunications against anyone found dealing with the missionaries themselves. The return on investment in missionary activities was a poor one. "The utter unprofitableness of these gentlemen cannot be sufficiently pointed out," wrote Slade. One tireless Scottish missionary, Mr. Crosbie, settled in Salonica in 1860 and opened a small school. When he died in 1904, it was doubted that he had made a single convert.[20]

CONVERSION: THE 1876 MURDERS

WITHIN THE EMPIRE CONVERSION was never a straightforward matter; it aroused strong feelings and needed to be handled with care. But it was not uncommon: Christian and Jewish girls often converted to Islam on marrying and entering a Muslim man's *haremlik*, not for theological reasons but to escape the disapproval of relatives. "The temptations of money, family dissensions, menaces, or it may be an amorous temperament are the principal motives which place Christian women and girls within the power of Mohamedans," noted an observer in 1858. Once apostasy from Islam no longer incurred the death penalty, Protestant missions again sought to target Muslims, and the authorities feared that some Muslim men would convert as a way of avoiding military service. In fact their fears were not groundless.[21]

But the climate of opinion was changing: a Christian woman who first embraced and then abandoned Islam was protected by the pasha from her vengeful Muslim husband who was wandering the city threatening to shoot her. Two young Jews—one a child of ten, the other sixteen—were also allowed to return to their original faith. Even Papa Isaiah, a would-be Christian Orthodox neo-martyr, turned out to be too late for martyrdom and despite his deliberate insults to the ruling faith was sentenced only to hard labour cutting stones.[22]

Since their primary purpose was to preserve the peace and ensure that the customary proprieties were observed, Salonica's pashas tried to ascertain that the half a dozen or so converts who came before them annually had good reasons for their decision. Those whose conversion to Islam was suspected to have been coerced—forced conversions in the villages at the hands of local Muslim land-owners were still a source of bitter feeling in the countryside—were sometimes sent to Constantinople to be examined at the Porte. Complainants also took cases there themselves. In June 1844, an Armenian couple officially lodged a complaint that their daughter, whom they had allowed to go to the local bath-house in Salonica with a Muslim woman, had not been returned to them on the grounds—which they angrily disputed—that she had converted of her own free will. The Porte dealt with the case and emphasized in its instructions to the authorities in Salonica that "if the illegal use of force has occurred, this is very damaging for the confidence of the population and can cause disruption of the order of the state."[23]

Other cases were scrutinized carefully on the spot. After a poor Jewish girl left her parents' house and took shelter in the home of Muslim friends, the pasha ordered her to discuss the matter with her parents in the *konak*. She told him that she had fled to escape the beatings her father gave her, but Rifaat Pasha responded that this was not a good enough reason to disown her parents and her religion, and ordered her to return. At the same time, however, he summoned the girl's father and told him to treat her kindly, pledging to protect her should he illtreat her again. It was a model of how to defuse a potentially explosive situation.[24]

A few years earlier, things had not been handled so well, and the result had been catastrophe. On the morning of 7 May 1876, a brief but alarming telegram from the British consul reached the embassy in Constantinople: "Both the Consuls killed, the Europeans much alarmed—struck with horror. The Greeks are arming, fearing general massacre." This was the first indication to reach the outside world of one of the most notorious—and misunderstood—episodes in the city's history, a conversion crisis which escalated rapidly into a double killing that made the headlines around the world.

What had happened was this. The previous afternoon a Christian girl called Stefana, from a village outside the city, had travelled into Salonica by train, already veiled, to register her conversion on entering the household of a Muslim land-owner. It was not an uncommon step, and as always, it left a trail of unhappy relatives in its wake. Her mother had followed her to the city to try to stop her—her father was dead—and at the train station she shouted out to some passing Christians for help. One of them seized the girl and tore off her veil—a most serious breach of Ottoman custom—before commandeering a carriage which belonged to the American vice-consul, the member of a well-known local Greek family, and spiriting the girl, and her mother, off into hiding. Police ran after the carriage as far as the town gate and then lost it.

The next morning, some Muslims called on the pasha to tell him the girl must be brought to his palace so that she could be properly examined, as convention demanded. But the American consul happened to be away, and his brother said the girl had left the consulate and he did not know her whereabouts; in fact she had been sent secretly to the house of another Greek notable. An angry crowd began to gather opposite the pasha's palace and warned him that if he did not act, they would attack the consulate themselves. "I went out of the pasha's room and told the chiefs or leaders they were wrong in collecting such a crowd, and asked them what they wanted," recalled Selim Bey, the chief of police, afterwards. "They said, 'The Girl.' I told them to wait a few hours and the girl would be surrendered, but they would not listen." Asked why he did not disperse the crowd, Selim Bey replied: "I had not sufficient force—only 20 men—and the crowd was composed of 100 men at least."[25]

News of the affair spread to the bazaar and armed Albanians joined the other protestors at the nearby Saatli mosque. Tempers soon began to fray and when told to disperse, the mob threatened members of the pasha's advisory council. Then the French and German consuls happened by ill luck to walk past the mosque on their way to try to see the governor. They were seized by the crowd and held in a small room. As they talked the matter over with the *mufti* and other members of the advisory council, it became clear that they were being detained as hostages for the girl's surrender. The pasha arrived on the scene but panicked as angry demonstrators forced their way into the room, despite the efforts of several policemen, and attacked the two men with chairs and iron bars. By the time the girl was found and handed over, they were dead. After her arrival at the *konak* the crowd dispersed, shouting in triumph and firing pistols and rifles into the air.[26]

Blunt, the British consul, was with the pasha barely one hundred yards from the mosque. "I was horrified and could not believe that the Consuls had been murdered." Hearing the sound of firing, he became alarmed and feared either that the police were shooting into the crowd, or that the latter had descended into the lower town and begun a general massacre. As he moved towards the window, the pasha cried after him: "Do not expose yourself. For God's sake don't let them see you: they are like mad wolves." So dangerous did the situation appear that the pasha let Blunt make his escape through his *haremlik*, from where "some members of his family, screaming and shrieking, attempted to rush out." Fearing a "great catastrophe," he went off to telegraph Athens to send a British man-of-war from Piraeus. Shortly after, he realized the girl had been handed over, and the mob had broken up.[27]

THE MURDER OF TWO EUROPEAN CONSULS was a tremendous blow to the prestige of the Great Powers and they quickly responded by sending warships to the city. There was talk of occupation, but in fact the ships simply trained their guns on the Upper Town and remained there in a show of force. While Europe buzzed with concern at what it regarded as another manifestation of Turkish religious fanaticism, urgent instructions came from Constantinople to punish those responsible. The pasha took his time making any arrests, since most of the troops available to him were sympathetic to the perpetrators. Nevertheless, more than thirty men were eventually held and on 17 May, six of the supposed ring-leaders were hanged in public on open ground by the quay walls.

Christians in mid-century Salonica remembered the events of 1821 and lived with the fear of massacre. Often the talk was nothing more than exaggeration, alarmist fantasy spread by those who should have known better. But at times, it was something more: in 1860, for instance, when "the fearful Syrian massacres were still thrilling men's minds," a traveller in the city noticed the spread of a vague sense of disquiet: "There was trouble of some sort, no one could define it—but there was alarm, and people hinted at Russian agency at work, to excite suspicions on the one side, and fanaticism on the other." For a few days, people slept uneasily at night and kept weapons to hand, and means of quick escape. But in the end "we all stayed quietly, nothing happened and the panic passed away."[28]

But 1876, when an angry, armed rabble was already descending on the Frank quarter to burn it, before they were told of the girl's delivery and dispersed, was the closest the city came to such a catastrophe. Aware of the need to reaffirm the values of communal harmony, notables from all sides made an effort in the days and weeks after the crime to show their solidarity. Less than a month later, in May, there was "indescribable" rejoicing for the accession of Sultan Murad and the return of the reformers to the capital. As one observer noted, the joy was not interrupted "by any act of disorder or ill-feeling; the quay, the principal streets, the Bazaars and the Coffee houses were crowded with Turks, Greeks, Jews, Levantines and Europeans all mingled together, men, women and children, as if their national and religious feelings had not been wounded and irritated by the latest horrid occurrences. Antipathy of race to race appeared to have been forgotten and forgiven."

The coronation festivities allowed for a very public display of harmony, led by the town's religious leaders. The Orthodox Metropolitan Ioacheim, a man greatly respected in the town, was seen to embrace the *defterdar*, the provincial treasurer, while the *mufti* "wept like a child." The metropolitan hailed "this glorious event," and when the chief rabbi offered prayers for the new sultan in the main synagogue, the ceremony was attended by four pashas, Turkish officers, the metropolitan himself and Orthodox, Catholic and Protestant priests. A few days later, they all assembled again for public prayers in the Mevlevi *tekke* outside the city walls: English, Greek and Austrian naval officers, as well as the consular corps added to the throng. The fears and rumours of massacre did not vanish—they emerged briefly again and led to what the British consul termed a "sort of panic" in October—by which time poor, mad Sultan Murad had already been deposed and replaced by his brother Abdul Hamid—but calmer heads knew that rumours did as much damage as the real thing, and needed to be dampened down for the good of the town. When Bairam came round, it was celebrated in an orderly manner after leading figures in the Muslim community urged the importance of taking account of the feelings of Christians and of "disproving all the rumours which are current here of a fanatical rising against the Christians." Christian notables reciprocated and the local Greek newspaper congratulated the authorities and "Muslim co-citizens" on the "great tranquillity" which prevailed and urged the Orthodox to follow their example at Easter. The proclamation of the first-ever Ottoman constitution that autumn was greeted in the city with prayers for a new era of common brotherhood and communal harmony.[29]

EASTERN QUESTIONS

IF THE GOVERNOR'S INEPTITUDE and the irresponsible behaviour of a few prominent Greeks had helped turn a minor dispute into an international incident whose reverberations rippled across the Levant, the real causes of the consuls' deaths lay elsewhere and had been building up for some time. Resistance had been evident among the city's Muslims to the Porte's insistence on measures that contravened the natural order of things. This opposition had not been confined to the landed beys. The poor of the city, who were—in Fanny Blunt's words— "an Allah-fearing people, eating a small quantity of yaghourt, smoking a few cigarettes, hard-working toilers," also found it difficult to stomach the notion that Christians should be placed on an equal footing with Muslims. The background of the thirty-five men convicted of involvement in the murders show how widespread such views were: they included servants, slaves, a butcher and a barber, several Albanian gunmakers, a Bosnian (described as a "card-player of no profession"), a coffee-house owner, food wholesalers, a carpenter, several masons and several young men who happened to be visiting from the provinces.[30]

Behind the Christians of the city, of course, lay the European Powers. The symbolic power of the 1876 murders lay precisely in the fact that the victims were consuls, members of perhaps the most privileged political class in Salonica. As the balance of power between the empire and the Great Powers tilted in the latter's favour, so the importance and confidence of the consular corps had grown. They began to receive return visits from the pasha—something unknown in the eighteenth century—and flew their national flags. Under what was known as the system of capitulations, they also acquired rights to try their own nationals and as they extended their protection and passports to more and more of the city's non-Muslim inhabitants, anxious to enjoy the immunities conferred by foreign citizenship, so they circumscribed the extent of Ottoman jurisdiction.

By the nineteenth century, the capitulations were clearly being abused. Neither the American nor the German consul in Salonica in 1876 was a national of the country he represented; the former was a Greek notable named Hadzilazaros, the latter was one of the Abbotts. Jews and Christians often declared their immunity before the authorities as Spanish, Tuscan, Neapolitan or Austrian subjects. Moses Allatini, the most influential Jewish businessman and philanthropist in Salonica, was an Italian. One local Christian escaped prosecution by claiming he was an "Ionian" (and therefore under British protection) despite never having been to the Ionian islands nor even knowing where they were. The system had become so corrupt that people changed nationality as it served their interests. James Roggotti was born in Macedonia as an Ottoman subject but acquired first a Greek and then, by the time of his return to the city as an adult, a British passport. "Signor Tavoulari" began life as a Bulgarian Christian, made his fortune under Russian and Swedish protection, importing counterfeit Turkish coin from Greece, and left the city with an "Ionian" passport (at that time the Ionian Islands were administered by the British) for Syra before finally returning as a "Hellene."[31]

The presence of a Greek consul in the city since 1835 particularly affronted Ottoman sensibilities, as did the deliberately assertive and hostile behaviour of the "Hellenes" who came there from Athens. In 1846 the Greek corvette *Ludovick* docked during joint Ottoman-Greek operations against pirates, and the British consul noted that "many of the Greek officers indulged openly in remarks in the Coffee Houses respecting the Turks which did them little credit." One man boasted openly that "in two years the Greek flag would fly upon the Castle of Salonica." In 1851 old Greek passports were supposedly circulating in the coffee-houses of the town, as part of a scheme—or so the Ottoman authorities suspected—of encouraging Christians to emigrate to the Kingdom. In 1863 the local authorities forbade any public demonstration or celebration after Prince George of Denmark was elected as King of Greece. Seamen were a predictable source of trouble. When a pasha of the old school ordered a Greek flag painted on the signboard of a wine shop by the port to be taken down, Greek sailors came on shore with their arms, and immediately replaced it.[32]

The 1876 crisis brought all these factors to the fore. For the Christians, there was the fear—later shown to be unfounded—that the woman was under-age and had not converted of her own free will: abductions, it should be noted, were commonplace in the countryside among both Christians and Muslims; nor, sadly, was it unknown for Muslim beys to carry off Christian women with impunity. For Muslims, on the other hand, there was anger at the thought that Christians now believed themselves so powerful that they could flout custom and the wishes of the pasha and prevent a potential convert from presenting herself at the *konak*. Both sides saw the woman as embodying the honour of the community, needing to be protected against their enemies. Above all, there was the presence of the consuls throughout: a consular carriage had been used to spirit the girl into hiding; it was rumoured—falsely as it turned out—that she had been hidden in the American consulate itself; and crucially, there was the presence of the French and German consuls on the scene, presenting themselves before the mob as intermediaries and bearing out popular Muslim suspicions of their role in the whole affair.

And one final factor played a decisive role: these events unfolded against the background of the most serious diplomatic and military crisis of the entire century—the Near Eastern crisis of 1875–78. Beginning with a peasant uprising in Bosnia-Hercegovina, the troubles spread in 1876 to Bulgaria and the Danubian provinces and ended with an invasion by the Russian army the following year. The Treaty of San Stefano, which Russia imposed on the empire early in 1878, created a vast new Bulgarian state which passed just to the north of Salonica itself and cut it off from its hinterland. Even after the other Great Powers forced Russia to back down and tore up the San Stefano agreement, there was no disguising the humiliation suffered by the Porte: at the Congress of Berlin, Serbia was declared independent, an autonomous (if smaller) Bulgaria was established under Russian control, Cyprus was occupied by British troops (as the price for supporting the Turks) and the Great Powers forced the Ottoman authorities to pledge a further programme of administrative reforms.

These events deeply affected Salonica. As always in time of war, the city was in a febrile state—filled with soldiers, requisitioning agents, tax-collectors and rumours. Muslim notables criticized the diplomacy of the Porte and feared for the first time "being driven out of Europe." The Bulgarian insurrection actually broke out just three days before the killing of the consuls in Salonica; rumours of the rising had reached the city, together with reports of outrages on Muslim villagers and of plans to drive them from their homes. At one point the authorities feared that Salonica's Christians too would rise to prompt a Russian advance on the city itself, and the Vali warned he would quell any insurrection in the harshest manner. "I know him to be of the party in Turkey," wrote the British consul, "who believe the Eastern Question can only be solved by the destruction, or at least the expatriation of all Christians from the European provinces of Turkey, and replacing them by Circassians and colonists from Asia."[33]

The spectacle of vast forced movements of populations crisscrossing the region was no fantasy. While the eyes of Europe were fixed—thanks to Gladstone's loud condemnation of the "Bulgarian horrors"—on the Christian victims of the war, thousands of Muslim refugees from Bosnia, Bulgaria and the Russian army were headed south. Added to those who had earlier fled the Russians in the Caucasus—somewhere between 500,000 and 600,000 Circassians and Nogai Tatars had arrived in the empire between 1856 and 1864—the refugee influx which accompanied the waning of Ottoman power was well and truly under way. A Commission for the Settlement of Refugees was created, and the figures provided by this organization show that more than half a million refugees crossed into the empire between 1876 and 1879 alone.[34]

In January 1878, the Porte ordered the governor of Salonica to find lodging for fifty thousand throughout the province. The following month it was reported that "the whole country is full of Circassian families, fleeing from the Russian army and the Servians, in long lines of carts . . . panic-stricken, they strive to embark for Asia Minor and Syria." While Albanian Ghegs and uprooted Nogai Tatars settled around the town, thousands more left weekly on steamers bound for Smyrna and Beirut. Many of these refugees had been settled in the Bulgarian lands only a decade earlier; now for a second time they were being uprooted because of Russian military action. Destitute, exploited by local land-owners, many—especially Circassian—men formed robber bands, and became a byword for crime in the region. Two years after the end of hostilities, there were still more than three thousand refugees, many suffering from typhus or smallpox, receiving relief in the city, and another ten thousand in the vicinity. The *Mufti* of Skopje estimated that a total of seventy thousand were still in need of subsistence in the Sandjak of Pristina. By 1887, so many immigrants from the lost provinces had moved to Salonica that house rents there had risen appreciably.[35]

The political outlook for Ottoman rule in European Turkey was grim. Only Western intervention had saved the empire from defeat at the hands of the Russian army; the consequent losses in Europe were great. The powers openly discussed the future carve-up of further territories, and Austrians, Bulgarians and Greeks fixed their eyes on Salonica. As discussions began at the Congress of Berlin on the territorial settlement, one observer underlined the need for a further sweeping reform of Ottoman institutions and the creation of an "impartial authority" to govern what was left. In view of the patchy record of the past forty years' reform efforts, few would have given the imperial system long to live. Indeed many expected its imminent collapse, especially after the youthful Sultan Abdul Hamid suspended the new constitution barely two years after it had been unveiled. But they had to wait longer than they thought. The empire had another few decades of life left, and in that time Salonica itself prospered, grew and changed its appearance more radically than ever before.[36]

PART II

In the Shadow
of Europe

AT THE ZENITH of Ottoman power, no Christian state could match it. In the sixteenth century, the French came to the Porte as supplicants and Elizabeth I was so desperate for an alliance that she told Sultan Murad III that Islam and Protestantism were kindred faiths. In 1623 a French political theorist placed the "great Turke" above all the rulers of Christendom, second in power only to the pope. Defeat at the gates of Vienna in 1683 is often taken as the moment when the rot set in, but in fact the empire performed respectably against its enemies for much of the eighteenth century as well.[1]

Only during and after the Napoleonic wars did the balance of power shift unambiguously against it, which was why successive sultans devoted so much energy to centralizing the state and modernizing its institutions. The main challenge they faced came from Christendom's successor, Europe. Initially the empire lay outside the so-called Concert of Great Powers. But in the Treaty of Paris which concluded the Crimean War in 1856 it was recognized for the first time as forming part of the "Public Law and System of Europe," a curious phrase that implied its entry into a broader civilization. Europe stood for a set of values and the Ottoman empire was being asked to sign up to these much as the European Union has recently required its successor to do. Another article of the 1856 treaty spelled out the price of membership, the sultan declaring his intention to improve the condition of his subjects "without distinction of Religion or of Race" *and* to make manifest his "generous intentions towards the Christian population of his Empire."[2]

As this odd combination of commitments suggests, "Europe" stood for a complex mixture of ideas—freedom of worship and equal treatment for all, on the one hand, and special solicitude for Christians on the other; respect for state sovereignty, and at the same time, concern for the rights of the individual. With time, other ideas bubbled out of Europe as well—the rights of nations to independence, as manifested in the rise of Italy, France and Germany; the expansion of free trade and the notion of an autonomous market; the redefinition of religion as a matter of private individual conscience. Into the Ottoman lands poured Europeans of all nationalities—businessmen and investors, soldiers and relief workers, reporters and government advisers. Salonica changed faster and more dramatically than ever before: as the nineteenth century progressed, it became simultaneously more European, and more "Oriental," more closely integrated in the empire, and more threatened by nationalist rivalries, more conscious of itself as a city and yet more bitterly divided. But all these paradoxes and apparent contradictions were nothing more than the manifestation of forces evident in the empire as a whole, an empire transforming itself in the shadow of Europe.

9

Travellers and the European Imagination

SEARCHING FOR THE PICTURESQUE

TOURISM CAME TO SALONICA in the middle of the nineteenth century and thereby created a new city—a city of the Western imagination. There had of course been the occasional visitor before that—monks, a curious diplomat or two and a few enterprising young gentlemen deviating from the usual Italian circuit. In 1751 James Stuart and Nicholas Revett were commissioned by the Society of Dilettanti to survey the ruins of classical Greece, and they made the first drawings of Salonica to survive. But the main land and sea routes between western Europe and Constantinople passed north or south of the city, and it figures in barely a dozen eighteenth-century travel accounts. Within fifty years all that changed, and a new image of it arose in books and articles which was eventually to exert a profound influence upon its own evolution.

The catalyst was steam. The first steam cruise in the Levant took place in 1833; a steam boat descended the Danube the following year. By the 1840s British, French and Austrian lines connected the city with the main ports of the Mediterranean. Steam changed time and space, imposing schedules and a degree of standardization unknown in an era when people simply relied on the weather and a friendly captain for a berth one day or the next. It also ushered in some familiar reactions to travel itself: on the one hand, sheer wonder that, for instance, the trip between the Austrian and Ottoman capitals had been cut from three weeks to one; on the other, fears that this acceleration would destroy travelling's very pleasure and purpose. When one German scholar

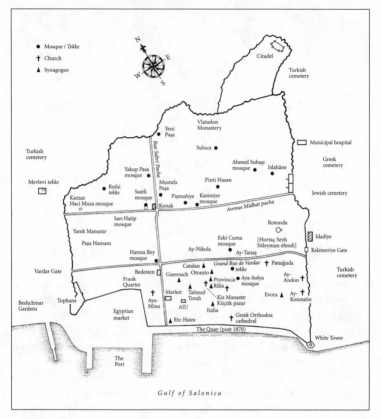

Inside the Ottoman City

spent a winter in Salonica in 1841, he boasted that he was "much more fortunate than other travellers, who are always in a hurry." The regrettable shortening of journey times was not be avoided "in our hurried century," warned one early guidebook. "Three days saved in the time for navigation, the railways and roads substituting for sail, these are the attractions against which the immense majority of travellers lack any defence."[3]

Yet even after the growth of tourism to Greece, Egypt and the lands of the Bible, the city and its Balkan hinterland remained off the beaten track. "I am the first American woman that has ever visited Salonica," one Southern belle wrote proudly to her sister in 1839. More than three decades later, travellers were still oddities. On a steamer from Constantinople, a German passenger fell into conversation with a French salesman. Why was he going to Salonica? he was asked. "For amusement? To Salonica? To this boring and most disconsolate of all Eastern one-horse towns? Can it be?" The pasha there complimented him on his enterprising spirit in venturing where few Europeans dared go, but recommended next time he try Crete instead "for a long stay in winter or spring."[4]

Not everyone thought the benefits outweighed the dangers of being captured by brigands, murdered by pirates or succumbing to plague, cholera or malaria. "I think the old motto 'Le jeu ne vaut pas la chandelle,' should have due weight with any Englishmen who are purposing to visit the interior of Turkey," wrote a journalist in 1881. Others felt drawn either by the risks, or by the sense of being at the centre of events. "The traveller in pursuit of the picturesque or in flight from the commonplace will find here what he seeks," wrote the correspondent-historian William Miller in 1898 as the Macedonian Question hotted up. "Tourists do not come to Macedonia," wrote a young American journalist in 1906, just before the Young Turk revolution broke out, "but if they did they would find a show that no other part of Europe can produce. Not only is the comic-opera stage outdone in characters, in costumes, and in complexity of plot, but the scene is set in alpine mountains on a vaster scale than Switzerland affords."[5]

Before the age of the guidebook, conscientious travellers to the Levant had been forced to pack a veritable library of tomes to help them make the most of whatever they encountered. "I am particularly in want of Wood's *Description of the Ruins of Palmyra and Balbec*, a work very valuable and very scarce, in two volumes in folio," John Tweddell wrote from the Greek archipelago to a friend in 1798. "There is also a book published lately by Robinson, in two volumes octavo—*View of the Ruins of Palmyra in the Desert of Syria* . . . Add to this, Anselm Banduri's *Imperium Orientale*, Du Cange's *Constantinopolis Christian*, Bryant's *Attack upon Homer's Topography* etc. etc."[6]

The nineteenth-century traveller was not supposed to escape the duty of extensive reading either. Murray's 1840 *Handbook*—the herald of a new age—sternly advised the traveller to the Levant to "refresh his memory by an attentive perusal" of Dr. Smith's *Dictionary of Antiquities*, and referred him to Gordon's *History of the Greek Revolution* for the recent background, to Neale's *History of the Holy Eastern Church* for ecclesiastical matters, and to Colonel Leake's *Researches in Greece* and

Thiersch's *Über die Sprache der Tzakonen* for those hoping to try out their classical Greek on the modern natives. But for the essentials the *Handbook* alone was intended to suffice. Here at last was a guide in the modern mode, with tips on how to travel, what to see and where to stay. Murray, Baedeker and Isambert all aimed, in the words of Isambert's 1861 *Itinéraire descriptif, historique et archéologique de l'Orient*, "to furnish the tourist with all the practical information necessary for a voyage which the new means of transportation facilitate."[7]

Inspired by "a scrupulous exactitude in details, a preoccupation with being always useful to the traveller," nothing was to be left to chance. From the construction of mosquito nets to the procuring of visas, obtaining letters of introduction, equipping oneself with provisions, employing servants and interpreters and bestowing appropriate gifts ("a few pairs of English pistols, knives, pocket-telescopes, toys for children, and ornaments for ladies . . . New periodicals, caricatures etc from London are most prized by English residents in the East")—all the practicalities of life on the road were covered. Travellers passed on tips of their own, especially regarding diet and disease. One advised dressing warmly in Macedonia, even in summer, to avoid chills. Another insisted on a morning coffee and a diet of cucumbers. The eccentric but highly erudite David Urquhart—among whose claims to fame was the introduction of the Turkish bath to England—advised shaving one's head to "prevent chills by cooled perspiration," taking as little liquid as possible (for the same reason), and just one meal a day—preferably nothing more than "pilaf, yaoort [a species of sour milk] and eggs . . . the first two form together a light, nutritive and not unpalatable diet." Everyone used quinine against the marshy fevers for which Salonica was notorious.[8]

Keeping as aloof as possible from the locals was also recommended. In 1798 John Morritt had ridden through Thessaly dressed like a janissary to avoid trouble; but by 1830 the janissaries were gone, and wearing European dress was the safest way to demonstrate power: the general attitude—though Urquhart for one would have disagreed—was that it was most important to avoid being taken for a native. "It is simply ridiculous in an English traveller to assume the Greek or any other Oriental dress," admonished Murray, "unless he is a *perfect* master of the local language and manners; and even in that improbable case he will still find an *English shooting jacket and wide-awake* the most respectable and respected travelling costume throughout the Levant." Caught up in a brawl in the streets of Salonica, one visitor escaped harm because "thanks to our clothes which allowed us to be taken for Franks, the *cawasses* [guards] let us enter the [Greek] consulate to . . . watch the riot from upstairs." It is an image—the frock-coated traveller standing above the fray on a consulate balcony—which perfectly expresses the attitude of superior detachment with which most travellers from Europe approached the mysteries of the Orient.[9]

ARRIVAL

COMING BY SEA, one left the islands behind and entered the calmer waters of the Gulf. To the right was the Halkidiki peninsula and the mysterious realm of the Holy Mountain, a mountainous presence falling away in the far distance; on the left, looming above the foothills, the home of the gods, Olympos itself, descended to the coastal flats of the Vardar plain. After another hour's sailing, the city walls gradually came into view. "The approach to this city from the sea is very imposing," wrote Henry Holland. "It is seen from a great distance, placed on the acclivity of a steep hill . . . surrounded by lofty stone-walls . . . and surmounted by a fortress with seven towers. The domes and minarets of numerous mosques rise from the other buildings, environed as usual by cypresses, and giving a general air of splendour to the place."[10]

From whatever angle it was viewed, the lovely setting inspired dreamy effusions. Having described the "glorious panorama of old red roofs, graceful minarets, green trees and the blue of the Aegean beyond," Goff and Fawcett paused before the "towering snow-capped 'Home of the Gods' "—Mount Olympus in the distance: "Such is the picture—so clear that it might almost be a fitting illustration by a fanciful artist to an Eastern fairy tale. For indeed is not the East one huge fairy tale? Are not the white minarets and the mysterious old houses, the storks on the roof, the beggar at the fountain, the very cobblestones and above all, the deep blue sky and the star-strewn night the very essentials of magic and romance?"[11]

One huge fairy tale? Tourists, it is clear, were seeing very much what they had come to see. Their own culturally determined appetites demanded to be satisfied—how could they not be?—inspired by a romanticism which valued new landscapes for the states of mind they induced. Victorian travel writers tried hard to convey the intense individuality of their experiences—even if they were often having much the same ones. The concrete realities and economic possibilities of the place no longer really interested them. They did not show much curiosity about the fertility of the soil, the range of local produce or the solidity of the city's fortifications, as earlier generations of visitors, less enmeshed in their own subjectivity, had done. Instead the East was now an aesthetic construct:

> So perfect is the composition of the picture that it seems to have been controlled and set out from the sea, just as the expert window-dresser directs his scheme from the pavement. The tiers of white, red-roofed houses, interspersed with graceful minarets, stretch in a vast amphitheatre from the upper gallery of the ancient walls down to a proscenium of deep blue sea. With a fringe of boats as the foreground, the mauve-tinted heights in the distance and a middle theme made up of the multi-coloured terraces of the town, the picture seems almost unreal in its perfection.[12]

What they found was that most-prized of nineteenth-century scenes—the picturesque. "It is one of the most picturesque cities from the water that I ever saw," wrote M. to her sister in 1839. Offering a different kind of beauty to that earlier favourite—the sublime—the picturesque prompted not terror or a sense of human insignificance but rather delicate musings on the harmonious interplay of nature and civilization, of a kind evoked by gentle inclines, graduated tones, and ruins. Edward Lear traversed the Balkans looking for such scenery and his sketches of the view across the gulf to Olympos are fine examples of the genre: in one, a small group of local men, their vermilion fezzes a contrast with their white Albanian fustanellas, sit on the bare slope of a hill within the walls of the Upper Town; below them, a broad dusty path winds lazily down past cypresses and minarets into the town itself, half-hidden in the lethargic haze of an August afternoon. A cholera epidemic was raging at the time of his visit, and Lear found inspiration even in the squalor of the lower town where, in his words, "I saw an infinity of picturesque bits, cypresses, and minarets, and latticed houses" before fear of the quarantine forced him out.[13]

The picturesque retained its grip on the sensibility of visitors for generations, long after the demolition of the old sea-walls had altered the prospect from the sea beyond recognition. According to the *Guide Joanne*, "the most agreeable promenade" in the city emerged as a result of these changes, but as modernity fringed the quay with hotels and warehouses, tramlines and street-lights, giving an "entirely European effect to this new quarter," searchers for the painterly landscape of the past encountered obstacles. "The walls which protected the city from the sea have unfortunately been removed in these days of peace," lamented the classicist J. P. Mahaffy, "more convenient no doubt but not half so picturesque." "Behind the quay," wrote R. H. Russell in 1896, "the modern tramway, with busy cars running to and fro, does much to destroy the Eastern atmosphere of the place, forcing you to close your eyes to this feature of the foreground ... before you can believe that you are really in an Oriental port." Yet for many foreigners Salonica remained an ideal place to glimpse those elements which had vanished in independent Greece, where in Lear's words, "war and change" had deprived her of "the charm of Oriental architecture, the picturesque mosque, the minaret, the fort and the serai." As Athens and Belgrade erased the traces of their recent Ottoman past, Salonica was turning into nothing more than a style—an "unmistakably Eastern look"—which became ever more pronounced, its anomalous character in a European setting ever more seductive. The more the world—and the Balkans—changed, the more Oriental the city was coming to seem. One or two commentators, trying to draw attention to its dynamism, reacted angrily to the tyranny of literary fashion: "One ought to flog the fanatics of the picturesque in public," thundered a frustrated journalist. His very irritation betrayed the continued resilience of an approach which lingered on beyond the First World War. Most European travellers screened out modernity and focused on what they had come to see.[14]

BRAVING THE REALITIES

AFTER THE ENCHANTMENT, a rude awakening invariably followed the discovery that the city had a life of its own. "It is the oriental city," wrote de Vogüé, "which one ought to pass from afar in a dream, without approaching it." This stance was in itself part of the aesthetic ideal of the picturesque for by definition, it kept humans at a distance, and guaranteed disappointment, irritation or at the least grudging readjustment, as what had been an enchanting prospect hove into closer view. Almost without exception, travellers to Salonica were shocked by the reality of a bustling, polyglot commercial port. "Few places can exhibit a greater discrepancy than here between external splendour and internal squalor," stated Murray's 1884 *Handbook*—a judgement which would carry more weight if it were not so easy to parallel with similar verdicts on Smyrna, Beirut and Istanbul itself.[15]

As the ship's lighters brought passengers to shore they felt disenchantment, revulsion and anxiety at the host of unruly gesticulating figures filling the foreground. Edward Lear, landing at the slippery wooden-planked quay, was fearful of the "crowds of black-turbanned Hebrews at the water's edge" who seized him, his *dragoman* and his luggage and carried them bodily out of the boat before fighting over who would have the right to carry his belongings to the hotel. Melville, who visited the town briefly a few years later, watched in fascination the "vast crowd and tumult" when the Austrian steamer arrived from Constantinople: "Imagine an immense accumulation of the rags of all nations, and all colors rained down on a dense mob, all struggling for huge bales and bundles of rags, gesturing with all gestures and wrangling in all tongues. Splashing into the water from the grounded boats." And before the sanctuary of consulate or hostel could be reached, the newcomer still had to brave the warehouses, customs sheds, taverns and muddy alleys of the city's docks.[16]

Once inside the harbour gate, the marvellous light-filled vista gave way to a grimmer, ill-lit reality—"suffocating streets, wretched wooden houses, leprous constructions, unmentionable cesspools." In a setting where even the main street was unimpressive in its dimensions, there were none of the broad avenues, spacious squares or vistas to be enjoyed in the increasingly sanitized and planned urban environments of northern and western Europe. Even the well-disposed German traveller Braun-Wiesbaden wrote that "the interior of the city is disappointing and . . . evokes in one an irritated disillusionment." "After telling you of the romantic appearance of the city from without," wrote M. to her sister, "I must not forget to say that the first object I encountered on entering was the *fish* market—a long dark, covered way, redolent with the most disgusting perfumes. Alas! for all romance in a Turkish city." The bazaar struck one unimpressed tourist as "quite large but filthy. Streets all narrow, like cow lanes, and smelling like barnyards." Another found the odour hard to bear, a strange, sweet "unpleasant and yet aromatic whiff like balsamine," mixed with damp wood and lamb fat. The open drains, which stank in all weathers, the effluent which collected against the walls in the lower town, the mean, crooked streets and poorly paved roads, harsh enough to tax the strongest feet on a day's sightseeing—this "sad labyrinth" tested the sympathies of all but the most open-minded visitor. The houses, so attractive from afar, looked jerry-built on closer inspection. "Aspect of streets like those of Five Points," noted Melville, alluding to a notorious slum back home. "Rotten houses. Smell of rotten wood." In the centre of the town, the throng of humans and packs of dogs worried such an experienced traveller as the Reverend Edward Clarke, who justified his cursory scrutiny of the Arch of Galerius on the implausible grounds—given that it was right by one of the main gates—that "it is situated in a very crowded part of the city, which made his stay dangerous, and would have rendered its examination difficult."[17]

But then Ottoman towns were hard for Western visitors to decipher. To many, as to generations of Western urban historians since, they did not really behave like towns at all. They lacked public spaces such as squares or boulevards; they were often curiously silent since there was little wheeled traffic; they were dark and deserted at night and there were no street names or numbers. The first detailed map for Salonica dates from 1882 and was almost immediately rendered out of date by the devastating fire of 1890. Even time failed to work as Europeans understood it, and the muezzins' calls to prayer did not help them much: there were few public clocktowers but there were at least three calendars in use (four if one counted the Jewish), and when one asked the time, one had to specify whether one meant *alla turca* (which began at dawn) or *alla franca*. Travellers were understandably thrown, wrote Lucy Garnett, by being asked: "At what time is noon today?" To add to the sense of disorientation, signs and shop placards could be written in one of four scripts and conversations overheard in more than half a dozen languages, or—more likely—an ever-varying amalgam of them all.

Manners were very different too: rooms lacked basic furnishings such as chairs or tables, and table manners were decidedly peculiar: how, for instance, could it be a mark of honour for the master of the house to stuff morsels in your mouth with his own hand? There were *chibouks* and *hookahs* to master, endless pilaffs, the ubiquitous cucumber, more salads than Europeans were used to, and meat stews peppered with strange spices, fruits preserved in syrup, sherbets, and the fermented millet drink known as *boza*, Albanian *halva* and yoghurt. Salonica was in fact renowned for its cuisine—it still is—but not among the Europeans. An early guidebook warned that "if culinary science is foreign to the Turks, the science of dining well is still more unknown."[18]

This daunting prospect made it imperative for the traveller to find a place where "amidst the dirt, decay and disorder of the Orient, one is surrounded by all the cleanliness and comfort of Europe." For Europe now stood for propriety in every sense, and Victorian travellers commented, as their predecessors never had, on differences in hygiene, noise and smell, and sought to create small islands of civilization for themselves to escape these. Staying in Turkish caravanserais and *khans*—as Ottoman subjects did—was too awful a prospect for most Europeans: they generally only endured them if already in the company of Turks—like geologist Warrington Smyth—or when venturing into the hinterland, where nothing else was available. "Travellers accustomed to the luxurious hotels of civilized Europe can form no idea of what must be endured in the search after the picturesque in the interior of Turkey," wrote Mary Adelaide Walker. Reaching the *khan* in Pella, just outside Salonica, she was reminded of the delights of travelling in Switzerland, Germany and France—the comfortable hotels, the bowing *maître d'*, carpeted staircases, smart chambermaids and warm, clean beds. In Pella what awaited her was a grumbling inn-keeper, clad in "a ragged caftan, greasy turban and tattered sheepskin cloak," crumbling walls, a broken staircase, rotten flooring and a mud floor spattered by the rain coming in through the roof. "One must be endowed with a certain dose of energy and courage to travel in the provinces of Turkey in Europe," cautioned the *Guide Joanne.*[19]

According to Boué, writing in 1840, inns with glass in the windows, beds, tables and chairs were only to be found in the capital, Scutari, the Danubian towns and Salonica; in the absence of separate toilet facilities, courtyards and windows served the needy, an additional hazard for travellers choosing to sleep outside at night. Most visitors of any standing lodged with their consul, until they found rooms of their own: Salonica possessed a single café, whose proprietor made available a living room, a bedroom and a gallery on the first floor. Edward Lear, passing through in 1848, records "a Locanda—a kind of hotel—the last dim shadow of European 'accommodation' between Stamboul and Cattaro." Later there was the Hotel Benedetti, where travellers could enjoy a coffee and cigarette over breakfast in the central courtyard, possibly the same establishment which the *Guide Joanne* sniffily referred to as "*une mauvaise auberge*" run by an Italian. In 1874 James Baker noted "two hotels, which are moderately comfortable." By 1890, however, with the coming of rail, things were much altered: the Colombo, the Splendid Palace, the d'Angleterre, the Imperial and the Grand Hotel stood in modern buildings on the new quay, or in the Frank Quarter.

Old Balkan hands were struck by the change: Who talked of Salonica fifty years ago? asked a French writer in 1888. "Only the antiquaries. Today her name is on every lip."[20]

With terrors ranging from dogs to stone-throwing little boys, walking around town unchaperoned was still only for the brave. Cultural intermediaries and protectors were needed, especially the interpreter (*dragoman*) and security guard (*cavass*). It was they who negotiated on the voyager's behalf for horses and provisions, dealt with Ottoman officials, and guided him or her through the narrow streets of the lower town to the sights. "I had to get organized, or what came to the same thing, to find someone to do it for me," wrote Auguste Choisy in August 1875. Nikolaos Hadji-Thomas was, in the words of his satisfied customer, "the model *dragoman:* a well-built man of open countenance, loyal, speaking Greek, Turkish, Bulgarian, Italian and able to make himself understood in French." The Romanian Hermann Chary, who was interpreter at the Hotel Imperial on five francs a day, spoke "nine or ten languages fluently" and had served Gordon in Egypt before being employed by Whitman of the *New York Herald* during the 1897 Greco-Turkish war.[21]

In fact, more or less the only activity which the average European undertook alone in the city was shopping for gifts in the *Kapalı Çarsi*—one of the largest and most impressive covered arcades in the Turkish provinces. "Sightseeing and visiting being accomplished, we had only to look if there was anything in the shops," wrote the Misses Irby and Mackenzie. Then, as now, obtaining souvenirs and presents took up time and energy—avoiding the pestering boot-blacks while browsing among the shoes, belt-knives, "gaudy pistols," silks, gold-embroidered trousers, rose oil and carpets. Shops were not organized as at home, and there were "no 'Stores' or general shops in which goods of various kinds are collected."

But the modern traveller's obsession—the search for authenticity—was already being obstructed by modern tourism's nightmare creation—consumerism—and local markets were gearing themselves to the visitors far more quickly than the visitors liked to realize. Local photographers began to churn out series of hand-coloured postcards of the main sights, and ethnographic street scenes, local trades and costumes—"the Lemonade Seller," "the Travelling Butcher," "Negro Slave chatting at her door"—appeared alongside views and vistas and the rich repertory of monuments. One traveller bought some local writing materials, a pair of white half-leather slippers, and an impressive dagger that looked "extremely Turkish"—only to discover too late that the blade was stamped with a German mark. "Ver'goot Johnnie, anyting you like, Sair, souvenir Salonik," rang in the ears. "The Saloni-cian quickly realized the Westerners' weakness for souvenirs," wrote another, "and it was not long before a number of shops were doing excellent business selling cheap modern jewellery and antiques, such as Turkish swords and pistols, Greek daggers, Albanian cartridge-cases and old coins dating from the Byzantine and Roman eras." The city was turning itself and its past into an object of consumption. What remained unchanged in the city was both despised and treasured for its difference; what adapted and modified itself to "European civilization" was both demanded by Europe itself and decried by it as depriving the "Oriental life" "of a large part of its colour and picturesque relief."[22]

MYSTERIES OF THE EAST

ONE AUGUST DAY IN 1828, an Austrian diplomat was amusing himself by pacing the circuit of the city walls—like Evliya Chelebi before him—and had reached the upland fields behind the citadel which served as a Muslim graveyard, when he noticed a small group of Turkish women sitting together under the plane trees and admiring the view. Even though they were not veiled, they called him over. The youngest got up and asked him if he was a medical man. When he said he was, they asked him to test their pulse, claiming they were all feeling feverish. Anton von Prokesch-Osten describes the scene:

A negress indeed, the companion of the young beautiful woman, was not at all surly. She listened attentively with her mistress to my advice and spoke in a friendly fashion. The younger woman's colouring was wonderful, her eyes bright and her hair deepest black. Her carriage was careless but her arms and hands were carefully made up. She did not bother about covering up her breasts and appeared interested in what impression this would make on me. "I love the Franks," she told me, while I took her pulse, and added, in a tone that would have done honour to a Parisienne, "because they are all doctors."[23]

To foreigners, Muslim women had always symbolized the unattainable mystery of their society and culture. Hidden behind their veils, they were remote figures, well guarded from Western eyes. When a French chaplain wanted to climb a minaret for the view of the town, local householders stopped him, saying he might be able to glimpse inside their homes. Similar considerations delayed the spread of glass windows, especially on high buildings. On the streets of the city, approaching women was no easier, unless they were slaves out on an errand. Bisani and his companions were foolishly attracted by a beautiful pair of eyes, until they were driven off by a little boy throwing stones at them. "Here comes trouble!" was the usual way in which Muslim women greeted the approach of unknown men. Doctors were in fact about the only kind of male strangers who might on occasion get closer.

Jewish women were similarly secluded, especially during the violent eighteenth century: many took to the veil as rabbis forced local custom on their congregations, and did not venture out unless accompanied by a man. Christian women also kept off the streets if they could, preferring the networks of paths and gates which inter-connected private houses. But, then as now, it was the Muslim woman who captured the imagination of the Western visitor. Or to be precise, of Western men, for there were a few women—especially if they could converse in Turkish, like Fanny Blunt or Lucy Garnett—who mingled socially with them and did not find them especially mysterious. Having spent many afternoons chatting politely and drinking coffee in the *haremliks* of the city, Fanny Blunt numbered among her acquaintances women like Besimé, originally a Circassian slave and a former member of the imperial harem, who lived in quiet retirement in Salonica and confided to her "all the sorrows of her adventurous life." For men, on the other hand, all remained fantasy where local women were concerned, especially when, as one visitor wrote, their "refined coquettishness piqued the curiosity and provoked desire."[24] Nowhere was this desire expressed more forcefully than in one of the most curious works ever to be inspired by an Ottoman city.

Salonica.
Loti's Journal. 16 May 1876

... A beautiful May day, bright and sunny, a clear sky ... When the foreign rowboats arrived, the executioners were putting the final touches to their work: six corpses hanging in front of the crowd underwent their horrible final contortion ... Windows, roofs were thick with spectators; on a nearby balcony the Turkish authorities smiled on the familiar spectacle.

Thus, with a characteristic blend of his favourite themes—death, Oriental despotism, voyeurism—did one of fin-de-siècle France's most popular novelists begin his first best-seller, *Aziyadé*, a book which appeared shortly after the murder of the two consuls, and showed Western self-absorption turning the Ottoman city from an object of aesthetic and sentimental contemplation into nothing more than a mirror for the individual psyche. There was only one ingredient missing, and this was soon supplied:

One fine spring day, one of the first that we were permitted to circulate in Salonica of Macedonia, a little after the massacres, three days after the hangings, around four in the afternoon, it happened that I stopped before the closed door of an old mosque to watch two storks fighting. The scene took place in a lane of the old Muslim quarter. Decrepit houses flanked tortuous little paths, half-covered by the projecting *shaknisirs*. Oats pushed between the paving stones, and branches of fresh greenery overhung the roofs. The sky, glimpsed at intervals, was pure and blue. One breathed everywhere the balmy air and sweet smell of May.

The inhabitants of Salonica still displayed a constrained and hostile attitude towards us. The authorities obliged us to carry a sword and full military kit. In the distance, some turbaned men passed the walls, and no woman's head showed itself behind the discreet grilles of the *haremlik*. One would have said it was a dead city.

I felt so perfectly alone that I felt a shock when I perceived near me, behind iron bars, at the height of a man's head, two great green eyes fixed on mine.

The brows were brown, lightly frowning, pushed together so that they nearly joined. The expression in that look was a mixture of energy and naivety. One would have said the glance of a child, it had so much freshness and youth.

The young woman whose eyes they were stood, and displayed to the waist a figure enveloped in a Turkish cape (*feredje*) with long, stiff folds. The cloak was of green silk, embroidered with silver thread. A white veil was carefully wrapped around her head, letting one see nothing but her forehead and her large eyes. Her pupils were green, that sea-green tint of which the poets of the East once sung. That young woman was Aziyadé.[25]

Pierre Loti—the "lotus"—was the pen-name of a young writer called Julien Viaud, acrobat, officer and adventurer, who was to become one of the most successful of Europe's Orientalists with his novels of decadent sensibility and exotic seduction. Many others, of course, had mined the same vein: the literature of Oriental fantasy erotica stretched back well before Loti's day. But if the earlier versions of the genre figured the lustful Turkish male able to exert his power over the helpless captives of his harem, the sexual balance of power was shifting. The once all-powerful Turk was reduced to impotence—his city was "dead"—and now it was the West that was penetrating the East. Of this moment Loti was the master storyteller, and it was in Salonica that his literary career took off with a tale of forbidden love, between a Frenchman, himself, and Aziyadé, a young woman in the harem of a Turkish bey.

Viaud was not making it *all* up. Writing from first-hand experience, he had actually spent some time in Salonica in 1876 as a naval cadet on a ship sent there after the killing of the two consuls. The novel opens with a scene showing the hanging of the supposed ringleaders of the mob—an event which did take place. What followed, however, showed how far the city had escaped even the loose moorings of picturesque romanticism to become nothing more than a foil for human subjectivity itself, a stage-set of imaginative possibilities in the mind of a talented writer.

Taking the form of a fictitious epistolary exchange between Loti and two young British naval friends in London, Brown and Plumkett, the story describes Loti's passionate but secretive affair with Aziyadé. They are assisted by a third person, a bearded man with "a very handsome head, a great sweetness in his eyes and resplendent with honesty and intelligence," the Jewish boatman Samuel. Of course this book is "about" Salonica only in the sense in which, say, D'Annunzio's writings are about Venice or Rome. The city serves as the stimulus for Loti's exploration of mood, sensibility, subjectivity and emotion. It is in its way a highly modern approach.

Everything, even the city itself, has become insubstantial and nothing is what it seems. Loti describes himself as "plaything of illusions . . . an illusion in Salonica, an illusion elsewhere." He escapes from the foreigner's trademark—visibility—by being dressed in Turkish costume by three elderly Jewish women, and this allows him to wander unremarked through "an absurd city, the Eastern bazaars, the mosques, the multi-coloured crowds." Embracing Aziyadé on a boat, draped in carpets, floating in the bay at night, is "drunkenness." "You will say that this wants a terrible egoism; I would not disagree," writes Loti. "But then I came to think that everything that pleases me is worth doing and that one should always spice up life's insipid stew." When he came to after the night's delirium, Salonica "presented a paltry picture. Its minarets had the air of a collection of old candles, set on a dirty, black city where the vices of Sodom flourished." The city's appearance mirrors the artist's mood: the world has shrunk to feeling and sensibility. All that matters is to keep away "the disheartening void and the immense *ennui* of life."

"It was at first nothing more than an inebriation of the imagination and the senses," Loti writes to his friend Brown in London. But gradually, the city's charms impress themselves on the lover. "It was happiness to take a stroll at sunrise. The air was so light, the freshness so delicious, that one had no trouble living. One was, as it were, penetrated by well-being. Some Turks began to circulate, dressed in red gowns, green or orange, in the vaulted lanes of the bazaar, hardly visible in the transparent half-glimmer . . . The evening was an enchantment of a different order for the eyes. All was pink or gold. Olympus was tinted as though smouldering or molten, and was reflected in the still sea like a mirror. No smoke in the air. It seemed as though there was no more atmosphere and that the mountains were floating in the void, so clearly delineated were the farthest ridges."

Curiously, Loti's novel was published at the same time as Gladstone—the liberal campaigner against Ottoman tyranny—was insisting on the importance (and the possibility) of Europeans acquiring real knowledge of the peoples of the Balkans in order to prepare them for civilization. Loti belonged to a younger, more mystical generation which embraced what could not be known: the Orient was not the origin of civilization, but its opposite, the mysterious spiritual alternative to Western rationalism. Knowledge was possible, but only of oneself. At bottom there was only *ennui* and excess. Loti simply carried the romantic style of travel writing—the voyage as internal exploration into the world of feeling, the escape from the conventions of sedentary, bourgeois Europe—to an unprecedented extreme.

By the outbreak of the First World War, he and Salonica had come to be equated in the minds of anyone with a knowledge of French literature and an interest in the Levant. He was increasingly popular in the city among the new middle classes and as for the French themselves, the memoirs and belles-lettres they produced when they visited during the war showed him to be inescapable. One wartime satirical squib—*A Salonique sous l'oeil des Dieux*—shows Loti's melancholic fascination with the Orient turning into contempt: Aziyadé has become a prostitute, Ayché, with "a chosen clientele of officers many of whom had read Loti" and are keen to meet a Turkish woman. "For the European man," the author continues ironically, "the Turkish woman is Mystery, Forbidden Love peppered with danger, the anticipation of variation in the unchanging melody of desire."[26] Another disillusioned new arrival wrote: "The Oriental woman! Well then, so [Loti] showed us one of these beautiful odalisques. Have you seen one yourself? In more than a year that we are at Salonica, behind the Villa of the Red Sultan, have you seen the sultanas? No, you have only been able to see those ugly women of the disgusting brothels in the Vardar, the three dancers of the Odeon." "But what of the Muslim women," wrote another, "the mysterious veiled women who sing in such a soft voice, behind their moucharabiehs? The voluptuous Aziyadé . . ."[27]

Sex-starved pilgrims searching for the scenes of Loti's infatuations retraced his steps much as others followed the Apostle: "I am at Salonica barely a week and since then I have been looking for the shadow of Aziyadé," wrote an infantry officer. "I know I shall never find her, but how not to be obsessed by that simple and marvellous story of love and death?"[28] The author was impressed by the affinities between himself and its hero—"the same way of feeling and of thinking, the same mix of scepticism and naivety, an identical need to love and be loved, a similar disgust of certain conventions, certain obligations, certain habits, the same desire for the infinite." And like Loti he found "all the charm of the Orient" working on his senses. "Behind those hermetically sealed blinds,"—he was strolling idly in the Upper Town—"no doubt pretty eyes shone and crimson lips smiled. Ah, mirage of the East! Aziyadé! Loveable fantasies of Loti!"[29]

Thanks to Loti, what had previously been regarded by travellers as the least knowable and inaccessible aspect of the city's life now became the centre of the Western erotic imagination; what was formerly regarded as worthy of description was reduced to the mundane and the banal. The European obsession with the city's Oriental nature had not died away; but now, it was concentrated in the fantasy of a Western conquest of the feminine East. And why not? Had not the West by this point conquered everything else?

10

The Possibilities of a Past

IN 1916 A WRITER for the *National Geographic* was struck by Salonica's seeming indifference to the needs of the tourists who came on the trail of its past. "So little indeed has she yet taken in, as the remainder of Europe has so profitably done, the possibilities of a past that I was unable to find there a map of the city . . . And as I went from shop to shop in search of photos of the churches, I was followed by an officer looking vainly for a Baedeker."[1] It was history, after all, which attracted the majority of visitors. What was the present for them but a backdrop to antiquity? Greece "has no modern history of such a character as to obscure the vividness of her classical features," asserted Murray's *Handbook.* "A modern history she does indeed possess, various and eventful, but it has been of a destructive not a constructive character. It has left little behind it which can hide the immortal memorials of the greatness of Hellenic genius . . . In all parts of the country, the traveller is, as it were, left alone with antiquity."[2]

The travellers' very guides were often the classics. "We passed from the gulf Syngiticus to that of Thermaicus, and anchored in the bay of Thermes, Thessalonica or Salonica, in the country of the Myrmidons," wrote Bisani. What the eighteenth century knew as "ancient geography" thus served a practical as well as a scholarly need. Crossing the Vardar on his way to the city, Edward Clarke noted that "it is the AXIUS of *Herodotus:* separating the *Mygdonian* from the *Bottioean* territory ["epi tin Axion potamon hos ourizei chorin tin Mygdonin te kai Bottiaiida, *Herodoti Hist.lib.vii.cap.123.p.418,* ed. *J.Gronov. L.Bat. 1715,*" a footnote helpfully confirmed], where Pella stood: and it is now called

Vardar. The same river is also mentioned, under the name of AXIUS, by the venerable *Scylax.*" The learned reverend could scarcely have guessed the enormous cultural and political power such scholarship would turn out to possess: entire landscapes would end up being re-named, and in the twentieth century an official government committee would celebrate the transfer of the region to Greek control by scrap-ping local Slavic, Albanian and Turkish place-names—the Vardar among them—and replacing them with classical alternatives.[3]

From the Upper Town, looking over the domes, minarets and rooftops across the bay to Olympos, one foreigner after another sought access to the spirit of the ancients. "From the mountain on which today the old citadel of Salonica stands, Xerxes saw some two thousand three hundred years ago what today any knowledge-thirsty tourist can see if he doesn't mind the effort of traipsing between debris and boulders, rocks and burned grass, thistles and especially weeds," wrote one, try-ing to recapture the thoughts of the Persian king, as he planned his invasion of Greece. For the high-minded Mary Adelaide Walker, "the sight which inspired Xerxes with the hope of other lands to conquer, may well elevate the mind of the Christian spectator to the world beyond the grave" to that "wondrous future when even the 'mountains shall pass away.' " "It is the same Olympus, empty now of its gods, but still full of its eternal loveliness, on which St. Paul must often have gazed," mused the Reverend Davies, "deep blue in the noonday, purple in the evening—seeing in it the work and beauty of Him who in His strength setteth fast the mountains, and is girded about with power."[4]

Primed by education, expectation and preparatory reading, the trav-eller thus came face to face with history itself—classical, biblical, or in the case of Macedonia, the two together. "It is history, which for him had till that point been no more than an ideal, an exercise of memory, or for some only a subject for meditation, the history of the first ages of mankind, which suddenly reveals itself in its proper theatre," wrote Isambert. "The East is the cradle of our civilisation . . . In the East, everything takes body, assumes its real proportions . . . not only in the sight of the ancient buildings which the hand of time has spared, but also by frequenting those peoples, those races conserved through the centuries which are still the most living monument, the most effective demonstration of what their ancestors bequeathed to us!" The task of civilization might have been passed to the West, but the East still offered its own unwitting enlightenment.[5]

Thus not only the landscape but also those who dwelled there—

their customs, their dress, sometimes their faces—helped conjure up the past. David Urquhart recommended experiencing the East for "what I would call the novelty of antiquity." Lost to "our times and in our portion of the globe," the "habits of ancient days still live and breathe" there, he asserted. Layard's recent excavations in Mesopotamia inspired the excited discovery that "the Assyrian type was widespread" in Salonica. "Certain lanes in the bazaar resemble a bas-relief from Nineveh and Babylon," readers were assured, "where magnificent Assurbanipals sell melons or watermelons." Choisy, who liked the Greeks and admired their fortitude and collective spirit, found that they had preserved "a physiognomy up till now which takes us back before the Turkish invasion, as far as the times of classical antiquity." Such attitudes turned Salonica into a kind of museum, its inhabitant into living fossils. "We set out through the streets of the sleeping town," recalled Demetra Vaka. "How teeming with history it was. Everything spoke of the past, not the present." The Jews in particular cast her mind back centuries. "But it is the same with all the other nationalities one sees in Saloniki: they represent the past not the present . . . The history of ages enveloped us." By 1905, as the lower town became ever more prosperous, noisy and Western in outlook, even the Muslim quarters on the slopes above could be enlisted, offering one American correspondent "truly a Biblical scene though the characters were Mohammedan."[6]

BUT SOME PASTS were more present than others. To the devotees of neo-classicism, the creed which had held sway in much polite European society since the late eighteenth century, the classical era represented a universal idea of beauty, and later epochs a sad degeneration in taste. It went without saying that the Islamic presence was not worth much in aesthetic terms. As a visiting British army officer put it: "There is very little to see in a mosque." The general assumption was that the Ottomans were squatters amid the faded glories of earlier architectural achievements. But many were equally dismissive of the Christians who had preceded them. "All that is of the pagan period had been byzantined and all that was Byzantine has been mohammedanized," wrote Misses Irby and Mackenzie after two days' sightseeing, "so that while much may be traced to interest the antiquary, there is scarce beauty enough left to delight the unprofessional traveller." How, after all, could beauty emerge from a civilization whose moral and religious principles were held in deep suspicion by the Victorians? As late as 1893, a Greek scholar noted "the unfavourable impression which even today is provoked by the name of Byzantium."[7]

But Western taste was changing, and its increasing appetite for the medieval past, for Genoa, Venice and the Italian city states, extended slowly to the Levant. The first architectural surveys of Byzantine remains were published, and the field of Byzantine studies emerged. Greek historians argued for the continuity of Hellenic culture from classical to modern times, a view which gave the Byzantine period enormous significance as a transmitter and protector of classical values. And there was also its role in the evolution of Christian architecture. Salonica's churches, wrote the scholarly Tozer in 1869, "are of the greatest value for the history of art." This was a novel view at the time, but others soon came to appreciate their importance. "The sole merit of the town," wrote de Vogüé in 1875, "is to have conserved a series of extremely ancient churches which allow one to follow step by step the evolution of architecture in the first centuries of Christianity . . . From this point of view Salonica is a unique museum in the Levant and has no equal except for Rome." By 1890, guidebooks boasted that there were to be found there "a group of Byzantine constructions of a richness which equals and even surpasses in certain respects the buildings of Constantinople."[8]

In the mosques—which otherwise interested them not at all—Christian visitors noted with relief that despite the carpets, painted columns and whitewashed walls, the basic outlines of the original structures allowed them to glimpse the "power of primitive Christianity." In Salonica, access turned out to be surprisingly easy, and very different from other Ottoman cities. "If the conquerors had showed everywhere the same moderation as at Salonica," wrote one, "the Orient would be nothing other than a vast museum of inexpressible interest . . . Imagine for a moment that one of our Eastern Catholic churches enclosed the tomb of some dervish, and that one allowed Muslims to make their prayers there."[9] But others were less impressed with what they found. The classicist J. P. Mahaffy thought the "empty and deserted churches show no care for religion, either in the Turks, who now own them, or in the Greeks, who are permitted on certain feasts to assemble in the basilica. All are in shameful neglect and decay." In the eighteenth century the Porte had several times ordered the repair of major church-mosques; by the late nineteenth, they seem to have been starved of funds. The eminent Russian Byzantinist Nikodin Kondakov found them "strewn with heaps of rubbish" left behind by refugees; their columns were cracked, the apses stained with soot and windows were boarded up or filled with stones. On the floor of Ayia Sofia, little children hunted for tiny cubes of gold mosaic amidst the rubble.[10]

To the majority of Christian travellers, in fact, Salonica's overwhelming significance lay not in its ecclesiastical architecture, nor its Byzantine art, but in its association with the Apostle Paul. With him they felt the kind of immediate connection they rarely felt with the holy men of Byzantium. "The early triumphs of the Gospel," wrote a publication of the Religious Tract Society, "have at least an equal share with any classical associations in the enthusiasm which leads the traveller to brave the perils of Macedonia and Achaia." To Salonica's classical connotations, wrote Bowen, was added "the more important Christian interest of St. Paul." Following in Paul's steps, Bible in hand, they walked the streets where he had preached. Guides showed them his actual pulpit—"the chief lion of Salonica," noted Melville, though this had miraculously multiplied. "No fewer than six places will be confidently pointed out to him as the identical spot," cautioned Mary Walker. "There are also clumps of trees in several parts of the plain," wrote Baker, "which are supposed to mark the spots where St. Paul stopped to preach."[11]

And Macedonia had a particular importance for the devout Victorian in the age of Christian imperialism, for did it not illustrate the truth of the maxim that "westward the course of empire takes its way?" Paul had heeded the call of the "man from Macedonia"—as the Bible said—and come over from Asia, thereby reversing that epic conquest of the East by the West which Homer had described with a "nobler conquest," the conquest of Christianity. It was in Macedonia, in other words, that Christianity first arrived in Europe. "Out of that expedition, and those words, CHRISTENDOM arose; and because of them England, America and Australia are great today." Proud of such a legacy, the traveller could feel that "strange, sad, fascination" brought by tramping the terrain of Apostolic triumph where "the name of Christ is blasphemed by those who still hold sway over these unhappy lands, and even where professedly honoured, it is amid perversions of a corrupt creed and of ignorant worship."[12]

Thus dismissive equally of Islam and Orthodox Christianity, confident that Victorian Protestantism was the true successor to the pure faith of the early fathers of the Church, the nineteenth-century mind unproblematically laid the biblical landscape over the modern. Literally too: Conybeare and Howson's great *Life of the Apostle*, like many a family Bible, was illustrated not by historical reconstructions but by engravings of the modern Macedonian port. "The physical features of a spot which was so dear to the man who once worked in its streets, and saw its scenery, are of interest enough to justify me in devoting the remainder of the chapter to a special description of the present aspect of Salonica," wrote the Reverend Davies. From afar, he went on, the city still looked as it once did to Paul: it was enough for him that walls, fort, towers conveyed an impression of antiquity, irrelevant that none of these features was less than several centuries too late for the Apostle to have clapped eyes on them. For this landscape was more than mere scenery for many of his readers: it was testimony to the Word of God, "to the truth of the Bible record, and to the wonderful and literal fulfil-ment of Bible prophecy."[13]

COLLECTING THE PAST

FROM THE VERY FIRST YEAR of Ottoman rule, visitors were struck by the abundant evidence of the city's ancient past. Roman gates still guarded the main approaches from east and west, and innumerable Greek and Latin inscriptions were embedded in the walls where gener-ations of Byzantine garrison commanders had used the old stones as filler. Crumbling, obscured by shops and homes, the city's remains attracted no special attention from the Ottoman authorities. The Turks, commented Boué in 1840, "even the most educated, are unable to comprehend the respect which we attach to a lump, however shape-less, of some beautiful architectural remain." Gazing on the ruins of the Arch of Galerius, a German tourist was struck by the futility of the pas-sion for monumentality, and felt "a shiver at the thought that our beau-tiful west European towns too might fall into the hands of barbarians, like Salonica today, and that in the future some Australian . . . of the 28th century will sit before our mutilated triumphal arch and contem-plate matters just as I do here."[14]

Not merely viewing, but saving the ruins of the Levant for scholar-ship and civilization therefore impressed itself as an urgent duty for educated Europeans. Already at the beginning of the eighteenth cen-tury, Jesuits were buying up coins and medallions, and tracking down ancient manuscripts through local agents and informers. A French antiquarian, Paul Lucas, spent most of his travels through the Levant collecting curios on behalf of his king. Nor were the French alone: they faced stiff competition from the English and the Venetians. "There are so many people here bidding for coins," wrote Father Souciet from Salonica in 1726, "that the prices have been driven up" even though most specimens, according to his experienced eye, were not rare.[15] Travellers collected what they did not sketch. "Went into the mosque . . . Tomb of an old Greek saint shown in the cellar . . . mosaic pieces falling. [Brought away several]," runs an entry in Melville's journal. He was not the only one. When one young British tourist was taken ill and died, his possessions (which the infamous Lord Elgin was later accused of taking) were found to include:

> *Eighteen* ancient vases, lamps of pottery-ware etc etc.
> A box covered with leather, containing (amongst other sundry items,)
> A book, entitled, "The Plains of Troy."
> A little journal, covered with green marbled paper, containing various annotations.
> A purse of blue-striped cotton, containing *eighty-seven* medals of brass, great and small, entitled, "Macedonia" 1 like to the former, containing *one hundred and fifteen* brass medals, great and small, entitled, Medals of Greece.[16]

Acquiring what could be transported, visitors also trained their eye on what could not. Ironically, the Western passion for the classical past means that we know much more about Salonica's ancient remains—which were extensively visited, sketched and copied—than we do about the buildings that were surrounding them. Our first visual records of the city focus on its arches, statues and other monuments: the living are included only for scale and colour. Or take the case of Jean-Baptiste Germain, the French consul in the 1740s, who spent much of his time copying fragments for publication back home by the Academie Royale des Inscriptions. His location notes—for he scrupulously identified where each inscription was to be found—act as a virtual map of the mid-eighteenth-century city:

1. Inscription on the entrance of a house in the Hippodrome quarter, at the beginning of a small street, on the left as you leave the large square to go to the Calamaria Gate.
2. One finds this inscription at the reservoir of the public fountain of the so-called Whirling Dervishes.

3. Inscription on the entrance of the hospice of the fathers of the Holy Mountain, in the old quarter of the Franks.
4. On the floor of the small back gate as you enter the mosque called *Eski Serai*—the Old Palace.
5. At the reservoir of the fountain outside the city facing the Vardar Gate.
6. On the side of a column painted green at the new monument of Ali Effendi.
7. Inscription under the first arcade of the guard-house on the left as you enter the gate called Vardar.
8. Piece of marble forming the corner of the traverse behind Manoli's tavern, in the old quarter of the Franks.

While the inscriptions themselves were subsequently confirmed and corrected by generations of scholars, the urban fabric itself was changing all the time so that without Germain's notes we would never know about Manoli's taverna, or the fountains outside the city gates, or the lines of shops, the *Kemerleré*, which led away into the country beyond the Vardar gate. Entering the historical record, solely in virtue of containing classical masonry in or near them, they also testify to the ubiquity of the past in the city, the stones used and re-used everywhere one looked.[17]

Above all, they show that the modern city existed for Western visitors as little more than a backdrop to what was left of its more significant ancient predecessor. Here, in the activity of amateur curio collectors, part-time classicists and antiquarian priests, one sees the beginnings of what was to develop from the middle of the nineteenth century onwards into a highly professionalized discipline which would ultimately have a huge impact on the shaping and re-shaping of the modern city. For it was at about this time that archaeologists began actually excavating the past on a much larger and more systematic scale. Between Layard's discoveries at Nineveh in the 1840s and Schliemann's great digs of the 1870s, a private passion grew slowly into a profession, in tandem with the emergence of great royal and state museums which constituted the primary customers for the resulting finds. Traveller-archaeologists—a new breed—were urged to do their bit for knowledge, not by carrying away mosaics, coins, sarcophagi fragments and shards but by serious work. The time had passed for picturesque views, insisted two scholars in 1876; measurement and analysis were now needed. Salomon Reinach's *Conseils aux Voyageurs Archéologues* advised travellers how to make rubbings of inscriptions, how to take advantage of the new techniques of photography, and in particular how to fill in the gaps in maps and charts by recording one's itinerary "simultaneously in two ways, by means of notes and by drawing." Many heeded the call. "The appended inscriptions are the outcome of a short visit to Salonica in April of this year," wrote a British classicist in the *Journal of Hellenic Studies* in 1887. "I copied or impressed as many Greek inscriptions as came to my notice in my short stay, the great majority being sepulchral of a commonplace order found in the foundations of houses in the Jewish quarter, and too frequently relegated to the stonemasons' yards to be cut up for modern gravestones." The pages of the *Archives des Missions Scientifiques*, the *Berliner Philologische Wochenschrift* and the *Mitteilungen des Deutschen Archäologischen Instituts* resounded with the clash of debate. Hogarth, the Frenchmen Duchesne, Bayet and Perdrizet, the Germans Wolters and Mordtmann and the Greek Papageorgiou—the only local among these savants—were part of the fraternity of scholars scouring the bazaars, drains, graveyards, and walls of the city.[18]

But it was not all the noble pursuit of disinterested scholarship. Archaeology may have been international in its research interactions, but there could be little doubt in late-nineteenth-century Europe that it was also a profession in the service of the nation. There was fierce jostling to grab the spoils for the new state museums springing up like mushrooms in western Europe. And while European professionals toured the Levant, there were growing signs that their predatory activities were angering local opinion. When Adolphus Slade, like many others, was shown round the verde-antico carving which was (one of the sites) claimed to be the pulpit from which St. Paul had preached to the Jews, he found the *imam* who was guiding him became irritated when Slade proposed to measure it. "The good priest might have thought that if he allowed me to measure it, I should make a corresponding aperture in the roof, and so convey it away at night," joked Slade. "It would be seen to much more advantage in London; and I dare say that the sultan would give it to an ambassador, if asked. He certainly does not know of it. A trifling gift afterwards to the pasha, and the Greek bishop of Salonica, would cause it to be embarked without opposition from the people."[19] Slade knew the empire well: this kind of enterprise was not so difficult to bring off.

LAS INCANTADAS

THE BRITISH MUSEUM'S MAN in the Levant, Charles Newton, had remarked after a visit that "the most interesting relic of classical antiquity" in Salonica was "the *Incantadas*." He went on to describe a colonnade "supported by Corinthian columns half-buried in the ground, above which are square pilasters, each of which has on two faces a figure sculptured in relief. Among these figures are Dionysos, Hermes, Ariadne, Ganymede, Leda, a Bacchante and a Victory." These spectacular statues, which were built into the walls of a house in one of the central Jewish quarters, were a well-known sight. A century before Newton, other British visitors sketched the house itself—a modest building with a verandah and courtyard—next to two of the colonnade's splendid Roman columns, the space between another two planked over with a small inset gate, the statues themselves clearly visible towering over the tiled roof of the house. Newton, who would shortly become Keeper of the Greek and Roman Antiquities at the British Museum, had his hands full with excavations in Anatolia; it does not appear that more than a half-hearted effort was ever made to bring them to Britain. But others too had felt the spell of the *Incantadas*—the Enchanted Ones—and eventually they were spirited out of the city for good.[20]

Salonica's Elgin was a fifty-one-year-old French savant called Emmanuel Miller, an expert palaeographer with a self-professed "passion for manuscripts." Miller had obtained the backing of Napoleon III to examine the holdings of the libraries of Ottoman Europe, especially the monasteries of Mount Athos—the Holy Grail of generations of French bibliophiles—in order to collect rare medieval and Byzantine manuscripts. At the time he was Librarian of the French National Assembly; later he would become Professor of Modern Greek in Paris. But that was after the publication of numerous articles, considerable academic politicking and, above all, the fruits of his successful mission to the East.

He teamed up in Constantinople with a photographer-artist compatriot called Guillemet, and the two men spent two months with the monks on Athos before making their first trip to Salonica. There Miller continued his search for manuscripts. "There is a doctor here," he writes, "very precious for me: he knows everything and no door is closed to him. In a short while he showed me all the antiquities. I also visited the library of the Tchaous monastery . . . I found there a large manuscript which I believe will greatly interest the emperor." Miller asked his Greek intermediary, well-connected in church circles, to obtain it and "various other antiquities for the emperor." Acquiring original medieval manuscripts was not only desirable as a means of impressing Napoleon III back in Paris; it would also help the homesick Miller since "if I am obliged to copy the manuscript, which is considerable, I'll have to stay in Salonica a long time."

But to Miller's chagrin, the monks would not part easily with their treasures: in Athos they remembered disagreeable experiences with his predecessor, a Paris-based Greek savant called Mynas; in Salonica, and in the rock monasteries of Meteora, where Miller took a hair-raising but ultimately fruitless ride, they were also suspicious and reluctant. Bargaining with the pasha was no easier: when Miller mentioned a handsome bas-relief, the pasha said he would need to get permission from Istanbul, and dropped heavy hints that he wanted a French decoration—"an impossible thing" which Miller hesitated to bother the emperor with. Then—good news: "They *will* lend me the manuscript. *Now*, if I can get some important stones," he wrote to his wife, "my mission will be worthy of my reputation, which between you and me, is a little burdensome, since they expect great things from me. There are many Greek monasteries in Macedonia, and I have a list: next spring I will make a tour."

In the summer of 1864 Miller paid a visit to Thasos, no less beautiful an island then than now, but considerably quieter. It was at this time a curious diplomatic anomaly—technically still part of the Ottoman empire and inhabited entirely by Greek Christian villagers, but a personal possession of the ruling Egyptian dynasty, whose founder, Mehmed Ali, had been born in the nearby port of Cavalla. An Egyptian engineer who was mapping the island proved useful to Miller since he "knows all the stones and monuments which might interest us." It was on Thasos, amidst its luxuriant vegetation and heavy-drinking villagers, that Miller discovered for the first time the joys of archaeology, its hard but simple life, the discovery of unknown fragments, the pride of the pioneer. The joys, but the sorrows as well: some of the locals, he discovered, were angry at his excavations even though "they burn the most beautiful marbles for building works."

Everywhere he found "traces of *une belle époque*," but everywhere, too, "traces of indescribable barbarism." The workers drank and shirked and only respected "someone with energy." And yet "the life of an archaeologist" he found "extremely attractive, despite all the suffering . . . What emotions one feels when an edge of marble pokes its head out of the soil! Will it be an inscription or a bas-relief? Perhaps a disappointment, merely a simple building block."

Miller's procedures were not very professional. Despite his fulminations at Turkish inefficiency and sloth, and his description of himself as "exactitude incarnate," he made no surveys, and gave no indication of the location of his finds. Guillemet took photographs, but soon ran out of glass plates. Yet Miller's "archaeological fever" drove him on and soon he had some fifty marbles. "You see it is a good harvest," he wrote to his wife proudly. "Sure, many are in poor condition, but where antiquities are concerned, nothing is to be ignored." The French consul from Philippoupolis who visited him was astonished at the haul. "You're not taking all this away!" he exclaimed. But then it struck him that "it is all interesting, and you should not leave anything otherwise the English will grab it."

Miller's biggest catch was to come, however. While he waited for the boat to be sent from France, his thoughts turned again to Salonica and the caryatids. "As obstacle, I foresee the jealousy of the Greeks and the foreign consuls," he wrote. "If Fortune wishes that I should take away those statues! Think then: eight statues, of a very fine period, mutilated it is true, but so what?" He was pessimistic, but news of the impending demolition of the city's fortifications made him dizzy with the thought of how much there was to be uncovered. "I know no longer where I am—past, present, future are all confused in my head." And then, to his wife:

Thasos, 10 October 1864

I rush to send you the good, the great news . . . The Sultan, through the Grand Vizier, Fuad Pasha, has authorized me to remove and ship to France the eight statues of Salonica which I so wanted . . .

French diplomacy had done its work: the rest was up to him. The local population was likely to be very angry, and it was not impossible that the Turks would change their mind. He made haste to the town, leaving behind on the beach at Thasos "two large sarcophagi with very remarkable inscriptions" which were too big for him to get on board. At the French consulate in Salonica, there was a despatch from Paris ordering him to take not merely the caryatids, but "the monument as a whole," a decision which left him perplexed since the boat he had been sent was not powerful enough to organize the transportation of five to six tonnes of marble. "Thus something which could have brought lively satisfaction to Paris," he fretted, "will be regarded as a job left unfinished."

The pasha of Salonica received Miller in a friendly fashion, and presented him with "an ancient vase" found during the road-building. He would, he said, provide Miller with everything he wanted—men, soldiers, carts. But the news of his plans was spreading and there was much upset. "Already the population is getting agitated and tormented," Miller wrote on 1 November, just two days after his arrival. "People are furious that I am going to remove these statues that have deteriorated so badly." He could not really understand why, when the janissaries had used to fire at them for fun, while the proprietor of the house which had been built around them used to break off pieces to sell to tourists. Having thus neglected them, how could the local inhabitants now feel angry if they passed into safer hands? It was the usual justification.

The statues were in an alleyway in the heart of the Rogos quarter and Miller planned to ring off the area with soldiers so that he and his men could work without interruption from the locals. But once operations began, the problems multiplied. First, the Jewish proprietor of the house where they stood tried to cause trouble and insisted on seeing Miller's firman. That problem was solved by the pasha pledging to recompense the owner for any damage. But the popular outrage did not subside. As his sailors prepared the carts which would take the marbles to the waterside, "the word got around, and the population reacted in an extraordinary fashion—wild rumours, gossip, incredible nonsenses. All the foreign consuls are going to telegraph Constantinople to prevent the removal of the statues." Offers also came flooding in of antiquities, bas-reliefs, sarcophagi; there was even a story that Miller was planning to cart off the Arch of Galerius as well.

Day after day, the operations went on, the crowds increased, and it became almost impossible to force a passage through. Miller was dreaming of bringing up a fire-hose to quench the spirits of the unruly onlookers. But signs of hostility did not end, either from the Jews or the Turks, who still hoped for a counter-order from the sultan. The French sailors were attacked and so too, at one point, was Miller himself. And there were less violent indications of the grief the operation was causing. "One of [the Turks] played a ridiculous comedy," wrote Miller. "A *cawass*, a servant, came up to the statue of Victory. He wept and tried to embrace it. Matting almost completely surrounded it; the sailors had left bare only the rear of the statue. Our chap, not seeing anything else, embraced it. Everyone roared with laughter . . . He must have been mad or a cretin."

Because the caryatids stood atop a marble colonnade, getting them down without smashing them was a delicate job and required machinery not easily to be found in Salonica. Eventually a large wooden derrick was brought through the narrow alleys on two buffalo carts. It looked alarmingly rotten, especially since "the pieces of marble are so immense!" But by 4 November the preparations had been completed and the operation of removing the statues could begin. Miller started with the massive slab which crowned them. A crowd watched from the street and hung out of the windows of adjacent houses as the first section was removed and brought to the ground; while it was halfway down, the derrick lost its footing, and the huge piece fell to the earth, fortunately without smashing. A couple of statues were removed and again there was a slight accident: "As it touched the ground, the group of two statues received a slight blow and the top section fell, happily, upon the upper part, which is to say that the figure of Victory was unscathed. The marble had evidently long been split, and the pieces were scarcely holding together as we could see from the break."

Although the upper pediment and the statues themselves were all eventually removed, bringing them to the port required a team of eight buffaloes to navigate the labyrinth of alleys, pitted with ruts and filled with slime and rubbish. Through the bazaar the team picked a way between rotting carcasses and their "foetid odours." Nauseous, riven with anxiety, suffering from lack of sleep, beset by the throng of onlookers who followed them everywhere, Miller and his team took an hour and a half before emerging at the port where the statues were embarked on *La Truite*, a transport ship, without difficulty, alongside his Thasos gains. The marble blocks on which the caryatids had rested were even heavier, and the Bulgarian carters became worried for their buffaloes. A sharp bend nearly defeated them; then, face to face with a deep, muddy cesspool which caused the animals to slip and lose their footing, they stopped. They were forced to leave one block in the bazaar overnight. Next day it took five teams of buffaloes to get it to the boat, and Miller began to despair of ever shifting the rest.

He had not given up thoughts of shipping the entire monument—"there is not, I believe, in Paris, another ancient monument of this size"—when word reached him that no more ships would be sent out from France. "That would have been fine," he complained, "at the start when the monument was still in one piece, but now the position is not the same, since all the marbles are in the street and we cannot leave them there. I'd have to break them to free the road but what a deplorable necessity! Then they would be justified in calling us barbarians. Better it would have been to leave the monument and rest content with taking only the statues. To destroy it, take down all the pieces which make it up, then smash them, that is the act of a Vandal." Winter was approaching: the rain had been followed by freezing cold, and the buffalo drivers were refusing to show up. He had the remaining marbles placed along the wall so as not to impede the traffic, and left four large slabs to one side. Either they could be fetched at a later date, or they could be given to help build the new church of Saint Nicolas, which was being constructed in the vicinity. By now Miller was exhausted, homesick and fed up. In the middle of December he sailed for Paris, having been forced to leave the larger pieces behind, most of the columns, and the dismembered remains of what had once been perhaps the most striking antiquity in the city.[21]

Over the next century, fires and urban redevelopment entirely erased all trace of the edifice. Because Miller failed to note its location or to draw a plan of the site, we have no means of knowing where it stood or what its function was. And the caryatids themselves? Initially intended to enrich the royal collection of Napoleon III, a latecomer to the museum business, they were only deposited in the Louvre once the idea of an imperial Musée Napoleon III was abandoned. Since Miller failed to number the pieces he did deliver, the curators had to reconstruct the ensemble blind. "When the Miller marbles were sent to France and brought to the Louvre," wrote the *conservateur des antiques* there in the 1920s, "they were unfortunately not accompanied by any kind of regular inventory." In fact, the Louvre's own initial catalogue made matters worse by mixing up pieces from Salonica with others from Thasos, and by failing to note that some pieces Miller had collected in Salonica had gone astray. After the Second World War, the reconstruction was dismantled, and the pieces were dispersed through the museum.[22]

The Miller affair left its mark on the Ottoman authorities and after it was over they tightened up their supervision of the foreign archaeologists. They did not prevent their activities; far from it, there were probably more serious investigations undertaken after 1880 than at any time previously. But, as one scholar reported, "they have become sufficiently alive to the possible value of archaeological finds no longer to allow the wholesale deporting that has often been practised, more especially by the French." In 1874 legislation controlled the foreign acquisition of antiquities for the first time, for officials had become conscious of their cultural and financial value. The regime began to collect on its own account, and major finds were reserved for the Imperial Archaeological Museum that Abdul Hamid established in 1880 in a fine neoclassical building in Istanbul. In Salonica the municipality began excavating the statues and sarcophagi uncovered in building works and stored finds in the courtyard of the governor's mansion, before sending the best pieces on to the capital. "In the past we did not appreciate the value of antiquities," declared Münif Pasha, minister of education, at the museum's opening. "A few years ago an American took enough [of them] from Cyprus to fill an entire museum. Today, most [objects] in European and American museums are from the stores of antiquities in our country."[23]

Despite these words, the traffic in real—and even more, in forged—goods continued. More worryingly, the sultan saw antiquities as a means of cementing international goodwill and was inclined to disregard the protests of his own museum director. In this way, Kaiser Wilhelm, a close ally of Abdul Hamid, acquired the marble ambo from which Saint Paul was said to have preached and had it brought to Berlin. It was only one of the many tangible benefits reaped by the Berlin Museum from the burgeoning German-Ottoman friendship. Although there were plans to build a museum in Salonica itself, these were still on paper only when the Greek army took the city in 1912.[24]

THE ARCHAEOLOGISTS WERE MORE INFLUENTIAL than perhaps they knew. For by bringing to light the extensive remains of ancient settlement, they reinforced the view, which as we have seen was so pronounced throughout the age of European travel, that the real city of Salonica lay beneath the Ottoman surface. After 1912, this led Greek (and foreign) planners to reshape the urban landscape, demolishing old seventeenth- and eighteenth-century buildings—today it is doubtful whether half a dozen survive—to clear space for new focal points—the Roman forum, the Arch of Galerius and the main churches—which would bring the ancient city into visual alignment with the modern one. Neo-Hellenic modernization was thus also an assertion of neoclassicism. The origins of this linkage lay in those Western attitudes exemplified by so many travellers and their obsession with antiquity.

Most of them had regarded the picturesque sight of the minarets to be the only positive aspect of Ottoman rule. Otherwise they blamed the Turks for the city's squalor, and openly doubted their ability to modernize or reform. "The Turks, although they have borrowed much and destroyed more, have built nothing," asserted Abbott. Even though they could not miss the signs of change which transformed the fin-de-siècle city—the demolition of the walls, the spread of new suburbs, the docks and railway—Europeans saw these only as ugly blots on the Oriental canvas they had come to admire. In the increasingly racialized vocabulary of the late nineteenth century, "Turks" were seen as Asiatic and essentially nomadic, the antithesis of European civilization and by implication, merely a transient presence on European soil. The idea that the empire might be modernizing itself, and transforming its cities and societies, struck only a few. Yet the great historical irony is that even as Victorian travellers were insisting more and more upon the hopelessly immobile character of late Ottoman Salonica, it was in the process of changing faster and more dramatically than at any other time in its history. Its population rose from around 30,000 in 1830 to 54,000 in 1878, 98,000 in 1890 and 157,900 by April 1913. The city was leaving the Western stereotypes far behind.[25]

The sea approach from the south-west, *c.*1860. The minarets and cypresses rising above the walls were what first struck visitors. The city is still entirely girded by its walls.

The sea approach from the south-east. The eastern wall divides the city from the uninhabited slopes outside.

The eastern walls in the early twentieth century. At the top is the stretch where Ottoman troops breached the Byzantine defences in the siege of 1430.

A Muslim graveyard in open country outside the fortress, early twentieth century.

right Mosque and minaret in the Upper Town in the early twentieth century.

below Surrounded by postwar apartment blocks, the Aladja Imaret is one of the few surviving mosques in the city.

An Ottoman tribunal in session.

Women collecting water from a street fountain in the Upper Town.

left Sabbatai Zevi, sketched by an unknown artist in Izmir, 1666.

below Sabbatians in Salonica performing penitential exercises.

left Ma'min boy in the robes of a Mevlevi oblate, Salonica, late nineteenth century.

below the Yeni Djami, the main Ma'min mosque, built in 1902 by the Italian architect Vitaliano Poselli.

The courtyard of the Mevlevi *tekke* shortly after the ending of
Ottoman rule, c.1917. A priest may be seen, with a group of refugees.

Mevlevi dervishes in Salonica, c.1900.

right Young Jewish man, wearing fur-lined robe, sash and fez, *c.*1900.

below Leading the mourners at a grave in the Jewish cemetery, *c.*1916.

I I

In the Frankish Style

DID ANYWHERE IN FIN-DE-SIÈCLE EUROPE offer the tourist such a taste of the Orient? Zepdji's postcards featured women in their *yashmaks* and *feredjés*, cafés with elderly turbaned men smoking their *narghilés*, belly-dancers, snake-charmers and street musicians. Early colour photographers posed Jewish women in their bright aprons and fur-lined jackets, their hair braided and cased in the traditional green silk snoods. Yet none of these ethnographic curiosities were particularly striking to local people. On the contrary, faced with a younger generation raised on a diet of Viennese operetta, buffet dances, aperitifs at the Café Olympos, balloonists, bicycles and moving pictures, many felt the city was changing bewilderingly fast. "The old dress has completely disappeared," wrote a local scholar in 1914. "The Greeks were the first to adopt the European style. The Jews were quick to follow their example. The Donmehs and Turks imitated the Jews . . . Today, apart from the occasional Albanian in his fustanelle and the hand-me-downs of some villager who has strayed into town, the quay at Salonica, with its cafés, hawkers, inns and cinemas, its passers-by rigged out in those dreadful bowler hats, is scarcely different from any European port in the Western Mediterranean."[1]

European visitors to the empire had not failed to notice the intrusion of their own values. "The immobile Orient is no longer immobile," wrote the *Guide Joanne*, "and in the presence of this peaceful invasion of the European spirit, the old world of Islam feels itself renewed." But most doubted that the consequences would ever be beneficial. The French engineer Auguste Choisy predicted the attempt to graft European civilization onto Ottoman traditions was doomed to failure: blending cultures, or races, would only foster degeneration.

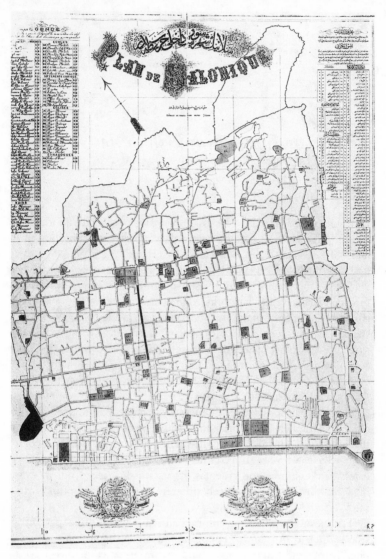

The first map of the Ottoman city, 1882, showing the new sea frontage

"Generally speaking, the Greek peasant degenerates in Asia, the Turkish in Europe," wrote Urquhart. "So the Turk in contact with Europeans and the Europeans among the Turks. The two systems, when in juxtaposition, and not under the control of a mind that grasps both, are mutually destructive . . . Ill-will and hatred are the result of intercourse without reciprocal sympathy and respect."[2]

Yet such opinions said more about the prejudices of Western visitors than they did about Ottoman realities. In the final third of the nineteenth century, "Frankish" values spread quickly throughout Salonica—more quickly perhaps than anywhere else in the empire. A wealthy Greek and Jewish "aristocracy" challenged the power of their own religious leaders: founding schools and newspapers, they subsidized European languages, learning and ideas. Their spreading influence rested on a new prosperity, the fruit of an extraordinary period of growth which saw the city treble in size as its trading activities boomed. For Salonica was escaping the gravitational pull of Istanbul and establishing profitable connections with western Europe. Entire stretches of its walls were demolished, exposing its frontage to the sea and allowing its harbour to be extended. And as the city opened itself to the outside world so its own appearance was transfigured by new suburbs, wide boulevards, factories, retail department stores and trams. For the first time, the city enjoyed municipal government. Indeed, it was perhaps only now that the city acquired a consciousness of itself. Under the leadership of its bourgeoisie, Ottoman Salonica embraced Europe.

COMMUNICATIONS

IN 1836 THE FIRST SMALL STEAMBOAT, the *Levant*, was sent by a British company. Shortly after this the British signed a commercial convention with the Porte to liberalize trade, and Abdul Mecid established a Ministry of Trade and a Council of Public Works. The abolition of monopolies and the freeing-up of the grain trade allowed the city to forge new trading linkages with the dynamic industrializing economies of western Europe. As the Austrian Lloyd Company, the Ottoman Steam Navigation Company and the French Messageries Maritimes established weekly steamer services linking Salonica to Istanbul and the Adriatic, the slow transformation of its prospects began.

They were not, initially, very bright. After the boom of the early nineteenth century, the Levant trade had stagnated. When an American frigate called into the port in 1834, the captain reported that the scenery was more enticing than its commercial potential. The wooden quay was mouldering away, the harbour itself was uncharted and sandbanks were slowly silting up the mouth of the Vardar. Piracy deterred movement by sea. "The outrages which the pirates commit in this gulf are of a nature beyond description," wrote the British consul in 1827, "and I am sorry to say that [as] their number increases daily, their inhumanity will prove very detrimental to our trade." "The Greek pirates still infest some Bays in this Gulf," reported his American counterpart six years later. The following year a Greek schooner from Smyrna was captured and the crew murdered. The advantages of getting rid of the menace were obvious. "There cannot be a doubt," wrote the American consul in 1834, "that when the advantages of the commerce of Salonica shall be better known, and our merchant vessels shall be protected from the Pirates which almost constantly infest the Gulf, a trade highly beneficial to the interest of the United States will be carried out."[3]

As a result of joint international naval operations, in which the Greek and Ottoman fleets worked together, the pirates were cleared from the northern Aegean over the next few years and the expansion of commerce got under way. The tonnage of shipping entering Salonica increased five-fold in just three decades. Sail gave way to steam, and regionally based Greek and Ottoman ship-owners lost out to the French and Austrians who dominated the traffic to and from the main European ports. The sea still carried voyagers eastwards—Adolphus Slade's fellow-travellers in 1830 to Izmir included five Albanians, a Greek tobacco trader, local Turkish women on the *haj*, a Maronite bound for Lebanon and an Egyptian slave dealer with nine "negresses" whom he had failed to sell in Salonica. Coffee and spices still came from Yemen, and the *Azizieh* steamer docked regularly from Alexandria. But the city's orientation was changing. The slave trade, which had linked the city with suppliers from Circassia and the Ukraine to Sudan, Benghazi and the Barbary coast, was targeted by British abolitionists: although it was not formally outlawed until 1880, even before then, slaves had to be smuggled in as domestic servants, or landed furtively outside the town before dawn on the wooden landing-stage in the Beshchinar gardens.[4]

Meanwhile, as local raw materials were exported to western Europe from the hinterland, European manufactures poured in: Manchester cottons and Rouen silks, beer from Austria, watches and jewellery from

Switzerland, wine and marble, worsteds and cutlery from Germany, French stationery and perfumes, drugs, billiard tables, cabinets and fancy upholstery. The British consul noted the growing demand for "British-made shoes and boots, felt and straw hats, men's flannels, cotton and linen shirts and vests, handkerchiefs, ties, stockings and socks." Between 1870 and 1912 the city's imports nearly quadrupled in value.

Land communications lagged behind. "Sometimes you overtake long strings of camels led by the invariable little donkey, and laden with bales of merchandise, passing slowly along the road," noted a traveller in 1860. "And occasionally a train of heavy Bulgarian carts drawn by buffaloes; the wheels of which are never greased, creaking, groaning and screeching in a manner quite inconceivable in civilized countries." After the Crimean War, the Ottoman authorities tried to improve or inaugurate new "imperial" roads. However, the cash-strapped central government could not afford to provide funds, and the provincial authorities were forced to conscript peasant labour and raise taxes locally. Quickly it became clear that no roads would ever be finished, or if they were finished maintained, by such methods. "My estate is only eight miles from Salonica," wrote one land-owner in 1877 "and five years ago the magnificent highway road to Serres was made and passes close to the property. The road has never been touched from that day to this and is now impassable for wheeled carriages. The result is that although I have an excellent market only eight miles off, I must send all my grain to it on pack-animals."[5]

It would take a long time before the regional road system was substantially improved—not until French and British technology arrived with the Army of the Orient in the First World War. In the meantime, what finally ended the city's isolation by land was rail. In 1852 the German scientist and traveller Ami Boué had proposed the construction of four major lines in the Ottoman Balkans, and over the coming years, local entrepreneurs and diplomats promoted the advantages of rail connections. In 1864 two English engineers surveyed the route between Salonica and Monastir, and finally in 1871, work finally began on a line from Salonica to Pristina: the first section of just over sixty miles was opened, after tortuous progress, in July 1872. The line was extended northwards to Skopje and more than a decade later it was linked up to the Serbian network and central Europe. "In a little while," wrote a local journalist in January 1886, "any one of us will be able, on the third night after leaving our city, to hear the finest musicians in the *Grande Opera* in Paris, and the merchant in a few days to equip his stores with

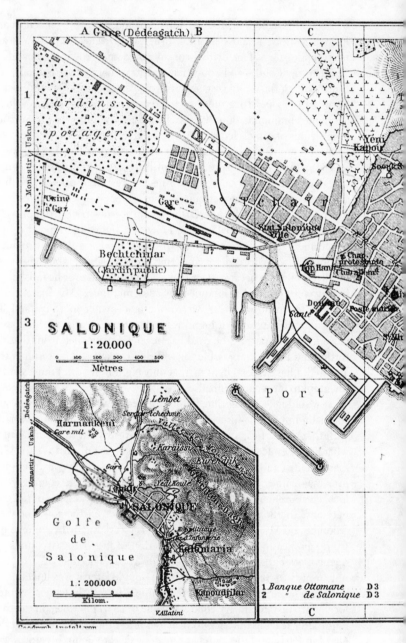

The late Ottoman city and its surroundings, *c.* 1910

t St Paul
des Derviches
eurs.

1

Yédi Koulé
(Heptapyrgion)
Prison

Jakoub Pacha Dj.

Porte

Porte

Porte

2

Seray Dj.

Nhamteh Monastic

Porte
Kouchakli
Koulé

Eski Seray Dj.

Minaret

Kassimié Dj.

Iskendistar Dj.

St Nicolas

3

Cimetière

Telli
Kapou

Eski Djouma Dj.

Cimetière
israélite

Française

Aya Sofia
Lycée
Arché Galère
Orhani Sultan Dj.
Isakieh

4

Eg. Metropolitaine

Karash Dj.

Cim

Béaz Koulé

5

Case..
d'infanterie
Hôpital
militaire

E
F
Kalamaria
G

Wagner & Debes, Leipzig.

Parisian or Viennese products." When, two years later, the connection with Europe was made, the train from Paris was greeted by a crowd of thirty thousand excited bystanders. "For half a mile before the train came to the main station the track was lined on both sides with dense rows of people," wrote a Prussian reporter. "Never in my life have I seen such an uproar, such a waving of shawls and hands. This reached a tremendous crescendo as the train finally came to a halt in the station, where the noise reached a fortissimo which literally deafened us. It is impossible to describe the shouting and the crush."[6]

A second track connected Salonica with the important administrative, commercial and military town of Monastir, and a third line later linked it to Istanbul. Abdul Hamid himself had hesitated before granting permission for this but the Ottoman general staff wanted to be able to move troops between Asia Minor and the Balkans. Opened in April 1896, the line proved its value the following year when it became "the right arm of the Ottoman government" in the war with Greece, and the secret of its unexpected victory. Keeping away from the coast, it meandered through the plains of Thrace and the foothills of the Rhodope mountains. Even today, the stretch after Xanthi that follows the Nestos River into its twisting roadless gorge—travelled now only by a few back-packers, gypsies and Turkish tobacco-merchants—makes one of the most dramatic rides in Europe.[7]

In just over twenty years, therefore, foreign speculators and engineers equipped European Turkey with more than seven hundred miles of track. The *shimen defair* as they were known in the city may have been a mixed blessing for Salonica's hinterland since they diverted traffic away from the roads, and probably helped the latter fall into even greater disrepair. On the other hand, they had a catalytic effect on the city itself, linking it more tightly than ever before to the world beyond.[8] A letter travelling from Salonica to Paris in the early part of the nineteenth century took a good month, no different from Roman times. By the 1860s this had been cut to about two weeks by steam-boat, and rail cut it further to sixty-three hours. By this point, the city was also in telegraphic communication with England, Austria, Italy and Istanbul. As a result, foreign reporters—a litmus test of international accessibility—started to arrive: first spotted in the Near Eastern crisis of 1877–78, their numbers increased during the Greco-Turkish war of 1897— Bigham of the *Times*, Gueldan of the *Morning Post*, Peel of the *Daily Telegraph*, Fetzer, the military correspondent for *Über Land und Meer*— and by the beginning of the twentieth century, they were coming in droves to report every twist and turn of the Macedonian Struggle. Later the trains would carry others too—troops heading inland, and refugees heading out. Without rail, it would scarcely have been possible to engineer the huge forced movements of entire peoples that were to transform the city beyond all recognition over the following seventy years.

All this had taken place thanks to the Ottoman economy's opening to European capital and expertise, and the speculative frenzy that accompanied this. "Travel where you will, in any part of Turkey," wrote James Baker in 1877, "and in every small town you will find many of the wealthiest people who can think and talk of nothing else but Turkish bonds; and there is quite a feverish excitement on the subject." Talked up, the prospects grew brighter and brighter, despite the imperial government's large debts. In the early 1880s, pundits predicted that the economy of Macedonia would be transformed by rail: the Serbian trade would be diverted southwards, perhaps even the India mail might be wrested from Brindisi. The British consul forecast that once the Skopje line was linked to the Austrian railway system, Salonica would become the leading centre of commerce in the Levant. "Is it necessary to recall how the entire press was publishing on the exceptional situation of this city, and on the importance which it must inevitably assume once in direct communication with the Balkan powers and central Europe?" wrote the French consul in 1892. In the event, Izmir, Alexandria and even Trieste outstripped the Macedonian port. Yet the dreams and ambitions were important, for they expressed the apparently boundless confidence that was turning a new force in the city—its bourgeoisie—into the motor of municipal change, cultural revolution and economic growth.[9]

SCHOOLING THE BOURGEOISIE

IN 1768 THERE WERE ONLY ONE HUNDRED European residents; by the end of the nineteenth century there were nearly ten thousand. The quarter where they had lodged since Byzantine times was close to the port and the new wheat market, with its warehouses and broking agents. In 1854, before the commercial boom had really got under way, Boué found "houses made of stone, two storeys high, with glass windows and painted blinds. In some of them you might well imagine yourself in Europe." By the end of the century, the district contained the French and German churches, the Deutsche Klub, the Théâtre Français, banks, post offices and expensive hotels, travel bureaux, consulates, bookshops and chemists. It was here that for much of the century lived the Charnauds, Chasseauds and Abbotts, bearers of a way of life which through inter-marriage and long residence combined European and Ottoman traditions, languages and occupations.[10]

More important (and richer) even than the Franks themselves were those local honorary Europeans—the prosperous Greek and Jewish merchants under consular protection—whose close commercial and intellectual connections with Europe and prominent position in their own communities within the city made them natural cultural intermediaries. In 1873, the cream of this elite—the Jews Hugo Allatini, Joseph Misrachi, Samuel Modiano and the Greek Perikles Hadzilazaros—combined forces with the British consul John Blunt and the Levantine banker John Chasseaud to found the *Cercle de Salonique* in order to provide facilities "for society and travellers." The idea had probably been Blunt's but the club clearly met a need for it lasted for more than eighty years. It provided a model of sociability that had not existed before—a luxurious meeting-place for the city's new cross-confessional upper class, and for important foreign visitors. By 1887 there were 159 members, including Jews, Greeks, Germans, Italians, Turks, Armenians and others. Among them were Alfred Abbott (Jackie Abbott's nephew), the tobacco-merchant and future mayor Husni Bey, Dimitris Zannas, a Greek doctor to the city's upper crust, the police chief Selim Bey, and the city's most famous lawyer, *maître* Emmanuel Salem, a long-standing member of the governing council of the Jewish community and secretary of the new Lawyers' Guild. These were the city's new masters—professional men, army officers, diplomats, bankers, land-owners and traders—and they insisted in the club regulations that political or other passions should not be allowed to disrupt the fundamental spirit of social harmony and comradeship.[11]

The chief battles they were waging—and from the 1870s winning—were with their own archbishops and rabbis. The Allatinis and Fernandes families among the Jews, the Hadzilazaros, Rongottis and Prasakakis among the Greeks, were not merely the presentable face of the city—its "society"—for Western visitors of standing, but more importantly, they were the architects of a shift of power within the city from the old elites to the new commercial class whose aspirations they embodied. It was the generation of Moses Allatini (1800–1882), educated at Pisa and Florence, the man described by one historian as the "real regenerator of the Jewish community of Salonica" and one of the city's first industrialists, which initiated the challenge of the moneyed classes to their own religious leaders.

This clash was produced directly by the contradictory consequences of the Ottoman legislative reforms. As we have seen, one effect of the 1839 Gulhané decree, which aimed to promote equality between the empire's religious communities, was to throw the weight of the Ottoman state behind the metropolitan and the chief rabbi, the recognized leaders of their communities. But at the same time, the freeing-up of trade, the consolidation of private property rights and the growth of the city's economy, especially after the Crimean War, increased the fortunes and the political weight of its traders and businessmen. Conservative religious leaders had not bothered much to bridge the cultural cleavage between them. Chief Rabbi Molho, for instance, had tried to play off his support among the poor to criticize the merchant notables for their religious laxity. He had excommunicated a youthful member of the Fernandes family for going hunting with the city's consuls and eating non-kosher meat; his successor locked up Jewish printers on charges of printing unauthorized books, in an effort to affirm the power of the rabbinical censors and stamp down on secular learning. But in 1856 an imperial decree introduced the principle of representative government within the empire's *millets*, leaving it to members of those communities to decide how they wished to govern themselves. Thereafter, the key issue for both Christians and Jews was to establish how much power religious leaders would be forced to hand over to the lay members of the new communal councils. When Abdul Mecid visited Salonica in 1859, he granted a personal audience only to those Jewish notables "with whom he could converse in French," leaving the rabbinate out in the cold. Under pressure from merchants, doctors and lawyers of liberal views, crucial changes were slowly made at the top of the religious leadership: the increasingly conservative Ascher Covo was replaced as chief rabbi on his death in 1874 by the more flexible Abraham Gattegno—elected for the first time by a vote of the new General Assembly of the community—and the wealthy stratum of the Jewish bourgeoisie eventually persuaded his successor—with the aid of the intervention of the Ottoman governor—to implement the administrative reforms agreed some fifteen years earlier, by adopting communal statutes which limited the chief rabbi's role in communal affairs. Similar struggles went on between "aristocratic" and "democratic" factions among the city's Greeks over the introduction of the General

Regulations for the Orthodox communities of the empire: there too the new influence granted to lay leaders of the community accompanied a narrowing of the juridical and fiscal powers of the religious hierarchy.[12]

The struggle for communal authority was fought out over many areas—care for the poor and sick, the upkeep of cemeteries, the administration of religious foundations themselves—but the key battleground was education. For religious learning alone was no longer enough. Ties with the West meant also that local merchants needed employees to be familiar with modern languages, mathematics and geography. The notable Jewish families pushed hard for the use of Italian and French books in the old Talmud Torah in the 1840s. When they got nowhere, they obtained a firman to found their own pilot school, run by a German rabbi whom the local rabbis regarded as an impious foreigner. But the real educational revolution among Salonican Jewry only came in 1873 when the same notables opened a branch of the Paris-based Alliance Israélite Universelle—the very embodiment of French Enlightenment liberalism—in the teeth of fierce opposition from the elderly chief rabbi. It was an extraordinary success: by 1912 the Alliance was responsible for educating more than four thousand pupils, over half the total number of children in Jewish schools. "I was once invited to an annual gathering of the Israelite Alliance," wrote a British journalist during the First World War. "There were many hundreds of Jews there, male and female, and a great many of them were once removed only from the street porter class. But they rattled off French as if they had been born to it." Not only were the majority of the city's Jewish children receiving an education outside the control of the religious authorities, but they were receiving it on the basis of the principles of contemporary French republicanism. Such a trend had a corrosive effect on the authority of the chief rabbi, and helped turn him slowly into more and more of a purely religious and spiritual figurehead.[13]

Within the Greek community similar shifts were taking place. In the old days, children learned reading and writing from the occasional literate priest or from the so-called *didaskaloi* who gave lessons as they passed through the city. But in 1828 the junior high school was re-established, and a girls' school was set up in 1845. The primary school population climbed from 1500 in 1874 to nearly 2000 in 1900 and 3900 by the time the Greek army arrived in 1912. An Educational Society was set up in 1872 with its own private library and a commitment to "useful knowledge," and in 1876 a teacher-training college followed. Salonica's Greek high school was recognized by the University of

Athens, a development of huge significance for the rise of Greek nationalism, and the control of school standards and appointments was also handled by representatives of the Greek state. Through education, in other words, the Greeks of Salonica gradually reoriented themselves towards the new national centre in Athens. The Patriarchate in Istanbul, which had once enjoyed unchallenged authority over the empire's Orthodox believers, found itself losing ground.[14]

Within the city's Muslim community, pedagogical arguments were also raging. Ali Riza, a minor customs official, quarrelled with his wife, Zübeyde, over how to educate their son, Mustafa. Zübeyde, a devout woman who was nicknamed the *mollah*, followed the older conception of education and wanted him to attend the neighbourhood Qur'anic school. His father, on the other hand, favoured the new style of schooling pioneered by a renowned local teacher, Shemsi Effendi, who ran the first private primary school in the empire. In the end, the young Mustafa started at the first and finished at the second, before moving to the military preparatory college. Helped by his education and by Salonica's new beer-gardens and nightlife, he became a pronounced secularist, thereby foreshadowing in his own upbringing the trajectory through which—by then better known to the world as Mustafa Kemal Ataturk—he would later lead post-Ottoman Turkey.

Mustafa Kemal's experiences were not unusual, for the spirit of Western education was transforming local Muslim cultures of learning. The *Ma'min* were setting up private schools like Shemsi's, and state officials like Mustafa Kemal's father shared their vision of a modernizing Islam. Investment in education had been a priority of the reformers in Istanbul, and in 1869 a new imperial Ordinance of General Education outlined a school system, based partly on the French lycée model, that would promote knowledge of science, technology and commerce among both boys and girls. Reaction from the long-established *medreses* was fierce but under Sultan Abdul Hamid this was overcome, in part by emphasizing the Islamic character of the new schools. A state schooling sector emerged in Salonica and the city's first vocational college, the *Ecole des Arts et Métiers*, trained orphans in typography, lithography, tailoring and music. Later came a teacher-training college, a junior high school, a commercial school and a preparatory school for civil servants—the *Idadié*—housed in an imposing neo-classical building standing just beyond the eastern walls. (Today it contains the chief administrative offices of the University of Thessaloniki.) In 1908 it was joined by a law school and by specialist colleges for farmers, gendarmes and army officers. By the century's end, there were at least nine public and private schools, teaching more than five thousand boys and girls, including a scattering of Christians and Jews as well as Muslims.[15]

Even the Great Powers were piling in to stamp their cultural predominance upon the city's schools. In addition to the *Alliance Israélite*, local Francophiles had the choice of the *Mission Laïque*, the *Lycée* and the Brothers and Sisters of St. Vincent de Paul; for Italophiles, there was the *Scuola Nazionale Italiana*, the *Principessa Iolanda* and the commercial college *Umberto I*. Romanians, Serbs, Germans and Armenians could all attend schools in their preferred tongue; there was even an International English School for Girls. A typical class at the Petit Lycée Français in 1904 had three French pupils, one Greek, four Jews, a Serb, a *Ma'min*, an Armenian, a Turk and a Montenegrin. This was the city's new cross-national cosmopolitan elite in embryo, for whom the ways of European bourgeois life were slowly erasing the old markers of religious and communal difference.

EUROPEAN FASHIONS WERE ALSO STEADILY INFILTRATING Salonica's middle-class homes. Around 1840 most people still lived in modestly furnished, almost Spartan surroundings. Perhaps poverty explained why a certain Abu Bakr, for instance, on his death in 1847 left only a wardrobe, two pistols, a bandolier, an amber pipe, a coffee grinder and a grey horse. But at that time even the well-off rarely handed on more than a few kilims and prayer carpets, some chests, a stove against Salonica's bitter winters, a mattress and a chair or two. By 1900 however, the carpets were often "European," and the furniture frequently included high marble-topped tables, sideboards, large clocks, mirrors and other signs of *alafranga* taste.

Having become commonplace in prosperous Greek and Jewish households, such items were now found also in Muslim homes. Emine, the well-off daughter of Osman Effendi, possessed two wardrobes, half a dozen salon chairs, mirrors and lamps; Iskender Pasha left a huge fortune to his children, as well as a mansion which contained sofas and settees, antique clocks and valuable "European" carpets. Huseyin Husni Effendi, a member of the provincial assembly, must have been among the wealthiest men in the city when he died in 1887; his home contained numerous sofas, glass-fronted *armoires*, pictures and photographs, two marble-topped side tables, nine large mirrors, eleven armchairs and no less than forty-two chairs. The transformation in attitudes and taste was rapid, and when a Jewish boy at the Petite Lycée was invited home by a Muslim class-mate, he was struck by what he found: "I was not a little surprised at first to find that the women in Shakri's household, his mother and two older sisters, admitted me to their apartment. But I was still more amazed to find myself in their midst without their making a pretence of covering their faces. They acted as if there was nothing untoward in their behaviour, greeting me in excellent French, and making me feel at home by resuming their sewing and embroidery work."[16]

Typical Salonican bourgeois homes preserved a mixture of European and Ottoman furnishings. The opulence of the Allatini household was certainly not typical—its palatial dimensions left one guest breathless when he stayed in 1888—but it too blended East and West: a "crowd" of magnificently tall servants dressed in the traditional Albanian *fustanella*, pistols and daggers tucked into their wide belts, offered newcomers the usual sugared fruits, coffee and cigars in a lavishly decorated and brightly lit reception room, before leading them to private apartments decked out with valuable old carpets, cushions and bedside tables equipped with drinks, sweetmeats and writing materials. The furnishings of the "grand old palace" of the British consul were slightly more modest: strewn with Turkish carpets, and adorned with old Spanish chests and what was described as "Chinese porcelain from Bulgaria," the house suited both Salonica's governor, Dervish Pasha, who felt comfortable enough to lay out his prayer mat and make his afternoon prayers in the presence of Mrs. Blunt, and the young British naval officers who danced the polka and played tug-of-war in the garden. Soon the European trademarks of success even invaded places of worship. The *sheykh* of the Mevlevi order had his own visiting cards. And in the synagogue attended by the Modianos, one of the wealthiest merchant families, the festival candles were "Europeanized by having donors' visiting cards neatly attached with silk ribbons."[17]

It was, above all, in matters of dress that the growing enthusiasm for European fashions hit the eye. When Stefana, the peasant girl whose conversion caused so much trouble, arrived at Salonica that fateful May noon in 1876 and was seized by Christian passers-by to prevent her abjuring her faith, their common religion was not the first thing she noticed; interrogated by the police shortly after, she described the men who had carried her off as *Franks*—frock-coated and with short beards. In her mind, the gulf in station between peasant and urban bourgeoisie was far greater than anything religion could bridge. Before long the *francos* were widely imitated. "Soft-hatted, his waist-coat unbuttoned beneath his garish cravat, trousers impeccably pressed, turned up at the bottom to reveal gaudy socks inside his polished shoes," wrote Nehama, the doyen of the historians of Salonica, satirizing the European style spreading through the new middle-class dandy. "He affects a knowing exoticism, getting himself up with exquisite care, he strains laboriously to set himself above the vulgar herd, to appear at all costs chic, smart, the last word in fashion." A decade later, an English visitor noticed "the young women copying Athens and Paris in short skirts and high-heeled yellow boots." Thus adorned, the city's young frequented the cafés, beer-gardens, clubs and theatres which were springing up to cater for them. They could watch a French balloonist ascend from the garden of the Hotel Colombo, catch the performing troupe of Ambrosio Botini, shop in the city's new department stores—Stein and Orosdi Back—or merely enjoy its carefully tended public parks and promenades.[18]

THE EUROPEANIZATION OF SPACE

IN 1868, ISTANBUL BECAME THE EMPIRE'S FIRST CITY to be granted a municipal council. Based upon the French model and equipped with powers to expropriate property for the public good, it demolished walls, widened and straightened roads and improved lighting, paving and sanitation. The next year the experiment was extended to Salonica, whose newly prosperous bourgeoisie—led mostly by Jews, *Ma'min* and Greeks—found a willing partner in the Muslim-led local government. The municipality directed the attention of the Muslim elite away from their landed estates in the hinterland and back to the city itself; hesitantly at first, then with greater confidence, it became the promoter and regulator of urban life.

In the old days, cities had chiefly been run by the pasha and the *kadi*—both of whom also had regional responsibilities—aided by guild chiefs, neighbourhood headmen and communal leaders. But pashas came and went almost annually, and lack of proper revenue-raising powers made investing in urban improvement impossible. Just how difficult this was, even when there was strong local pressure for change, had been demonstrated in the sporadic and largely ineffectual attempts to ward off plague and cholera. To fight fires, Salonica traditionally relied on levies of youths drawn from the twelve main trade guilds.

Individual householders were assigned the responsibility for keeping roads, gutters and pavements outside their homes clean and in good repair, and could be reported by their *imam* or neighbourhood head if they neglected their duties. Now these tasks began to be seen as the responsibility of the state.[19]

In 1869 Sabri Pasha came as governor from Izmir, where he had carried out an ambitious modernization of the port. His strategy for Salonica was very similar—to open it up by demolishing stretches of the walls and extending its commercial and harbour facilities. Up to then, the old sea-wall had stood as a barrier to the outside world. "I never remember before to have seen a town so closely walled along the seafront," noted a traveller, shortly before work began. Throughout late-nineteenth-century Europe, urban growth was bringing down the medieval walls—1860 in Antwerp and Barcelona, 1870 in Amsterdam and 1878 in Vienna. Sabri Pasha was thus scarcely behind the times when he took his silver hammer to the sea-wall and cast the first stone into the water. His timid taps marked the start of the most ambitious building programme in Salonica's history.[20]

In order to enlarge the port, Sabri Pasha proposed to use the rubble from the old walls as landfill to build out into the bay. The new frontage would then be sold off to developers to finance badly needed improvements, as well as providing space for new public buildings, and even a public park. He also envisaged a waterfront avenue with tramways to allow traffic to traverse the city without snarling up the main road through the town. It was a brilliantly imaginative scheme which permitted expansion into the flatter land on either side of the walls. With the demolition of the old Vardar gateway, and the stretch of the eastern walls running up from the White Tower, the city for the first time in its history lay open to the outside world and began the process of suburban growth which has continued with virtually no interruption up to the present.

Although the Porte approved the scheme, it had to be self-financing and thus its success depended on the willingness of the city's new mercantile elite to participate. Following an advertising campaign, individual entrepreneurs and state organizations such as the new Imperial Ottoman Bank and the Imperial Post bought up many plots; European investors acquired nearly half. Bounded by the port at one end, and the White Tower at the other, Salonica's new face to the world included "hotels and modern houses, warehouses and magazines, in the uninteresting style of European civilization." The Splendid Palace Hotel, the

Olympos and the d'Angleterre hosted visitors, and their balconies offered future orators and politicians a new setting: crowds gathered, for instance, to hear the speeches made from the first floor of the Olympos Hotel in July 1908, at the start of the Young Turk revolution. Along the quay were the cafés, cabarets, beer-gardens and music-halls that carried noise deep into the night—"red frocks and shrill music, Turkish guitars, gypsy violins, Greek melodies and dirty French songs," noted Berard on arriving in 1896. Caiques moored along the front next to the new marble embarkation point, and from 1894 horse-drawn trams carried passengers from the railway station to the garden and restaurant which had been established next to the White Tower.

Larger public works projects were delayed by financing difficulties. Schemes to improve the harbour passed from one group of private capitalists to the next, obliging most ships to lie at anchor off-shore and transfer their merchandise by lighter. Even when the port was completed, its dues were so high that shippers were put off from using it. But on a smaller scale the combined forces of the market and the local authorities functioned much better. Sabri Pasha himself opened up the main shopping street which led from the governor's *konak* down to the quay. Rue Sabri Pasha, as it became known, marked the boundary between two worlds. On one side, down twisting narrow lanes, lay the Talmud Torah, the centre of Jewish religious life, and the old flour market, the *Oun Kapan*, set in a large square surrounded by low rickety buildings and dilapidated stalls. In the late nineteenth century it was crowded with Vlach shepherds selling off their lambs, villagers bringing in barrows of limes, cucumbers and watermelons, "tinware and earthenware, rice and lentils, live poultry and mutton, prints and calicoes, sea urchins and squids." Here one found the wandering Albanian *yogurtdjis*, local ice-sellers, and the aproned Muslim butchers whose mules carried chopping boards to cut joints, entrails and—a great delicacy—entire lambs' heads. Under the huge plane trees nearby, buying and selling went on as it had done for centuries.

On the other side of Sabri Pasha, however, lay a very different world, marked with the grand monuments to capitalist power—the new headquarters of the Banque de Salonique, the Imperial Ottoman Bank and the Passage Lombardo. And whereas elsewhere shopkeepers squatted on platforms at the front of their windowless stalls, in the old style, down Sabri Pasha itself retailers displayed their merchandise behind glass windows. "Montres Omega, or, argent et metal," advertised Mallah Frères at number 78. Further along were military outfit-

Saint Dimitrios and his city. A sixteenth century icon.

left The Greco-Roman-Christian synthesis: Saint Dimitrios flanked by the bishop and the prefect, the patrons of his church, seventh century mosaics, Church of Ayios Dimitrios.

below The Slavic threat: Byzantine forces drive a Bulgarian army away from the city, miniature from the chronicle of Ioannis Skylitzes, eleventh–twelfth century AD.

opposite Ottoman officials supervise the forced levy of Christian children from a Balkan town. In the foreground the children wait to be registered and to receive a stipend. Relatives and a priest watch from behind a wall. Sixteenth century Ottoman miniature.

کسی را که باشد و فرزند نیا | همیشه بود از نیکی بی‌نیاز | کنون شاه را در سرِ مهر سپال | چنین است قانون فرخنده فال

که سازد به حظّ از دریا | روانی نیکی که دارد وقار | کند مهر او و فرخنده‌ای | بروبر نوازش پی بندکی

گل‌های سپنج و فتادای ال | فراوانت ز برگِ سبز نهال | زگلگونه نوع لالۀ دهست | چو گل بیه برسرِ اند و هسته

گرد و به گردِ ولایت تمام | ستانذ زمر خانۀ نیکِ غلام | پولاد کلامی به بهر برکش | پُرنجه قبایی کنند در برش

above Sultan Murad II (*c.*1403–1451) the conqueror of Salonica, and father of Mehmed II, who finally captured Constantinople two years after Murad's death. Sixteenth century Ottoman miniature.

left A Jewish merchant and doctor in Ottoman dress. Istanbul, 1574.

Visitors arrive at the home of a Jewish merchant to examine Las Incantadas. Their host offers coffee to the British consul watched by his wife and daughters from the balcony. In the background are James Stuart and Nicholas Revett, British antiquarians, the consul's son (the only one in European dress) and the consul's Greek interpreter. Sketched in 1754, this picture is the first life drawing of the city to survive. The statues themselves were carted off to the Louvre a century later.

The Arch of Galerius at the end of the main street as drawn by Edward Lear, 1848.

left Jewish singers and musicians, late nineteenth century.
below left Jewish marriage contract, 1790.

opposite Jewish wet-nurse (*left*) and Bulgarian peasant bride (*right*), *c.*1860.
below The picturesque city: the panorama from the fortress slopes, Edward Lear, 1848.

above Greece triumphant: Prince Constantine takes the Ottoman surrender of the city, in 1912, as depicted in a popular lithograph.

right A backstreet near the Rotonda, 1913.

ters, boot-makers, confectioners, fur shops, Molho's bookshop, stationers and money-changers. In 1907 the *Fils de Mustafa Ibrahim* opened *Au Louvre*, a large store which sold chandeliers, large brass and copper lamps and other adornments for the home. At its upper end, Rue Sabri Pasha was covered by a traditional wooden canopy but lower down this ended, the road opened out and one came to Salonica's first department stores, and a small piazza flanked by cafés and hotels, the fashionable heart of the town, with a view of the bay and the landing-stage.

The municipal council itself was set up during Sabri Pasha's tenure but only began really to stamp its authority on the city under the dynamic leadership of Galib Pasha, who served on and off as governor between 1882 and 1891. Helped by railway fever, the new quay and the wheat market were paved with stone, the Rue Egnatia was straightened, and a grand Haussmanian avenue, the Boulevard Hamidié, running parallel with Sabri Pasha on the east side of the city, was built along the line of the demolished walls: its elegant neo-classical villas proved immediately popular with the new elite. After the 1890 fire, which destroyed a large part of the southeastern section of the old city, more central streets were widened and straightened. Four years later, foreign investors brought horse-drawn trams—the cars themselves Belgian, the horses Hungarian, the engineers Italian—which careered hazardously around the curving streets of the old town. Other investors modernized the water supply, and introduced gas lighting into the heart of the city. The urban map was being redrawn in the interests of regularity, accessibility and predictability while the centres of governmental power—the governor's new *konak*, the barracks, the municipal hospital and the vast customs house—were connected by new or enlarged roads. They, and the bastions of commercial success from Allatini's giant flour mills in the east to Saias's textile factory on the front and the railway stations in the west, now defined the city and pointed to the new coalition of forces—the autocratic central Hamidian state and the wealthy local capitalist class—which ran its affairs.

Naming the *Mahala*

WHAT A BREAK THIS REPRESENTED with a past, and what a radical shift in the way the city's inhabitants understood their own surroundings, can be conveyed by looking at place-names. The old streets within the walls were tortuous, narrow and mostly unnamed. There were no maps and navigation was difficult for strangers. "How useful the minarets are," commented one visitor, "for guidebooks are not to be had at Salonica." Residents were classified by Ottoman officials, and identified themselves, by their neighbourhood (*mahala*) whose nicknames made no sense to outsiders. Kaldigroç was a corruption of the Judeo-Spanish *Kal de los Gregos*, the Street of the Greeks; Bedaron, an abbreviation of the synagogue *Beth Aron*. There was the "Quarter of the Three Eggs"—named after a decorated marble slab on the façade of an old house—"At the Fire" (after an especially bad one) and "Defterdar," because a treasurer of the province had once lived there. Other neighbourhoods were known after local places of worship and their nicknames. There was the "Red Mosque," the "Mosque of the Clocktower" and the "Burned Monastery" district, from the destruction caused by a Venetian bombardment two centuries earlier. The Ashkenazi synagogue was known as "Russia" or "Moscow," Poulia as *Macarron*, from its members' supposed fondness for pasta; the salt-farmers' synagogue, Shalom, was called *Gamello*, after the camels who carried the salt (but also local slang for a dullard or idiot).

In such a society, directories and maps were neither known nor needed. Jewish men were called to prayer each morning by street criers, who were also paid to call out invitations to weddings and funerals and to spread news of public importance. The *muezzin* could see the entire quarter beneath him when he made the call to prayer. Nightwatchmen were supported by each neighbourhood, and kept an eye out for strangers—for if they misbehaved or got into trouble, all the residents round about could end up worse off—and street fountains acted as magnets for local women, or *mahalushas*, to exchange gossip and rumours. "People live and work with their doors open, on the streets," noted a visitor. "It is in the streets that they cook, hammer and beat. Workshop, shop, display—all is one."[21]

Places thus acquired names according to an entirely locally generated logic. Many small alleys and cul-de-sacs were nameless, or known by such helpful terms as "Rocky Place," or "Behind the Square of the Graveyard." Larger streets changed name several times as they wound their way past mosques and shrines. What today appears on maps as Muses Street, in the Upper Town, at this time lay mostly in the quarter of Two Balconies (*Iki Serife*, named after the minaret of the local mosque which was noted for this unusual feature), and was known in successive stretches as Hizir Baba, Iki Serifeli Cami, Ali Baba Turbe, Kasimiye Binari, Zafer Baba Dergahi and Kara Tas. Other streets were named after trees—Black Mulberry Street, the School by the Plane

Trees Street, Plane Tree Mosque, the Street of the Burned Plane Tree—and springs (Elm Spring, the Place of Water, Bitter Spring, Salty Water, Fresh Water, even the Well of Malaria).

But at the very end of the nineteenth century, this localized way of naming space was challenged by new conceptions of what place-names should do. "The Sadikario house, situated in the Arnaout-Fournou (Albanian bakery) quarter, is providing unpleasant competition to the Tower of Pisa," wrote a journalist in September 1896. "The wall of its external façade makes an acute angle with the street . . . But don't enquire after the precise location of the quarter, the street or the house . . . A number, a street sign, a name would quickly inform you, but the municipality still refuses to give us these indispensable markers which are found in the most humble village abroad."[22]

The municipality eventually issued the first street names in May 1898, although their usefulness for strangers was initially limited by being written only in Turkish. A more fundamental problem was that those choosing the new names had not properly understood the logic which was supposed to lie behind them. It was as well they had only been in Turkish—for what would Europeans have made of the "Street that leads to Miltiades' Coffeeshop," or the "Street of the Greengrocer Constantine?" Local journalists tried to explain to the authorities the error of their ways:

> We know that in Europe streets are given names of celebrated men whose memory it is wished to honour or those of noble citizens who have rendered useful services to their country. But we do not see how the said Constantine with his plums and his bad coffee, or M. Miltiadis, pouring out his raki, can raise the prestige of the city so far as to be honoured by the municipal scribe.
>
> In Europe, squares and wide avenues carry as an honorific title the dates of national triumphs, the names of cities where the national army covered itself in glory, or where great generals are illustrated: the Boulevard Magenta and the Avenue de la Grande Armée in Paris, the Strada Manin in Venice, Trafalgar Square in London, are monuments which speak to the hearts of patriots. Each crossroads is a lesson and History is written on the walls. And is the history of our dear country so lacking in these glorious occasions?[23]

One conception of the past—the past which linked the city dweller's pride in his country to that in his city—was coming to impose itself on another—the past as local memory. No longer was it thought appropriate to commemorate random fires, the Old Horsemarket, the Old Quarantine, the Pasha's Baths or the Old Telegraph Station. Emperors, notable officials and elevated political values would be written over the plane trees, the bath-towel makers and the religious benefactors of the past who had made the city their own. These names were stamped with the authority of the new municipal bodies and conformed to European norms. Ironically, although they were more transparent than those they replaced, they proved far less durable. In the twentieth century, wars, revolutions and sudden changes of regime led names to be discarded and replaced with ever-increasing frequency. The civil servants and bureaucrats were kept busy, but the city's inhabitants were left little if any better off than they had been before.

MUNICIPAL IMPROVEMENT AND THE PRESS

THE PRESS APPEARED LATE IN SALONICA compared with other ports in the Levant, held back by the obstructive attitude of the local rabbinate. In fact, its birth coincided with that of the municipality itself. In 1869, Sabri Pasha founded an official weekly gazette called *Selanik*, which carried news, decrees and proclamations in four languages. There followed a Turkish weekly, *Rumeli*, and two major independent newspapers, the Jewish *La Epoca* and the Greek *Ermis*. In 1895 they were joined by the *Journal de Salonique* and the *Ma'min*-owned *Asr* (whose successor still appears in Turkey today).

Newspapermen were, by definition, non-conformists and sceptical of their own religious authorities. They had often suffered at the latter's hands and saw themselves on the side of progress, supporting the democratization of their own communities and cooperation with others. *Ermis*, for instance, identified Constantinople, not Athens, as the centre of Hellenism, and preached the necessity for the co-existence of Greeks and Turks. When the Jewish community leapt to the defence of the city's Greeks, following a derogatory article abroad, *Ermis* welcomed that too. Operating under the watchful censorship of the Hamidian regime, journalists publicized the civic-mindedness of the city's leaders and private benefactors and acted as mouthpieces for the state's Ottomanist ideal.[24]

Where they did feel free to strike a more critical and forceful note was in municipal affairs. The journalists were satirists of the old ways and proselytes for the new. Starting in 1880 they unleashed a barrage of criticism against the municipal council for its incompetence, and actually forced the resignation of the then mayor. The governor shut them down for three weeks for insulting public officials, a penalty which had to be repeated at intervals over the next few years.[25] It did not stop them in their self-appointed task of educating the members of the municipal council, and encouraging them to ever-further intervention and regulation. A sample of the areas in which the authorities were being urged to assume responsibility over just a few months in 1896 would include:

safety: "Saturday evening, on the quay opposite the Olympia, a distracted pedestrian bumped into a coil of mooring ropes and fell into the sea. The crowd, dense at that time, managed to drag him out safe and sound. These accidents could have been easily avoided if the municipality had taken up the giant iron rings set into the paving and placed them along the sea-wall itself."[26]

public health: "The construction of sewers in the fire zone [of 1890] has finally begun a few days ago; after a year of useless discussions, the municipal council has finally decided to act on this project of incontestable public utility."[27]

keeping the streets clean: "In the last month, mud has become a permanent feature of most of our roads, making circulation painful and even dangerous. We are truly pained to see our municipal counsellors left absolutely indifferent before this deplorable state of affairs."[28]

juvenile delinquency: "Some urchins belonging to the lower classes of the population, are not ashamed to undress on the quay and bathe shamelessly before the scandalized eyes of passing men and, especially, women. If these individuals apparently do not know the most elementary notions of decency, the agents of the police should remind them."[29]

bathing: "It is incontestable that Salonica is growing day by day in density of population. The more the city expands, the more bitter the struggle for existence. These rude daily assaults weaken the constitution, they bring exhaustion and illnesses most of which are capable of being cured by sea bathing . . . The building of a bathing station, comfortable, large, well-placed and presenting the dual advantages of hygiene and modern comfort, has been a necessity for years past."[30]

begging: "Perhaps it is time to deal with the problem of begging which has become a scourge in Salonica . . . The municipality alone can give a favourable solution to this question."[31]

Other, perhaps more sensitive, subjects were raised as items of news, with no further commentary: the plague of pickpockets, stabbings, shootings and street robberies; the issue of drunkenness leading to assaults in cafés and tavernas; and the question of prostitution. Here the authorities were more likely to be commended than criticized, brave policemen praised for their public-spiritedness; nevertheless, the necessity of official action was once again underlined.

In the pages of the press, a new balance is struck between public and private interest, between the enclosed space and the open. Widening the main street is greeted with enthusiasm, for it will give Salonica "the physiognomy of a grand European city." Openness—to the world, the surrounding countryside, to the street outside one's door—is a virtue. There is no longer any need, readers are reminded, not only for city walls, but even for the courtyard walls which still surround many houses. These are a sign of past times when security could not be guaranteed. If Salonica's inhabitants want a "new and light city," then they should demolish them and have more "trust" in each other. They should be "more sociable, leaving behind all unnecessary barriers more fitting for fields than houses, since day by day civilization spreads its beneficent wings."[32]

Civilization meant running water piped to the home by the Compagnie des Eaux de Salonique rather than long waits in the open air around communal wells and springs. The surge in Salonica's population had placed a huge strain on local water supplies and in the 1880s the newspapers had criticized the authorities for their indifference to the city's needs. Successive mayors had invested in the traditional solution of new public wells, but by 1893 Belgian investors had won the contract to establish a modern piping system. The journalists now directed their fire at the city's water carriers, from whom people used to buy their drinking water in the past: they were written off as fossils from a more primitive age, and those who could afford it were encouraged to subscribe to the Compagnie des Eaux—though subscription rates were well beyond the means of most. Modernity meant also not being afraid of gas lighting and of leaving behind the memories of a time when the nocturnal city was wrapped in darkness. It meant keeping the roads clean, not urinating in the streets now that public urinals had been constructed, taking action against the vile smells generated centrally by the fish market, local factories, oxen, donkeys and horses, and training housewives not to throw their slops outside the door.

Valuing business enterprise the city's press sometimes turned in their pages to the vast realm of investment possibilities. Why, one journalist urged, did not some clever businessman open up a building for wedding receptions: he would make much money, and passers-by would be freed from the crowds of guests that milled around and blocked the narrow streets whenever people got married. The owners of the private seashore villas were criticized for allowing people through their gardens for free swimming, since by doing so they were depriving investors who had set up special bathing areas of an income. But some kinds of entrepreneurs were clearly preferable to others. Wandering street-sellers were "the phylloxera of local trade": one ought not to buy from them because they offered unfair competition to shopkeepers and defrauded the public purse by not paying taxes. Between the old bazaar and the new shops along Sabri Pasha, there was no doubt which the journalist "Diogenes" preferred: the spectacle of the former was "truly repugnant—a real human morass of vendors of all sorts, bread, fruit, vegetables, set up in the best part of the road with no thought to the pedestrians whose passage they block."

Staying true to "Europe"—the ultimate goal—thus meant encouraging some activities and discouraging others. Mme. Evangelia Paraskevopoulou's performance of *La Dame aux Camélias* was highly praised. Tennis matches and the events of the White Star Cycling Club were covered in loving detail. Wrestling, on the other hand—one of the city's favourite sports—was condemned for its primitivism. "While Paris, London and everywhere else get excited about horse-racing, bicycling, yachting and a mass of other fashionable sports, Salonica, faithful to the cult of the past, will hear only about the fights of the *pehlivans*. At the news of a bout between famous wrestlers, the Salonican feels the same frisson of pleasure as the Catalan at the corrida." The epic bouts of Kara-Ahmed and Dramali Ali attracted crowds of eight thousand or more and were still talked about fifty years later; gypsy musicians, drums and clarinos blaring, heralded the fighters' parades through the streets; beys gave the victor live sheep, and belts of gold. Yet all this was mere embarrassment for the journalists of the *Journal de Salonique*. They would have been astonished to learn that the heroic Jim Londos and Timonides "the Macedonian" would be fighting it out with Mehmed Mustafa, Black Demon and John Patterson before huge crowds of appreciative Salonicans well into the 1960s.[33]

RICH AND POOR

IN THE 1890S, THE TRAMLINE which ran eastwards out of the city beyond the White Tower facilitated the emergence of a pleasant leafy new suburb along the shoreline of the bay. The municipality lined the avenue with acacias and provided a police station for the protection of its residents. Gradually many of the city's wealthiest families moved out and built themselves "towers" and villas with views over the sea to Mount Olympos. From their verandahs the fortunate residents could enjoy the evening breeze, watch the spectacular sunsets and see the lights come on in the city itself, a short distance around the Gulf. Here lay the city's future, at least as imagined by devotees of liberalism and progress—a future defined not by religion or language but by class.

At the avenue's end stood the imposing Villa Allatini, behind its park of pines. Sultan Abdul Hamid was exiled there in 1909, following the Young Turk revolution, and was shocked, on entering its doors, to find its owners had been so Westernized that they had omitted to build a Turkish-style bathroom. The road back into town was lined with the palatial homes of prominent Greek, Bulgarian, *Ma'min*, Jewish and Turkish families—the Château Mon Bonheur, for instance, the Villa Ida and the Villa Bianca—some of which still survive, though their once extensive gardens have shrunk, and their sea frontage has disappeared with postwar infill. Vitaliano Poselli, the elite's favourite architect, designed the new *Ma'min* mosque, the Yeni Djami, in a solid bourgeois Orientalizing style, and the Beth Saul synagogue, which survived until blown up by German troops in the summer of 1943. (He was also responsible for the Catholic and Armenian churches.) The merchant Osman Ali Bey constructed a renaissance villa with a magnificent sweeping staircase to the main door; Piero Arrigoni devised the *Ma'min* industrialist Mehmed Kapanzis a chalet-like residence complete with tower; the popular Greek architect Paionidis built a villa for a Turkish army officer which combined a baroque façade with neo-Orthodox onion-domes at its corners. More conservative Muslims and Jews preferred to remain in the older, crowded city centre where they could hear the familiar chant of the muezzin, the town crier and the nightwatchman. But others sought to avoid the diseases and over-crowding of the town, and enjoyed the distance from poverty, crime and disease the new suburb provided.

Yet if Kalamaria, with its "marble palaces," its "fashionable drive by the sea, screened by flowering acacias and garlanded with roses," was the preserve of the rich, the railway lines on the other side of the city were a magnet for the ever-growing numbers of indigent refugees and newly arrived peasants from villages in the interior. Between the station, the gas works and the new warehouses by the port lay the notorious Bara district, an area which had been a poisonous malarial swamp until it was partially drained in the 1870s. Thereafter as an industrial zone grew up around it, it became a muddy quarter of cheap wooden shacks, taverns and inns. Nearby was the humble Hirsch neighbourhood, an encampment of single-storey homes built thanks to the generosity of foreign benefactors, and the miserable rotten huts of the Mustafa Effendi and Simtov Nahmias quarters where the unheated dwellings were "unfit even for dogs."[34]

By the end of the century, poverty—always a feature of Salonican life—was becoming an overwhelming challenge to the municipal authorities and communal leaders. The city's rapid population growth—from roughly 30,000 in 1831 to more than 150,000 by 1913—had brought down the cost of wage labour and facilitated the economic boom. The power of many of the old guilds had been broken by the flood of cheap imports, while the new socialistic ideas which frightened some notables were slow to make their appearance; the mass of small artisanal concerns which made up the bulk of the city's manufacturing did not encourage unionization. When the governor Reouf Pasha shared the first tram ride in the city in 1893 with the company's Belgian manager, and commented on the cheapness of local labour compared with the cost of horses, the latter replied: "Had I known men cost so little here, I would not have bought horses to pull the cars."[35]

Communal bodies had always handled poor relief among their own brethren; there was, after all, a powerful local charitable tradition, and wealthy Christians, Jews and Muslims generally left bequests for the city's poor and needy. But the end of the nineteenth century saw private philanthropy applied in what one journalist called a "fever of charity." New hospitals, orphanages and clinics testified to the concern of community leaders—the colossal Greek Papapheion orphanage was easily the largest building in the city. There were dances, recitals and subscriptions to raise money for flood victims, refugees and the feeding of poor schoolchildren. For its part, the municipality provided free drugs and serums to fight diphtheria and its fledgling medical services attempted to regulate the activities of the many unlicensed doctors and pharmacists who operated there. But as the municipality could not even keep the streets clean, or the garbage collected promptly, the state and smell of the backstreet slums can be imagined, especially as the lack of fresh and safe drinking water in the homes of the poor allowed disease to spread. Out in the western suburbs, several hundred could fall victim to malaria in a bad summer.

Poverty had always plagued the Jews in particular; the 1835 census reveals a far higher proportion of Jews coming from poor households than anyone else, and their high birth rates (compared with the Christians and Muslims) and low average age of marriage intensified the problem. Towards the end of the century it was clear that despite the impressive wealth of a few, the vast majority of Jews lived in great misery. More than twenty thousand of the poorest of them were rendered homeless by the fire of 1890, and when another two thousand Ashkenazim arrived fleeing pogroms in the Tsarist lands, the "homeless turned the city into a camp." After the 1911 cholera epidemic which left hundreds dead, mostly from among the residents in the rotten and airless tenements of the centre of town, there was bitter criticism of both municipality and communal leaders. Nearly half the community was in receipt of welfare assistance by this point, and the new bourgeois leadership did not appear to have any more satisfactory answers to the plight of the poor than the rabbinate had had.

SALONICA'S NEW LINKS TO EUROPE did not strike everyone as an unmixed blessing. Writing in 1888 at the time of the first Paris train's arrival in the city, a Greek journalist had questioned the prevailing euphoria. "Even fearing lest we be denounced as pessimists," he wrote, "we cannot hide our opinion and declare that, in part at least, we do not share in the joy which this event has prompted." He went on to warn of the importation of "political ideas and opinions which scarcely serve the interests of our empire and which were not till now able to develop on account of the difficult and indirect state of communications." As for the moral aspect, he frankly anticipated the worst—"the poisonous seeds of social dissipation and corruption which we euphemistically call European civilization."[36]

Visitors greeted at the quay by the prostitutes from the *Alcazar di Salonico*, or surrounded by crowds of young Jewish men offering "every kind of encounter we might desire," knew what he meant. The city's flourishing prostitution trade was merely a symptom of social immiseration, however. For bringing the values of Europe to Salonica turned out to mean bringing its divisions too. The new cosmopolitan elite sought to bridge the gap between Christians, Muslims and Jews, but as they did so other, more fundamental social chasms opened up, between the rich and the poor, between factory-owners and workers. In the days of the old, walled city, rich and poor had lived as neighbours, sharing membership of congregations, and suffering Salonica's misfortunes together. But after 1880, as it expanded, they grew further apart.[37]

12

The Macedonia Question, 1878–1908

CATEGORIES

TRUSTING IN CAPITALISM and the prestige of the sultan to create common interests and allegiances, the leaders of fin-de-siècle Salonica promoted the idea of an Ottoman identity uniting the city's different communities. But how far were these really becoming more integrated? After all, Muslims still dominated the public sector, and there were hardly any non-Muslims employed by the municipality, or indeed the army. Because the 1856 Ottoman reforms had led each non-Muslim community to develop its own regulations for self-government, they seemed more rather than less self-contained at a time when the absolutist rule of Abdul Hamid stifled moves towards representative government in the country as a whole: in the words of historian Niyazi Berkes, they turned into "little non-territorial republics and incipient nations." "The most diverse civilizations shared [the city] but did not penetrate one another," wrote a local scholar in 1914. "The city was not one. Jews, Orthodox, Donmehs, Muslims, lived side by side, without mixing, each shut in its community, each speaking its language." Or as the city's main workers' newspaper wrote in 1911: "Salonica is not one city. It is a juxtaposition of tiny villages. Jews, Turks, Donmehs, Greeks, Bulgarians, Westerners, Gypsies, each of these groups which one today calls 'Nations,' keeps well away from the others, as if fearing contagion."[1]

As European visitors arrived to "form an accurate opinion on that most important question—the present state and future destinies of the Levant," they were struck by the bewildering variety of languages and religions the city contained: it was, in the words of two British travellers, "historically Greek, politically Turkish, geographically Bulgarian and ethnographically Jewish." "The population is hotchpotch," wrote another, "but you have to note the features, the eye, the walk, the general manner, to decide whether this man be a Turk, a Greek, an Armenian, a Bulgarian or a Jew. The shifty eye tells the Armenian, the swagger of demeanour proclaims the Greek, the quiet alertness reveals the Jew."[2]

Victorian theories of anthropology encouraged foreigners to see character, costume, physiognomy and physical beauty or ugliness not as the property of individuals but as the attributes of the race. Most visitors had their favourites—the Jews in the case of Braun-Wiesbaden, the Greeks for Choisy. The Slavophile Misses Irby and Mackenzie thought the Greeks compared badly with the Bulgarians: "The one is commercial, ingenious and eloquent, but fraudulent, dirty and immoral; the other is agricultural, stubborn and slow-tongued, but honest, cleanly and chaste."[3]

But whether positive or negative, the assumptions of racial nationalism which shaped most European travel accounts were highly misleading when applied to the Ottoman context for they did not fit how people inside the empire saw themselves. Despite the prejudices of Irby and Mackenzie, for instance, most Slav Christian peasants in the Salonica countryside probably did not count themselves as either "Greeks or Bulgarians" at the time of their visit. Moreover "Turk" was a term which made little or no sense when applied to a Muslim population which ranged, as a German visitor noted, from "the black of Ethiopia" (in reality, slaves brought over from the Sudan and beyond), to fair-skinned Circassians, blue-eyed Albanians, and Hungarian, Prussian and Polish converts.[4]

To understand the forces of nationalism and their impact on the late-nineteenth-century city we need above all to appreciate their novelty. Much time, money and effort was required by disciples of the new nationalist creeds to convert its inhabitants from their older, habitual ways of referring to themselves, and to turn nationalism itself from the obsession of a small, educated elite to a movement capable of galvanizing masses. The Macedonian Struggle, which swept across the city and its surroundings, started out as a religious conflict among the region's Christians but quickly turned into a way for activists to force national identities—"Greek" or "Bulgarian" or even "Macedonian"—on those who refused them. By the first decade of the twentieth century, thanks to years of fighting, there were indeed Greeks, Bulgarians and even Turks in a national sense, and their rivalries were threatening to undermine Salonica's cosmopolitan Ottomanist façade.

The late Ottoman Balkan peninsula

BEYOND ORTHODOXY

To the Ottoman authorities what had always mattered were religious rather than national or linguistic differences: Balkan Christians were either under the authority of the Patriarch in Constantinople or they were—more rarely—Catholic or Protestant. The Patriarchate shared the same outlook; it was indifferent to whether its flock spoke Greek, Vlach, Bulgarian or any other language or dialect. As for the illiterate Slav-speaking peasants tilling the fields, they rarely felt strongly about either Greece or Bulgaria and when asked which they were, many insisted on being known simply, as they had been for centuries, as "Christians."

In Salonica itself, the growth of the Christian population had come from continual immigration over centuries from outlying villages, often as distant as the far side of the Pindos mountains, where many of the inhabitants spoke not Greek but Vlach (a Romance language akin to Romanian), Albanian or indeed various forms of Slavic. The city's life, schools and priests gave these villagers, or their children, a new tongue, and turned them into Greeks. In fact many famous Greek figures of the past were really Vlachs by origin, including the savant Mosiodax, the revolutionary Rhigas Velestinlis, as well as the city's first "Greek" printers, the Garbolas family, and the Manakis brothers, pioneers of Balkan cinema. "Twenty years ago there was nothing in Balkan politics so inevitable, so nearly axiomatic, as the connection of the Vlachs with the Greek cause," wrote Brailsford in 1905. "They had no national consciousness and no national ambition ... With some of them Hellenism was a passion and an enthusiasm. They believed themselves to be Greek. They baptized their children 'Themistocles' and 'Penelope.' They studied in Athens and they left their fortunes to Greek schools and Greek hospitals." So many Vlachs settled in Salonica that in 1880 a Romanian paper claimed, to the fury of the Greek community, that there were no genuine Greeks there at all. Changing—or rather, acquiring—nationality was often simply a matter of upward mobility and a French consul once notoriously boasted that with a million pounds he could make Macedonians into Frenchmen.[5]

Money affected nationality in other ways as well. In the Ottoman system, the Orthodox Church was not merely a focus of spiritual life; it was also a gatherer of taxes. Peasants in the countryside, just like wealthy magnates in Salonica itself, chafed at the power and corruption that accompanied these privileges. But while most bishops and the higher ecclesiastical hierarchy spoke Greek—the traditional language of the church and religious learning—and looked down on the use of Slavic, most Christian peasants around Salonica spoke Bulgarian—or, if not Bulgarian, then a Slavic tongue close to it. This started to matter to the peasants themselves once they identified Greek with the language not merely of holy scripture but of excessive taxation and corruption. In 1860, the Bishop of Cassandra's extortions actually drove some villagers under his jurisdiction to threaten to convert to Catholicism: French priests from Salonica contacted the families concerned, promising them complete freedom of worship and a "Bishop of your own creed who will not take a single piastre from you." Other villagers from near Kilkis demanded a bishop who would provide the liturgy in Old Church Slavonic, and got one after they too started to declare themselves for Rome.[6]

Yet what these peasants were talking was about shifting their religious not their national allegiance and it took decades for the discontent of the village tax-payer to be further transformed into nationalism. Greek continued to be the language of upward mobility through the nineteenth century. As for Bulgarian self-consciousness, this was slow to develop. Sir Henry Layard visited Salonica in 1842 to enquire into "the movement which was alleged to be in progress amongst the Bulgarians," but he did not find very much. "The Bulgarians, being of the Greek faith," he wrote later, "were then included by the Porte in classifying the Christian subjects of the Sultan, among the Greeks. It was not until many years afterwards that the Christians to the south of the Balkans, speaking the Bulgarian language, were recognized as a distinct nation. At the time of my visit to Salonica no part of its Christian population, which was considerable, was known as Bulgarian."[7]

What led Slavic speakers to see their mother tongue in a new light was the influence of political ideologies coming from central and eastern Europe. German-inspired romantic nationalism glorified and ennobled the language of the peasantry and insisted it was as worthy of study and propagation as any other. Pan-Slavism—helped along perhaps by Russian agents—gave them pride in their unwritten family tongue and identified the enemy, for the first time, as Greek cultural arrogance. "I feel a great sorrow," wrote Kiryak/Kyriakos Durzhilovich/Darlovitsi, the printer, "that although I am a Bulgarian, I do not know how to write in the Bulgarian language."

For the Patriarchate, the priority was keeping its Slav-speaking worshippers within the fold. It realized that many of them might leave the church if forbidden to use the old Slavonic liturgy, and it tried to ward off this danger by proposing its introduction in areas where there was a clear majority of parishioners in favour. In 1870, however, before an Ecumenical Council could meet to approve the proposal, the Ottoman authorities pre-empted it and established a Bulgarian autonomous church—known as the Exarchate—by imperial decree: this demarcated the area within which the Exarchate was to operate but also allowed for inhabitants elsewhere to join "if at least two-thirds of them should wish to be subject" to it. The way was open for an epic "battle for souls" between the Patriarchate and the Exarchate which would last more than four decades and turn quickly into a struggle between Greeks and Bulgarians.[8]

Within the Greek-speaking world, a divergence of views now emerged between the Patriarchate and Greek nationalists. Many senior clergymen like Salonica's metropolitan, Ioacheim, wanted to conciliate the Slavs since they feared the fragmentation of their power and saw the Bulgarian Exarchate as a blow to the unity of the Orthodox *millet* and the purity of the creed. Lay Greeks, on the other hand, were more concerned about land than souls. To them the Bulgarians were less a religious threat than a national one in the struggle which the Near Eastern crisis of 1876–78 had unleashed for the territorial spoils of the Ottoman empire.

The rift between the "Hellenes" (as supporters of the new kingdom of Greece were known) and the Patriarchate was latent rather than overt, for even Greek nationalists realized that combating the Bulgarians would be helped by fostering good relations with the Ottoman authorities themselves. In October 1880, the Salonican Greek newspaper *Ermis* wrote that Ottoman Turkish ought to be obligatory in Greek communal schools since it would enable "a strong and sincere tie [to] more closely unite Greeks and Turks." The Greek consul in the city, Logothetis, maintained very cordial relations with the governor Galib Pasha: as a result he managed to get anti-Greek Ottoman officials dismissed, and to have spies watch suspected Russian agents on Mount Athos. But Logothetis was also highly critical of many of the Greek clergy themselves. Close acquaintance persuaded him that it was their venality, nepotism and indifference to education which was responsible for turning so many of their flock away from the true path. Salonica's doctors and teachers were more reliable advocates of Hellenism, and it was to them that the Greek state would increasingly turn: Athens was beginning to flex its muscles.[9]

LATE OTTOMAN VIOLENCE:
FROM ECONOMICS TO POLITICS

IN THE MACEDONIAN COUNTRYSIDE, before the struggle between Patriarchists and Exarchists really boiled over, the chief problem for the Ottomans was of a different, and older, kind. Around 1870, "bands of Robbers" were reportedly "plundering and committing acts of bloodshed" in "nearly every part of this extensive Vilaet," much as they had been doing for centuries. The 1878 Congress of Berlin created new borders across which the brigand could retreat when necessary, which made the problem worse. That year, three Jewish sheep-buyers were seized near the city, and a ransom note demanding fifteen hundred pounds was delivered to the chief rabbi; a prominent Turkish land-owner was another victim; so was one of the Abbott boys. Salonica's hinterland was as unsafe as ever: the gangs of Caloyero and Karabatak controlled the slopes of Mount Olympos, the Karahussein band infested the hills near Kilkis, while army deserters and Circassians based themselves in the Kassandra peninsula.[10]

Because foreigners made lucrative targets, the consuls became used to dealing with ransom demands. In 1880 John Blunt, the British consul, tackled a kidnapping made more difficult because the victim was a friend of his, Colonel Synge, a deer-hunting sportsman who had retired to Macedonia, where he kept busy helping Muslim refugees and organizing his estate. The perpetrator was one of the most notorious and vainglorious of the Greek brigands in the region, Kapetan Niko, a man who was, wrote Blunt's wife in her memoirs, "well known for his savage cruelty. He would commit a murder or two in a town or village and carry off boys of tender age, and then barter the noses and ears of his victims for cash with the helpless parents; or he would send the heads of the boys to horrified relations in cases where the stated amount was not forthcoming."[11] Synge's letter, most of which had evidently been dictated by his captors, went straight to the point:

My dear Blunt

Send 15,000 liras, 15 Martini rifles, 500 cartridges for each rifle, 15 gold watches with gold chains, 15 revolvers with 500 cartridges for each; 15 Palles [swords], Damascus blades . . . these must be of the best description and fifteen cigarette holders of amber, and fifteen Comboloya [worry beads] of Amber and fifteen gold rings, one to have Niko written on it, another Nikina, another Vassil *adelfos tou Niko* [brother of Nikos] and fifteen Salpingas [trumpets] and don't leave me to be lost ... The Almighty made Niko, neither Panayia neither Mahomed does he believe in, he has no religion in him, wickeder and worse than Niko there is not in the world.[12]

The "bloodthirsty ruffian" himself opened with the usual threats. If the deadline was not met, he warned, he would send first Synge's nose, then his ears and finally his head. "I do not write to you at length because few words are useful," he told Blunt. Eventually, after some haggling, the price dropped by one-fifth. Even so, it was a huge sum of money: Europe was enriching the local economy in more ways than one.

As businessmen, the brigands had their own code of honour, and could be relied upon to stick to their side of a bargain: when the ransom was delivered, Synge was produced, rather the worse for wear—"so overcome with emotion that he recognized nobody and could not speak a word"—offered cognac as a restorative, shaved (by one of the brigands) and given back his valuables. The twelve thousand Turkish pounds were carefully counted by Niko himself, who exchanged any defective coins. Finally, he handed fifty pounds over to Synge, "saying to him that it was the commission which rightfully belonged to him from the ransom." This kind of brigandage was a means of earning money but it was also, at least in the eyes of the brigand, a matter of honour.[13]

On his release, Synge described the band as best he could. It was—like many local trades at that time—a family business, and Niko's brother and brother-in-law both helped him. The manpower was provided by deserters from the Greek army (including a former monk from Mount Athos), and Christians who had been involved in insurrections against the Turks.

From other sources we learn that the bands typically treated their victim well; so long as he kept off the subject of his release, he was free to discuss any topic with them. Not only did brigands enjoy good intelligence of what was happening around them; they were also able to read the shoulder-blade of a roasted sheep or goat to predict the outcome of their venture: a small hole in the flat portion represented the grave of the prisoner—bad news for all concerned—while small lines running towards the leg bone indicated that everything would turn out well and the ransom would be paid. Brigands were curious about modern marvels such as the telephone and the phonograph, but they were also prone to boasting in bloodcurdling terms of "the most atrocious and brutal deeds of which they have been guilty." Of these, of course, Niko had more than his fair share. Like most of his kind, he was not able to enjoy the fruits of success for long. Despite making a typically daring visit disguised in European dress to a Salonica theatre, two years passed before he could return to his native village and he was killed a short while later. Instilling fear was an indispensable part of professional success in his line of work, as was proclaiming his credentials as a Christian. Even so, when one reads of the unfortunate peasant quartered with a *yataghan* before his mother's eyes, the villager who was rubbed in oil and set alight because he refused to hand over a small silver cross, or the *hodja* forced to climb a tree and call the people to prayer as though from the minaret, it is hard to feel much regret at the brigand's often violent end.[14]

Most of them liked to dress up their activities with noble rhetoric, justifying their violence either by pleading poverty or by boasting of their ability to humiliate the authorities. But as the century progressed and Greek nationalists cast their eyes northwards, some brigandage acquired a political tinge. Would-be liberators of Macedonia's Christians had been making forays across the Greek border since before the time of the Crimean Wars, usually meeting with a disappointing lack of interest from the objects of their concern. In 1866, Leonidas Bulgaris—"a well-educated but half-crazy enthusiast"—was captured by Turkish troops at the head of "what they supposed to be brigands." Having hoped to incite the local Greeks to rise up, Bulgaris admitted that the latter had not sympathized with their "would-be liberators" but had actually helped the Turks capture them. But once an autonomous Bulgarian state emerged in 1878, Macedonia became a battle-ground for insurgent bands. Secret guerrilla units, supported from Sofia, were formed by intellectuals aiming to restore the greater Bulgaria of the San Stefano Treaty. Kidnapping rich foreigners now provided a way of bringing much-needed cash into revolutionary coffers while simultaneously shining the unwelcome spotlight of international attention on the deficiencies of Ottoman administration.[15]

In 1901 the new political brigandage made international headlines in the so-called Miss Stone affair when a redoubtable American missionary was kidnapped in a narrow valley north of Salonica. Ellen Stone was, in fact, the first American victim of twentieth-century terrorism. Her kidnappers had spoken Turkish when seizing her in order to throw the weight of suspicion on the Ottoman authorities, and to encourage Western opinion to believe that the latter could no longer guarantee law and order in their European provinces. But the ring-leader was a young Bulgarian-Macedonian activist, Yane Sandanski, and his profile in no way fitted that of the typical brigand of yesteryear: literate, a socialist, and a schoolteacher, he was a leading figure in an underground political grouping called the Internal Macedonian Revolutionary Organization. Violence was no longer merely a means to a livelihood; in the hands of activists, it was becoming an instrument of nationalist politics in what the world came to know as the Macedonian Question.[16]

BULGARIANS AND MACEDONIANS

IN SALONICA A SMALL NUMBER of Bulgarians broke away from the Greek community and joined the Exarchate in 1871; by 1912 they numbered about six thousand. They were stonemasons, traders, shopkeepers and teachers—practical men drawn from the Macedonian hills—with no one of any great wealth to lead them and little influence in municipal affairs. They were supported, however, by the Russian consul, and once a Bulgarian state was founded, by its representatives as well. They were greatly heartened by the remarkable outcome of the 1876 uprising against Ottoman rule, and encouraged further by the territorial provisions of the Treaty of San Stefano which would—had it been allowed to stand—have handed over most of Salonica's hinterland to Bulgaria. Schooling was one of their priorities, and in 1880 they founded a gymnasium—many of whose pupils soon found their way into the ranks of new pro-Slav political movements.

To be "Bulgarian" initially meant to support the Exarchate: it was a linguistic-religious rather than a national category. But after the creation of an autonomous Bulgarian principality in 1878, irredentist politicians in its capital, Sofia, started demanding autonomy for "the Macedonians" as well. Meanwhile, in Salonica itself, a militant new organization was incubating: in November 1893 the "Bulgarian Macedo-Adrianopolitan Revolutionary Committee" was founded by a group of men reared on the ideas of Russian anarchism, and proclaimed open to any who wished to fight for liberation from the Turks and autonomy for Macedonia. Sofia-based activists regarded it with suspicion and did not trust its commitment to Bulgarian interests. Eventually the committee dropped any reference to Bulgaria from its name, and it became known simply as the Internal Macedonian Revolutionary Organization (IMRO) with the slogan "Macedonia for the Macedonians."[17]

Most of IMRO's youthful members were not much bothered about the old disputes over dead sacred languages. What was the difference between the Greek of the liturgy and Old Church Slavonic? After all, hardly anyone understood either of them. Between these youthful secularists—whose motto was "Neither God nor Master"—and the devout supporters of the Bulgarian Exarchate a gulf emerged.[18] Even within its own ranks, IMRO was deeply factionalized. Sandanski's band—which was responsible for the abduction of Ellen Stone—was barely under its control. Moreover, although the kidnapping bought rifles and explosives for the cause, and IMRO units killed beys, tax-collectors and gendarmes, the peasants were often reluctant to follow them. The province was heavily policed and when a pro-Bulgarian leader crossed the border in 1902 with two hundred band members to start a general revolt, he was driven out by the local inhabitants. It might be going too far to say that IMRO was a more coherent and efficient force in the minds of its enemies than it was in reality but it certainly made little impact on the Ottoman state.

Politically IMRO was no more successful. Autonomy for Macedonia—which was the name Balkan Christians (and Europe) gave to the Ottoman *vilayets* of Salonica, Monastir and Uskub (Skopje)—was the goal: a "Bulgarian" governor would rule the province from Salonica, all officials would be "Bulgarian" Slavs, and Bulgarian would be an official language on an equal footing with Turkish. But faced with such a prospect, Greeks lent the support of their intelligence networks to the Ottoman authorities, and in Salonica itself Greek agents in the Hamidian police helped track IMRO sympathizers. Even more important an obstacle was the opposition of the Great Powers. Russia was now focused on central and east Asia—the conflict with Japan was only a few years away—and Britain and Austria saw the Balkans as one area where they could all work in harmony to support the status quo. They pushed—as Great Powers often will—for incremental reform rather than revolutionary change, and merely urged the Porte to take steps to improve the administration of the province.

Frustrated with the impasse which faced them, and believing that targeting the symbols of European capitalism might force the Powers to intervene, some young anarchists in Salonica took matters into their own hands, and decided to blow up the Ottoman Bank, in the European quarter. Under the influence of their beloved Russians, they called themselves the "Troublemakers," and later adopted the term "the Boatmen"—by which they identified themselves with those "who abandon the daily routine and the limits of legal order and sail towards freedom and the wild seas beyond the law." They bought explosives in Constantinople and smuggled them as cases of "sardines" into Salonica. Then they rented a grocer's shop opposite the Bank, dug a trench under the street and packed it with explosives. In January 1903, a meeting of IMRO activists was held in the chemistry lab of the Bulgarian gymnasium, and the older men denounced the plotters for their "stupid childish games." It had little effect.

By April, rumours of the plot were circulating in the town and Panayiot Effendi, a Greek secret agent with the local police, was on their trail. When the manager of the Hotel Colombo, which stood next to the Ottoman Bank, reported that his drains were blocked, the plotters feared discovery and accelerated their plans. They also decided to magnify the impact of their campaign by simultaneously blowing up the French steamer *Guadalquivir* which had arrived in the port, and one of them went on board as a passenger with twelve kilos of dynamite. Another plan was to destroy the main electricity generating station, a fourth to set fire to the *Bosniak Han*, and—at the last moment—the harbour-front cafés and the branch-line of the train running into the city were added to the list.

At 11:20 on the morning of 28 April 1903, a huge explosion rocked the city as the *Guadalquivir* was holed. Smoke and flames rose from the stricken steamer, and although the bystanders who gathered along the quay to watch believed the boilers had burst it was quickly evident from the gap in its side that the damage had been caused by a bomb. The same evening, while the town still speculated over the identity of the perpetrators, another bomb went off beneath the branch-line train pulling into the central station. Fortunately, the explosives had been poorly laid and little damage was done. The next morning Pavel Shatev, the man responsible for bombing the *Guadalquivir*, slipped out of town. When he failed to appear with the other passengers in the shipping company offices that lunchtime, the police were notified. Within a few hours, he had been arrested at Skopje station.

But the attack on the bank was still to come. At dusk, another of the conspirators blew up the main pipeline leading from the gas station, and all the lights in the city went out. This was the signal: bombs were thrown at the generating station itself, causing little damage, and another explosion rocked the *Alhambra* café on the front, killing a waiter. The bar on the ground floor of the popular Hotel d'Angleterre was also attacked, and Vladimir Pingoff tried to set fire to the *Bosniak Han*. Panic spread through the city. Outside the Ottoman Bank, two members of the group pulled up in a carriage, jumped out and scattered bombs and grenades, killing a guard and a passing soldier, and wounding two others. Hiding in the grocer's shop across the road from the Bank, Yordan Yordanov also took his cue from the sudden power failure and set off the fuse in the tunnel leading under the building. The tremendous explosion left only its outer walls standing, with several people buried under the rubble.

In the confusion which followed, troops began firing wildly at one another, and the exhausted sailors of the *Guadalquivir* rushed to help pull survivors out of the ruins. Foreign consuls cabled their governments to send naval vessels—many remembered the events of 1876 and feared an indiscriminate massacre of the town's Christians by the enraged soldiers. The terrorists had succeeded in making the Ottoman authorities look helpless and drawn international attention back to Macedonia. As soldiers made house-to-house searches, hunting down suspects and killing several summarily in gardens and courtyards, people cowered inside their homes, hoping that what they remembered as a "night of terror" would soon pass. A curfew was declared and troops patrolled the streets. Fearing the explosions were the preliminary to a more general uprising, they scoured the Bulgarian quarters and arrested scores of men. According to some officers, more than one hundred were summarily executed. The next day, Hassan Fehmi Pasha, aware of the need to calm public anxieties, circulated with his entourage through the city's neighbourhoods, promising his protection and warning Muslims not to take the law into their own hands. The mayor was instructed to clean up the streets around the bank and convicts scrubbed the bloodstains off the walls.[19]

In fact there was, as the French consul noted, no reaction from the Muslim population. (Another of the anarchists had planned earlier to blow up a mosque during Friday prayers in order to provoke a massacre of Christians, but had been arrested beforehand.) The prisons were overflowing—by early May nearly eight hundred prisoners were held—and a court-martial tried those responsible. The chief culprits were sentenced to death, and the ring-leaders were transferred to the notorious jails of Fezzan in the Libyan Sahara where several of them died.

The two surviving members of the plot, Shatev and Bogdanov, returned to Macedonia in the amnesty of 1908: Bogdanov died a few years later, but Pavel Shatev lived until 1952, becoming a lawyer in interwar Bulgaria and then minister of justice in the postwar Yugoslav republic of Macedonia.[20]

IMRO sputtered on, although the bombers had dealt a near-fatal blow to the organization in the city. The better-known Ilinden uprising which took place on St. Elias's Day a few months later was the IMRO leadership's own anxious attempt to arouse a peasant revolt against Turkish rule. But its chief consequence was that several thousand more Christian peasants were killed by Ottoman troops in reprisal. The only success IMRO could claim after this series of bloody failures was a further diplomatic intervention by the Great Powers—their last significant involvement in the tangled Macedonia question before the Balkan Wars. The Ottoman authorities were forced to swallow the appointment of European officials to supervise the policing of the province. Among the younger army officers stationed there, resentment and a sense of humiliation led to the first stirrings of conspiracy against the Porte. On the other hand, Macedonia remained part of the empire and Hilmi Pasha continued as inspector-general. The one conclusion to be drawn from the rise and fall of IMRO was that ending Ottoman power in Europe would not come that way: the use of terrorism to embroil and involve the Great Powers was futile when the Powers upheld the status quo.

THE MACEDONIAN STRUGGLE

MANY GREEKS HOWEVER FELT Macedonia was slipping from their grasp. From their point of view, the situation looked desperate. Serbian and Romanian propaganda was having an effect among the Slavs and Vlachs, and Bulgaria seemed to be in the ascendant. "I myself imagined there could be no doubt that the northern littoral of the Aegean is Greek," wrote an informed British observer. "But a few years ago the Greek Archbishop of Gürmürjina complained to me that his flock were all turning Bulgarian and speaking that language." "Is your village Greek . . . or Bulgarian?" the British journalist H. N. Brailsford asked a wealthy peasant in the Monastir market. " 'Well,' he replied, 'It is Bulgarian now but four years ago it was Greek.' " By 1904, according to the Ottoman census of that year, which gives an approximate picture of

the ethnography of the disputed provinces, there were 648,962 Patriarchists to 557,734 Exarchists. Figures based on language groups gave a
more alarming impression—896,496 Bulgarians compared to 307,000
Greeks, 99,000 Vlachs and 100,717 Serbs. Either way, Greek activists
decided that if they did not enter the fray, they would lose the hearts
and minds of the Christians in the countryside. Thus the stage was set
for what would come to be known in Greece as "the Macedonian
Struggle."[21]

Between 1904 and 1908 the Greek bands—often in fact Hellenized
Slav or Albanian brigands loyal to the Patriarchate—went about their
patriotic work in the hills. Forced to declare themselves for one side or
the other, reluctant peasants were encouraged by beatings as well as
money. Exarchists were shot. "Hostile" houses and some entire villages
were burned—by both sides.[22] New battle-lines were being drawn. The
"Bulgarians" were the Greeks' main enemy, the Antichrist, heretics,
against whom anything was permissible. Villagers were warned that
Exarchist priests were schismatics and that those they buried would not
lie at peace. At the Greek gymnasium in Salonica, a priest taught his
classes that the Bulgarians were "murderers, criminals, infidels and
should be cleared from the face of the earth." Those who did this were
"naturally heroes, protectors of our Church." In retrospect, it seems
obvious that the Greek strategy simply reproduced the flawed assumptions of the Bulgarians before them; nor indeed is there any indication
that the gallant patriots who stirred up trouble in the Macedonian villages contributed very much to the ultimate triumph of Greek arms in
1912. But that was not how it seemed at the time: according to the
over-heated logic of fin-de-siècle national rivalries, every thrust had to
be answered with counter-thrust, and passivity was a sign of weakness
not wisdom. "By the autumn of 1905," noted Brailsford, "a reign of terror had settled down on the whole of central Macedonia."[23]

The centre of operations was Salonica's Greek consulate whose elegant neo-classical building today houses the Museum of the Macedonian Struggle. An energetic new consul, Lambros Koromilas, had been
posted there to build up a network of activists and bands. Patriotic
activity was organized through "the Organization," an underground
movement led by a young army cadet called Athanasios Souliotis-
Nikolaides. His agents collected information on enemies of the Greek
cause, and carried out assassinations of leading members of the Bulgarian community. They also engaged in more peaceful propaganda activities—Souliotis wrote a brochure entitled *Prophecies of Alexander the*

Great which he circulated among the peasantry in a Slavic translation to persuade them that only the Greeks could liberate them from Turkish rule. He also tried to make Greek shopkeepers in the city alter their shop signs so that the Greek lettering was largest, placing Turkish and French in subsidiary positions. Greek was not usually set first, and Souliotis thought the change would impress "the Slavophones who came into the Macedonian capital from the villages" and help "Hellenize" the city.[24]

In 1907, Souliotis urged Greeks to boycott Exarchist or Bulgarian businesses, and Greek employers were told not to hire Exarchist workers. One man was killed when he ignored these instructions, and an Exarchist priest's house was burned down when he tried to build in a Greek neighbourhood. Later the practice of ethnic boycotts spread to other communities: Turks and Jews boycotted Austrian products after the Habsburg annexation of Ottoman Bosnia, Greek goods after the uprising on Crete, and Italian goods in 1911 at the time of the Italian invasion of Ottoman Tripolitania. This last episode drove away the city's richest family, the Allatinis, who had Italian citizenship. What thus started on a small scale as part of the Macedonian Struggle became something much more pervasive: indeed one might view the boycott—as indeed the Struggle itself was in a wider sense—as the moment when nationalist politics imposed its own logic upon interactions in the Ottoman city. Before then, politics had been a limited affair which concerned only municipal elites; now it affected everyone and demanded total participation. Against its power, even a family as influential and wealthy as the Allatinis was helpless.

13

The Young Turk Revolution

AT THE START of the twentieth century, Salonica became a hive of plotting against Abdul Hamid. A branch of the émigré Ottoman constitutionalist organization, the Committee of Union and Progress (CUP), had been founded there as early as 1896. But it was only a decade later that it was invigorated by growing discontent among the officers of the Third Army Corps which was stationed in the city. The loss of Greece, Serbia, Bosnia and Bulgaria, and the growing interference of the European Powers in the life of the empire, alarmed many Muslims and renewed demands, dormant for nearly thirty years, for reform, constitutional liberties and imperial revival. For Ottoman society too was entering the era of mass politics and the same institutions—the schools and the army—which were politicizing young men in neighbouring states were doing so in the empire itself.

The Young Turks behind the revolution of 1908 were youthful figures who aimed to break the hold of the traditional grey-bearded Istanbul statesmen. They were practical men such as Selanikli Nazim, the director of Salonica's municipal hospital, who succeeded in unifying the Paris and Salonica branches of the Committee of Union and Progress in 1907; Talaat Bey, a civil servant in the telegraph office; and a charming young army officer in the service of Hilmi Pasha, Enver Bey, the son of an Anatolian bridge-keeper and an Albanian peasant, who would become the most famous Young Turk of all. Many of them were freemasons, for the city's masonic lodges formed a useful means of making secret contacts and shared the plotters' progressive goals. They cultivated close ties with local Greek notables and used Greek agents to help them get in and out of the country. There were also numerous young army officers like Salonica-born Mustafa Kemal. In 1907 Kemal succeeded in getting himself reassigned from a cavalry expedition in Syria to the staff of the Third Army Corps in his home town. There he tried to organize a local branch of a rival party but was forced to give up when he realized how strong the CUP had become in his absence.[1]

Even outside the ranks of the army and the civil service, many supported the idea of restoring the 1876 constitution—Mustafa Rahmi, a member of the Evrenos land-owning dynasty; *Ma'min* such as Mehmed Djavid Bey, the economics professor and future finance minister; as well as Salonican Jews like the journalist Nissim Rousso or Hilmi Pasha's adviser on legal matters, the constitutionalist Nissim Mazliah. Hilmi Pasha himself was whispered to sympathize with the plotters. Many commentators then and since even saw the Young Turk revolution as a product of the city, holding its cosmopolitanism, its close links with Europe, for some also its large Jewish and *Ma'min* population, responsible for the dramatic changes forced on the empire in 1908. This was flattering to the city's image of itself as the place where Ottoman and European values and aspirations met. But it is probably closer to the truth simply to say that it was in European Turkey that external meddling was most troublesome and that imperial authority was most sharply thrown into question.

THE YOUNG TURK REVOLUTION

WITHIN THE CITY, the spring of 1908 was filled with assassinations. An unknown gunman shot the interpreter at the Greek consulate; then Greek gunmen took revenge, first shooting a Bulgarian chemist in his shop on Vardar Kappesi, the main street, and then, a few days later, killing a prominent Bulgarian notable, Hadji Mischeff, "a highly respectable and inoffensive old gentleman of 67," as he was going to his office. The cycle continued: a seventeen-year-old Greek youth attacked a Bulgarian workman with an axe on his way to the Allatini brickyards, and someone else fired at the *dragoman* of the Bulgarian consulate. "The rapid succession of these outrages, most of which have occurred in broad daylight and in one or other of the most frequented thoroughfares of the town," noted the British consul, "is attracting universal attention to the inadequacy of the Police."[2]

In June, even more troubling and unusual events took place suggesting the ferment was spreading beyond the familiar Greco-Bulgarian bloodletting. On 3 June, the vice-consul in Monastir reported that he had received a memorandum "which is clearly the work of the 'Young Turk' party and bears the signature and seal 'Comité d'Union et de Progrès Ottoman.' " He took little notice at first. But then a few days later, there was a sensational attempt on the life of the military commander of Salonica—sensational because the would-be assassin was apparently a Turkish officer, who had made his attempt in the centre of the town, close by the gardens of the White Tower where "half of Salonica society were assembled at an open-air concert." More such shootings followed: a regimental chaplain narrowly escaped, and Lt.-General Shemsi Pasha was killed in Monastir. The sultan sent his senior intelligence officer from the capital to investigate rumours of disaffection in the Third Army Corps, and as he uncovered details of the CUP network in the city, the plotters brought forward their plans.[3]

At dawn on 23 July, news reached the city that proclamations were being distributed in Monastir calling for the satisfaction of the Young Turks' demands. In Salonica itself crowds started to gather outside the prefecture building and discussed what was happening. Then, at ten in the morning, the Greek archbishop, the president of the local Bulgarian Committee and the *mufti* came out onto the balcony, embraced one another and called on the onlookers to do the same in the name of fraternity. A great shout of joy erupted, and an enormous flag was held up with the words "Long Live the Constitution!" in Turkish, and "Liberty, Equality, Fraternity and Justice" inscribed in its four corners. Standing in front of it, an excited *hodja* raised the cry "Long Live the Constitution!" The crowd responded immediately. "There was indescribable delirium," wrote a French officer watching the scene. Soon army officers and civilian CUP supporters—including Jews, Greeks and Bulgarians—were speechifying from the steps of public buildings, on café tables and hotel balconies, "enthusiastically cheered by crowds of all nationalities." The streets were filled late into the night with groups waving the Ottoman flag as well as the red and white stripes of the CUP.[4]

The government's capitulation the next day—the plotters had threatened to march on Istanbul if a commitment to restore the constitution was not immediately forthcoming—produced further public jubilation. Hilmi Pasha presented himself on the steps of the town hall in front of a crowd estimated at fifteen thousand and announced the reconvening of the General Assembly in the capital. Few were aware of the astute way in which this experienced bureaucrat had brought his master into line; all they could see was that the sultan had finally brought back the constitution he had scrapped three decades earlier. "The rest of the day was given up to demonstrations of popular rejoicing of which I doubt the like has ever been seen in Turkey," wrote the British consul. "The whole town was dressed in flags, processions paraded the streets, speeches were delivered in every public place— the populace, half-intoxicated with a sense of unwonted freedom applauded uproariously on every possible occasion. At nightfall the city was illuminated and the wildest enthusiasm prevailed when Enver Bey . . . who had fled from Salonica to form one of the earliest insurgent bands, returned about nine o'clock from Ghevgheli and was conducted in triumph through the town to the Garden of the Tour Blanche."[5]

A few days later, the same Enver Bey, a dapper mustachioed figure, addressed a large crowd outside the cafés in what had just been renamed Place de la Liberté. "Citizens!" he began. "Today the arbitrary ruler is gone, bad government no longer exists. We are all brothers. There are no longer Bulgarians, Greeks, Serbs, Romanians, Jews, Muslims—under the same blue sky we are all equal, we are all proud to be Ottomans!" Europe, he continued, would be forced to recognize that its mandate over the empire was finished, for the empire had been reborn, as a state belonging not to the sultan but to all its citizens. This was the official ideology of nineteenth-century reform pushed to its limits. "Yesterday massacre and words of hate, today the unanimous joy of liberty and fraternity," wrote a French observer. "We could hardly believe our eyes and ears. After having witnessed five years of carnage and horrors, we believed we were living in a dream. And yet it was unquestionably reality. This new situation, created by the committee, responded well to the secret sentiments of all the populations whatever their race and religion. Everyone thirsted for a little peace and tranquillity."[6]

Enver himself stood at the beginning of the dizzying ascent which took him in just a few years from the post of staff officer to pasha, ruler of the empire and husband of an imperial princess. Later there would be the disastrous decision to enter the Great War on the German side, the ensuing military catastrophe in the Caucasus, the Armenian genocide and eventually his flight and death on the battlefields of central Asia during the Russian civil war. That lay in the future, but his astonishing talents were already on display. For a moment it seemed as though the vision of social harmony he had conjured up might bring peace even to Macedonia. Brigands and band leaders made their way down from the hills to pay homage to the empire's new masters. Sandanski—the man responsible for kidnapping Ellen Stone a few years earlier—delivered an anarchist speech from the balcony of the Hotel d'Angleterre and declared his loyalty to the CUP. Under pressure from the Young Turks, the men of violence were being diverted temporarily into the path of peaceful politicking. Electioneering began for the new assembly.

The main obstacle to reform was the sultan himself. On 1 September, the anniversary of his accession, *Yeni Asir*, a loyalist Turkish newspaper, declared that "the Ottoman CUP has torn down the curtain which separated the sultan from his people. July 11th has opened a new horizon of happiness to the Nation and the State." But few people saw things that way. "Long Live the Sultan!" cried Hilmi Pasha, after he had read out the firman announcing the restoration of the 1876 constitution to a large crowd: there was no answer. Twice he repeated the traditional formula: the crowd remained stubbornly silent. Abdul Hamid himself resented the humiliation the revolution had caused him, and believed he could eventually marginalize and dispose of these new opponents as he had with others so often in the past.

This time, however, they controlled a powerful section of the army as well. Or did the army control them? In April 1909, news came in of an attempted counter-revolution in the capital. Fearing that the sultan was scheming to suspend the constitution again, the "Salonica Army" advanced on the imperial capital. General Mahmoud Shefket Pasha—Hilmi Pasha's successor as inspector-general of Macedonia—assumed control, not in the name of the CUP, but "in the interests of the Army and . . . of the Nation . . . whose constitutional liberties the Army had been the principal instrument in defending and remains the only power capable of defending from the threatened reaction." The struggle had begun for the right to lead the nation, a struggle between the men on horseback and those in frockcoats that would bedevil Turkey (and for that matter Bulgaria and Greece) long into the twentieth century.[7]

The counter-revolution was quickly put down and Constantinople was soon under the control of the "Salonicans." Suspected Hamidian sympathizers and plotters were arrested, and a more compliant government was installed. Abdul Hamid himself was forced by the revolutionaries to hand over power to his younger brother Reshad. At first he refused, believing he would be killed; then he learned he was to be sent into exile to the birthplace of the revolution. On the night of 28 April 1909 a special train from the capital pulled up at the military station outside Salonica's city limits. Rumours had been circulating all day that the sultan—who had last visited the town as a child with his father, Abdul Mecid, half a century earlier—was arriving. Stepping down from the train, he spurned the automobile offered by General de Robilant, the Italian inspector of gendarmerie, and climbed into a hired landau instead. Escorted by thirty mounted gendarmes, he and his entourage rode through the backstreets of the Upper Town and along the avenue that ran by the sea beyond the White Tower before reaching his desti-nation—the Villa Allatini—shortly before midnight. "Although a good many people were still in the streets in consequence of the illumina-tions that were in progress," wrote an observer, "yet the passage of the cortege attracted remarkably little attention and gave rise to no sort of demonstration whatever." "Half-awed amazement" was how the British consul described the public reaction. With time the awe decreased and the sultan became a tourist attraction. In 2002 one cen-tenarian in Istanbul still recalled being taken as a boy by his father and glimpsing a stooped figure on a balcony in the distance through the railings. Salonican newspapers published unkind snippets of informa-tion about the comings and goings at the Villa Allatini, for like Napoleon in exile, the heavily guarded Red Sultan remained "an enigma and an object of curiosity."[8]

His entourage was confined to his two small sons, three sultanas, four cadines, four eunuchs and fourteen other servants. In the capital, the rest of his staff were dismissed. The First Eunuch—the former Guardian of the Gates of Felicity—was hanged from the Galata Bridge, while the Second Eunuch, Nadir Agha, having won the faith of the Young Turks by showing them how to enter the treasury of Yildiz, remained alive to conduct visitors round the imperial palace which he knew better than almost anyone else. More than two hundred surplus members of the imperial harem were brought by carriage—more than thirty were needed—from Yildiz to the Top Kapi, to be met by their relatives and taken home. Elderly Circassian mountaineers were escorted to the palace where they scrutinized the faces of the unveiled women and tried to recognize daughters they had last seen years before.[9]

In the Villa Allatini the former sultan made no effort to escape. He passed his time doing carpentry, listening to his wives reading him the newspapers, and playing in the garden with his Angora cat. He demanded a Turkish rather than a European bath, and this was built for him. But his efforts to attend mosque were rebuffed with warnings that he might be assassinated. And when his brother, now Sultan Mehmed V Reshad, visited the city in 1911, no direct contact was allowed between the two men, although the new sultan did send his private secretary to enquire after his brother's health. Abdul Hamid requested that one of his sons be allowed to study in Istanbul, and asked for information about a bag of jewels left behind on his departure from the Yildiz palace. Gradually he fell into a state of melancholia, irritability and incoherence. Even astrology and predicting the future through cards lost their charm. Perhaps it was just as well: otherwise the ex-sultan would have foreseen the disasters to come—the losses of the Balkan Wars, which virtually ended Ottoman power in Europe and brought him back to his final gilded cage in the Beylerbey palace in Istanbul; the First World War and its catastrophic consequences; the occupation of Istanbul itself by Allied soldiers only a few months after his death in 1918; and the ignominious end of the last sultan of the Osmanli line, who died in exile in San Remo pursued by his creditors.

OTTOMANISM

THE YOUNG TURK REVOLUTION started out as an assertion of the values of cosmopolitan loyalty to the empire over the divisive power of nationalism. It replaced the old version of Ottomanism—shared allegiance to the person of the sultan—with one which stressed common participation in a constitutional government acting in the name of the "People" or the "Ottoman nation." Today it is easy to wonder at the naivety with which the population rejoiced at the CUP's triumph. But the ideology of what was officially termed the Unity of the Elements (*Ittihad-i Anasir*) seemed attractive for a time, especially in places like Salonica where nationalism offered no sure future for either the Muslims or the Jews.[10]

The trouble was that the CUP's Ottomanism hid competing and contradictory impulses. For some, the restoration of constitutional government was an end in itself. For others it was a way of warding off Western meddling and a means of reasserting Ottoman sovereignty and the dignity of the state. Some wanted to dismantle the capitulations which immunized foreign residents from Ottoman law and to replace the numerous privileges enjoyed by different communities with a single source of authority. For the Christians on the other hand, it made no sense to abolish their privileges unless they were allowed a greater say in the running of the state. The CUP itself talked the language of liberalism and representative government; yet in its origin it was a conspiratorial organization, modelled on the example provided by underground Russian and Bulgarian revolutionary committees, and with an equally suspicious attitude towards the forms of parliamentary democracy. Following the success of the revolution, its instincts led it to act as puppet-master behind the scenes rather than to form a government of its own, for its leaders regarded parliaments as instruments of symbolic importance to be shaped and guided by those who held real power. In October 1909 it decided to cease operating as a secret society; in practice, its behaviour did not change.

At first there was a widespread desire to give it a chance. Although some of its Muslim opponents disliked its secularism—in the spring of 1909, for instance, an opposition "Mohammedan Committee" was formed in the town of Serres by a group of *hodjas*, theology students and teachers—many more Muslims supported its defence of the constitution. Macedonian *komitadji*, hoping for a social upheaval which would give more power to the peasantry, saw the CUP and the continued existence of the empire as the only alternative to falling under the tyranny of Greece or Bulgaria. The Patriarchate looked to the preservation of its traditional privileges (which it would lose if the empire disappeared) and some Greek deputies argued that only an Ottoman constitutionalist framework would safeguard the Orthodox communities scattered throughout Asia Minor. Several Greeks in Salonica echoed this line, demanding support for the CUP and even joining its ranks. When one of the city's main Greek papers came out for the CUP—there were rumours of bribes and subventions—the community was deeply split.

Soon, however, it was clear that the CUP did not have the solution to the empire's problems. Indeed these became altogether more serious when, in a sudden series of humiliating body-blows, Bulgaria declared its independence, Austria-Hungary annexed Bosnia, and Cretan insurgents proclaimed union with Greece. The new government was shocked by its territorial losses and clamped down hard in the Macedonia *vilayets*, for if these were lost, it would mean the end of five centuries of Ottoman rule in Europe. Greek, Bulgarian and Serb national organizations were outlawed, new laws were passed against brigand bands and the population was ordered to hand in its arms.[11]

THE NEW TURK

BY 1910 THE IDEOLOGY OF OTTOMANISM had more or less collapsed as a way of holding the empire together, and as nationalism
spread among its Christian population, it gained ground among Muslims too. Arguments between Ottomanists and Turkish nationalists had
been raging within the ranks of the CUP for some years. But who, or
what, was a Turk? Although Europeans had been talking about "Turks"
for centuries, it had not been a term much used within the empire. The
ruling language was an amalgam of Turkish, Arabic and Persian, with a
smattering of Greek, Slavic and Italian, and its ruling class—like all
imperial ruling classes—included individuals from an astonishing array
of different backgrounds—Albanian, French, Venetian, Arab, Jewish
and Circassian. Mehmet Nazim—better known as the great Turkish
communist poet Nazim Hikmet—was descended on his mother's side
from the Polish Count Borzenski and from the German Huguenot
Karl Detroit, who left Hamburg as a poor cabin-boy and rose to
become a field marshal of the Ottoman army. If "Turk" meant simply
Muslim, then in the Balkans alone, there were Albanian, Cretan, Bosnian, Bulgarian, Jewish and other Muslims in addition to a scattering of
Sudanese slaves, Egyptian market gardeners and the long-established
peasant descendants of nomadic Turcoman tribes.

The main issue—how to define a Turk—was explored by the
Salonica-based Turkish nationalist Tekin Alp in a series of articles in
1912 on *The Nature and Historical Development of the Turkish National
Movement*. According to him, a mere three years earlier, Ottoman
Turks had regarded themselves "simply as Mohammedans and never
considered their nation as having a separate existence. The Anatolian
peasant took the word 'Turk' as synonymous with *Kisilbash* (one who
wore a red fez). Even among educated classes there were persons who
did not know that members of the Turkish race were living outside
Turkey." Popular consciousness changed with the triumph of the CUP
and supported its effort to base the empire on the creed of Ottomanism.
But as the "Greeks, Bulgarians and Serbians" gradually returned "to
their mountains and their arms, to resume their struggle against Turkish authority," the dream of Ottomanism was dispelled. Some at this
point advocated Pan-Islamism—"the union of all the Mohammedan
elements in the kingdom"—but their arguments were shaken by the
rising of Muslim Albanians and by revolts in the Arab peninsula. These

developments strengthened the position of those who "regarded the Turkish element as the saviour of the Ottoman Empire." In CUP circles, Tekin Alp went on, this idea had gathered ground and was propagated through Salonican newspapers which preached the "foundation of a new language, a new literature and a new purely Turkish civilization." The old Arabic and Persian elements in Ottoman Turkish would be eradicated and its literature consigned to the past. Ziya Gökalp, often regarded as the founding father of the nationalist movement, had settled in the city where he was the first man to teach sociology in the Ottoman empire. He inspired youthful intellectuals, armed with ammunition drawn from the European theoreticians of romantic and racial nationalism; they founded journals and clubs to promote the use of Turkish and tried to ignore the political limitations of their nationalist vision in a multi-national empire.[12]

Tekin Alp, though a far less important figure than Gökalp, had been in the thick of these discussions, and had made the transition himself from Ottomanism to Turkish nationalism. Subsequently he became a productive intellectual in the interwar Turkish republic. In a work he published in 1928, he preached the Turkification of minorities in Turkey on the basis of patriotic commandments such as: Turkify your names! Speak Turkish! Mingle with Turks! All of this was very much in keeping with nationalist ideology around the world. But one thing about Tekin Alp is worth mentioning: it was not his real name. For this apostle of Turkish nationalism had been born into an orthodox Jewish family in nearby Serres in 1883, and it was as Moise Cohen that he had been known when he first went to Salonica to study to become a rabbi: indeed one of his brothers eventually became rabbi of Serres. So the story of Turkish nationalism is more complicated than appears at first sight and raises the question of how the Jews of Macedonia—in the face of growing Greek and Slavic nationalism, and the rise of the CUP— also chose to define their political identities and fortunes.

JEWS, ZIONISTS AND TURKS

THE YOUNG MOISE COHEN was active within the city's branch of the CUP since, like many Jews there, he initially saw Ottomanism as the perfect expression of his community's interests. Few Jews believed they would be better off in one of the Christian successor states than they were in an empire where their loyalty made them trusted, and none can have thought that Salonica in particular—the city they dominated—would develop to their benefit if it became part of Greece or Bulgaria. The rise of Balkan nationalism thus increased the intensity of the Jews' identification with the Ottoman state. Indeed, Jews from Thessaly had made their way *into* the city in the 1890s after the latter province was handed over to Greece, and Jews from Bulgaria had resettled in Constantinople and Smyrna. Cohen was therefore preaching to the converted when he wrote articles promoting the idea of harmony between Turks and Jews. In May 1910 he established a *Ligue d'Ottomanisation* in the city.

Given this strong support for Ottomanism, it is not surprising that many of Salonica's Jews were unsympathetic to the idea of Jewish nationalism, nor that emissaries of the new central European creed of Zionism found the going hard there. In 1908 the energetic Zionist ideologist Vladimir Jabotinsky came to Salonica and called for Jews in the Ottoman empire not to follow the errors of their Austrian brethren; they must show that they were proud of their own culture and cultivate a sense of Jewish nationhood:

> As a flower with petals, Turkey today as a garden and the Turkish Empire as a gardener must assure all flowers can conserve their own sweetness and flourish. The Turkish people have proven their spirit of tolerance for religions. When they will learn that nationality has also to be tolerated, they will also respect this.[13]

But Salonica's Jewish elite did not need an Ashkenazi outsider to lecture them on communal self-pride and although some members of his audience believed it was possible to combine Ottomanism and Zionism, most did not. The chief rabbi, Jacob Meir, who arrived in 1907 from Palestine—the first-ever not to have been born in the city—was sympathetic, and the following year a breakaway group founded a pro-Zionist newspaper. But a deep sense of allegiance to the empire and its rulers was still the norm. Moise Cohen himself attended the Ninth World Zionist Congress in Hamburg the following year and tried to explain to his audience why he did not share their beliefs. When the future David Ben-Gurion came to study in Salonica, the local Zionist movement was in the doldrums. According to one of his biographers, although he found the city enchanting, he was "as a Zionist ill at ease," and he left after several months.[14]

In fact, had some Salonica Jews had their way, there would have been no Jewish colonization of Palestine at all. They did not oppose the idea of settlement, just the Zionists' choice of destination since they believed that Jewish immigration, properly directed, could bolster their own position in Macedonia. In Salonica Jews predominated; but in the countryside they were few and far between. Colonization could help change that. At the time of the 1891 Russian pogroms, Abdul Hamid had sounded out the chief rabbi about the merits of settling Jews *en masse* in the empire. Although an organized policy did not materialize, east European Jews continued to arrive in Istanbul and Salonica. The prominent journalist Saadi Levy, editor of the *Journal de Salonique*, entertained the idea of resettling colonists in Macedonia itself and Moise Cohen even advocated the policy at the 1909 Zionist Congress, though the bulk of the delegates can hardly have been pleased to hear it.[15]

In CUP circles, too, Jewish immigration was being discussed as part of a broader scheme for solving the Macedonia problem through demographic engineering. The decline of Ottoman power had been accompanied for at least a century by the immigration of waves of Muslim refugees—more than one million of them—uprooted from their old homes. Latterly, thousands had been arriving from Bulgaria, Serbia and Crete, many settling in the city. After the Habsburg annexation of Bosnia, the 1909 Austro-Turkish peace settlement guaranteed the religious rights of Bosnian Muslims and made the sultan, as caliph, responsible for their welfare. But some in the CUP saw the Muslims of the lost provinces as a national rather than a religious resource and an official CUP committee proposed encouraging them all to leave their homes. If sufficient numbers emigrated into the empire, they could be used to colonize Macedonia and increase the proportion of non-Christians.[16]

On the eve of the 1909 Zionist Congress, Nazim Bey, a senior figure within the CUP, told a Jewish journalist that two hundred thousand Bosnian Muslims were ready to emigrate "at the first signal," and suggested that within a short space of time more than one million Muslim settlers might be brought into Macedonia—not only from Bosnia, but also from Bulgaria, Romania, the Crimea and central Asia; Jewish colonists, he went on, would be a welcome addition. Romanian Jewish farmers were to be settled in the Vardar valley and subsidized: five thousand had already arrived and there was room for more "right up to the doors of Salonica itself." "Upon this Judeo-Muslim project," he told the journalist, "rested the life or death of European Turkey." Lobbied by senior Zionist officials, the CUP repeated its line: it was opposed to the idea of Jewish colonization in Palestine and the national aspiration this represented but Jewish settlers were a different matter entirely in places where they would not predominate. To Jabotinsky, Nazim gave this response: "There are no Greeks and no Armenians, we, all of us, are Ottomans; and we would welcome Jewish immigration—to Macedonia." The Zionists were disheartened by such ideas, not least because they appeared to meet with approval in Jewish circles in Salonica itself.[17]

The CUP policy was already in its early stages. In Kosovo and Skopje several thousand Bosnian immigrants were being prepared for rural resettlement. Nazim Bey purchased land for them in Macedonia. In November 1910 the first seven hundred families passed through Salonica en route to the slopes of Mount Olympos: hundreds more were not far behind. The new arrivals took over common lands and drove out Christian peasants; Bulgarian and Macedonian groups objected bitterly, but could do nothing except bide their time until they got their chance for revenge. Only Habsburg counter-propaganda to persuade Bosnian Muslims to stay, and the latter's own reluctance to leave their homes, limited the success of the CUP's scheme.[18] Yet they were only a little ahead of their time. In just a few years, Balkan states would be pushing populations around on a huge scale, the Habsburgs and their way of thinking would vanish, and Macedonia would indeed be colonized, though not by Muslims or Jews.

THE EMERGENCE OF WORKER POLITICS

NATIONALISM WAS NOT THE ONLY SUCCESSFUL CREDO to make its appearance in the political ferment which followed the Young Turk revolution. Salonica was the most industrially advanced city in the Ottoman Balkans and after 1908, a vigorous workers' movement, led chiefly by Jewish and Bulgarian intellectuals, exploded into life. It placed itself at the head of the city's numerous labouring classes and became in a short space of time so active and militant that it turned into the chief political concern of the city's new masters who—like the other astonished inhabitants—had to familiarize themselves with the sight of union marches, sit-ins, strikes, lock-outs and parades.

Behind the unrest lay the plight of the city's workforce. The fishermen and boatmen who plied the bay, the porters, *hamals* and dockworkers all earned a pittance; often they could not afford to send their children to school. In the cotton mills, employees were expected to work a fifteen-hour day in summer with only thirty-five minutes for lunch. They were almost all girls, working to save up for their dowry. "No recognized scale of wages exists," reported a British observer, "and it is needless to say that there is no Factory Act in force to protect the operatives against their harsh task masters." Local work was often only available for a few months each year, for the city's economy as a whole still rose and fell according to the seasonal rhythms of the agriculture in the Macedonian hinterland. "Business runs normally during the first four months, reduced in January and February, which happens every year owing to conditions in communications in Macedonia in winter time." This was written in 1928, but things were just the same twenty years earlier.[19]

Children were pressed into work from an early age—as shoe-blacks, shop attendants, newspaper sellers and street vendors—and many more were left unsupervised on the streets where they fought for *baksheesh* from foreign visitors, pestering sailors and living outdoors. Domestic service was still the main way poor girls earned their dowry. And prostitution was a major industry for local women as well as foreigners. Scattered references in the archives make it clear that it was not unknown in the seventeenth and eighteenth centuries. But at the end of the nineteenth century—with the rise of a new culture of public parks, cafés, beer-gardens and dance-halls—it assumed new proportions. In 1879 journalists denounced the "depraved women" who haunted the city's beer-halls, and demanded they be driven away. The following year Christian, Jewish and Muslim community leaders protested to the municipality at their presence in the heart of the city. But by 1910, girls of all races and religions were working its more than one hundred brothels in a separate quarter near the railways. Neither the rabbis nor the other notables of the city seemed very concerned about the problem. "What do you expect?" one told a visiting investigator. "The Jews sell their children like chickens!"[20]

One way out was emigration. Large numbers of peasants were flooding into the city. But tens of thousands more were going straight on overseas, and more and more of the city's workers were following them. Reliable statistics do not exist, but the numbers were considerable enough at the turn of the century to start affecting wage levels inside and outside the city. In the early 1900s as wages began to rise, the first successful strikes took place—by tobacco and textile workers, shoe-makers, and workers in the Allatini brickyards. Even so, few would have predicted the pent-up anger and fierce activism of the labour force which erupted as soon as the Hamidian autocracy was overthrown.[21] It was as if the revolution in the summer of 1908 had unleashed the genie of mass political mobilization and brought the city to a standstill. Even before any kind of political movement had been formed, a series of strikes and work stoppages disrupted the summer months: first the port, then the telegraph, the tobacco factories, brewery workers, brick-makers, shop assistants, tailors, carpenters, ironmongers, the railways—one strike followed another. "The strikers rule the city," noted the French consul.[22]

Transforming this ferment of grievances into an organized force was complicated by the novelty of the very idea of political mobilization. As was noted in 1910, "there is no public opinion in Turkey, and the indifference of the popular masses to economic and social questions of the greatest importance is the reason for the limited impact of local protests." Within Bulgarian circles, Russian Marxist and anarchist thought had long been intensively discussed. But leftist discussions spilled over into the Jewish community too. A young Bulgarian Jewish printer and schoolmaster called Avraam Benaroya founded a group called the Sephardic Circle of Socialist Studies which was connected to one of the Bulgarian socialist factions in the city. The fewer the members, the greater the in-fighting: groups coalesced and splintered, denunciations followed proclamations.

The key question of whether workers should be organized on national lines rather than in a single unified movement—exactly the same question which preoccupied socialists in the Habsburg and Russian empires at the same time—caused violent disagreement. Greek workers in the city kept mostly to themselves. The Bulgarian Narrows were ardent internationalists: they stuck to *their* reading of Marx and attacked any recognition of the principle of nationality among workers or any dilution of the coherence of a revolutionary vanguard party. In the middle were Benaroya and his Jewish followers who believed that the idea of federating like-minded activists of different national groups was better suited to the conditions of the empire. "The Ottoman nation is composed of different nationalities living in the same territory and each having its own language, culture, literature, habits and character," they later explained. "For these ethnic and philological reasons we believed it best to form an organization to which all the nationalities can adhere without having to abandon their language or culture."[23]

Events seemed to justify Benaroya's tactics. His largely Jewish workers' circle first met above an Albanian taverna and attracted a membership of thirty activists. But its impact on the city was quickly magnified after a large demonstration of workers took place on 1 May 1909. When the Ottoman government declared that it planned to limit the right to strike and curb trade-union activity, the movement grew. That summer Benaroya's association held a "great international workers' fair" in the Beshchinar gardens and sold thousands of tickets to raise money for a newspaper which appeared in Turkish, Greek, Bulgarian and Judeo-Spanish versions on 15 August: the *Amele gazetesi*, the *Efimeris tou ergatou*, the *Rabotniceski vestnik* and the *Journal do laborador* bore eloquent witness to the ethnic complexities of worker politics in Ottoman society.

By now the group had a name—the Workers' Solidarity Federation. The Ottoman authorities had passed a law banning organizations established on a national basis, but allowed the Federation because it was loyal to the empire and professed cross-confessional unity. However, Greek, Muslim and Armenian workers were gravitating towards their own communal organizations instead. Soon the Greek and Turkish language editions of Benaroya's paper folded, leaving just the Judeo-Spanish and Bulgarian. Despite the activism of Bulgarian intellectuals, the vast majority of the rank-and-file membership of the Federation were Jews. In fact, it would not be going too far to say that worker internationalism became one of the main political expressions of early twentieth-century Salonica Jewry.[24]

Initially the movement's leaders shared in the general enthusiasm for the Young Turks: Vlahov, the Bulgarian, had stood on the CUP list and served in the Ottoman parliament as a deputy until 1912; Benaroya was among the volunteers who marched on Istanbul with the "Army of Freedom" to quash the counter-revolution in 1909. But the amazing success of the workers' movement, and the display of its power to disrupt the city and force concessions from employers and state alike, soon alarmed the government. It issued a battery of anti-labour decrees, banning popular demonstrations, establishing press censorship (the Hamidian censorship had been scrapped months earlier), and prohibiting strikes in publicly sensitive sectors. As a result, the workers distanced themselves from the CUP. The latter imprisoned Benaroya, and passed a raft of anti-socialist measures and arrests, mostly directed against left-wing Muslim journalists and political activists in the capital.[25]

On the other hand, the thousands of Jewish workers in the city constituted a social base from which the WSF could not easily be dislodged. And their staunch Ottomanism too was not easy for the

Ottoman café in the Upper Town.

European officers witness the hanging of the alleged murderers of the two consuls following the disturbances of 1876. The artist is Pierre Loti.

Ottoman street life: *left* hamal, or porter; *right* vendor of lemonade;
below sellers of leeches

The old konaki [pacha's palace].

The new konaki with the Saatli mosque visible to the left. It was from the balcony on the first floor that Hilmi Pacha announced the restoration of the constitution in 1908.

Ottoman modern: *above* the municipal hospital, built outside the eastern walls.

below a classroom in one of the city's new state schools.

The Macedonian
Struggle:
above the staff
of the Greek
consulate, 1905.

right Greek and
Albanian band
members, *c.*1904.

above left Sandanski: brigand, kidnapper and fighter for Macedonian autonomy.

above Hilmi Pacha: General Inspector of Macedonia and Grand Vizier, 1909.

left Ioacheim III: Metropolitan of Salonica, and later Ecumenical Patriarch – he saw nationalism as a threat to the integrity of the Orthodox Church.

left Albanian Ottoman
irregulars.

below Regular Ottoman
infantry arrive in
Macedonia.

The city's new masters: *above* Cretan gendarmes.

below Venizelos arrives by sea to lead Greece into the First World War, 9 October 1916.

authorities to disavow or ignore. In 1911 when news of the Italian war in Tripolitania arrived, it was the WSF which successfully organized the largest demonstrations in support of the empire: six thousand people attended the first, ten thousand the second. The workers of Salonica heard speeches in favour of the fraternity of working peoples throughout the Balkans, and arguments for confederation as a means of bringing peace to the region. In the summer of 1912, on the eve of the First Balkan War, socialist groups in the region issued a pacifist manifesto. The wars of territorial expansion planned by the empire's hostile neighbours would "simply change the names of our masters and the degree of oppression." Only socialist internationalism, they insisted, would respect cultural difference and allow all nations to express themselves. But this vision of an empire ruled in the name of socialism was overtaken by events and eventually forgotten by all except a few scholars of Balkan history. Instead, the defeat of the Ottoman armies in the First Balkan War of 1912–13 meant the triumph of the principle of nationality in southeastern Europe.[26]

Afterwards, the key figures in Salonica's political awakening scattered far and wide. In 1913, the CUP assumed power directly in Istanbul: Talaat and Enver led the Ottoman empire into war, presided over the loss of its Arab provinces, and helped organize the Armenian genocide before themselves meeting a violent end. Finance Minister Djavid Bey was hanged in 1926 for his part in a supposed conspiracy to assassinate Ataturk while Emmanuel Carasso, another key CUP member from Salonica, emigrated to Trieste where he died a rich man in 1934. Of the city's socialists, the former IMRO activist Dimitar Vlahov published articles on Balkan federation from exile in Weimar Germany, while Sefik Hüsnü became the head of the Turkish Communist Party. Benaroya for his part became one of the architects of Greek socialism, instrumental in founding the Greek Socialist Party and the General Trades Union Federation. He remained an influential labour organizer in interwar Salonica, survived German occupation and imprisonment in the Greek civil war, before being exiled to Israel where the old anti-Zionist ran a newspaper kiosk until his death in 1973. Even for Benaroya, a man whose political vision at the start of the century had extended across confessions, languages and states, the forces of nationalism had proved too strong. But the stakes had been clear from the start. "Each of these groups which one calls today 'Nations' keeps well away from the others, as if fearing contagion," the worker's newspaper he edited had written in 1911. "Is this a good thing or not? This can never be good!"[27]

PART III

Making the City Greek

14

The Return of Saint Dimitrios

THE BALKAN WARS

Come my friends and sit around
And listen to my new song,
A poem pious and well-composed
Festooned with the flowers of 1912.
Of our Thessaloniki I shall sing
What happened there I'll set before you
How our Thessaloniki was enslaved
And returned thereafter to her mother's arms.
It was God's will, the intervention of the Saints
Which put the Beast so miserably to flight.[1]

ONLY A FEW YEARS AGO, a Greek folk-song collector recorded this lengthy oral epic about the defeat of the Turks. Chanting into the tape-recorder, a couple of women sang how the night before the Greek advance into Ottoman Macedonia during the First Balkan War, the city's patron saint Dimitrios came to the Greek commander-in-chief, Prince Constantine, in a dream to give him "a lion-heart and courage, and superhuman strategic insight." Five hundred years earlier the saint had been so disappointed with the sinful behaviour of the city's Christians that he had abandoned them. Now he was returning, terrifying the enemy with his threats and giving his divine assistance to the Greek army so that it could enter the city in triumph, led by its "new Alexander," the Prince.

For the Ottoman empire the First Balkan War was an unimaginable disaster. In just six weeks in the autumn and winter of 1912 a coordinated offensive by the Balkan states resulted in the loss of almost all its

European territories, most of which it had held for five hundred years, and brought invading armies to the very edge of the capital itself. But to many Greeks, the incredible string of victories their forces enjoyed—Salonica, the Aegean islands, Epiros—seemed little short of miraculous. "It was unhoped-for in the year 1912," wrote a pro-Greek band leader from Macedonia in his memoirs, "that there would be a war with Turkey and that we would win."[2]

That spring and summer, events had moved very fast. Parts of Ottoman Macedonia seemed about to fall into the hands either of Italy (which had gone to war with the empire over Tripolitania) or of Albanian rebels who were demanding a state of their own. This was perhaps the one threat capable of bringing the Balkan states together, and in a whirlwind of diplomacy, Montenegro, Serbia, Bulgaria and Greece signed a series of bilateral treaties and decided upon an autumn offensive against the Ottomans. In September they demanded radical reforms in Macedonia—the appointment of a Christian governor, the creation of a locally recruited militia and a provincial legislature. When to no one's surprise they failed to get their way, they ignored the Great Powers, who insisted that they should not fight, and declared war.

What no one had anticipated was the extent of their success. The Ottoman forces were beaten back on all fronts. The Bulgarian army invaded Thrace, laying siege to Edirne and threatening the imperial capital itself. The Serbs pushed south into Kosovo and Skopje, reaching as far as Lake Ohrid and Monastir, and then, together with the Montenegrins, besieged Durazzo on the Albanian coast. The Greek navy controlled the Aegean. A few daring Greek aviators flew their "Blériot machines" over Olympos. As for the Greek army, it laid siege to Jannina and, after overwhelming Turkish resistance at Yannitsa, marched unopposed into Salonica just in time to celebrate Saint Dimitrios's Day.

"It is not a dream. Salonica is truly Greek," wrote a philhellenic French journalist who had accompanied the army on its march across the Vardar. "Byzantium is awakening once more!" His disbelief was matched by that of many Greeks themselves. After living with humiliation and failure, they now had to adjust to success. "I like this city enormously. I can't believe it is ours!" was the reaction of one prominent Athens politician, visiting for the first time. Yet as the conquerors awoke from their dreams of Byzantine revival, the challenges ahead sobered them. "The unhoped-for happiness did not cause me the joy I might have expected," recollected Alexandros Mazarakis-Ainian, one of the first into the city. "We were hemmed in by uncertainty and wondered what the occupation of the city held in store for us and what the destiny of the Macedonian provinces would be." The place made some Athenians positively uneasy. Writing home to his wife, a well-connected staff officer called Hippocrates Papavasileiou confessed that "Salonica doesn't excite me" despite its "beautiful park by the sea with a cinema, music, *café chantant* and restaurant." Soon his tone became more bitter: "14 May 1913: I am totally fed up. I'd prefer a thousand times to be under canvas on some mountain than here in this gaudy city with all the tribes of Israel. I swear there is no less agreeable spot." "19 May: How can one like a city with this cosmopolitan society, nine-tenths of it Jews. It has nothing Greek about it, nor European. It has nothing at all."[3]

This was how Old Greece expressed its disdain for what it termed its New Lands with all their Balkan heterogeneity, an ambivalence about the fruits of victory which would, if anything, only intensify in the future. It would take years to change the city's Ottoman character, and the rivalry and comparisons with the Greek capital were there from the start. But Papavasileiou was perhaps unfair to Salonica's existing Greek inhabitants. They might not have been as numerous or prominent as he had expected—after all, they were less than one-third of the population—but they had turned out in force to greet the conquering heroes. Blue-and-white Greek flags festooned every street. "Our entry was a triumphant progress," wrote a British journalist with the Greek troops. "The streets were packed and the Pioneers' Regiments were obliged to force a way with the butts of their rifles. The Greeks of Salonika, whose tongues had been muzzled for weeks past, gave free vent to their joy at seeing the Greek uniform." The grand marble fountain at the top of the Hamidié boulevard which a year earlier had welcomed Sultan Mehmed V Resad was now draped with slogans hailing "The Victorious Greek Army."[4]

In the days before the Greeks arrived, the authority of the Ottoman state had been dwindling fast. On 17 October, the former sultan, Abdul Hamid, was quietly embarked on the German *Lorelei* and whisked away to a new island exile in the Sea of Marmara (and thence to Istanbul itself). News of his departure provoked nervousness within the city, as did the arrival of thousands of refugees fleeing the fighting in the countryside. With the Ottoman army in retreat, large numbers of soldiers deserted, taking their pack-animals with them. On 22 October, the municipal council met in emergency session and sent a resolution to the overall military commander, General Taksin Pasha, urging him for the sake of the city not to resist further. He was not initially sympathetic to the idea, but the Greek army's crossing of the Vardar River on 24 October brought home the hopelessness of the situation. The city was surrounded by hostile forces and thoughts of a last-ditch stand vanished in the rain and mud. Back in Istanbul, news of the surrender was greeted with dismay. "How could you leave Salonica, that beautiful home-town of ours?" Mustafa Kemal berated a friend of his. "Why did you hand it to the enemy and come here?"[5]

Once in possession of the city, the Greeks seemed unconcerned by the possibility of Ottoman revanchism and permitted the imperial gendarmerie to continue to help police it. For several weeks incoming troops were astonished to see armed Turks still patrolling the streets. They also allowed many of the mosques which had been converted from Byzantine churches to remain in Muslim hands, at least for the initial weeks. "What good to have conquered the Turk?" wrote an outraged philhellene in the first days of Greek rule, "to be obliged still to wander through a mosque of Allah when one wanted to go and pray to Saint Dimitrios?"[6]

In fact it was not the Turks but the Bulgarians who were provoking the Greeks' anxiety. Having sparred over Macedonia for several decades, Greece and Bulgaria had been unable to agree on how to carve it up and the treaty they had reached earlier in 1912 was an essentially defensive alliance eloquent in its silence on this critical issue. Once hostilities began, both armies headed for the city, but the Bulgarians were bearing the brunt of fighting against the Ottoman forces elsewhere and the Greeks got there first by just eight hours. Sixteen thousand Bulgarian troops, accompanied by numerous *komitadjis*, were streaming down the Langada road and insisted on making their own entry two days later. They did not disguise their dissatisfaction at the course of events. "The hatred and loathing felt by the Bulgarians for the Greeks are only intensified by the war," reported a journalist. "If they hated each other before, they now loathe each other a hundred times as much as they did in the past."[7]

Over the next few months, the tension built up. The Greeks had made it clear that the city was under their sole control and to underline the point, King George and his court transferred themselves there from Athens. Meanwhile, Sofia was presenting Salonica's liberation as *its* achievement. Most of the Bulgarian troops were soon withdrawn under Greek pressure, while an influx of civilian administrators, gendarmes and fresh troops strengthened the Greek hand. Nevertheless, even the reduced Bulgarian presence constituted a daily challenge to the legitimacy of Hellenic rule at a time when internationally the Great Powers had still not determined the city's future. There were almost daily incidents involving Greek and Bulgarian soldiers, while the *komitadji* bands themselves stirred things up further. In March 1913, the two sides clashed openly about thirty miles northeast of Salonica. It was a harbinger of worse to come.[8]

When the First Balkan War ended formally in April 1913, the diplomats gathered in London to discuss the terms of peace. Greece and Serbia had won far more than they had dared hope for; Bulgaria had ended up with much less. Greece's population and territory both nearly doubled, as did Serbia's, and Ottoman Macedonia was largely partitioned between them. Bulgaria's gains, on the other hand, were largely confined to Thrace, even though it was not Thrace for which it had gone to war. Feeling cheated of the spoils of victory, the Bulgarians prepared to fight for what they wanted. A second conflict, this time among the former Balkan partners, was clearly in the offing, and Greece and Serbia hastened to conclude a defensive alliance. "Trains are being hurried to Salonica, packed full of men, guns and horses," reported the *Manchester Guardian* at the start of June 1913. "There are all the signs of a very pretty quarrel."[9]

On 29 June, the Second Balkan War broke out, when Bulgaria launched an attack on the Serbs. The following morning the atmosphere in Salonica was electric: shopkeepers boarded-up their stores, and patrols of Cretan gendarmes "passed slowly up and down the deserted tramway lines." Fighting broke out the same afternoon and ended—after a night's worth of "the incessant din of musketry and the churning crackle of machine guns, punctuated by the boom of the deeper-throated artillery fire"—with the outnumbered and surrounded Bulgarians surrendering; thirteen hundred soldiers and over five hundred *komitadji* were transferred by steamer to the prisons of Old Greece where they sat out the end of the war.[10]

The repercussions went further than this. Hundreds of long-time Bulgarian residents of the city were arrested by the Greek authorities; others left on Bulgarian steamers. The Bulgarian gymnasium, which had been a base of operations, was looted by Greek soldiers, and the Exarchate was banned. The Second Balkan War—over in barely a month—brought, in effect, the end of Salonica's Bulgarian community. By April 1914 the British consul was writing that "almost all those who wished to go have gone. Those who remain have either conformed to the Patriarchate or are living as best as they can as Exarchists." Saint Dimitrios had triumphed again—over the Slavs. In November 1913, the Greek claim to the city finally received international recognition and the Bulgarians, who had been roundly beaten on all sides, were forced to acknowledge their defeat. But the threat they posed never really went away. In both world wars Bulgarian troops crossed the frontier, and both times the city's inhabitants trembled that they might take their revenge for the events of 1912–13.[11]

THE GREAT POWERS were not overjoyed at the thought of Salonica becoming Greek either. Their subjects had enjoyed a privileged status under the Ottomans, and many questioned whether the small Balkan state was capable of rising to the challenge of effectively administering such a potentially important city and guaranteeing its prosperity. Austria-Hungary coveted Salonica for itself, and continued to criticize the Greek administration there for some time. Italy, Germany and France, while not making direct claims of their own, hoped to extend their influence by offering their protection and passports to the city's Jewish merchants. Britain was concerned about its holdings of the Ottoman debt, and wondered whether the Greeks would be ready to take this over.

Within hours of Greek forces assuming control, a French naval commander in the port was threatening to sink their two vessels unless he received a public apology for an incident with Turkish ships he claimed were under his protection. The Greeks had to comply but the humiliation smarted. The consuls themselves not only brokered the Ottoman surrender but tried to throw their weight around as well. The German consul sought to take all the city's Muslim subjects under his protection and distributed passports to several Turkish officials before he was forced to back down. On the streets, German, British and Habsburg flags challenged the primacy of the Greek blue-and-white as the city's foreign nationals publicly proclaimed their own divided allegiances. In six months, 2400 Jews changed nationality to avoid Greek citizenship—Spain and Portugal being, alongside Austria, the preferred options, while prominent Muslims took French and Austrian papers, and investigated the chances of emigrating not only to Anatolia but also to Tunisia, Marseilles, Belgium, Egypt and India. The vogue for changing citizenship allowed local fraudsters to enrich themselves by offering new passports in return for large fees. Only after it abolished the Ottoman capitulations, which had allowed foreigners sweeping immunities from domestic law, was the Greek state finally able to enjoy full sovereignty in the city.[12]

SALONICA'S JEWS HAD GIVEN the victorious Greek army a cool welcome as well. "It must be said that the Jew was not in a mood for celebration," wrote a Jewish schoolteacher shortly afterwards. "He adopted a correct and appropriate stance, as befitting someone who had lost . . . Only when we lose what we have do we value it truly, and the Jews who had never forgotten the rare virtues, the patience and generosity, of the Turkish people, feel today . . . that they have just lost their most secure and stable foundation." Many had serious doubts about a future Greek administration. Warning that annexation by Greece would be economically disastrous, cutting off the city from its traditional markets, some Jewish leaders proposed instead that Salonica and its environs should, in effect, become an autonomous statelet guaranteed by the Great Powers, a Jewish-run metropolis detached from the rivalries of its Balkan neighbours. The internationalization project was discussed with émigré Young Turks in Vienna, with Salonican *Ma'min* acting as intermediaries. In Istanbul a Turkish-Jewish-Vlach Macedonian Committee was formed to promote the idea. Some prominent Jewish Ottoman sympathizers may have gone even further and promised the Ottoman government financial support if it continued to fight against the Balkan states.[13]

None of this went anywhere—the Great Powers were not going to reverse the Greek *fait accompli*—but it was more than enough to anger many Greeks. The local Greek press whipped up anti-Jewish feelings and there were incidents, widely reported abroad, of troops breaking into houses and assaulting civilians. In March 1913 the city was transfixed by the news that the much-loved elderly King George had been assassinated while out for his daily stroll in the city suburbs. Suspicion immediately fastened on the Jews and Muslims, and fuelled new assaults before the authorities clarified that the culprit was a deranged Greek with a history of mental disturbance.[14]

The soldiers' disorderly conduct, however, contrasted with the liberal aspirations of the Greek leaders. Proclaiming martial law on the morning after his entry into the city, the military commander, Prince Constantine, issued a statement—in the city's four languages, Greek,

French, Turkish and Judeo-Spanish—in which he hailed the "will and courage of the Hellenic army" which had spent "glorious Hellenic blood" in order to "safeguard the rights of nationalities and of Man considered as individual and citizen."[15] Gradually, as the troops were brought under control, the solicitous policies of the Athens government bore fruit. After all, the maltreatment of non-Greeks—whether Muslims, Bulgarians or Jews—undermined its own international standing and jeopardized the position of Christians in the Ottoman empire itself. The country's leadership, led by the royal family, endeavoured to reassure Salonican Jewry in particular of its good intentions. In a policy it defined as "hyper-semitism," it proclaimed its willingness to protect Jewish interests in particular and the country's new minorities in general. The Jewish community, for its part, came to accept that the Greeks were there to stay: Greek flags hung outside Jewish homes on state festivals; rabbis and bishops attended each other's holiday ceremonies. The last Ottoman mayor, a Ma'min called Osman Said Bey, was kept in his post and the town council continued to include members drawn from the city's non-Greek confessional groups.

HELLENIZATION

THE TASK OF INCORPORATING THE CITY into the Greek state was entrusted to Constantine Raktivan, the new civilian governor-general of Macedonia. Raktivan was a leading jurist and the minister of justice in the Liberal government of Eleftherios Venizelos—itself perhaps the most energetic and reformist administration in Greek history. In his first proclamation, Raktivan declared that the war had been waged to remove "the tyranny and poor administration which the existence [of the Ottoman Empire] had allowed to last for centuries, and to bring the benefits of liberty to all the inhabitants of the country." Genuine liberty, he continued, presupposed "a complete equality between the different races living under the aegis of the same state" and he promised an administration "worthy of a civilized State, strong and impartial at the same time."[16]

Building up a modern bureaucracy would take time, however. There was no direct rail link between Salonica and Old Greece (it only arrived in 1916), and the post which should have taken no more than a day sometimes took weeks or even months. Raktivan remained in ignorance of the negotiations taking place in London and even lacked the drachmas with which to pay his civil servants. Turkish currency, law, weights and measures continued to be used alongside the Greek for several more years, and it was not until 1915 that the International Financial Control, which had supervised Greek money issue since the bankruptcy of 1897, permitted the National Bank of Greece to issue drachmas to the New Lands in the north. The capitulations were abolished but the "Company"—as the Belgian firm which ran the gas and tram concessions was known—retained its powerful position in the town. The new governor of the northern territories was getting a first frustrating taste of what rule from Athens—by a state at once centralizing and distant—really implied: it was a problem with which his successors, and the inhabitants of the city, would quickly become familiar.

Some elements of Salonica's Ottoman legacy were easily targeted. War was waged on the fez (though less than a century earlier it had been seen in Ottoman society as a dangerous sign of modernity), and the local authorities instructed railway, tram and electricity managers to dismiss employees who wore it to work. Those who refused Greek citizenship were fired: many Muslims, choosing to remain Ottoman subjects, quit; most Jewish workers conformed. Greek became the language of administration, and Greek customs tariffs replaced the Ottoman. Meanwhile boats arrived daily from Piraeus bringing a new ruling class of policemen, gendarmes, judges and lawyers—the first wave of Greek officialdom. Some came from Athens, many more from Crete and the Peloponnese. Their new posting—hardly a plum—was regarded as tantamount to being "exiled to Bulgaria." Even so, many settled and put down roots. Eighty years later, Elias Petropoulos noted that "in practice Salonica has been ruled for decades by the Pan-Cretan Brotherhood and the Union of Peloponnesians."[17]

Changed street names now testified, as an observer ironically put it, to "all the most beautiful glories of Hellenism." Aristotle, Alexander and the city's favourite Byzantine emperor—Basil the Bulgar Slayer—were inscribed on the small French-style enamelled plaques. The Hamidié, the main thoroughfare from the earlier phase of Ottoman modernization, and home to most of the city's consulates and administrative headquarters, was named Union Avenue, then Prince Constantine, then King Constantine, National Defence (twice) and Queen Sofia. Shops signs were re-painted with prominent Greek characters, often in blue and white—indeed many patriotic shopkeepers and householders painted their entire shop-fronts and even the pavement so that the city itself seemed to some "an unreal landscape." But for the next few years, more substantial plans for urban renewal remained on paper, building work "started and ended with the baptism of streets" and the roads were paved "with good intentions." Rainstorms still made it impossible to cross what was now known as Rue Salamina, except on the back of a Jewish porter. The nightwatchmen continued, as in Ottoman times, to make their rounds, and the fire service was still manned by volunteers. Moving from the devolved—even uninvolved—state apparatus that had served the city for centuries to the Prussian-style bureaucracy that liberals like Raktivan believed was appropriate would not be achieved any time soon. The completion of a small new pleasure garden around the White Tower was the most visible fruit of municipal activity. Writing in 1914, an Italian journalist summed up the changes that had taken place in the preceding two years: "There are no more Bulgarians, the *donmehs* have disappeared into their lanes and the cafés of the Upper Town, the Jews have adapted themselves to the new authority, the colonies of remaining Europeans—Italians, French, Germans, keep to themselves . . . The capitulations have been abolished, and what is worse, so have the foreign mails of the city."[18]

One important matter *was* quickly seen to, however. Since one could scarcely govern a city whilst remaining in ignorance of its composition and size, Raktivan organized a census, the first of any accuracy since the sixteenth century. Although there had been two more recent Ottoman efforts, no one familiar with the procedures they had employed placed much confidence in their results. The Greek governor created local subcommittees to visit householders, and groups of literate Jews, Muslims and Greeks patrolled their neighbourhoods, knocking on doors (rather than inviting householders to come to them, as had been done in the past). The aims behind the operation were lofty. "As is well known," wrote the organizers, "the first concern of every civilized State aiming at its overall progress, is to ascertain its population in all its varied aspects."[19]

In fact, though never published, and soon rendered out of date by huge wartime shifts of population, the 1913 census gives us a first reasonably accurate snapshot of the modern city's ethnographic composition and a last view of the Ottoman confessional balance which was to vanish in the months and years that followed. The overall population came to 157,889, of whom just under 40,000 were listed as Greeks, 45,867 as "Ottomans," in other words Muslims, and 61,439 as Jews. The Greek population probably included those street-traders, refugees and others who had entered the city since the previous October, from

Old Greece, Egypt or the Ottoman empire, as well as some who had previously been registered as "Bulgarians." Among those categorized as "Ottoman" must also have been several thousand refugees from the countryside. The predominance of the Jews is thus strikingly confirmed: there were more Jews in the city than in the whole of Serbia, Bulgaria or Istanbul. "Even today," wrote an Italian journalist in 1914, "when for three years Greece as master has left no means neglected for Hellenizing Salonica . . . when 1908 seems so remote in the city's history, she still at certain moments, almost everywhere gives one the impression of being a strange Jerusalem, very modern, very Macedonian, a little international, but Jerusalem to be sure, because of the great quantity of Jews who inundate her, so much so that they make all the other nationalities of secondary importance."[20]

At this point, more than two-thirds of the inhabitants lived within the old walls; suburbanization was in its infancy. The Upper Town remained, even after 1912, largely Muslim, while much of the lower town nearest the sea was between 60% and 90% Jewish, and the Greeks lived mostly in their traditional quarters on its eastern and western sides. But perhaps more striking and unexpected was the high degree of residential mixing the figures revealed. There were no ghettoes in Salonica and few neighbourhoods belonged exclusively to one religion or another: in fact less than one-third of the city's inhabitants lived in such quarters (defined as more than 80% of one faith). The tendency to stick together was most pronounced among Muslims, but even so, under half of them lived in exclusively Muslim areas. In short, the census shows how intermingled the religious communities of the late Ottoman city were. Thanks to the remarkable performance of her armies, Greece had required less than three weeks to bring Ottoman rule in Salonica to an end. But after nearly five centuries under the sultans the city would need longer than that to become truly Greek.

15

The First World War

Is she Greek yet, in these days, Salonica? On the new maps, sure; in the colours of the houses and the street signs, yes. But anywhere else? At its heart, the city is not and has never been Greek... This is an international city, par excellence. Or, rather, a denationalized city. Even after its annexation to Greece, the Greeks of Salonica are but a fraction, and not even the largest, of its inhabitants.

A. Fraccaroli (1916)[1]

THE NATIONAL SCHISM

IN THE 1940s a statue of Prince Constantine on horseback was put up on the shady side of Vardar Square. Today buses flash past as they carry passengers from the train station into town. The commander-in-chief of the Greek army is riding in from the western suburbs along the route he led his troops when they made their triumphant entry in 1912. Perhaps half a mile away along the central thoroughfare, not one hundred yards from Sultan Murad II's *hamam*, stands another statue, this time of the charismatic Greek prime minister Venizelos. The man who started out as a rebel leader in Ottoman Crete, and then became Greece's most visionary and controversial statesman, the architect of both its domestic modernization and external expansion, bestrides the main square in the heart of the city, stepping forward confidently and looking down towards the sea. The distance between the two men is not accidental. Constantine and Venizelos acted in partnership as Greece's military and diplomatic leaders during the Balkan Wars and continued to do so when Constantine became king in 1913 after his

father's assassination. But the outbreak of the First World War the following year led to an irreparable breach between them. King Constantine was convinced of the superiority of German arms and wanted
Greece to remain neutral; Venizelos, equally convinced that the
Entente would triumph, argued for intervention alongside the British
and French. Their clash threw into question the constitutional position
of the Greek monarchy and plunged the country into the worst political crisis of its history. Eventually the Entente powers intervened with
little regard for the niceties of international law, and in 1917 Constantine was forced into exile. Salonica itself played no small part in these
events for in 1916 Venizelos formed his own provisional government
there, and the city's rivalry with Athens took on a deadly new meaning.

BRITAIN AND FRANCE had done their bit to contribute to the
imbroglio. When the Ottoman empire entered the war on the side of
the Central Powers, they sent their own forces into the Aegean. In early
1915, they tried to attack Istanbul by sea, and when that failed, by land,
via the Gallipoli peninsula. Nearly a year later, they were still confined
to their beach-heads as Ottoman troops, led by Mustafa Kemal,
blocked the way. Seeking to extricate their forces without abandoning
their entire position in the eastern Mediterranean, officials in London
and Paris debated the strategic merits of Salonica. Here, some argued,
was a convenient port at which to disembark the troops from Gallipoli:
from there they could bring aid to their hard-pressed Serbian allies,
who had already rebuffed two Habsburg attacks. A waste of time and
lives, rejoined those for whom it was axiomatic that the war would be
decided on the Western Front. While they dithered, Germany and
Austria decided to eliminate Serbia as a military threat, and signed a
secret agreement with Bulgaria. At the end of September 1915, the
Bulgarians mobilized their forces for the impending joint offensive.

Facing disaster, the Entente decided to compromise and land a
small force at Salonica to march north to help the Serbs. Venizelos welcomed the plan. On 3 October he confidentially told the British and
French ambassadors they could use Salonica, even though Greece was
still formally neutral. At the same time, confusingly, he covered himself
against his domestic opponents by issuing a formal protest. The king
was not taken in and on 5 October, as the first contingent of Allied
troops sailed into the harbour, forced his prime minister to resign.
Brigadier-General Hamilton, commander of the advance party of the

British Salonika Force, was understandably baffled by events. Sitting amid his baggage in the Hotel de Rome, he tried to work out what to do next. "Damn. What the devil have they sent us here for?," he muttered to a fellow-officer. "Here I am—and not a word of instructions. What the devil do they want me to do?"[2]

Constantine's sympathies were certainly not with the Entente. Greek officials gave the Entente troops a frosty welcome, and allowed them to camp on a patch of marshy ground several miles outside the city along the Langada road. Later they ceded the use of the port, and grudgingly made the post, telegraph and railways available. But it was a tense and anomalous situation: the Greeks felt they were being forced into the war against their will, and the consuls of the Central Powers remained at liberty within the city. Much of the population was more sympathetic to them than to the Entente and an army of spies monitored every movement of the British and French troops.

Barely two months later, things got even worse: in the winter of 1915 the Serb army was pushed back over the snow-bound mountains of Montenegro to the Adriatic sea, Serbia was occupied by the Central Powers and the original reason for sending British and French soldiers to Salonica vanished. The units that had gone north returned, and relations between them and the Greek authorities deteriorated. Once Bulgarian troops had invaded Yugoslav Macedonia, nothing seemed to prevent them descending on Salonica too. They were only six days from the city and could probably have taken it had the Germans not vetoed the idea. Berlin knew that both the Bulgarians and the Austrians coveted Salonica, and they had no intention of allowing their allies in the Balkans to quarrel with each other over it.[3]

The British dithered, but the French were determined to stay. Christmas 1915 saw all the remaining troops at the Dardanelles evacuated to Salonica, and within a fortnight one hundred and fifty thousand men had landed there. Outside the city they built up a proper ring of defences; inside, General Maurice Sarrail, the French commander, decided to throw international protocol to the winds. Following a Zeppelin attack, he arrested the consuls of the enemy powers and shut their agents and spies in the mouldering dungeons of the old fortress; these were acts appropriate to a colonial or occupying force rather than an uninvited guest in a neutral state. Next he seized the fort that guarded the entrance to the bay.

The French and British governments protested they had no intention of restricting Greece's sovereignty, but this was only because they still hoped to persuade Constantine to come over to their side. Yet there was little chance of this happening, and the king had even threatened that if their troops did not leave Salonica, he would order the Greek army to allow the Bulgarians in. Here he over-reached himself, for this turned his constitutional dispute with Venizelos into a question of Greece's territorial integrity and national honour. Rolling back the victories of 1912–13 was something not even loyal Greek officers could easily accept and voices of dissent were soon heard in the ranks. In January 1916, anti-royalist posters appeared on the streets. And in March, the Cretan gendarmerie—traditionally loyal to their fellow-Cretan Venizelos—declared themselves ready to support an insurrection against the king.

With the arrival of spring, the conflict came to a head. Constantine—who had stood firm against Bulgarian pressure in 1912–13— actually carried out his threat and Bulgarian and German troops were allowed to take over Greek border fortifications without a fight, enabling them to occupy eastern Macedonia. Most of the Greek Fourth Army Corps was taken prisoner. But would the Bulgarians stop there, or were all the New Lands gained for Greece four years earlier now at risk? In Salonica, rumours ran riot—the Germans were coming down from Monastir; another three days and they would wipe out the Franco-British force. Outraged at Constantine's action, the Entente demanded the immediate demobilization of the Greek army.

On 3 June 1916, Constantine's birthday, Sarrail declared martial law in Salonica. French troops trained their machine guns on the town hall and took over the main government buildings. What price Greek sovereignty now? Barely four years after the ending of Ottoman rule, the city was once again effectively under military occupation. Noticing a Greek sentry missing outside the White Tower, a member of Sarrail's staff wrote that he saw "vanishing thus simply one of the last vestiges of Greek sovereignty in Macedonia . . . just as one had seen so many go before it." "Whatever happens," confided one official to a journalist, "we will not see Salonica in Greek hands any more." "It is a city with a great future," wrote an experienced British commentator at this time. "But no one knows what that future will be."[4]

It was this alarming prospect that impelled Venizelos's supporters to act. There had been demonstrations as the Bulgarians' entry through the Rupel Pass became known, denunciations of the government's policies and cries of "Long Live Venizelos!" In the summer, news reached Salonica of the way the Fourth Army Corps, known for its Venizelist sympathies, had been abandoned to its fate. Following angry speeches in the gardens by the White Tower, a committee of army officers raised a volunteer force, made up mostly of Cretan gendarmes and Greek refugees from Asia Minor, and soon claimed a strength of 1400–1500 men. On 30 August 1916, the pro-Entente "revolution" finally broke out and Macedonia was declared "independent" of the Athens government. Token resistance by royalist officers in the city was easily crushed. Several thousand men who had fled Cavalla to escape the Bulgarians joined the ranks of the self-styled new Venizelist Army of National Defence. In early October, Venizelos himself arrived in the city—having journeyed by sea to raise support in Crete and the eastern Aegean—and he immediately established a provisional government of National Defence to control the city and its hinterland. More troops arrived and a Greek battalion was established and left for the Struma front. Ministers were appointed, and political opponents thrown into prison. By the end of 1916, Greece had two governments and two armies: the "Greece of Salonica" faced the "Greece of Constantine."[5]

The City and the Revolution

But these fractious twists and turns left much of the city's population unmoved. Antoine Scheikevitch, a French intelligence officer serving Sarrail, was struck by the locals' passivity: "Nothing in the attitude of the Salonican population allowed one to suppose that it was capable of the slightest gesture which could do violence to the fatal course of History." The Jewish community at this stage was largely for the Central Powers, Muslim residents tended secretly to support the Ottoman empire, and many Greeks remained loyal to the king, whom they still thanked for the glorious victory of 1912. People generally were tired of war.

Watching the brief stand-off between the Venizelists and their opponents, a British war correspondent was perplexed to see "how little attention the ordinary population of Salonica paid to these happenings. They went streaming past on foot and in trams along the street at the bottom of the parade-ground, hardly turning their heads to notice the blue-coated revolutionaries and the khaki-coated royalists facing each other with arms in their hands at the side of the street. A population," he concluded, "that has seen so many uprisings and disorders within the last few years could hardly be expected to give great attention to so haphazard a bickering as this."[6]

Sometimes it all seemed rather like a scene from an operetta. At the party he attended to celebrate the success of the revolution, in the Beau Rivage restaurant, Scheikevitch noted the portraits of King Constantine and Queen Sofia turned to the wall, and pictures of Venizelos, cut out of the local newspapers, pasted on the back. The writer William McFee thought the whole affair resembled a "soap opera." Venizelos himself could see the humorous side. "Well, Mr. Wratislaw, here I am again; in revolt as usual," he remarked wrily to the British consul, an old friend, who had known him since his days as an insurgent in Crete fighting against the Turks.[7]

Yet the stakes were high. By providing a diplomatic fig-leaf for the Entente presence in Greece, Venizelos aimed to give his country a voice when the spoils of war were eventually divided up. And there was appreciable military assistance too: his provisional government eventually sent two hundred thousand recruits to the front. From this point of view, Scheikevitch, for all his sneering dislike of "the immense buffoonery" of "the Venizelist masquerade," surely hit the nail on the head. Criticizing his fellow-Frenchmen for feeling the need to take sides between Venizelos and the King, he pointed out that both men "sought the same goal—the realization of a Greater Greece. The Venizelist revolt was necessary to preserve Greek control over a Macedonia which threatened to escape them"; the "Army of M. Venizelos is destined much less to fight than to permit the servants of the "Great Idea" to count in the decisions of the arbiters of the peace." Initially merely tolerated by the Entente powers, and scarcely encouraged even to build on his position, Venizelos's patience was eventually rewarded by full international recognition at the start of January 1917. Six months later, King Constantine was forced to abdicate and Venizelos left the Macedonian capital for Athens again. With the "union of the two Greeces," Salonica's "short heyday" in the political limelight came to an end. But the political consequences for Greece were lasting, and the so-called "national schism" divided royalists and republicans for many years.[8]

THE ARMY OF THE ORIENT

THE ARRIVAL OF THE ARMY of the Orient—or as the British termed them back home, the "Gardeners of Salonica"—transformed the city into "one of the busiest hives of humanity in the world." "A magic wand," wrote a local journalist, "seemed to have awakened from its sleep this city which had enjoyed calm and a perfect tranquillity."

Between 1912 and 1916, an influx of Greek refugees, officials, street-traders and businessmen had already lifted the population to close to 170,000. With several hundred thousand soldiers soon camped in and around it, Salonica's population more than doubled in just over a year. In this period of "feverish activity," wrote a British journalist, "the great transports that came into the splendid bay discharged troops or munitions daily. There were docks, camps, offices, transport, telephones, dumps, hospitals." By the summer of 1916, it struck him as "probably the most crowded city in the universe." Demetra Vaka, a Greek writer who knew the city well from prewar visits, could scarcely recognize it in its new incarnation: "The amount of traffic was incredible to me, who had last seen the city and the bay when it seemed to have been left over, asleep from the Middle Ages. It was now a new city, in which I was completely lost and in which nothing looked familiar."[9]

The war accelerated the growth and expansion of settlements where ten years before there had been estuarial marshlands, abandoned fields and swamp. A French officer arriving by sea in 1917 was startled to discern—on either side of the minarets and city walls of the old town—"Allied camps which extend along the horizon into infinity... thousands and thousands of marabouts and tents which look like white points under the burning sun." To the west, on the edges of the Vardar plain, the troops were housed in wooden barracks and yellow-brown canvas tents. A new "Avenue de la Base" was cut from the quays directly to the Vardar Gate, where the unprecedented traffic was controlled by British military policemen. Beyond lay fair stalls, cafés and military canteens, then a settlement of Serb refugees, another straggling row of small shops, the Italian camp and the original encampment of Zeitenlik itself—"an entire city of wood and canvas." "The immense undulating district between Zeitenlick and Salonika is peopled with an army," a doctor wrote home. "Formerly it was a desert. Now there are fantastically long lines and groups of tents—towns under canvas; there are masses of munitions, a conglomeration of motor cars of every model and form, a hundred motor-ambulances in a line, rows of wagons thirty or forty deep." To the east, beyond the cemeteries and the villas and tree-lined boulevards of Kalamaria, lay the aerodromes, the military hospitals, the Anzac camps amid the woods by the shoreline and the British staff headquarters in the Depot and on the slopes of Mount Hortiatis. By night, their lanterns shone upon what one described as "the Lilliputian, ephemeral and powerful city of an army."[10]

To an already multi-lingual town, the newcomers added numerous new shades and tongues. Even today visitors to the military cemetery at Zeitenlik—now hard to locate amid the urban sprawl of postwar tenements—will find the remains of the hundreds of French Senegalese troops who died there of malaria. Both the British and French armies included colonial units drawn from Africa, Asia and the Dominions. Vietnamese tents were pitched just behind the White Tower, and the red-fezzed Senegalese lodged in the suburb of Karagatsia. There were Italians, Russians—fifteen thousand of whom landed in 1916, just before revolutionary slogans started circulating among them—Albanians and the remnants of the Serb army, led by the ageing King Peter. Off-duty, they crowded together in the narrow streets by the waterfront. Weaving their way amid the street-sellers, they shopped for trinkets, or muscled their way to a table at Floca's, Roma or the Bristol. On the Rue Venizelos—formerly Sabri Pasha—in the early evening where "the agitated fever among the main cafés was so intense that one could not move"—one discerned "many hundreds of warriors gathered festively round those little tables. French, Russians and Cossacks, Italians, British, Serbian, French colonials, Senegalese, Zouaves, and men from Madagascar—Indians, Annanese, Albanians, Macedonians and Greeks" in a kaleidoscope of bemedalled uniforms.[11]

The city itself bemused the soldiers with its ambiguities and its sheer commercialism. One saw it as a "coquette" surrounded by cemeteries. "She babbles all the tongues of Europe and speaks none of them aright," wrote the novelist William McFee. "She has nothing to give but death, yet the nations fling themselves upon her." Other, less literary types, were not so melodramatic. In the best-selling epic parody of *Hiawatha*—"Tiadatha"—which an officer in the 6th Wiltshires wrote while there:

> *Tiadatha thought of Kipling,*
> *Wondered if he's ever been there*
> *Thought: "At least in Rue Egnatia*
> *East and West are met together."*
> *There were trams and Turkish beggars,*
> *Mosques and minarets and churches,*
> *Turkish baths and dirty cafés,*
> *Picture palaces and kan-kans:*
> *Daimler cars and Leyland lorries*
> *Barging into buffalo wagons,*

French and English private soldiers
Jostling seedy Eastern brigands.[12]

And, for the majority of working-class recruits, war provided their first opportunity to travel. "From the boat deck, the rising of the morning was a very lovely sight," wrote Ned Casey, an Irish working-class boy from Canning Town, six decades later, "so different to the Albert Dock." The contrast with the "cold hard world" of East London hit him at once, as he caught sight of

> a great big bearded man, his legs scraping along the ground, riding a very small Donkey, while his woman with a bit of rope over her shoulder seem[ed] to drag the old [thing] along. I had pictures in my prayer book that looked exactly like the people I saw in this Greek City. I knew that our Lord, who was a carpenter, had a donkey but he let his wife who was the Virgin Mary ride the Donkey. All my Mates remarked look at that lazy bugger, he ought to be ashamed of himself, treating a tart like that. Christ if that bloke did that along the Barking he would be pinched, and the Cockney Tarts would cut his love affair off. I was to see many such sights while stationed in Greece.[13]

The presence of a huge modern fleet in the bay, the camps springing up on the city's edges, the influx of lorries, bureaucracies, languages had replaced the Turkish past with a "feverish, make-believe pleasure." "Salonica since the war has lost a little of its *Orientalism*," wrote an officer. In this jostling dusty chaos, ranks, tongues and races intermingled in a bewildering fashion. Riding the trams, an American journalist noted that "one of our 'Jim-Crow' street-cars would puzzle a Turk. He would not understand why we separate the white and the black man." This was what one serviceman called "the disagreeable disorder" of the wartime city, though another regarded it as simply "living in the present." English or French soldiers were astonished at the locals' ability to speak four or five languages. But even though they could converse in many languages, shopkeepers and shoe-blacks could rarely speak the important ones fluently enough to escape the visiting officers' ridicule or contempt. The latter particularly disliked the "Hello, Johnny!" with which enterprising local street-sellers greeted officers and men alike. Fighting the summer dust and winter mud, constantly assailed by "intolerable" assaults, the taps on the shoulder of the youthful *loustroi* (shoe-blacks) and sellers of the *Balkan News*, the "Gardeners of Salonica" struggled to preserve that tidy, dignified and disciplined appearance to which they attached such importance.

CIVILIZING MACEDONIA

MAKING ORDER OUT OF CHAOS was how many British and French officers saw their task. "One has above all to be organized," a French officer insisted in his discussion of what he termed "this colonial war." Steeped in an imperial tradition—proud of their civilizing mission in India and North Africa—they were out not only to defeat the enemy on the battlefield, but to demonstrate, before the eyes of the locals, the benefits of European civilization. War could be a "creator of the future, the powerful agent of renovation," wrote a British war correspondent, and armies could serve to bring progress, method and modern technology to those benighted regions which had suffered from ages of neglect and ignorance. Since 1915, wrote the author of *The Civilizing Work of the French Army in Macedonia*, Macedonia "will have breathed again, worked, learned many things which she knew not and will not forget." The British too extolled what one journalist termed "the stimulus of the Great War"; "Our labours," wrote another, "if they have done nothing else, have stretched the framework of civilization across the country."[14]

Military necessity, after all, demonstrated how "human energy" and force of will could impose themselves on a land and its people. Macedonia—a word pregnant with associations for the Europeans—lay before them, a land of enormous potential fertility gone to waste through misrule and passivity, transformed over the centuries from ally of man to obstacle and impediment. This was not only war "against man alone, but also against Nature—Nature neglected, misused, spurned," wrote Harold Lake in 1917. One instance of this was the campaign against malaria, which was rife in the marshy plains around the city. Indeed in the first year, the mosquito was a more deadly foe than the enemy himself, and thousands of soldiers died. No sooner had they dug trenches, gun emplacements and fortified concrete bunkers to defend themselves against the Bulgarians than they had to assemble a vast armoury of fly-strafers, whisks, swatters, guns, curtains, nets and papers against the lethal insects. Most of the men who waded through the shallows and reeds of the Vardar River to recover the wreckage of a Zeppelin came down with fever within hours. At one point, no less than twenty per cent of the entire British force was hospitalized. An intense programme of medical research began into the causes of malaria, and quinine was widely distributed, both to the troops and to the civilian population. The water-level was lowered, thanks to the construction of new drainage canals stretching for miles, and ponds were drained, filled in or sprayed with paraffin. In the spring of 1917 troops were pulled back from the valleys to new positions on higher ground. As a result, losses from malaria dropped sharply in the last two years of the campaign and the foundations were laid for the more extensive public works which the Greek state would undertake in the region after the war was over.[15]

Drinking water was the other key health problem, especially as the increase in demand had led to an unbearable strain on the city's supply. General Sarrail created a water service to tackle the problem, built a new aqueduct from Hortiatis, eleven kilometers away, bored hundreds of new wells and restored large numbers of disused fountains and springs. The food crisis that was created by the sudden influx of the Entente forces led him to establish a special provisioning service to take control of the local harvest. A farm school was set up to train peasants in modern methods—metal ploughs, modern mechanized threshing and reaping—and model farms demonstrated the superior productivity of the results. Meantime, fresh vegetables and fruit were brought from southern Italy, and refrigeration ships kept the troops supplied with meat. Special factories producing beer and ice for the men arose on the outskirts of the city; others provided the bricks and planks they needed for their housing. Thousands of civilian labourers laid hundreds of miles of new roads to carry men and munitions to the front as well as new rail lines, in and around the city. For the first time, the hills echoed to the sound of three-ton trucks and occasional aircraft.

Even the region's past could be transformed by the new civilizers. "Faithful to the French traditions of Egypt and the Morea," wrote a propagandist in 1918, "the Army of the Orient will have the honour to establish the foundations of a scientific study of Macedonia." A wartime French archaeological service was set up which by 1919 had identified more than seventy proto-historic sites in the area, conducted numerous excavations, collected the finds and displayed them to the troops. Not to be outdone, the British ordered all their men to report finds to head-quarters as well. Many artefacts were uncovered in the digging of trenches, dug-outs and gun emplacements, while officers and men scavenged among the prehistoric tumuli that dotted the landscape.[16]

Ever since the eighteenth century, local tomb-robbers and grave-diggers had been busy supplying Europe's antiquities markets. This time, however, it was not *andarte* bands who were rifling the sites in Salonica's hinterland, but officers of the Black Watch, the Leinsters and the Wiltshires. Major T. G. Anderson, a man with some experience of excavating in Egypt, reported a coffin containing bones, dishes and jewellery; the Cheshires sent in funerary objects, while the construction of dug-outs near the Bulgarian frontline at Doiran revealed a prehistoric cemetery (though continuous shellfire hampered detailed investigation).

The beleaguered Greek inspectors of antiquities sought the support of their allies in setting up a museum locally. In December 1918, they proposed that the Louvre and the British Museum make a grant of prehistoric objects from their collections "as recognition of the interest and love which the British and French Army of the Orient displayed throughout the war for the history and culture of our country." Traffic was moving in the other direction, however, and strict orders came from London that holdings in British hands were to be shipped back to England. The Greeks were outraged but could do nothing about it as they were hoping to tap the British and French for loans and long-term investment funds to rebuild their new territories. In the 1919 *Annual of the British School at Athens* we find a scholarly note written by Ernest Gardner, sometime naval intelligence officer and head of the wartime Salonica Headquarters Museum, alluding to the fact that the objects formerly displayed there "have now very generously been given by the Greek Government to the British nation" and placed in the British Museum.[17]

16

The Great Fire

AUGUST 18, 1917, was a typically hot and sunny summer's day. That afternoon a strong north wind was blowing across the city, as it had done for two or three days continuously. Henry Collinson Owen, a journalist serving with the British forces, was sitting down to tea when his Greek maid informed him that a cloud of smoke was billowing above the houses in the Turkish quarter. Fires were commonplace in Salonica; curious rather than alarmed, he went onto the roof from where he could see over the entire city. Looking through field glasses, he observed that in the northwestern corner of the Upper Town, on the hill above the port, the fire had set a considerable area alight and was being fanned towards him by the wind. Gradually, the columns of smoke over the old town grew denser, and by dusk the roads and alleys leading down the slopes were congested with refugees fleeing the blaze, crossing the Rue Egnatia to the open spaces of the lower town by the seafront. Those soldiers who battled their way up through the crowds encountered a frantic throng of Muslims and *Ma'min*, elderly Jews wearing fezzes, slippers and their long gabardine *intari*, women clutching their children by the hand, sobbing, shouting and imploring for help. British troops burst into a Turkish house, in response to frantic knocking, and found that the master had fled, leaving his veiled wives locked inside their *haremlik*. Some noticed the strange calmness that fell over people once their homes were burnt: "up to that point they wept, blasphemed, prayed and ran hither and thither wringing their hands; once the house was burnt, however, they made their way in silence out of the district."[1]

"It was an amazing and sad scene," wrote Collinson Owen, "the wailing families, the crash of falling houses as the flames tore along,

Area destroyed by the 1917 fire

swept by the wind; and in the narrow streets, a slow-moving mass of pack-donkeys, loaded carts, *hamals* carrying enormous loads; Greek boy scouts (doing excellent work); soldiers of all nations as yet unorganized to do anything definite; ancient wooden fire-engines that creaked pathetically as they spat out ineffectual trickles of water; and people carrying beds (hundreds of flock and feather beds), wardrobes, mirrors, pots and pans, sewing machines (every family made a desperate endeavour to save its sewing machine) and a general collection of ponderous rubbish."[2]

The refugees, as they made their way down to the sea and sat on the quay, would not be parted from their belongings. Soldiers, working continuously to transfer people to the British lighters, found that the only way they could be shifted was to throw their possessions onto the lighter first—the owner then followed. By nightfall the blaze had spread into the lower town and buildings were being blown up in a futile attempt to stem the course of the fire. Streams of red wine flowed into the gutters from bursting barrels of French army claret; at Floca's café, directly in the line of the inferno, perspiring officers were invited by the owner to help themselves to whatever they found. Returning to his roof for one last look, Collinson Owen saw a sea of vivid red, out of which were thrust the long, white needles of the minarets. Clouds of smoke, streaked with enormous tongues of flame, hung over the city. Towards midnight, the buildings fronting the sea caught fire and within minutes the entire three-quarters of a mile of the front was one vast cliff of orange and white flame raining incandescent ash down onto the quay, setting ablaze cars, carts and several caiques, which had to be hurriedly pushed off from the sea-wall where they had been moored.

Thereafter the fire, albeit slowly, passed its peak. Some buildings were still burning two days later when soldiers re-entered the town to inspect the devastation. The damage was almost incomprehensible. No less than three-quarters of the old city had been destroyed, according to an official report—"all the banks, all the business premises, all the hotels and practically all the shops, theatres and cinemas were reduced to ashes. Most of the churches fortunately escaped, but of the beautiful Byzantine church of Demetrios, only the bare walls remain." The strong wind, the shortage of water, the difficulty posed to fire-fighters by the narrow roads had all contributed to the scale of the devastation. Ninety-five hundred buildings were destroyed and over seventy thousand people had lost their homes. The Jewish community was worst affected for the fire had consumed its historic quarters: most of its thirty-seven synagogues were gone, its libraries, schools, club buildings and offices. Many mosques were also burned, as were most of the great *khans*—Ismail Pasha, Eski Youmbrouk, the Pasha Oriental—which had housed travellers through the centuries.

In the immediate aftermath, Allied military personnel helped the Greek authorities find shelter for the homeless. Many were settled provisionally in tents, huts and sheds around the city; those who could stay with relatives elsewhere were encouraged to leave. Five thousand Greeks moved to Athens, Volos and Larissa, and several hundred Jews—mostly very poor—emigrated to France, Italy, Spain, the USA and Old Greece. Soup kitchens were set up and fed thirty thousand daily. By September, there were only seventy-five hundred still in tents. Yet rebuilding would take very much longer. Two months after the fire, wrote a British soldier, "Salonica was a city of the dead. Its streets were deserted, its cafés and restaurants were no more, and at night the gibbous moon cast its silvery light over a waste land of ghostly ruins, projecting hanging girders and the blackened shells of houses . . . The slender but solidly built minarets had in most cases survived . . . and as one carefully picked his way through that stricken town, wailing on the still night air sounded the muezzin's calls: 'Alla-hu-akbar!' "[3]

In 1917, the brick frontier advancing slowly southeastwards over centuries from the seaboard of northern Europe had not yet reached the Balkans, where wood still remained the chief means of construction. In Salonica, fires were such a regular occurrence that prayers against them formed part of the local Yom Kippur service. With the increase in the town's population in the nineteenth century, and the growing shortage of water, they seem to have got worse. "The French consul," reported Ami Boué in 1854, "told us that he was always obliged to safeguard his most precious papers before going to the countryside for fear of fire." Forty years and three major fires later, an American scholar, hoping to add to his collection of Judaica, was repeatedly told in his book-hunting expedition round the town: "We had books, but they were burned." The great fire of 1890 had done huge damage to the centre of the Hamidian city, especially near the Christian quarter round the Hippodrome. But this was dwarfed by the impact of the 1917 fire which destroyed the essence of the Ottoman town, and its Jewish core. Out of the ashes, an entirely new town began to emerge, one moulded in the image of the Greek state and its society.[4]

REBUILDING THE CITY

"The fire has created the chance to build a new Salonica, a showpiece of business and commerce, commanding the foreigners' respect," wrote a British journalist in *The Comitadji* on 2 September. But officialdom was ahead of the journalists and moving with astonishing speed. Within five days of the fire, a meeting had been convened in Athens to discuss the government's response, and the important decision was taken to expropriate the whole of the fire-affected city centre, and to rebuild the area on a new basis. General Sarrail offered his assistance, and recommended the architects and engineers on his own staff

After the fire: the 1918 plan

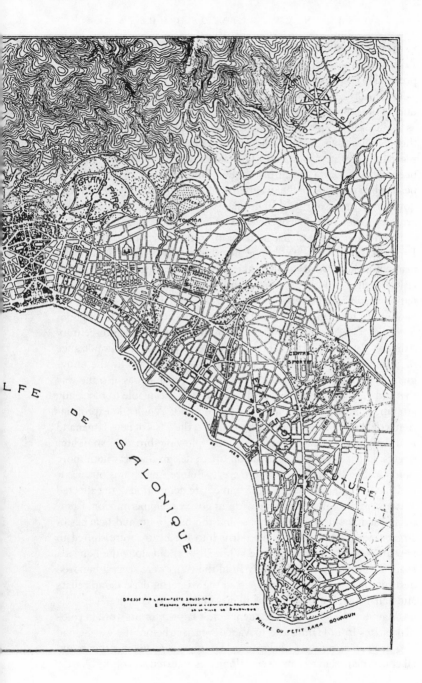

GRAN PARC

GOLFE DE SALONIQUE

CENTRE SPORTIF

FUTURE

DRESSE PAR L'ARCHITECTE BRUXELLOIS
E. HÉBRARD

POINTE DU PETIT KARA BOURNOU

to the Greek authorities. As a result, a committee of Greek, French and British experts was quickly established. Prime Minister Venizelos had previously felt frustrated at his inability to force through what he considered badly needed aesthetic and hygienic improvements to Salonica during the previous four years. The fire, as he put it later, came "almost as a gift of divine providence" and he told the committee's chairman, the distinguished British landscape architect Thomas Mawson, to regard the city as a blank slate. The results were far-reaching, and have been described by a recent historian as "the first great work of European urban planning of the twentieth century." They eradicated the last downtown traces of the old Ottoman town and substituted the modernizers' vision of a city conceived as an integrated whole.[5]

Both Venizelos and his minister of communications, Alexandros Papanastasiou, were capable and decisive men who believed—in the prime minister's words—in "thinking big," and regarded the Ottoman city they had inherited as unworthy of the progressive and modern nation they wished Greece to become. Over the previous century, the ending of Ottoman rule had led to new towns being built throughout much of Greece, but nowhere—not even mid-nineteenth-century Athens—had these settlements come close to the size and importance of Salonica. For Papanastasiou, the problem was not only the unhygienic and uneconomic character of the old town; it was also the way that individual property owners had previously been able to block any attempt at improvements for the general good. Wholesale expropriation would allow the government to plan on the basis of new, larger and more regularly shaped building plots, allowing broader, straighter streets, larger squares and, in all, an urban design that was both more functional and more pleasing to the eye. Before August was out, a law had been passed providing for the immediate demolition of the affected area and prohibiting rebuilding without government permission. Engineers carried out the demolitions, and the huts, tents and benches of street-traders who had begun to drift into the centre were shifted to new areas on its outskirts, by the White Tower, and along the Langada road. The only living beings left amid the ruins were several hundred destitute Jewish refugees, who passed the winter in dark, damp cellars and half-rotten burned-out synagogues in danger of collapse.[6]

Mawson was a landscape gardener, best known for his work in colonial estates from Hampstead to Vancouver. But before the war he had also been advising the Greeks on urban improvements in Athens, and all concerned seem to have seen Salonica as an extension of this. Barely three months after the planning committee first met, a preliminary study had already been exhibited to the public and an exhausted Mawson had been sent back to England to recuperate. Filling his place was a Frenchman, Ernst Hébrard, a younger man, who had been excavating Roman and Byzantine sites in the city for the army's archaeological service. Hébrard was an architect too. Some years earlier he had published a study of the "world city" of the future; later he would go on to design towns in French Indochina. Like Mawson, he was a creature of the colonial era, only in his case, Salonica was an important stepping-stone near the start of his career and the plan that emerged bore his imprint.[7]

Putting theory into practice, the Hébrard Plan fundamentally changed the character of the historic heart of the city for it envisaged a chiefly administrative and business quarter, with residential space relegated to the outskirts and the new suburbs. A new industrial zone was to be established behind the port, condemning the old Ottoman pleasure gardens to a slow demise. The open slopes beyond the eastern walls were to be turned into parkland and the campus of a new university, displacing the vast cemeteries there. Space in general was identified on the basis of its use and function, something quite alien to the city that had preceded it. Streets were to be widened and straightened and the rectangular plot became the norm; the winding narrow alleys which had obstructed Emmanuel Miller's efforts to carry off *Las Incantadas* in 1864 were banished for ever. Long vistas down regular thoroughfares would carry traffic, views, light and air into the very heart of what had been the most insanitary, crowded and unregulated part of the Ottoman town. Even architectural forms themselves were to be regulated, and the plan, with a typical mixture of authoritarianism and naivety, proposed a uniformity of building styles (functional for the workers and lower-middle classes, neo-Byzantine for the downtown municipal buildings), height and colours ("unaesthetic" shades were to be prohibited). A wide avenue was to be cut running down the hill from a large central square on the Via Egnatia to the sea, flanked by grand public buildings, with traffic carried through the city on intersecting roads which ran parallel with the shoreline.

There remained, however, the question of what was to be done with the former inhabitants of the fire-affected zone themselves. Where were they to live and what claim should they have, if any, on the expropriated land? Here was perhaps the most controversial aspect of the entire scheme. Desiring to preserve for itself as much room to manoeuvre as possible, the government stuck fast to its original intention of compensating the owners with certificates which they could use to bid for building land under the plan when it was made available. Most refugees were housed temporarily in shelters and army barracks around the outskirts of the city. Gradually it became clear to them that they would not be returning home.

As the overwhelming majority of these were Jews, there was little doubt in the minds of the leaders of the Jewish community that one of the goals of the plan was to drive Jews from the city's centre. Protests were sent almost immediately to international Jewish organizations to solicit their support. The government denied that "it sought to displace the [existing] population of Salonica and settle another in its stead." Its goal was modernity and civilization, not ethnic engineering. Yet the two were not incompatible and it is striking that most of those entrusted with the plan itself appear to have assumed that its impact on the ethnic balance of the city was not a secondary consideration. "Mawson did state," reported Hetty Goldman to the American Jewish Joint Distribution Committee, "that the fundamental purpose of the plan was to deprive the Jews of complete control of the city." But, she went on, he added "that there was no desire to oust them completely. On the contrary, the Greeks wished to retain the Jewish element of the population and . . . those who could afford to buy back the larger ground plots would doubtless be able to do so. The man with the small property would be the one to suffer."[8]

This was an accurate assessment. The Jews were not an accidental target for they were, at any rate in their traditional pattern of settlement, an integral part of the fabric of the Ottoman city: one could not Westernize Salonica without uprooting the Jews. On the other hand, Jews were not barred from the new plots in the heart of the city, nor prevented from buying there. On the contrary, the Jewish community invested heavily in land in the central zone, and a number of Jewish businessmen did likewise, alongside their Christian counterparts and competitors. The Stoa Modiano was built to house the fruit and vegetable market and a new central synagogue provided the public face of the new, highly centralized religious community. What happened was as much a socio-economic change as an ethnic one. With the government relying on private investors to bear the costs of rebuilding, the wealthiest former inhabitants of the centre benefited most and returned, while those who sold their certificates early or lacked funds were pushed to the shanty-towns on the outskirts. Jewish workers settled on the slopes to the east and west of the city, while the Jewish middle classes enjoyed sea frontage from their villas on the way to Kalamaria. In fact, some of the poorest Jews in the city may well have been better off as a result of the forced relocation. Noting that 2700 poor Jewish families had been rehoused by February 1920, a report from a committee representing their interests concluded that "on the whole the Jewish families have now been provided with better housing than those they had before the fire. As a matter of fact, in the old city, thousands of persons formerly lived in basements and cellars, where light entered in most instances, through very small shafts only, in narrow, humid and filthy alleys. In nearly all of the new quarters, the rooms are well aired. Nothing has been neglected to assure good hygienic conditions."[9]

Continuing the trend evident since the 1890s, the city was separating on class rather than ethnic lines; workers were to be kept apart from the bourgeoisie, and their places of entertainment were separated too. But there was in fact a deeper truth to the complaints of Jewish leaders: the plan's primary purpose—and here it surely succeeded—was to assert the control of the Greek authorities over the very heart of the city, and that goal was incompatible with the old spatial organization of Ottoman Salonica where the densely packed Jewish quarters had dominated its core. Today not even the lay-out of the streets betrays where exactly among the downtown boutiques the numerous sixteenth- and seventeenth-century synagogues were once situated.

FROM A LOCAL PAPER at the end of December 1918 came the following comment, entitled "Papa's Sketches":

"You see Thessaloniki, how beautifully she has been rebuilt?"
"Where?"
"On paper, for now."
"Let's see."
"Look! A first-class city, with everything. With areas for the rich and separate ones for the workers."
"And have they really built somewhere specially for us workers?"
"Have they built it? It's paradise."
"And where are our neighbourhoods, then?"
"You can't see them. They are behind the page."[10]

The pretensions and ambitions of the planners quickly attracted comment from satirists and journalists even before Mawson's preliminary plan was published. One "proposal" at the end of November 1917 suggested helpfully that

> The piers should be turned into a hill where a *téléférique* transports people into the air.
> The trams should be turned into boats, and canals built everywhere.
> The harbour should become a square, the forum of Thessaloniki.
> The Arch of Triumph, which is not pretty, should be demolished and the bits used to build an Eiffel Tower.
> Eleftheria Square should be removed from the new plan and turned into a cemetery.
> We should preserve some ruined houses from the fire and declare them historic monuments.[11]

And indeed, reality—as is its way with town planners and architects—soon modified and whittled down the initial proposals. How could it not have done when there were no less than ten changes of government between 1920 and 1924, the most turbulent period in Greece's history? Within the city centre, Mawson's original plan to unify the railway termini into one grand new station was quickly abandoned: the various lines and stations continued to confuse visitors for several more decades. And after 1920 a new government made more changes, reducing the size of secondary squares, narrowing roads, doubling the number and cutting the size of the plots in order to appease the discontented owners.

Money—or the Greek state's lack of it—was the key obstacle. Even the socialist Papanastasiou soon realized that without private investors, the centre would never get rebuilt. Thus most of the actual construction was left to individual property-owners and well-connected private developers, who did their best to thwart Hébrard's visions of a regulated and uniform aesthetic approach. The hotels, office blocks, apartment buildings, cafés and cinemas of the interwar years ended up in a bewildering variety of styles—pseudo–Louis XV, neo-Renaissance, -Venetian and -Moorish, Art Deco, "Mauritarian-Islamic" and even the occasional glimpse of Bauhaus—alongside the rather stolid Byzantine-Italian mode that Hébrard had deemed most suitable for the city as a whole. There were also gaps and lags: the central waterfront square, Plateia Aristotelous, was finished only in the 1950s and 1960s, and Plateia Eleftherias was just one of the planned open spaces to be turned into a car-park.

Even the city's Byzantine character was emphasized in a slightly absent-minded fashion, as if the planners were more interested in the future than the past. Mosques were converted back into churches, and restored—or, in the case of the fire-ravaged Saint Dimitrios, rebuilt—in a way that cleansed them of the accretion of centuries and brought out what the architects regarded as their "highest value." Sheds, shops and other unworthy elements were removed from the main sites, allowing them to be appreciated in a sanitized environment stripped of all distractions and encumbrances. Yet apart from the use of a few well-known churches as visual reference points, the planners appear to have attached little importance to the city's monumental past. The Arch of Galerius still sits as an afterthought near the eastern end of Egnatia; had Hébrard had his way, it would have been dwarfed by an entirely new colossal Arch of Triumph—never, as it turned out, to be built. To the fury of the inspector of antiquities, no provision was made for an archaeological museum, and he had to struggle to get permission to house his collection in the Yeni Djami, the *Ma'min* mosque.

Downtown, the basic layout of streets remained surprisingly close to the plan's original conception. But outside the city centre the plan's impact fell away sharply. Grand schemes for garden towns remained on paper, and many refugees either housed themselves in shacks made of beaten-out tin, planks and board, or were housed in the army barracks and military hospitals left by the departing French, Italians and British. A model workers' settlement was only half-finished. Mawson's vision of a new university campus adjacent to the eastern walls would have to wait till after the German occupation in the Second World War. And, as we shall see, with the arrival of hundreds of thousands of new refugees in 1922–23, the city expanded rapidly in all directions, too quickly and too haphazardly for the hard-pressed municipal and national authorities to do much more than monitor what was happening.

But back in 1917 the planners could have been forgiven for failing to anticipate the new challenges the city would face. Between 1917 and 1923 the Greek-Turkish antagonism reached a new pitch, climaxing in a further war, the Greek landing and occupation of Izmir, and the invasion of Anatolia; this was followed by catastrophic defeat at the hands of

Mustafa Kemal's new Turkish army, and a forced movement of populations without any precedent in history. More than thirty thousand Muslims were obliged to leave the city. At the same time, nearly one hundred thousand Christian refugees arrived from eastern Thrace, Anatolia and the Black Sea, and turned Greeks back into a majority of Salonica's population for the first time since the Byzantine era. In 1913, Greeks had been a minority of the city's 157,000 inhabitants; by 1928 they were 75% of its population of 236,000. Thanks to war, the fire and the displacement of hundreds of thousands of people, this was now a new city, organized on new principles and populated by newcomers. By 1930, only a small proportion of Salonica's inhabitants could remember the city as it had existed in the days of Abdul Hamid.[12]

17

The Muslim Exodus

AN OLD COLOURED POSTCARD shows a vast Muslim cemetery stretching into the distance, shaded by cypresses and guarded by a low parapet. Hundreds of tombstones, some turbanned, others unadorned, peep through the high grass. In the background there are larger, more distinguished graves, decorated with marble columns, clusters of grapes and wreaths, and behind them a long building of some kind. The message on the back reads:

22 Juin 1916

Mon cher Papa. Voici encore une curiosité de Salonique, un des rares cimetières turques à peu près. Au fond se trouve la mosque des dervishes tourneurs dont il ne reste plus qu'un seul specimen, par contre des familles musulmanes refugies y sont établi leurs campements . . .*

The author was probably a French soldier, and the card is one of the last images we have of the cemetery adjoining the main Salonica *tekke* of the Mevlevi dervish order, among the loveliest spots in the city. Perched on rising ground outside the northwest corner of the walls with a view over the gulf and the Vardar plain, it marked, according to legend, a place of conspicuous piety. In the early seventeenth century, the vizier Ahmed Pasha had been forced out of Istanbul by his enemies, and was living in disgrace in Salonica, when he went for a stroll and fell

*Dear Papa. Here is another of Salonica's curiosities, one of the rare Turkish cemeteries. In the background is the mosque of the whirling dervishes, of whom only one is left. On the other hand, Muslim refugee families are camped out there . . .

into conversation with a Mevlevi hermit inhabiting the boughs of a huge tree. The hermit prophesied his return to power and after this came to pass, Ahmed Pasha endowed a *vakf* to support the Mevlevis and built a monastery on the spot of their encounter. The hermit became the *tekke*'s first *sheykh* and over the centuries the monastery itself became renowned throughout the empire for its wealth.[1]

A wall fortified it against intruders, and behind its large iron gate a garden of cypresses shaded the tombs of the faithful. The main building was fronted by a curving wooden façade of colonnaded porticos with a verandah and huge overhanging timbered eaves that ran its entire length. Inside there were reading rooms and cells for the monks, giving on to a richly decorated central hall which greatly impressed the seventeenth-century traveller Evliya Chelebi: "It has a remarkable cupola, more beautifully constructed than the Mevlevi dervish monastery in Besiktas. Even Habib-Noutzar, the patron himself of carpenters, could not make a dome like this one. The paintings are like magic." Here was the space where adepts performed the ecstatic whirling dance which brought them closer to the divine. But the *tekke* was also a place of learning, where the *Mesnevi* of the founder Djelal-adin Rumi was recited and the Qur'an discussed, a place of charity, which fed the poor and lodged pilgrims, as well as a centre for festivities at the start of each summer.[2]

In Salonica itself, the Mevlevi order enjoyed great prestige. With revenues from the salteries around the gulf, and from other duties, the *sheykh* ran a foundation of considerable local power. In the early nineteenth century the incumbent was known locally as "Talleyrand" for his political acumen. It was a Mevlevi *hodja* who admitted pilgrims to Salonica's most important shrine—the chapel of Ayios Dimitrios—in whose miraculous powers he believed no less than anyone else. Many notables, including governors of the city, belonged to the order and Sultan Mehmed Resad V attended a service in 1911, during the final imperial tour of the European provinces. The visiting card of Ali Eshref, the last *sheykh*, gave his traditional Mevlevi title—Head of the *Sheykhs*—but he was also known to have liberal and constitutionalist sympathies, and was widely respected by the population as a whole. Today, the only trace of the Mevlevis in Salonica is the name they have given to the neighbourhood where they once were based. Nothing remains of the monastery, nor of the cemetery, and a school now stands on the site. When our French visitor penned his postcard in 1916— barely five years after the Sultan's visit—the building was crumbling through neglect, and was being used to house Muslim refugees from the hinterland.

Between 1912 and 1924 its fate mirrored that of Islam in the city as a whole. Emigration—first voluntary, then forced—depleted the place of Muslims; the cemetery was desecrated, its walls were torn down, the tombstones and urns sold off for building materials. When the bones of distinguished former *sheykhs* were threatened with being disinterred, a Greek priest sympathetic to the order helped gather and transport them to the safety of their sister-*tekke* in Istanbul. But to have required Christian help was already a sign of the order's weakness. Deprived of both the living and the dead, the Muslim presence in Salonica was brought to an end.

REFUGEES, 1912–1914

THE EXODUS BEGAN during the Balkan Wars themselves. International observers described the first campaign as a "war waged not only by the armies but by the nations themselves"—a war whose aim was "the complete extermination of an alien population." The judgement may have been excessive, for many hundreds of thousands of Muslim peasants were still farming their land in Macedonia a decade later: massacre and extermination are not the same thing. But perhaps it was not so much excessive as premature, for all the protagonists in the conflict saw that what the Balkan Wars involved was a historic reversal of the prevailing balance of power between Muslims and Christians.[3]

As it marched towards Salonica across the Vardar valley, the Hellenic army was far less violent towards Muslim civilians than its Serbian and Bulgarian allies (in fact, many Muslim peasants fled *into* Greek-held territory to get away from the other armies, and, especially, from the bands of irregulars which accompanied them), and for the most part it preserved its discipline. When Bosnian Muslims, recently settled by the Young Turks in villages in the plain, greeted the troops with the traditional gesture of surrender by offering them bread and salt, there was no trouble. Nevertheless, there was plundering, looting and killing elsewhere, and when the first Greek troops marched into the city, Salonica's Muslim inhabitants kept off the streets, avoiding the assaults and robberies that accompanied the first hours and days of the transition. Once the civilian administration established itself, calm was restored and the initial anxieties were assuaged.[4]

In the countryside, however, it was a different story. During the fighting, the peasants rose in what was described as "a species of Jacquerie . . . throwing themselves ravenously upon the property of the land-owners . . . and destroying much of what they could not carry away." The violence there was more intense from the start, fuelled by a combination of religious and economic resentments. Memories of the Macedonian Struggle—of Greeks and Bulgarians killing each other, of Ottoman soldiers killing both—were still vivid. Outside Kilkis, Christian sharecroppers killed Muslim land-owners as soon as the Bulgarian army approached, and when others attempted to return several months later to reclaim their estates they too were murdered—their bodies were found by the roadside—or warned off. This was a war of the poor against the rich, and Christian as well as Jewish land-owners' homes were also ransacked. Nevertheless, the Muslim beys were the most vulnerable and the least able to protect themselves. In Salonica a group of them requested British assistance in regaining possession of their estates; the governor of Izmir, Rahmi Bey, tried to exchange his properties around Salonica for Greek-owned estates in Anatolia.[5]

As for the hundreds of thousands of poor Muslim villagers, tobacco-farmers, carters and vegetable gardeners, they were vulnerable even after the fighting ended, and for all the fine words of Athens politicians, they experienced Christian rule very differently. Soon their cemeteries were being ploughed over, their *medreses* requisitioned, and sheep and pigs were being sheltered in village mosques. In Serres, the mausoleum of Yusuf Pasha was destroyed and the great mosques were turned into hay lofts by the Bulgarians. Villagers began to leave. According to an observer:

> One needed to be at the Serres market last Tuesday to see with one's own eyes how the business is being done. It was impossible not to cry seeing villagers from the purely Muslim villages . . . emptying their stores and coming into Serres to sell up without thinking about the price. I asked all of those who were preparing to emigrate why they were going and they told me, with tears in their eyes and weeping that "We're used to living freely and in honour, but seeing how they seize our fields and even enter our homes, we feel life has become impossible for Muslims."[6]

With shops, warehouses, fields and public buildings being requisitioned before their eyes, more and more villagers abandoned their homes and made their way to Salonica, from where steamers carried them to lands still under Ottoman control.

It was not only soldiers who were intimidating them. Gendarmes—many of them from Crete, which itself had only recently escaped Ottoman rule—found the reversal of power going to their heads. In one village a "law" was passed ordering all Turks who passed a gendarme to dismount and say "Yassou Effendi": a beating was the punishment for those who failed. Gendarmes threatened any Greeks who were still in the employ of Turkish beys, and ordered them to quit their jobs. Muslims were forced to subscribe to the Greek Naval League and to wear a cross in their buttonhole to show they had paid. All the while, brigands and local farmers enriched themselves—men like Yorgios Papadoulis, a land-owner near Kilkis, who reduced the local bey to penury and behaved "like the absolute master of the region, the tyrant who disposed of the life and person of the entire Turkish population of which today none is left but two people like slaves in his lands."

Much of this could be attributed to the excitement and the aftermath of the war itself. What kept tensions high was the arrival some months later of Greek refugees from Thrace. From late 1913, more than one hundred thousand Greeks suffered ethnic cleansing of their own: driven out of their homes by Bulgarian and Ottoman troops, they fled westwards. Once safely on Greek-controlled soil, they wanted revenge, occupying Muslim properties and trying to drive out their owners. Others were resettled in Muslim communal buildings. With no diplomatic representation of their own (at least before the arrival of an Ottoman consul in Salonica in 1914), and no political representation in Greece before the elections of 1915, Muslim grievances and remonstrations fell on deaf ears.

The Greeks claimed this was the fault of the Ottoman government and its unspoken policy of forcing through an exchange of populations after the war. They pointed to the influx of Greek refugees as proof that the Ottoman authorities wanted to expel Greeks from the last remaining Turkish-controlled lands in Europe and replace them with Muslim settlers. The Greek police claimed Ottoman agents were touring the villages telling Muslim peasants to sell up and leave. This may even have been happening in some places. Just four years earlier the Young Turks had responded to the loss of Ottoman territory in Bosnia by urging Bosnian Muslims to settle in Macedonia. Bringing them out of Macedonia into Thrace to resettle the strategically crucial lands just west of Istanbul with a loyal population would have been a logical continuation of this policy. Ottoman diplomats did in fact propose a partial exchange of populations to the Greeks, though this was never implemented because of the outbreak of the First World War. But as an explanation for why Muslims were leaving, the idea that the Turkish authorities were to blame was a convenient over-simplification. The real reasons for the exodus, wrote the British consul, were not patriotic or religious feelings but "widespread massacres, forced conversions and the wholesale robbing of Muslim goods," mostly by "Macedonian Christians," in other words Slav peasants.[7]

By the spring of 1914 tens of thousands of Muslim villagers had passed through Salonica en route to Izmir and Istanbul. "Vast numbers of Moslems arrived on the outskirts of Salonica during our stay there," wrote an international team of observers. "We saw them camped to the number, it is said, of 8000 in the field and by the roadside. They had come with their bullock carts, and whole families found their only shelter in these primitive vehicles. They had left their villages and their fields, and to all of them the future was a blank." Refugees crowded into the courtyards of mosques, sheltering behind makeshift carpet partitions; others were put temporarily in unoccupied houses. The Greek government fed many, and the city's Muslim Committee looked after the rest, and organized their transportation: as under the Ottomans, care of refugees was still regarded as primarily a communal matter. But of the 140,000 who had left by April 1914, only 24,000 were from the newly conquered Greek territories: the vast majority had fled the Serbs and Bulgarians, many in anticipation of future troubles.

The Turkish press had its own mirror-image of the Greek allegations: it was all the fault of the Greeks and their "systematic plan to force the Muslims to emigrate." In reality there was no plan. The brutality of lower-ranking Greek officials and the anti-Muslim outlook of many of the men were unmistakable. But the government at higher levels was concerned at losing the "sober and hardworking" Muslim farmer through emigration, for who would then till the new lands? No one dreamed in 1914 that more than one million Greeks might eventually be forced to leave Anatolia. On the contrary, the need to make sure that *they* were properly treated was a major curb on any officially sanctioned Greek anti-Muslim policy. The Ottoman government did not bother to hide the link, and there was a clear relationship between the expulsions of Greeks and Turks. The arrival of Muslim refugees from Macedonia in Anatolia led to the formation of irregular *chetté* bands which wreaked *their* revenge on the Christian peasants there. Turkish officials began organizing their own deportations in May 1914 and forty thousand Anatolian Greeks fled the Turkish mainland for the safety of Chios. Not for the first or last time, victims were becoming perpetrators, adding another twist to the spiral of nationalist war. To the British consul in Salonica the pattern of events was horribly clear:

> The result of the massacre of Muslims at the beginning of the war, of the looting of their goods in the ensuing months, of the settling of Christians in their villages, of their persecution by Christian neighbours, of their torture and beating by Greek troops, has been the creation of a state of terror among the Islamic population. Their one desire is to escape from Macedonia and to be again in a free land.
>
> They arrive in Turkey with the memory of their slaughtered friends and relations fresh in their minds, they remember their own sufferings and the persecutions of which they have been victims, and finding themselves without means or resources, encouraged to some extent by their own government, they see no wrong in falling on the Greek Christians of Turkey and meting out to them the same treatment that they themselves have received from the Greek Christians of Macedonia.[8]

THE MUSLIM COMMUNITY: THE FINAL PHASE

SALONICA REPRESENTED SAFETY in comparison with the violent countryside, but life for Muslims there did not return to anything close to normality. Most Muslim residents in the city kept their Ottoman citizenship after 1912, and the new authorities followed the old Ottoman model by creating what they termed an "Ottoman community" to represent them, headed by a newly appointed *mufti*. Unfortunately, it was not always clear whether the rents on certain properties—the legacy of the old *vakf* system—belonged to the municipality as a whole, or specifically to the city's Muslims. With the municipality laying claim to buildings and lands, revenues formerly dedicated to the upkeep of mosques, *tekkes*, schools and orphanages dried up. The presence of an Ottoman consul afforded some diplomatic protection. But the community remained very weak, and it was unable to get the local authorities—despite the fact that the mayor at this time was a Muslim, Osman Sait Bey—to protect them. Cemeteries were desecrated, and the pattern of violence which had already driven villagers from their homes began to manifest itself in the city too.

Gangs of axe-wielding Greek refugees ransacked Muslim shops, and broke into houses. Following protests by Muslim community leaders and the local Turkish press, the governor-general tried to get the squatters to leave; but often the best the real owners could hope for was to obtain some form of rent from the new occupants. There were also constant humiliations. Cretan gendarmes assaulted non-Greeks for such petty infractions as speaking French instead of Greek. Fezzes were torn from people's heads and in June 1914 the muezzin in the Mes'ud Hasan district was mocked whenever he made the call to prayer.[9]

In a couple of years, more than fifteen thousand Muslims left their homes. The mother, sister and cousin of Mustafa Kemal made their way to the refugee camps of the Turkish capital. Also departing was Nazim Pasha, the last governor of the city: he was a distinguished associate of the great reformer Midhat Pasha, a poet and a Mevlevi adept. His eleven-year-old grandson, who had grown up in the neighbourhood of the Aladja Imaret, wrote a poem lamenting the loss of the city; later he would become famous as Turkey's best-known modern poet, Nazim Hikmet. "I was born in 1902/I never went back to my birthplace/I don't like to turn back"—this from his poem *Autobiography*, which he wrote in East Berlin in 1961, shortly before his death—"Some people know all about plants, some about fish/I know separation."

But at the highest levels of the Greek state, there was no desire to provoke a large-scale emigration, and had it not been for the pressure exerted by incoming Greek refugees, the persecution of Muslims in Greece would have subsided more quickly. As it was, experienced observers in Salonica in the spring of 1914 were impressed by the extent to which the Greek authorities were trying "not to offend the susceptibilities of their Moslem subjects" and predicted that "in time Greek rule may benefit them." In 1915 national elections took place in which Muslims could vote. They were considerably freer than the 1912 elections to the Ottoman parliament had been, and sixteen Turkish MPs took their seats in Athens supporting the anti-Venizelist camp.[10]

IN FACT, AS GREECE ENTERED THE WAR on the Entente side, there were still some thirty thousand Muslims in Salonica, and more than ten times that number in the provinces. Their sympathies were mostly with the Central Powers of course. When a German Zeppelin was shot down and its carcass was re-assembled and put on display by the White Tower, the local Turks mourned the loss of an ally. And in 1918, when Greeks celebrated the end of the war, Christian schoolboys mocked Muslims, by reminding them they had lost.[11] For a time, it looked as if having picked the winning side, Greece would soon be governing Muslims in Asia Minor as well. Venizelos was one of the stars of the Paris Peace Conference and when he received the green light to occupy and administer the Izmir region, it seemed that his great gamble on the war had paid off. The great Cretan had brought his small country within sight of the "Greece of Five Seas"—the modern resurrection of the Byzantine empire—which Greek nationalists had been dreaming of for a century. Ottoman authority lay in tatters, and Mustafa Kemal was only beginning to reorganize the army on a new basis. In 1919 Greek troops disembarked in Izmir, and Salonica's Muslims faced the greatest test of their loyalties so far.

But the following year Venizelos was ejected from office by a war-weary electorate. It was the biggest shock in Greek political history and Muslim and Jewish voters in northern Greece were crucial to the anti-Venizelists' success. When the news reached Salonica, delighted Greek soldiers—for there were huge numbers of Greek anti-Venizelists too—swapped their caps for Muslim fezzes, and Turks and Jews joined in the celebrations.[12] Although the formation of a royalist government in Athens did not lead to any radical change of policy in Asia Minor, for a year and a half Salonica's Muslims enjoyed a more sympathetic and supportive administration. Under the presidency of a Muslim government deputy, a congress on the use of the Turkish language in education was convened in the city. New Turkish-language newspapers and satirical journals emerged, textbooks were imported from Allied-controlled Istanbul, and travel restrictions on Muslims were lifted. At Ramadan in 1921, the *iftar* and *sahur* cannonades were fired once more to mark the points between dusk and dawn when Muslims might break their fast: for the last time in Salonica's history, they entertained their friends and relatives during these festive evenings.[13]

The Greek military debacle in Anatolia and the successful Turkish counter-attack brought this Indian summer to an end. When the Greek army rashly advanced hundreds of miles eastwards towards Ankara in a bid to crush the Kemalist forces, it suffered a decisive defeat in a bloody battle at the Sakarya River. Afterwards, the Turkish national assembly named the commander-in-chief, Mustafa Kemal, Field Marshal and *Ghazi*: it was a decisive step on his road to absolute power. The Greek army fell back to new lines, but the following summer a successful Turkish offensive forced them towards Izmir and the coast. Retreat turned into a rout, as military discipline broke down and Turkish irregulars harassed their flanks. First the French and then the British withdrew their backing from the Greeks and sought terms with Turkey's new leadership. The culmination of these dramatic events—which ended a Greek presence in Asia Minor dating back more than two thousand years—came in September 1922 when the city of Izmir went up in flames, tens of thousands of civilians were killed, and an overwhelming mass of refugees fled before the advancing Turkish troops. Two months later, Ataturk proclaimed the abolition of the Ottoman empire.

Although Venizelos had begun the invasion of Asia Minor, it was the royalists that succeeded him who took the blame for defeat. In Athens, a group of patriotic young Venizelist army officers seized power in a military coup, deposed the anti-Venizelist government and after a show trial executed the prime minister and five others whom they held responsible for the catastrophe. Martial law was declared in Salonica, its Muslim mayor was ousted (having held the position on and off since 1908), and a leading supporter of the Revolutionary Committee was named governor. For the city's Muslims, the prospects immediately darkened. Venizelists were again in power, but this time the military were in charge and the atmosphere was uglier than at any point in the past. Greece had just suffered the worst disaster in its history, and thousands of destitute refugees were arriving daily at the Salonica docks on a scale which dwarfed any previous influx. Bewildered, angry and frightened, the Revolutionary Committee and its supporters were in a paranoiac frame of mind. They purged the ranks of royalists and threw many into prison. But they still found it hard to explain the scale of the catastrophe that had befallen their country. "We wonder why and how we have so many enemies, we Greeks," wrote the ardently Venizelist Penelope Delta. Izmir had been lost; was even Macedonia safe?[14]

Seeing conspiracy everywhere, the search for secret agents began. The *mufti* was arrested and so was the former mayor. Muslim villagers in the countryside were believed to be celebrating the Turkish victory, and were said to be waiting for the Kemalist army to liberate them too: how, after all, could Mustafa Kemal resist the chance of marching to free Salonica, his own birthplace? There were stories of a Kemalist underground in Salonica itself, collecting money to buy arms. A rising could not be ruled out, nor even a replay of the old Macedonian Struggle, this time with the Turks as the underdogs. Agents reported that "fanatical Kemalists," mostly drawn from the *Ma'min* community, had made contact with royalist anti-Venizelists. Others indicated that Muslims—directed from Istanbul—were cooperating with prominent Jews and with Bulgarian *komitadjis*. By December 1922, Salonica's chief of police was at his wits' end: the city's population had swollen to 350,000, among them "all the worst elements, common criminals and propagandists."[15]

The Venizelists now decided to rule out any chance of a repetition of their 1920 defeat. They cordoned off the Muslims and Jews in separate electoral colleges so that national minorities could never again become arbiters of the country's political fortunes. Then they took advantage of a botched royalist counter-coup to arrest and exile scores of their opponents. Greek politics was now set for another round of the interminable struggle between royalists and republicans, but this no longer mattered to Salonica's Muslims. For at the end of 1922 Greek and Turkish delegates meeting in Lausanne had negotiated an end to the war and agreed at the same time to a comprehensive exchange of populations. There had been voluntary exchanges before but for the first time in history this one was to be compulsory and sanctioned by international law. Norwegian diplomat Fridtjof Nansen, who had been entrusted by the League of Nations with organizing refugee relief, probably made the original suggestion but both Venizelos and Ataturk were already thinking on similar lines. The two leaders were seeking to build nation-states on the ruins of the Ottoman empire and both were supervising a policy of national and religious homogenization. Venizelos himself had been born in Ottoman Crete; Ataturk had grown up in Hamidian Salonica. But for both, the world of their childhood had vanished, the time for fighting was over, and a new society and a new state now needed to be constructed, on national principles. With some minor exceptions, Greece would receive all the Orthodox Christians of Asia Minor, Turkey the Muslim population of Greece. A total of more than one and a half million lives were affected, the Muslims of Salonica among them.[16]

THE EXCHANGE OF POPULATIONS

IN APRIL 1914, following the Balkan Wars, the French ambassador in Constantinople had already seen the writing on the wall. Minorities were a source of conflict, he instructed Paris, and since they could not live together in peace, they must be eradicated by being moved to their proper homelands:

> The Balkan peninsula in its entirety is at this moment the theatre of horrors comparable to those which accompany the great migrations of peoples; these horrors are the logical consequence of recent events, and, sad to say, perhaps the only means of putting an end once and for all to disorder and anarchy, to the murders and depredations which ravage European Turkey lies in redistributing the Balkan populations by nationality among each of the states among whom European Turkey was divided at Bucharest. It is a sad but definitive liquidation of a situation which neither Turkey nor Europe has found a remedy for in more than a century.[17]

A limited population exchange, affecting villages along the new Turco-Bulgarian border, had been agreed by the two governments in November 1913. The following spring, after the Ottoman authorities had attempted to clear part of the Asia Minor coastline, by expelling and deporting Greek residents, diplomats discussed the idea of a partial population exchange, covering the Muslims from Macedonia and the Greeks from around Izmir. The initial idea was for a compulsory agreement, though the Greek side watered this down and the discussions ended with the outbreak of the First World War. Venizelos was evidently struck by the concept because the following year he sketched out a plan for a reciprocal scheme with Bulgaria. But even at the time many resisted the logic of exchange and saw it as a capitulation to mankind's worst instincts. When news of the Greco-Turkish talks reached Archbishop Chrysostomos of Izmir—eight years later he would be among the first of the thousands of Greeks to be killed in the sack of his city—he angrily denounced the very idea of this "counting and exchange of human beings—incomprehensible, unheard-of and unprecedented in the chronicles of History—as is done by animal dealers with horses, livestock and cattle." And many of those affected later—both Muslim and Christian—shared his sentiments: a large refugee meeting in Salonica in January 1923 reacted to news of the Lausanne agreement by protesting the decision as "a disgraceful bartering of bodies to the detriment of modern civilization."[18]

But at the end of 1922 Venizelos was in no mood to listen. The truth was that more than one million refugees had already arrived in Greece from Asia Minor by the time the agreement was signed, and there was no earthly chance they could ever return to their homes. The imperative for the Greek side was to find ways to house them, and in his mind this meant expelling the country's remaining Muslims so that their property could be utilized. That suited the new regime in Turkey too: not only would their control of the much larger quantity of Christian property in Anatolia be thereby legitimated; but they would also need Muslim immigrants to resettle the land and help cushion the huge economic disruption which the loss of so many Christians must cause. As a Turkish deputy put it to the Ankara assembly: "The arrival of every individual is a source of richness for us; and the departure of every individual is a blessing for us!" For both sides, it was evident that if Greece's Muslims would not go by themselves, they must be forced to leave.[19]

For Salonica, therefore, the 1923 population exchange completed what 1912 had begun—the dispossession and disappearance of the group which had dominated its life over the preceding five centuries. Although the city was by this point predominantly—and increasingly—Greek, as of July 1923 there still remained a Muslim community of at least eighteen thousand people. They were deeply attached to their birthplace and according to the local Greek authorities, only a "few fanatics" among them actually wanted to depart. The sisters of the departing mayor were said to be "inconsolable" at having to leave their home. "When our people asked those caught up in the exchange if they were happy to be going to Turkey," remembered Kostas Tomanas, "they replied sorrowfully, 'We don't know.' "[20]

Yet there were all-too-evident incentives to pack. By 1923, Muslim peasants in the villages were being required to supply newly arrived Christian refugees with everything from food to bedding. Their fields and oxen were confiscated and some refugees broke into mosques to steal the carpets. Destitute and bitter at their own treatment in Anatolia, others made Muslim peasants fetch water, firewood or stones for them. As a result, many of the Turkish-speaking peasants were said to be "longing to leave Greece."

In the city the authorities kept a closer eye on things, but the pressure of the tens of thousands of new arrivals was irresistible. In the neighbourhood of Mes'ud Hasan, on the eastern side of the Upper Town, for example, where the religious properties administered by the *mufti* amounted to one-third of all real estate, most of this was immediately occupied by refugees. Property-owners hired guards to stop the attacks but the numbers were overwhelming: The boyhood home of Reshad Tesal, son of a Muslim politician, was attacked one afternoon by fifty refugees who burst in and began to allocate the rooms among themselves. His father protested to the governor-general himself who sent a dozen Greek soldiers to evict the squatters, but the remedy was only temporary and the family had to share the house after another break-in, using the newcomers as a protection against further incursions. "We had to accept these people to prevent further attacks," recalls Tesal. "We were lucky that these were very decent people. They spoke Turkish and respected our customs and way of life. We lived together with this family at peace until we left Salonica." If this was the situation which confronted a former MP in the Greek parliament, we can guess how less well-connected Muslims fared. "Houses which the Muslims departing for Turkey are leaving and which have been occupied illegally and without the permission of the authority must be vacated," ran an announcement in January 1924. It had little effect.[21]

While refugees took matters into their own hands, the bureaucracy established under the population exchange agreement began to function. The end of 1924 was set as the terminal date for Muslims to leave the country and mixed committees of Greek, Turkish and international bureaucrats supervised the process of emigration in as orderly a fashion as they could. Valuation committees received property declarations from departing house-owners, and trains from western Macedonia began arriving in the city with hundreds of peasants at a time, carrying an estimated twelve tons of luggage per train before the Turkish government announced a weight limit for what emigrants could bring with them. From November 1923, steamers began to ship out the 350,000 Muslims affected—first peasants and then city-dwellers.

At the port there were chaotic scenes: one minute, Muslim householders were being told they were not allowed to sell those goods they could not take with them—then that they could. The agreement was clearly intended to be definitive, but the Turkish consul was making fiery speeches at the dockside telling the emigrants that "in two months they would be back in their homes." Fraudsters took advantage of the emigrants' anxieties and there was a flourishing market in fake travel documents. Among the thousands who arrived at the docks there were numerous Yugoslav Muslims, who had sold their homes and were hoping to obtain lands in Anatolia left behind by the departing Greeks. In the end, there were so many of these that the Turkish government ordered captains not to admit them on board. Meanwhile the schedule of departures was delayed as the Kemalist government tried to find Turkish ships to carry out the embarkations.[22]

Salonica itself saw relatively little violence, though the threat hung in the air; on the other hand, amid the desperation, acute poverty, political uncertainty and urban disorder, criminal gangs flourished. Greek refugees broke into a Turkish-owned dairy and stole some large cheeses, leaving behind an apologetic note: "It isn't death that frightens us, only hunger/and our children, who are starving too." After other refugees bought cows from a Muslim householder—for in these days, farmers still sold fresh milk within the city walls—the seller boasted too loudly in the local taverna of the high price he had got, and the following night he and his wife were killed in their beds.[23]

Such killings were rare and even today elderly Muslims from Greece remember the exodus as a largely peaceful matter. Mixed Greco-Turkish commissions did try to protect emigrants, allowing them to sell off property prior to departure, and to record their valuations of what they were leaving behind. Indeed, many of the Greek refugees in the city reacted angrily to this, for the violent turmoil of their own hasty exodus from Anatolia had not permitted such an orderly winding-up of their affairs. "When we see the Turks of Salonica leaving the country, music playing and carrying all their possessions, money and preferred objects," one refugee group protested, "we don't understand the reasons for this difference in treatment." Others complained that the departing Muslims were allowed "to bring their donkeys and even their dogs, the doors and windows of their houses and in general everything they can carry away with them." In their minds, the exchange agreement had made the stock of Muslim housing in the city theirs: anything subtracted from it meant less for Greeks. Their own organizations put the local authorities under pressure to speed up the Muslims' departure, and they threatened the members of the committee which regulated the exodus that if they took too long a summer holiday they might find the refugees taking matters into their own hands. "Let the Turks be gone," they demanded in August. "Every delay of the exchange is a heavy blow to the refugees and all Greeks. We should not have to pass a third winter in such misery." In fact the steamers were embarking 7,000 weekly and 111,000 had left Salonica by the end of December. Arriving in Izmir or Istanbul, they were greeted with "tea and cakes, speeches and flags" before being sent up-country. Ataturk's government tried to plan for their coming, assigning them places of settlement and providing loans for the poorest. Even so, disappointment often awaited them and they found "they had neither houses, food, money nor any means of procuring the necessaries of life."[24]

Desperate to stay, some "exchangeables" (as they were termed) tried to take advantage of Greek contacts they had built up over the years of the Macedonian Struggle. One bey vainly solicited the help of a former Greek band leader whom he had helped hide from the Ottoman authorities years earlier: the latter tells in his memoirs how he sought to obtain his friend's exemption only to find he had already been embarked for Turkey. Other Muslims emphasized their anti-Kemalist credentials, for things were happening in Turkey itself that many of them disapproved of, including the abolition of the empire and the exiling of the last sultan. (The last Ottoman *sheykh-ül-Islam*, an outspoken anti-Kemalist, actually fled *into* Greece.) For these "old Turks," the term "Ottoman" was much more than merely a synonym for Muslim, and they did not like the look of Ataturk's new secular republic. Under the pressure of their impending departure, bitter rows broke out between "old" and "Young Turks." In the Hamza Bey mosque Kemalists were angered by the *mufti*'s Ottomanist sympathies—praying for the deposed sultan—and accused him of being a Greek puppet and against what they called "the Ottoman republic."[25]

Historians have had little to say about those Muslims who mourned the passing of the empire and opposed the founding of the new Turkish state. The extraordinary lengths to which the anti-Kemalist opposition could go is illustrated by the case of Ali Sami Bey, a fifty-year-old former colonel, court photographer and adjutant to Sultan Abdul Hamid. Sami Bey had apparently followed his exiled sultan to Salonica, and stayed there after 1912, publishing a newspaper called *Justice* which proclaimed itself during the war to be "the supporter of the Entente and protector of Islam and the Greeks." During the Asia Minor campaign, he actually fought for the Greeks and organized an underground anti-Kemalist resistance organization. Back in Salonica in October 1924 he resumed publication of his newspaper. That same month—with the deadline for final evacuation fast approaching—he approached the governor of the city to complain that the departing *mufti* planned to take with him the carpets of the Hamza Mosque: Sami Bey requested that they and the mosque itself should be kept in the city for the benefit of the "many Ottomans of foreign nationality, as well as anti-Kemalists, Circassians, Albanians and others" who would stay behind. But plans to appoint an Albanian *mufti* were squashed after Greek refugees protested that the mosque itself should count as "exchangeable property"; it remained open for a little while after the last Muslims had been embarked but by June 1925 there was no one left to pray there, and it was turned into a telephone exchange. Sami Bey himself was one of the very few Muslims permitted to remain. He opened a photography studio—a photograph of a dervish with a needle through his cheek decorated the shop-window—and between 1925 and 1927 he took a remarkable series of panoramic photographs of the monasteries on Mount Athos. Shortly afterwards he appears to have left Salonica for good and moved to southern Greece.[26]

RIGHT ON SCHEDULE, the exodus was completed. "Excellency!" the governor-general of Macedonia was informed by the French official in charge. "We have the honour to bring to your attention that the last convoy of exchangeable Muslims from this city left for Turkey on 26 December and that the evacuation of the city of Salonica of all Muslims may be considered as completely terminated from said date."[27] All that was left was to count how many Muslims were still there. A little later, the local press announced:

> Since the term for exchangeable Muslims to leave the city of Thessaloniki expired on 26 December, we are informed that there will be a detailed census of those remaining after that date . . . Those who do not have a special permit to remain for a specified period of time will be forced to leave quickly. Those in possession of passes are granted no more than 5–6 months.[28]

At the end of January 1925, the head of police summarized the results. Of the 97 names on his list, 78 were foreign nationals, chiefly Serbs who worked as food-sellers, and Albanians (mostly consular security men, or *cavasses*); 12 were liable for removal, and had been delayed for "unknown reasons," and 7 were of unknown citizenship or making special cases for exemption—mostly rich land-owners or industrialists trying to obtain Albanian papers which would allow them residency in Greece. The question of who counted as Albanian tormented the Greek authorities, not least since a very high proportion of the Muslims in the city could legitimately have made such a claim. In the end it was decided that residence in Greece, the Muslim faith, a father born in Albania and lack of what was termed a "Turkish self-consciousness" were the key criteria. In this way a handful of notable *Ma'min* managed to wangle a reprieve, including Ahmed Kapanji, scion of one of the leading families of the late Ottoman city, whose magnificent fin-de-siècle villa was converted into the local NATO headquarters after the Second World War. Three months on, the police were still trying to chase up stray Muslims: Saki Abdoulah and Saim Ekrem were not exempt and were instructed to leave the city within ten days; Ali Terzi was away in Vodena, Fais Mustafa was in Athens, and Haki Bekir could not be found. Some had left for Albania. Two claimed to be "Circassians"—a category which left the police confused and asking for further instructions. But by this point virtually everyone else had departed for Turkey, where the new republic of Kemal Ataturk would turn them from Muslims, as most had once identified themselves, into Turks.[29]

The City Without Muslims

UNDER THE TERMS OF THE POPULATION EXCHANGE, the properties they left behind—they had been forbidden to sell their homes privately since late 1922—were due to be taken over by the state for the benefit of the incoming Christian refugees. In the old city, this amounted to a very considerable collection of real estate since Muslims, despite their depleted numbers, possessed much more property than Greeks or Jews. At least one-third of the burned zone, for instance, had been owned by them. In the Upper Town, the proportion was much higher, and entire streets and neighbourhoods were emptied of the former owners. It is not surprising that for years after the Greek refugees had settled there, the ghosts of local dervishes and Muslim saints were reported around their old haunts, clustering in particular by old fountains, shrines and former mosques: exorcists were much in demand as new house-buyers moved in. From January 1925, the first formerly Muslim commercial properties were auctioned off in a *kafeneion* by the Syntrivani fountain: Rifaat Efendi's shop on Markos Botsaris Street, and Ahmed Hussein's on Army Avenue were the first to go under the hammer; by April, the new tenants of these properties had already formed an association to protect their interests.[30]

As if to erase any indication that there had ever been Muslims in the city, the municipality decided almost immediately to demolish the city's minarets, which had been the defining feature of Salonica's skyline, and invited building companies to bid for the work. "One after the other, the symbols of a barbarous religion fall crashing to the ground," wrote one journalist. "The forest of white minarets is thinning out . . . The red fezzes are leaving, the yashmaks vanish. What else remains? Nothing. Nothing after some months will remind us that the occupier swaggered through here, shamelessly raising emblems of his faith, sullying magnificent temples of Orthodoxy! . . . Their threatening height will no longer intimidate us, nor remind us of the former misfortunes of our race, the frightful slavery and the sufferings of their subjects. The voice of the muezzin will no longer bother our ears, and he and his voice will disappear in the depths of their new country . . . Nothing, nothing at all must remind us again of the epoch of slavery."[31]

The demolitions followed the pattern set over the past century in Old Greece and elsewhere in the Balkans where the departure of Muslims was often followed swiftly by the destruction of their places of worship. But not everyone agreed: "I accept as correct and logical the demolition of the minarets of former Christian churches which had been turned into mosques," declared the former prime minister, Alexander Papanastasiou, in a press interview. "But the demolition of the minarets of other mosques is a coarse act stemming from mindless chauvinism. Those issuing the decree imagined that they could thus make the traces of Turkish occupation disappear. But history is not written with the destruction of innocent monuments which beautified the city." For Papanastasiou, the minarets too were a "national resource." Typically, he argued that "the disappearance of the traces of the occupation should come about only through the elevation of our own civilization." But his opinion came too late to affect the outcome, and anyway in the circumstances it was unlikely he would have been heard with sympathy.[32]

Even the few religious buildings that survived aroused angry attacks in the press. Leading the charge was Nikolaos Fardis, a journalist whose ardent nationalism would lead him down the path of collaboration in the Second World War:

Who can tell me why that disgusting Hamza mosque remains on the key corner of Venizelos and Egnatia streets? Architectural value? None! Historic value? Less than none! The square building is simply ugly . . . And the state uses part of this miserable mass of stones as . . . cabins of the telephone exchange where everyone goes when they want to call Athens! And yet around the mosque huge blocks have gone up, and the road, prepared for the double set of tram lines, with its luxurious lamps, looks

almost European. As soon as we can we must tear down the
Hamza mosque which someone paid two or more millions for.[33]

Fardis's spite was turned equally against other such remnants—the
"miserable baths" by the White Tower (which were eventually demolished), another old bath-house by the Stoa Modiano, and even the covered market, the *bezesten*, whose survival he attributed to a mania
among the urban planners for "local colour." Thanks to such attitudes,
almost all the city's *medreses*, mosques and *tekkes* disappeared and today
only the hundred-foot-high minaret of the Rotonda survives out of the
dozens which once punctuated the skyline.[34]

Outside the heart of the city, the story was slightly different. The
old Turkish cemetery, beyond the city walls, was soon occupied as
"exchangeable property" and gave birth to the shanty-town of Ayia
Foteini. In the Upper Town, however, where most of the 4700 vacant
private properties were to be found, less was destroyed. Its villas were
large and often possessed spacious courtyards and grounds: refugee
families built over the gardens and moved into the existing homes,
many of which survived for decades with their characteristic overhanging storeyed *sachnisia*, wooden frames and shuttered windows. Tall
Ottoman town houses, their façades faded in washes of pink, pale blue
and ochre, preserved by their inhabitants' poverty, still commanded the
curving lanes of the Upper Town in the late 1970s. Today few are left;
most have been torn down and replaced with modern versions in concrete and glass.

Ironically it was more or less as soon as the fire-affected centre was
rebuilt in the new modern vein that the back-streets of the Upper Town
came to seem repositories of a kind of authenticity. There one could
find an urban landscape which by its popular and anonymous tradition-
alism, its simple charm, challenged the pretensions of modernist architects, bureaucrats and entrepreneurs. Stripped of their unwelcome
political overtones, the "old days" acquired a new appeal. "[The Upper
Town] shows us whatever remained standing from former times,"
wrote a journalist in 1931. "There is rhythm and order there . . . Its
streets are more poetic and the trees which flower among the square
houses give a romantic tone to the spot." In May 1935, the city's new
tourism office organized the first walking tour of the city which consisted almost entirely of the sights of the Upper Town. Even the names
of its neighbourhoods—Chinar, Tsaous Monastir, Yedi Kulé, the
Islachané—preserved the charm of bygone times. Yet the romanticism

offered by the Upper Town could not be separated from the fact that its creators and former occupants were no longer there. This was a romanticism of ruins, or at least of absence.[35]

IN RECENT YEARS, books, monuments, museums and conferences have contributed to a new interest in the deportation and extermination of the city's Jews during the Second World War. After a lengthy silence, the subject emerged from the shadows to become a legitimate topic of discussion. As yet, however, no such debate has opened concerning the departure of Salonica's Muslims. Their experiences are still overshadowed in the public mind by the simultaneous suffering of the Greek refugees who took their place. Yet their exodus was an event of the first importance for the city and its subsequent history for it marked the real break with the Ottoman past, the moment in which the twentieth century imposed its values and practices upon an older world.

In this process of nation-making through force there were two deadly novelties in operation. The first—visible during the Balkan Wars—was what a much later generation termed ethnic cleansing, that is to say, the use of war to alter the ethnographic balance of particular regions. Greeks, Turks, Serbs and Bulgarians had all—to one degree or another—seen the wars of 1912–18 in such terms. Yet ethnic cleansing was usually hesitant, partial, and incomplete, and the hatreds and bullying of soldiers, gendarmes and peasants were often counter-balanced by the very different priorities of political elites. In Salonica—and in the surrounding countryside—the majority of the Muslim inhabitants had not moved: they had withstood the threat of violence just as they had proved deaf to the calls of Turkish politicians and agents to uproot themselves for the good of the homeland.

To get them to leave in their totality required a diplomatic agreement drawn up between states in the aftermath of war, which forcibly uprooted these people for the sake of geopolitical stability and nation-building. This time—in 1923–24—they had to depart whether they wished to or not. Their nationality was of no relevance; their religion alone marked them out for removal. And it was just here that the awesome power and ambition of the twentieth-century state left its nineteenth-century Ottoman precursor in the shade. Populations could now be moved on an unprecedented scale, and every aspect of the operation—from the evaluation of properties to transportation and resettlement—was, at least on paper, the responsibility of the state. Under such pressure, the Muslims of Salonica had no choice, and within a year and a half, Muslim life in the city came to an end. For the Greek authorities, keen to Hellenize the city and the northern new lands as a whole, their departure was a vital step forward in shifting the ethnographic balance and making properties available for the Christians flooding in from the East. The Muslims from Salonica settled in places like Izmir and Manisa and helped those towns become Turkish, while their old home-town for the first time in five centuries became predominantly Greek.

18

City of Refugees

WITH JUSTICE the writer Giorgos Ioannou once called Salonica "the capital of refugees." In the late nineteenth century alone, it had welcomed Russian Jews, Tatars, Circassians and Muslims from the lost Ottoman provinces of Thessaly, Bosnia and Crete. Armenians found shelter from both Bolsheviks and Turks, and remnants of General Wrangel's White Russian army squatted in abandoned First World War barracks until the 1960s. Today a new generation of Greeks from the former Soviet Union have also made their home there, as well as Georgians and Kurds. No group of refugees, however, has had an impact—either on the city, or on the country itself—remotely comparable to the huge, panic-stricken immigration of over one million Orthodox Christians who arrived during the final death-throes of the Ottoman empire. In Greece this event is still known simply as the Catastrophe. At its height, in 1922 and 1923, boats docked daily, unloading thousands of starving homeless passengers. It was, by any standards, an overwhelming humanitarian disaster. But in the longer run, it was also the means by which the New Lands and their capital, Salonica, finally became Greek. The refugees fled an empire, and helped build a nation-state.[1]

CATASTROPHE

EVEN IN 1912–13, Muslims (and Bulgarians) leaving Greek territory were outnumbered by the Greeks coming in. Every army, and every state, was driving out civilians. At least forty thousand Greeks fled the Bulgarians, while the Turks expelled about one hundred thou-

The Balkans after 1918

sand from eastern Thrace, and by 1916 the demographic balance in Salonica had been fundamentally changed.

Soon there were many more. In 1920–21, another 20,000 fled fierce fighting in the Caucasus. In their tented encampment on Cape Karaburnu, typhus was rife, and there was little water, fuel or shelter from the harsh winter winds and rain. Amid the stench of human waste and dying children, American Red Cross workers battled to avert a "natural disaster."[2] Yet almost immediately they were engulfed in the human tidal wave which followed the Greek defeat in Asia Minor as nearly one million refugees, at least half of them in need of urgent assistance, clogged the roads and ports heading west. "In a never-ending, staggering march, the Christian population of Eastern Thrace is jamming the roads towards Macedonia," wrote Ernest Hemingway, reporting for the *Toronto Star* in October 1922. "The main column crossing the Maritza river at Adrianople is twenty miles long. Twenty miles of carts drawn by cows, bullocks and muddy-flanked water-buffalo, with exhausted staggering men, women and children, blankets over their heads, walking blindly along in the rain beside their worldly goods." The height of the panic followed the final evacuation of the Greek army from Smyrna, when the city was burned to the ground and Kemalist forces massacred 30,000 Greek and Armenian civilians in cold blood, while an estimated quarter of a million terrified refugees crowded the waterfront. By May 1923, the date when the Greco-Turkish exchange agreement was supposed to come into force, another 200,000 had fled as well and only 150,000 were left, in effect hostages for the proper treatment of Greece's Muslims.[3]

The Greeks had at least escaped the fate of the Armenians—hundreds of thousands of whom had been killed since 1915. But they had their own grim stories of forced marches, starvation, imprisonment and massacre; women and children had faced the threat of forced conversion and rape. The refugee camps outside Istanbul—if they succeeded in reaching them—were death-traps of typhus and cholera; the rains poured down, there was little to eat. They packed themselves into the ships carrying them across the Aegean to safety, but many did not make it alive. When one ten-year-old boy, whose father had already died, crossed from Prince's Island (outside Istanbul), his journey to Salonica took eleven days: "We starved. The boat stopped in Cavala for water only. Older people and younger ones, about four or five of them, died. Their bodies were thrown into the sea."[4]

An American diplomat despairingly watched a steamer carrying seven thousand dock at Salonica—"a squirming writhing mass of human misery." It was November, and the refugees had spent four days at sea, many on the open deck, without space to lie down, or food, or toilet facilities. "They came ashore in rags," he noted in shock, "hungry, sick, covered with vermin, hollow-eyed, exhaling the horrible odor of human filth." Interviewed many years later, another woman was so overcome by her memories of that journey she could not describe how she had got to Greece; before leaving Turkey she had buried two of her children in the camp near Istanbul, and the journey itself was too distressing to recall. "We landed at Salonica. Some people were lucky to get homes to stay in. We didn't. We stayed in a yard. We put down some handmade carpets and sat down on them. For three or four weeks we stayed there. Some people would give us food to eat. Then we registered for the villages we wanted to settle down . . . We were sent to a village where we really didn't want to go. However we had no choice."[5]

Refugees ended up in every part of the country. But the departing Muslims had left properties in northern Greece, and this was where their demographic impact was greatest. More than a quarter of a million people passed through the quarantines and tented encampments of Salonica before being transported into the countryside to be settled in agricultural colonies. The demographic dominance of Greeks in Greek Macedonia was thus finally achieved through what one observer at the time called a process of "contemporary colonization"—something close to what the Young Turks had envisaged in 1910, only now with Christians not Muslims.[6] Neat new village settlements with orderly straight streets and whitewashed red-tiled single-storey homes stamped the impress of Hellenism on Macedonia's erstwhile ethnographic kaleidoscope. "What a miracle!" wrote a French scholar, "The country round Salonica, which was formerly pasture for sheep . . . is now transformed into orchards and vineyards." Salonica itself was affected deeply too, for as many as 92,000 refugees eventually made it their home.[7]

The refugees themselves were not a homogeneous group, however, and only their suffering united them. They had originated from all over the Greek world—from the Asia Minor seaboard, the Black Sea, the Caucasus and eastern Thrace—places where their communities had existed, in many cases, since antiquity: the "Greece" that now called itself their homeland was generally unknown to them. Some were from prosperous urban backgrounds, merchants from Izmir who looked on in astonishment at the primitive ways of the Macedonian villager; others were Anatolian peasants themselves, who found it hard to adjust to the life of the city. They brought strange clothes and unfamiliar customs, harsh dialects and even, ironically, the Turkish language, which many of them spoke much more fluently than Greek. In fact, many still only understood Turkish, and thought of themselves as "Anatolian Christians," or "Christians from the East" rather than "Greeks." Political appeals to the refugees often had to be printed in Turkish as well as Greek. Salonica's Muslims were astonished. "They didn't know Greek and spoke Turkish," recalled the young Reshad Tesal in surprise. "[They] sang in Turkish in our *makams* [musical scales]." With their arrival, the market for Turkish records quickly expanded and Greek cinemas screened Turkish melodramas well into the 1950s. They had insults hurled at them by Greeks from the Peloponnese or the islands—they were "Turkish-seed" and "the yoghurt-baptized"—for to the existing population of Old Greece they scarcely seemed Greek at all. In fact the population exchange was not about bringing a nation together so much as assembling the component parts from which one would emerge. Two or three generations passed before their descendants stopped referring to themselves as refugees, and felt more at ease in their new homeland.[8]

At the height of the influx—in the weeks and months which followed the fall of Smyrna—Salonica was stretched to breaking point. Relatives were separated, and the shortage of adult men was noticeable for many had been killed or were still in Turkish captivity. The city's wealthier residents were invited to sponsor newcomers, or to adopt orphans, and notices requesting news of family members appeared frequently in the press. From 12 September 1922: "The husband of Anastasia Iliadakis from Niflis is sought, and their children, Constantinos, Ilias, Evangelos and Minas Iliadakis." "Emmanuel Xydopoulos from Yiayiakoi seeks his father, Efstratios Xydopoulos, his mother and three brothers, Constantinos, Sotirios and Dimosthenes." Pelagia Konstantinou, dwelling at 74 King George St., "seeks her sister Partheni Konstantinou, from the village of Atslaga near Samsun. Anyone in possession of information please contact her." For years people wandered the country, still hoping to trace their loved ones.[9]

Evicted from their homes, many of them were penniless, with only what they had been able to carry. A journalist was appalled to see newly arrived old men and women dragging their belongings from the docks to the encampments. Another was furious when refugees were evicted from the church of Ayia Paraskevi because the archaeologists wanted the space for a museum: "Thus numerous destitute families are thrown onto the pavement so that some stones of dubious archaeological value may be placed there." As so often in the past, churches, mosques and schools were pressed into service, and refugees were crammed in "like sardines." Local newspapers identified vacant houses to be taken over—"various public buildings on V. Olgas and V. Georgiou," the Villa Kapanji, the Villa Ismail Pasha on Allatini Street. "7 October 1922: In the stoas of the harbour offices on Salamis street there are 15–20 refugee families who have been abandoned . . . lying on the cold cement without even bedding." "26 October 1922: the refugees who remained in the open air, by the quay, fearing they might die of the cold and rain, managed yesterday to transfer themselves to the Ayios Dimitrios quarter, bursting into various Turkish and Greek houses and settling themselves in there. We are informed that with many cafés, churches and cinemas requisitioned, the temporary housing of refugees in them will begin."[10]

But as they tried to make a more permanent home for themselves, the refugees found themselves in a bureaucratic labyrinth. They had left their homes so fast they generally lacked the necessary documents to claim compensation. Now they needed a certificate describing the property they had left behind, and they had to make the rounds—this committee, that directorate, tracking down notables from their village—to get their claim certified and declared eligible for some form of paltry remuneration. It was to help with such tasks that an incredible number of refugee associations, guilds and clubs sprang up, providing them with identity cards, property certificates, nationalization papers and—crucially—contacts with politicians. They formed associations—Refugees from the Region of Bursa, the Smyrneans—to stick together, against hostile natives (with whom fights were common, especially in the villages) and against the bureaucracy. In response to a law of July 1923, which decreed that land would only be distributed to legally constituted groups rather than individuals, the main refugee groupings—representing members from Asia Minor, Thrace, the Caucasus and the Black Sea—banded together to form a single umbrella organization, whose political weight was immediately demonstrated in elections, where the majority of the Venizelist candidates were refugees. For the rest of the interwar period and indeed afterwards, refugee votes shaped the city's electoral profile. But rather like the first generation of Holocaust survivors after 1945, they did not talk much about what they had endured, and it was only much later that their sufferings were officially recognized. In 1986 the Greek government declared a national day of mourning to commemorate the destruction of Smyrna, and from that point the old silence belatedly began to lift.[11]

RESETTLING THE CITY

CONSCIOUS OF THE DANGER that might be posed to social stability and political order by large numbers of impoverished refugees settling in the towns, the Greek authorities tried to direct the majority to the countryside. With the aid of the League of Nations, a Refugee Settlement Commission began constructing villages and farms, and so-called "refugee fathers" bargained with civil servants in the ministry of agriculture for the land they wanted. Those who came from mountain villages were settled in sensitive border areas, and given financial incentives to remain there. Urban reconstruction, with fewer resources behind it, was a less important consideration—especially for Salonica, which tended to take second place in politicians' minds behind the more crucially located suburbs of Athens and Piraeus. Yet the demographic impact upon the northern city was far greater than it was around the capital. By 1928 the refugees made up more than one-third of its population. How could an impoverished government, already struggling to rebuild it in the aftermath of the fire, possibly find shelter for all the newcomers?[12]

Residential housing, after all, was in very short supply. Departing Muslims—far fewer in number than the incoming refugees—had not left more than 4600 buildings behind them and most of the 50,000 Jews and 10,000 Greeks who had lost their homes in the 1917 fire still needed housing. Because the burnt-out central zone was off-limits, and subject to the slow pace of the urban planners, refugees headed towards the Upper Town, where the city's Muslim population had mostly lived. They settled themselves in abandoned houses, and built another 2500 dwellings in courtyards, empty plots and open spaces. By 1925 virtually all the inhabitants of the narrow streets above Ayios Dimitrios were refugees, and many remained there for years to come. The fields and pastures which had characterized the Upper Town since the fifteenth century disappeared under the weight of this new population.[13]

The change wrought by the refugees was staggering. As late as 1913, 73% of Salonica's population had lived within the walls in a space dominated by Jews and Muslims; by 1932 more than half—and they were now mostly Christians—lived in the 36 refugee settlements, 7

Jewish quarters, and 13 mixed ones which stretched in a vast sixteen-kilometre arc from north to south around the historic centre. A "second" city had grown up encircling the old one. "There exist few examples of cities," wrote a French architect, "partially or utterly destroyed, so rapidly reconstituted . . . through the form of new extended neighbourhoods." It was mostly the wealthy who could afford the high prices of a location in the newly remodelled streets south of Egnatia; the poor—whether refugees, local Greeks or an estimated 25,000 working-class Jews, were displaced and forced into the Upper Town or to the periphery from where they trudged in to work, cursing inadequate public transport and the unfinished roads.[14]

ATHENS AND PIRAEUS were surrounded by shanty-towns, but in Salonica, the planners talked of "anarchy" with even more reason than usual. Refugee organizations demanded exemption from planning provisions, while slums hindered traffic and jeopardized public health. A 1921 city plan had envisaged Salonica growing to a size of 2400 hectares with a population of 350,000 over the next fifty years; in fact the city reached 2000 hectares and a population of 274,000 even before the Second World War broke out.[15] The extreme political instability of the time—the coups, counter-coups, revolutions, and no less than five changes of government in 1924 alone—and the country's poverty did not help. Few wealthy states could have easily afforded to handle an influx amounting to an additional fifth of their total population and Greece was not rich. The government's distribution of loans to refugees, though a burden on the state budget, alleviated their plight slightly and the League of Nations helped with money and advice. Occasionally, the ministry of welfare organized the building of a new neighbourhood itself, or provided land to private developers. But as it turned out, homes actually constructed by the state for the refugees amounted to a fraction of their total housing needs.

In the end, the primary means of salvation for the impoverished Greek state were land expropriation and the remarkable energy of the refugees themselves. Plots were handed over to numerous self-forming groups who then built their own homes. Thirty members of the Smyrna Refugee Group, for instance, another body of sixty Refugee Tramdrivers, and a group of Refugee Army Officers were all allocated land on the estate of Hamdi Bey, the former mayor of the city (and architect of its tramway system). Dozens if not hundreds of estates were similarly broken up.[16] In many cases, refugees simply squatted in buildings or began occupying land which did not belong to them. Some of these illegal settlements were being dismantled as late as the 1950s, but many others were legalized retrospectively and the new claimants allowed to stay. If the land's original owners were not affected by the population exchange agreement and demanded compensation, the resulting lawsuits could drag on for decades. Right through to the end of the century, the courts were being asked to adjudicate on such claims, and among those using the city's rich and well-ordered Ottoman archive one still finds lawyers chasing up their clients' documentation.

The necessity for continued reference to Ottoman land titles—for from the legal point of view, the empire remained very much alive—created all kinds of complications. In 1925 for instance, the Salonica Cooperative of Vegetable Growers, a non-refugee association, protested to the prime minister that they had been unjustly deprived of their gardens in order to settle refugee families—one of many cases which was leading to what they termed "fatal hatred between natives and our brother refugees." The problem was that the growers themselves had no freehold title to their land—they had cultivated it for generations under a Turkish arrangement called *yediki*, according to which they passed down the usufruct to their children in return for regular payments to the land's Muslim owners. Because the owners had gone, they too were in danger of being evicted, even though they were Greeks. They asked for recognition of their claim, and if not for the return of their gardens then at least for compensation for the value of the *yediki* payments they had made over the years. (Perhaps fearful that this line of argument would not work, they also reminded the authorities of the great contribution they had made in the final years of Ottoman rule to the Greek guerrilla struggle in Macedonia, smuggling weapons in from the coast, hidden in their carts under piles of vegetables.)[17]

The point is that legal uncertainties of this kind allowed cases to be influenced by political factors, and with the refugees now in a majority in the city, their political weight was substantial. Because there was no cadastral survey for the city as a whole, it was hard, if not impossible, for former owners or their heirs to establish definitively that they had indeed once held the land in question. What looked at first sight therefore like bureaucratic confusion and incompetence possessed a logic of its own: it helped the state, with relatively little outlay of its own, to settle its priority group, the Greek refugees, as quickly and permanently as it could.[18]

TROGLODYTES AND SUBURBS

THE TROUBLE WAS that even if such a strategy may have been pretty much all that was open to the cash-strapped Greek authorities, it still left many refugees in penury, making the city's old problem of poverty infinitely worse. In 1928 the governor-general of Macedonia painted a grim picture of conditions in the "other Thessaloniki." What he called "the city of the wretched and the miserable" extended into the heart of the fire zone, where next to "the city of magnificent apartment buildings" more than 2000 people still shivered through icy winters in makeshift shacks—"piteous, ramshackle constructions made out of corrugated iron sheets, mud-bricks and cheap materials of any kind." Out to the east, the suburb of Kalamaria, home to 20,000 refugees, was sandwiched between the middle-class villas which lined the shore and the "truly European suburb" of Toumba on the hills above. The state appeared to have done nothing for the inhabitants of Kalamaria other than providing them with a few petrol lamps to break the nocturnal darkness, and its half-finished streets and tiny half-ruined wooden huts resembled a "gypsy encampment" alongside its more respectable neighbours. As for the Café Koulé quarter in the Upper Town, people feared to walk home at night lest in the darkness they "drown in one of those lakes which the rains have created."[19]

Things were even worse in the grim and dirty slums around the railway station. "There are troglodytes in Thessaloniki," claimed a local reporter describing conditions in the Tin Neighbourhood (Teneké Mahala), which got its name from the flattened tins which formed the basic building material of its Lilliputian homes. These primitive hovels consisted of "one or two rooms, like large cans of sardines which come up to one's waist, a minute window, misshapen, with a bit of a window pane, an ill-fitting front door, narrow and low . . . And all this from blackened cans of petrol." Between the shacks snaked constricted alleys carrying smells, vermin and sewage; paper-thin walls made sleep and privacy rare commodities.[20]

The Tin Neighbourhood was among the poorest and most wretched quarters of all, a zone of disease, over-crowding and poverty which the state appeared to have forgotten. In fact the only sign of

Greek officialdom there was the nightwatchman, a former prison inmate with repeated convictions for smoking hashish and gambling. Other new districts, situated on higher ground, were more desirable. Toumba, a vast eastern suburb in the foothills, enjoyed the advantage of a slight elevation above the malarial low ground immediately surrounding the old city. Its roads were wide and straight, and spacious building plots allowed the new residents to expand their homes as their wealth grew. "Settlement! What am I saying? Suburb, yes, suburb is the proper term for this section of our city," wrote one visitor impressed by its changed appearance within a couple of years. By 1933 Toumba had a population of 32,000—almost the size of the city itself a century earlier.[21]

Similarly fortunate, the small cooperative settlement of Saranta Ekklisies (Forty Churches), one of the few quarters to be settled almost entirely by refugees from one locale (in this case from Eastern Thrace) was perched immediately above the Jewish cemetery on the old city's eastern flank, utilizing land expropriated by the state in 1926. New homeowners commissioned local architects and built houses and gardens from which they could look down towards the White Tower and the sea. In Top Alti, up against the northwestern walls, settlers whitewashed their tiny homes and tilled the surrounding fields after their work in the lower town had ended. In neighbouring Neapolis, the neat rows of one-storey blocks were built by their owners—mostly working on the railways, the trams and in the tobacco factories—without any real state assistance. Even the Upper Town, though it remained without electricity or properly paved roads long after these had appeared in the streets of the commercial centre below, preserved its rural character and allowed its new inhabitants far more space and more abundant light and fresh air than they would have enjoyed in the grimy backstreets of Bara, Vardari or Teneké Mahala.

New Jewish working-class quarters—Campbell, 151 to the east, Regie and the older Hirsch on the west—were also a level above the degradation of these. Yet many of their inhabitants spent years in draughty converted First World War barracks, or in sheds and cabins which had little of the charm of their former haunts in the city centre. Once they had hung out their laundry in the common *cortijos* of their homes; now it was in the grassy, open spaces between their half-built shacks. The elderly reminisced about life as it had been before the fire, but this was already a lost world to the younger generation. "Their language," wrote one young Jewish journalist, "with its coarse words, con-

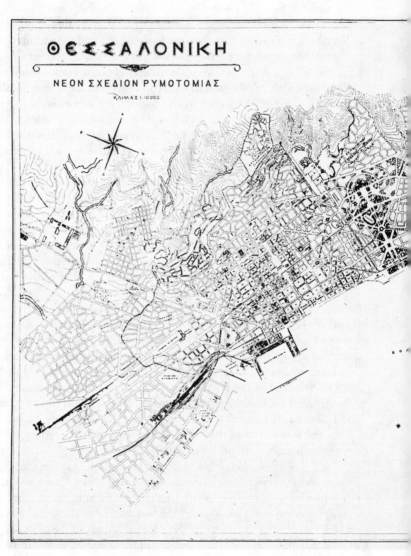

The 1929 municipal city plan

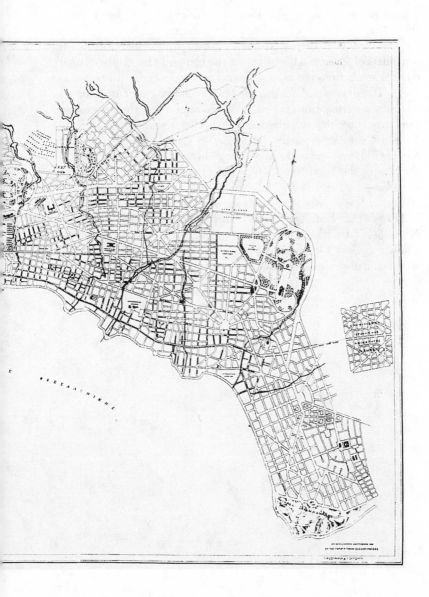

stitutes an old-fashioned style that piques one's curiosity. Just hearing the old names of the Jewish quarters leaves me amazed."[22]

The fire had destroyed the original synagogues with their reminders of Spain and Portugal, and the Hébrard Plan displaced their congregations from the heart of the town they had come to regard as theirs. Time-honoured Turkish and Jewish names for the city's quarters were disappearing from the map. At the same time, the newcomers were baptizing the suburbs with their own reminders of home— Neapolis, for the town of Nef-Shehir in Cappadocia, Troiada and Saranta Ekkliseis—after the places they had been forced to abandon. In the villages, the Turkish and Slavic Ottoman names—Arapli, Verlantza, Kirtzilar—were also being Hellenized as the refugees moved in. The *Alcazar di Salonico* was long gone; the new tavernas, ouzeris and cafés had names like "Lost Asia Minor," "Smyrna Betrayed" and "Dreams of Nicomedia." Under the pressure of refugee nostalgia—a nostalgia for another faraway Ottoman past—the signposts of Ottoman Salonica were being discarded.

19

Workers and the State

PROSPERITY HAD ALWAYS COME to Salonica through its command of far-flung trading routes. At one time, these linked it to Venice and Egypt; later, to France, Russia, Britain and central Europe. It was, wrote William Miller in 1898, "one of the most flourishing commercial towns of Eastern Europe . . . intended by nature to be the outlet for the trade of the whole Peninsula on the Aegean." Any partition of the region among the nation-states of the Balkans threatened to cut it off from its key markets. Economic self-interest therefore helps explain why the city's Jewish population in general, and its mercantile class in particular, remained loyal to the Ottoman sultans. Like many at the end of the nineteenth century, Miller thought that empires fostered trade more successfully than small states. He was one of the first commentators to suggest that as Ottoman power waned, so Austria-Hungary should " 'run down' to Salonica and occupy Macedonia as she has already occupied Bosnia and the Hercegovina, to the general advantage of mankind." But the nation-states of the Balkans proved more power-ful than the great empires of the past, and Greece's triumph left inter-war Salonica in the unfavourable position many commentators had feared—cut off from its Balkan hinterland, the Black Sea, Asia Minor, and the Levant, and enclosed within the confines of a small country. The timing too could not have been worse: opportunities for emigra-tion—a regional safety-valve before 1912—were curtailed by American immigration quotas; the country was bankrupted by the war and strug-gling to regain international financial respectability, and to add to the gloom, the global economy was growing more slowly than ever before or since. The result was proletarianization, poverty and political unrest.[1]

With the coming of the refugees, the city acquired a new workforce, desperate for jobs, expecting help now not from its communal or religious leadership as in Ottoman times, but rather from the highly bureaucratic if disorganized state. The Greek government turned itself into a major employer, and the number of civil servants rose. But it found itself too in the middle of a series of increasingly bitter conflicts between workers and management. To the north the Bolsheviks were triumphant, and a new vocabulary of *agitatsia*, *lockoutarisma* and *provocatsia* started to be heard. For interwar Salonica was the cockpit of violent class struggle and a powerful labour movement built on the foundations laid by the old Workers' Solidarity Federation. Venizelos and his generation, one-time revolutionaries, now became guardians of what they themselves called "the bourgeois status quo." Labour militancy threatened the authority of the state, brought the city to a standstill, and eventually provided the pretext for the establishment of an anti-communist dictatorship in 1936.

A City of Workers

AFTER HALF A CENTURY of industrialization, Salonica had become a city of workers. Two-thirds of the labour force of 105,000 recorded in 1928 worked for someone else; another 25,000 were self-employed or assisting relatives. But this was a world of tiny operations and small family firms, not giant combines or industrial plants. The manufacturing sector was mostly producing foodstuffs, textiles and leather goods just as under Abdul Hamid. Only 5000 men belonged to firms of any size. The rest were shoemakers, bakers or confectioners—much prized in the city—tailors, metal-workers and carpenters, odd-job men who owned carts and, later, cars. Heavy industry was virtually non-existent and regular wages the privilege of a few.

Too many hands and changing tastes made most of the old trades precarious and uncertain. Jewish *hamals* still shouldered huge loads for shoppers and traders, and carters stabled their oxen and horses in the burnt-out ruins in the fire zone. But furriers, fez makers, organ-grinders and tinsmiths were on the way out. The lamplighters, street-butchers, sellers of salted fish and Albanian *halvades* slowly disappeared; so did the wandering vendors of *salep* and lemonade. Refrigeration and electrification eliminated the ice-sellers of Hortiatis. As a result, state-run soup kitchens at the bottom of the slump were feeding as many as fifty thousand people daily.

As early as February 1922, before the flight from Asia Minor had begun in earnest, businessmen in Athens were already being alerted to the fact that refugees in Salonica, unable to find work there, were "ready to come to Piraeus, Athens or other cities in Greece to work in factories at a wage advantageous to their employers." Thousands of men were sitting in the *kafeneia* waiting for a job to turn up. "I turned right and left looking for work. There was nothing," recalled Petros Pasalides, a shepherd from Konya in Asia Minor. He worked on the railways for a time, tried the mines, then fell in with a market gardener. Over the next few years he tramped all over Greece, partly driven by the need to earn his living, partly in the hope of finding relatives and "compatriots" from his birthplace.[2]

Some refugees set themselves up as traders, pedlars and shopkeepers. But once mild inflation gave way to prolonged deflation the real value of their debts increased and many faced bankruptcy. Not coincidentally, there were fires at the oil storage depot of the Asiatic Oil Company in 1923, while another the following year in the commercial district destroyed sixty shops. A wary bank manager in the city noted in 1929, at the onset of the real commercial crisis, that there were "frequent, almost daily fires in shops, several of which proved to be not casual." The local Lloyd's agent reckoned that 90% were caused deliberately.[3]

Politicians in far-away Athens, having fought so hard to conquer the New Lands, were too busy to pay much attention to their economic needs: they were overwhelmed by the refugee issue, and obsessed by constitutional arguments between republicans and royalists. The horizons of the "political world" in the capital seemingly petered out before they ever reached the city. Few Salonican firms were listed on the Athens Stock Exchange and no minister of national economy was ever appointed from Macedonia: the paucity of figures from northern Greece in the upper echelons of power in Athens was a constant local complaint. An International Fair was founded in the city in 1926, but although it provided publicity for regional firms, its benefits were limited, its flashy kiosks good for a day out but little more. The city's businessmen felt marginalized and ignored.[4]

Tobacco processing was still the most important "industry," just as it had been in Ottoman times. By 1940 at least one hundred companies, mostly Greek but including Jewish, American and Armenian houses, were based in Salonica and traded in the preparation and export of tobacco leaf, and in a few cases, the manufacture of cigarettes themselves. For a brief period, the market boomed, and in the mid-1920s production soared well above the levels known in former times. But Greek tobacco was an expensive commodity, and as world prices began to fall, they took tobacco with them. By the end of the decade, the sector was in serious crisis.

Even before the slump kicked in, the well-organized tobacco workers were the main source of labour militancy in the city. The Tobacco workers Federation of Greece fought hard over pay, working conditions, unemployment benefits and the regulation of exports and in 1919 they won the right to an eight-hour day. These gains were the fruit of more or less constant struggle with employers—demonstrations, shut-downs, factory occupations and lock-outs, punctuated by clashes with police and army. In August 1924, workers intercepted deliveries of tobacco bales to the docks which exporters were trying to ship before they had been processed: the bales were cut open and the bundles of leaf tossed into the sea. Three months later, strikers occupied the Florentin warehouse and fortified it against the police. Even though the Federation was forcibly disbanded in 1930 as a communist front, the power of its members was far from broken, as would be seen most impressively in their nationwide strike six years later.

But the tobacco workers were not alone and in the 1920s the city was hit by a wave of stoppages. After a nationwide general strike in August 1923, the government responded nervously by temporarily dissolving *all* unions. The following June the docks came to a standstill. Key services such as water, railways and trams were also hit; printers, leatherworkers, bakers, butchers and even civil servants took industrial action while the Union of Ex-Servicemen shouted pacifist slogans and got into fights with the nationalists of the Macedonian Youth movement. In short, throughout these years the city streets saw incessant protest, and the White Tower, the Pantheon cinema and even the Skating Palace—anywhere in fact where orators could harangue a sympathetic crowd—became the scene of violent clashes. In the eighteenth century, it had been the plague that brought Salonica to a standstill; in the early twenty-first, it was traffic. But for much of the twentieth, it was the strikes and demonstrations of organized labour and mass politics.

Ironically, Venizelos himself had encouraged the formation of a nationwide Greek union movement in the hope that it would back him up at the peace talks in Paris after World War One. It was his wartime administration that had founded the Workers' Centre in Salonica. But the wave of strikes and demonstrations which hit the country alarmed him deeply. From 1919—with Greek troops committed to the Allied intervention in the Russian civil war—pro-government newspapers called for labour unions to be banned, and Venizelist army officers formed units against the "Bolsheviks" and "anarchists" at home. The workers themselves meanwhile were moving rapidly to the left; in Salonica the Workers' Centre became the focus of socialist life. With a claimed twelve thousand workers under its command, the large centrally located two-storey villa had its own library and reading room, and acted as a kind of college for working men and women, where the victories of the Red Army in Poland, Ukraine and Siberia were chalked up daily on a large blackboard. In 1922, a gun battle in the street outside ended with a gendarme shot dead and after the Centre was searched for weapons, the police announced that they had uncovered thirteen boxes of explosives with which "the Bolshevik anarchists" planned to attack the authorities and "set up a state like that which the Communists have in Russia." Later it transpired that the explosives were in fact fireworks, left behind by Serbian army engineers who had used the building during the war.[5]

COMMUNISTS AND ANTI-COMMUNISTS

THE WORKERS' CENTRE testified to the potency of a Marxist subculture in a city where large numbers of workers were increasingly disillusioned with what they saw as the rule of the "bourgeois state." Many were illiterate but deeply conscious of the value of self-improvement. "Take a newspaper not a coffee in the mornings," the *Workers' Voice* reminded comrades. The *Biblioteka Sosyalista* distributed Marx and Engels in Judeo-Spanish among the Socialist Workers' Youth groups in the poorer quarters down by the rail stations. The KKE (Communist Party of Greece) set up its Lenin Upper School in the Café Byzantion, another pro-labour hangout with a conveniently large basement. When the First of May was celebrated in the Beshchinar Gardens, thousands of onlookers were treated to poetry recitals, gymnastic displays and speeches.

By this point, the authorities were afraid that Salonica had turned into a major centre of communist activity in the Balkans. The police—mostly peasant boys recruited from the villages of Crete and the Peloponnese—were suspicious of the multi-ethnic character of local labour activism. "No separate activity is carried on by Jewish, Armenian, Turkish, French, Bulgarian and Greek communists," agents observed. "All work together for the cause." Jews as well as Orthodox Greeks were put under surveillance and imprisoned or sent into internal exile, just as they would be during the civil war too. Armenian activists were deported to Soviet Armenia "since they scandalously propagandize among their co-nationals for communism and give significant backing to Greek and Jewish communists." The refugees too were widely accused of being responsive to the communist "virus," much to the annoyance of their leaders.[6]

As old anxieties about the activities of Kemalist and Italian fascist agents subsided international communist policy itself gave ample new grounds for police fears. In Moscow in 1924, the Comintern, hoping to promote revolution in Bulgaria, adopted the Bulgarian Communist Party's slogan of "a united and independent Macedonia" (one which would unite the lands taken by Yugoslavia, Greece and Bulgaria in 1912–13 in a larger communist Balkan federation). The Greek Communist Party publicly declared its adherence to the new line and although many party members resigned in protest, the party itself stuck to this deeply unpopular position for a decade. As a result, in the following year high-ranking party cadres were put on trial for treason as "autonomists." In the minds of the authorities, they had become pro-Bulgarian and anti-Greek protagonists in a new round of the Macedonian Struggle. Far-fetched claims circulated in police headquarters that leading international Bolsheviks had descended from Vienna to make the Macedonian capital their base as they prepared to overthrow Greek rule. Under the shadow of the Russian revolution, the old Slav peril thus resurfaced in a new guise. "With . . . the development of industry, especially tobacco, the tram-drivers, docks and the railways," noted the police in 1927, "Thessaloniki brings together a great mass of workers upon whom communist propaganda finds fertile soil, given the lack of any kind of countervailing anti-communism to forestall its attacks, and given the absence of preventative measures able to hinder the impact of the nation-destroying activity of certain rootless blind organs of the Third International and the Russian Communist Party."[7]

Inside the movement, however, the tensions, disagreements and limitations were unmistakable. The KKE split almost immediately after its formation into several factions who detested each other as much if not more than they detested the representatives of "the bourgeois state." Benaroya, one of the founders of the Greek labour movement, was expelled, while rival groupings such as the Trotskyite

"Archive Marxists," who gave priority to worker education over revolutionary activism, rejected the Comintern line over Macedonia: their fights with party members were every bit as frequent and violent as those with the police.

The party's Macedonia policy damaged it deeply. It disturbed relations between the Salonica branch and the central committee in Athens, and led to many defections. In 1926 the party lost control of the trades union federation, and marginalized itself further by recruiting primarily factory workers and ignoring the villages. Although it did fairly well in the general elections of November 1926, winning 4 per cent of the vote nationally, and nearly 11 per cent in the city itself—which returned three of the ten communist deputies to parliament—it was a false dawn. By 1927 the Salonica branch had run out of funds. A decade later, in the critical elections of 1936, when the communist vote rose substantially over its 1926 levels in most of the country, it slipped in Salonica, the centre of labour activism. In fact, what is surprising is how limited the party's appeal remained within the Greek working population for most of the interwar period.

Worker militancy was fed far more by heavy-handed official repression—and by the poverty of the city's refugee masses—than it was by communist tactics. In the early 1920s, when the authorities had little manpower to spare, they hired thugs and bravos, known colloquially as "cudgel-carriers" (though they were equally fond of using knives, guns and explosives), to help the gendarmerie sort out labour problems.[8] These brawlers, often themselves working men in employer-financed "yellow unions," clashed enthusiastically with leftist groups. In April 1921, bakery workers were assaulted by them, while armed members of a monarchist gang beat up the general secretary of the Workers' Centre. The Allatini flour mills—one of the largest factories in the Balkans—were the scene for repeated attacks of this kind. In October 1921, royalist bravos accompanied the police to the Beshchinar Gardens: together they broke up a gathering of the guild of bootmakers which was having its evening dinner there. Gendarmes turned a blind eye, and often continued to make the victims "eat wood" [as the Greek expression has it] in the privacy of police cells.

These gangs eventually formed the nucleus of a network of anti-communist, nationalist groups which flourished in close conjunction with the military authorities over the next half a century and played a deeply baneful role in Greek politics. Through the civil war and the 1950s the presence of this so-called "para-state" dominated the city's streets and exploded into prominence with the murder of a leftist deputy in 1963—an episode which shocked the country and inspired the film Z. But once the Asia Minor war ended, their role against organized labour diminished. The Greek police became better organized, and city policing in particular was professionalized and placed in the hands of a special force.

The city police, and especially the feared Special Security branch, saw the fight against communism—which for them meant much the same thing as the repression of the union movement—as their main task. It looked like an uphill struggle in a place where, as the police directorate notified Athens, the worst elements "more than in any other city in Greece find fertile ground." Special agents were described by their own bosses as "useless and unskilled, lacking disguises and sufficient funds." When foreign spies jumped into cars and sped away, their pursuers could not afford the taxi fare to follow them. Understaffed—there were only a hundred policemen in Salonica, less than one for every two thousand inhabitants and less than a third of what police officials judged the necessary minimum—they relied on informers. Following the Ottoman tradition—the Venizelist head of the security section had started in the gendarmerie on Ottoman Crete in 1901, and the Ottoman term for these stoolpigeons, *hafies*, passed into Greek—the city's police chiefs ran large networks of spies, often placing two in the same organization to report—unwittingly—on one another.[9]

As any police chief knows, intelligence is no use without the means to act on it, and the nervous political elite of Athens was only too happy to provide this. Activists and their relatives were initially punished under old anti-brigandage laws. Crimes of opinion had been punishable since 1924, the year the republic was founded, and more than 1000 labour activists were exiled during the short-lived dictatorship of General Theodore Pangalos. A further draconian step forward came in 1929 when the Venizelos government legalized the repression of suspected communists through its so-called Special Law, which punished people simply for having beliefs that aimed at the overthrow of what the law itself described as "the bourgeois status quo." There followed over 16,000 arrests and perhaps 3000 supposed leftists were sent into internal exile. Yet despite these measures, communism was still gaining ground—at least according to the experienced head of the Salonica city police, a long-time Venizelist from Crete called Georgios Kalochristianakis. Reporting in 1932 to Venizelos himself, Kalochristianakis noted gloomily that although the KKE had been hit by the use of the

Special Law, as well as by its own internal disputes, and although any increase in its recent vote was to be attributed to the effects of the economic depression rather than to the party's own tactics, nevertheless

> Both [the party and the Archive Marxists] have as many conscious elements as ever who ceaselessly and daily proselytize for new recruits, especially the Archive Marxist faction which by its system of educational circles has instilled in the souls of the young the microbe of Marxist theory. And to this we must also add the psychological state of young people who have been naturally inspired by Liberal and revolutionary tendencies and easily embrace these.

Kalochristianakis had fought with Venizelos against the Turks to liberate Crete and Greece. Faced with the Red menace, however, and its threat to the country's national integrity, the policeman's older revolutionary sympathies were being whittled away. As he saw it, the Communist Party might be relatively weak but its message was attractive. The emergence of a sympathetic body of students at the new university provided a depressing indication of a future shift to the left. As for the workers, one thing—he warned Venizelos—was clear: "Most are communists because they lack even their daily bread."[10]

Days of 1936

In Salonica's tavernas, during the cold days of early 1936, a new song made the rounds:

> *All those who become Prime Minister are sure to die*
> *The people hunt them down for the good they do.*
>
> *Kondylis is dead, Venizelos gone.*
> *Demertzis died too, when he might have found the way.*
>
> *I'll put down my name for the PM's job*
> *So I too can sit like a bum and eat and drink.*
>
> *And get up in the House and give them their instructions,*
> *I'll force the* narghilé *on them, and get them stoned.*[11]

An unexpected sequence of deaths that spring suddenly transformed the Greek political landscape: the first to go was the strongman General George Kondylis, who had put down an attempted Venizelist coup the previous year, and brought back King George from exile; then, out of the blue, he was followed by Venizelos himself. The greatest and most controversial Greek statesman of the twentieth century had plotted that last coup to regain power, fled after it failed, and died in exile in Paris. And the month after him the macabre series continued with the death of Prime Minister Konstantinos Demertzis, a minor figure who had been appointed by the king as caretaker to guide the country into calmer waters.

New elections in January 1936—the first since the restoration of the monarchy—had shown how deeply the country was split. The antagonism between Venizelists and anti-Venizelists which had emerged during the First World War lingered on, a matter of loyalty, memory and affiliation rather than ideology or policy. Each camp polled over 40% of the votes and ended up with 47% of the seats. Holding the balance was the Communist Party, with 6% of the vote and just fifteen seats. It was the nightmare scenario for the "bourgeois world." The Venizelists declared their acceptance of the monarchy, but even so they and their opponents were unable to agree to terms for a coalition. In March the leader of the Liberals was elected president of the Chamber thanks to communist support. The latter, obediently following the popular front strategy laid down in Moscow, were now closer to real influence if not power than ever before.

This perspective scared many conservatives, and on 13 April, after Demertzis's death, King George appointed a faithful royalist army man, Ioannis Metaxas, as prime minister. General Metaxas had been a brilliant staff officer but an undistinguished politician: in the last elections, his Free Opinion Party had polled less than 4% of the votes. What mattered to the king, however, was first his loyalty—which was unquestioned—and second, that Metaxas could control the army, always an unpredictable factor in Greek political life. Within two weeks, Metaxas had called for and received a vote of confidence, and parliament itself broke up early for its summer recess. It was not to convene again for another ten years.

The spring of 1936 was a time of great tension in and beyond Europe: the international battle-lines between right and left were emerging in Germany, where the troops of the Third Reich marched into the Rhineland that March, and in France, where a Popular Front government was formed the following month. On 5 May, Italian troops captured Addis Ababa, dealing a death-blow to the prestige of the League of Nations. But it was on 9 May, the day that the Italian king Victor Emmanuel was declared Emperor of Ethiopia, that dramatic events took place in Salonica itself which showed the depth of unhappiness within its working classes and the scale of the crisis which faced the country.

After a bitterly cold winter, labour unrest had grown, bringing fresh intimidation in its train. At the end of April, tobacco workers struck for higher wages and union rights and the strike quickly spread elsewhere over the next few days. In Cavalla, workers called for an end to "the state of terror," and shopkeepers closed their shops in sympathy: the local prefect responded by arresting and deporting union and guild leaders. By 8 May, the Salonica tobacco workers had grown tired of waiting for serious negotiations to begin, and the trades union federation called its members out on strike. When crowds headed for the town hall, the police fired over their heads to try to stop them, scuffles broke out, and several workers who had been arrested were freed by their comrades. Then another 3000 workers ignored police road blocks and made their way from the warehouses near the Beshchinar into the centre. Feeling they were losing control of the streets, the authorities called up reinforcements, mounted gendarmerie and army conscripts. The latter were mostly local boys and unreliable in their sympathies, in some cases siding with the workers rather than the police. That evening, more guilds came out: cab and tram drivers, workers at the electricity plant, the docks and the railways. With at least 25,000 on the streets, the city was paralysed. The response of Prime Minister Metaxas was uncompromising: he forced the rail-workers and tram drivers back to work under martial law—and gave the police "freedom of action."

Next day, an anticipatory silence hung over the city: shutters were drawn down over the shops, there was no traffic on the streets. Groups of protesters gathered in clusters, watched by patrols of police and soldiers and ignoring orders to disperse. Strikers stopped a police car containing men who had been arrested for refusing to work and released them. Others put up barricades across Egnatia. Then, as the crowd grew and tens of thousands gathered in the heart of the city, shouting such slogans as "Long Live the Strike" and "Down with the Police," the police themselves opened fire. On the very corner where, nearly thirty years earlier, Young Turk gunmen had marked the start of their revolution by assassinating Abdullah Bey, the local head of the Hamidian police, the gendarmerie now claimed several victims of their own. By the time the masses of protestors had dispersed, several hours later, the police had shot twelve people dead and left another thirty-two badly wounded. The victims included two chauffeurs, and four tobacco workers; three of the twelve were Jews. The verdict of the British consul was that "the police acted with unnecessary brutality as was their custom." And he continued: "The town at that time certainly looked and sounded as if it had been invaded by an enemy."[12]

Fearing the crowd's revenge, the police were confined to quarters, control of the streets was handed over to the army and fresh units were ordered in. Thousands of workers turned out to mourn the dead, whose corpses were carried through the streets on biers, and flowers were strewn where they had fallen. There was, however, no further violence. After a few days in which the government's authority appeared to have almost completely broken down, the demands of the tobacco workers were granted, and the general strike was called off. The American ambassador, Lincoln MacVeagh, who had been in the city throughout these events, was quite clear that their underlying cause was the government's neglect of labour conditions in northern Greece, and of the economic plight there in general. "The region as a whole feels itself in a hopeless situation," he wrote. "Is the Greek Government going to heed these lessons? Or is Salonica destined to become another Barcelona and spread the infection of economic revolt throughout the whole rotten body politic of this country?"[13]

MacVeagh was not blind to the possibility of communist agitation behind what had happened, but it was not, for him, the real reason for such widespread protest. After all, had the unrest been revolutionary in its aims, it would not have subsided so quickly. Prime Minister Metaxas, however, was of a different mind and played up the threat of subversion. When the trades union federation announced a general strike for 5 August, he was given the pretext he had sought. He told the king the country faced a communist plot to overthrow the political system, and with the latter's approval, he declared martial law the day before the strike was due to begin and assumed dictatorial powers.

Technologies of war: *above* a German biplane attracts crowds along the front.

below A refugee camp inside the city, 1916.

Devastation in the town centre following the 1917 fire.

First meeting of the town planners, 1917.

Wartime excavations: Ernest Hebrard leads a dig in the precinct of the Rotonda.

above The new city: A straightened and widened Egnatia runs alongside the Arch of Galerius.
right Huts of Asia Minor refugees beneath the old walls, *c*.1960.
below Last remnants of the Ottoman city: the Upper Town, *c*.1960.

opposite left Rosa Eskenazi, Dimitrios Semsis (violin) and Tomboul (bouzouki), *c*.1930.
right An interwar dandy.
below The Hamza Bey mosque, in its postwar incarnation as the Alcazar Cinema, *c*.1960.

The round-up of Jewish men by German troops, July 1942.

University buildings going up on the site of the old Jewish cemetery, 1950s.

The city expands: *above* the Ottoman city is still divided from the new suburbs along the coast by cemeteries and open ground, *c.*1910. The new Idadié building is visible in the middle distance.

Below The same view half a century later: the campus and International Fair grounds flank the Idadié. Arterial roads link the old city with the suburbs. The minarets and cypresses have vanished from the centre; high-rise construction dominates.

The Cold War nation-state triumphant: during 1962 parades marking a half-century of Greek rule, school-children hold up a globe, flanked by personifications of ancient and modern Greece (*below*) and (*right*) military vehicles pass down Egnatia.

The planned city centre: the new street grid carves channels between post-war apartment blocks, leading down into Plateia Aristotelous and the seafront road.

20

Dressing for the Tango

IN THE IMMEDIATE AFTERMATH of the Asia Minor catastrophe, the Greek state could scarcely maintain its authority beyond Athens. Brigands ruled Samos, ransacking the island treasury, and unlocking the prisons. In Salonica, the Salikourtzis gang, refugees from Asia Minor, terrorized the city for two years, robbing merchants with impunity before they were caught and shot. But perhaps most notorious of all was the brigand Giangoulas who roamed the slopes of Mount Olympos. Occasionally he ventured into the plains and in June 1925 he was reported to have entered the city disguised as a priest, taken a coffee at the *zaharoplasteion* Doré, and then strolled off towards the White Tower, with the police close behind him. Giangoulas was a worthy descendant of those robber bands that had terrorized Salonica and its hinterland for centuries. Like his forebears, he boasted in grandiose terms about making "his own justice," and styled himself in letters in half-literate Greek as "King of the Mountains." But like them he too depended on the protection of powerful local politicians, and as the nature of politics changed, his way of life was jeopardized. Worried about the impact of his activities on Greece's image abroad, Athens ordered him to be hunted down. In September 1925 he was killed, and in the usual way a photograph of his severed head was published in the press to confirm his death before being sent to the University of Athens for criminological study.[1]

We can therefore imagine the shock felt three years later when the driver of a car crossing the hills just beyond Salonica's walls caught sight of Giangoulas and his gang in triumphant mood. Reversing fast, he drove off to the nearest police station; half an hour later a troop of cavalry arrived and chased after their man. Only in the nick of time did the soldiers realise that the fustanella-clad band of brigands they were about to attack was in fact a bunch of film extras. An enterprising local producer had been inspired by the hero's life and exploits: Giangoulas himself was being played by a Salonican journalist, his "wife" by a well-known actress. All was explained, a new pursuit scene was quickly added and the officers enthusiastically joined in.

CHANGING TIMES

TIMES WERE CHANGING and a previously endemic threat to public order had been turned into a concept which would make Salonica—at least in the minds of the men responsible—"the Hollywood of the North." It might be lagging behind Athens in literature and the fine arts, but perhaps Greece's northern metropolis could become a centre for the new art of the twentieth century. That at least was the hope. Unfortunately, brigandage was not so far in the past that the nervous authorities felt happy heroizing these public enemies, and anti-brigandage laws stopped the movie being shown. Salonica's own film industry never really got off the ground, though an academy which claimed to train students for a career in front of the cameras did good business for a time.[2]

But no one ever accused Salonica's inhabitants of not knowing how to enjoy themselves. Entertainment was a vital part of daily life, a distraction from the anxieties of exile, separation and displacement common to virtually every family there. Offering *cowboïka*, Charlie Chaplin and Hollywood tearjerkers, cinemas like the *Dionysia*, the *Pallas*, the *Athinaion* and the *Royale* attracted crowds of regulars. The *Attikon*, on the western end of Egnatia, with its White Russian pianist—briefly accused of being a Bolshevik spy—was a favourite of leftists, being situated close to the end of town where the tobacco sheds and the union offices were to be found: political meetings were frequently held in its hall. The *Pantheon* played mostly "erotic" films—by which were meant, according to Aimilios Dimitriades, not the sex films of a later, less innocent era, but rather melodramas, adventure films—anything with women and without cowboys. On the quay, the *Modern* offered more Westerns, this time mostly to appreciative Jewish families who littered the floor with the traditional *pasatempo* (roasted pumpkin seeds) and drank *gazosa* through two or three viewings.[3]

The cinema-owners would try any trick to keep their clientele. In the intervals, singers performed arias from operettas. Others added cabaret and circus acts and called themselves "variety cinemas." Child prodigies were a favourite—the "Miniature Little Devil, Nini Zaharopoulou," or five-year-old Louisa Bellini, who "dances exotic dances in imitation of Josephine Baker." The *Pathé* ran a lottery in the interval, with a prize—alarm clocks were popular. And when a long-forgotten masterpiece entitled "What Giannis Suffered" came to town, the same cinema announced free entry to anyone of that name.

Of course the cinema was not the only modern form of entertainment linking the city to worldwide tastes and fashions. The craze for speed made the first motorcycles an object of neighbourly amazement. During the First World War, airmen became symbols of human daring and technological wonder, much as the electric tram—*chaitan arabasi* (the devil's carriage) the city's older inhabitants had called it—had done earlier still. The air was starting to play its part in city politics too: in April 1922 the royalist government—in its final phase—had dropped leaflets over the city announcing the imposition of a forced loan, and a few months later, another plane brought in members of the Revolutionary Committee. In 1930, fifteen years after the first Zeppelin attack on the city, an English hydroplane, named "City of Salonica" for the occasion, landed in the bay and taxied to a stop in front of the Hotel Méditerranée, where it became an instant sensation and was blessed publicly by the Metropolitan Gennadios, "in front of the city authorities and a large crowd." The owners recouped their expenses by charging 250 drachmas for a flight above the town, and their many customers later founded a Society of Friends of the Air in order to popularize the delights of air travel.[4]

IN THE OLD DAYS, the best-known street sport had been wrestling, and well-known *pechlivanides* remained popular figures at fairs and on public holidays. One of them, Prodromos Tsaousakis, was later discovered as a singer by the great *rembetika* player Tsitsanis and became one of his finest interpreters. But strength was now being overshadowed by fitness. Soccer had arrived in the city even before the Balkan Wars, but exploded in popularity with the coming of the refugees, whose clubs formed its most important teams. Testifying to the interwar cult of the healthy body, new pitches were laid out on the edge of the Jewish cemetery, where they hosted professional matches and athletic competitions. Sports entered the school curricula, and the founding of the city's

YMCA, housed in a massive neo-Byzantine building, popularized basketball and baseball. The Pan-Thessalonican athletics competitions—including sections for "classical athletics"—became a fixture, and by the 1930s the government had established an inspectorate of gymnastics for northern Greece. For unlike the old-fashioned individualistic strongman, gymnasts, athletes and football players matched the new collectivist ethos of the times. Massed healthy bodies were a national priority.

Other kinds of exercise were less obviously useful to the nation. Probably even more popular than athletics was dance, and dance halls and academies proliferated. "Luxemburg was the most popular entertainment centre of those days, and it was in full swing," recalls Erica Counio-Amariglio in her memoirs. "Many big names were singing or bringing their orchestras there. One summer the very famous Eduardo Bianco came with his orchestra. The centre was bursting with people every evening."[5] Dancing was no longer just a cabaret act for the pleasure of the viewing male; it was a way for young men and women to meet and touch, out of sight of their parents. "One cannot imagine how clearly on the faces of the dancers shows the enchantment and an aesthetic satisfaction which comes from the pleasure of whirling around," wrote a journalist in 1927. "Especially the coquetteish expressions of the young ladies, all red and shining from a kind of extreme pleasure." It was, wrote another, "the instinct of necessity, the same instinct which brings the starving traveller outside the kitchen, the thirsty man to the spring, the lover beneath the window of his loved one."[6]

As for the sexually charged content of the new style of dancing, what attracted the crowds was exactly what alarmed more old-fashioned souls. In the interwar period, an anonymous composer tacked on a new ending to the well-known Judeo-Spanish "Song of the Fire." In the song's original version the catastrophe of 1917 had been attributed to *los pecados de sabat* (the sins of the Sabbath); but according to the new version God had punished the city because *Los mocicas de agora/todas visten de tango* (The young girls of today/all dress for the tango). Angeliki Metallinou, defender of civic virtue, warned that in the dance halls "poor young women learn to dance and proceed to worse." Driven on by conservative commentators and churchmen, vice police raided dance halls, and harassed owners so much that one at least was driven to suicide. As a result, popular spots like the Ramona, or the Aaron in the Jewish 151 neighbourhood, tried to highlight their respectability. Katakolos's dance hall assured parents that "inside the school of dancing the rules of order and morality are strictly observed."[7]

In 1929, following suggestions in the press, the mayor inaugurated the first Miss Thessaloniki competition in the Hotel Méditerranée. The short-listed candidates danced a tango with their partners, then a waltz. (The competition struck a chord in the city, and the gay men in Koufos's taverna organized their own "Miss of the Evening" in homage.) The second year's winner, a twenty-one-year-old refugee from Bursa called Roxani Stergiou, was the strong favourite to go on and win the Miss Greece title, but was deprived of that title after some behind the scenes manoeuvring by the mayor of Athens. As ever, the nation's capital knew how to sabotage the prospects of its northern rival. The eventual winner, Aliki Diplarakou, went on to win Miss Europe in Paris too, before returning to Greece and hitting the front pages a second time when she aroused the anger of the church by secretly visiting Mount Athos with the help of a celebrity-struck priest.[8]

MODERN WOMEN

A NEW KIND OF COMMERCIALISM was dissolving the grip of tradition, and women, especially younger women, found themselves challenging older ideas of what was proper. "If only someone would help me escape from this *modernizmo de mujer* [modernism of woman]," complains the elderly Uncle Bohor, in a popular satirical series in the Jewish press. In the old days, a respectable Jewish housewife—like her Muslim or Christian counterpart—stayed at home, let the man do the shopping and was not seen out unless properly attired and even veiled. In the suburbs and refugee quarters, neighbours and relatives still made sure young people did not get up to mischief. But in the city centre women were as visible—or so it seemed to some—as men, showing off like Frankish "madmwazeles," or "devilish coquettes/with elegance, and chic" (diavlas koketas/kon la elegansa, el shik), as the composers of the fox-trot "Salonik sivilizado" complained.[9]

This was not so much a question of politics—although there were feminist groups in the interwar city calling for an extension of the suffrage, to little avail—as economics. Among the refugees, in particular, there were far more women than men, forcing the former into the workplace. Women had always been wet-nurses and domestic servants. They now also served in tavernas and cafés, as shop-assistants, singers and dancers in variety shows; the *Beau Rivage* promised "extraordinary hospitality at the hands of Russian ladies." In Salonica, sang Tsitsanis,

"I was loved by refugee girls/Blue-eyed, brown-haired and refined *modistroules.*"

The *modistra*—or dressmaker—was the icon of new femininity in the interwar city. Called into being by female spending power, she was also herself a symbol of economic independence. Together with the hat-maker, she passed into the city's consciousness and the "little dressmaker's apprentice" became the heroine of a popular song of the period:

> *Oh, my* modistroula, *mincing and flirtatious,*
> *With your needle how you pierce my heart*
> *When you pass before me with such a posture*
> *Bir boza bir boza—clicking your heels with such elegance.*

Working alongside men, freed from parental supervision, female tobacco-handlers were a tougher breed, with a reputation for free-minded behaviour. The tobacco industry had traditionally offered employment to girls for a few years in order to earn their dowry, and between the wars, nearly half of all tobacco workers in the city were women. "Our suffragettes," as their defenders called them, were prominent from the 1914 strike wave onwards. Not only did they often take a leading role in industrial action, to the consternation of the authorities, but they also lived by their own rules. "Regina"—a well-known Jewish worker—lived openly with a Christian man, something highly unusual at that time. The police, who were less comfortable beating up women than men, were often perplexed, then shocked. Outraged by the behaviour of one female worker, a police officer warned her that her conduct was suspicious and she would be sent for medical examination, "and if this shows anything she will be sent to the brothels."[10]

HANOUMAKIA

AN UNUSUAL THREAT, no doubt, and one which testified not only to the authorities' repressive instincts where women were concerned, but also to the important place occupied by prostitution in the interwar economy of the city: there were no less than forty-eight licensed establishments in 1928 and street-walkers outnumbered civil servants. The traffic in sexual pleasures had existed in the city since Ottoman times, when more than one visitor had been invited by an apparently respectable Jewish youth to visit his "sister." With the Russian revolution and the Asia Minor catastrophe came a new supply of impoverished White Russian aristocrats and abandoned Greek refugees. Some (male) writers might talk glibly about the "charm" and the "traditional erotic sensibility of the East" that the newcomers brought with them, but what spurred on many of these "unprotected and orphaned girls" was economic need or vulnerability. Chrysoula T., for instance, had "erotic relations" with Panayiotis Peiridis after he promised to marry her, but then found herself being led, not to their new home but to the brothel of an old friend and partner of his, Angela Machaira ("the Knife"). She went to the police but this was surely not the first time the device had been used, and many in her situation were too ashamed to do this.[11]

In 1915 the arrival of the Army of the Orient had turned the back-streets of Bara into the largest red-light district in the Balkans. It "was drab, dirty, the women nearly 30 years old, and sitting on the steps of their shops with no drawers on, legs wide open, showing everything they had," recalled a young Cockney soldier. "This sight put me off. Saying in their broken [English] 'Very good for the jig a wig,' they pulled out their tits, shaking them. I was disgusted, they were all sizes and shapes, some hanging down, all were flabby. My mates tried to entice me to go into a house. The tarts looked younger, and had smaller and firmer tits. Not this time mates." Others were less squeamish. Even after the war there were over one thousand prostitutes working in one-room wooden shacks, and the district attracted droves of soldiers, farmers and merchants. It was so busy by night that in the adjacent quarter of Regie—where six thousand Jews had been re-housed after the fire—irate householders, fed up with being disturbed, patrolled the streets and hung signs outside their door: "Attention: this is a family home," or simply "Family House."[12]

Never far from the girls, as they sat outside their huts waiting for customers, were the quarter's pimps, card-sharps, hashish-dealers, *narghilé*-smoking "dervishes" and horse-traders. The all-night Ottoman-era café of Malik Bey, who owned several Bara brothels, survived until 1930 with its old-fashioned large mirrors, its *narghilés* and torn leather armchairs. The flashily dressed Alkis Petas, the "king of Bara," and leader of the Constantinople gangs in their perennial feud with rivals from Smyrna and Crete, had two pictures in his more modest establishment—one of "beautiful Constantinople," where he had grown up, and the other an icon of Venizelos, flanked by two angels, accompanied by the legend "Saviour of the Race." It was there, in Afroditi Street, opposite the brothel of Madame Erasmia, that he was shot dead by Smyrniot rivals in 1932 and succeeded as neighbourhood boss by a thuggish former henchman, Christos Papadopoulos, better known as Kerkyras—the Corfiot. The latter opened a bouzouki joint round the corner in Irini Street, and eventually, during the German occupation, joined the collaborationist Security Battalions before he too was shot dead outside his café in 1944.

The *putanes*—*pornes* in more proper Greek, "little ladies" or *hanoumakia* in the slang (from the Turkish)—lived amid the violence of their pimps and customers. In some high-class establishments the *patrona*—"mama" to her girls—might preside over a cosily domestic arrangement. Jean-Jose Frappa described the "simple, almost familial" atmosphere of a larger wartime brothel, its prostitutes drawn from Corinth and Cyprus as well as Greek, Jewish and Muslim women from the city itself, the clients Scottish, French and Senegalese soldiers. But even in such establishments women were vulnerable. "The day before yesterday," wrote one journalist, one of those women found herself in the street because she'd been kicked out of the house after a customer got angry. She was blind drunk, half-naked and unkempt with black bruises from being beaten. She was covered in make-up and her eyes were blackened. Blood ran from her nose and teeth." As for the grubby *maisons de tolérance* round Vardar Square, these were nothing more than a short step literally and figuratively from the degradation of Bara itself. Young women who had started out consorting with "aristocrats" and those of "other fine classes" were liable to find themselves quickly reduced to the level of street-walkers, or *kalderimidzoudes*—those who walked the cobbled *kalderimia* and turned a trick amid the rubble of the Great Fire.[13]

After the Second World War, the church, the ministry of public order and the UN all demanded a clamp-down. The new postwar seafront was supposed to give "another lung" to "this asphyxiating city," except that so many prostitutes gravitated there that tourists and respectable families kept away. Outside Bara, most brothels were closed by 1949, but those allowed to stay open—"to cure the needs of the Army and the visiting population"—profited from their new monopoly. In 1951 most of the dives in Bara itself were shut down for the opening of the new main railway terminus nearby. But as local police warned, this drove prostitution underground and when an American warship docked in the winter of 1952, "the central areas of the city and especially the seafront were filled with women of all kinds of suspect morals." By the mid-1950s, more than one hundred "dishonourable women" were still in the business. It was a far cry from the one thousand sex workers of the First World War; but now all the women involved were Greek. Even prostitution had been Hellenized.[14]

As the seedy western quarters slowly disappeared after the war, so they inspired Salonica's poets and writers. Bars and cafés, the deserted cemeteries and burned and bombed-out ruins in the city centre all featured in their accounts of "the erotic city." "To enter the city coming from the station," wrote Georgios Ioannou, for example, "it is a virtual necessity that you cross the erotic Vardari Square." The grimy backstreets which led into it, the ruins of the old Ottoman fortifications behind the Law Courts, the shabby remains of the old Frankish quarter round Ladadika, became part of this nocturnal literary vista of solitary and melancholy pleasures.[15]

These were the postwar hymns to vanished neighbourhoods which had been transformed as Ioannou put it into "places of archaeological tranquillity." But between the wars, when prostitution was ubiquitous—an eloquent testimony to the deep social crisis and impoverishment provoked by the Asia Minor catastrophe—there had been little time for romanticism. Anxiety about society's moral crisis, and in particular the fragile and vulnerable honour of its young women, raised issues of regulation and control. Some called for charitable work among the girls on the street; but most people were more concerned with protecting the public. "The secret dwellings of debauchery number in the hundreds," wrote *Makedonia* in 1934. "So many that they make it difficult for honest families to remain and the evil gets worse." "Other cities have managed to clean themselves up," complained another columnist. "Only here must the unfortunate inhabitants of one of the larger neighbourhoods, Vardari, continue to suffer this curse." In the First World War, the military authorities of the Army of the Orient had kept a close watch on the brothels. Prostitutes had to undergo weekly medical inspections, and were prevented from circulating freely in the town. After the war, the Greek authorities tried, less successfully, to keep the same checks. Medical inspections remained routine, but it was no longer possible to confine the women and girls to specific areas. In June 1921 "common women" were barred from entering the King George Gardens before midnight; it had become notorious for the Russian "countesses" who frequented it at all hours. A few years later a new police Section of Morals busted housewives for entertaining men when their husbands were away, and mounted so-called "virtue operations" in the city's parks, woods and cemeteries—all favoured trysting places. Even hotels were raided to catch couples who could not provide proof of marriage.[16]

Journalists poured scorn on the absurdity of the police harassment, "these moralologists [*ethikologoi*] interfering everywhere, in the suburban places of entertainment, roads, cinemas—anywhere a romantic couple flees to be alone." For as everyone knew, the police and the madames—"Cleopatra," "Giselle" and their Greek, Jewish, French and Armenian competitors—were closely linked. Madame Dede, who ran a brothel staffed with refugee girls in Angelaki Street, was even godmother to the child of the police chief Nikos Mouschountis. He and his colleagues protected the brothels in return for information; word from the street travelled to them quickly and any new faces were soon reported to the authorities.[17]

In his memoirs, the musician Markos Vamvakaris gives a vivid picture of the close relations between Salonica's head of police and the underworld. He had come north to play because his haunts in Piraeus and Athens were being closed down. His first night in town was spent with a prostitute, but early the next morning a policeman was hammering at the door, ordering the newcomer to the station to meet the chief. Mouschountis's attitude took him aback:

> I sat there quite a while . . . Markos, you get around, he says, I know. Of course I get around, I say, I wouldn't tell you lies. You go to this joint, then that. Sure, I go, Mr. Nikos, I say, I wouldn't lie to you. Then he tells me: For your sake, I won't disturb them so long as you are around. You go where you want, he says, it is fine, O.K.[18]

And in fact for all the frequent knife-fights in the tavernas where he played, Vamvakaris had fond memories of his trips to the "beautiful city"—where everyone was "well-dressed," the women "very *chic* . . . as if you were in Europe." Mouschountis loved *rembetika;* he followed Vamvakaris and he became so close to Greece's most famous *bouzouki* player, Tsitsanis, that he was best man at the latter's wedding. Athens, with its puritanical obsessions, was a different world: Salonica was small enough, and far enough away from the capital, for the police to make their own rules and set their priorities: Bara and the underworld served their purposes and never really escaped their control.

MUSICIANS

In the hamam *in the City, a harem is swimming*
Guarded by Arabs, who take them to Ali Pasha.

He orders his guards to bring them before him
To set them dancing and play bouzouki.

To smoke narghilés *with Turkish hashish*
And the little ladies dancing the gypsy tsefteteli,

That's how all the pashas of the world enjoy themselves,
With bouzoukia *and* baglama, *embraces and kisses.*

In songs like Tsitsanis's 1935 *In the Baths of Constantinople*, the Ottoman past was evoked and transformed. *Rembetika*—the swaggering, plangent music of the underworld of the Eastern Mediterranean—flourished in Salonica's bars and tavernas, despite the efforts of the state to clamp down on it. Using melancholic modes with Arabic and Turkish origins—the *hijaz*, the wailing *ouzak*—these songs were certainly not for those overly concerned with respectability, and were condemned by officialdom as decadent remnants of an Oriental age contaminated by non-Greek influences, unlike the supposedly purer folksongs of the mountains. In the smoke-filled cafés, a stern line-up of mustachioed *bouzouki* and *baglama* players, their faces impassive, laid down the harsh, strict, metallic rhythms against which their female leads sang tales of broken love, easy morals and above all drugs:

Like an Orthodox Christian, in this society
I get ready, old chum, to take the service.

I shop around for cigarette butts and a piece of hash
And get ready, old chum, to head to St. Mama.

In the church I go, into the rounded rooms
And start to puff away as if I was lighting candles.

And the archangel rushes down in front of me
The smoke has made him high.

He says, "Listen, man, it's no sin
That you came to church for your devotions."

But lo, a monk starts telling me: Get out!
It's my turn to be smoking now.[19]

With lyrics like these—written by Tsitsanis during his time in Salonica—*rembetika* spread rapidly through the country. Its popularity is often attributed to the influence of the Asia Minor refugees, and it had probably grown out of the improvised café singing sessions—in the so-called Café Amans—which were beloved by Turks and Greeks alike. But in fact it had been very popular in Greece itself before the Smyrna refugees in particular brought a far more emotional, highly orna-mented style with them and turned Piraeus into the recording centre for the genre. In Salonica, one of the finest of all interwar *rembetika* singers, Rosa Eskenazi, had been active since before the First World War when she made a spectacular appearance at the age of twelve—unknown to her parents—at the Grand Hotel. Eskenazi was from a central European Jewish family, who had emigrated first to Constan-tinople and then to Salonica. By the time she left for the recording stu-dios of Athens, others—like Vamvakaris and Tsitsanis—were heading north to the welcoming tavernas of the city's refugee quarters.

They could not be missed—for tavernas, in addition to orchestras and live bands, were now relying on amplification too. "Woman is like a gramophone," ran a song of this time. "And the man is the dynamo/which makes her sing." In an era when few people yet owned cars, when the most familiar sounds in the streets were still the braying of donkeys, cock-crows at dawn, the trumpet reveille in the barracks and the sing-song cries of passing traders, the "murderous instrument" introduced the city for perhaps the first time to the eminently modern problem of noise. The silence of the Ottoman city was becoming a thing of the past. As one journalist wrote sadly:

Once, when the gramophone was not so widespread probably it was a means of enjoyment and musical delight. But now, alas! . . . It is a monster which tears apart your ears, beats the nerves, turns your intestines upside down, unscrews your brain, kills relaxation, sleep, beauty, our very humanity . . . Just when you are dying of heat and stop at a café to cool off with a lemon-ade and relax, the moment when you need quiet and flee to the suburbs, where you think that all is asleep, unmoving, suddenly you leap up terrified, as if from a nightmare . . . What is it? The hoarse, asthmatic, apoplectic, crippled loudspeaker hangs from some tree or from the entrance . . . and without excuse or by your leave, attacks you and crushes you with the lament from Traviata or informs you that the young lady is asking her mother for "a young man/sweet and tasty," who with everything else will be "handsome and an Athenian" and she can't restrain herself.[20]

One of the reasons why the tavernas flourished was Salonica's insatiable appetite for music of all kinds. Before 1912, musical contacts with Istanbul had been very close, and musicians in the sultan's service used to give concerts at the Café Mazlum on the waterfront. "Spring in Salonica," ran one popular Judezmo song, "at Mazlum's café/a black-eyed girl sings the *amané* and plays the *oud*." Music united all tongues and faiths. "There was not a Salonican who did not run to hear the voice of Karakas Effendi which set the great old Mazlum Café in a tremble," remembered an enthusiast. Backed by violin, clarinet, *oud* and *kanun*, Karakas Effendi—"an elderly man, tall as a pine, his 75 years hidden in a black frock-coat"—was an Istanbul Jew who moved easily, like many musicians, between the café and the synagogue, challenging the cantors to see who could chant the blessings more beautifully. Ottoman Salonica itself boasted the gifted *Ma'min* vocalist "Kyor Ahmet"—a member of the aristocratic Kapandji clan—described later as "master of the pashas, beys and Ottoman colonels of high society; and the Caruso of the common folk." Dimitrios Semsis—sometimes known as "the Salonican" or "the Serb"—had been a youthful violinist in Abdul Hamid's entourage before he settled in the city. Later he became an important record producer for both Columbia and His Master's Voice.[21]

Mazlum's café was burned down in the fire, and the upper-class Hotel Méditerranée was built in its place, but some of Kyor Ahmet's Jewish students continued to develop and adapt his Ottoman legacy. "Maestro Sadik"—the blind Jewish *oud* player Sadik Nehama Gershon—collaborated with the song-writer Moshé Cazés who paid tribute to his partner as "truly an 'international musician' who plays many instruments and sings in Turkish, Greek, *Judezmo* and Arabic. The excellent traditional musicians who reached Salonica from Istanbul during the period of the population exchange categorize Master Sadik as a 'gramophone'; it suffices for him to hear any piece of music just once in order to learn it; and if it contains mistakes, he will correct them." In the cafés, players clustered round as Sadik taught them new songs "freshly arrived from Istanbul. Since all the musicians take the lesson together, you can easily imagine how the café turns into a veritable dervish centre, Sadik with his *oud* and everyone else beating rhythm, some on their clothes, others with their feet." And it was not only the musicians and their songs which still came from Turkey, but record producers and devotees, like another student of Kyor Ahmet's, the Turkish poetess Madame Aziz, who frequented the café where Sadik played.[22]

On the street, too, the old-established musical styles could be heard—the gypsy drummers, *klarino* players from the mountains inland, the mandolin bands and the love songs or *kantades* with which musicians and lovers still serenaded girls outside their homes. Christians like the Vlach violinist Mikos Salonikios played alongside Jewish bands, and hung out in the musicians' cafés—the Dolma Batché, and the Nuevo Mundo (New World) where cantors, tobacco workers and professional players adapted the old Ottoman modes—*hijaz*, *segah* and *shetaraba*—for a new clientele. This was also the last generation of the uninhibited, sharp-tongued Jewish entertainers, men of local renown like Moshiko el Mentirozo (the Liar), the Fratelli Nar, Los Ratones (the Mice), Nataniko, Daviko el Chiko (Little Dave) and Baruh el Dondurmadji (Baruch the Icecream Man)—whose scabrous rhymes and songs were the highlights of any wedding.[23]

These performers were nothing if not adaptable. Just as the *café chantant* gave way to the *café variété*, so the violin and the *kanun* were slowly being replaced by the bouzouki and guitar. Old-time musicians occasionally deplored the headlong rush into "European" fashions. "Everything goes out of style, even the traditional Turkish music ensemble. The piano, bass and violin have defeated the Eastern violin, *oud* and tambourine. The fox-trot has beaten the Eastern-style love song," wrote Sadik and Gazoz. But they were, after all, businessmen too, and they managed to adapt tangos and other European dances in their repertoire with little fuss and much humour. " 'Having a good time' today means dancing, and dancing without end. The old people say, 'The good ones go, the bad ones stay.' But *we* say, 'The old routine has gone; the new ways are here to stay.' " Sadik himself was said to be able to handle songs "en turko, en grego, en ewspanyol i franko/mezmo los tangos ed Edwardo Byanko [in Turkish, Greek, Spanish and French/Even the tangos of Eduardo Bianco]."[24] And there was still an insatiable demand for music in "the Oriental style," with all the memories this conjured up. A journalist described the evening bedlam of one street in the Upper Town which was lined with tavernas, all loudly competing to attract customers: "One tries to present the best singer who can hold the wail of the *amané* highest and play the tambourine, another the best players who can charm up, with the *oud* and the *santouri*, nostalgia for the much-mourned East." In the city's tavernas, at least, the Ottoman world remained alive.[25]

BACKLASH

NOISE, SEX, BRASH MATERIALISM and immorality—it is perhaps not surprising that the disappearance of the old ways produced a backlash of nostalgia and condemnation. "We went to bed mules and woke up Franks," complains Auntie Benuta in a popular satirical series in the Jewish press. Its elderly protagonists railed against the "snot-noses," "little Franks," the "messieurs" as they were ironically called, who used fancy words like "progress," "coiffeur" and "hypertension." Yet of course even in the old days, "when fruit stones were sweet," according to the saying, the entertainments and pleasures of city life had come under attack. In the nineteenth century, the rabbis had denounced "frivolous gatherings," and warned parents not to let their boys become musicians or dancers "for these professions expose one to meetings between unmarried men and maidens at weddings and dinner parties and in coffee-houses or hideaways and such, and this can cause one to engage in forbidden behaviour such as profanation and frivolity, jesting and lightheadedness." Both rabbis and *hodjas* inveighed against the evils of the coffee-house in particular, though the incessant stream of prohibitions is probably a clue to their lack of effectiveness. The city was known for its cafés, and most men went to pass the time in dominoes and backgammon, if nothing worse.[26]

Between the wars, antipathy to the city's pursuit of modernity was as strong as it had been in the mid-nineteenth century. The refugee crisis and the near-disintegration of the state prompted a mood of something close to panic at the nation's collective moral health. General Pangalos banned short skirts, while churchmen and police authorities closed down the city's first open-air gymnastics society, founded by an Italian devotee of sunlight and naturalism. And at the beach by the Beshchinar gardens, guards in boats tried to patrol the space between the male and female bathing cabins to prevent any mixing of the sexes, something which bewildered many of the refugees from the Asia Minor coast, for whom mixed bathing had been customary.

What was new in the 1920s was not the fact of protest but its source: religious authorities could still make their presence felt—especially the church—but it was the organs of state who now assumed the primary responsibility for the enforcement of social norms. The police adjudicated on propriety, checked dress and even reported on civil servants spotted in gambling dens. As we have seen, however, the police's ability and even willingness to perform this task was often in doubt. Sure enough, before long mixed bathing was commonplace and as for sex outside marriage that, so far as some commentators were concerned, appeared to be taking place in every nook and cranny of the city, churches not excepted. The boundaries of respectability were constantly being redrawn, in no small part because of the needs of commercial profit and the media. Society was policing itself as much as it allowed itself to be policed, and groups defined their own terms of acceptability. The shoemaker's guild, for instance, had no difficulty accepting "Simonetta," a gay man much prized by his fellow-guild members for his designs as well as his wit during their weekly parties; he in turn kept out of their interminable political rows—they were Archive Marxists and used to have regular brawls with members of the Communist Party—insisting that "these matters are not for women." In the cinemas, the dance-halls, the streets and the tavernas, a new topography of pleasure was emerging: through the experiences it generated, and the memories and places it claimed, it was establishing the city in the affections of a new generation of inhabitants. The taverna, claimed one journalist, was drug-store in daytime, refuelling stop in the evening, and theatre of political and personal passions at night, when it became a "parliament, a session of the League of Nations, a conference to solve all outstanding social problems." "The Beshchinar is your life, your lungs, your joy," proclaimed an advertisement for the city's oldest public park in 1934. It was no longer strictly true: the oil refineries which surrounded the once elegant Garden of the Princes where Sultan Abdul Mecid held court in 1859, the rail tracks, slums, tanneries and meat yards whose refuse polluted its beach, all pointed to its imminent and sad demise. But in a wider sense it was so: Salonica's pleasure gardens, parks, suburban and seaside centres of entertainment and distraction were, in times of exile, unemployment, poverty and political unrest, the places that people would remember, that made the city itself not only bearable but, to an ever-larger proportion of its inhabitants, home.[27]

21

Greeks and Jews

AUNTIE DJAMILA: You don't want to hear anything that has
to do with modernism.

UNCLE BOHOR: Doesn't "modernism" mean . . . "anti-
Semitism"?[1]

LANGUAGE AND IDENTITY

BEHIND THE GRECO-TURKISH population exchange of 1923 lay an
apparently simple logic: Muslims should be made to settle in Turkey
and Orthodox Christians in Greece. But where were Salonica's Jews to
go? No one in Madrid or Lisbon (or Salonica for that matter) suggested
they return to Iberia. Only a minority considered Palestine. Some did
emigrate to France and the USA. But for the vast majority, their home
was the city, and if asked they would have naturally described their
nationality—as one emigrant did to the French authorities in 1916—as
"Salonican."[2]

As a result of its conquests in the First Balkan War, Greece's total
Jewish population had shot up from ten thousand to well over eighty
thousand, of whom around seventy thousand lived in Salonica. The
tiny communities of Old Greece spoke Greek and were highly assimilated whereas the Sefardic Jews of the north, who played a highly influential role in what was now the country's second-largest city, were quite
distinct from the Greeks in both language and culture. Lucien Wolf, a
British Jew who helped draw up the post-WWI minorities treaties of
Eastern Europe, wanted Greece to guarantee many of the traditional
rights which the city's Jews had enjoyed under the Ottomans. But when
he discussed the idea with the Greek ambassador in London, the latter

saw such concessions as preserving all the humiliations of an Ottoman system of capitulations, and retorted that "to ask us to make special distinctions or grant special privileges would be to upset the very principle of equality which is on the other hand demanded of us." It was a fair point; Ottoman diplomats had been making it for decades before him.[3]

At the Paris Peace Conference, however, the idea of guaranteeing minority rights in law won the day and most states in eastern Europe were forced to accept the principle. In 1920, the Venizelos government passed legislation defining the constitutional position of Greek Jewry and this came into effect two years later. The rights and duties of the rabbinate were spelled out for the first time, the old property qualifications for voting in communal elections were scrapped, and all adult males over twenty-one were granted the vote. Jewish traders were allowed to make Saturday not Sunday their day of rest, and to keep their accounts in Judeo-Spanish.[4]

From the Greek point of view, the key to turning Jews into full citizens of their new country was language. Before 1912, few Jews in Salonica had bothered to learn Greek. From 1915, however, all Jewish (and Muslim) community schools in receipt of public funds were obliged to teach it. Jewish children were not forced to attend what Greek civil servants called "our schools"—whose instruction was described as "rather classical" and "incompatible with Jewish customs and nature"—and instead Athens invested in the Jewish schools themselves, providing language teachers, and later actual buildings. In this way, the younger generation learned Greek quickly and by the Second World War, many Jewish children were fluent, having taken part in school productions of such Greek classics as "Golfo the Shepherdess," or the stirring story of Leonidas and the three hundred. After one school play, a Judeo-Spanish paper proudly reported in 1932: "Many Christian friends who followed the performance assured us that they could not tell that the actors were Jews, so beautiful and correct was their Greek. We single out Miss Emilia Nachmia, who played with naturalness the role of Syrmo, Miss Esther Habib, daughter of our chief rabbi, who played Froso, Miss Matilda Almosnino, who moved us in the role of Krinio . . ."[5]

For the older generation it was harder, of course. According to the satirists, Uncle Ezra would take the wrong bus because he didn't know how to read the name of the destination, while Auntie Benuta's Greek was so poor that when the postman arrived with a registered letter, she had to seek help from her niece, Sunhula. But even Judeo-Spanish changed with the times, and Greek phrases rushed in. Albert Molho, a leading Jewish journalist, wrote in 1939: "Our assimilation to Hellenism is to be noted not only in the thousand and one manifestations of our public and private life. One sees it in our language as well: even when we speak *Judesmo*, one still sees we are Hellenes. Judeo-Spanish, which once overflowed with Turkish words . . . today shows clear signs of Greek influence." By the late 1930s readers of some *Judesmo* publications wanted a page in Greek: "in my opinion," wrote one, "the idea is not bad because as things are going, in time readers of Judeo-Spanish will be rare, since the younger people are reading Greek newspapers more, and in the schools [Judeo-]Spanish is no longer studied."[6]

The language question reflected the spectrum of attitudes to assimilation more generally among the city's Jews. French remained the language of the cultured elite, especially among those wealthy enough to send their children to the foreign schools. Local communists stood up for the continued use of Judeo-Spanish, the vernacular of the workers. But a middle-class minority stressed the need for fluency in Greek in order to "give Greece good Greek citizens who will, at the same time, be no less good Jews." In the view of the Alliance Israélite Universelle, religion was a matter of private conscience, Judeo-Spanish a backward dialect holding up intellectual progress, and cultural assimilation a necessity. "If I speak about assimilation," wrote one,

> I do so not out of Greek patriotism but for the sake of Jewish interests. I believe that in order for the Jews to be able to live here, they need to assimilate to the environment in which they live. The fewer barriers there are between Greeks and Jews, the easier it will be for us to live here. Our purpose is not to be ostentatiously patriotic, but to safeguard the existence of the Jewish population. If assimilation is not the correct means of doing this, let us suggest another way.

This view was opposed chiefly by the Zionists. They accused the Alliance of betraying Judaism and demanded a prominent place in the school curriculum for Hebrew. Relatively unimportant before the First World War, Zionism became far more popular in the 1920s. The 1917 Balfour Declaration had been hailed with enthusiasm in the city, and Vladimir Jabotinsky's visit in 1926—unlike his earlier, pre-war one—elicited exuberant demonstrations outside his hotel.[7] But while many sympathized with the Zionists' desire for an assertion of Jewish ethnic identity, they felt there was little point wasting "hour after hour learn-ing a language such as Hebrew, which is of no use to anyone here." As a Greek analyst of these language battles remarked:

> Even now, when no restrictions are placed on the teaching of Hebrew . . . Hebrew is neither learned properly nor is there any need for it in the everyday lives of the Jews.[8]

The truth was that behind these struggles over language lay new atti-tudes to politics. By eliminating the old property qualification from community elections, the Greek authorities had unwittingly under-mined the old Ottoman Jewish notable class and reduced the power of its assimilationist message. Both the communists and the Zionists prof-ited from this and were able to draw upon the votes of the thousands of the poor, including those who had suffered most from the fire and its aftermath. In addition, for much of the interwar period the post of chief rabbi was vacant and this meant that there was no one to play the kind of unifying role which Saul Modiano or Ascher Covo had done half a century earlier.

The first communal elections in 1926 were a two-way fight between the communists and everyone else—Zionists and assimilationists alike—who banded together into a so-called Jewish Union to stop the left. They elected fifty-eight candidates as opposed to twelve commu-nists. But deep ideological divisions existed among the opponents of the latter—chiefly over how far to accommodate Greek demands for assimilation. In 1930, while the communist vote stayed constant, the Zionists split into different factions. At this point, Zionism, though internally divided, was undoubtedly the leading political force within the community. Yet four years later, in the last communal elections of the interwar period, both the communist and the assimilationist votes held steady, while the vote of the pro-Jabotinsky radical Zionists col-lapsed. The truth was that Salonica's Jews were so deeply divided along ideological lines that they were more or less incapable of unified action. Communal democracy and the collapse in the power of the old Ottoman-Jewish bourgeois elite made administering community affairs harder rather than easier. Many voters evidently felt alienated from politics, and in 1930 there was an abstention rate of perhaps 50 per cent. But the accusation that the city's Jews were a hot-bed of socialism was misplaced: the extreme left was always a minority cause, though it was a larger minority—typically between 15 and 20 per cent—than among non-Jews. The main trend was that a large part of the community first embraced and then lost faith in Zionism.[9]

The idea of founding a Jewish national home in Palestine gained currency in the city only from the start of the twentieth century. After Chief Rabbi Jacob Meir arrived from Jerusalem in 1907 the movement acquired a network of clubs, schools, newspapers. The 1917 fire, by destroying the old neighbourhood synagogues around which local networks of power and authority had formerly been based, also helped to foster the new kind of ethnic (rather than strictly religious) definition of community which the Zionists espoused.[10]

Yet even though Jews began to emigrate from 1910 onwards, they went mostly to France and Italy, or across the Atlantic. The figures are uncertain, but by 1930 thousands of Salonican Jews had settled in Paris, and there were smaller communities everywhere from New York to Naples. Some dock-workers, *hamals* and fishermen did make their way to Haifa and Tel Aviv, and there was a spurt of departures after anti-Semitic disturbances in Salonica in 1931. But the actual numbers involved were probably relatively small. As many as 20–25,000 Jews emigrated from the city before the war but probably only about a quarter of these, if that, ended up in Mandate Palestine.[11]

Well before the Arab Revolt of 1936, the sense had grown that Zionism did not have the answer to the problems of Salonican Jewry. The economic slowdown was just as acute in Palestine as in Greece, and the British were only issuing about two hundred entry permits annually. Moreover, the Greek authorities themselves did not want the Jews to leave. Emigration "would *not* be in our interests," noted a civil servant, for it was the rich and the enterprising who tended to go first, making unemployment worse.[12] By the end of 1933 Greek sources reported that the numbers of those who wished even to visit Palestine had fallen away. The Revisionists' disappointing performance in the 1934 communal elections was an indication of the changing mood.[13]

Not that there had been any shortage of critics of the Zionists within the community. On the left, Jewish communists distinguished themselves by the ferocity of their attacks, perhaps because they were competing for the same votes. They called the Zionists in charge of communal affairs a "filthy clan of gangsters," termed others "Jewish fascists," and castigated the "criminal politics" of those who had thoughtlessly encouraged the masses to dream of emigration. One Judeo-Spanish Marxist weekly, *The Staff*, defined its outlook at the top of its front page as "extremist communist tendencies, clear and open, with no mercy or personal favours right or left, against the Jewish religion and the bourgeoisie, against Zionism and the Jewish colonization of Palestine."[14]

But a no less impassioned critique came from so-called moderates like the historian, writer and educator Joseph Nehama. By the 1920s Nehama was convinced that mourning the "good old days" of Ottoman rule was a waste of time. It was necessary now to work positively with the Greek authorities and Zionism was a distraction, if not worse. Some "assimilationists" put forward a theory of Greco-Judaism and argued that patriotism and the preservation of one's own ethnic identity were not incompatible. They stressed their common bourgeois credentials in the fight against communism, and in December 1928 they founded the Association of Jewish Assimilationists whose goal was "to create and develop amongst Salonica Jews feelings utterly identical with those of their fellow-citizens irrespective of religious persuasion, without however distancing themselves from the Jewish faith, the Jewish tradition and the spirit of Jewish solidarity."[15]

Yet Zionists and anti-Zionists alike faced the same problem. The Jewish community did not exist in a vacuum, but in a state shaped by the twists and turns of mass politics. Political success and failure did not lie only in their hands but depended as much if not more upon the attitudes and policies of the Greek authorities. Jewish affairs were a marginal matter in Greek national life. But the great issues of the day—the monarchy versus the republic, refugees against natives, Venizelos versus his enemies—left their imprint upon all Salonica's inhabitants, not least its Jews.

THE IMPACT OF GREEK POLITICS

THE 1917 FIRE and the plan that followed it had left the Jewish community fragmented, impoverished, marginalized and resentful at what it regarded as discriminatory treatment by the Greek state. These feelings were somewhat allayed three years later by the relatively favourable provisions on schooling, language and self-government in the law on Jewish communal life. But with the arrival of the refugees, a frontier note crept back into Greek-Jewish relations. The 1920 law had explicitly allowed traders to close on Saturdays instead of Sundays in order to observe the Jewish Sabbath. But after the Asia Minor disaster the issue was reopened when Prime Minister Papanastasiou urged young Jews to emancipate themselves from old "narrow religious conceptions," and refugee representatives asked for obligatory Sunday closing. Some guilds, with mixed Greek and Jewish memberships, proposed the "English working week" as a compromise. The struggle was a bitter and public one, but eventually the Sunday trading law was passed. Its proponents used the language of equality before the law to justify the same day of rest for all, but as contemporary observers noted, the only plausible reason for abandoning the 1920 agreement was to give the newly arrived refugees in Salonica an economic advantage over their Jewish competitors. The latter—if observant—would be obliged to close two days of the week, the former only one. But the refugees were now a greater power in the city than the Jews, and held its future in their hands.[16]

While the government could at least nominally justify the ban on Sunday trading on the basis of its desire to treat Jew and Christian alike, it could not argue that way in defence of its decision to make Salonica's Jews vote in a separate electoral college. This was deliberate political ghettoization. In elections before the Asia Minor catastrophe Jews had always voted alongside Christians for the same candidates. But in 1920 the Liberals marked out special electoral districts in the city for Jewish voters, and three years later, in the elections for the constituent assembly, a separate electoral college was set up. Supporters of the scheme claimed this was needed to stop Jews disproportionately affecting Greece's fortunes. They supposedly lacked patriotism, and had contributed to the country's misfortunes by voting against Venizelos in his shock 1920 defeat—a move which in the eyes of his devoted followers was equivalent to treachery: "Thanks to the Thessaloniki Jews," wrote one, "we lost Eastern Thrace, and the Asia Minor disaster occurred, which was terrible for our nation."[17] The truth was that the separate Salonica college made sense only in terms of the interests of Venizelos's Liberal Party—"for reasons of party and electoral calculation," as Venizelos himself actually admitted later.[18]

In the critical elections of 1928, which marked Venizelos's triumphant return to the political stage and ushered in four years of Liberal rule, the system was fully implemented for the first time. Venizelos claimed disingenuously that it was needed—if only temporarily—to guard "the traditions and special interests" of this "ethnic grouping." Jewish voters gave him the benefit of the doubt and returned two deputies who both declared their willingness to adhere to the Liberal line. But after the elections, Venizelos said that until Salonica's Jews felt themselves to be Greek citizens, the system would be retained by the state "to defend itself against a possible abuse of the vote." It was against this background that the pro-Liberal Jewish League for Assimilation was founded.[19]

When Venizelos fell from power in 1932, under the impact of the economic depression, however, a new anti-Venizelist administration declared the separate Jewish electoral college unconstitutional and scrapped it.[20] Relations between Venizelos and Salonican Jewry now reached an all-time low. When many Jews again voted against the Liberals, Venizelos himself interpreted the move as "an act of hostility against half of Greece." "Do you want war, Israelites? You will have it!" declared a Venizelist newspaper in 1933. Venizelos was finally adopting the intransigent positions his supporters in the city had been urging on him. In 1934, he told a journalist from the *Jewish Post* that "the Greeks do not want the Jews to influence Hellenic politics . . . The Jews of Salonica follow a national Jewish policy. They are not Greeks and do not feel as such. Hence they ought not to involve themselves in Greek affairs." And he went on to say: "The Salonican Jews are not Greek patriots but Jewish patriots. They are closer to the Turks than to us . . . I will not allow the Jews to influence Greek politics." It was a far cry from the conciliatory statesman of twenty years earlier, and one further sign that the great politician was losing touch with his country. In 1912 he had combined ardent nationalism with a belief in Hellenism's power to incorporate and assimilate its minorities. Now that confidence had waned, and a harsher, shriller tone emerged.[21]

THE CAMPBELL RIOT

THE PRONOUNCEMENTS of national politicians were what made the headlines, but on this issue local activists were driving the Liberal machine. Venizelists in Salonica were far more outspoken than their leaders in Athens. The need to be sensitive to international opinion weighed less with them, and they spoke directly for interest groups in the city who saw the Jews as competitors or threats. Febrile hostility towards communists, Bulgarians and Jews combined with a sense of economic competitiveness among the refugees pushed some nationalists in an increasingly vicious direction.

One of their main weapons was the local press. Greek journalists had greeted the 1914 strike of tobacco workers as a sign of the dangers of letting "foreign races," with no sense of loyalty to the blue-and-white flag, flourish in the city. In those days Venizelos himself, despite exiling two prominent Jewish labour leaders, had deplored gutter press anti-Semitism. But with the coming of the refugees, some newspapers again singled out the Jews for attack. *Makedonia*, in particular, a leading Venizelist broadsheet, was supportive of the separate electoral college, and critical of the community's supposed reluctance to assimilate. In fact, the paper did its best to whip up animosities and played a prominent role in the one outbreak of anti-Jewish violence the city (and country) witnessed before the Second World War—the Campbell riot.[22]

After the 1928 elections, relations between the Liberal Party and the Jewish community had seemed cordial enough. Indeed in December 1930, a Liberal mayor was elected in the city with strong Jewish support. Nevertheless, it was in this period that a translation of the *Protocols of the Elders of Zion* was carried in local Greek newspapers, while *Makedonia* publicised "scandals" which, as they put it, revealed "the eternal hate of the Jews for Hellenism." According to them, the city's Jews were a compact and highly organized group, conspiring to take over the municipality and the other organs of state, and seeking to undermine Greece. Referring to the country's minorities, in the aftermath of a row over the teaching of Greek history in the local *Mission Laique* school, the paper warned: "Either they will acquire a Greek consciousness, identifying their interests and expectations with ours, or they will have to seek a home elsewhere, because Thessaloniki is not in a position to nurse in its bosom people who are Greeks only in name whereas they are the country's worst enemies." Such intemperate language, deployed month after month, carried more than a whiff of violence, and soon led to worse.[23]

In June 1931 a new athletics hall was built by the local branch of the Zionist Maccabi sports organization, and the opening ceremony was attended by representatives of the city's other sports and scouting organizations, both Jewish and Christian. Immediately after this, however, *Makedonia* published what turned out to be an explosive revelation: it claimed that Salonican Maccabi delegates had participated in a congress of Bulgarian *komitadjis* in Sofia where they had denounced Greek rule in Macedonia and called for autonomy. The accusation was nonsense, but it was dangerous nonsense, linking Jews and Bulgarians in a way calculated to inflame Greek nationalists. A farrago of half-truths and falsehoods sufficed to allow *Makedonia* to raise the temperature and to accuse the Jewish community as a whole of lack of patriotism, cosmopolitanism and indeed treachery.

Makedonia was just one newspaper, of course, and by itself could have had little influence. Even inside the city, where it played a powerful role, it was known for its extremism on this issue and criticized by other papers, Venizelist and anti-Venizelist alike. However, nationalist groups combining anti-communism and anti-Semitism were emerging for the first time in Greek politics. An organization of army officers stationed in northern Greece circulated pamphlets that accused the Jews of responsibility for Bolshevik crimes as well as for the Asia Minor disaster. In 1923, the Central Union of Anti-Jewish Youth was established in the city, and joined later by groups like the rightward-leaning All-Students Union and the Anti-Communist Youth Organization of Macedonia. Another nationalist students' association at the university warned Greeks not to be fooled by Jewish professions of loyalty and patriotism. Reprising the tactics of the previous generation, it called for "a savage boycott":

> The Jews are those who edit three French language papers and one in Greek; those of whom three quarters are foreign subjects getting rich in Greece; those whose paper *Avanti* calls on honest Greek soldiers to turn their arms against their officers . . . those who work as hard as they can to make Salonica a free city run by the Jews; those, finally, who denigrate everything Greek and calling themselves Maccabis participate in congresses of *komitadjis* and declare themselves in favour of the autonomy of Macedonia.[24]

In June 1931 the campaign in *Makedonia* intensified and ethnic violence erupted. A mob ransacked the Maccabi offices, stones were thrown at Jewish homes and synagogues, and cases of attempted arson were reported. Jewish shopkeepers closed their shops in protest, Jewish students tried to prevent the distribution of inflammatory pamphlets, whilst in parliament government and opposition alike denounced the troublemakers.[25]

Delegates from the Jewish community appealed to the local authorities to step up security around some of the outlying Jewish settlements. But the government under-estimated the gravity of the situation. On Sunday 28 June, squads of nationalists attacked one Jewish neighbourhood, only to be beaten off by the locals. The next evening a crowd estimated at nearly 2000 people, drawn largely from the adjacent refugee quarters of Toumba and Kalamaria, rampaged through the so-called "Campbell" settlement, home to 220 poor Jewish families who had moved there after the 1917 fire. They were expecting trouble and many had barricaded themselves inside their dwellings. But they were forced to flee when the mob set fire to their shops and houses. In unsuccessful attacks on two other neighbourhoods, the inhabitants managed to drive off the attackers.

The "Campbell riot," as it became known, shocked public opinion in a country where such events were unknown. There were few fatalities—one was the Christian baker of the quarter, whose premises had been attacked by the rioters—but the neighbourhood was abandoned by its former residents and eventually sold off to the Greek authorities. The government ordered army and police patrols onto the streets, promised compensation to the Jewish community and pledged a full-scale investigation into the affair. Yet the parliamentary debate that followed was far from reassuring. Deputies with strong refugee connections protested that "men filled with patriotism and nationalism cannot be characterized as bands of malefactors." Stylianos Gonatas, the governor-general of Macedonia, declared that he could not see what there was to censure in a group set up "to exalt national sentiment" and to defend the "established social order."[26]

Not surprisingly, many Jewish families began to feel that the outskirts of the city were no longer safe, and moved nearer the centre, lodging in schools and other community buildings. Others made plans to emigrate, or visited the foreign consuls to ask for protection and permission to raise foreign flags above their houses. It was a huge psychological blow to a community already reeling from the effects of depression and discrimination. "The largest part of the Jewish population," wrote a journalist, "already so hard hit economically, sees itself today ambushed by misery, an irremediable, despairing misery."[27]

The trial, the following year, of those responsible illuminated Salonica's shadow world of extremists. Among the defendants was the editor-in-chief of *Makedonia*, Nikolaos Fardis, whose inflammatory articles had done so much harm. But the key defendants were the organizers of a previously little-known militant fringe party called EEE—the National Union of Greece. Founded in 1927 by refugee merchants who resented Jewish competition, this was registered as a mutual aid society whose members—Christians only, according to the statutes—helped each other find work. In reality it was an ultrapatriotic paramilitary organization. Georgios Kosmidis, who set it up, was an illiterate Turkish-speaking refugee trader, a small-timer best known for his impressive moustache. Predominantly Venizelist, EEE nevertheless prided itself on standing above party politics and organized its members on quasi-military lines. Most of its three thousand members in Salonica were refugees who saw the Jews as old allies of the Ottoman Turks, and hated communists as much if not more. Its shock-troops wore uniforms and helmets, and some would go on during the German occupation to become members of the collaborationist Security Battalions.[28]

Like other such groups, EEE was the kind of marginal political force which needed violence and publicity. Campbell was their moment in the limelight: their work otherwise involved scrawling anti-Jewish graffiti and slogans on walls, throwing stones, and making the occasional attack on cinemas, cafés and bookstores frequented by the left. Standing in municipal elections in February 1934, it won few votes and despite the support provided by visiting fascists from Germany and Romania, it collapsed later that year as a result of factional in-fighting. But it was part of a more enduring network of right-wing groups whose activities were to make a deep impact in the coming decades.

What really made them significant was the support of mainstream politicians. It was not merely that the defendants at the 1932 trial were acquitted, nor that the organization was never closed down by the authorities. The links were closer than that. Representatives of EEE had met with the governor-general of Macedonia on the eve of the troubles, and he was clearly sympathetic to their aims as his comments in the subsequent parliamentary debate showed. Welfare Minister Iasonides, a leading interwar refugee politician, also backed them. They took part in official parades on national holidays and received subventions from the municipality and major banks. And there were rumours that neither the police nor the army had showed much energy in pursuing them at the time.[29]

The truth was that Venizelist Liberals especially, and many others in the civil service and the army, shared some of the attitudes that motivated the rioters. They were more sophisticated in their expression, and more conscious of the need to consider the impact of anti-Semitism upon Greece's international image. Nevertheless, Greek nationalism—riven with anxiety in the aftermath of the Asia Minor disaster—operated through an ethnocentric view of the world, much as Zionism did. It saw Jews in communal terms, and under-estimated the variety of views and opinions that existed among them. And despite their public statements, few people really believed that Jews, however assimilated, could become Greeks.

A startling illustration of how deeply such attitudes had penetrated the administrative elite is provided by the confidential memoranda of the director of the Thessaloniki press bureau, an intelligence service set up (revealingly) in the foreign ministry to monitor the city's Jewish press. On 5 July 1931, he analysed the background to the Campbell riot. Its root cause he attributed to Jewish "provocation" to Greek sentiment over many years. The very formation of the Maccabi groups was one such act; as for the press, no one could deny, he wrote, "that the Jewish newspapers have always been provocative." He went on to imply that it was the failure of leaders of the Jewish community to reply publicly to *Makedonia*'s original allegations that had led to the "sad and bloody actions against the Jewish population" when, as he put it, "Greek public opinion—rightly or wrongly—took to the streets and engaged in acts of violence."[30]

And yet it was not always simply a matter of being for, or against, Jews. In early April 1933, special services were held in some synagogues to protest anti-Jewish persecution in the Third Reich, and Salonica's rabbis ordered Jewish shopkeepers to shut their premises. Although the governor-general of Macedonia tried to persuade the president of the community not to go ahead with the shop closures, the police took a different line: their view was that since the matter had arisen during synagogue services, the closures were a matter of individual conscience and should not be blocked. In the event, they went even further than that and actually enforced the shop closures in one or two cases where Jewish proprietors had either deliberately or through misunderstanding failed to comply, provoking angry protests from fellow-Jews. The main concern of the city police in this case was simply to preserve public order and to forestall fights between Jews which might cause a disturbance. They patrolled the streets and kept watch outside synagogues where well-attended services were in progress. Their interest was thus local and quite different from that of the political elite, who were far more concerned about the impact of the protest on relations with the new German government. By and large, the police succeeded in their aim, though later that night nationalist youths paraded through the deserted market quarter singing patriotic songs and hailing Hitler, while others painted the letters "EEE" on the central Monastirioton synagogue, and scrawled large red swastikas on walls and pavements.[31]

Yet after the tensions of the post-1922 crisis decade, the steam was going out of organized anti-Semitism. In national elections in 1932 and 1933 the city's Jews—disillusioned with Venizelos and shocked by the aftermath of the Campbell riots—swung overwhelmingly behind the anti-Venizelists. The latter relied on Jewish votes (as they had in 1920) and were vehemently against the refugees, whom they regarded as the main cause of Greece's troubles. Anti-Venizelists wanted to gerrymander Salonica's electoral districts to marginalize the latter rather than the Jews. In January 1934, one anti-Venizelist deputy even described Salonica's Jews as "more Greek" than the refugees—a remark which was hardly meant to be taken seriously but did point to the fact that the process of Hellenization had more than one target: after all, the leader of EEE spoke Turkish better than he did Greek. The following month, the anti-Venizelist mayor Manos was elected for a second time, a man with a well-founded reputation for pro-Jewish sympathies.[32]

The failed Venizelist coup of 1935, the return of the king, the collapse of parliamentary democracy and the establishment of the Metaxas dictatorship all weakened those political forces which had been most inclined to agitate against the Jews. EEE was among the many political organizations disbanded under the dictatorship, which lacked the racial dimension of central European fascism. A new chief rabbi was appointed—an Ashkenazi called Zvi Koretz—with a reputation for a modern outlook, and he established close relations with the Greek authorities. King George made his feelings towards the Jews clear by visiting Salonica's Beth Saul synagogue. The decade after 1931, in short, was more harmonious in terms of Greek-Jewish relations than the preceding one had been. It would not be much of an exaggeration to suggest that an authoritarian regime saved the Jews from the tensions and dangers to which parliamentary politics had exposed them.[33]

ATTITUDES AND MENTALITIES

THE GREEK STATE might have formalized the structure of the Jewish community, and treated it for most of the interwar period as a collectivity, distinct from the Christian majority, but at the level of daily life the boundaries between the two religions and communities were permeable, and becoming more so with time. Political affiliations created ties across the ethnic divide. And even more than in Ottoman times, the city made its own demands, and created realities quite different from those established by law or imagined by the political elite. In the large mostly Jewish 151 quarter, for instance, Avramatchi, the Jewish grocer, sold his *kezo blanko* (white cheese) to Greek and Jewish housewives alike. The very language of shopping combined Turkish words which everyone still used—*bakkal* for grocer, the *bakkal defteri* for the book containing his customers' accounts—Judeo-Spanish and Greek. Jewish women talked of going home to their *sinyor* (husband) but were themselves known as *nikotcheras*, after the Greek word for housewife (*noikokyria*). Greek and Jewish children played games like *aiuto* together in the streets, shouting *Judesmo* terms that refugee kids were quick to pick up.[34]

Few Greeks, it is true, ever acquired more than a few words of Judeo-Spanish. One of the few who were fluent was the so-called "Jewish" Panayiotis Constantinidis, who had worked from a young age for Jewish customs-brokers near the docks. "Panayiot" liked to play practical jokes such as dressing up and impersonating the rabbi who went round on Fridays at dusk telling the Jewish stallholders to close for the Sabbath, or, on another occasion, alarming local women at their prayers by entering the church where he served on the administrative committee dressed as a Jewish salesman and pretending to sell them candles. Stories of his pranks circulated for years precisely because his skill was so unusual.

On the other hand, even though *Judesmo* remained in use at home, most male Jews and younger females knew enough Greek to pursue a living. Elderly wandering street-sellers advertised their wares—shirts, tumblers, oranges, tomatoes—in a broken Greek which amused their clients. Poor Jewish women worked as wet-nurses for the Ayios Stylianos orphanage, while seamstresses like Luna Gattegno had "Jewish and Christian clients." Although many of the city's trade guilds were exclusively Christian Orthodox or Jewish, a surprising number had a mixed membership: in 1922, for example, the Praxiteles guild of marble carvers had four Greek, eleven Jewish and one Muslim member; the old vegetable-sellers' guild included fourteen Greeks and thirty-three Jews, while fishmongers, street porters and traders in the central market all promoted their interests together. Ethnic homogeneity was certainly not the rule even for the small businessmen, traders and sellers who dominated the city's economy. Among the workers in its factories and warehouses there was a strong vein of inter-communal association and solidarity, especially in the unions and left-wing political groups. For the city's business elite, the exclusive *Club de Salonique*, which had been

founded in the late nineteenth century to provide a place to receive foreign visitors, still provided a discreet and civilized setting for influential
Greek businessmen and officials to meet Jewish fellow-members. The
balance of power was shifting, and the Greek membership now outnumbered Jews. But like most clubs it was proud of its rules and traditions, and continued to accept Jewish members even after the German
occupation began in 1941.[35]

Faith remained the key marker of ethnic difference. Greek liberals
and socialists accused Jews of preserving what they called their
"Ottoman mentality," by still seeing themselves as a separate collectivity. And indeed among Jews the term "Greek" was often used as a synonym for "Christian"—as when one man described his sister, who had
converted, as having "become Greek." Similarly, for the elderly Uncle
Bohor in the *Judesmo* press satire, a man with a rather traditional outlook, a Greek barber is simply "one of them." But then in his eyes Jewish "atheists," like his neighbour upstairs who had shaved off his beard,
were not much better. The older generation was still devout, atten-
dance at both church and synagogue was high, and families paid regular
visits to the cemetery. A handful of weddings each year took place
across the religious boundary, but this remained a fraught business for
both faiths. When a refugee priest baptized a young Jewish woman
without having first consulted Metropolitan Gennadios, his action provoked an angry response from the chief rabbi, and Gennadios, who was
himself a product of the old Ottoman system and well understood the
sensitivity of the matter, ordered the priest to be punished. The city's
diocesan archives contain at least seventy-eight applications from Jews,
mostly young women, seeking to marry Greek Orthodox men during
the interwar period. But in the old days, converts had risked ostracism
by marrying out; by the late 1930s this was less of a worry.[36]

And the much-maligned "Ottoman mentality" was not to be found
only among Jews. Greek society itself still harboured deeply rooted
prejudices against them. As *Judaioi* they were linked in the popular
imagination to the figure of Judas, the betrayer of Christ. The journalist who translated the *Protocols of the Elders of Zion* into Greek in 1928
also published *Judas through the Ages*, an equally nasty tract welcomed
by none other than the Archbishop of Athens. Had the Jews not crucified Christ, after all, and had they not desecrated the corpse of the
Greek Patriarch in Constantinople in 1821? Their supposed religious
and national crimes were thus easily merged. In the summer of 1931,
Makedonia serialized a fictional story of unhappy love between a Jewish

girl and a Christian boy: the moral—that befriending Jews led Christian families to ruin—was powerful enough to be taken up in one of Greece's most popular post-war novels, *The Third Wedding Wreath.*[37]

Religious anti-Semitism and a sense of ethnic rivalry and competition coloured the atmosphere of the interwar city. But as we have seen, they only became a recipe for violence when politicians sought to use an anti-Jewish policy for their own electoral advantage. Stereotypes facilitated but did not cause the Campbell riot. Nor did stereotypes prevent the Greek authorities from recognizing and supporting Jewish life in various ways. Indeed, an anti-Venizelist administration made Yom Kippur a public holiday in Salonica—to the consternation of Nazi diplomats. Although the anti-Semites fulminated, there is no indication that this was an unpopular move among a majority of the city's inhabitants for whom co-existence and increasing interaction were facts of life. The metropolitan, Gennadios, and the chief rabbi, Koretz, preserved cordial relations, and tried to ensure that their subordinates did too. Thus in the mid-1930s, the sources of communal tension were largely fading even as official anti-Semitism intensified in Germany, Poland and Romania. Left to themselves, Greeks and Jews might well have sorted out their differences. In the Second World War, hundreds of young Jewish men from the city fought in the ranks of the Greek army, and some of these went on to join the resistance. But they found themselves now up against an infinitely more deadly and highly organized form of anti-Semitism—not the petty discrimination of Greek officials, nor the mob violence of provincial right-wing louts, but the genocidal capabilities of the most advanced state in Europe.

22

Genocide

On 6 April 1941, German troops attacked Greece from the north, and three days later, they entered Salonica. By the end of the month, the king and his government had fled Athens, the British expeditionary force had been pushed back to Crete, and a puppet government had been formed. The country was partitioned. The Germans assigned the Peloponnese, central Greece and most of the islands to the Italians, and the Bulgarians were allowed to take over eastern Macedonia. Salonica and its region were among the strategically vital areas which remained under the control of the German army.

Military occupation need not have brought the city economic distress for in the First World War, fortunes had been made there and business flourished. But in 1941 it had still not recovered from the depressed conditions of the 1930s, and unemployment was high. To make matters worse, 48,000 refugees now fled into the city from the Bulgarian zone. Fifty thousand were being fed in soup kitchens in October 1940; a year later, the number had probably doubled. Housing was scarce, for many homes had been damaged in Italian bombing raids.[1]

Very quickly the authorities found the city was running out of food. There was little they could do about it. Requisitioning crops was hard when the drachmas and occupation marks given to farmers were made worthless by inflation. As winter approached, even the armed convoys sent out to collect grain encountered resistance; the villagers preferred to sell their produce through the black market. "My mother sold whatever valuables she had," wrote one child of Smyrna refugees. "The roads and footpaths that led to the villages were crowded with people coming from the towns to give jewellery, clothes, salt, soap, empty bags, glass, porcelain, pictures, carpets, sewing machines . . . just to find something to eat and above all some flour to make bread." Some left to settle in the countryside where food could be found more easily, but neither the refugees nor the Jews had strong family links to the villages.[2]

Within an astonishingly short time, therefore, hunger began to spread through the streets on an alarming scale. "The causes of this economic disintegration are known," the French consul informed Vichy six months into the occupation. "They are the war, defeat, pillaging, the entry of the victorious armies, the Greek demobilization, then inflation coinciding with the scarcity of foodstuffs, the almost absolute control of the Aegean by the English navy which prevents the provisioning of Greece by sea, the influx of refugees chased out by the Bulgarians and finally and above all the massive requisitions effected by the Occupation authorities in a poor country deprived of a part of its production and all its imports." By November, shop shelves were bare and black-market prices had soared.[3]

The wife of the Swiss consul, who returned home at the end of 1941, painted a grim picture of city life. Emaciated adults were collapsing on the pavements; their bodies were later removed on open carts "drawn by gaunt horses, staggering in their traces from the effects of hunger. Subsequent burials are carried out without coffins owing to the lack of wood." As the death toll rose, fear of famine gripped the population. The Greeks, she reported, blamed the Germans for their plight and called them "locusts." "The spectre of a contrived extermination of a whole population," she concluded, "cannot be dismissed as a hallucination conjured up by starved stomachs but rather viewed as a logical appraisal of German behaviour in Greece since the invasion of Russia."[4]

In fact, the Germans certainly did not plan to exterminate the population and even imported a little food from other Balkan countries. Yet in the spring of 1942 hundreds of people were still dying of hunger, and that summer, malaria—the city's traditional scourge—killed many more. Not until the spring of 1943 did death rates return to something close to normal levels or births begin to outnumber deaths. In all, more than five thousand people died of starvation—far fewer than in Athens, or the islands, but a catastrophe without parallel for Salonica. And yet, frightening as this was, for the city's Jews it was only the beginning.[5]

THE ROSENBERG COMMANDO

THE FIRST SIGN that the Jews might be singled out came right at the start of the occupation when representatives of the communal council called on the German commander and were dismissed without being seen. A few days later, the entire council was arrested, and Chief Rabbi Koretz was sent to Vienna. Gestapo officials raided Zionist clubs, while the previously banned anti-Semitic EEE party was re-formed. On 29 June, a week after the invasion of the Soviet Union, Jewish homes on two streets—Miaoulis and Misrachi—were requisitioned for the use of German families fleeing Allied bombardment; Christian-owned homes were not touched.

More damaging than this were the activities of Hitler's ideological commissar, Alfred Rosenberg, who was setting up a research centre in Frankfurt for the study of world Jewry. When Greece fell, he immediately sent a team to Salonica—"one of the main Jewish centres, as you yourself know," he told Martin Bormann. Led by a German Hebraicist, the Sonderkommando Rosenberg plundered its Jewish libraries, clubs and synagogues, seizing tens of thousands of books, archives, manuscripts and rare objects to send back to Germany. To men more habituated to the world of East European Jewry, Salonica was unfamiliar territory: in August, one enquired where the ghetto had been located, only to be politely informed by a local scholar that after more than twenty years of his own historical research, "he had never encountered in any manuscript, or any document of whatever kind, the least indication allowing one to believe that there existed at any time a ghetto in Salonica."[6]

The Rosenberg commando left Greece laden with looted Jewish goods, some of which would turn up, many decades later, in the KGB special archive outside Moscow. But after appointing a new, more pliable president of the community, the Germans apparently lost interest in the Jews. Jewish businesses continued to play an important part in the life of the town, and at school and university Jewish and Christian children found that life went on little changed. The members of the pre-war communal council were released, Chief Rabbi Koretz returned to Salonica, and the quisling Greek prime minister stated publicly that "there is no Jewish question in Greece." The Sonderkommando Rosenberg agreed; its final report concluded with evident disappointment that "for the average Greek there is no Jewish question. He does not see the political danger of world Jewry."[7]

Others did, of course. The German consul had been sending detailed information about the community back to Berlin since 1938, and local German agents and collaborationist Greek anti-Semites were constantly suggesting anti-Jewish measures. Heinrich Himmler himself warned Hitler in October 1941 that the city's large Jewish population posed a threat to German security. Yet no plans for further persecution were drawn up. The military authorities understood the economic importance of the Jews for the city, and felt the famine was not a good time to disrupt trade further. They were also aware of the Jews' irrelevance to anti-German resistance. Suggestions from Berlin to introduce the yellow star were dismissed.[8]

LOCAL ANTI-JEWISH MEASURES

IT WAS THUS A SHOCK when out of the blue—on 8 July 1942—the local Wehrmacht commander in Salonica instructed all male Jews aged between eighteen and forty-five to present themselves for registration. "Whoever belongs to the Jewish race is considered a Jew, regardless of what religion he professes today": with these words, meaningless in the absence of prior legal definition, racial categories entered Greek administrative life. The announcement gave no reasons for the registration, but it soon became known that the men were to be used as civilian labour building roads and airstrips. From eight in the morning the following Saturday, nine thousand Jewish men stood in lines in Plateia Eleftherias while their names were taken down. Huge crowds gathered to watch, and from the balconies overlooking the square some Germans took photographs. The men were forbidden from taking refreshment; some were humiliated and made to do gymnastic exercises. In the daily *Apoyevmatini*—the one local pre-war paper still published—the Jews were accused of being "parasites" and black-marketeers, who would now be put to productive use.[9]

The German army urgently needed civilian workers. Volunteers had already been recruited locally, and there had been tentative efforts to conscript the able-bodied population of the city by year-group. In the first week of July, Greek men were being put to work at the docks, building air defences. With public resentment growing, a senior gendarmerie officer in Salonica had suggested to the local military commander, General von Krensky, that the Jews be singled out. In this sense, the round-up of 11 July helps us to realize how the Final Solution unfolded: not only through instructions from Berlin, but also via the accretion of local initiatives taken by authorities such as the German army, their civilian labour contractors and politically astute local officials.

What most struck the onlookers were the scenes of deliberate humiliation that accompanied the registration. In Salonica, German soldiers and officers had sometimes targeted Jews for ridicule, just as they had done more frequently in Poland. One rabbi had half his beard shaved; another was forced to discuss the Talmud whilst being beaten. But the events of 11 July—discussed at gleeful length the next day in the quisling press—were of a very different order. The cruelty which the Germans had displayed preyed on people's minds. The Italian consul Zamboni noted that "unlike what has happened in other occupied countries, there were no clear anti-Jewish orders issued until now here. Now, suddenly, after a few previous indications which passed almost unnoticed by most people, the question has been raised in full."[10]

This was confirmed when the quisling daily *Nea Evropi* published a series of articles on the history of the local Jewish community. The story they described was of Greek suffering at Jewish hands: since 1890, according to the author, Nikolaos Kammonas (from an old, respected Salonica family, he later became a founding member of Salonica's branch of the Friends of Adolf Hitler), "the Jews managed with infernal perversity and venomous perfidy to secure their financial and racial empire on the corpse of Macedonian Hellenism." Others joined in denouncing this "danger to our health." One journalist described the Jews as "a sort of epidemic" and called on the authorities to remove traders near the Hirsch hospital, and "to force them to wash themselves, and their houses, and stop their bazaars." Nor could anyone doubt the ultimate backing for such sentiments. On 9 November 1942, the Greek papers carried a speech by Hitler under the headline: "International Jewry will disappear from Europe."[11] All of this was being orchestrated locally by a new military propaganda office run by the Germans. Its Greek underlings included well-established journalists such as Alexandros Orologas, the owner of *Apoyevmatini*, and Nikolaos Fardis, whose inflammatory writings in *Makedonia* had played such an important part in the Campbell riot. In the 1920s, the same Fardis had been vociferous in calling for the destruction of remaining Ottoman buildings. What drew men like him to collaboration was not racialism so much as an extreme nationalism that allowed them to accept any measures necessary to weaken the role played by other ethnic groups in the life of the city.[12]

One of the buildings Fardis had wanted destroyed in 1925 was the Hamza Bey mosque on Odos Egnatia which had been turned into a telephone exchange and then into a cinema. In 1942, as the "Attikon" cinema, it was one of three properties owned by a Jewish businessman. That September he was arrested and thrown into the Pavlos Melas camp on the northern outskirts of the city. This camp was run by the SS and it chiefly housed political prisoners to be shot in reprisal executions. The cinema owner was told that he would be released only if he appointed new managers nominated by the press and propaganda office. Eventually the contracts were drawn up by Greek lawyers in the presence of Max Merten, the Wehrmacht official in charge of the administration of the city, and the cinemas were rented out to a refugee from Serres. The transfer of Jewish properties to beneficiaries of the Germans had thus begun. Within weeks, people understood: Jewish businesses faced expropriation by the Germans and their agents, and their owners could be arrested or otherwise coerced into releasing them.[13]

In December 1942 came the strongest indication to date that even the municipal authorities themselves might find the plight of the Jews impossible to resist. The Jewish cemetery, which occupied a very large area outside the eastern walls, had been the object of controversy between the community and the municipality for decades. It had obstructed the implementation of the interwar town plan from its inception, for it lay squarely where Hébrard had envisaged green recreational spaces at the heart of the new modern city, and where others, more practically, wanted to build a new university campus. The university, which had started out in the old Villa Allatini, had been penned for most of the interwar period into the old Ottoman Idadié building on the cemetery's edge. Negotiations between the Greek authorities and the Jewish community had progressed slowly. But in 1937 they had agreed that in return for ceding the western part, the rest would be planted with trees, while new Jewish graveyards would be constructed elsewhere. In 1940 further burials were forbidden in the old cemetery, though in fact they continued to take place because no action was taken to build new ones.[14]

Now, however, the municipal authorities saw the chance to resolve the cemetery issue for good, and they raised it with the Germans. Negotiating the release of Jewish forced labourers that October—they were eventually ransomed by the community, which paid the Germans a large sum—Merten mentioned to his Jewish interlocutor, the lawyer

Yomtov Yacoel, that he had received many suggestions from Greeks that the expropriation of the cemetery should form part of their negotiations. Although this idea was instantly rejected by the Jewish side, it resurfaced a few days later. On 17 October, Vasilis Simonides, the governor-general of Macedonia, informed the Jewish community that it should transfer the existing cemetery and construct two new ones on the city's outskirts: any delay would lead to the cemetery's immediate demolition. When the chief rabbi asked for the work to be postponed until after the winter, the municipality ordered the demolition to begin.

Thus in the first week of December, instructed by the chief municipal engineer, five hundred workers destroyed thousands of tombs, some dating back to the fifteenth century, and piled up the marble slabs and bricks. Relatives of those buried there hurried to collect the remains of their dead before it was too late. "My parents and I rushed to the cemetery," recalled a survivor:

> The sight of it was devastating. People were running between the tombs begging the destroyers to spare those of their relatives; with tears they collected the remains. In my family vault there were the remains of my brother, aged twenty, who died during a journey to Rome. His body was brought back from abroad and put in two coffins, one in metal and the other in wood. When the second coffin was opened my poor brother appeared in his smocking and his pointed shoes as though he had been put there yesterday. My mother fainted.[15]

The cemetery covered a vast area of nearly thirty-five hectares (in comparison, the Jewish cemetery in Prague is about one hectare) and contained hundreds of thousands of graves. German military authorities requisitioned some of the marble for road-building and to construct a swimming-pool. Greek organizations and individuals carted off more: indeed even a few years ago, tombstones could still be seen stacked in the city's churchyards or set in the walls and roads of the Upper Town. "A few weeks sufficed for this army of workers to achieve the task of destruction for which it had been engaged," wrote an eyewitness. "The vast necropole . . . now presented the spectacle of a violently bombed city, or one destroyed in a volcanic eruption." One of the oldest and largest Jewish cemeteries in Europe had been uprooted; the Germans had given the green light, but the initiative had not come from them. After the war, the Greek authorities took the view that the land had been definitively expropriated, and today the university campus stands on the spot.[16]

WISLICENY AND BRUNNER

DURING LATE 1941 highly secret discussions on the Final Solution took place in Berlin as the innermost circles of those concerned with "the Jewish question" came to terms with the vast dimensions of the task they had set themselves. Neither emigration out of Europe, nor resettlement inside it, now seemed to provide the answer, and near the end of 1941 Hitler decided upon "biological annihilation." After that came the building of extermination camps, and the coordination of the complex diplomatic, financial and transportation arrangements for bringing hundreds of thousands of Jews to them. The spring of 1942 saw mass deportations from Vienna, Prague and many towns in Germany itself. Jews from Croatia, Slovakia and occupied France, including many hundreds who had emigrated from Salonica before the war, were killed in Auschwitz, which was rapidly being expanded into the largest combined concentration- and death-camp in the SS system.[17]

Extending the Final Solution to Greece ran up against the problem that the Italians, who controlled much of the country, did not share the German desire for action. Salonican Jews with Italian citizenship were reassured that they would be protected from German racial policies if these were introduced and in May 1942, the Italians told the Germans that they saw no need to make Jews wear a star. That July, the SS complained about the Italians' attitude, and the foreign office was told that if agreement with Rome were not possible, the Germans would press ahead and "show the way."[18]

Months went by, the SS grew impatient and in January 1943, Adolf Eichmann sent his trusted deputy, Rolf Günther, to Salonica. It was the first time an official from the infamous department IV B 4 for Jewish affairs of the Main Reich Security Office had come to Greece, and Jewish officials he met there were struck by his "harsh and disdainful" attitude. He demanded information on the community and left for Berlin almost immediately. Some days after, Eichmann ordered one of his closest aides, Dieter Wisliceny, to go to Salonica "to make arrangements with the military administration to find a Final Solution for the Jewish problem there." Wisliceny had already sent women and children from Slovakia to the gas chambers, and was fully briefed on the newly comprehensive Final Solution now under way. In Vienna he was joined by Hauptsturmführer Alois Brunner who had been entrusted with the technical aspects of the deportations. Their instructions were to have the whole matter wrapped up in six to eight weeks.[19]

SATURDAY, 6 FEBRUARY 1943: Wisliceny and Brunner, accompanied by about one hundred German police, arrived in Salonica and installed themselves in a suburban villa outside which they draped a large black SS flag. That Monday they told Chief Rabbi Koretz that Salonica's Jews would have to wear the yellow star, mark their shops and dwell in a ghetto. Instructions issued a few days later were more specific: the star must be ten centimetres in diameter and have six points. It was to be worn by all Jews over the age of five on the left breast. New identity cards were to be issued. For the first time, a racial definition of being Jewish was provided, based on the Nuremberg laws. Then came further prohibitions—on changing residence without permission, on using the trams or telephones and on walking in public places after dark. By 25 February, all Jewish homes had to be marked as well.[20]

Trying to carry out all these instructions led to a frenzy of activity for Koretz insisted that the German orders must be obeyed in full. "At the head of this multifarious and multifaceted organization," wrote Yacoel, the community's legal adviser, "stood the Chief Rabbi, Dr. Koretz, occupying himself personally, from morning to late at night, with the smallest and least important details, neglecting the examination of the greater problem: the fate that awaited the Jewry of Salonika." Koretz was persuaded, against his will, to ask Wisliceny whether it would be possible to create two Jewish quarters instead of one. This was accepted, and so one area was marked out for Jewish settlement on the west of the city above Egnatia Street, and another in the eastern suburbs. The almost entirely Jewish working-class districts on the outskirts were not affected, and the SS agreed that for the time being their inhabitants could remain in their homes. Everyone else had to move into one of the two designated zones by 25 February. Since Christian inhabitants in these areas were not evicted, they quickly became extremely crowded. Although they were not enclosed, large black six-pointed stars were drawn on walls to mark their boundaries. "Finally!" exclaimed *Apoyevmatini* on 25 February. "Did you see Thessaloniki this morning? The streets were filled with bright stars worn by filthy Jews."[21]

In January and early February, those who could transferred assets to Christian friends and associates in order to save them from the Germans. In front of the Hirsch hospital, crowds gathered as Jews sold off their possessions for food, clothing, rucksacks and handcarts. Eventually they were prohibited from selling their belongings at all. Meanwhile, a Jewish police force was made up of young men, mostly from well-off families, under the control of the SS's Greek collaborator Laskaris Papanaoum. Led by their Jewish heads, Hasson and Albala, they went around with German guards closing up shops, expropriating them and terrorizing people. At their trial after the war, the president of the court intervened to say to Hasson: "I heard many things about you . . . The whole neighbourhood of Ayia Triada had to deal with you. You went about on horseback, whip in hand, and threatened them." Another witness, a leather merchant, watched helplessly as Hasson's men "took out anything they liked from his house for the Germans and loaded it up onto carts."[22]

Next the Germans ordered all clubs, unions and professional organizations to dismiss their Jewish members, effectively cutting them off from municipal and state allocations of goods, allowances and pensions. On 1 March, all Jews were instructed to make a declaration of their assets. Meanwhile, Jewish workmen were ordered to turn the Baron Hirsch quarter, down by the station, into an enclosed camp with barbed-wire fences and lighting for the guards. It was a sad irony that this neighbourhood had originally been built in the late nineteenth century to house Ashkenazi refugees from Tsarist pogroms. Wooden fences went up around its perimeter and left it with only three tightly guarded exits—two onto adjacent roads and the third leading directly to the station. Without warning, its impoverished inhabitants were cut off from the world, and went two days without food before the community managed to organize a soup ration for them. Brunner's idea was that once its original inhabitants had been deported, it would become the transit camp from which the rest of the city's Jews could be easily put onto the trains nearby. Yet even at this stage, few people realized what the Germans planned. When one of the Jewish engineers involved in the lighting of the Hirsch encampment learned that the Jews were not merely to be subjected to the Nuremberg laws and confined, but also deported, the news struck him "like a bombshell." On 5 March, Koretz—who denied there was any truth in the rumours of deportation—felt obliged to call for calm and to remind people "not to give credence to alarming rumours, entirely unfounded."[23]

Friday, 6 March: All the areas designated for Jewish settlement in the city were suddenly blocked off with checkpoints. Greek and Jewish policemen checked papers and did not permit Jews to exit, though Christians could come and go. The next day, Brunner called a meeting of Jewish notables. His message was a harsh one. Through Koretz, who translated, he warned his audience that had not the chief rabbi guaranteed their obedience with his life, they would all be in a concentration camp as hostages. He demanded their full cooperation and told them that the community was now responsible for organizing soup kitchens and distributing clothing. After Brunner left, Koretz announced that no Jews were allowed to work any longer outside the specified Jewish zones. Their shops would only be opened to allow them to retrieve possessions. Otherwise they would be kept shut and the keys handed over to the occupation authorities who were creating an organization to find caretakers to run them.[24]

With almost all the city's Jews confined to their new "ghettoes," the disruption to trade was immense. As services previously provided by them became unavailable, prices soared. Debts could not be collected; shoes and watches awaiting repair could not be collected by their owners. Vegetables, eggs and perishable goods began to rot. Stalls and shopfronts, especially in the commercial districts, were shuttered and closed and factories lay idle. "Following the closure of very many Jewish shops, the diminished circulation in the streets and the lack of a public in cinemas and restaurants and cafés," the Italian consul wrote, "the city has suddenly acquired an unexpectedly sad appearance."[25]

On 14 March, Koretz was ordered by the Germans to call a public meeting inside the barricaded Hirsch quarter. There, for the first time, he told people that they were to be deported to Cracow. He attempted to put a brave face on what awaited them—work according to your aptitude, a new life on the land in a Jewish settlement—but the meeting dissolved into catcalls, wails and cries of outrage and despair. The next day there was a train waiting with more than thirty carriages on the tracks and the deportations began. It was just over five weeks since Wisliceny and Brunner had arrived.

THE DEPORTATIONS

SUNDAY, 15 MARCH: Approximately 2800 people left on the first train, around 80 tightly packed into each carriage, guarded by a contingent of German policemen. They could carry 20 kilos of baggage each but no valuables, jewellery or other money. Previously they had been made to exchange their drachmas for what were in fact fake zlotys. What they left behind was supposed to be deposited in the administrative offices in the Hirsch camp; in fact many simply abandoned their possessions in the muddy streets or threw them away. As the overcrowded train began the five-day journey to Auschwitz in southern Poland, the camp lay temporarily empty.

Just a few hours later on the same day, however, it filled up again. The adjacent neighbourhood of Ayia Paraskevi was surrounded by soldiers, and its inhabitants were given 20 minutes to gather in the streets before they were marched there under guard. The following day, the residents of the nearby settlement of the Stazion Chiko, or Little Station, were made to join them. These two groups were sent in the second convoy, which left Salonica on 17 March. Then it was the turn of Regi Vardar—better known as "Ramona"—whose nearly 15,000 inhabitants were evicted in less than an hour shortly before dawn. The working-class Jewish neighbourhoods on the city's western outskirts were now deserted. Despite a police warning against looting, the empty homes and shops were quickly plundered by Greek gangs looking for valuables which had been left behind. Robbers were shot by German soldiers.[26]

Among the Jews who remained in the centre and in the eastern suburbs, a rumour spread that it was only the "communist" workers' quarters in the west that had been destined for deportation. But on 17 March Koretz appeared at the central Monastirioton synagogue and dispelled this illusion. He told a crowded gathering that there was no alternative for the Jews but to resign themselves to their fate. Their behaviour was worthy of praise—he cited the selflessness of the rich who were assisting the poor, the wonderful number of marriages which were being contracted on the eve of departure—and this would help to ensure that when they arrived in Poland they would be able to preserve "the good name of Salonica." But his words no longer sounded plausible or reassuring: there were shouts of "traitor," and Koretz was attacked and only escaped without injury thanks to his Jewish guards who bundled him into a waiting car and sped him out of the ghetto.[27]

OPTIONS

WHEN ASKED BY THE ITALIAN CONSUL on 27 March, Merten said that the Jews were being deported to "a locality near Warsaw where there is a coal mine. They will live together, administer themselves and work in a synthetic rubber factory." This was the official line. In fact, without necessarily knowing the precise details, Italian diplomats realised many of the deportees would be killed. Another consular official, Lucillo Merci, noted in his diary on 21 March that in Poland "the physically fit among them are put to work, whereas the rest are eliminated. In the end, the physically fit will be eliminated too."[28]

We do not know how widely such suspicions were circulating in the spring of 1943. A Jew with Turkish citizenship who left the city for Istanbul in early July knew nothing more than that the deportees had been sent in the direction of Nish. Others knew even less. On the other hand, an escapee from Salonica reported in mid-August not only that German officers when asked where the Jews had gone, reportedly answered "Heaven," but also that one officer had told him that "they were forced in large groups to enter an empty cleaning establishment, [and] the gas was then turned on until all perished."[29]

Nothing as precise as this has surfaced for the spring months themselves. But there had been vague indications and warnings of what lay in store. The BBC's broadcast in December 1942 accusing the Germans of massacres in Poland had reached some. Yet when one elderly Jewish man from central Europe heard this in Salonica he remembered the First World War and dismissed it angrily as "English atrocity propaganda." Jewish shopkeepers were sometimes alerted indirectly by German soldiers: one advised Alberto Saoul to "go to Athens where the air is better." Another German told a Jewish acquaintance of his Christian girlfriend: "Why don't you flee?" A third hinted to a Jewish photographic goods dealer that "the air of Thessaloniki will become very bad for the Jews," and when asked what he meant said that the Nuremberg laws would shortly be introduced. A fourth bought some soap from a shopkeeper and then told him: "You aren't doing well just staying here. I was in Romania and saw them drown Jews in a lake; all the Jews from one town they drowned in a lake." The shopkeeper listened, and discussed it with his friends and came to the conclusion that "he was making propaganda to frighten us—how could they have drowned all the Jews?"[30]

Vague warnings such as these left most people in a state of deep anxiety. "One day they sent some carts to Ptolemaion Street to load up the belongings of the Jews who were going to be sent to Germany," recollected Sarina Beza in 1945. "Until that point there had not been any cordon around the area. The Jews gathered in the streets in groups and began to talk uneasily about the future that awaited them." Many were worried by the especial "brutality" and the "particularly harsh circumstances" of the "German persecutions." Salonica's inhabitants remembered the forced population exchange which had led to the departure of the city's Muslims; some had fled from Russian pogroms themselves before the First World War, and of course many Asia Minor refugees had their own deeply traumatic experiences of deportation at Turkish hands. These historical memories encouraged people to believe the German stories that they were going to be resettled elsewhere, but also added to the sense of foreboding. The Muslim emigration, after all, had extended over more than a year following the population exchange agreement; but the Germans were trying to move many more people, in a far harsher manner, in a matter of weeks.[31]

One of the most remarkable documents to have survived from this period is a series of letters sent by a woman called Neama to her sons in Athens. In the first letter, dated from 5–7 March 1943, when the cordons were placed for the first time round the Jewish zones, she writes: "When God will unite us, we do not know . . . Will God have pity on me not to fall ill if they do not exterminate me? What we are seeing is not very encouraging." The next day she answered a letter from her sons: "I see you are not very well informed about what we are going through. This week we are enduring scenes that we have seen only in the cinema and in history books . . . For two nights we sat on the bed, dressed, waiting for the knock on the door to wake us and take us away. Everyone is selling things in the streets to buy food . . . The cries, moans and tragedy cannot be described . . . The streets are crowded with people who are falling upon the others like hyenas on a dead horse to steal their things from them."[32]

It was not just the German SS officials whose harsh behaviour seemed so frightening. The Hirsch camp became notorious as a place where the leaders of the Jewish police tortured, extorted and killed their fellow-Jews in order to force them to reveal where their possessions were kept. The ring-leaders escaped in the summer of 1943 to Albania and survived the war, only to be captured and brought back to Salonica to be put on trial at the demand of what remained of the Jewish community in 1946. At this extraordinary event, survivors told tale after tale of how they had been interrogated, tortured and tricked into giving up their valuables. So overwhelming was the sense of desperation that many Jews decided it was better to depart as quickly as possible to escape the hellish conditions they faced in Salonica itself. "Forty-eight hours in those conditions were enough to make us wish to leave one hour earlier for Krakow," remembered one.[33]

The obvious alternative—fleeing the city—was a highly risky option. On the night of 18 March, the Germans played a cynical trick to deter would-be escapees: they kidnapped a well-known Jewish doctor who worked for the International Red Cross—his status and Italian citizenship had allowed him immunity from the restrictions imposed on other Jews—and put him and his wife straight on a waiting train. The next day they announced that he had escaped, and declared that twenty-five Jews had been immediately taken as hostages and would be shot if there were any further escape attempts. And with large sums of money changing hands, many efforts to flee failed at the first hurdle. Some policemen got Jews to pay them to get out of the ghetto, and then handed them over. A Greek fisherman betrayed three Jews who had hoped to flee south; they had contacted him through his wife, but the couple turned out to be unreliable.[34]

Nevertheless, many Christians were urging Jews to go underground. Eleftheria Drosakis's grandfather, himself a refugee from Smyrna, visited an old Jewish friend in the town ghetto—Christians could enter without hindrance—and offered to hide him. The postman told Erika Kounio's father to give him his two children: they could stay with his mother outside Verria. Railway workers, sometimes for money and sometimes out of sheer compassion, hid Jews in goods wagons heading south. Leftists organized a network which spirited more than seventy out of the city, and offered help to many more.[35]

Yet going underground put the helpers at risk as well: Anastasios Maretis was imprisoned in the Pavlos Melas camp for hiding Jews and was interned in the Hirsch camp—this happened to several Christians—and beaten up. It is therefore not surprising that Christians hesitated to help Jewish friends. "The day before yesterday the chemist's daughter came to see me and I pleaded with her to tell her father that I want to visit him and to rest there for a while," wrote Neama on 8 March. "He refused. Today she came again and gave me a small jar of marmalade and a small *tsoureki* [bread] and asked me to forgive him for his refusal." Leon Hayouel "tried to remain in Salonica but was unable to." "To flee to the mountains," recalled Leon Perahia, "I had to find a contact with the men in the mountains . . . Obviously I didn't bother with the star. I went to Kalamaria where most of my comrades were hanging out. For three days I came and went until I found the right guy."[36]

Opportunities to get away did sometimes present themselves which were rejected for fear of splitting up the family. Most of the actual and potential escapees were relatively young, mobile and usually single: they spoke fluent Greek and had many Christian friends and work-mates, whereas the older people spoke Greek, if at all, with a heavy and easily recognizable accent. Young people turned down chances to escape when their parents decreed the family should stay together. Others chose to stay, because they felt that abandoning their older and younger relatives was irresponsible. Sam Profetas was urged by his boss to head for Athens, and told he could get him false papers. Then he heard that the Germans had rounded up the inhabitants of Regi Vardar, where his mother and sisters lived, and taken them to the Hirsch camp. "Thank you for your suggestion," Profetas told him. "But you must bear in mind that we Jews have two religions: first comes the family, and after that God. I can't leave my mother who has struggled hard all her life to bring me up." And he presented himself voluntarily at the camp entrance.[37]

Yet hundreds of Jews did escape—on foot, by boat and by rail, into the villages of the Chalkidiki peninsula, the mountains of western Macedonia, the Greek islands, Turkey and above all Athens, which remained still under Italian occupation. They were helped by scores of individuals, as well as the burgeoning left-wing resistance movement— still in its infancy in the Macedonian hinterland—and even by the Italian consular authorities in the city, who negotiated strenuously with the SS to issue as many passports as they could. In the early hours of July 15—after all but the final 2000 Jews had already been deported to Auschwitz—the Italian consulate managed to transfer a train with 320 Jews under its protection to Athens. In Salonica there were left only the "privileged" Jewish elite, several hundred Jews with Spanish papers, and more than 1,000 men who had been building roads for a military con-tractor in central Greece. These men made up the last transport. The communal leadership, including Koretz and the Spanish Jews, were sent at the beginning of August to the "privileged" camp of Bergen-Belsen. Having seen the bulk of the deportations through, Brunner had already gone at the end of May. Wisliceny followed him in August.

Almost no Jews now remained in Salonica. Fifteen or so were exempted because they were married to non-Jews—some well-connected Greek men with Jewish wives had protested angrily to the Germans and managed to save their families—and up to one hundred were hiding with friends. Two women were helped by men they later married; another older woman was hidden by a Christian relative. An unknown number of children were adopted—five of these were returned by the city orphanage in 1947—despite stringent German prohibitions against doing this. All those left faced a terrifying underground existence in the city itself where searches for hidden Jews continued until liberation. At least three Jewish men, married to Christian women, were later arrested and deported. Evgenia Abravanel, a Christian shopkeeper, was blackmailed by one of her customers. "She was taking my dresses, she was taking my robes," she recalled. "Every time she wanted more money so that she would not reveal that I have a Jewish husband and that I am hiding him."[38]

REACTIONS

ON THE STREETS, many Greeks showed their revulsion at the German measures from the moment Jews were forced to wear the yellow star. Yacoel noted the relief Jews felt when they observed "the decent conduct of the Christian population" and their "many expressions of compassion and sympathy." He tells a revealing story from 25 February, the first day the star had to be displayed:

The writer's housemaid, a young Jewish girl, whose speech and external appearance could in no way betray her religion, went out on the balcony above the street for a household chore, without having worn the distinguishing Jewish sign. While there, she observed a scene involving a Jewish woman wearing the Jewish sign going down the street, timidly passing a Christian woman going up the street. The Christian, probably seeing that sign for the first time, addressed a comforting word to the Jewess. Perceiving then the writer's housemaid on the balcony smiling and assuming her to be a Christian, she raised her head and chided her for her behaviour, saying: "Why are you laughing, child? You ought to feel compassion for them over their plight. They are people just like us. Can you be sure that perhaps tomorrow it won't be our turn?"[39]

Solidarity was shown by many friends and neighbours when the Jews were forced out of their houses and confined to the ghettoes. They went to make their farewells, promised to look after property and valuables—though this too would become a risky matter—and exchanged gifts and tears. "Everyone was out and crying," recalled one. "The Christians were sad we were leaving our homes; we sat with the Greek women who wept as we left."[40] As long lines of hundreds of people, all ages, pushing carts and carrying heavily laden rucksacks, trekked through the centre of town to the Hirsch camp, many Christians gathered on the pavements to see them go. Leon Perachia noticed the sad faces of those watching as he went past. Another recalled that "we walked down Leoforos Stratou and Egnatia. On the way there were many people, Christians, and they looked on helplessly. Some cried."[41]

"By the station, my path was interrupted by a river of Jews coming down from the camp to the train," recollected Eleftheria Drosakis, then a young girl from a refugee family. Living near the station, she witnessed several such forced marches, and would rush out hoping to see the friends she used to play with. "And my joy was great when I didn't see one of them, because we hoped they would escape." On the other side of the city, among the Pontic refugees in the suburb of Kalamaria, someone greeted the apparently endless line of Jews trailing past with the comment "They deserve it for having crucified our Lord." But Georgios Andreades, then only seven, asked himself what the poor people he saw before him—"for me the sight was a painful one"—had to do with Christ's crucifixion.[42]

Whereas individuals displayed their unhappiness at what was happening, there was little sign of this on the part of the city's professional associations and organizations. The one exception was the Greek ex-servicemen's association which reacted angrily when disabled Jewish war veterans were made to take part in the forced registration in July 1942. On several occasions after this, the leaders of the Christian association of war wounded tried to intervene on behalf of their Jewish comrades. Eventually the Germans threatened to execute them if they went ahead with planned demonstrations. They were the only ones to take protest so far. Yacoel, the community's lawyer, could not hide his disappointment with the frostily detached attitude of men he had long known and had assumed would feel differently. As he wrote in his 1943 memoirs, written shortly before his own deportation and death, the city's professional classes, in particular, the major merchants and businessmen, showed "a total lack of comradely solidarity." Following the forced dismissal of Jews from Salonica's guilds and associations, Yacoel called on "the president of the largest and most outstanding economic organization of the city"—presumably a reference to the Chamber of Commerce. Despite the man's many and strong ties to Jewish firms—so strong indeed that he spoke Judeo-Spanish—he remained "cold and passive" and refused to do anything.

In this respect, Salonica was very different from Athens. There Archbishop Damaskinos condemned the deportations in no uncertain terms in formal letters sent to the prime minister and Gunther von Altenburg, the Reich plenipotentiary for Greece. His many fellow-signatories in this remarkable protest included the representatives of all the chief professional and public institutions of the capital. Athens business associations proposed that Salonican Jews should, if necessary, be concentrated internally rather than sent out of the country. By contrast, the Metropolitan of Salonica, Gennadios, appears to have confined himself to a private protest. When a handful of city notables visited Simonides to try to forestall the deportations the governor-general simply referred them to the Germans, who expressed their astonishment that the Greeks did not understand the favour that was being done them. Thereafter, the silence from Salonica's professional classes was deafening. From the university professors and students, the businessmen and lawyers' associations, there was barely a whisper. The municipality enquired of the governor-general when it should advertise vacancies for the jobs previously filled by Jews, and renamed the few streets in the city which commemorated Jewish figures. Simonides himself, far from protesting the deportations, raised no objections, failed to report what was happening to his own government in Athens and provided gendarmes and other civil servants to assist Eichmann's men. "The rumour circulated insistently in Salonica," writes Michael Molho, "especially among the Jews, that the Government was not entirely opposed to the idea of deporting the Jewish element, and this because the Government thought thus to attain a double end, that of assuring the racial homogeneity of the population, and of facilitating the settlement of the refugees from Thrace and Macedonia who had flooded into the city."[43]

This lack of reaction could not be put down to the impossibility of protest itself. In 1942 there had been strikes and demonstrations against civil mobilization, and these were renewed in April 1943—in the middle of the deportations. There were further labour protests in August and September 1943 mounted by students, union workers, and war veterans against food shortages and profiteers. But the biggest public protest of all came in July 1943 when the Germans decided to expand the Bulgarian occupation zone in northern Greece, allowing a Bulgarian division into the vicinity of the city. In fact, the prime concern of Simonides, Archbishop Gennadios and a range of political figures from across the spectrum in 1943 was to prevent the gains of 1912–13 being rolled back and seeing the Bulgarian army enter Salonica. To stop this happening, they formed a semi-official National Macedonian Council to persuade the Germans to keep faith with the Greek administration. They believed Max Merten, the chief Wehrmacht administrator in the city, was sympathetic, and an advocate for the Greek side in discussions with his pro-Bulgarian military superiors. No senior Greek political figure in the city was thus prepared to forfeit his support and waste valuable political capital by speaking out on behalf of the Jews, not least since Merten had already made it clear to everyone that this was a matter decided at higher levels in Berlin and out of his hands.[44]

Something less than 5 per cent of Salonica's Jewish population escaped deportation compared with perhaps 50 per cent in the Greek capital a year later. This was partly because the Jews of the Macedonian capital were far more numerous, more obtrusive and less assimilated than in Athens; helping a few thousand mostly Greek-speaking Jews in a city of nearly half a million was considerably easier than helping 50,000 Sefardim in a city half the size. Timing explains a lot too: much more was known by 1944, not least because of what had happened earlier. Perhaps more could have escaped from Salonica had families been willing to split up, or if Chief Rabbi Koretz had been a different personality, and obstructed German wishes—as the Chief Rabbi of Athens did: by 1944 the resistance was fully operational and better able to help than it had been the previous year. But a crucial part was also played by the different priorities and sentiments of the elites in Greece's two main cities. According to the German records, approximately 45,000 people reached Auschwitz from Salonica. Within a few hours of arriving, most of them had been killed in gas chambers.[45]

23

Aftermath

IN THE SUMMER OF 1943, an undercover British agent called Nicholas Hammond, disguised as a Vlach shepherd, made the hazardous journey *into* Salonica from the mountains to establish contact with the resistance. He was taken to a hideout in what he was told was the safest part of the town, a quarter recently vacated by the Jews. "My man explained the merit of the Ghetto to me. The Germans had recently deported the . . . Jews of Salonica, and they had no check on who was now living in the Ghetto, which swarmed with squatters and refugees." Hammond's testimony is a reminder that although the Jews were gone, their presence lived on in the tangible shape of empty homes, communal buildings, shops, factories and entire quarters. In a matter of weeks nearly one-fifth of the population of a large city had been deported, leaving their property and possessions behind them.[1]

THE SERVICE FOR THE DISPOSAL OF JEWISH PROPERTY

AS SOON AS THEY WERE MARCHED AWAY, people rushed into their houses, tore up floorboards and battered down walls and ceilings, hoping to find hidden valuables. "The poor folk of Ayios Fanourios and Toumba who wanted their share of the Jewish inheritance were fired upon by the bravos and guards of the thieving pair Nikos Stergiades and Peri Nikolaides . . . who had been assigned the dwellings and the huts of the deserted Jewish quarters," wrote a Greek newspaper shortly after Liberation. "Youthful, daring raiders managed to grab small bits and pieces." But the same thing happened in smarter quarters. Giorgos

Ioannou's short story "The Bed" describes the instant looting of tables, chests of drawers, mirrors and sheets from his neighbour's apartment. Within hours it was stripped bare: the floor was covered in paper, mattress stuffing and feathers, the bath was filled with discarded books, and the tiles in the kitchen had been broken away in the search for hidden treasure. There was a "complete breakdown of order" wrote an official at the time, and the second-hand shops of the city began to fill up with stolen goods. The Germans themselves looted the villas of the elite and Jewish-owned warehouses; vans took away "pianos, wardrobes, furniture, carpets, electric lights and clothing of all kinds" to Germany. It was, in the words of one journalist, a "general and shameless pillaging."[2]

Experience in Germany and Austria had taught the SS the importance of organizing the takeover of Jewish property properly. "Wild" looting was inefficient and dangerous—inefficient because it did not allow the authorities to distribute the gains from Jewish property as they wished, and dangerous because it contributed to a breakdown of public order and easily led to a free-for-all. Thus even before the deportations began, Wisliceny and Brunner ordered Governor-General Simonides to set up a new department to administer Jewish property on behalf of the Greek state. The Service for the Disposal of Jewish Property (YDIP) was headed by a dutiful civil servant called Ilias Douros, head of the city's mortgage office. Above him there was a raft of worthies including a university law professor as legal adviser, the branch directors of the main local banks, the president of the Chamber of Commerce, and representatives of professional and craft guilds. German policy implicated much of the city's business elite in the disposal of Jewish property and created a powerful incentive for them to work with Berlin.

Residential property in the western suburbs was invaded by squatters after YDIP removed furniture to its warehouses: twenty-seven were needed to store all the chairs, tables and other goods. Because there was so much Jewish-owned residential housing elsewhere in the city, the welfare service was told to settle refugees there, as it had done in Muslim property after 1923. But German intervention made this plan impossible to fulfil, and many homes were stripped by occupation troops and then squatted by refugees themselves, much as had happened after the population exchange. Meanwhile, YDIP was, in the words of its director, "continually bombarded" with requests for its stored furniture from government and municipal departments and individuals.[3]

Using lists supplied by the Jewish community itself, Douros decided to narrow down a Herculean task by concentrating on the commercial properties. Where the nearly two thousand abandoned offices, stockrooms, shops and factories were concerned, he planned to bring their owners out from the ghettoes, and to send them together with stocktakers and representatives of YDIP to inventory and seal their own premises. The keys safely returned to him, he could then allocate caretakers to manage and look after each property. These caretakers would pay rent to YDIP—benefiting the Greek state—and account for their use of the premises and their contents.

It was a neat scheme but ambitious in the circumstances. After all between the setting-up of YDIP and the first transports to Auschwitz, no more than a few weeks elapsed, not nearly enough time to allow some two thousand Jewish businessmen and shopkeepers to be brought out of confinement to inspect their shops. Even working round the clock, only some six hundred—less than one third of the total—were ever inventoried in the presence of their owners.

A big problem was the lack of qualified and trustworthy personnel to check inventories. There was, to be sure, no shortage of candidates. Indeed queues of prospective stock-takers formed outside the YDIP offices: Douros was inundated by their requests and called the police to keep them out. However, most people only wanted to be nominated for "substantial concerns, preferably jewellers, textile merchants and fancy goods," making excuses if they were assigned to something more modest. Another problem was the never-resolved issue of what constituted "Jewish property" in a city where Jews and Christians owned businesses in common, and rented properties from one other. And finally there was the biggest headache of all—the Germans. If the Greek civil servants had really thought the occupation authorities would resist the temptation to interfere in the work of YDIP, they were quickly disabused. What unfolded—at least to judge from the fragmentary minutes of YDIP's meetings through the spring and summer of 1943—was an extraordinary story of greed, coercion and fraud.

People were pulling strings, competing to get the plums. On 9 April, for instance, a certain Dimitris V. complained to YDIP that he had submitted a request to the Chamber of Commerce, which was handling many of the staffing issues, to be assigned a position as stock-taker, and had been allocated the shop of Solomon Florentin in Ermou Street. He had run around the city looking for the keys to it, being sent from one office to another. Yet in the end he was turned away from the shop itself by another man and told "to get lost, because my brother-in-law has been nominated and is preferred to you." Signing himself "an unemployed head of family," he was upset at having wasted so much time on this, especially as "the shop in question is full of goods and will need many days' work to count them."[4]

For some, there were quicker and more effective routes than YDIP. A beautician called Evi P. was one of dozens who went straight to the Germans. She called into the offices of the Wehrmacht administrator and informed a certain Inspector Kuhn—in German—that "I studied at the Vienna cosmetics school for three years on a Humboldt scholarship and passed with distinction. I would like to let you know of my request for one of the shops left by the Jews. I suggest either 107 Tsimiski Street (formerly owned by Haim Mano), or 33 Ermou Street (owned by Greta Almaleh)." Three days later, Kuhn assigned her the Tsimiski Street premises, and two men accompanied her there to evaluate the property and its contents.[5]

Questions about the legality of all this initially took a back seat. The pressing problems of public order, trade and hygiene created by the suddenness of the deportations were the priority as debts went unpaid and vegetables, fruits and fish-roes mouldered in the late spring heat. Item 3 of the meeting of the YDIP supervisory council on 5 May noted that "worried about the possible decay of stocks of foodstuffs in Jewish properties [it is agreed] to proceed to the formation of a sub-committee to examine the problem and to see how to bring these goods to auction."[6] The question of YDIP's own legal standing was not addressed until June when the Greek government finally got around to passing the necessary decree. For the first three months of its operation, therefore, the sole basis for YDIP's actions was administrative fiat. Wehrmacht administrator Max Merten, who was an expert on property law in the Reich, advised Simonides to use existing Greek legislation on the expropriation of enemy assets which had been invoked to seize Italian-owned property in the city in 1940, and English the following year. But of course the Greek Jews were not enemy subjects. When legislation was eventually published, it talked of "caretakers" and "trustees," as if to imply that the arrangement was provisional and that the caretakers themselves had no claims to ownership. The real owners were referred to as "having settled abroad."

What opened up was a difference of opinion between the legally minded Douros, who wished to follow the law to the letter, and the occupation authorities who could not have cared less for the legal niceties but were impatient at the slow pace of hand-overs. Other things were making Douros unhappy too. Stock-takers and caretakers were doing deals to carve up the contents of shops, submitting inventories to his office that fell far short of the truth. The nightwatchmen guarding the store-rooms, warehouses and factories were helping themselves. Above all, there was the way the Germans kept going around him to hand properties out. By 23 June, the organization had placed only 300 caretakers, and of those 256 were German nominees.

In July 1943, when Bulgarian troops marched further into Greek territory, the German army decided to place the civil administration of the Salonica region under their direct control, and YDIP came under the oversight of Merten's deputy Kuhn. Kuhn and Douros rowed about whether caretakers were entitled to sell off the goods they found in the shops. Douros insisted that they were not; the Germans, keen to spread the benefits of the expropriations further around the city, disagreed. Pro-German armed gangs burst into shops and made their new proprietors, who had been sticking to the terms of the original contract, sell off whatever was there. On 3 August, to Douros's dismay, the Germans ordered all the locked properties in the west half of the city—from Ayia Sofia to the Hirsch district—to be opened up, with predictable consequences. Two weeks later, Douros tried to resign on health grounds but was ordered by Simonides to stay in his job. Next month, the supervisory council was dissolved.

By the autumn of 1943 the whole question of what one YDIP official called "the dirty business that went on around Jewish property" was an open secret in the city. Only 160 properties had been handed over to YDIP-nominated caretakers. Some refugees from towns in the Bulgarian zone had been taken care of: 296 from eastern Macedonia and Thrace, 242 from Simonides's home-town of Serres, and 169 from Drama, according to the YDIP files. But the bulk of the refugees had certainly not felt the benefits. German officers and firms had confiscated buildings—sometimes for personal gain, sometimes not. Others had gone to their Greek agents, or to Greeks whose own properties had been requisitioned. Proceeds from the sales of Jewish shops were financing stool-pigeons, interpreters and the collaborationist militias which were terrorizing the city. The Association of Friends of Hitler—whose members included local journalists, businessmen and gendarmerie officers—acquired new offices; the Bulgarian Club was allocated sixty properties. The collaborator Pericles Nikolaides was handed over four formerly Jewish-owned cafés in order to set up gambling dens and casinos and bought up the Baron Hirsch quarter, now "silent and deserted," on the cheap, before demolishing it and selling off the rubble at a handsome profit. Laskaris Papanaoum, who later lived quietly in retirement in West Germany, was rewarded for his help in rounding up Jews in hiding by being given the largest tannery in the Balkans, as well as Jack Juda's shop on Egnatia, the Nar fish-shop, and the premises of Amir and Mevorah at no. 57, 26th October Street. The Germans also auctioned off the concessions to demolish the other outlying Jewish quarters—151 and Kalamaria to the east, Regi Vardar and Ayia Paraskevi to the west—and acres of the city's outskirts were reduced to rubble and ruins. Against six Jewish-owned groceries on the YDIP lists, an official has pencilled in: "All the premises found in the 151 Settlement have been demolished." The same note accompanied the sixteen properties—greengrocers, cobblers, dairy products, tavernas, a barber and a chemist—listed along one street in the Hirsch quarter. The buildings left behind by the deported Jews had thus rewarded local collaborators. "In Thessaloniki it was widely known," stated a collaborationist civil servant after the war, "that many people were saved by Merten and praised him because he gave them Jewish properties."[7]

Little of this reached the ears of the authorities in far-off Athens for some time, but when it did they were horrified. In October 1943 a Greek civil servant reported to the ministry of the interior that the treatment of Jewish property was "alarming and scandalous." The housing shortage in the city was as serious as before, and many refugees continued to live in awful conditions. Most Jewish apartments and dwellings had become uninhabitable following the plundering of their walls, roofs and floor materials. Others had been blown up—like many of the city's synagogues—depriving the needy of further shelter. "My personal impressions of the general treatment of this stupendous problem are sorrowful," he concluded. Shortly after liberation, a Jewish survivor visited the two remaining YDIP warehouses and described what he found there: "Their total contents were some old closets, some old tables, some typewriters mostly destroyed, empty jars for perfume manufacturing, everything of insignificant value."[8]

Survivors

THE GERMANS finally pulled out at the end of October 1944, more than two weeks after the liberation of Athens. The previous month eight Jews had been discovered in hiding and shot. Another five or six survived until liberation. Several hundred, who had escaped into the mountains, or gone to fight with the partisans, now made their way back. Hundreds more had survived in hiding in or around Athens and many of these also gradually returned. But first-hand news of the fate of the tens of thousands who had been deported to Poland did not come until March 1945 with the appearance of the first survivors from Auschwitz.[9]

The first to arrive was an Athenian Jew called Leon Batis who reached Salonica from the north on 15 March. That evening, tired, irritated and suspicious, eager to get on to Athens to see whether his family was still alive, he told his story over ouzo to a large audience in a café. Journalists demanded the facts, the Jews who had come wanted to know about their relatives and friends. "This was the first time we heard those terms: gas chambers, selections. We froze and dared not ask for details," wrote one of the listeners. "Batis spoke coldly, without regard for our emotions . . . He thought everyone knew [these things]." The next day, his account was in most of the city's newspapers. It was a precise and largely accurate description of the fate of the community. "They burned all the Jews from Thessaloniki in the crematorium," was one headline. A few weeks later others brought further details, including for the first time reports of the sterilization and other medical experiments performed on many women. By August, two hundred had returned and more were on the way. One year after liberation, there were just over one thousand "Poles"—as the others called them—who had come back from the camps.[10]

The survivors found Salonica transformed and unrecognizable. Yehuda Perahia, a tobacco merchant who had gone through the war in hiding, recorded his feelings in verse:

> *How into rusty iron pure gold has been transmuted!*
> *How what was ours has been changed into a foreign symbol! . . .*
> *I walk through the streets of this blessed city.*
> *Despite the sun, it seems to stand in darkness.*[11]

Jewish tombstones were to be found in urinals and driveways, and had been used to make up the dance-floor of a taverna built over a corner of the former cemetery itself. Because graves had been ransacked for the treasure that had been supposedly hidden there, "many Jewish skulls and bones are visible." The Hirsch quarter was demolished except for the synagogue and lunatic asylum which were being used as ware-houses. Other synagogues had been dynamited by the Germans, and lay in ruins. Trying to cope with an acute housing shortage—there were sixty thousand refugees from eastern Macedonia in the city in mid-1945—the over-stretched local authorities did not provide any special assistance to Jewish returnees. Without homes, for the most part, or work, the survivors faced destitution. Relief workers reported an urgent need for clothing, mattresses and blankets. Many were sleeping on benches or on the floor in the remaining few synagogues.[12]

The overwhelming short-term priority—as throughout Greece at this time—was for food, shelter and medical assistance. The UN Relief and Rehabilitation Agency (UNRRA) was active in the city helping Jews and Christians alike and one of its officials, Bella Mazur, who had been seconded from the American Jewish Joint Distribution Commit-tee (better known simply as the "Joint") spent her spare time "trying to help organize the community so that it can have the semblance of a for-mal and official set-up." Like many in the city, Jewish survivors were dependent on UNRRA for food and clothing. Mazur gave each former concentration camp inmate, most of whom lacked anything other than the clothes they had returned in, underclothes and double blankets which served as mattresses. Some received old pairs of shoes. Several communal buildings were cleaned up, renovated and whitewashed—refugees from the Bulgarian zone had squatted in them during the war—to house the most needy occupants.[13]

There was no disguising the disappointment, anger and bitterness many felt on their return. "The deportee was filled with hopes glamor-izing his return home to friends, some relatives, a place in which to live, a job and the future," wrote one observer. "These hopes are shattered on arrival." Unexpected though it might be for us, those returning from Auschwitz were "greeted coldly" by those who had survived the war in Greece itself; they were asked why they, and no others, had made it through the camps alive—the unspoken and sometimes not so unspo-ken implication being that they had collaborated and allowed the oth-ers to go to their death. "The question is almost always asked: why are you alive and not my relative—my mother, my father, sister and so forth," wrote an aid worker in December 1945. "This led to the untrue generalization on the part of the leading people . . . that in the main only the worst elements of the Jews survived the concentration camps."[14]

Angered by such charges, many returnees claimed that "they had been better treated in Germany than here," and accused those who had stayed of hoarding their wealth and failing to help them out. An unemployed former camp inmate threw a stone through the glass window of Haim B.'s shop, and then shouted to the crowd of onlookers that men like the shop's owner "had taken all the millions of the world while men like these die of hunger." To the police he declared that he had wanted "to take revenge on all the rich Jews who did not care about the fate of the poor and never set foot in the community except when they need certificates of the death of their relatives or other favours." For his part the shopkeeper blamed the community authorities for not doing more both to help the needy, and to clamp down on such incidents—of which this was evidently not the first.[15]

The 1157 "Poles" formed their own party for the communal elections early in 1946 and thanks to their numbers won the largest share of the vote. Yet in truth, their programme scarcely differed from that of their rivals—the Zionists, and the so-called (mostly left-wing) Resurrectionists. All in practice wanted greater control over the communal assets, a more active welfare programme and pressure on the Greek authorities to give back their property. Even after the "Poles" won, they spent most of their time attacking the foreign Jewish relief agencies for their condescending approach. This aggressiveness was really an outward manifestation of the suspicion, individualism and anxiety that harrowed survivors' lives. But such attitudes made it frustrating for outsiders to work with them. Relations deteriorated as the new communal authorities tried to insist proudly on their right to handle all funds from abroad; by 1947 the quarrel had got so bad that the main Jewish relief agency actually withdrew from the city. Its subsequent verdict on the way the survivors were handling their affairs was that they were poorly led, lacked any communal solidarity, and allowed party politicking—the old curse—to get in the way of proper organization.[16]

RESTITUTION

NONE OF THIS HELPED in the battle to get Jewish property back. On liberation, the new Greek government had repudiated the wartime legislation passed by its predecessors and thus, in theory at least, committed itself to restoring Jewish properties to their former owners. But in the city itself such a policy collided with the interests of the wartime beneficiaries and their patrons, and it soon became clear that they were not going to give up without a fight.

At first things went well. For four months the city was run by EAM/ELAS—the left-wing national resistance movement—which was broadly sympathetic to the plight of Salonica's Jews. Its officials had lists of collaborators who had taken properties, and warned them to hand them back or face charges: several dozen complied. But in the winter of 1944–45 relations in Athens between EAM/ELAS and the British-backed government broke down and the crisis eventually led to the "December events" in which the two sides fought openly in the streets, and RAF planes strafed leftist suburbs. In Salonica an uneasy understanding was preserved but this conflict and the victory for the right that followed entirely altered the balance of power. After February 1945 the once-powerful EAM/ELAS was gradually marginalized, the middle ground in Greek politics disappeared, and the British-backed government (and its successors) came to rely on anti-communists and former collaborators. In far-off Athens, governments were weak and changed frequently. Despite making all the right noises for international consumption on the issue of Jewish property, they found it hard to combat the increasingly organized opposition to restitution in Salonica itself.

After March 1945, the hand-over slowed down to a trickle. Under EAM/ELAS, forty to fifty properties had been restored, and others had been reclaimed through various forms of direct action as the old owners simply evicted the new ones, confident that the police would not intervene. But over the following year only another thirty-seven were handed over, and the police started to behave less sympathetically. By spring 1946, there were stories of claimants being assaulted, and of the wartime caretakers appealing to the courts to try to get eviction orders rescinded, demanding "their" shop back. A vegetable merchant who had thrown a Jewish grocer out of his shop across the street in 1943 challenged an eviction order three years later and managed to persuade the court of appeal to find in his favour.[17]

One reason why the courts were reluctant to intervene was the severe housing shortage afflicting the city as a whole. At least ten thousand refugee families were still living in the primitive huts they had inhabited since the 1920s and many of the newcomers who had come during the war were worse off still. Cement worker Georgios D., his wife and his six children lived in a large damp hole within the Byzantine walls. The family of Constantine T. inhabited a one-room shack three and a half metres square; another family, refugees from the Bulgarians, lived in an "old half-destroyed wooden hut" with no mattresses, blankets, clothing, plates or utensils—at least according to the relief workers that visited them: for meals they boiled wild herbs. One downtown shop was shared between seven families; another group of eight families, again wartime refugees, camped out in a vacant house near the station. There were hundreds of such stories.[18]

The housing shortage also provided an excuse to protect politically well-connected clients; and even when courts did issue restitution orders little was done. YDIP continued to function in 1945 and 1946, under a new director, and remained part of the governor-general's office: on several occasions the governor-general, a political appointee, instructed it to ignore court instructions to hand properties back. Douros was reassigned to his old job running the city's mortgage office and publicly protested accusations of collaboration, claiming he had been threatened by the Germans as a "saboteur," and insisting he had never wanted the job in the first place. Alexandros Krallis, the former president of the Chamber of Commerce, and Simonides were arraigned as collaborators at the end of 1945, but the trial against them was suspended. Wartime YDIP personnel were tried later and mostly acquitted.[19]

Legally speaking, too, restitution was not a straightforward matter. It was not just survivors who were claiming their properties; others made claims on the basis of kinship to, or even business associations with, a deceased owner. Children and siblings were usually considered to inherit automatically; but survivors demanded that more distant degrees of consanguinity be accepted as well. Lack of witnesses to the death of most of the Jews meant that lawyers and religious authorities found themselves having to make the macabre adjudication on whether parents and children had been gassed simultaneously or not in order to rule on whether claimants really were justified in presenting themselves as the heirs of the dead. To prove kinship applicants needed special certificates from the town hall, a process which the local authorities began to obstruct to slow down the rate of return. "If the citizen is called Nikolaos, Georgios or Ioannis," wrote one journalist angrily, "he is freely given the certification of kinship which he needs to inherit the property of his parents or more distant relatives. But if he is called Avraam, Isaac or Iakov, it is not issued. Fine logic!" By the spring of 1949, the mayor's office had been blocking the issue of such certificates for more than a year.[20]

At bottom, the problem was a political one. In the spring of 1945 many of the wartime caretakers were sufficiently worried at being branded collaborators to pass on their properties to third parties; but by the summer, as the political climate changed, they had lost these fears and were already beginning to mobilize in a more overt fashion. In fact, they formed a "Union of Trustees" to put pressure on the governor-general's office, and built up close ties with the Venizelist Liberal Party in particular; the pre-war link between Salonica's Liberals and anti-Jewish sentiment had survived the war, and intensified as the party did well in elections locally. In late 1945 a judge decided that since the Jews had "abandoned" their properties during the war, they had no automatic right of return. Then a new governor-general froze all transfers. "We haven't the strength to control ourselves any longer and keep quiet about this scandal," wrote one Jewish journalist in 1946. "Our interest is also that of Greece as a whole: the country cannot identify itself with a handful of collaborationist caretakers."[21]

But others disagreed. As elsewhere in Europe, post-war arguments over the restitution of properties intensified anti-Jewish feelings. One public prosecutor in the city exclaimed that "the persecution which the Jews endured at the hands of the Germans has now turned since Liberation into a persecution of Christians by Jews." A local Liberal politician complained it was "not fair that every Jew should inherit fifteen shops." The governor-general—and then the Athens government—advised the community to restrict its demands lest it create what they described as a "social problem" in the city. By the summer of 1947 there was a full-scale press campaign in Salonica against Jewish claims. The poverty of the refugees was contrasted with the supposed wealth of the surviving Jews. "To get rid of my boredom and sorrow I bought a newspaper. To my great astonishment I read that I'd become stinking rich," commented a survivor in a satirical Jewish sketch. "All the Jews have become filthy rich, it said. I am a Jew—what I went through in Hitler's camps proves it—so I must be filthy rich too."[22]

The contrast in the way Athens and Salonica approached these issues was as apparent after the war as it had been during it. In February 1945 Salonica welcomed Archbishop Damaskinos, the most senior figure in the Greek church, who was then serving as regent of the country. Damaskinos and his counterpart in the city, Gennadios, both made speeches at a ceremony to celebrate liberation. But while Damaskinos included explicit references to the suffering of "our Jewish fellow-citizens," Gennadios did not mention the deportations at all, even though they had affected his flock far more directly.

Meanwhile, the municipality's pursuit of its own interests continued to cause conflict. The inauguration of the new university hospital "on top of Jewish bones" (as one newspaper put it) was boycotted by the Jewish community's officials. The old cemetery was still being looted for buried treasure and, more alarmingly, despoiled by council workers; carts were carrying away gravestones daily. The mayor promised a Jewish delegation that they would be collected and returned to the community, but eleven months later little had been done. There were further painful negotiations both locally and nationally over the expropriation of the Hirsch hospital, and the rubble-strewn area where the 151 neighbourhood had once stood. In January 1949, a Jewish newspaper published an open letter to the mayor accusing him not merely of a "lack of interest" but actual discrimination against Jewish claims.[23]

Weakness forced Salonica's Jews to seek support outside the city, and the newly formed Athens-based Central Jewish Council (KIS) lobbied ministers on its behalf and liaised with American Jewish organizations and U.S. government officials. But KIS's very creation—and location—was a reminder of how far the fortunes of Salonican Jewry had fallen. Before the war, the city had housed two-thirds of the country's total Jewish population and had been the centre of its intellectual and cultural life; after 1945, however, only one-fifth of the approximately eleven thousand Greek Jews who had survived the war lived there and the spotlight shifted to the nation's capital. The Salonicans were suspicious of the Jews in Athens, claiming they were less educated and politically inexperienced: they had formed KIS to protect their own interests, they were slow to worry about the plight of their fellow-Jews in Salonica, and they were led by Zionists, who would compromise with the Greek government on the property issue in order to facilitate emigration to Palestine. There may have been some truth on all counts; far more important was that KIS itself, like the Salonican community, was racked by political infighting.[24]

In the end, after several years of hard bargaining and thanks to behind-the-scenes American intervention, an agreement was reached with the Greek government by which a new, Jewish-run successor to YDIP would administer the large amount of property left unclaimed after the war. Greece had been quick to recognize the need for restitution in principle, noted one Salonica journalist, but slow to implement it in practice. YDIP was wound up in 1949, and the new organization started to negotiate directly with the caretakers and the municipal government. By 1953 it had regained control of 543 homes, 51 shops, 67 plots of land and 18 huts.[25]

The political repercussions of the wartime property free-for-all had not, however, been laid entirely to rest and the quick rehabilitation of collaborators in the conservative climate of post-war Greece created many hostages to fortune. In 1957 Max Merten, the wartime military administrator of the city, visited Greece to testify at the trial of his former interpreter. To the shock of the West German embassy—which had assured him he would be safe—and the Greek government itself, which was taken entirely by surprise, a zealous public prosecutor in Athens had him arrested and charged with war crimes. On trial for his activities in Salonica, as one survivor after another recounted the events of 1943, Merten made the explosive allegation that among his wartime contacts had been members of the current Greek government, and other individuals very close to the prime minister, Konstantine Karamanlis. The timing could not have been worse, for Greece was in the middle of negotiations to enter the Common Market. Karamanlis could not prevent the trial from going ahead, but he quietly agreed with the Germans that, in return for Bonn's backing of his country's membership application, Merten would be transferred to the Federal Republic as soon as the trial was over. The sordid bargain was struck, and after a perfunctory second trial there, Merten was released.

In Greece, there was speculation that Merten's real motive for returning had been to recover his loot. Even today divers scour the rocky sea-bed off the south of the Peloponnese for the treasure Merten supposedly sank there. So far they have not found anything. In any event, to focus exclusively on Merten is something of a distraction. He was a career bureaucrat, whose real responsibility had been to allow the city to run smoothly in the interest of the German war effort throughout the 1943 deportations. To the extent that he had done this, it had been with the help of other bureaucrats among the local and regional Greek authorities, and the network of other interest groups they had brought into play. *Their* priority had been to keep out the Bulgarians, and to ensure that Greek control over Salonica was unimpaired. They had not sought the deportation of the Jews, but they had not obstructed it either since it enabled them to complete the process which had started twenty years earlier—the Hellenization of the city.

Vanished Pasts, New Problems

The drawn-out post-war quarrel over the restitution of Jewish property can only be understood against the backdrop of the infinitely more urgent political problems Greece as a whole faced in the late 1940s. After months of tension, fighting broke out again between leftist guerrillas and the government in 1946, and the country was plunged into a bitter civil war which turned it into the first international battle-ground of the Cold War. The resulting damage was in some ways even greater than had been caused by the Germans. Thousands died and hundreds of thousands of villagers were forcibly relocated as government troops with British and American advisers battled against a highly effective guerrilla insurgency organized by the communist Democratic Army of Greece. Only in August 1949 did the government regain control; by then, it had rounded up tens of thousands of suspected leftists, executed several thousand by firing squad, and built up a new network of shady anti-communist paramilitary units on whom it relied for several decades afterwards. Never before or since had the authority of the Greek state looked so fragile. Compared with this, the issue of Jewish property was a side-show.

In what novelist Nikos Bakolas called "the season of fear," Salonica itself was deeply traumatized. Thousands more refugees fled there for shelter, and the city was rocked by assassinations, round-ups, mortar fire and occasional gun-fights between left and right. The insurgents were in the hills and in January 1949, they kidnapped a group of schoolboys from the nearby American Farm School. With a strong left-wing presence in the worker suburbs, the authorities felt nervous and hundreds of people were incarcerated. Fear of the communists blended with memories of the long-running struggle with the Bulgarians; the rebels were written off as a Slav fifth column, fighting once again to tear Greek Macedonia away for incorporation in a Balkan communist federation.

Anti-communists who had worked alongside the Germans in the early 1940s now gave their services to the British and Americans: in no country in Europe were the trials of collaborators wound down so soon. As Cold War fever reached its height, UFOs were spotted over the city and there were rumours of Russian planes on their way from the north. The church was drawn into the fray, and Christian youth groups warned the city's residents not to be tempted by the godless left. Saints—one was "well dressed, freshly shaved, wearing blue clothes and a white shirt"—were reported politely getting into taxis at the station and being driven to local churches before vanishing: once again, they seemed to have taken the city under their protection. Ghostly images of the Virgin Mary appeared in the windows of department stores and apartment blocks. In 1951, barely a year after the fighting ended, the funeral of Metropolitan Gennadios, the religious leader who had shepherded his flock ever since 1910, provided a show of strength for the church and the right. His corpse was dressed in the regalia of office, and after lying in state for several days in Ayios Dimitrios, it was paraded through the crowded streets on a throne draped in the national flag. Through the celebration of Gennadios's remarkable life, the defeat of the left was linked to Hellenism's other triumphs over Turks, Bulgarians and Germans alike.[26]

The 1940s left the city polarized politically and economically destitute. Even in 1951 its population was not much larger than before the war. But in the decades which followed, the country's economy took off and Salonica grew faster than ever. The refugees who had landed in 1922 now became the old guard as thousands of new migrants arrived from the countryside looking for work, part of the drift out of the rural economy which was transforming post-war Greece, and Europe. They packed into the old buildings and land densities soared. Salonica's population increased faster than Athens's, and by 1971 it had risen to over half a million. Most of the newcomers had no knowledge of the city as it had existed before the war, and did not remember its now-vanished mosques and synagogues.

The little that did survive from those days was quickly being sacrificed to the bulldozers. As land became more valuable, the old low houses were torn down and replaced with multiple-storeyed apartment blocks. Constructors and developers were the city's new rich. Within not much more than a decade in an unregulated orgy of construction, what remained of the Ottoman urban fabric was largely demolished and gardens and greenery gave way to concrete. The tramlines were torn up overnight and replaced by buses, a cheaper form of public transport which allowed the suburbs to spread in all directions and killed off the ferry-boats that used to carry passengers across the bay. Bara and the Beshchinar gardens disappeared under new warehouses and factories. As the roads leading into town were widened, Vardar Square was modelled and remodelled, and the last of the faded Ottoman cafés was torn down. Workers' apartments spread over the hills and pushed up against the old walls. In-fill created a new seafront promenade. The elegant Royal Theatre by the White Tower disappeared under the bulldozers, as did the neo-classical mansions along the old Hamidié, and the Alliance Israélite headquarters in the centre of town which was replaced by a tourist hotel. New faculty buildings, a swimming pool and observatory went up on the site of the Jewish cemetery, where tens of thousands of students now studied. Kalamaria, remembered one local author, was transformed from a muddy village into a "luxury suburb which justified . . . the effort and the tears of the refugee element." Only in the Upper Town, still inhabited by the poorest, did lack of money protect the old gable-fronted Ottoman homes.[27]

When a British foot-soldier who had slogged through the Macedonian mud in 1915 returned nearly half a century later he was struck by the change. The seafront villas that survived were mostly empty and had a "sinister air"; the minarets (bar one) had vanished and the Muslims with them, and all around he saw "blocks of offices and flats . . . indistinguishable from their counterparts in Lisbon, Stockholm and London." A Turkish woman, who had grown up on endless stories of the Hamidian city told her by her mother, found it impossible to reconcile these with the reality: "The great houses had been torn down and the gardens destroyed . . . It was all gone."[28]

For returning Jews the experience was a haunting one. Jacques Stroumsa was a young engineer who had helped construct the Hirsch camp, and had survived Auschwitz, where his parents and his pregnant wife had been killed. After the war, unwilling to return home, he had left for good. When eventually he came back for a brief visit, he spent hours sitting on his hotel balcony and looking out over the sea: "I was smoking cigarette after cigarette for fear the tears would come. A Greek Orthodox friend found me alone around midnight and said: 'I understand you, Jacques, you don't really know any more where to go in Salonica, the city where you once knew every stone.' And that's how it was."[29]

Conclusion

The Memory of the Dead

We are turned to hollow bones, shall we be restored to life? A fruitless transformation![1]

—QUR'AN

BEFORE THE FIRST WORLD WAR, the dead were to be found, not only in the weed-strewn cemeteries which lined the approaches to the walls, but also within the city itself, crammed into the small railed enclosure by the Saatli Djami, under the trees of the Vlatadon monastery, in dervish *turbes* and roofed family mausoleums on street corners. A tiny graveyard of richly carved turbaned tombs stood near the Hamza Bey mosque, surrounded by pastry-shops, watch-menders, bakeries and general stores in the busy commercial quarter where the *Kapali Çarsi*—the main shopping arcade—met the old *Bezesten*. When they drew water at the fountain, or entered their church, mosque or *hamam*, the living saw inscriptions which reminded them of how much they owed to those who had gone before them. But they remembered them too in public pilgrimages to the cemetery like the Jewish *Ziyara grande* which took place thirteen days before Yom Kippur. Women paid visits to their relatives' graves to pray for domestic advice and tied small pieces of paper or ribbons to tomb railings.

The dead, with their powers and demands, thus formed part of the world of the living. When a rabbi died, a note was often placed in his hand prior to burial asking for some important favour from God: this was done when Rabbi Levi Gattegno passed away in the middle of a dry spell, and the rains came within hours. Bodies which had not decomposed indicated the presence of a restless spirit; bodies laid the wrong way or face down would rest uneasily in the ground. Sometimes tombs were re-opened to check that all was well. But people also visited cemeteries for picnics and conversation. The dead watched the living enjoying themselves as well as lamenting their passing. Above the graves the city's inhabitants worked, begged, grazed their animals and indulged in a variety of activities which Ottoman legislators vainly tried to curb.[2]

In the middle of the nineteenth century, however, the dead and the living began to move apart. Following the 1866 International Sanitary Conference in Istanbul, Ottoman regulations proscribed burial within the capital. Graveyards had to be moved to a sufficient distance from the walls to avoid their "putrid emanations" endangering public health. Similar measures were introduced in Salonica, and the occupants of some of the small neighbourhood graveyards within the city were incorporated in the larger ones outside. City burial became an exclusive matter: only spiritual leaders could still be buried in their places of worship, a privilege which was sometimes extended to religious benefactors as well. Was this a mark of honour for these men of distinction, or a sign that their remains radiated a special power that helped those living among them?[3]

After the 1917 fire, Hébrard's plan for the modern city envisaged radical changes in the use of urban space, and relegated the dead definitively to the margins. Where the Jewish cemetery was concerned, German occupation in the Second World War simply provided an opportunity for the municipality to carry out its own modification of Hébrard's ideas. Today the area is dominated by the massive Corbusier-style faculty blocks, concrete plazas and landscaped avenues of the Aristoteleion University; but the ground had been prepared in the winter of 1942 when council workers turned the old cemetery into a rubble-strewn waste-land of vandalized graves, with shattered fragments of marble, brick and human bones everywhere. "Desecration of the graves is forbidden," wrote the Salonica novelist Nikos Gabriel Pentzikis in his stream-of-consciousness *Mother Thessaloniki*. But whose graves?[4]

MADAME SARA, one of the last exponents of a powerful Ottoman tradition, was born in Edirne in 1926 and now lives in Istanbul. She is Jewish and is much in demand as a spirit medium, communicating with the dead at the request of the living. She first realized the gift God had given her when she was a child, and used to collect water from a fountain near a Muslim cemetery. There she saw others praying to a wise man, and soon heard him calling her over. Sadik, a Muslim holy man who had died more than a century earlier, became her spiritual guide, and has helped her ever since, in her own life and in her work.[5]

Not so long ago this kind of story was less exceptional than it is today. For over many centuries the power of the dead remained an ecumenical one. The Ottoman authorities acknowledged the potent sanctity of the blood of Christian martyrs. Saint Dimitrios's tomb was guarded by a Mevlevi dervish who advised Christian pilgrims how its holy earth should be used. But as the empire fell apart and nation-states came into being, something changed in people's minds. The age of mass migrations began, waves of refugees came and went, and the dead who stayed behind suddenly became just another target for the living whose political passions and enmities brought them humiliation, desecration and eviction.

In Salonica, it was not only the Jewish dead who were treated as though they were less valuable than the land they occupied and the slabs that covered them. The city's Muslim and *Ma'min* graveyards had already vanished under new roads and buildings. With the exception of the mausoleum of Mousa Baba, a couple of tombs in the precinct of the Rotonda, a sarcophagus stored on the west side of Ayia Sofia, and another grander one in the garden of the Yeni Djami, there is virtually no resting-place for the Muslim dead in the city today. General Taksin Pasha, the Greek-speaking Ottoman general who surrendered Salonica to Prince Constantine in 1912, is said to have been buried on the city's outskirts on his death a few years later, but no trace of his tomb has survived. The Bulgarian cemetery was expropriated after the Bulgarians were expelled in 1913, and graves with inscriptions in Slavic lettering are hard to find, though one or two remain in the grounds of the old Catholic seminary in Zeitenlik.[6]

The compulsory population exchange of 1922 was the turning-point. For like the departing Muslims, the Greek immigrants had been forced by the catastrophe that befell them to leave their own forebears behind. Since the dead who counted to them lay far away, often in unknown graves, why should they have attached importance to those who happened to be buried in their new places of settlement? Some refugee women—having chatted with the Turkish women of the neighbourhood before the latter left—continued to pray at the graves of Muslim holy men in the upper town. But these practices became rare. Feeling at home in Salonica meant turning it into an entirely new city, building settlements on the outskirts that had not even existed in Ottoman times. It meant re-baptizing it, with names that created ties to their own homelands (much as the Jewish refugees from Spain had done four centuries before them), and finding new homes for the precious icons they had managed to bring with them. Nostalgia for the lost lands of Christian Orthodoxy thus meshed with the city's expansion and modernization.

The rising death toll and mass violence of the twentieth century also played their part in this devaluation of the dead. The era of political assassination had come to the city as the century began, but politically motivated killings soon multiplied. At its murderous apogee, the 1940s brought not only the genocide of the Jews and the destruction of their graves, but also the loss of hundreds of civilians shot by the Germans in mass executions, and hundreds more in the civil war that followed. "Our city is full of dead people whom nobody escorted to their final resting-place," wrote Pentzikis, who lived through it all. "The lovely dawn, which best shows off the flowers, often brings corpses to light on the roads. Mutilated faces. With no nose or ears. Blood on the steps of the garden gate. On the pavement."[7]

To many Greek writers after 1912, the generation of the new arrivals, Salonica seemed suspended in the present, cut off from any recognizable past. Brought up on Pound, Eliot and Joyce, they inhabited a melancholic wasteland of alienation and anomie. But in the meantime, the archaeologists were helping to restore a past they could connect with, creating new forms of historical memory to bolster local Hellenic pride. Digging deep into the earth, they exhumed long-forgotten paleochristian tombs, and brought to light old gods, temples and shrines. Some decades earlier they had turned the Athens Acropolis into a contemporary icon of antiquity by ridding it of its medieval and Ottoman buildings. Salonica did not have the Acropolis, but it had its churches. In 1914, a Greek scholar declared it the "Byzantine city *par excellence*," and described it as the symbol of "the new great historical horizon" that the victories of the Greek army had made possible. "Athens represents, embodies better, antiquity in our history and in our consciousness," writes the novelist Ioannou. "Salonica Byzantium." An inspectorate of Byzantine monuments was established in 1920, and the restoration of the city's churches, with islands of space carved out around them to allow them greater prominence, indicated how much importance was being attached locally to this historical legacy. After the Second World War, an old Byzantine festival in honour of Saint Dimitrios was revived, and eventually the city even acquired its long-promised Byzantine museum.[8]

Byzantium's material re-emergence helped Greeks to feel confident the city was theirs, a place of resurrection and of miraculous Orthodox renewal. But much as in Athens earlier, recovering the memory of one past meant forgetting or even destroying another. The centuries of Ottoman rule were written off as a long historical parenthesis, a nightmare of oppression and stagnation. Any surviving remains associated with them not only lacked historical value but potentially threatened the new image the city was creating for itself. This was the primary explanation for the demolition of the minarets and the total destruction of the Jewish cemetery, and why Greek archaeologists published learned articles on the ancient inscriptions that came to light on the reverse side of many uprooted Jewish tombstones, whilst ignoring their Hebrew, Portuguese or Judeo-Spanish epigraphs. Anything post-Byzantine in the city was at risk, except for the White Tower which had quickly achieved such symbolic status that most people refused to believe it was an Ottoman construction. It took the 1978 earthquake to get surveys made of the remaining fin-de-siècle villas on Queen Olga Street, and only in the 1980s did state funds begin to be assigned to Ottoman monuments.

Today, it is true, a few grand Ottoman houses have been converted into libraries or museums. The old mill has become a busy complex of bars, jazz clubs and galleries and the streets behind the long-neglected lumber yards are jam-packed with parked cars till the early hours; the Yedi Koulé fortress—where leftists were held to be executed in the civil war—has been smartened up and turned into a cultural space, and Ladadika, the last remaining pre-1914 downtown quarter, has seen the warehouses on Odos Egyptou turned into restaurants. In fact, there is a far greater willingness than ever before to find historical value across all periods and in all kinds of buildings. But much of this is less the indication of a new cultural consciousness than a reflection of the scarcity of old buildings of any kind in Salonica today. The anxiety that globalization will soon eradicate whatever particular charm the city possesses has put new wind in the preservationists' sails. As a result, prestige is now attached to anything dating back more than a few decades.

History itself had not always been seen as a handmaiden of the nation: indeed, in 1880, when Mihail Hadzi Ioannou published the first description of Salonica in Greek, he deliberately called his work a "Description of the City" (*astugrafia*), preferring this to the clumsy term "Description of the Fatherland" (*patridografia*), since as he put it, he wished to write something "for everyman." But after 1912 this kind of cosmopolitan outlook became uncommon. As Greece's rulers set up new institutions of learning to shape the national consciousness of the city in fundamentally new ways and with a different kind of authority—the authority of historical science—they found they could rely on scholars to fulfil their side of the bargain.[9]

Through research institutes, publishing programmes and higher education, those in command of the twentieth-century Greek state showed they were fully conscious of "the possibilities of a past"—that consciousness which seemed so strangely lacking in the city when the century began but which came to be indispensable to its emergent national identity. In 1939, a Society of Macedonian Studies was founded, with support from the municipality. During the Cold War struggle with the communist Slavs to the north, this enjoyed government backing, moving into spacious premises in a prime location just opposite the White Tower. The Society played a crucial role in developing historical research into the city and embarked on a major publishing programme of its own, giving birth to two important new institutions—the Institute of Balkan Studies in 1953, and the Historical Archives of Macedonia the following year. All three have since generated many scholarly works—without the society's journal *Makedonika*, for instance, this book could not have been written. But they were also closely connected with local centres of power. The governing committee of the archives had the metropolitan as chair and the mayor on the board. The Society of Macedonian Studies itself was founded by the president of the city's Federation of Merchants: fifty years later, his successor boasted that the society had been able to promote scientific research "within the framework of our national identity." That much good work emerged did not alter the fundamentally instrumental conception of history which motivated their backers.[10]

It was not only the "Turks" and "Bulgarians" that suffered as a result. The myth of eternal Hellenism flattened out the past of the Greeks themselves and made it less interesting. Instead of showing how Orthodox Christian villagers speaking Vlach, Albanian and Slavic tongues had come over time to see themselves as Greeks, the history books described a sense of Greekness that had been there from the start. There was, in other words, no Hellenization, only Hellenes. Such a denial of the past could not easily accommodate the real role the church had played in Ottoman times. It could not even deal with the experiences of the refugees, many of whom, as we have seen, had been ignorant of Greek and needed time to understand why they should stop calling themselves simply "Eastern Christians." In fact, despite the unmistakable contribution of the refugees to the life of the city, and despite their numbers, the refugee experience too was a kind of taboo, and for many years their own stories and sufferings were rarely discussed. "Today no one says he is a 'refugee,' " declared Ioannou in 1982. "And at most perhaps, if pressed, that he is 'of refugee origins.' "[11]

Then, in 1986, the Greek state set aside a day—14 September—as a "national day of remembrance" to commemorate the destruction of Smyrna and the exodus from Asia Minor.[12] By now, the refugees were power-brokers in the city; they had broken the hold of the Peloponnesians and the Cretans, and stood for something more than funny accents and peculiar music. The identity politics of the second and third refugee generations began to chip away at the smooth façade of official Hellenism and broke down the emphatic nationalism of the Cold War era.

With the collapse of communism, the city and the world around it were transformed even more rapidly. Bulgaria was no longer the archenemy; with Turkey too a rapprochement was conceivable. True, bloodshed, war and ethnic antagonisms were what made the headlines whenever the Balkans were discussed internationally. But just as important in the long run was the fact that Salonica was connected again—for the first time in generations—to older markets, breaking out of the economic strait-jacket which had shut it in since 1912. Its businessmen were looking north and east to invest, for they were now the wealthiest and most experienced capitalists in the region. Coming the other way were thousands of migrants searching for work. By 1997 the city housed an estimated 100,000 of them, some 10 per cent of its population, and Albanian could be heard in the coffee-houses round the railway station. Others streamed in from Poland, Turkey, Moldova and Bulgaria. Pushed by Western Europe on the one hand, and Eastern Europe on the other, Greek society was changing fast, and the old historical truths (which in truth were not that old) no longer escaped criticism.

IN 1994 A BITTER PUBLIC ROW swirled around the Rotonda, one of the city's most ambiguous and unusual buildings. Roman in origin, it had been a Byzantine church before being converted to a mosque in 1591 when Hortaç, *sheykh* of the nearby Halvetiye monastery, engineered its conversion by a demonstration of his miraculous powers. In 1912 it was returned to Christian use, and the following year it was declared a "national monument." When the city's other twenty-six minarets were demolished by contractors in 1925, its was left standing and still survives.[13]

Although the dispute between Greece and the former Yugoslav republic of Macedonia rumbled on, Salonica had been nominated as Cultural Capital of Europe and European funds were pouring in for the restoration of its antiquities. The ministry of culture planned to use the Rotonda for concerts and exhibitions, and so at the end of 1994 it permitted the church to organize a display of icons there and allowed a prayer service to be held for the exhibition's opening. The Sunday after the exhibition closed, however, worshippers gathered outside once again, and tried to get in to pray. This was evidently more than a mere misunderstanding, because the following day local church leaders called for an all-night vigil. Police had to be called to guard the building as a large crowd began to chant slogans: "Not a synagogue, nor a mosque but a Greek church!" and "This is not Greece, not Albania; onwards for Macedonia and Orthodoxy!" Eventually hundreds of the protestors forced their way through the gates, and the local church hierarchy demanded that the Rotonda be returned to religious use, and even brought a lawsuit against the Archaeological Service for plundering and desecrating it.

This ferocious row over the competing claims of culture and religion went to the heart of the very character of the Greek state. Both had traditionally been utilized in the name of Hellenism; now they were pitted against one another. As the crowd's slogans suggested, it was not only the strong feelings generated locally by the Macedonia question that had prompted the stand-off: arguments over the city's complex cultural identity were also involved. The demonstrators outside the Rotonda had equated control of the building by the ministry of culture with the return of Jews and Muslims to a Christian place of worship. And indeed there was a kind of symbolic truth behind the rumour, for Salonica's designation as Cultural Capital of Europe had led many local commentators to stress its ethnically mixed past as a way of marking it out from, and perhaps proclaiming its superiority to, Athens. It was against these developments that the crowd had been protesting. "The people of God have triumphed," asserted their ringleader Canon Tassias, after they disrupted a piano recital there the following October. "They tell us that Thessaloniki is a multi-historical city. If they mean that many conquerors passed through here, then I agree. But the Orthodox character of the city was never altered."[14]

The politicians who opened the festivities of the Cultural Capital two years later did their best to smooth things over. There was much mention of "European values" and speakers underscored the historical significance of the Orthodox legacy for Europe as a whole. The mayor talked about "Greeks and Europeans" being initiates in the same mysteries, about being "re-baptized" in a "feast of cultural delights" and he declared that history was important in showing the 2300 years of a Greek Macedonian past in "one of the most multi-cultural cities in Europe." The Commissioner of the European Union discussed Europe's common future, and reminded his audience that Salonica was a place that had always welcomed refugees. The public debate about "multiculturalism"—a concept much in vogue at this time—reflected awareness of the recent wave of immigration. But the term itself was just a buzz-word and gave a very misleading impression. For all its newcomers Salonica at the end of the twentieth century remained predominantly Greek in culture and Orthodox in religion—and clung to this image of its past.[15]

TODAY, ACKNOWLEDGING ITS OTTOMAN LEGACY still appears to be as unimaginable to most people as when the historian Kostas Moskof first proposed the idea, more than twenty years ago. The city's older museums cover classical antiquity, Macedonian folklore and the Macedonian Struggle; newer ones, created in a recent frenzy of museological activity, cater for interests in Byzantium, photography, the cinema, modern art, water supply and musical instruments. The White Tower hosts a charming exhibition of the city's history and art which begins with its foundation but ends emphatically at the Ottoman conquest of 1430. The Bey Hamam is being restored, but the sixteenth-century Pasha Hamam, which had been in use until 1981, remains in disrepair and the Hamza Bey mosque stands forlornly in the centre of town like an unwanted guest. The Yeni Djami, the quiet of its leafy courtyard barely disturbed by visitors, is used as an annex to the Archaeological Museum and an occasional venue for art exhibitions. Ironically, the best surviving example of nineteenth-century Ottoman architecture is probably Ataturk's well-guarded birthplace, now the Turkish consulate.

The Jewish community—that other reminder of Ottoman times—recently opened a small museum of its own and at the end of the 1997 celebrations, a Holocaust memorial was unveiled, something the community had been seeking since 1945. Yet its eventual location was suggestive of unease in the municipality. A proposal to set it somewhere central—perhaps in the square where the Jewish men had been rounded up in 1942—was rejected, and it was finally erected on a distant suburban intersection on the road out to the airport. The so-called Square of the Jewish Martyrs, one of the few street-names which makes any reference to the city's Jews today, languishes in obscurity, unknown to all but the most experienced taxi drivers. And despite recent demands by many professors, successive administrators of the university have refused to mark the site of the Jewish cemetery.[16]

If all this mattered, it was only because by the late twentieth century, official monuments had become the way the living re-affirmed their connection to the dead. The Holocaust memorial joined the Giacometti-like cluster of Macedonian Fighters erected on a square in front of the Acheiropoietos church, Alexander the Great on the waterfront, an unknown Mother of Refugees, Venizelos, Prince Constantine and various ministers and mayors. What they had in common was their public character and their lack of any organic connection with the precise spot where they stood. None of them signified the presence of physical remains, like the mausolea of the past, nor that those they honoured had actually died there, like the humble paveside memorial put up in 1913 to King George at the place of his assassination, which has long since disappeared in its turn. Venizelos stood in the heart of the city he had rebuilt. Alexander the Great could have gone anywhere since the city did not exist in his lifetime.

Location was no longer about the site of a spiritual connection between living and dead so much as a reflection of electoral calculus. Salonica had turned into a symbolic space to be defined and redefined by its political masters. But there was no mystique in marble when the bones were not there, and the age in which people paid attention to monuments, if it had ever existed, was rapidly passing. All that could be said for them, like street-names, was that they helped establish the identity of those figures who the authorities regarded as important enough to be brought to the public's attention. By the end of the twentieth century, therefore, the city's relationship with the dead had been radically transformed. Although the churches remained, the Ottoman network of synagogues and mosques had vanished and the streets had been so comprehensively realigned that it was often difficult to know where they once stood. The cemeteries had long gone too and in their place a new archipelago of arts centres, museums, monuments and carefully preserved sites of historical value provided the living with their entrance to the past, with curators and scholars serving as their guides.

Today nearly one million people inhabit this ever-expanding city. Its transport system is stretched, though there is talk of an underground train line—and the traffic, parking and pollution are, if anything, a worse headache than in Athens. In 1900 the waters of the bay were so clear that one could look down and see the fish; a century later, they are a murky grey-green, and diners at waterside tavernas risk their meal being spoilt by the stench of sewage when the wind is in the wrong direction. The city centre is bursting, prices even in the Upper Town are sky-high, and younger couples are being forced further and further into the suburbs. With all these problems to cope with, what use to them is the history of a small city, with a complex polyglot population, which disappeared many decades before?

And yet that older city may turn out to serve the living in new ways only now coming into view. Nation-states construct their own image of the past to shore up their ambitions for the future: forgetting the Ottomans was part of Greece's claim to modernity. But today the old delusions of grandeur are being replaced by a more sober sense of what individual countries can achieve alone. As small states integrate themselves in a wider world, and even the largest learn how much they need their neighbours' help to tackle the problems that face them all, the stringently patrolled and narrow-minded conception of history which they once nurtured and which gave them a kind of justification starts to look less plausible and less necessary. Other futures may require other pasts.

The history of the nationalists is all about false continuities and convenient silences, the fictions necessary to tell the story of the rendezvous of a chosen people with the land marked out for them by destiny. It is an odd and implausible version of the past, especially for a city like Salonica, most of whose inhabitants cannot trace their connection to the place back more than three or four generations. They know that whatever they are taught at school, their own family experiences suggest a very different kind of story—a saga of turbulence, upheaval, abandonment and recovery in which chance, not destiny, played the greater role.

It is just such a history that I have tried to show unfolding, a history of forgotten alternatives and wrong choices, of identities assumed and discarded. In this city, the dominant group for centuries was a people who clung to the medieval language of the country from which they had been expelled, yet who felt in Salonica, as Rabbi Moses Aroquis put it in 1509, that "to them alone the land was given, and they are its glory and its splendour and its magnificence." As it happened, God had already given it to the Ottoman sultans so that, in the words of the fifteenth-century chronicler Asikpashazadé, "the metropolis of unbelief should become a metropolis of Islam." Before that he had given it to Christians, and in 1912, the city's Greeks once again gave thanks to God for the triumph of their army. They all claimed the city for themselves in God's name. Yet is it not said: where God is, there is everything?[17]

Notes

ABBREVIATIONS

AJDC American Joint Distribution Committee

EIE Elliniki Istoriki Etaireia

ELIA Elliniko Laografiko kai Istoriko Archeio (Athens)

FO Foreign Office archives (Public Record Office)

GDM Geniki Dioikisis Makedonias

IAM Istorika Archeia Makedonias (Thessaloniki)

IWM Imperial War Museum

Mertzios *Mnimeia Makedonikis Istorias* (1947)

NA U.S. National Archives (Washington, D.C.)

PRO Public Record Office (London)

UNRRA United Nations Relief and Rehabilitation Agency

Vasdravellis *Istorika Archeia Makedonias*, I (1952)

YDIP Yperisia Diacheiriseos Israilitikon Periousion (Jewish Museum of Greece)

Where no place of publication is given,
it should be assumed to be Thessaloniki.

Introduction

1. Italo Calvino, *Invisible Cities* (London 1974), 30–31.
2. E. Petropoulos, *La présence Ottomane à Salonique* (Athens, 1980), foreword.
3. L. Sciaky, *Farewell to Salonica* (London, 1946); N. Kokantzis, *Gioconda* (Athens, 2001); A. E. Yalman, *Turkey in My Time* (Norman, Oklahoma, 1956), 11.
4. P. Risal, *La ville convoitée: Salonique* (Paris, 1914), x.
5. M. Fischback, *Records of Dispossession: Palestinian Refugee Property and the* *Arab-Israeli Conflict* (Columbia UP, 2003).

1 / Conquest, 1430

1. *The Mosquito*, 53 (March 1941).
2. K. Mertzios, *Mnimeia Makedonikis Istorias* (1947), 410.
3. M.A. Walker, *Through Macedonia to the Albanian Lakes* (1864), 34; J. Murray, *Handbook for Travellers in Greece* (London, 1854), 415; G. Marindin, ed., *The Letters of John B. S. Morritt of Rokeby* (London, 1914), 158.

4. H. F. Tozer, *Researches in the Highlands of Turkey* (London, 1869), 1, 149.

5. On Jews converting thanks to St. Dimitrios, see the fifth-century miracle cited by R. Cormack, "Mosaic decoration of S. Demetrios, Thessaloniki," *Annual of the British School at Athens*, 64 (1969), 17–52.

6. Procopius, *De bello gothico*, iii. 14.22–30, cited in S. Vryonis, "The evolution of Slavic society and the Slavic invasions in Greece: the first major Slavic attack on Thessaloniki, AD 597," *Hesperia: Journal of the American School of Classical Studies at Athens*, 50:4 (Oct.–Dec. 1981), 378–390, quotation from p. 385.

7. P. Lemerle, *Les plus anciens recueils des miracles de Saint Démétrius*, 1 *Le Texte* (Paris, 1979), 134, translated by Vryonis, op. cit., 381–382.

8. Emphasized by R. Browning, "Byzantine Thessalonike: a unique city?," *Dialogos*, 1:2 (1995), 91–104.

9. P. Sugar, *Southeastern Europe under Ottoman Rule, 1354–1804* (Seattle, 1977), 19–22; M. Balivet, *Byzantines et Ottomans: Relations, Interaction, Succession* (Istanbul, 1999), 4; H. Inalcik, *The Ottoman Empire: The Classical Age, 1300–1600* (London, 1994).

10. H. Lowry, *The Nature of the Early Ottoman State* (Albany, NY, 2003).

11. G. G. Arnakis, "Gregory Palamas among the Turks and documents of his captivity as historical sources," *Speculum*, 26:1 (Jan. 1951), 104–118.

12. Balivet, *Byzantines et Ottomans*, 33, 65–69.

13. Ibid., 39.

14. "The Travels of Bertrandon de la Brocquiere, AD 1432 and 1433," in T. Wright, ed., *Early Travels in Palestine* (London, 1848), 346–347; M. Letts, ed., *Pero Tafur: Travels and Adventures, 1435–1439* (London, 1926), 126.

15. G. Tsaras, *I teleftaia alosi tis Thessalonikis (1430)* (1985), 50–57, 96, 172;

K. Mertzios, *Mnimeia Makedonikis Istorias* (1947), 45–90.

16. F. Miklosich and J. Müller, *Acta et Diplomata Graeca Medii Aevi*, iii (Vienna, 1865/1968), 282–283.

2 / Mosques and Hamams

1. "Bertrandon de la Brocquiere," 347; Tsaras, *I teleftaia alosi*, 62.

2. M. Kiel, "Notes on some Turkish monuments in Thessaloniki and their founders," *Balkan Studies*, 11 (1970), 129–131.

3. Tsaras, *I teleftaia alosi*, 66–67.

4. E. D. Bodnar, ed., *Cyriac of Ancona's Later Travels* (Harvard UP, 2003), xi, 12–13; "The travels of Bertrandon de Brocquiere, AD 1432 and 1433," in T. Wright, ed., *Early Travels in Palestine* (London, 1848), 349–355.

5. M. Vickers, "Cyriac of Ancona at Thessaloniki," *Byzantine and Modern Greek Studies* 2 (1976), 75–82; Vryonis, "Thessaloniki in 1430," in A. Bryer and H. Lowry, *Continuity and Change in Late Byzantine and Early Ottoman Society* (Birmingham, 1986), 314–315.

6. Vryonis, "Thessaloniki in 1430," 299, 316–317.

7. Bisani, *A Picturesque Tour*, 36; H. F. Tozer, *Researches in the Highlands of Turkey* (London 1869), II, 141.

8. H. Lowry, "Portrait of a City: The Population and Topography of Ottoman Selanik [Thessaloniki] in the Year 1478," *Diptycha*, 2 (1980–81), 254–292.

9. N. Beldiceanu, *Recherche sur la ville Ottomane au XVe siècle* (Paris, 1973), 159–160.

10. J. de Hammer, *Histoire de l'empire Ottoman depuis son origine jusqu'à nos jours* (original ed. Paris, 1835, new edition Istanbul, 1994), iii, 112; M. Kiel, "Notes on some Turkish monuments in Thessaloniki and their

founders," *Balkan Studies*, 11 (1970), 125.

11. M. Kiel, "Notes on some Turkish monuments in Thessaloniki and their founders," *Balkan Studies*, 11 (1970), 132–134.

12. Ibid., 139–141.

13. E. Ginio, " 'Every soul shall taste death'—Dealing with death and the afterlife in eighteenth century Salonica," *Studia Islamica* (2001), 113–132.

14. But on the dating of the *bezesten*, see S. Curcic and E. Hadjitrifonos, eds., *Secular Medieval Architecture in the Balkans, 1300–1500* (1997), 286–288; T. Stavrides, *The Sultan of Vezirs: The Life and Times of the Ottoman Grand Vezier Mahmud Pasha Angelovic (1453–1474)* (Brill, 2001), 285–288.

15. A. Zombou-Asimi, "To Bey Hamami (Loutra Paradeisos) tis Thessalonikis," *Thessaloniki*, 1 (1995), 341–376; N. Moschopoulos, "I Ellas kata ton Evlia Tselebi," *Epetiris Etaireias Byzantinon Spoudon*, 16 (1940), 348.

16. N. Moschopoulos, "I Ellas kata ton Evlia Tselebi," 337.

17. S. Tzortzaki-Tzaridou, "Ideikotera provlimata efarmogis tou Othomanikou yaioktitikou sistimatos sti Makedonias," in KITh., *Christianiki Thessaloniki: Othomaniki periodos, 1430–1912* (1994), 259–277, 269–270.

18. Cited in P. Atreinidou-Kotsaki, "Leitourgia ton bezestenion stin agora tis Othomanikis periodou," *Makedonika*, 30 (1995–96), 169; V. Dimitriades, *Topografia tis Thessalonikis kata tin tourkratia, 1430–1912* (1983), 180–182; Dimitriades, "Problems of land-owning and population in the area of Gazi Evrenos Bey's wakf," *Balkan Studies*, 22:1 (1981), 43–46; Dimitriades, "*Vakifs* along the Via Egnatia," in E. Zahariadou, ed., *The Via Egnatia under Ottoman Rule, 1380–1699* (Heraklion 1996), 85–97;

H. Pernot, ed., *Voyage en Turquie et en Grèce du R.P. Robert de Dreux* (Paris, 1925), 35.

19. I. Vasdravellis, *Istorika archeia Makedonias*, I (1952), 2–5; N. Beldiceanu, *Recherches sur la ville Ottomane au XVe siècle* (Paris, 1973), 144–146.

20. H. Inalcik, *The Ottoman Empire: The Classical Age, 1300–1600* (1973), 70–75.

21. Ibid.; N. Todorov, *The Balkan City, 1400–1900* (Seattle, 1983), 98.

22. E. Ginio, "Aspects of Muslim culture in the Ottoman Balkans," in D. Tziovas, ed., *Greece and the Balkans: Identities, Perceptions and Cultural Encounters since the Enlightenment* (Ashgate, 2003), 120.

23. "Viaggio di un ambasciatore veneziano da Venezia a Constantinopoli nel 1591" in L. Firpo, ed., *Relazioni di ambasciatori veneti al Senato*, XIII (1984), 201.

3 / The Arrival of the Sefardim

1. N. Moschopoulos, "I Ellas kata ton Evlia Tselebi," *Epetiris Etaireias Byzantinon Spoudon*, 16 (1940), 321–363.

2. M. A. Epstein, *The Ottoman Jewish Communities and Their Role in the Fifteenth and Sixteenth Centuries* (Freiburg, 1980), 178–180; H. Lowry, "Portrait of a City: the Population and Topography of Ottoman Selanik (Thessaloniki) in the Year 1478," *Diptycha*, 2 (1980–81), 254–292.

3. Y. Yerushalmi, "Exile and expulsion in Jewish history," in B. R. Gampel, ed., *Crisis and Creativity in the Sephardic World, 1391–1648* (New York, 1998), 3–22. As Yerushalmi notes, Jews had suffered temporary expulsions in France at the end of the twelfth century.

4. Cited in H. Kamen, "The Mediterranean and the Expulsion of Spanish

Jews in 1492," *Past & Present*, 119 (May 1988), 53–54.

5. A. Hess, "The Moriscos: an Ottoman fifth column in sixteenth-century Spain," *American Historical Review*, 74:1 (1968), 1–25.

6. A. Marx, "The expulsion of the Jews from Spain: two new accounts," in his *Studies in Jewish History and Booklore* (New York, 1944), 96.

7. Cited in A. Levy, *The Sephardim in the Ottoman Empire* (Princeton, 1992), 26.

8. V. Demetriades, "*Vakifs* along the Via Egnatia," E. Zahariadou, ed., *The Via Egnatia under Ottoman Rule, 1380–1699* (Rethymnon, 1996), 91; M. A. del Bravo, "The expulsion of Spanish Jews as seen by Christian and Jewish chroniclers," in I. Hassiotis, ed., *The Jewish Communities of Southeastern Europe* (1997), 70.

9. H. Lowry, "Portrait of a city: the population and topography of Ottoman Selanik [Thessaloniki] in the Year 1478," *Diptycha*, 2 (1980–81), 293; Epstein, *The Ottoman Jewish Communities*, 45–46; E. Ginio, "The administration of criminal justice in Ottoman Selanik [Salonica] during the eighteenth century," *Turcica*, 30 (1998), 197.

10. J. Hacker, "Superbe et désespoir: l'existence sociale et spirituelle des Juifs ibériques dans l'empire ottoman," *Revue historique*, 578 (April–June 1991), 261–295; Yerushalmi, "Exile and Expulsion," 21.

11. A. Danon, "La communauté juive de Salonique au XVIe siècle," *Revue des Etudes Juives*, 40 (1900), 207; M. A. Cohen, *Samuel Usque's Consolation for the Tribulations of Israel* (New York, 1964), 211–212.

12. Y. Yerushalmi, "Exile and expulsion in Jewish history," 8–14; N. Stavroulakis, *Cookbook of the Jews of Greece* (Athens, 1986).

13. P.C.I. Zorattini, ed., *Processi del S.*

Uffizio di Venezia contro Ebrei e Giudaizzanti (1608–1632) (Florence, 1991), IX, 76–77.

14. Danon, "La communauté juive," 209; *Cautiverio y Trabajos de Diego Galan, 1589–1600* (Madrid, 1913), 120; the primary source is J. Nehama, *Dictionnaire du Judéo-Espagnol* (Madrid, 1977/Gordes, 2003).

15. A. Hananel and E. Eshkenazi, eds., *Fontes Hebraici*, 42–43.

16. M. Rozen, "The corvée of operating the mines in Siderokapisi and its effects on the Jewish community of Thessaloniki in the 16th century," *Balkan Studies*, 34:1 (1993), 29–47.

17. M. Delilbasi, "The Via Egnatia and Selanik in the 16th century," in E. Zahariadou, ed., *The Via Egnatia under Ottoman Rule, 1380–1699* (Heraklion, 1994), 67–85.

18. S. Andreev, ed., *Ottoman Documents on the Balkans: Sixteenth to Seventeenth Centuries* (Sofia, 1990); A. Shmuelevitz, *The Jews of the Ottoman Empire in the Late Fifteenth and Sixteenth Centuries* (Leiden, 1984), 110.

19. B. Braude, "Venture and faith in the commercial life of the Ottoman Balkans, 1500–1650," *International History Review*, 7:4 (Nov. 1985), 519–542; R. Segre, "Sephardic settlements in sixteenth-century Italy: a historical and geographical survey," in A. M. Ginio, ed., *Jews, Christians and Muslims in the Mediterranean World after 1492* (London, 1992); B. Ravid, "A tale of three cities and their *raison d'état*: Ancona, Venice, Livorno and the competition for Jewish merchants in the sixteenth century," in ibid.

20. Epstein, *The Ottoman Jewish Communities*, 29.

21. Danon, "La communauté juive," 223; M. Russo-Katz, "Jewellery," E. Juhasz, ed., *Sephardi Jews in the Ottoman Empire: Aspects of Material Culture* (Jerusalem, 1990), 122, 173, 177.

22. V. Dimitriades, "O kanunname kai oi christianoi katoikoi tis Thessalonikis gyro sta 1525," *Makedonika*, 19 (1979), 328–349.

23. A. Shmuelevitz, *The Jews of the Ottoman Empire in the Late Fifteenth and Sixteenth Centuries* (Leiden, 1984), 23 n44.

24. J. Nehama, *Histoire des Israélites de Salonique*, iii: *L'Age d'Or du Séfaradisme Salonicien (1536–1593)* (Salonica, 1936), 53; P. Belon, *Les Observations de Plusieurs Singularitez et Choses Memorables, trouvées en Grèce, Asie, Iudée, Egypte, Arabie et autres payes estranges* (Anvers, 1555), I, 94.

25. M. Rozen, "Individual and community in the Jewish society of the Ottoman empire: Salonica in the sixteenth century," in A. Levy, ed., *The Jews of the Ottoman Empire* (Princeton, 1993), 218.

26. Ibid., 218.

27. A. Asher, ed., *The Itinerary of Benjamin of Tudela* (New York, nd), I, 49; D. Kaufmann, "L'incendie de Salonique du 4 Ab 1545," *Revue des Etudes Juives*, 21 (1890), 293–297; Danon, "La communauté juive," 230.

28. M. Rozen, "Individual and community," 222.

29. M. Goodblatt, *Jewish Life in Turkey in the Sixteenth Century as Reflected in the Legal Writings of Samuel de Medina* (New York, 1952), 61–68.

30. J. Hacker, "Jewish autonomy in the Ottoman empire: its scope and limits. Jewish courts from the sixteenth to the eighteenth centuries," in A. Levy, ed., *The Jews of the Ottoman Empire* (Princeton, 1993), 152–202.

31. Shmuelevitz, *The Jews of the Ottoman Empire*, 45–49.

32. Epstein, *The Ottoman Jewish Communities*, 72–73; cf. J. Hacker, "Jewish autonomy in the Ottoman empire," 161 seq., esp 174.

33. Ibid., 156.

34. B. Rivlin, "The Greek peninsula. A haven for Iberian refugees: effects on family-life," in Hasiotis, ed., *Jewish Communities*, 443–452.

35. J. Hacker, "The intellectual activity of the Jews of the Ottoman empire during the sixteenth and seventeenth centuries," in I. Twersky and B. Septimus, eds., *Jewish Thought in the Seventeenth Century* (Harvard UP, 1987), 120.

36. A. Shmuelevitz, *The Jews of the Ottoman Empire*, 34; J. Hacker, "The intellectual activity of the Jews of the Ottoman empire," 105 n20, 119.

37. N. Todorov, *The Balkan City, 1400–1900* (Seattle, 1983), 86–87, 470–471; A. P. Fernandez, *Españoles sin patria: la raza Sefardi* (Madrid, 1905).

4 / Messiahs, Martyrs and Miracles

1. H. Lenowitz, *The Jewish Messiahs* (New York, 1998), 179.

2. N. de Nicolay, *Dans l'empire de Soliman le Magnifique* (Paris, 1989), 257; Tournefort cited by B. Lewis, *The Jews of Islam* (Princeton, 1984), 138.

3. B. Nicolaides, *Les Turcs et la Turquie contemporaine* (Paris, 1859), ii, 45.

4. J. de Hammer, *Histoire*, xii, 28.

5. E. Ginio, "The administration of criminal justice in Ottoman Selanik," *Turcica*, 30 (1998), 185–209.

6. S. Senyk, "A man between East and West: Philip Orlyk and church life in Thessalonica in the 1720s," *Orientalia Christiana Periodica*, 60 (1994), 159–185.

7. O. Subtelny, ed., *The Diariusz Podrozny of Pylyp Orlyk (1720–1726)* (Harvard UP, 1989), 458. My thanks to Maria Wojcicka for her help with the translation.

8. B. Netanyahu, *The Marranos of Spain* (Cornell, 1992 ed.).

9. P.C.I. Zorattini, ed., *Processi del S. Uffizio di Venezia contro Ebrei e*

Guidizzanti, iii [1570–1572] (1984), 38–43; P.C.I. Zorattini, ed., *Processi del S. Uffizio di Venezia contro Ebrei e Guidizzanti*, x [1633–1637] (1992), 127–128; B. Pullan, "'A ship with two rudders': Righetto Marrano and the Inquisition in Venice," *Historical Journal*, 20:1 (1977), 25–58.

10. Y. Yerushalmi, "Messianic impulses in Joseph ha-Kohen," in B. D. Cooperman, ed., *Jewish Thought in the Sixteenth Century* (Harvard, 1983), 460–487.

11. S. Sherot, "Jewish millenarianism: a comparison of medieval communities," *Comparative Studies in Society and History* (1980), 394–415; G. Scholem, *Sabbatai Sevi: the Mystical Messiah* (Princeton, 1973), 562–563.

12. H. C. Lukach, "The False Messiah," in his *The City of Dancing Dervishes and Other Sketches and Studies from the Near East* (London, 1914), 189–190.

13. G. Saban, "Sabbatai Sevi as seen by a contemporary traveller," 112.

14. Lukach, 191.

15. Ibid., 200; Pernot, ed., *Voyage en Turquie et en Grèce de R.P. Robert de Dreux* (Paris, 1925), 42.

16. J. Freely, *The Lost Messiah* (London 2002), 120–122.

17. Freely, 135–137.

18. J. Nehama, *Histoire des Israelites de Salonique*, v: *Période de Stagnation—la Tourmente Sabbatéenne (1593–1669)*, (1959), 144–145.

19. E. Eden and N. Stavroulakis, *Salonika: A Family Cookbook* (Athens, 1997), 42–43.

20. G. Scholem, "The crypto-Jewish sect of the Dönmeh (Sabbatians) in Turkey," in his *The Messianic Idea in Judaism and Other Essays in Jewish Spirituality* (New York, 1995), 142–167.

21. A. Danon, "Une secte Judeo-Musulmane en Turquie," *Revue des Etudes Juives*, 35 (1897), 271.

22. S. Deringil, *The Well-Protected Domains: Ideology and the Legitimation of Power in the Ottoman Empire, 1876–1909* (London, 1999), 81.

23. A.E. Yalman, *Turkey in My Time* (Norman, Okl., 1956), 11–13; See also F. Gorgeon, "I 'Selanik' ton Mousoulanon kai ton donmedon," in G. Veinstein et al., eds., *Thessaloniki, 1850–1918* (1994), 129–130.

24. E. Eden and N. Stavroulakis, *Salonika*, 20–53. My thanks to Nikos Stavroulakis for his guidance on this subject.

25. Freely, *The Lost Messiah*, 239.

26. V. Kolonas and P. Papamalthaiakis, *O architektonas Vitaliano Poselli* (1980).

27. I. Melikoff, "Les voies de pénétration de l'hétérodoxie islamique en Thrace et dans les Balkans aux XIV–XVe siècles," Zahariadou, ed., *The Via Egnatia under Ottoman Rule, 1380–1699* (1994), 158–170.

28. J. Baldick, *Mystical Islam: An Introduction to Sufism* (New York, 2000).

29. A. Little, "Salonica," *Fortnightly Review*, 100 (July/Dec. 1916), 426–435; N. Clayer et al., eds., *Melamis-Bayramis* (Istanbul 1998), 180.

30. A. Bisani, *A Picturesque Tour through Part of Europe, Asia and Africa* (London, 1793), 48; "Odysseus," *Turkey in Europe* (London, 1900), 200–201.

31. F. W. Hasluck, *Christianity and Islam under the Sultans*, ii (Oxford, 1929), 500–551.

32. Hasluck, *Christianity and Islam under the Sultans*, ii, 493; W. Leake, *Travels in Northern Greece*, I, 495; E. Zengini, *Yenitsaroi kai Bektasismos* (2002), 269–271.

33. N. Moschopoulos, "I Ellas kata ton Evliya Tselebi," *EEBS*, 16 (1940), 360; L. de Launay, *Chez les Grecs de Turquie* (Paris, nd), 183–184.

34. Cited in A. Dimitriades, *"Phoinix Agiros": I Thessaloniki tou 1925–1935* (1994), 205–206.

35. G. F. Abbott, *Macedonian Folklore* (Cambridge, 1903), 211.

36. F. J. Blunt, *The People of Turkey:*

Twenty Years' Residence among Bulgarians, Greeks, Albanians, Turks, and Armenians, by a Consul's Daughter and Wife (London, 1878), ii, 224; M. Molho, *Usos y Custombres de los Sefardies de Salonica* (Madrid, 1959), ch. 6.

37. M. M. Bourlas, *Ellinas, Evraios kai aristeros* (2000), 25.

38. "Description de la ville de Salonique, par le père Jean-Baptiste Souciet," in *Lettres Edifiantes et Curieuses écrites des Missions Étrangères, Mémoires du Levant*, i (Lyon, 1819), 501.

39. G. Tsaras, *I teleftaia alosi tis Thessalonikis (1430)* (1985), 150; A. Vacalopoulos, *The Greek Nation, 1453–1669* (Rutgers, 1976), 141.

40. G. Ziakas, "Pnevmatikos vios kai politismos tis Thessalonikis kata tin periodo tis Othomanikis kyriarchias," *Christianiki Thessaloniki: Othomaniki periodos, 1430–1912* (1994), 89–167.

41. E. Ginio, "Childhood, mental capacity and conversion to Islam in the Ottoman state," *Byzantine and Modern Greek Studies*, 25 (2001), 90–119; for the nineteenth-century evidence, see M. Anastassiadou, "Des musulmans venus d'ailleurs: les 'fils de 'Abdullah' dans la Salonique du XIXe siècle," *Anatolia Moderna*, ix (2000), 113–171.

42. Vacalopoulos, *The Greek Nation*, 139–140.

43. H. Inalcik, "The status of the Greek Orthodox patriarch under the Ottomans," *Turcica*, 21–23 (1991), 406–433; J. Kabrda, *Le Systeme Fiscal de l'Eglise Orthodoxe dans l'Empire Ottoman* (Brno, 1969), 142–143.

44. S. Runciman, *The Great Church in Captivity* (Cambridge, 1968), 201; S. Senyk, "A man between East and West: Philip Orlyk and Church Life in Thessalonica in the 1720s," *Orientalia Christiana Periodica*, 60 (1994), 159–185.

45. Kabrda, *Le Systeme Fiscal*, 139–140; M. Gedeon, "Thessalonikeon palaiai koinotikai dienexeis," *Makedonika*, 1 (1941–52), 1–24.

46. "Description de la ville de Salonique, par le père Jean-Baptiste Souciet," *Lettres Edifiantes et Curieuses*, 495–497.

47. Senyk, "A man between East and West," 176.

48. E.g., H. Pernot, ed., *Voyage en Turquie et en Grèce du R.P. Robert de Dreux* (Paris, 1925), 98.

49. Senyk, "A man between East and West," 170.

50. I. Vasdravellis, *Istorika Archeia Makedonias*, I (1952), 42–43; Senyk, "A man between East and West," 174–175.

51. I. Anastasiou, "Oi neomartyres tis Thessalonikis," *Thessaloniki*, 1 (1995), 485–500.

52. *New Martyrs of the Turkish Yoke* (Seattle, 1985), 284–285.

53. M. L. Aimé-Martin, ed., *Lettres Édifiantes et Curieuses concernant l'Asie, L'Afrique et l'Amerique*, I (Paris, 1875), 94; *New Martyrs of the Turkish Yoke*, translated by L. J. Papadopoulos, G. Lizardos et al. (Seattle, 1985), 251.

54. *New Martyrs of the Turkish Yoke*, 284.

55. Ibid, 138–144, 234–235.

56. Senyk, "A man between East and West," 184.

57. H. T. Norris, "The history of Shaykh Muhammad Lutfi Baba and Shaykh Ahmad Sirri Baba," in his *Islam in the Balkans* (London, 1993), 218–227.

5 / Janissaries and Other Plagues

1. E. M. Cousinéry, *Voyage dans la Macédoine*, I (Paris, 1831), 45.

2. Moutsopoulos, "Evliya," 333; K. Mertzios, *Mnimeia Makedonikis Istorias* (1947), 104–106, 142; M. Kiel, "A note on the exact date of construction

of the White Tower of Thessaloniki," *Balkan Studies*, 14:2 (1973), 352–357.

3. K. Vasdravellis, *Istorika Archeia Makedonias*, vol. 1: *Archeion Thessalonikis, 1695–1912* (1952), 200–202; C.S. Sonnini, *Voyage en Grèce et en Turquie* (Paris, 1801), ii, 365; J. J. Best, *Excursions in Albania, Comprising a Description of the Wild Boar, Deer and Woodcock Shooting in that Country; and a Journey from Thence to Thessalonica and Constantinople and up the Danube to Pest* (London, 1842), 205–206.

4. Anon., "De Salonique a Belgrade," *Revue des Deux Mondes*, 85 (1888), 109; W. M. Leake, *Travels in Northern Greece* (London, 1835), iii, 235; FO 195/685, Calvert-Constantinople, 24 June 1861; E. Ginio, "Migrants and workers in an Ottoman port: Ottoman Salonica in the eighteenth century," in E. Rogan, ed., *Outside In: On the Margins of the Modern Middle East* (London, 2002), 126–148.

5. N. Svoronos, *Le commerce de Salonique au XVIIIe siècle* (Paris, 1956), 26.

6. N. Svoronos, *Le commerce de Salonique*, 44–45; Mertzios, 437, 451.

7. Mertzios 409; D. Iliadou, *Inventaire des documents des archives de la Chambre de Commerce de Marseille: Lemme Salonique (XVIIe–XVIIIe siècles)* (1981), 94; Leake, *Travels in Northern Greece*, III:I, 257.

8. Mertzios, 419.

9. Ibid., 323, 383–385.

10. Ibid., 413; D. Iliadou, *Inventaire*, 93–94.

11. P. Rycaut, *The Present State of the Ottoman Empire* (1668), 196–197.

12. *Memoirs of the Baron de Tott on the Turks and the Tartars Translated from the French by an English Gentleman at Paris* (London, 1785), ii, 368.

13. Iliadou, *Inventaire*, 42; Mertzios, 448; Arasy in M. Lascaris, "Salonique à la fin du XVIII siècle," *Les Balkans*,

10:iii (1938), 46; *Memoirs of the Baron de Tott*, ii, 369; Mertzios, 458–459.

14. Bisani, *Picturesque Tour*, 43.

15. Mertzios, 319.

16. Ibid., 343, 352–356.

17. Ibid., 392.

18. R. Dankoff and R. Elsie, eds., *Evliya Çelebi in Albania and Adjacent Regions (Kosovo, Montenegro, Ohrid)* (Leiden, 2000), 45.

19. Lascaris, "Relation des troubles qui regnent aux environs de Salonique," 391.

20. E. Ginio, "Migrant workers in an Ottoman port: Ottoman Salonica in the eighteenth century," E. Rogan, ed., *Outside In: On the Margins of the Modern Middle East* (London, 2002), 136.

21. Lascaris, "Relation des troubles qui regnent aux environs de Salonique," 37–41; N. Svoronos, *Le commerce de Salonique au XVIIIe siècle* (Paris, 1956), 8–9.

22. Sonnini, *Voyage en Grèce*, ii, 369.

23. Mertzios, 462; Ginio, "Migrants and workers," 141.

24. M. J. Zallony, "Essay on the Fanariotes," in C. Swan, *Journal of a Voyage up the Mediterranean* (London, 1826), ii, 416–417.

25. K. Vasdravellis, *Istorika Archeia Makedonias*, vol. 1: *Archeion Thessalonikis, 1695–1912* (1952), 111–112; E. Ginio, "The administration of Criminal Justice in Ottoman Selanik (Salonica) during the Eighteenth Century," *Turcica*, 30 (1998), 185–209, here 202–203.

26. E. S. Forster, ed., *The Turkish Letters of Ogier Ghiselin de Busbecq* (New York, 1927), 102; E. Brown, *A Brief Account of some Travels in Hungaria, Servia, Bulgaria, Macedonia, Thessaly, Austria etc. etc.* (New York, 1971), 74–75; Mertzios, 429; Iliadou, *Inventaire*, 27.

27. Mertzios, 290; K. Vasdravellis, *Istorika Archeia*, 291–294.

28. Mertzios, 395, 412–413; K. Vasdrav-ellis, *Istorika Archeia*, 154–155; Iliadou, *Inventaire*, 8; Svoronos, *Commerce*, 157.

29. E. Ginio, "Living on the margins of charity: coping with poverty in an Ottoman provincial city," in M. Bon-ner et al., *Poverty and Charity in Middle Eastern Contexts* (SUNY, 2003), 170; Ginio, "Migrants and workers," 138.

30. Mertzios, 412–413; O. Subtelny, ed., *The Diariusz Podrozny*, 213–217.

31. E. Ginio, "Aspects of Muslim culture in the Ottoman Balkans," in D. Tzio-vas, ed., *Greece and the Balkans: Identities, Perceptions and Cultural Encounters since the Enlightenment* (Ashgate, 2003), 121.

32. On the Shah of Persia's brother, Mertzios, 286; On Sherif of Mecca, K. Vakalopoulos, "Pos eidan oi evropaioi tin katastasi sti Makedonia ton perasmeno aiona," *Makedonika*, 20 (1980), 73, and G. de Gaury, *Rulers of Mecca* (New York, 1954), 206–207, 238, 241.

33. O. Subtelny, ed., *The Diariusz Podrozny*, xvii–xxx; K. Vasdravellis, *Istorika Archeia*, 169.

34. M. G. Brennan, ed., *The Travel Diary of Robert Bargrave Levant Merchant (1647–1656)* (London, 1999), 87.

35. *The Negotiations of Sir Thomas Roe in his Embassy to the Ottoman Porte from the Year 1621 to 1628 Inclusive* (London, 1740), 420–444; Bisani, 36; D. Panzac, *Population et Santé dans l'Empire Ottoman (XVIIIe–XXe siècles)* (Istanbul, 1996), 35.

36. Mertzios, 304–307; A. Vacalopoulos, *A History of Thessaloniki* (1993), 106; D. Panzac, *La peste dans l'Empire Ottoman, 1700–1850* (Louvain, 1985), 215, 359.

37. O. Subtelny, ed., *The Diariusz Podrozny*, 507.

38. *Lettres Edifiantes et Curieuses*, II, 27–28, gives an account of negotia-tions between city-dwellers and vil-lagers during a prior outbreak of plague.

39. Mertzios, 323–326, 426–427; Bren-nan, *Robert Bargrave*, 87.

40. J. Howard, *An Account of the Principal Lazarettos in Europe* (London, 1791), 64–65; Mertzios, 426.

6 / Commerce and the Greeks

1. Mertzios, *Mnimeia* 453.

2. D. Hemmerdiner-Iliadou, "Thessa-lonique en 1726: (La relation du moine russe Basile Barskij)," *Balkan Studies*, 2:2 (1961), 294–295.

3. V. Aksan, *An Ottoman Statesman in War and Peace: Ahmed Resmi Effendi, 1700–1783* (Brill, 1991), 39; H. Hol-land, *Travels in the Ionian Islands, Albania, Thessaly, Macedonia etc. during the Years 1812 and 1813* (London, 1815), 310.

4. Figures from F. Beaujour, *A View of the Commerce of Greece* (London, 1800); V. Aksan, *An Ottoman States-man in War and Peace*, 40; D. Panzac, "International and domestic mari-time trade in the Ottoman empire during the 18th century," *IJMES*, 24:2 (May 1992), 189–206.

5. Mertzios, 305–306.

6. Nehama, *Histoire des Israélites de Salonique*, VI–VII, 318–320.

7. E. M. Cousinéry, *Voyage dans la Macé-doine* (Paris, 1831), I, 156–157; Beau-jour, 241–243, 383–384.

8. N. Svoronos, *Le Commerce de Salonique au XVIIIe siècle* (1956), 347; W. M. Leake, *Travels in Northern Greece*, III:1 (London, 1835), 249.

9. S. Lambros, "To en Thessaloniki Venetikon proxeneion kai to meta tis Makedonias emporion ton Veneton," *Makedonikon Imerologion* (1912), 227–241.

10. J. Galt, *Voyages and Travels in the Years 1809, 1810 and 1811* (London, 1812),

235; H. Holland, *Travels in the Ionian Islands*, 319–323; Mertzios, 351.

11. Beaujour, 430–431; M. Rozen, "Contest and rivalry in Mediterranean maritime commerce in the first half of the eighteenth century: the Jews of Salonika and the European presence," *Revue des Études Juives*, 147: 3–4 (July–Dec. 1988), 335–336.

12. Mertzios, 338.

13. G. Hekimoglou, "Ioannis Gouta Kaftantzoglou: to prosopo stin epochi tou," *Grigoris o Palamas*, 758 (May–Aug. 1995), 417–418; E. Horowitz, "The early eighteenth century confronts the beard: Kabbalah and Jewish self-fashioning," *Jewish History*, 8:1–2 (1994), 94–115; "Description de la ville de Salonique par le père Jean-Baptiste Souciet," *Lettres Edifiantes et Curieuses*, I (Lyon, 1819), 504.

14. Mertzios, 340; M. Rozen, "Contest and rivalry," 309–352; Y-J. Dumont, "To metroon vaptiseon tis Katholikis Ekklisias Thessalonikis," *Makedonika*, 11 (1971), 42–43.

15. Rozen, "Contest and rivalry," 339–341.

16. Beaujour, 285; Rozen, "Contest and rivalry," 329.

17. C.G. Pitcairn Jones, *Piracy in the Levant, 1827–28* (London, 1934), 138.

18. Mertzios, 422–423; Nehama, 307.

19. K. Mertzios, "Emporiki allilografia ek Thessalonikis (1742–1759)," *Makedonika*, 7 (1966–67), 94; Hekimoglou, "Ioannis Gouta Kaf tantzoglou," 407–437.

20. Mertzios, 370–371.

21. "De l'establissement et des progrès de la mission de Thessalonique," *Lettres Edifiantes et Curieuses*, II (Memoires du Levant) (Lyon, 1819), 24–25; P. Kitromilides, "War and political consciousness: theoretical implications of eighteenth-century Greek historiography," in his *Enlightenment, Nationalism, Orthodoxy* (1994), II; J. Nicolopoulos,

"From Agathangelos to the Megale Idea: Russia and the emergence of modern Greek nationalism," *Balkan Studies*, 26:1 (1985), 41–56.

22. Mertzios, 407–412.

23. Ibid., 419–420.

24. A. Papazoglou, "I Thessaloniki kata ton Maio tou 1821," *Makedonika*, 1 (1940), 417–428.

25. A. Papazoglou, "I Thessaloniki," 423.

26. W. M. Leake, *Travels in Northern Greece*, III:1 (London, 1835), 202.

27. A. Karathanasis, "Thessaloniki pendant la première année de la Résurrection Hellénique vue par le consul François Bottu," *Thessaloniki*, 1 (1995).

28. A. Karathanasis, "Thessaloniki," 101.

29. M. Lascaris, "La Révolution Grecque vue de Salonique: Rapports des consuls de France et d'Autriche (1821–1826)," *Balcania* (1943), 161.

30. Vasdravellis, *Istorika Archeia Makedonias*, 500–501.

7 / Pashas, Beys and Money-lenders

1. PRO 30/22/88 (1859–60), p. 63; FO 195/586, 1 August 1859.

2. A. Cunningham, "Stratford Canning and the *Tanzimat*," in E. Ingram, ed., *Eastern Questions in the Nineteenth Century: Collected Essays*, vol. II (London, 1993), 118–119.

3. K. Karpat, "*Millets* and nationality: the roots of the incongruity of nation and state in the post-Ottoman era," in B. Braude and B. Lewis, eds., *Christians and Jews in the Ottoman Lands*, I (London, 1982), 141–171.

4. FO 195/176, Blunt-Ponsonby, 9 April 1840; FO 78/531, "Mr. Consul Blunt's report upon the commerce of Salonica during the year ending the 31 December 1842."

5. FO 195/176, Blunt-Ponsonby, 13 Nov. 1840; G.F. Bowen, *Mount Athos*,

Thessaly and Epirus (London, 1852), 127–128; K. Braun-Wiesbaden, *Eine türkische Reise*, ii (Stuttgart, 1876), 87–100.

6. Vakalopoulos, 88; FO 195/371, Blunt-Canning, 29 Sept. 1853; 195/100, Blunt-Ponsonby, 18 Dec. 1839; 195/1196, Barker-Layard, 25 Nov. 1878.

7. FO 195/649, Calvert-Constantinople, 28 Feb. 1860; FO 78/612, Blunt-Canning, 28 March 1845; 195/811, Wilkinson-Stuart, 11 Sept. 1865; 195/176, Blunt-Ponsonby, 30 Sept. 1840.

8. FO 78/651, Blunt-Wellesley, 24 Nov. 1846.

9. FO 195/952, Wilkinson-Rumbold, 16 March 1872; FO 195/240, Blunt-Stratford Canning, 16 Oct. 1845.

10. FO 195/952, Wilkinson-Rumbold, 16 March 1872.

11. FO 195/723, Calvert-Bulwer, 20 Sept. 1862; 195/371, Blunt-Canning, 22 July 1851.

12. FO 78/651, Blunt-Canning, 8 April 1846.

13. A. H. Midhat Bey, *The Life of Midhat Pasha* (London, 1903), 67; D. Urquhart, *La Turquie: Ses resources, son organisation, son commerce* (Brussels, 1837), ii, 150–151.

14. L. Stavrianos, *The Balkans since 1453* (1958), 382–383; FO 195/100, Blunt-Ponsonby, 27 June 1837; 195/176, Blunt-Ponsonby, 24 July 1840.

15. K. Vakalopoulos, "Pos eidan oi evropaioi tin katastasi sti Makedonia ton perasmeno aiona," *Makedonika*, 20 (1980), 65–71; on Bekir Pasha see also the memoirs of his doctor, Zallony, M. P. Zallony, "Essay on the Fanariotes," in C. Swan, *Journal of a Voyage up the Mediterranean* (London, 1826), ii, 391–394.

16. FO 78/57, Leake-Howick, 25 Jan. 1807.

17. FO 195/100, Blunt-Ponsonby, 30 Jan. 1838; 195/176, Blunt-Ponsonby, 9 April 1840.

18. 195/100, Blunt-Ponsonby, 20 July 1837; 195/176, Blunt-Ponsonby, 23 April 1840.

19. K. Karpat, "The transformation of the Ottoman state, 1789–1908," *International Journal of Middle East Studies*, 3:3 (July 1972), 263.

20. F. Ahmad, *The Young Turks: The CUP in Turkish Politics, 1908–1914* (Oxford, 1969); A. Mango, *Ataturk* (London, 1999), 67–8, 81, 412; FO 371/1997, Elliot-Grey, 8 Oct. 1914.

21. FO 286/874, Henderson-Bentinck, 29 Jan. 1923.

22. FO 195/176, Blunt-Ponsonby, 16 Sept. 1840.

23. FO 371/371, Blunt-Stratford Canning, 28 Oct. 1851.

24. FO 195/371, Blunt-Canning, 10 Dec. 1857.

25. K. Vakalopoulos, "Pos eidan oi evropaioi," 91.

26. FO 195/477, "Lord Napier's Mission to Salonica," passim; S. Levy, *Salonique à la fin du XIXe siècle* (Istanbul, 2000), 72; Urquhart, *La Turquie*, 155.

27. Levy, *Salonique*, 72–73.

28. J. M. Wallace, "Urendjik—and all that!," *Mosquito*, 74 (June 1946); V. Colonas, "Nouveaux éléments sur l'histoire du bâtiment de la Banque Ottomane à Thessalonique," *Makedonika*, 11 (1971).

8 / Religion in the Age of Reform

1. C. V. Findley, *Bureaucratic Reform in the Ottoman Empire: the Sublime Porte, 1789–1922* (Princeton, 1980), 7; E. Ginio, "Aspects of Muslim culture in the Ottoman Balkans" in D. Tziovas, ed., *Greece and the Balkans: Identities, Perceptions and Cultural Encounters since the Enlightenment* (Ashgate, 2003), 117.

2. D. Urquhart, *La Turquie* (Brussels, 1837), ii, 28; Stavrianos, *The Balkans since 1453*, 316; H. Temperley, *The Crimea: England and the Near East* (London, 1936), 22–23; D. Quataert, "Clothing laws, state and society in the Ottoman empire, 1720–1829," *International Journal of Middle Eastern Studies*, 29 (1997), 403–425.

3. S. Mardin, *The Genesis of Young Ottoman Thought* (Princeton, 2000 ed.), 128; B. Abu-Manneh, "The Sultan and the bureaucracy: the anti-Tanzimat concepts of Grand Vizier Mahmud Nedim Pasha," *IJMES*, 22 (1990), 257–274.

4. H. Temperley, *The Crimea: England and the Near East* (London, 1936), 89; FO 195/176, Blunt-Ponsonby, 30 July 1840.

5. FO 195/371, Blunt-Stratford Canning, 29 April 1851; FO 195/526, Blunt-Canning, 20 March 1856; FO 195/586, Ioannides-Calvert, 1 August 1858; FO 195/685, Calvert-Constantinople, 2 July 1861.

6. FO 195/811, Wilkinson-Stuart, 1 April 1867; 195/952, Wilkinson-Rumbold, n.d. [1872]; A. L. Tibawi, *American Interests in Syria, 1800–1901* (Oxford, 1966), 173.

7. FO 195/1107, *Selanik*, 18 May 1876.

8. FO 78/700, Blunt-Cowley, 22 Sept. 1847; FO 195/1065, Blunt-Elliott, 1 Jan. 1875.

9. J. Nehama, *Histoire des Israélites de Salonique*, vi–vii (Thessaloniki, 1978), 565; *Missionary Register* (Feb. 1850), 83.

10. FO 195/100, Blunt-Ponsonby, 11 April 1839.

11. FO 195/100, Blunt-Ponsonby, 20 June 1839.

12. FO 195/240, Blunt-Stratford Canning, 18 June 1846.

13. FO 195/371, Blunt-Porter, 28 Dec. 1852.

14. FO 195/371, Blunt-Porter, 25 Jan. 1853.

15. P. Dumont, "La structure sociale de la communauté juive de Salonique à la fin du dix-neuvième siècle," *Revue Historique*, CCLXIII/2, 352–393.

16. Sir Henry Bulwer in A. L. Tibawi, *American Interests in Syria, 1800–1901* (Oxford, 1966), 173.

17. *Missionary Register* (Sept. 1826), 423–424; J. Brewer, *A Residence at Constantinople in the Year 1827* (New Haven, 1830), 294.

18. *Missionary Register* (Jan. 1831), 24; J. Wolff (G. Wint, ed.), *A Mission to Bokhara* (New York, 1969), 1–5; A. Slade, *Records of Travels in Turkey, Greece, etc. and of a Cruise in the Black Sea with the Captain Pasha* (London, 1854), 514.

19. K. Vakalopoulos, "Pos eidan oi evropaioi tin katastasi sti Makedonia ton perasmeno aiona," *Makedonika*, 20 (1980), 88; "Narrative of facts and incidents in the Life of John Meshullam," in A. B. Wood, *Meshullam! Or Tidings from Jerusalem. From the Journal of a Believer Recently returned from the Holy Land* (Philadelphia, 1851), 96–97.

20. S. I. Prime, *The Bible in the Levant; or The Life and Letters of the Reverend C. N. Richter, agent of the American Bible Society in the Levant* (New York, 1859), 89–90; *Missionary Register* (Dec. 1851), 514; Slade, *Records of Travels in Turkey, Greece, etc.*, 516.

21. FO 195/586, Calvert-Constantinople, August 10, 1858.

22. FO 195/240, Blunt-Canning, August 20, 1845; FO 195/1196, Barker-Layard, 11 May 1878.

23. S. Deringil, " 'There is no compulsion in religion': on conversion and apostasy in the late Ottoman empire," in his *The Ottomans, the Turks and World Power Politics* (Istanbul, 2000), 122.

24. FO 195/240, Blunt-Canning, August 20, 1845; 195/1255, Blunt-Layard, 30 June 1879.

25. FO 195/1107, "Preliminary deposition of Colonel Selim Bey".

26. FO 195/1107, Blunt-Elliott, 7 May 1876.

27. FO 195/1107, Blunt-Elliott, 6 June 1876.

28. 195/526, Blunt-Canning, 20 March 1856; Mary Adelaide Walker, *Through Macedonia to the Albanian Lakes* (London, 1864), 77–80.

29. 195/1107, Blunt-Derby, 31 May 1876; 195/1108, Blunt-Elliott, 5 Oct. 1876, 23 Oct. 1876.

30. F. Blunt, *My Reminiscences*, 211; 195/1107, "List of individuals regarded as guilty in recent events in Salonica," 383.

31. J. J. Best, *Excursions in Albania etc.* (London, 1842), 227–228; FO 195/1007, Blunt-Elliott, July 7, 1873; 195/176, Blunt-Ponsonby, 23 April 1840, and 22 Oct. 1840.

32. FO 195/240, Blunt-Canning, 20 August 1846; 195/371, Blunt-Stratford Canning, 28 Oct. 1851; 195/756, Wilkinson-Bulwer, 5 May 1863; 195/723, Calvert-Constantinople, 23 April 1862.

33. 195/1108, Blunt-Elliott, 5 Oct. 1876; 195/1149, Barker-Layard, 26 Oct. 1877; 78/2994, Blunt-Layard, 21 Sept. 1879.

34. A. Toumarkine, *Les migrations des populations musulmanes balkaniques en Anatolie (1876–1913)* (Istanbul, 1995), 27–29.

35. A. Uner Turgay, "Circassian immigration into the Ottoman empire, 1856–1878," in W. Hallaq and D. P. Little, eds., *Islamic Studies Presented to Charles J. Adams* (Brill, 1991), 193–217; FO 195/1196, Barker-Layard, 5 Jan. 1878; B.N. Simsir, ed., *Rumeli'den Türk Göcleri* (Ankara, 1989), 226; B. Gounaris, *Steam over Macedonia, 1870–1912* (New York, 1993), 257.

36. 195/1196, Barker-Layard, 5 July 1878.

9 / Travellers and the European Imagination

1. F. Baumer, "England, the Turk and the Common Corps of Christendom," *American Historical Review* (1944).

2. A. Oakes and R. B. Mowat, eds., *The Great European Treaties of the Nineteenth Century* (Oxford, 1930), 176–177.

3. E. Isambert, *Itinéraire descriptif, historique et archéologique de l'Orient* (Paris, 1881), xxii.

4. Anon. "Letters to my Sister: Letter III: Turkey-Salonica, 1839," *Southern Literary Messenger* (July 1840), 550; Karl Braun-Wiesbaden, *Eine türkische Reise* (Stuttgart, 1876), ii, 96–97, 129–130.

5. *Appleton's Journal*, 11:65 (Nov. 1881), 469–472; W. Miller, *Travels and Politics in the Near East* (London, 1898), xiv; F. Moore, *The Balkan Trail* (London, 1906), 88.

6. R. Tweddell, ed., *Remains of the Late John Tweddell* (London, 1815), 272–273.

7. E. Isambert, *Itinéraire*, xxvi; cf R. Schiffer, *Oriental Panorama: British Travellers to Nineteenth Century Turkey* (Amsterdam, 1999), 35–38. Also J. Buzard, *The Beaten Track: European Tourism, Literature and the Ways to "Culture," 1800–1918* (Oxford, 1993).

8. J. Baker, *Turkey* (New York, 1877), 371; E. Miller, *Le Mont Athos, Vatopedi, L'île de Thasos* (Paris, 1889), 234; D. Urquhart, *Spirit of the East* (London, 1838), 208.

9. *Handbook for Travellers in Greece* (London, 1854), 7; B. Nicolaidy, *Les Turcs et la Turquie Contemporaine. Itinéraire et Compte-Rendu de Voyages dans les Provinces Ottomanes* (Paris, 1859), I, 49–50.

10. H. Holland, *Travels in the Ionian Islands, Albania, Thessaly, Macedonia*

etc during the Years 1812 and 1813 (London, 1815), 310; G. S. Davies, *The Heathen World and St. Paul: St. Paul in Greece* (London, n.d.), 123.

11. A. Goff and H. Fawcett, *Macedonia: A Plea for the Primitive* (London, 1921), 155–157; H. F. Tozer, *Researches in the Highlands of Turkey* (London, 1869), ii, 140–141; G. F. Abbott, *The Tale of a Tour in Macedonia* (London, 1903), 35; John Foster Fraser, "Adrianople, Salonika and Monastir," in E. Singleton, ed., *Turkey and the Balkan States* (New York, 1908), 148; R. Schiffer, *Oriental Panoramas*, ch. 8, is excellent background.

12. A. Goff and H. Fawcett, *Macedonia: A Plea for the Primitive*, 128–129.

13. E. Isambert, *Itinéraire*, xxxv; E. Lear, *Journals of a Landscape Painter*, 25. See generally, J. Buzard, *The Beaten Track*, ch. 1.

14. *Handbook for Travellers in Greece* (London, 1854), 1; J. P. Mahaffy, *Greek Pictures* (London, 1890), 218; W. Miller, *Travels and Politics*, 365; R. H. Russell, *On the Edge of the Orient* (New York, 1896), 191.

15. E.-M. de Vogüé, "La Thessalie," *Revue de Deux Mondes*, 31 (1879), 6; Murray cited in B. Gounaris, "Salonica," *Review: Fernand Braudel Center*, 16:4 (Fall, 1993), 499–518.

16. Lear, *Journals*, 18–19; H. Melville, *Journals* (Evanston, Ill., 1989), 56; Walker, *Through Macedonia*, 31–32.

17. E.-M. de Vogüé, "La Thessalie," 7; H. Melville, *Journals*, 55; Braun-Wiesbaden, "Letters," 550; Clarke, *Travels*, 360.

18. A. Boué, *La Turquie d'Europe* (Paris, 1840), ii, 326–327.

19. Lear cited by J. Pemble, *The Mediterranean Passion* (Oxford, 1988), 50; anon., "Letters to My Sister: Letter III: Turkey-Salonica, 1839," *Southern Literary Messenger* (July 1840), 550; M. A. Walker, *Through Macedonia to the Albanian Lakes* (London, 1864), 86.

20. E. Lear, *Journals of a Landscape Painter* (London, 1848), 18; anon., "De Salonique à Belgrade," *Revue des Deux Mondes*, 85 (1888), 108.

21. A. Choisy, *L'Asie Mineure et Les Turcs en 1875: Souvenirs de Voyage* (Paris, 1876), 13; Braun-Wiesbaden, 135; S. Whitman, *Turkish Memories* (New York, 1914), 40–41.

22. G. Muir Mackenzie and A. P. Irby, *Travels in the Slavonic Provinces of Turkey-in-Europe* (London, 1877, 2nd ed.), I, 63; A. Goff and H. Fawcett, *Macedonia: A Plea for the Primitive* (London, 1921), 138–140; E. Isambert, *Itineraire, I,* (1873 ed.), 475.

23. A. E. Vakalopoulos, "I Thessaloniki kai i perochi Pellas-Yenitson sta 1828," *Makedonika*, 26 (1987–88), 187.

24. F. Blunt, *My Reminiscences*, 234; Nicolaidy, I, 43–44.

25. P. Loti, *Aziyadé* (Paris, 1886), 1–7.

26. J.-J. Frappa, *A Salonique sous l'oeil des Dieux* (Paris, 1917), 137–138.

27. Doctor Gelibert, *Avec les Poilus d'Orient* (Lyon, 1936), 161–162.

28. P. Roussel, *Salonique au temps de la campagne d'Orient* (Paris, 1925), 167.

29. Roussel, *Salonique*, 99.

10 / The Possibilities of a Past

1. H. G. Dwight, "Saloniki," *National Geographic*, 30:3 (1916), 221.

2. J. Pemble, *The Mediterranean Passion: Victorians and Edwardians in the South* (Oxford, 1987), 267; *Murray's Handbook*, 1.

3. Bisani, *Picturesque Tour,* 35; Clarke, *Travels*, 335–337.

4. Braun-Wiesbaden, 263; Davies, *St. Paul in Greece*, 129; Walker, *Through Macedonia*, 66.

5. E. Isambert, *Itinéraire descriptif, historique et archéologique de l'Orient* (Paris, 1881), xviii.

6. Urquhart, *The Spirit of the East* (London, 1838), i, 11; Choisy, *L'Asie*

Mineure, 16–22; anon., "De Salonique à Belgrade," 115; D. Vaka, *The Heart of the Balkans* (New York, 1917), 228; Moore, *The Balkan Trail,* 87.

7. J. J. Best, *Excursions in Albania etc.,* (London, 1842), 209; Irby and Mackenzie, *Travels,* 56; D. Bikelas, *La Grèce Byzantine et Moderne* (Paris, 1893), 4.

8. Tozer, *Researches,* 145; de Vogüé, "La Thessalie," 7.

9. D. Placide de Meester, *Voyage de deux Bénédictins aux monastères du Mont-Athos* (Paris, 1908), 25.

10. Mahaffy, *Greek Pictures,* 219; N. P. Kondakov, *Makedon'iia: arkheologicheskoe puteshetvie* (St. Petersburg, 1909).

11. M. A. Walker, *Through Macedonia,* 51; Bowen, *Mount Athos, Thessaly and Epirus,* 28; S. G. Green, *Pictures from Bible Lands* (London, n.d.), v, 171–174; J. Baker, *Turkey* (New York, 1877), 349.

12. Bowen, *Mount Athos, Thessaly and Epirus,* 28; S.G. Green, *Pictures,* v, 171–174.

13. Davies, *St. Paul in Greece,* 120–125; S. G. Green, *Pictures from Bible Lands,* vii.

14. A. Boué, *La Turquie d'Europe* (Paris, 1840), ii, 307; Braun-Wiesbaden, 241–242.

15. H. Omont, ed., *Missions Archéologiques Françaises en Orient aux XVIIe et XVIIIe siècles,* ii (Paris, 1902), 725–727.

16. *Remains of the late John Tweddell,* 343–345.

17. H. Omont, "Inscriptions grecques de Salonique," *Revue Archaeologique,* xxiv (1894), 196–214.

18. S. Reinach, *Conseils aux Voyageurs Archéologues en Grèce et dans l'Orient Hellénique* (Paris, 1886), 108–109.

19. A. Slade, *Record of Travels in Turkey, Greece etc.* (London, 1854), 512.

20. C.T. Newton, *Travels and Discoveries in the Levant* (London, 1865), 121.

21. The entire story has been reconstructed from E. Miller, *Le Mont Athos, Vatopedi, L'île de Thasos* (Paris, 1889).

22. P. Perdrizet, "L'Incantada de Salonique," *Monuments et Mémoires,* 31 (Paris, 1930), 51–90.

23. W.M.K. Shaw, *Possessors and Possessed: Museums, Archaeology and the Visualisation of History in the Late Ottoman Empire* (California, 2003), 94; FO 195/1196, Barker-Layard, 21 Dec. 1878.

24. Ibid.

25. Abbott, *Tale of a Tour,* 13.

11 / *In the Frankish Style*

1. F. Moore, *The Balkan Trail* (London, 1906), 90; P. Risal, *La ville convoitée: Salonique* (Paris, 1914), 352.

2. E. Isambert, *Itinéraire,* xx; D. Urquhart, *The Spirit of the East* (London, 1838), ii, 61; Choisy, *L'Asie Mineure,* 1–2.

3. J. Field, *America and the Mediterranean World, 1776–1882* (Princeton, 1969), 187; C. G. Pitcairn Jones, *Piracy in the Levant, 1827–28: Selected from the papers of Admiral Sir Edward Codrington* (London, 1934), 138; T-46/9 (Despatches from US Ministers to Turkey, 1818–1906), vii, Porter-Washington, 10 Aug. 1833; ibid., 12 Sept. 1834.

4. E. Toledano, *Slavery and Abolition in the Ottoman Middle East* (Princeton, 1998), ch. 1.

5. Mary Adelaide Walker cited by B. Gounaris, *Steam over Macedonia, 1870–1912* (Columbia UP, 1993), 35; J. Baker, *Turkey* (New York, 1877), 389.

6. K. Tomanas, *Chroniko tis Thessalonikis 1875–1920* (1995), 69, 77; Paul Lindau cited in P. K. Enepekidis, *I Thessaloniki sta chronia 1875–1912* (1988), 316–317.

7. W. Miller, *Travels and Politics in the Near East* (London, 1898), 363.

8. B. Gounaris, *Steam over Macedonia*, 35–58.

9. J. Baker, *Turkey*, 392; M. Anastassiadou, *Salonique, 1830–1912: Une ville ottomane à l'âge des Réformes* (Brill, 1997), 100.

10. A. Boué, *Receuil d'Itinéraires dans la Turquie d'Europe* (Vienna, 1854), 154.

11. R. Molho, " 'Le Cercle de Salonique' 1873–1958: Leschi thessalonikeon: symvoli sti meleti tis astikis taxis tis Thessalonikis," in Etaireia Meletis Ellinikou Evraismou, *Oi Evraioi ston elliniko choro: zitimata istorias sta makra diarkeia* (Athens, 1995), 103–131.

12. R. Molho, *Oi evraioi tis Thessalonikis, 1856–1919* (Athens, 2001), 82–84.

13. H. Collinson Owen, *Salonica and After* (London, 1919), 83.

14. V. Gounaris, "Thessaloniki, 1830–1912: History, economy and society," in I. Hassiotis, ed., *Queen of the Worthy: Thessaloniki, History and Culture* (1997), 118.

15. P. Valsamides, "Ta tourkika scholeia sto santzaki tis Thessalonikis kata to 1901–1911," *Makedonika* (1997–98), 345–355.

16. Anastassiadou, *Salonique, 1830–1912*, 260–264; L. Sciaky, *Farewell to Salonica* (1946), 145, 152.

17. Enepekidis, 319–320; F. Blunt, *My Reminiscences*; E. Adler, *Jews in Many Lands* (Philadelphia, 1905), 141.

18. Risal, *La ville convoitée*, 352–353; "Sita," *The Cornhill Magazine* (April 1917), 451–460.

19. A. Themopoulou, "Epidimies sti Thessaloniki," EIE, *IZ' Panellinio Istoriko Synedrio: Praktika* (1997), 286–300; Vasdravellis, *Istorika Archeia*, 389, 421.

20. R. Arthur Arnold, *From the Levant* (1868), 327.

21. Enepekidis, *Thessalonikis*, 353.

22. *Journal de Salonique*, 21 Sept. 1896.

23. "Les noms des Rues," *Journal de Salonique*, 26 May 1898.

24. P. Kokkas, "I oikoyeneia Garbolas kai i proti elliniki efimerida tis Thessalonikis," *Makedonika*, 21 (1984), 234.

25. A. Yerolympou and V. Colonas, "Mia kosmopolitiki poleodomia," in G. Veinstein, ed., *Thessaloniki, 1850–1918* (1994), 174.

26. Ibid.

27. *Journal de Salonique*, 23 July 1896.

28. *Journal de Salonique*, 28 Dec. 1896.

29. *Journal de Salonique*, 23 July 1896.

30. *Journal de Salonique*, 20 July 1896.

31. *Journal de Salonique*, 27 July 1896.

32. *Journal de Salonique*, 26 Oct. 1896; A. Karadimou-Yerolympou, "O typos kai i diamorphosi mias 'syneidisi tis polis' sta teli tou 19ou aiona," KIS, *I neoteri istoria tis Thessalonikis kai o typos* (1993), 116.

33. *Journal de Salonique*, 24 August 1896; *Tamarix*, 3 (March 1997): "To kats mechri telikis ptoseos."

34. Molho, *Oi evraioi*, 117–120.

35. Tomanas, *Chroniko tis Thessalonikis, 1875–1920*, 104.

36. Tomanas, *Chroniko tis Thessalonikis, 1875–1920*, 77–78.

37. Tomanas, *Chroniko tis Thessalonikis, 1875–1920*, 104; Enepekidis, *Thessaloniki*, 342.

12 / The Macedonia Question, 1878–1908

1. N. Berkes, *The Development of Secularism in Turkey* (London, 1964/1998), 158; P. Risal, *La ville convoitée* (Paris, 1914), x, 203; "Les races sont des troupeaux," *La Solidaridad Ovradera*, 2 June 1911, cited in N. Cohen-Rak, "Salonique en 1911 à travers *La Solidaridad Ovradera*," *Revue des Études Juives*, CXL VIII (July–Dec. 1989), 477–485.

2. Fraser, "Adrianople, Salonika and Monastir," 149; Abbott, *Tale of a Tour*, 21–22; anon., "De Salonique à Bel-

grade," 114–115; de Meester, "Voyage," 20.

3. Choisy, *L'Asie Mineure*, 22; Mackenzie and Irby, *Travels*, 69.

4. Braun-Wiesbaden, *Eine türkische Reise*, 213–214.

5. H. N. Brailsford, *Macedonia: Its Races and their Future* (London, 1906), 103, 184–185.

6. FO 195/649, Calvert-Constantinople, 24 March 1860; 195/685, 10 June 1861.

7. H. Layard, *Early Adventures in Persia, Susiana and Babylonia* (London, 1887), ii, 379–380.

8. D. Dakin, *The Greek Struggle in Macedonia, 1897–1913* (Thessaloniki, 1966), 14–16; V. Papageorgiou, "Oi mikres ethnikes koinotites sti disi tis othomanikis Thessalonikis," *EIE, IZ' Panellinio Istoriko Synedrio: Praktika* (1997), 297–316.

9. Cited in FO 195/1324, *Ermis*, 1 Oct. 1880; Ch. Kaldaras, "Symvoli sti meleti tis drasis tou Genikou Proxeniou Thessalonikis Petrou Logotheti (1881–1885)," *EIE: Praktika* (1994), 414–432.

10. FO 195/1007, Blunt-Elliot, 11 Nov. 1872; Blunt-Elliott, 28 Nov. 1874; FO 195/1196, Wilkinson-Layard, 15 July 1878.

11. F. Blunt, *My Reminiscences* (London, 1918), 149.

12. FO 195/1322, "Letter from Captive Col. Synge."

13. "Details concerning the release of Colonel Synge, captured more than twenty years ago by the Greek band of Captain Nico in the district of Caterini, Salonica," *FRUS 1902* (Washington, 1903), 1012–1013.

14. "Brigandage in Macedonia," *Appleton's Journal: A Magazine of General Literature* (Nov. 1881), 469–472.

15. FO 78/1939, Wilkinson-London, 14 May 1866.

16. R. B. Woods, "Terrorism in the Age of Roosevelt: The Miss Stone Affair, 1901–1902," *American Quarterly*, 31:4 (Autumn 1979), 478–495; T. Carpenter, *The Miss Stone Affair: America's First Modern Hostage Crisis* (NY, 2003); L. B. Sherman, *Fires on the Mountain* (Boulder, Colo., 1980).

17. D. Livanios, "Bulgar-Yugoslav controversy over Macedonia and the British connection, 1939–1949," D. Phil. thesis, Oxford 1995, pp. 17–20; V. Vlasidis, "I avtonomisi tis Makedonias: apo tin theoria stin praxi," in V. Gounaris et al., ed., *Taftotites sti Makedonia* (Athens, 1997), 63–89.

18. G. Megas, *Oi "Varkarades" tis Thessalonikis: I anarchiki voulgariki omada kai oi vomvistikes energeies tou 1903* (1994), 47–51.

19. Steeg—Paris, 7 May 1903, in Bulgarian Academy of Sciences, *Macedonia: Documents and Materials* (Sofia, 1978), 483–490.

20. On the mosque plot, Brailsford, *Macedonia*, 135–136; I. Banac, *With Stalin against Tito: Cominformist Splits in Yugoslav Communism* (Cornell, 1988), 198.

21. "Odysseus," *Turkey in Europe* (London, 1900), 344; Brailsford, *Macedonia*, 102; Figures in Livanios, "Bulgar-Yugoslav controversy over Macedonia," 7.

22. J. Koliopoulos, "Brigandage and insurgency in the Greek domains," in D. Gondicas and C. Issawi, eds., *Ottoman Greeks in the Age of Nationalism* (Princeton, 1999), 143–160.

23. Zannas, *O Makedonikos Agonas*, 39; Brailsford, *Macedonia*, 218.

24. A. Souliotis-Nikolaides, *Apomnimonevmata* (1959), 43–45.

13 / The Young Turk Revolution

1. I. and M. Orga, *Ataturk* (1962), 9–47.

2. FO 195/2297, Lamb-O'Connor, 28 March 1908, Lamb-Barclay, 2 May 1908.

3. Ibid., Lamb-Barclay, 12 June 1908, 10 July 1908.

4. A. Sarrou, *La Jeune Turquie et la Révolution* (Paris, 1912), 19–21.

5. FO 195/2298, Lamb-Barclay, 24 July 1908.

6. A. Sarrou, *La Jeune Turquie et la Révolution*, 25.

7. FO 195/2298, *Yeni Asir*, 1 Sept. 1908; 195/2328 Lamb-Lowther, 21 April 1909.

8. Ibid., Lamb-Lowther, 29 April 1909.

9. F. McCullagh, *The Fall of Abd-ul-Hamid* (London, 1910), 274–277.

10. K. A. Vakalopoulos, *Neoturkoi kai Makedonia (1908–1912)* (1988), 282; R. Olson, "The Young Turks and the Jews: A Historiographical Revision," *Turcica: Revue d'Etudes Turques*, xviii (1986), 219–235.

11. K. A. Vakalopoulos, *Neoturkoi kai Makedonia (1908–1912)*, 246–247, 297.

12. J. Landau, *Tekinalp, Turkish Patriot, 1883–1961* (Istanbul, 1984), 91–107; S. J. Shaw and E. K. Shaw, *History of the Ottoman Empire and Modern Turkey*, Vol. II: *Reform, Revolution and Republic: the Rise of Modern Turkey, 1808–1975* (Cambridge, 1977), 301.

13. Eugene A. Cooperman, "Turco-Jewish Relations in the Ottoman City of Salonica, 1889–1912: Two Communities in Support of the Ottoman Empire," NYU, D.Phil.: 1991, *passim*, esp. pp. 104–144; J. Schechtman, *The Life and Times of Vladimir Jabotinsky* (no date), 1, 150–152.

14. J. Landau, *Tekinalp*, 9–10; M. Edelman, *David: The Story of Ben-Gurion* (New York, 1965), 52.

15. E. Benbassa, "Presse d'Istanbul et de Salonique au service du sionisme (1908–1914). Les motifs d'une allégeance," *Revue Historique*, 560 (Oct.–Dec. 1986), 337–367; A. Galanté, *Recueil de nouveaux documents inédits concernant l'histoire des Juifs de Turquie* (Istanbul, 1949), 36–39; J. Landau, *Tekinalp*, 21, 57–58.

16. K. A. Vakalopoulos, *Neoturkoi kai Makedonia*, 289: S. J. Shaw and E. K. Shaw, *History of the Ottoman Empire and Modern Turkey*, 277.

17. "Conversations avec le Nazim Bey," *Journal de Salonique*, Nov. 1909.

18. D. Dakin, *The Greek Struggle in Macedonia*, 405; *Nea Alithia*, 12 Nov. 1910.

19. Ionian Bank Archives (LSE), Half-yearly Report of the Salonica Branch, 1928.

20. K. Tomanas, *Chroniko tis Thessalonikis 1875–1920*, 34, 42; B. Pappenheim, *Sisyphus-Arbeit* (Leipzig, 1924).

21. K. Moskof, *Thessaloniki: tomi tis metapratikis polis* (Athens, 1978), 169.

22. M. Tremopoulos, "To syndikalistiko kinima ton trochiodromikon tis Thessalonikis," *EIE, IZ' Panellinion Istoriko Synedrio: Praktika* (1997), 395–420; P. Dumont, "A Jewish, Socialist and Ottoman Organisation: the Workers' Federation of Salonica," M. Tuncay and E. J. Zürcher, eds., *Socialism and Nationalism in the Ottoman Empire, 1876–1923* (London, 1994), 49–75.

23. G. Haupt, "Le début du mouvement socialiste en Turquie," *Le mouvement social*, 45 (Oct.–Dec. 1963), 121–137, 131–132.

24. P. Dumont, "Sources inédites pour l'histoire du mouvement ouvrier et des courants socialistes dans l'Empire Ottoman au debut du Xxe siècle," *Études Balkaniques*, 3 (1978), 16–34; I. Yalimov, "The Bulgarian community and the development of the socialist movement in the Ottoman empire during the period 1876–1923," in M. Tuncay and E. J. Zürcher, eds., *Socialism and Nationalism*, 89–108.

25. P. Dumont, "Une organisation socialiste ottomane: la fédération ouvrière de Salonique (1908–1912)," *Études Balkaniques* (1975), 76–88.

26. P. Dumont, "Sources inédites," 27.

27. "Les races sont des troupeaux," *La Solidaridad Ovradera*, 2 June 1911

cited in N. Cohen-Rak, "Salonique en 1911 à travers *La Solidaridad Ovradera*," *Revue des Études Juives*, CXLVIII (July–Dec. 1989), 477–485.

14 / The Return of Saint Dimitrios

1. C. Antonopoulos, "I apeleftherosis tis Thessalonikis apo ton Ayio Dimitrio to 1912," in Ch. Bakirtzis, ed., *Ayiou Dimitriou Thaumata* (Athens, 1997), 337–343. My thanks to Peter Brown for bringing this to my attention.
2. Memoirs of Lakis Dailakis, cited in K. A. Vakalopoulos, *Neotourkoi kai Makedonia*, 404.
3. J. Leune, *Une revanche, une étape: campagne de l'Armée Hellénique en Macedoine, 1912* (Paris, 1914), 308; Papanastasiou in Ch. Papastathis, "O Alexandros Papanastasiou kai i Thessaloniki," in his *Thessalonikeia kai Makedonika Analekta* (Thessaloniki, 1999), 157–167; A. Mazarakis-Ainian, *Mémoires* (Thessaloniki, 1979), 100; Papavasileiou in L. Tricha, ed., *Himerologia kai grammata apo to metopo: Valkanikoi polemoi, 1912–1913* (Athens, 1993), 307–310.
4. On flags, K. Tomanas, *Chroniko tis Thessalonikis, 1875–1920* (Thessaloniki, 1995), 168, 171; R. Rankin, *The Inner History of the Balkan War* (London, 1914), 345.
5. V. Nikoltsios and V. Gounaris, eds., *Apo to Sarantaporo sti Thessaloniki* (2002), 48–61; A. Mango, *Ataturk* (London, 2001).
6. Leune, 369–373.
7. "Bulgarians and Salonica," *The Orient*, 4 June 1913.
8. A. Buonaiuti, *Salonicco* (Milan, 1916), 62–63.
9. A. H. Trapmann, *The Greeks Triumphant* (London, 1915), 155–158.
10. Ibid.
11. Carnegie Endowment for International Peace, *Report of the International Commission*, 188–195; B.

Gounaris, "Doing business in Macedonia: Greek problems in British perspective (1912–1921)," *European Review of History*, 5:2 (1998), 169–180.
12. L. Maccas, "Salonique occupée et administrée par les Grecs," *Revue de Droit International Public*, 20 (1913), 207–242; K. Skordyles, "Réactions juives à l'annexion de Salonique par la Grèce," in I. Hassiotis, ed., *The Jewish Communities of Southeastern Europe* (1997), 503 note 10.
13. R. Molho, *Oi Evraioi tis Thessalonikis, 1856–1919* (Athens, 2001), 3242–3243; K. Skordyles, "Réactions juives à l'annexion de Salonique par la Grèce," 503–516.
14. R. Molho, *Oi Evraioi tis Thessalonikis, 1856–1919*, 244–245.
15. Maccas, 214–217; S. Marketos, "I ensomatosi tis sefaradikis Thessalonikis stin Ellada: to plaisio, 1912–1914," in n.a., *O ellinikos evraismos* (Athens, 1999), 69.
16. K. Raktivan, *Eggrafa kai simeioseis ek tis protis Ellinikis dioikiseos tis Makedonias* (1951).
17. H. Petropoulos, *I onomatothesia odon kai plateion* (1995), 128–129.
18. A. Scheikevitch, *Hellas? . . . Hélas! Souvenirs de Salonique* (Paris, 1922), 34–36; Buonaiuti, 100.
19. E. Hekimoglou, "Dyo anekdota keimena apo ti neoteri istoria tis Thessalonikis: ta paraleipomena tis apografis tou 1913," in Hekimoglou, ed., *Thessaloniki: Tourkokratia kai Mesopolemos* (Thessaloniki, 1995), 330–345; Tomanas, 176.
20. Buonaiuti, 141.

15 / The First World War

1. A. Fraccaroli, *Dalla Serbia invasa alle trincee di Salonicco* (Milan, 1916), 113–114.
2. J. Reed, *War in Eastern Europe: Travels through the Balkans in 1915* (London, 1999), 173.

3. A. Palmer, *The Gardeners of Salonika* (London, 1965), 45–46.

4. A. Scheikevitch, *Hellas? . . . Hélas!*, 143; J. Ancel, *Les Travaux et les Jours de l'Armée d'Orient (1915–1918)* (Paris, 1921), 78–87; Fraccaroli, 211; "Odysseus," "The Scenes of War—1," *Blackwood's Magazine*, 200 (Oct. 1916), 536.

5. P. Petrides, "I prosorini kyvernisi tis Thessalonikis apenanti sto aitima yia rizikes politeiakes kai koinonikes metarrythmiseis," in Dimos Thessalonikis, *Symposio: I Thessaloniki meta to 1912* (Thessaloniki, 1986), 139.

6. A. Scheikevitch, *Hellas? . . . Hélas!*, 143; G. Ward Price, *The Story of the Salonica Army* (London, 1918), 111–112.

7. A. C. Wratislaw, *A Consul in the East* (London, 1924), 332.

8. A. Scheikevitch, *Hellas? . . . Hélas!*, 183–185.

9. Pol Roussel, *Salonique au temps de la campagne d'Orient* (Paris, 1925), 78–79; L. Abastado, 52; H. Collinson Owen, *Salonica and After* (London, 1919), 19, 20, 89; D. Vaka, *In the Heart of German Intrigue* (Boston, 1918), 247.

10. Pol Roussel, *Salonique au temps de la campagne d'Orient*, 113; (J. M. Vassal), *Uncensored Letters from the Dardanelles* (London, n.d.), 250; Canudo, 83.

11. E. P. Stebbing, *At the Serbian Front in Macedonia* (London, 1917), 33–34.

12. W. McFee, *A Six-Hour Shift* (New York, 1920), 35; O. Rutter, *Tiadatha* (London, 1935), 41.

13. "The Misfit Soldier: A War Story 1914–1918 by . . . John William Roworth" [Edward Casey], Imperial War Museum 80/40/1. See also J. Bourke, ed., *The Misfit Soldier: Edward Casey's War Story, 1914–1918* (Cork UP, 1999). My thanks to my colleague Joanna Bourke for showing me this source.

14. Ancel, *Les travaux*, 136; E. Thomas,

L'Oeuvre Civilisatrice de l'Armée Française en Macedoine (Salonica, 1918), 3; "Odysseus," "The scene of war," 543; Lake, 277.

15. H. Lake, *In Salonica with our Army* (London, 1917), 17.

16. E.A.G., "Antiquities found in the British zone, 1915–1919," *Annual of the British School at Athens*, 23 (1918–1919), 10–43, and C. Picard, "Les recherches archéologiques de l'Armée Française en Macedoine, 1916–1919," *Annual of the British School at Athens*, 23 (1918–1919), 1–9.

17. Ibid., 6–7.

16 / The Great Fire

1. R. Preece, "Great Fire Impressions," *The Mosquito*, 119 (Sept. 1957).

2. Collinson Owen, 90–104; other eyewitness accounts include Harry Pierce in T. Mawson, *Life and Works of an English Landscape Architect* (London, 1927), 281–282; S. Luck, in the *Jewish Chronicle*, 5 Oct. 1917.

3. F. H. Smart, "The Great Fire," *The Mosquito*, 93 (March 1951).

4. A. Boué, *Receuil d'Itinéraires dans la Turquie d'Europe* (Vienna, 1854), 154; V. Adler, *Jews in Many Lands* (Philadelphia, 1905), 147.

5. *The Orient Weekly*, 2 Sept. 1917; A. Karadimou-Gerolympou, *I anoikodomisi tis Thessalonikis meta tin pyrkaia tou 1917* (Thessaloniki, 1995), 35.

6. Hetty Goldman-AJDC, New York, 22 Dec. 1918, AJDC (American Joint Distribution Committee), 1921, Reel 15/146, Greece.

7. *The Life and Work of a Northern Landscape Architect: Thomas Mawson* (Lancaster, 1978).

8. Hetty Goldman-AJDC, New York, 30 Nov. 1918, AJDC 1914–1918, file 110a, Greece.

9. Committee of JDC of America: Funds for Jewish War Sufferers—

JDC, 20 Feb. 1920, AJDC, 1919–1921, Greece, file 146.

10. Tomanas, *Chroniko*, 241.

11. Karadimou-Gerolympou, 139.

12. A. Pallis, "Racial migrations in the Balkans during the years 1912–1924," *Geographical Journal*, 315–317; R. Darques, *Salonique au XXe siècle* (Paris, 2000), 68–78, 103.

17 / *The Muslim Exodus*

1. N. Clayer, "Trois centres Mevlevis Balkaniques au travers des documents d'archives Ottomans: Les Mevlevihane d'Elbasan, de Serez et de Salonique," *Osmanli Arastirinalari* [*Journal of Ottoman Studies*], xiv (1994), 11–28.

2. N. Moschopoulos, "I Ellas kata ton Evlia Tselebi," *EEBS*, 16 (1940), 346–347.

3. Carnegie Endowment for International Peace, *Report of the International Commission to Inquire into the Causes and Conduct of the Balkan Wars* (Washington, DC, 1914), 106, 148–151; A. J. Toynbee, *The Western Question in Greece and Turkey* (London, 1922), 138–141; FO 371/1997, Morgan-Mallet, 20 July 1914.

4. A. Zannas, *O Makedonikos Agonas: Anamniseis*, 80–81, 84.

5. FO 195/2453, Lamb-Lowther, 14 May 1913, 29 April 1913.

6. IAM/GDM (*Istorika Archeia Makedonias: Geniki Dioikisis Makedonias*) 76, "Oi logoi tis metanastevseos".

7. IAM/GDM 776, Astynomiki diefthynsis Thessaloniki—GDM, 9 April 1914; FO 371/1997, Morgan-Mallet, 20 July 1914; Bompard-Doumergue, 26 April 1914, Ministère des Affaires Étrangères, *Documents Diplomatiques: Affaires Balkaniques*, I: 1912 (Paris, n.d.), 125.

8. *Le Jeune Turc*, 11 March 1914; FO 371/1997, Morgan-Mallet, 20 July 1914.

9. FO 371/1997, Mallet-Grey, 22 June 1914.

10. FO 371/1996, Morgan-Mallet, 21 March 1914; G. Mavrogordatos, *Stillborn Republic: Social Coalitions and Party Strategies in Greece, 1922–1936* (California, 1983), 237.

11. R. Tesal, *Selanik'ten Istanbul'a* (Istanbul, 1998): my thanks to Alexandre Toumarkine for giving me a copy of this book, and to Sukru Ilicak for translating passages for me.

12. P. S. Delta, *Eleftherios Venizelos: Imerologio-Anamniseis-Martyries-Allilografia*, I (1988), 75–76.

13. Tesal, *Selanik'ten Istanbul'a*, 47–49.

14. P. S. Delta, *Eleftherios Venizelos*, 137.

15. IAM/GDM 87/1, Anotera dioikisis chorofylakis Makedonias, "Egklimatikotitos minos Sept. 1922," 20 Oct. 1922; 87/1, Astynomiki diefthynsis Thessalonikis, 22 Dec. 1922.

16. S.P. Ladas, *The Exchange of Minorities*, 335–338.

17. Bompard-Doumergue, 26 April 1914, Ministère des Affaires Étrangères, *Documents Diplomatiques: Affaires Balkaniques*, I: 1912 (Paris, n.d.), 126.

18. Y. Mourelos, "The 1914 persecutions and the first attempt at an exchange of minorities between Greece and Turkey," *Balkan Studies*, 26:2 (1985), 389–413; G. Anastasiades, *I Thessaloniki ton efimeridon* (1994), 234; S. P. Ladas, *The Exchange of Minorities*, 28–29.

19. S. Marketos, "I ensomatosi tis Sefaradikis Thessalonikis stin Ellada: to plaisio," *O ellinikos evraismos* (1999), 77; A. Aktar, "Homogenising the economy: Turkifying the economy," in R. Hirschon, ed., *Crossing the Aegean: An Appraisal of the 1923 Compulsory Population Exchange between Greece and Turkey* (New York, 2003), 87.

20. S. Loukatos, *Politeiografia tis Nomarchiakis Periferias tis Thessalonikis,* I (Athens, 1987) 37–38; Tomanas, *Dromoi,* 141.

21. On western Macedonia, FO 286/874, Hasluck-Bentinck, 22 April 1923; Tesal, *Selanik'ten Istanbul'a,* 60–63; Anastasiades, *I Thessaloniki ton efimeridon,* 244.

22. FO 286/902, Crew-Bentinck, 16 Jan. 1924; K. Tomanas, *Chroniko tis Thessalonikis, 1921–1944* (1996), 39–41; S.P. Ladas, *The Exchange of Populations,* 428–429.

23. Tomanas, *Dromoi kai yeitones tis Thessalonikis,* 141.

24. T. Köker and L. Keskiner, "Lessons in refugeehood: forced migrants in Turkey," in Hirschon, *Crossing the Aegean,* 198; FO 286/874, "Council of Elders of Kirk-Kilissi," 7 Dec. 1923; R. Darques, *Salonique au XXe siècle* (Paris, 2000), 271; *Makedonika Nea,* 25 May 1924; Anastasiades, *I Thessaloniki ton efimeridon,* 244; S. Pelagides, "Metra kai antimetra meta tin ellinotourkiki symvasi tis antallagis," *Thessaloniki,* 3 (1992), 121–142; FO 286/898, Edmonds-Lindsay, 27 Feb. 1924.

25. FO 286/902, Crew-Bentinck, 16 Jan. 1924.

26. Ayioreitiki Fotothiki, *Thessalonikeis Fotografoi tou Ayiou Orous: O filellinas Othomanos fotografos Ali Sami* (1996); *Efimeris Valkanion,* 3 June 1925, "To temenos Hamza Bey".

27. IAM/GDM 69, President of the 1st Sub-Committee/Mixed Committee for the Exchange of Greek and Turkish Populations—Governor-General of Macedonia, 29 Dec. 1924.

28. *Makedonika Nea,* 3 Jan. 1925.

29. Hekimoglou, "Oi teleftaioi mousoulmanoi fevgoun apo ti Thessaloniki," *Thessaloniki: tourkokratia kai mesopolemos,* 377–386.

30. S. Loukatos, *Politeiografia,* 36; R. Darques, *Salonique au XXe siècle: de la cité ottomane à la métropole grecque* (Paris, 2000), 187–193; A. Dimitriades, *"Phoinix agiros": I Thessaloniki tou 1925–1935* (1994), 205, for an example of ghostly activity.

31. *Makedonika Nea,* 22 March 1924, "Minaredes".

32. Hastaoglou and K-G, "Thessaloniki, 1900–1940," interview 8 Nov. 1925, *Thessaloniki meta to 1912,* 465.

33. Cited in Dimitriades, 45.

34. Ibid., 62–63.

35. Ibid., 73–77.

18 / City of Refugees

1. A. Galiropoulou, "I parousia ton Roson sti Thessaloniki kata ton Proto Pankosmio Polemo," 141–153, and I. Hasiotis and G. Kasapian, "I armeniki paroikia tis Thessalonikis: Idrysi, organosi, ideologia kai koinoniki ensomatosi," 257–284, in *Thessaloniki meta to 1912.*

2. H. A. Shaw, "Greek refugees from the Caucasus and the work of the American Red Cross at Salonique," *Journal of International Relations,* 12 (1921–22), 44–49; S.P. Ladas, *The Exchange of Minorities: Bulgaria, Greece and Turkey* (New York, 1932), 16.

3. Hemingway reproduced in K. Andrews, *Athens Alive* (Athens, 1979), 306.

4. http://manila.djh.dk/Stella/stories/storyReader$19.

5. H. Morgenthau, *I was Sent to Athens* (New York, 1929), 101; http://manila.djh.dk/Stella/stories/storyReader$19.

6. J. Ancel, *La Macédoine: Etude de colonisation contemporaine* (Paris, 1930).

7. Ibid.; Ladas, *Exchange of Populations,* 660.

8. R. Clogg, "A millet within a millet: the *Karamanlides,*" in D. Gondicas and C. Issawi, eds., *Ottoman Greeks in the Age of Nationalism* (Princeton, 1999), 115–143.

9. Anastasiades, *I Thessaloniki ton Efimeridon,* 238–239; G. Anastasiades and

E. Hekimoglou, *I fotografia stin Thessaloniki tou mesopolemou* (1998), 27.

10. Anastasiades, *I Thessaloniki ton Efimeridon*, 224–225.

11. Tesal, 61; G. Mavrogordatos, *Stillborn Republic: Social Coalitions and Party Strategies in Greece, 1922–1936* (U. California, 1983), 194–195.

12. J. Ancel, *La Macédoine: Etude*, 291.

13. A. Anastasiadis and P. Stathakopoulos, "I fysiognomia tis Pano Polis stin istoria, poleodomia kai architektoniki typologia," *I Thessaloniki meta to 1912* (1986), 525–526.

14. J. Playber, *La problème de l'habitation à Salonique et à la campagne* (n.d.), 14.

15. A. Karadimou-Gerolympou, "Prosfygiki enkatastasi kai o anaschediasmos ton voreionelladikon poleon (1912–1940)," in n.a., *O xerizmos kai i alli patrida: oi prosfygoupoleis stin Ellada* (1999), 89–109; V. Hastaoglou, "Metaschimatismos astikou chorou sti Thessaloniki," in ibid., 331.

16. *Efimeris Valkanion*, 10 Nov. 1925.

17. Alexandros Svolos files, author's possession; also *Efimeris Valkanion*, 31 March 1925.

18. Darques, passim.

19. Cited in Dimitriades, 91, 104–105; *Phoni ton Ergaton*, 14 Nov. 1923.

20. Ibid., 93–95.

21. Dimitriades, 106; Hastaoglou, 326.

22. Bunis, *Voices*, 317.

19 / *Workers and the State*

1. W. Miller, *Travels and Politics in the Near East* (London, 1898), 364–365, 388.

2. P. Pizanias, *Oi ftochoi ton poleon* (Athens, 1993), 79–84, 140.

3. Dangas, *Symboli stin erevna yia tin oikonomiki kai koinoniki exelixi tis Thessalonikis* (1998), 306; M. Mazower, *Greece and the Interwar Economic Crisis* (Oxford, 1991), 136.

4. See E. Hekimoglou, "Thessaloniki, 1912–1940: Economic Develop-

ments," in I. Hassiotis, ed., *Queen of the Worthy: Thessaloniki, History and Culture* (1997), 147–148

5. K. Tomanas, *Chroniko*, 16–17.

6. A. Dangas, *O hafies: to kratos kata tou kommounismou* (Athens, 1995), 154, 271.

7. Cited by A. Dangas, *O hafies: to kratos kata tou kommounismou*, 270–271.

8. Ibid., 51–52.

9. IAM/GDM, file 87/1, Astynomiki diefthynsi Thessalonikis—Archigeion Chorofylakis, 22 Dec. 1922.

10. Cited in Mazower, "I synkrotisi tou antikommounistikou kratous," 83.

11. "Osoi ginoun prothypourgoi," by Vamvakaris, in G. Holst, *Road to Rembetika* (Athens, 1975), 104.

12. FO 371/20389 R 3310/220/19, Lomax [Salonica]-Athens, 27 May 1936.

13. J. O. Iatrides, ed., *Ambassador MacVeagh Reports: Greece, 1933–1947* (Princeton, 1980), 86.

20 / *Dressing for the Tango*

1. *Efimeris Valkanion*, 23 Sept. 1925.

2. A. Dimitriades, *"Foinix Agiros": i Thessaloniki tou 1925–35* (1994), 119–121.

3. Ibid., 112–113.

4. Tomanas, *Chroniko*, 131–132.

5. E. Counio-Amariglio, *Peninta chronia meta . . .* (1995), chapter 1.

6. Dimitriades, *"Foinix Agiros,"* 134–135.

7. Tomanas, *Tavernes*, 121–122.

8. Dimitriades, *"Foinix Agiros,"* 158–164.

9. Bunis, *Voices from Jewish Salonika* (Jerusalem, 1999), 45; 288–289.

10. E. Avdela, "Thessaloniki: o sosialismos ton 'allon'", *Ta Istorika* (June-Dec. 1993), 189; Dangas, *Hafies*, 73 n. 33.

11. *Efimeris ton Valkanion*, 29 May 1925.

12. N. Casey, IWM ms. 80/40/1, page 38. My thanks to Joanna Bourke for

bringing this remarkable document to my attention.

13. Dimitriades, *"Foinix Agiros,"* 35–37.
14. IAM/GD V. Ellados, B/26/1: various documents.
15. G. Ioannou, *Protevousa ton prosfygon,* 15.
16. *Efimeris ton Valkanion,* 1 April 1925.
17. *Efimeris ton Valkanion,* 30 April 1925.
18. M. Vamvakaris, *Avtoviografia,* ed. A. Vellou-Kail (1978), 164–165.
19. "Litaneia." In G. Holst, *Road to Rembetika* (Athens, 1975), 110–112. I have adapted the translation.
20. Dimitriades, *"Foinix Agiros,"* 87.
21. Bunis, *Voices,* 330.
22. Ibid., 294–297, 334–335.
23. Ibid., 278.
24. Ibid., 326, n.75.
25. Dimitriades, 87 seq.
26. Bunis, 117, 325.
27. Tomanas, *Katoikoi,* 130–131; Dimitriades, *"Foinix Agiros"* 143–144.

21 / *Greeks and Jews*

1. Bunis, *Voices,* 119.
2. E. Morin, *Vidal et les siens* (Paris, 1989), 87.
3. M. Levene, *War, Jews and the New Europe: The Diplomacy of Lucien Wolf, 1914–1919* (Oxford, 1992), 171–173.
4. Text in F. Constantopoulou and T. Veremis, eds., *Documents on the History of Greek Jews* (Athens, 1998), 103–110.
5. A. Nar, "I theatriki drastiriotita ton Evraion tis Thessalonikis mesa apo ta dimosievmata tou typou tous," in his *"Keimena epi aktis thalassas": meletes kai arthra yia tin Evraiki Koinotita tis Thessalonikis* (1997), 205.
6. Bunis, *Voices,* 120–121.
7. F. Constantopoulou and T. Veremis, eds., *Documents,* 127.
8. Ibid.
9. Ibid., 174.
10. S. Raphael, "The longing for Zion in Judeo-Spanish [Ladino] poetry," M. Rozen, ed., *The Jews in Turkey and the Balkans, 1808–1945* (Tel Aviv, 2002), 217.
11. M. Vassilikou, "Politics of the Jewish Community of Salonika in the Inter-War Years: Party Ideologies and Party Competition," D. Phil. thesis, UCL (Oct. 1999), 158–159, has a good discussion; for 20,000 in Paris, see I. Skourtis, "Metanastefsi ton Evraion tis Thessalonikis sti Gallia," *Makedonika,* 243; other figures in N. Abravanel, "Paris et le séphardisme ou l'affirmation sépharadiste à Paris dans les années trente," in W. Busse, ed., *Sephardica: Hommage à Haim Vidal Sephiha* (Frankfurt, 1996), 497–523; see also Gennadios Library, Dragoumis Papers: 38:2 (General Directorate of Macedonia: Jews/Thessaloniki [1932–35]).
12. Gennadios Library, Dragoumis Papers: 38:2, memo from Press Office, 13 Dec. 1932.
13. Constantopoulou and Veremis, eds., *Documents,* 222–223; 231.
14. Vassilikou, 277–285; Bunis, *Voices from Jewish Salonika,* 271.
15. P. Dumont, "La correspondance du Joseph Nehama avec l'Alliance Israélite Universelle," in *Oi Evraioi ston Elliniko Horo* (1995), 131–146; Vassilikou, 200–205.
16. B. Pierron, "Histoire des relations entre les Grecs et les Juifs de 1821 à 1945," Thèse de doctorat, INALCO, Paris, Oct. 1993, 598; K. Foundanopoulos, "I glossa tou syndikalismou: ta katastatika ton ergatikon somateion tis Thessalonikis (1914–1936)," *Ta Istorika,* 18–19 (June–Dec. 1993), 205–227.
17. Cited in G. Mavrogordatos, *Stillborn Republic: Social Coalitions and Party Strategies in Greece, 1922–1936* (California, 1983), 238–239.
18. Venizelos cited in Pierron, 569.
19. Pierron, 558–560.

20. G. Mavrogordatos, *Stillborn Republic*, 260.

21. Pierron, 574–575.

22. Avdela, "Thessaloniki: o socialismos ton 'allon,' " 199–200.

23. Pierron, 668 seq.; P. Constantopoulou and T. Veremis, eds., *Documents*, 142.

24. Vassilikou, 96–98; text in Pierron, 688–689.

25. Pierron, 697.

26. Ibid., 716–718.

27. Ibid., 705.

28. See K. Tomanas, *Oi katoikoi tia palias Thessalonikis*, 48–50; Dim. Sfaellos archive, "EEE" file, ELIA; Mavrogordatos, *Stillborn Republic*, 258.

29. T. Tsironis, "I organosis Ethniki Enosis 'I Ellas' sti Thessaloniki tou mesopolemou (1927–1936)," *Thessaloniki*, 6 (2002).

30. Constantopoulou and Veremis, 175–192.

31. Articles in *To Fos*, 4 April 1933, and *Le Progres*, 3–4 April 1933.

32. G. Mavrogordatos, *Stillborn Republic*, 231.

33. On anti-Venizelist strategies, see G. Mavrogordatos, *Stillborn Republic*, 203–214.

34. D. Benbassat-Benby, "Haim 'la sousta,' " *L'Arche* (Feb. 1998), 59.

35. A. Brouskou, "Evraies trofoi sto christianiko vrefokomio 'Ayios Stylianos' stis arches tou 20ou aiona," in *Oi evraioi ston elliniko choro*, 33–42; E. Counio-Amariglio and A. Nar, eds., *Proforikes martyries evraion tis Thessalonikis yia to Olokavtoma* (1998), 54; A. Dangas, *Symvoli*, 529–571.

36. A. Karathanassis, "The relations between the Jewish community and Metropolitan Gennadios of Thessaloniki (1912–1951)," in I. Hassiotis, ed., *The Jewish Communities of Southeastern Europe from the 15th Century to the End of World War II* (1997), 223–228; E. Counio-Amariglio and A. Nar, 188, 316.

37. F. Ambatzopoulou, "The image of the Jew in the literature of Salonika," in P. Mackridge and E. Yannakakis, eds., *The Development of a Greek Macedonian Cultural Identity since 1912* (New York), 220–221.

22 / Genocide

1. Kentro Istorias Thessalonikis, *Thessaloniki, 1917–1967: I taftotita tis polis mesa apo to Dimotiko Archeio* (1995), 51; V. Gounaris and P. Papapoliviou, eds., *O foros tou aimatos stin katochiki Thessaloniki: xeni kyriarchia-antistasi kai epiviosi* (2001), 17.

2. E. Drosaki, *En Thessaloniki . . .* (1985), 44, 57.

3. H. V. Sephiha, "Dernier Pessah à Salonique (1942)" in *Société des études juives*, 465–470; Archives Diplomatiques, Nantes. Box 33 (Salonique): "Situation en Grèce du Nord," 28 Oct. 1941.

4. FO 371/33175 R 610/281, "Conditions in Salonica," 7 January 1942.

5. Monthly births and deaths from Red Cross sources in FO 371/42366 W13768/75, Mallet-London, 15 Sept. 1944; cf. the similar figures provided in Gounaris and Papapolyviou, eds., *Foros tou aimatos*, 138–141.

6. Rosenberg-Bormann, 23 April 1941 in FO 645, box 303/USA-371 [IWM]. M. Molho, *In Memoriam: Hommage aux Victimes Juives des Nazis en Grèce* (1973), 67.

7. M. Molho, *In Memoriam:* 47–51; Bundesarchiv Koblenz, NS 30/75, "Abschlussbericht," 15 Nov. 1941.

8. On Himmler, H. Fleischer, *Stemma kai swastika* (Athens, 1995), ii, 303.

9. *Apogevmatini*, 11 July 1942.

10. D. Carpi, ed., *Italian Diplomatic Documents on the History of the Holocaust in Greece (1941–1943)*, (Tel Aviv, 1999), 82.

11. Kammonas in Pierron, 865–866; *Apoyevmatini*, 16–22 October 1942, 9 November 1942; Yiacoel, 87.

12. On Fardis, see Special War Crimes Court Martial (Athens), *Praktika*, 11 Feb–5 March 1959, testimony of Coen, pp. 31–33.

13. Zentrale Stelle der Landesjustizverwaltungen (Ludwigsburg): AR-Z 139/59 (Merten proceedings), B13–420, pp. 260–262 is the most thorough account; Molho, *In Memoriam*, 70–71.

14. Molho, *In Memoriam* 383–385; Yiacoel, 72–75

15. M. Novich, *The Passage of the Barbarians* (Hull, 1989), 56–57.

16. Yiacoel, 58, 75–76; Molho, *In Memoriam*, 386; Special War Crimes Court Martial (Athens), *Praktika*, 11 Feb–5 March 1959, testimony of Kyriakides, pp. 94–96.

17. C. Browning, *The Origins of the Final Solution* (London, 2004).

18. Politisches Archiv Auswärtiges Amt (PAAA) (Bonn), "Judenfrage in Griechenland: 1941–1943," R 100870, Suhr-Rademacher, 11 July 1942; D. Carpi, ed., *Italian Diplomatic Documents*, 69–72.

19. Yiacoel, 82; Wisliceny affidavit, 611; PAAA "Judenfrage in Griechenland: 1941–1943," R 100870/057, Luther-Athens, 25 January 1943; ibid., 059, Altenburg-Berlin, 26 Jan. 1943.

20. Molho, *In Memoriam*, 76–80.

21. *Apoyevmatini*, 25 Feb 1943.

22. *Praktika*, 70, 82, 108 (see note 12).

23. J. Stroumsa, *Geiger in Auschwitz: Ein jüdisches Überlebensschicksal aus Saloniki 1941–1967* (Konstanz, 1993), 36–37.

24. Yiacoel, 119–120.

25. D. Carpi, ed., *Italian Diplomatic Documents*, 136–137; *Apoyevmatini*, 8 March 1943.

26. S. Levy, "I apagogi ton katoikon tou Rezi," *Israilitikon Vima*, 4 July 1947; *Apoyevmatini*, 16 March 1943; Carpi, ed., *Italian Diplomatic Documents*, 152.

27. Molho, *In Memoriam*, 99–100.

28. D. Carpi, ed., *Italian Diplomatic Documents*, 145; "Excerpts from the Salonika diary of Lucillo Merci (Feb.–Aug. 1943)," *Yad Vashem Studies*, XVIII (1987), 303–304.

29. A. Kitroeff, "The Jews in Greece, 1941–1944: Eye-witness accounts," *Journal of the Hellenic Diaspora*, xii:3 (Fall 1985); A. Apostolou, " 'The exception of Salonika': Bystanders and collaborators in northern Greece," *Holocaust and Genocide Studies*, 14:2 (Fall 2000), 165–196, 180.

30. Kounio, 39; E. Kounio-Amariglio and A. Nar, eds., *Proforikes martyries evraion tis Thessalonikis yia to Olokavtoma* (1998), 367, 399; *Praktika dikis Hasson, Albala ktl.*, 42.

31. D. Carpi, ed., *Italian Diplomatic Documents*, 178–179; *Praktika dikis Hasson, Albala ktl.*, 36.

32. "Letters from Salonika, 1943," *The Jewish Museum of Greece: Newsletter*, 33 (Autumn 1992), 4–8.

33. I. Matarasso, "And yet not all of them died . . ." in S. Bowman, ed., *The Holocaust in Salonika*, 192; E. Kounio-Amariglio and A. Nar, eds., *Proforikes martyries*, 23.

34. *Praktika dikis Hasson, Albala ktl.*, 37–39, 65; Molho, *In Memoriam*, 101–102.

35. Kounio, *From Thessaloniki*, 43.

36. *Praktika dikis Hasson, Albala ktl.*, 57; "Letters from Salonika, 1943," *The Jewish Museum of Greece*, 5–6; Ambatzopoulou, *Holokavtoma*, 158–159; E. Kounio-Amariglio and A. Nar, eds., *Proforikes martyries*, 387.

37. Ambatzopoulou, *Holokavtoma*, 142–143.

38. B. Spengler-Axiopoulou, "Allilengyi kai voitheia," in R. Benveniste, ed., *Oi Evraioi tis Elladas stin katochi* (1998), 20; J. Weber, *Prosopa*, 10; *Praktika dikis Hasson, Albala ktl.*, 109.

39. Yiacoel, 108–109.

40. E. Kounio-Amariglio and A. Nar, eds., *Proforikes martyries*, 94.

41. Ibid., 45.
42. Drosakis, *En Thessaloniki*, 90; G. Andreades, *Kalamaria mou axechasti* (1994), 71–72.
43. Apostolou, " 'The Exception of Salonika,' " 175; Molho, *In Memoriam*, 127–131.
44. Gounaris and Papapolyviou, eds., *Foros tou Aimatos*, 101.
45. D. Czech, *Kalendarium der Ereignisse im Konzentrationslager Auschwitz-Birkenau, 1939–1945* (Rowohlt, 1989), 445–480.

23 / *Aftermath*

1. N. Hammond, *Venture into Greece: With the Guerrillas, 1943–1944* (London, 1983), 64–65.
2. *To Fos*, 21–26 April 1945; Douros report to Simonides, 13 June 1943, YDIP files; Kounio, *From Thessaloniki*, 159–160.
3. Douros-Simonides, 13 June 1943, YDIP files.
4. YDIP files, Dimitrios V.-YDIP, 9 April 1943 (Some names have been changed).
5. Zentrale Stelle der Landesjustizverwaltungen (Ludwigsburg): AR-Z 139/59 (Merten proceedings), B13–420, pp. 241–248 (Douros testimony).
6. YDIP files.
7. ASKI K411, 23/4/23; ELIA, Archeio Voulgarikis Katochis kai Propagandas sti Makedonia, 14/313; Matarasso, 164–165; Special War Crimes Court Martial (Athens), *Praktika*, 11 Feb–5 March 1959, testimony of Chrysochoou, pp. 65–66, 99–100.
8. NA RG 59/868.00/1324, Berry (Istanbul)-State, 6 Dec. 1943, enclosing "Memorandum of Dim. Andreades, Nomarch of Drama, Concerning the Situation in Macedonia," 18 Oct. 1943; Matarasso, 223.
9. ASKI 23/4/121.
10. Matarasso, 178–192; *To Fos*, 16 March 1945; Israel Jacobson (AJDC), Salonica, August 1945; Omiron Israeliton Polonias—AJDC, 17 Nov. 1945, AJDC archives, gives a figure of 1,157.
11. "Despoues de la catastrofa en Salonique," I. J. Levy, ed. and translator, *And the World Stood Silent: Sephardic Poetry of the Holocaust* (Urbana, Ill., 1989), 162–163.
12. Israel Jacobson (AJDC), Salonica, August 1945 (AJDC archives).
13. B. Mazur-Louis Sobel (JDC), 20 March 1945 (AJDC archives).
14. I. O. Jacobson-Phillip Bernstein, 12 Nov. 1945 (AJDC archives); Wiener Library, HA 15-1/2/7/C, "Greece," April 1946 (Henriques Collection); "Greece," 20 Dec. 1945, AJDC files.
15. *Israilitikon Vima*, 3 Oct. 1947.
16. Jewish Community of Salonica-AJDC (New York), 24 July 1946 (AJDC: file 455, AR 45/64), ibid., "Country director's report on Greece," 5 Sept. 1950.
17. *Israilitikon Vima*, 22 Feb. 1946; ibid., 15 March 1946; ibid., 22 March 1946, 10 Oct. 1946.
18. UNRRA archives (New York), PAG-4/3.0.12.0.1:4.
19. *Fos*, 19–20 May 1946.
20. *Evraiki Estia*, 28 Jan. 1949.
21. *Israilitikon Vima*, 1 Feb. 1946, 24 May 1946.
22. *Fos*, 28 February 1945; *Israilitikon Vima*, 18–19 July 1947; 3 Oct. 1947; "Zaploutos!," *Israilitikon Vima*, 29 Nov. 1946.
23. *Israilitikon Vima*, 7 Feb. 1947, 9 May 1947; ibid., 28 Jan. 1949.
24. J. Jacobson—AJDC (New York), June 25, 1949 (AJDC 467, AR 44/64).
25. *Evraiki Epitheorisis*, 6 Feb. 1953.
26. Serefas, *Ptomata*, 80–87.
27. N. Kokallidou-Nahmias in *I Thessaloniki sti dekaetia tou '60* (1994), 35.
28. C. Packer, *Return to Salonika* (London, 1964), 3; E. Eden and N.

Stavroulakis, *Salonika: A Family Cookbook* (Athens, 1997), 34–35.

29. J. Stroumsa, *Geiger in Auschwitz*, 74.

Conclusion / The Memory of the Dead

1. Qur'an, Sura 79: 10–14.
2. M. Molho, *Usos y costumbres de los Sefardies de Salonica* (Madrid, 1959), ch. 6; N. Vatin and S. Yerasimos, "Documents sur les cimetières Ottomans, II," *Turcica*, 26 (1994), 169–187.
3. E. Kakoulidou, "Ta ellinika orthodoxa nekrotafeia tis Thessalonikis to 190 aiona," *Makedonika*, 22 (1982), 391–420.
4. N. G. Pentzikis (translated L. Marshall), *Mother Thessaloniki* (Athens, 1998), 113.
5. I. J. Levy and R. L. Zumwalt, "Madame Sara: a spirit medium between two worlds," in Y. Stillman and N. Stillman, eds., *From Iberia to Diaspora: Studies in Sephardic History and Culture* (Brill, Leiden, 1999), 331–345.
6. E. Kakoulidou, "Ta ellinika orthodoxa nekrotafeia tis Thessalonikis to 19° aiona," *Makedonika*, 22 (1982), 391–420; V. Dimitriades, *Topografia tis Thessalonikis kata tin epochi tis Tourkokratias, 1430–1912* (1983), 449–452.
7. Pentzikis (translated by L. Marshall), *Mother Thessaloniki*, 23.
8. A. Adamantiou, *I Vyzantini Thessaloniki* (Athens, 1914), I; G. Ioannou, *I protevousa ton prosfygon* (1985), 105.

9. M. Hadzi Ioannou, *Astygrafia Thessalonikis* (1880), β.
10. Etaireia Makedonikon Spoudon, *Eortastikos Tomos: 50 Chronia, 1939–1989* (1992), 27.
11. Ioannou, *Protevousa ton prosfygon*, 46.
12. A. Kyriakidou-Nestoros, "I Thessaloniki tis psychis mou," in *Logotechnia tis Thessalonikis* (1989), 278–281.
13. C. Stewart, "Immanent or eminent domain? The contest over Thessaloniki's Rotonda," in R. Layton et al., eds., *Destruction and Conservation of Cultural Property* (London, 2001), 182–198; V. Dimitriades, *Topografia tis Thessalonikis kata tin epochi tis Tourkokratias* (1983), 299–300; C. Hadzantoniou-Delivoyiatsi, "O minares tis Rotontas," *Makedonika*, (1995), 59–74.
14. Stewart, "Immanent or eminent domain?" 190; G. Agelopoulos, "Political practices and multiculturalism: the case of Salonica," in J. Cowan, ed., *Macedonia: The Politics of Identity and Difference* (London, 2000).
15. G. Angelopoulou, "Politikes praktikes kai polipolitismikotita," *O Politis*, 35–43.
16. B. Lefkowicz, "The Jewish community of Thessaloniki: An exploration of memory and identity in a Mediterranean city," Ph.D., University of London, 1999, 18–19.
17. J. Hacker, "The Sephardim in the Ottoman empire," in H. Beinart, ed., *The Sephardi Legacy*, ii (Jerusalem, 1992), 111; G. Tsaras, ed., *I teleftaia alosi tis Thessalonikis (1430)* (1985), 119–120.

Glossary

agha	janissary commander
ayan	provincial landed notables
ayios/ayia	saint
bazaar	open market
bedesten/bezesten	covered market for valuables
beratli	beneficiaries of the capitulation agreements (thus, clients of a European state)
bey	high military title
boza	drink made of fermented barley and millet
caique	long, fast boat
caravanseray	a hostelry for travellers
cavass	bodyguard
cortijo	courtyard
defterdar	treasurer
dervish	member of Muslim mystical order
devshirme	child slave levy
djami	large mosque
Dönme	see Ma'min
dragoman	interpreter
Effendi	title of respect
fetva	advisory opinion issued by mufti
firman	imperial decree
gavur	infidel (used of Christians) (also giaour)
ghazi	warrior fighting for Islam
halvades	sellers of halva
hamal	porter, carrier
hamam	bath-house
haremlik	women's/family quarters
Hatt-i-Humayun	imperial decree/rescript
herem	a decree of excommunication
hodja	teacher

Glossary

imam	Muslim prayer-leader
imaret	a complex of public buildings associated with a mosque
intari	gabardine overcoat worn by Jewish men
janissary	member of imperial infantry corps
Judesmo	Judeo-Spanish (lit. "Jewish")
kadi	judge
kahal	congregation of a synagogue
kahya	agent, representative
khan	hostelry
komitadji	armed band member (lit. "committee-man")
konak	villa, governor's building
limonadji	lemonade-seller
loustros	shoe-black
mahalla	neighbourhood, district
Ma'min	followers of Sabbetai Zevi who converted to Islam
Marrano	Iberian Jews who converted to Catholicism
medrese	religious school attached to a mosque
mesjid	small mosque
millet	religious community
modistra	seamstress [dim. modistroula]
mollah	Muslim judge and senior member of the ulema
mufti	Muslim jurisconsult
muqarna	honeycomb combination of miniature squinches
narghilé	hookah
odos	street
orta	a janissary battalion
oud	musical instrument
pasha	governor, or high-ranking military officer
pasvant	neighbourhood watchman
pechlivanides	wrestlers
plateia	square
sarraf	personal banker, money-lender
shaknisirs	projecting covered windows
shari'a	Muslim canonical law
sheykh	elder, head of a religious order
sheykh-ul-Islam	Chief Mufti of the Ottoman empire
tekke	Sufi lodge
tseftiteli	belly-dance
turbe	mausoleum

ulema	the doctors of Muslim canon law, tradition and theology
vakf	charitable endowment
vilayet	province
yataghan	a long dagger, sword
yürük	Turkish nomad
zaharoplasteion	patisserie
ziyara	pilgrimage to the tomb of a holy man

Index

473

ALSO BY MARK MAZOWER

*"This splendid book makes a convincing case for a
different version of twentieth-century European history."*
—The New York Times Book Review

DARK CONTINENT

Europe's Twentieth Century

Dark Continent provides an alternative history of the twentieth century, one in which the triumph of democracy was anything but a forgone conclusion, and fascism and communism provided rival political solutions that battled and sometimes triumphed in an effort to determine the course the continent would take. Mark Mazower strips away myths that have comforted us since World War II, revealing Europe as an entity constantly engaged in a bloody project of self-invention. Here is a history not of inevitable victories and forward marches, but of narrow squeaks and unexpected twists, where townships boast a bronze of Mussolini on horseback one moment, only to melt it down and recast it as a pair of noble partisans the next. Unflinching and intelligent, *Dark Continent* provides a challenging vision of Europe's past, present, and future—and confirms Mark Mazower as a historian of valuable gifts.

History/0-679-75704-X

THE ANATOMY OF FASCISM
by Robert O. Paxton

What *is* fascism? Robert O. Paxton answers this question by focusing on the concrete: from the first violent uniformed bands beating up "enemies of the state," through Mussolini's rise to power, to Germany's fascist radicalization in World War II.

History/1-4000-3391-8

THE FIRST WORLD WAR
by John Keegan

In this magisterial narrative, John Keegan has produced a definitive account of the Great War. He sheds light on weaponry and technology; shows us the doomed negotiations between the monarchs and ministers of 1914; takes us into the verminous trenches of the Western front, to the council rooms of Haig, Hindenburg, and Joffre, and to key conflagrations from Gallipoli to East Africa to the Carpathians.

History/0-375-70045-5

HITLER AND STALIN
Parallel Lives
by Alan Bullock

Hitler and Stalin, a dual biography of the two most destructive figures of the twentieth century, examines its subjects' origins and personalities, traces the arc of their careers, analyzes the methods by which they seized and clung to power, and assesses the scars they left on their world with clarity and mastery of detail.

History/0-679-72994-1

EUROPE'S LAST SUMMER
Who Started the Great War in 1914?
by David Fromkin

In a riveting re-creation of the run-up to war, Fromkin shows how German generals, seeing war as inevitable, manipulated events to precipitate a conflict on their own terms. Moving deftly between diplomats, generals, and rulers across Europe, he makes the complex diplomatic negotiations accessible and immediate.

History/0-375-72575-X

THE AGE OF EMPIRE
1875–1914
by Eric Hobsbawm

In this third volume of his history of the modern world, as it has been produced by the development and expansion of the West, Eric Hobsbawm combines vast erudition with a graceful prose style to recreate the epoch that laid the basis for the twentieth century.

History/0-679-72175-4

A SHORT HISTORY OF BYZANTIUM
by John Julius Norwich

In this magisterial adaptation of his epic three-volume history of Byzantium, John Julius Norwich chronicles the world's longest-lived Christian empire. Beginning with Constantine the Great, who in A.D. 330 made Christianity the religion of his realm and then transferred its capital to the city that would bear his name, Norwich follows the course of eleven centuries of Byzantine statecraft and warfare, politics and theology, manners and art.

History/0-679-77269-3

FAREWELL ESPAÑA
The World of the Sephardim Remembered
by Howard M. Sachar

In *Farewell España*, Sachar follows the Sephardic diaspora in its passage across the Old and New Worlds and from the golden age of *convivencia* to the Holocaust. He weaves together the narratives of merchants and mystics, physicians and philosophers, a British prime minister (Benjamin Disraeli) and a false Messiah. The result is a major work of Jewish history, formidable in its scholarship and filled with bravura storytelling.

History/0-679-73846-0

VINTAGE AND ANCHOR BOOKS
Available at your local bookstore, or call toll-free to order:
1-800-793-2665 (credit cards only).

THE SEDUCTION OF PLACE
The History and Future of the City
by Joseph Rykwert

In *The Seduction of Place*, Rykwert argues that cities display and represent the *personal* desires of their inhabitants. Insisting that they are the physical constructs of communities, he travels through history to trace their roots in ancient times and outlines current attempts and future possibilities to improve the metropolis.

Urban Studies/0-375-70044-7

BARCELONA
by Robert Hughes

In *Barcelona*, Hughes scrolls through the city's often violent history; tells the stories of its kings, poets, magnates, and revolutionaries; and ushers readers through municipal landmarks that range from Antoni Gaudí's sublimely surreal cathedral to a postmodern restaurant with a glass-walled urinal.

History/0-679-74383-9

MAXIMUM CITY
Bombay Lost and Found
by Suketu Mehta

Mehta approaches Bombay from unexpected angles, taking us into the criminal underworld of rival Muslim and Hindu gangs; following the life of a bar dancer raised amid poverty and abuse; opening the door into the inner sanctums of Bollywood; and delving into the stories of the countless villagers who come in search of a better life and end up living on the sidewalks.

Travel/0-375-70340-3

LONDON
The Biography
by Peter Ackroyd

Here are two thousand years of London's history and folklore, its chroniclers and criminals and plain citizens, its food and drink and countless pleasures. In this unique thematic tour of the physical city and its inimitable soul, London comes alive.

History/0-385-49771-7

SEVEN AGES OF PARIS
by Alistair Horne

From the rise of Philippe Auguste through the reigns of Henry IV and Louis XIV; Napoleon's rise and fall; the Belle Epoque and the Great War; the Nazi Occupation, the Liberation, and the postwar period—Horne brings the city's highs and lows, savagery and sophistication, and heroes and villains splendidly to life.

History/1-4000-3446-9

A HISTORY OF VENICE
by John Julius Norwich

A History of Venice traces the rise of the empire of this city from its fifth-century beginnings all the way through 1797, when Napoleon put an end to the thousand-year-old Republic. This book will be treasured by all those who share the author's fascination with "the most beautiful and magical of cities."

History/0-679-72197-5

FIN-DE-SIÈCLE VIENNA
Politics and Culture
by Carl E. Schorske

Fin-de-Siècle Vienna is a landmark book from one of the truly original scholars of our time: a magnificent revelation of turn-of-the-century Vienna where out of a crisis of political and social disintegration so much of modern art and thought was born.

Intellectual History/0-394-74478-0

CAIRO
The City Victorious
by Max Rodenbeck

Rodenbeck provides a cultural excavation of this ancient and multi-faceted city—from its Pharaonic beginnings to its heyday as the glittering metropolis of the Middle Ages, from its subjugation by the Turks and British to its emergence as the capital of Arab nationalism.

Travel/History/0-679-76727-4